ANTHONY & BERRYMAN'S

2007 Magistrates' Court Guide

F G Davies

BA, Barrister

Deputy Clerk to the Justices, North Cambridgeshire

LexisNexis®

® Butterworths

Members of the LexisNexis Group worldwide

United Kingdom	LexisNexis Butterworths, a Division of Reed Elsevier (UK) Ltd, Halsbury House, 35 Chancery Lane, London, WC2A 1EL, and RSH, 1–3 Baxter's Place, Leith Walk Edinburgh EH1 3AF
Argentina	LexisNexis Argentina, Buenos Aires
Australia	LexisNexis Butterworths, Chatswood, New South Wales
Austria	LexisNexis Verlag ARD Orac GmbH & Co KG, Vienna
Benelux	LexisNexis Benelux, Amsterdam
Canada	LexisNexis Canada, Markham, Ontario
Chile	LexisNexis Chile Ltda, Santiago
China	LexisNexis China, Beijing and Shanghai
France	LexisNexis SA, Paris
Germany	LexisNexis Deutschland GmbH, Munster
Hong Kong	LexisNexis Hong Kong, Hong Kong
India	LexisNexis India, New Delhi
Italy	Giuffrè Editore, Milan
Japan	LexisNexis Japan, Tokyo
Malaysia	Malayan Law Journal Sdn Bhd, Kuala Lumpur
Mexico	LexisNexis Mexico, Mexico
New Zealand	LexisNexis NZ Ltd, Wellington
Poland	Wydawnictwo Prawnicze LexisNexis Sp, Warsaw
Singapore	LexisNexis Singapore, Singapore
South Africa	LexisNexis Butterworths, Durban
USA	LexisNexis, Dayton, Ohio

ISBN 10: 1 4057 1091 8

ISBN 13: 978 1 4057 1091 6

Printed and bound in Great Britain by William Clowes Ltd, Beccles, Suffolk

Visit Butterworths LexisNexis direct at www.butterworths.com

Preface

I would like to take this opportunity to thank Terry Moore who was editor of Anthony & Berryman's for the last 12 years. The quality and style of his editorship has made my task markedly easier.

My opening remarks mirror those of Terry Moore from the 2006 edition: 'What a year it has been for changes and legislation'. Speaking for myself, the pace of change is inexorable. I think it is fair to observe that the vast majority of practitioners who appear in magistrates' courts are on the verge of 'information overload' or 'information disorientation'. A pause for breath would be welcome, but the current Government shows no sign of abating its statutory and legal reform programme. That conclusion is based on the publication of several bulky documents during the summer vacation including one entitled 'Simple, Speedy, Summary Justice' (DCA, July 2006).

The Criminal Defence Service Act 2006 received the Royal Assent in March 2006. The Act comes into force on October 2, 2006 and brings about a major change in the way in which legal representation [legal aid] is granted and administered in the criminal courts. The Act transfers the power to grant 'rights to representation' from the courts to the Legal Services Commission. The decision is now regarded as an administrative rather than a judicial one. The second change is the reintroduction of means testing. These changes have been incorporated into the text at section **I[7]**. Secondary legislation will add flesh to the bones of the 2006 Act. At the time of writing three statutory instruments are in draft form only and have yet to be published.

At the same time 2006 has been a year of frustration. As editor I spent a good deal of time preparing to amend the text to take account of the 'allocation' and 'custody plus' provisions which are to be found in the Criminal Justice Act 2003 (CJA). The anticipated timetable was that the second tranche of the CJA 2003 would be brought into force on 6 November 2006. During May 2006 rumours began to spread that the said legislation would be deferred and this was finally confirmed in July 2006. The Government has now indicated that the allocation provisions will not be brought into force until probably the first half of 2007 and there is speculation that the custody plus provisions may never be brought into force.

The Government's drive to increase the number of anti-social behaviour orders made by magistrates' courts was achieved in part via the introduction of a new s 1C into the Crime and Disorder Act 1998 ('Orders on Conviction'). The temptation has been for the prosecution to apply for such orders despite the statutory requirement that an individual was caused 'harassment, alarm or distress' and/or that such an order was necessary. The rise in the number of orders sought explains the consequent increase in judicial activity. We now have the benefit of guideline judgments emanating from the higher courts, notably *R v Boness; R v Bebbington* (2005).

I have endeavoured to proof read the whole of the text in an effort to eliminate the typographical errors and the gremlins which can afflict any major work such as Anthony & Berryman's. I will leave the reader to judge whether my attempts have proved successful. Notwithstanding, any errors are attributable to me. I have also sought to keep the reader abreast of any changes resulting from primary and secondary legislation, and judgments of the higher courts including relevant pronouncements of the European Court of Human Rights.

The law is as stated as that of 1 October 2006, unless otherwise noted in the text.

F G Davies

Cambridgeshire

Contents

Table of Statutes

Paragraph references printed in **bold** type indicate where the Statute is set out in part or in full.

Table of Statutory Instruments

Paragraph references printed in **bold** type indicate where the Statutory Instrument is set out in part or in full.

Table of Cases

A

B

C

D

E

F

G

H

I

J

K

L

M

N

O

P

R

S

T

U

V

W

X

Y

Z

Section A

Criminal offences dealt with in magistrates' courts

Index to criminal offences and table of maximum penalties

Set out below are a number of maximum penalties for some common offences. If an offence is dealt with more fully in this book the relevant paragraph is stated.

† or + Penalty on summary conviction of an offence triable either way.
* Indicates that the police may issue a fixed penalty ticket
** Revised penalties in brackets denote changes in relation to offences committed on or after a date to be appointed by virtue of the CJA 2003

For index and penalties for road traffic offences, see **C[1]**

Absconding level 5 and 3 months **J[1.82]**

Abusive words or behaviour level 5 and 6 months (**51 weeks) **A[80]**

Actual bodily harm level 5 and 6 months (**12 months) **A[1]**

Affray level 5 and 6 months† (**12 months) **A[2]**

Aggravated vehicle-taking level 5 and 6 months (**12 months) **A[3]**

Air gun in public place (FA 1968, s 22(5)) level 3 forfeiture **A[4]**

Airports (Aviation Security Act 1982)
false statements relating to baggage, cargo, etc (s 21A) level 5
false statements in connection with identity documents (s 21B) level 5
unauthorised presence in restricted zone (s 21C) level 5
unauthorised presence on board aircraft (s 21D) level 5
intentionally obstructing an authorised person (s 21E(1)(a)) level 5
impersonating an authorised person (s 21E(1)(b)) level 5

Ammunition (FA 1968, s 1) (*See* Firearms) level 5 and 6 months (**51 weeks), forfeiture† **A[36]**

Animal (cruelty to) level 5 and 6 months (**51 weeks) **A[17]**

Animals straying on highway level 3

Anti-social behaviour order – breach level 5 and 6 months (**12 months)†

Article with blade or point in public place (CJA 1988, s 139) level 5 and 6 months (**12 months) † **A[5]**

Assault (*See* Actual bodily harm, Common assault, Indecent assault, Grievous bodily harm, Wounding)

Assault on police constable or person assisting police constable level 5 and 6 months (**51 weeks) **A[6]**

Avoiding customs duty (*See* Customs duty) **A[19]**

Bankrupt (undischarged, obtaining credit) level 5 and 6 months (**12 months)†

Begging level 3

Blade, article with, in public place (CJA 1988, s 139) level 5 and 6 months (**12 months) **A[5]**

Breach of peace (*See* Insulting words, and *see* **B[10]** for Binding over) **A[80]**

Brothel level 3 and 3 months; level 4 and 6 months (**51 weeks) (second or subsequent offence in relation to a brothel)

Builder's skip
depositing on highway level 3
not complying with a condition level 3
unlit on roadway level 3

Burglary level 5 and 6 months (**12 months)† **A[7]**

Car dumping (*See* Litter) **A[60]**

Children (cruelty to) level 5 and 6 months (**12 months)† **A[18]**

Chimes level 5 **A[34]**

Common assault level 5 and 6 months (**51 weeks)**A[8]**

Computers (Computer Misuse Act 1990)
unauthorised access to computer material (s 1) level 5 and 6 months (**51 weeks)
unauthorised access with intent to commit or facilitate further offences (s 2) level 5 and 6 months (**51 weeks)
unauthorised modification of computer material (s 3) level 5 and 6 months (**12 months)†

Contempt of court level 4 and 1 month **I[3]**

Controlled drugs Penalty varies with classification of drug **A[25]**

Copying false instrument level 5 and 6 months (**12 months)† **A[40]**

Court security officer
assault level 5 and 6 months (**51 weeks) **A[6]**
obstruction level 3 **A[62]**

Criminal damage Penalties vary with value of property **A[9]**

Crossbow (draw weight 1.4kg or more) (Crossbows Act 1987)
sell or lease to person under 17 level 5 and 6 months (**51 weeks), forfeiture
buying or hiring by person under 17 level 3, forfeiture
possession of by person under 17 level 3, forfeiture

Cruelty to animals level 5 and 6 months (**51 weeks) **A[17]**

Cruelty to children level 5 and 6 months (**12 months)† **A[18]**

Customs duty (avoiding) 3 times value of goods or £5,000 and 6 months (**12months)† **A[19]**

Damaging property Penalty varies with value of damage **A[9]**

Dangerous dog A[20]

Dangerous drugs (*See* Controlled drugs) **A[25]**

Dangerous machinery level 5†

Deception (obtaining by) level 5 and 6 months (**12 months)† **A[21]**, **A[22]**

Dishonestly handling level 5 and 6 months (**12 months)† **A[49]**

Disorderly conduct (Public Order Act 1986, s 5) level 3 **A[23]**

Displaying indecent matter level 5

Disposal of property in police possession A[66]

Dogs

Dangerous Dogs Act 1991

- breeding or parting with, etc, fighting dogs (s 1(2)) level 5 and 6 months (**51 weeks)
- fighting dog in public place without muzzle and lead (s 1(2)) level 5 and 6 months (**51 weeks)
- dog dangerously out of control in public place level 5 and 6 months (**12 months)+ (if aggravated offence)

control order (Dogs Act 1871) **A[20]**

dog worrying livestock level 3 **A[24]**

Drugs (controlled) Penalty varies with classification of drug **A[25]**

Drunk and disorderly level 3* **A[33]**

Drunkenness level 2 **A[33]**

Drunk at, or on the way to, a football match level 2 **A[76]**

Earnings of prostitution (living on) level 5 and 6 months (**12 months)†

Enclosed premises (found on) level 3 or 3 months (**level 3 only) **A[46]**

Evasion of liability, obtaining by deception level 5 and 6 months (**12 months)† **A[21]**

Excessive noise (nuisance order) level 5 **A[34]**

Exclusion order (licensed premises), breach of level 4 and 1 month (**51 weeks) **B[32]**

Failure to maintain oneself or a dependant

level 3 or (and, depending on the facts) 3 months (**51 weeks) (National Assistance Act 1948, s 51)

level 4 and 3 months (**level 4 only) (Social Security Administration Act 1992, s 105)

False instrument, using level 5 and 6 months (**12 months)† **A[40]**

False statement to obtain social security level 5 and 3 months (**51 weeks) (Social Security Administration Act 1992, s 112)

False trade description
applying level 5+ **A[35]**
supplying goods with level 5+ **A[40]**

Firearm (forfeiture for each of the following) (Firearms Act 1968)
air weapon in public place level 5 and 6 months (**51 weeks) (s 19) **A[36]**
firearm (other than air weapon) in public place level 5 and 6 months (**12 months)† (s 19) **A[36]**
purchasing, possession, etc, without certificate level 5 and 6 months (**12 months)† (s 1) **A[37]**
trespassing in a building level 5 and 6 months (**51 weeks) **A[38]**
trespassing on land level 4 and 3 months (**51 weeks) **A[38]**

Food (selling food not of quality demanded) (Food Safety Act 1990, s 14) £20,000 and 6 months (**12 months)†

Football spectators (may attract a football banning order) A[39]
throwing of missiles level 3
indecent or racialist chanting level 3
going on to the playing area level 3

Forgery level 5 and 6 months (**12 months)† **A[40]**

Found on enclosed premises level 3 or 3 months (**level 3 only) **A[46]**

Fraud (*See* Obtaining pecuniary advantage by) **A[21]**

Game (trespassing on land in day time in search of game) level 3; level 5 if 5 or more trespassers (Game Act 1831, s 30) **A[65]**

Glue sniffing, supplying level 5 and 6 months (**51 weeks)

Going equipped to steal level 5 and 6 months (**12 months)† **A[47]**

Grievous bodily harm level 5 and 6 months (**12 months)† **A[48]**

Gross indecency level 5 and 6 months (**12 months)†

Handling stolen goods level 5 and 6 months (**12 months)† **A[49]**

Harassing residential occupier (Protection from Eviction Act 1977, s 1) level 5 and 6 months (**12 months)†

Harassment (Protection from Harassment Act 1997, s 1) level 5 and 6 months (**51 weeks)

Harassment (Protection from Harassment Act 1997, s 4) level 5 and 6 months (**12 months)† **A[50]**

Harassment, alarm or distress/disorderly behaviour (Public Order Act 1986, s 5) level 3* **A[23]**

Health and Safety at Work Act 1974
to fail to discharge a duty imposed by ss 2–6 fine not exceeding £20,000 **A[51]**
contravention of ss 8 or 9 level 5
contravention of any health and safety regulations or any requirements or prohibitions imposed under health and safety regulations level 5
contravention of any requirement imposed by or under regulations under s 14 level 5

or intentionally to obstruct any person in the exercise of his powers under that subsection level 5
contravention of any requirement imposed by an inspector under ss 20 or 25 level 5
prevention or attempt to prevent any other person from appearing before an inspector or from answering any question to which an inspector may by virtue of s 20(2) require an answer level 5
contravention of any requirement imposed by an improvement notice or prohibition notice (including any modified on appeal) £20,000 or 6 months (**51 weeks)
intentionally to obstruct an inspector in the exercise or performance of his powers or duties or to obstruct a customs officer in the exercise of his powers under s 25A level 5
contravention of any requirement imposed by a notice under s 27(1) level 5
use or disclosure of any information in contravention of ss 27(4) or 28 level 5
knowingly or recklessly to make false statements
(i) when required to provide information; or
(ii) to obtain the issue of documents level 5
intentional falsification of books, registers, notices or documents or making use of false entries, with the intention to deceive
using authorised or issued documents with the intent to deceive or making or having false documents in your possession with the intent to deceive level 5
pretending to be an inspector level 5
failure to comply with an order made by a court under s 42 (failure to remedy) £20,000 or 6 months (**51 weeks) **A[51]**

Highway
builder's skip (depositing or leaving unlit) level 3
straying animals on level 3
wilful obstruction level 3

Housebreaking implements (*See* Going equipped to steal) **A[47]**

Indecency and photographs level 5 and 6 months (**12 months)†

Indecent display level 5

Insulting magistrate, etc level 4 and 1 month **I[3]**

Insulting words or behaviour level 5 and 6 months (**51 weeks)**A[80]**

Interference with vehicle level 4 and 3 months (**51 weeks) **A[82]**

Intoxicating liquor
possessing at, or on the way to, a designated sporting event level 3 and 3 months (**51 weeks) **A[76]**
selling outside permitted hours level 3
selling to persons under 18 level 3 and forfeiture of licence (on second or subsequent conviction within 5 years)
selling without a licence level 4 and 6 months (**51 weeks); forfeiture of liquor and containers. For a subsequent offence defendant can be disqualified from holding a licence

Intoxicating substance, supplying level 5 and 6 months (**51 weeks)

Kerb crawling level 3 **A[59]**

Landlord and tenant (unlawful eviction or harassment) level 5 and 6 months (**12 months)†

trading without certificate (Pedlars Act 1871, s 4) level 1

Poaching (For hunting wild mammals with dogs and hare coursing see the Hunting Act 2004, ss.1–5)
day time offence level 3; level 5 if 5 or more trespassers (Game Act 1831, s 30) **A[65]**
night time offences level 3; level 4 and 6 months where violence is used or offered (Night Poaching Act 1828, ss 1 and 2) or 3 or more being armed (s 9) **A[65.9]**
pursuing game without a licence level 2 (Game Licence Act 1860, s 4) **A[65.23]**

Point, article with, in public place (CJA 1988, s 139) level 5 or 6 months (**12 months)+ **A[5]**

Police (Property) Act 1897 A[66]

Possessing certain false documents level 5 and 6 months (**12 months)† (Forgery etc Act 1981, s 5)

Property (damaging or destroying) Penalty varies with value **A[9]**

Property (obtaining property by deception) level 5 and 6 months (**12 months)† **A[22]**

Property in possession of police A[66]

Prostitutes
living on earnings of level 5 and 6 months (**12 months)†
soliciting by prostitutes level 2/level 3

Public telephone (see **Telephone**) (Telecommunications Act 1984 – Communications Act 2003
fraudulent use of (s 42) level 5 and 6 months (**12 months)†
indecent or false telephone calls (s 43) level 5 and 6 months (**51 weeks)

Racially or religiously aggravated offences
wounding level 5 and 6 months (**12 months)+ **A[48]**
actual bodily harm level 5 and 6 months (**12 months)+ **A[1.2]**
common assault level 5 and 6 months (**51 weeks) **A[8.2]**
criminal damage level 5 and 6 months (**12 months)+**A[9.16]**
threatening behaviour/intentional harassment alarm or distress level 5 and 6 months (**12 months)+ **A[80.3]**
disorderly behaviour level 4 **A[23]**
harassment level 5 and 6 months (**51 weeks) **A[50]**

Railway offences
avoid fare level 3 or 3 months(**51 weeks) **A[67]**
giving false name or address level 3 or 3 months (**51 weeks) **A[67.2]**

Resisting a constable or a person assisting a constable level 3 and 1 month (**51 weeks) **A[62]**

Scales (unjust) level 5 (and 6 months (**51 weeks) if fraud), and forfeiture (Weights and Measures Act 1985, s 17)

School attendance, parent not ensuring (Education Act 1996, s 444) level 3 Aggravated offence level 4 and 3 months (**51 weeks) **D[17]**

Selling food not of quality demanded (Food Safety Act 1990, s 14) £20,000 and 6 months (**12 months)†

Sexual activity with child level 5 and 6 months (**12 months)† **A[53]**

Sexual assault level 5 and 6 months (**12 months)† **A[54]**

Shotgun
purchasing or possessing, etc, without certificate level 5 and 6 months (**12 months)+, forfeiture **A[70]**
loaded shotgun in a public place level 5 and 6 months (**12 months)+, forfeiture **A[36]**

Skip
depositing on highway level 3
not complying with condition level 3
unlit level 3

Smuggling 3 times value of goods or £5,000 and 6 months (**12 months)† **A[19]**

Social security
false statement to obtain level 5 and 3 months (**51 weeks) (Social Security Administration Act 1992, s 112)
persistently refusing or neglecting to maintain oneself or a dependant level 4 and 3 months (**no longer imprisonable for offences from a date to be appointed) (Social Security Administration Act 1992, s 105)

Soliciting by prostitutes level 2/level 3

Soliciting women for prostitution level 3 **A[59]**

Solvent, supplying for intoxication level 5 and 6 months (**51 weeks)

Sporting event
football banning order **B[32]**
intoxicating liquor, possessing at/on the way to level 3 and 3 months (**51 weeks) **A[76]**
drunk at/on the way to level 2 **A[76]**

Statutory nuisance (noise) A[61]

Stealing level 5 and 6 months (**12 months)† **A[79]**

Taking motor vehicle or conveyance level 5 and 6 months (**51 weeks), disqualification **A[77]**

Tattooing a minor level 3

Telephone (Telecommunications Act 1984 – Communications Act 2003)

NB: Ss 42, 42A and 43 below were replaced by ss 125–127 of the Communications Act 2003 effective from 25/7/03 by virtue of SI 2003/1900 as amended.
fraudulent use of public telephone (s 42) level 5 and 6 months (**12 months)†
indecent or false calls (s 43) level 5 and 6 months (**12 months)*

Television licence level 3 **A[78]**

Terrorism offences (Terrorism Act 2000, ss 15–18) level 5 or 6 months†

Theft level 5 and 6 months† (**12 months) **A[79]**

Threatening to damage or destroy property level 5 and 6 months (**12 months)† **A[80]**

Threatening letters level 4

Threatening words or behaviour (Public Order Act 1986, s 4) level 5 and 6 months (**51 weeks) **A[80]**

Threats or intimidation of witnesses level 5 and 6 months (**51 weeks)**A[81]**

Trade description
applying false trade description level 5† **A[35]**
supplying goods with false description level 5† **A[35]**

Trespassing on land during day time in search of game, etc level 3/level 5 (if 5 or more trespassers) (Game Act 1831, s 30) **A[65]**

Trespassing with firearm in a building level 5 and 6 months (**12 months)+ (if not an air weapon) forfeiture **A[38]**

Trespassing with firearm on land level 4 and 3 months (**51 weeks), forfeiture **A[38]**

Unauthorised taking of motor vehicle level 5 and 6 months (**51 weeks), disqualification **A[77]**

Using false (or copy of false) instrument level 5 and 6 months (**12 months)+ (Forgery etc Act 1981) **A[40]**

Vehicle interference level 4 and 3 months (**51 weeks)**A[82]**

Violent disorder level 5 and 6 months (**12 months)† **A[83]**

Weighing equipment (unjust) level 5 (and 6 months (**51 weeks) if fraud), and forfeiture

Wilful obstruction of highway level 3 **A[63]**

Wilful obstruction of police constable (or person assisting police constable) level 3 and 1 month (**51 weeks) **A[62]**

Wounding level 5 and 6 months (**12 months)† **A[48]**

A[1]

Actual bodily harm and racially/ religiously aggravated assault occasioning actual bodily harm

Charge

A[1.1]

Assault occasioning actual bodily harm

Offences Against The Person Act 1861, s 47

Maximum penalty – Fine level 5 and 6 months (**12 months). Triable either way. Violent specified offence under sched.15, Part 1, CJA 2003.

Crown Court – 5 years' imprisonment and unlimited fine.

A[1.2]

Racially or religiously aggravated assault occasioning actual bodily harm

Crime and Disorder Act 1998, s 29

Maximum penalty - Fine level 5 and 6 months (**12 months). Triable either way. Specified violent offence under sched.15, Part 1, CJA 2003

Crown Court - 7 years' imprisonment and unlimited fine.

Mode of trial

A[1.3]

Consider first the general notes at **I[4]**.

A[1.4]

In general, except for the presence of one or more of the following factors, an offence of assault occasioning actual bodily harm should be tried summarily.

(a) Use of a weapon which was likely to cause or which did cause serious injury.
(b) Serious injury caused by kicking or headbutting.
(c) Victim in the 'front line', eg police officer, taxi driver, bus driver.
(d) Victim particularly vulnerable.
(e) The offence has a motivation which is based on racial, religious or perceived sexual orientation.

The same considerations apply to assaults in a domestic setting.

A[1.5]

Owing to the nature of charges of assault it is particularly important that magistrates hear an outline of the facts before making their decision.

Legal notes and definitions

A[1.6]

Assault. See under 'Common assault' at **A[8]**.

A[1.7]

Intent. The defendant must intend to cause his victim to apprehend immediate and unlawful violence, or be reckless whether such apprehension be caused (*R v Venna* [1976] QB 421, [1975] 3 All ER 788, CA). This constitutes an assault. The offence of assault occasioning actual bodily harm is made out upon proof of an assault together with proof of the fact that actual bodily harm was occasioned by the assault. The prosecution are not obliged to prove that the defendant intended to cause some actual bodily harm or was reckless as to whether such harm would be caused (*R v Savage* [1992] 1 AC 699, [1991] 2 All ER 220, CA; affd [1992] 1 AC 699, [1991] 4 All ER 698, *R v Parmenter* [1991] 4 All ER 698, HL).

A[1.8]

In *DPP v K (a minor)* [1990] 1 All ER 331, [1990] 1 WLR 1067, a schoolboy who put acid in a hot air dryer recklessly but in a mindless panic rather than with any intention to cause harm was nonetheless guilty of assault. In *DPP v Santra-Bermudez* [2003] EWHC 2908, [2003] All ER (D) 168 (Nov) the offence was made out when a police officer pricked her finger on a needle while carrying out a lawful search of a man who had told her that he had no needles in his pocket.

A[1.9]

Actual bodily harm. This is less serious than grievous bodily harm. There need not be permanent injury. Any hurt or injury calculated to interfere with health or comfort can be actual bodily harm, so can an assault causing unconsciousness or an hysterical or nervous condition (*R v Miller* [1954]

2 QB 282, [1954] 2 All ER 529), ie some psychiatric damage and not just distress or panic (*R v Chan-Fook* [1994] 2 All ER 552, [1994] 1 WLR 689, CA). Significant psychological symptoms caused by a series of telephone calls, followed by silence can constitute an assault causing actual bodily harm (*R v Ireland* [1997] QB 114, [1997] 1 All ER 112, , CA; affd [1998] AC 147, [1997] 4 All ER 225, HL). Where a victim suffered great pain immediately and for some time thereafter suffered tenderness and soreness, that was sufficient for the court to infer that there was actual bodily harm notwithstanding that no physically discernible injury had been occasioned. This would include the victim's unconsciousness without the appearance of physical injury (*T v DPP* [2004] EWHC 183 (Admin), [2004] All ER (D) 278 (Jan)). Where there is evidence that a blow was struck, the justices are entitled if they see fit to infer that some bodily harm, however slight, has resulted.

Cutting off a substantial part of the victim's hair was capable in law of amounting to an assault which occasioned actual bodily harm (*DPP v Smith (MR)* [2006] EWHC 94 (Admin), [2006] 2 All ER 16).

A[1.10]–A[1.15]

Racial, religious, disability or sexual orientation aggravation. This means that at the time of committing the offence, or immediately before or after doing so, the offender demonstrates towards the victim of the offence hostility based on the victim's membership (or presumed membership) of a racial or religious group or their disability or presumed sexual orientation; the offence is motivated (wholly or partly) by hostility towards members of a racial or religious group based on their membership of that group, or persons of a particular sexual orientation or disability.

A[1.16]

When considering whether an offence was racially motivated for the purposes of the CDA 1998, s 28 (1)(a) in the light of words uttered immediately prior to the offence, the following matters were irrelevant: (i) victim's perception of the words used; (ii) any additional reason unrelated to race, for uttering the words (CDA 1998, s28(3)(b)); and (iii) the fact that in the defendant's frame of mind at the time he uttered the words, he would have abused anyone by reference to an obvious physical characteristic (*DPP v Woods* [2002] EWHC 85 (Admin), [2002] All ER (D) 154 (Jan)).

It is immaterial whether or not the offender's hostility is based, to any extent on any other factor not mentioned above. See **A[1.34]** for sentencing.

A[1.17]

Provocation is not a defence but can be taken into consideration when deciding sentence.

A[1.18]

Self-defence. A person may use reasonable force to defend himself, his property or another. Where self-defence is put forward to justify the use of violence, the onus is on the prosecution to disprove the defence beyond reasonable doubt. A person must not use force in attacking or retaliating, or revenging himself. It is permissible to use force not merely to counter an actual attack but to ward off an attack honestly believed to be imminent. The reasonableness or otherwise of the belief is only relevant in ascertaining whether he actually held the belief or not (*Beckford v R* [1988] AC 130, [1987] 3 All ER 425, PC).

A[1.19]

Proof that the accused tried to retreat or call off the fight might be a cast-iron method of rebutting the suggestion that he was an attacker or retaliator or trying to revenge himself. It is to be stressed, however, that this is not the only method of doing so, and it depends on the circumstances of the particular case (*R v Bird* [1985] 2 All ER 513, [1985] 1 WLR 816, CA).

A[1.20]

A man who is attacked can defend himself but can only do what is objectively reasonable in the circumstances as the defendant believes them to be (*DPP v Armstrong-Braun* (1998) 163 JP 271, [1999] Crim LR 416). A man cannot rely on a belief of fact which was induced by voluntary intoxication (*R v O'Grady* [1987] QB 995, [1987] 3 All ER 420, CA).

A[1.21]

Misadventure. See **A[8.8]**.

A[1.22]

Consent and reasonable chastisement. See **A[8.10]–A[8.17]**.

A[1.23]

Lawful sport. See **A[8.18]**.

A[1.24]

Trespasser on of property. See **A[8.22]**.

A[1.25]–A[1.30]

Execution of legal process. See **A[8.24]**.

Reduction of charge/alternative verdict. The court cannot reduce this charge to common assault or consider an alternative verdict but, if a separate charge of common assault is preferred, a conviction for that may be possible. The legal adviser should be consulted. See **A[8.31]**.

Sentencing

A[1.31]

Structure of the sentencing decision. See **B[3.6]**.

Guideline: Are the magistrates sentencing powers appropriate?

A[1.32]

Available sentences. See Table A at **B[4.1]**

A[1.33]

In considering sentence a helpful starting point is to consider factors which are relevant to the mode of trial decision. Aggravating factors include:

(a) the use of a weapon;
(b) kicking or headbutting;
(c) assaults on public servants doing their duty or members of the public going to their aid when attacked, eg assaults on police officers and traffic wardens usually merit an immediate custodial sentence (eg *R v Robertson* (1990) 12 Cr App Rep (S) 278, CA). 'Public servants' include such people as bus drivers, taxi drivers and hospital workers. (*R v McNally* [2000] 1 Cr App Rep (S) 535, CA).
(d) a vulnerable victim, eg an old person;
(e) aggressors outnumbering the victim;
(f) unprovoked assault;
(g) racial violence or motivation;

together with statutory aggravating factors such as hostility towards disability, sexual orientation or an offence committed whilst on bail.

Apart from general mitigation such as previous good character the court might consider whether the accused was provoked by the victim and also the absence of any aggravating features.

A[1.34]

Custodial sentence. Racially aggravated assault will usually be committed to the Crown Court: see *R v Saunders* [2000] 1 Cr App Rep 458, [2000] Crim LR 314, CA where a sentence of two and a half years' imprisonment was upheld. See **B[2]** and **A[8.33]**.

A[1.35]

Community sentence. See **B[3]**.

A[1.36]

Fines. See **B[33]**.

In *R v Best* [2004] EWCA Crim 483, [2004] All ER (D) 315 (Mar) a fine costs and compensation totalling £3,000 was upheld for a headbutt which fractured a cheek bone of an opponent in the course of a rugby match.

A[1.37]

Compensation. This may be ordered in respect of the victim's injuries or any other loss he may have suffered (e g broken dentures). Maximum is £5,000. It may be ordered in addition to another sentence, or as a substantive penalty by itself. If a monetary penalty is appropriate and the defendant's means are limited, preference must be given to ordering compensation instead of a fine.

Licensed premises

A[1.38]

An assault committed on licensed premises will enable the court to make an exclusion order. See **B[32]**.

Husband and wife

A[1.39]

These cases present especial difficulty. There has been a tendency amongst police and magistrates to treat the violent husband with leniency. This was probably based on a general reluctance to interfere in matrimonial disputes. However, a wife, like a policeman, is entitled to the protection of the law from those most likely to assault her. When wives are murdered it is usually by their husbands. When there are children in the family the effect of paternal violence should be considered and so should the ramifications of children seeing a violent father go unpunished by the law.

A[1.40]–A[1.45]

In a case decided in 1986 Mr Justice Michael Davies said that it was high time that the message was understood in clear terms by courts, by police forces, by probation officers and, above all, by husbands and boyfriends of women, that it was no mitigation of a serious assault that it had occurred in a domestic scene. The idea that in some way serious assaults were rendered trivial because of a relationship of marriage or friendship was completely outdated (*R v Cutts* [1987] Fam Law 311, CA). Subject to the principle of totality, there is no reason why consecutive prison sentences should not be imposed for assault on the same victim. Violence in a domestic context was aggravated by the betrayal of trust: *R v McNaughton* (2004) Times, 15 January, CA.

A[2]

Affray

Charge

A[2.1]

Using or threatening unlawful violence towards another such that the conduct would cause a person of reasonable firmness present at the scene to fear for his personal safety

Public Order Act 1986, s 3

Maximum penalty – Fine level 5 and 6 months (**12 months). Triable either way. Specified violent offence under Sch 15, Part 1, CJA 2003

Crown Court – 3 years' imprisonment and unlimited fine.

Mode of trial

A[2.2]

Consider first the general notes at **I[4]**.

A[2.3]

In general, except for the presence of one or more of the following factors, affray should be tried summarily:

(a) the violence was organised;
(b) significant injury to victims;
(c) a racially aggravated offence;
(d) violence towards people called to the scene, eg ambulance men or policemen.

Legal notes and definitions

A[2.4]

The charge. Only one offence is created.

A[2.5]

Using or threatening. Where two or more persons use or threaten the violence, it is the conduct of them taken together that must be considered for the purpose of the offence.

A[2.6]

Threats. Cannot be made by way of words alone, there must be at least a physical gesture towards someone.

A[2.7]

Person of reasonable firmness need not actually be or be likely to be present at the scene, it is the hypothetical reasonable bystander who has to be put in fear for his personal safety, not just the victim himself (*R v Sanchez* (1996) 160 JP 321, [1996] Crim LR 572, CA). In *R v Plavecz* (2002) it is made clear that an assault does not turn into an affray because it is in a public place. There must be evidence that anyone watching would have been put in fear themselves.

A[2.8]

Violence. Violence does not include violence justified in law (self-defence or prevention of crime).The violence must be directed towards another, ie not property – such as kicking a door. However, the violence is not restricted to violence causing or intended to cause injury and includes violent conduct such as throwing a missile of a kind capable of causing injury even though it misses or falls short.

A[2.9]

Intent. The accused must intend to use or threaten violence or be aware that his conduct may be violent or threaten violence.

A[2.10]–A[2.15]

Intoxication. See under the offence of violent disorder at **A[83]**. Affray can be committed in a public or private place.

Sentencing

A[2.16]

Structure of the sentencing decision. See **B[3.6]**.

Guideline: Are the magistrates sentencing powers appropriate?

A[2.17]

Available sentences. See Table A at **B[4.1]**.

In assessing the gravity of the offence the court may consider the factors which are relevant to mode of trial. Affray was formerly considered to be a more serious offence than now. More serious offences are charged as violent disorder, see **A[83]**. An affray on an aircraft in flight should be treated more seriously than an affray in a public place on the ground (*R v Oliver* [1999] 1 Cr App Rep (S) 394, [1998] 40 LS Gaz R 37, CA). Personal mitigation may allow for a sentence well within the magistrates' court powers (*R v Benson* [2005] EWCA Crim 1107, [2005] All ER (D) 336 (May)).

A[2.18]

Custodial sentence. See **B[2]**.

A[2.19]

Community sentence. See **B[3]**.

A[2.20]

Fines. See **B[33]**.

A[2.21]

Compensation. See **B[18]**.

A[3]

Aggravated vehicle-taking

Charge

A[3.1]

Taking a mechanically propelled vehicle without the owner's consent or other lawful authority (or driving, or allowing oneself to be carried in or on it, knowing it to have been taken without the owner's consent etc) and at any time after it had been unlawfully taken and before it was recovered:

> **the vehicle was driven dangerously on a road or public place; owing to the driving of the vehicle an accident occurred by which (injury was caused to any person) (damage was caused to property other than the vehicle);**
>
> **damage was caused to the vehicle.**

Theft Act 1968, s 12A(1)

Maximum penalty – Fine level 5 and 6 months' (**12 months) imprisonment+. Specified violent offence under Sch 15, Part 1, CJA 2003 if the offence involves an accident causing the death of any person.

Mandatory disqualification for one year and endorsement. Penalty points 3–11.

Crown Court – 2 years' imprisonment (14 years where death has been caused) and unlimited fine.

Mode of trial

A[3.2]

Where no allegation is made other than damage to property or the vehicle concerned, the offence is triable only before magistrates where the total value of the damage concerned does not exceed £5,000 (*R v Kelly* [2001] RTR 45, CA). The value of the damage to property other than the vehicle involved in the offence is what it would probably have cost to buy the property in the open market at the time of the offence. The value of the damage to the vehicle taken is assessed in a similar manner to that where property has been damaged. Otherwise the offence is triable either way.

A[3.3]

For the procedure where it is not clear whether the damage is above or below £5,000, see **A[9.4]**. Although no mode of trial guidance has been issued it is apparent that these will be serious offences by their nature and that justices will accept jurisdiction only after careful consideration. Cases involving death should go to the Crown Court for trial.

A[3.4]

Seriousness factors, such as prolonged high speed chases with the police, disregard for passenger pleas to stop and alcohol, may indicate a custodial sentence outside the powers of a magistrates' court for a single offence (*R v Bird* (1993) 14 Cr App Rep (S) 721, CA; *R v Ore and Tandy* (1993) 15 Cr App Rep (S) 620, [1994] Crim LR 304, CA).

Legal notes and definitions

A[3.5]

Mechanically propelled vehicle ie a vehicle intended or adapted for use on a road.

A[3.6]

Vehicle recovered ie when it is restored to its owner or to other lawful possession or custody.

A[3.7]

Owner includes a person in possession under a hiring or hire-purchase agreement.

A[3.8]

Dangerous driving ie driven in a way which falls far below what would be expected of a competent and careful driver and it would be obvious to a competent and careful driver that driving the vehicle in that way would be dangerous.

A[3.9]

Road or public place. See **C[22.5]**, **C[22.6]**.

A[3.10]

Defence. The defendant is not guilty of this offence if he proves that the driving accident or damage occurred before he committed the basic offence or that he was neither in, nor on, nor in the immediate vicinity of the vehicle when that driving etc occurred. The defendant does not have to establish one of these defences beyond reasonable doubt. He need only establish that it was probably true. (It is suggested that the burden and standard of proof legitimately lies with the accused because the facts giving rise to the defence are peculiarly within the knowledge of that person. Accordingly, the legal burden of proof appears compatible with the European Convention on Human Rights (ECHR).)

A[3.11]–A[3.15]

Reduction of charge/alternative verdict. The court may find the defendant guilty of the basic offence if it decides to dismiss the aggravated version. (*H v Liverpool City Youth Court* [2001] Crim LR 897)

Sentencing

A[3.16]

Structure of the sentencing decision. See **B[3.6]**.

Guideline: Is it so serious that only custody is appropriate?

A[3.17]

Available sentences. See Table A at **B[4.1]**. This offence was created to deal with the spate of offences of taking vehicles without consent accompanied by dangerous driving and damage to property or injury to persons.

Mitigation may be found for a non-driving co-defendant who asks the driver to desist. (*R v Wiggins* [2001] RTR 37, CA). However elements of racing and risk of injury will indicate the use of custody. (*R v Akram* [2002] All ER (D) 44 (Jun), CA)

A[3.18]

Custodial sentences. See **B[2]**.

A[3.19]

Community sentences. See **B[3]**.

A[3.20]

Fines. See **B[33]**.

A[3.21]

Disqualification is mandatory for a minimum period of one year unless special reasons exist (see **C[5.2]**). However the fact that the defendant did not drive the vehicle at any particular time or at all cannot amount to a special reason for not disqualifying (Road Traffic Act 1988, s 34(1A)).

A[4]

Air guns

Charge

A[4.1]

1 Being a person under 17 having with him an air weapon or ammunition

Firearms Act 1968, s 22(4)

2 Person under 17 making improper use of air weapon on private premises

Firearms Act 1968, s 23(4)

Maximum penalty – Fine level 3 or any other adjudication to which a young person is liable, bearing in mind the offence is not punishable with imprisonment.

Forfeiture of the air weapon or ammunition can be ordered.

Legal notes and definitions

A[4.2]

Possession, a close physical link and immediate control over the firearm but not necessarily that he had been carrying it. It is not an offence where he is under the supervision of someone of or over 21 years.

A[4.3]

Air weapon means an air rifle, air gun or air pistol of a type which has not been declared to be specially dangerous in rules made by the Home Office. See *Street v DPP* [2004] EWHC 86 (Admin), (2004) Times, 23 January, [2004] All ER (D) 70 (Jan) where a low powered ball bearing gun was included in the definition.

A[4.4]

Public place includes any highway or premises or place to which at the material time the public had access whether for payment or otherwise.

A[4.5]

It is not an offence for a person of 14 or over to have with him an air weapon on private premises with the consent of the occupier.

A[4.6]

He does not commit an offence if he is engaged in target practice as a member of a club approved by the Home Office or if the weapon and ammunition are being used at a shooting gallery where only air weapons or miniature rifles of 0.23 calibre or less are used (Firearms Act 1968, s 23(2)).

Sentencing

A[4.7]

Available sentences. See Table C at **B[4.3]**.

A[4.8]

Fines. See **B[33]**.

A[5]

Article with blade or point in public place

Charge

A[5.1]

Having an article which has a blade (or is sharply pointed) namely a [ ] in a public place or on school premises

Criminal Justice Act 1988, s 139 and s 139A

Maximum penalty – Fine level 5 and 6 months (**12 months). Triable either way.

Crown Court – 2 years' imprisonment (4 years for school premises) and unlimited fine

Legal notes and definitions

A[5.2]

For other provisions concerning the carrying of offensive weapons in public places see **A[64]**.

A[5.3]

For the offence described here, the prosecution merely has to prove that the accused had an article to which this offence applies and it is then up to the accused to justify its possession. The prosecution has a lesser burden of proof, than in the offence described at **A[64]**. The defendant does not discharge this burden merely by providing an explanation uncontradicted by prosecution evidence if the justices disbelieve his explanation (*Godwin v DPP* (1992) 96 Cr App Rep 244, 157 JP 197). However the prosecution must prove the defendant had knowledge of his possession of the blade (*R v Daubney* (2000) 164 JP 519, CA).

It is suggested that having regard to the legitimate aims of the legislation the legal burden of proof which rests with the accused is ECHR compliant.

A[5.4]

Mode of trial. Consider the general guidelines at **I[4]**. In general the offence will be tried summarily.

A[5.5]

Exceptions. This offence does not apply to a folding pocket knife except if the cutting edge of its blade exceeds 3 inches. Folding knife does not include a knife where the blade is secured in the open position by a locking device (*Harris v DPP* [1993] 1 All ER 562, [1993] 1 WLR 82).

A[5.6]

Public place includes any place to which at the material time the public have or are permitted access, whether on payment or otherwise. See *R v Roberts* [2003] EWCA Crim 2753, [2003] All ER (D) 325 (Oct).

A[5.7]

School premises includes any land used for the purposes of a school but excludes a dwelling occupied by a person employed at the school.

A[5.8]

Defences. It is a defence for the accused to prove that he had good reason or lawful authority for having the article with him in a public place. The defendant does not have to prove this beyond all reasonable doubt, only that it is more probable than not. (*L v DPP* [2001] EWHC Admin 882 [2002] 2 All ER 854). This burden is held not to be incompatible with the presumption of innocence in Article 6(2) of the ECHR (*R v Matthews* [2003] EWCA Crim 813, [2004] QB 690).

See also **[A66.7]**.

A[5.9]

Good reason or lawful authority includes cases where the accused had the article with him:

(a) for use at work;
(b) for religious reasons (e g a Sikh) but not where the reason was connected with a martial art ancillary to a religious practice (*R v Wang* [2003] EWCA Crim 3228, [2003] All ER (D) 299 (Dec)); or
(c) as part of any national costume (e g a Scotsman's dirk).The defendant cannot rely on forgetfulness as constituting a good reason for having a weapon with him even where at an earlier period he was in lawful possession of the article (*DPP v Gregson* (1992) 96 Cr App Rep 240, 157 JP 201);

or, in the case of the school offence:

(d) for educational purposes.

Sentencing

A[5.10]–A[5.15]

Guideline: Is it so serious that only custody is appropriate?

Available sentences. See Table A at **B[4.1]**.

This offence is punishable with imprisonment and so sentences such as a detention in a young offender institution, community service or attendance centre are available.

A[5.16]

Structure of the sentencing decision. See **B[3.6]**.

A[5.17]

Custodial. See **B[2]**.

A[5.18]

Community sentence. See **B[3]**.

A[5.19]

Fine. See **B[33]**.

A[6]

Assaulting a police constable (or a person assisting the police) Assaulting a court security officer

Charge

A[6.1]

Assaulting a constable in the execution of his duty

or

Assaulting a person assisting a constable in the execution of his duty

Police Act 1996, s 89

and

Assaulting a court security officer in the execution of his duty

Criminal Justice Act 1991, s 78 [from 1 April 2005 contrary to Courts Act 2003, s 57]

Maximum penalty – Fine level 5 and 6 months (**51 weeks). Triable only summarily.

Legal notes and definitions

A[6.2]

Assault. See under Common assault at **A[8]**.

A[6.3]

Constable. Includes a special constable and any member of the police irrespective of actual rank. Offences against designated and accredited persons acting in the execution of their duty ie community support officer, investigating officer, detention officer or escort officer are catered for under the Police Reform Act 2002, s 46. Assaults carry a maximum penalty of a level 5 fine and/or six months imprisonment (**12 months).

A[6.4]

Court security officer. A person appointed by the Lord chancellor or provided under a contract and designated by the Lord chancellor as a court security officer (s 51 Courts Act 2003).

A[6.5]

In the execution of his duty. The constable must be carrying out his duty at the time of the assault. If he goes beyond his duty, for example by catching hold of a person whom he is not arresting, then this offence is not committed by a person resisting him with reasonable force. The line between duty and what lies beyond is not easily discernible. This needs reference to many decided cases in the higher courts – see, for example, *Donnelly v Jackman* [1970] 1 All ER 987, [1970] 1 WLR 562 and *Osman v DPP* (1999) 163 JP 725. Police acting on a reasonable expectation of a breach of the peace are acting within their duty (*Wragg v DPP* [2005] EWHC 1389 (Admin), [2005] All ER (D) 131 (Jun)).

A[6.6]

A court security officer shall not be regarded as acting in the execution of his duty unless he is readily identifiable by a badge or uniform (powers of court security officers are found in the Courts Act 2003, s 51(3)).

A[6.7]

The burden of proof that the constable was acting in the execution of his duty rests on the prosecution but the prosecution does not have to prove that the defendant knew that the constable was a constable, nor that the defendant knew that the constable was acting in the execution of his duty. The offence may be established even if the court accepts that the defendant (who must take his victim as he finds him) did not know that his victim was a police officer. Where the accused is unaware that his victim is a police officer and believes there are circumstances which would justify the use of force, eg self-defence, he should have a defence (*Blackburn v Bowering* [1994] 3 All ER 380, [1994] 1 WLR 1324, CA) (see **A[8.8]** for defences).

A[6.8]

If a police officer touches a person to draw his attention that contact must be acceptable by ordinary standards and for no longer than necessary to remain within the execution of the officer's duty (*Mepstead v DPP* (1995) 160 JP 475, [1996] Crim LR 111).

Plain clothes officers carrying out a drugs search are not acting in the execution of their duty if they fail to comply with the requirements of s 2(3), PACE 1984 (*Bonner v DPP* [2004] EWHC 2415 (Admin), [2004] All ER (D) 74 (Oct)).

A[6.9]

Reduction of charge/alternative verdict. The court cannot reduce this charge to common assault, but if a separate charge for common assault is preferred, a conviction for that offence may be possible.

Sentencing

A[6.10]–A[6.15]

Structure of the sentencing decision. See **B[3.6]**.

Guideline: Is it so serious that only custody is appropriate?

A[6.16]

Available sentences. See Table B at **B[4.2]**.

A[6.17]

This is a serious offence and will frequently attract a custodial sentence. The Court of Appeal has upheld immediate custodial sentences for deliberate assaults on police officers, even where the offender has been of previous good character. An aggravating feature appears to be assaults on officers in order to prevent them arresting other offenders, particularly in the context of violent disorder (*R v Coote* (1992) 14 Cr App Rep (S) 40, CA). Gang attacks will invariably attract a custodial sentence if the sentencing guidelines of the Court of Appeal are followed.

A[6.18]

Conversely, some police assaults may be more technical than injurious, no actual bodily harm may have been caused and sometimes the defendant may not have been aware that the victim was a police officer.

A[6.19]

The surrounding facts must be considered carefully when deliberating on the seriousness of the offence.

A[6.20]

Custodial sentence. See **B[2]**.

A[6.21]

Community sentence. See **B[3]**.

A[6.22]

Fines. See **B[33]**.

A[6.23]

Compensation. This may be ordered up to £5,000 in respect of the victim's injuries or other loss he has suffered as a result of the assault. It may be ordered as part of a wider sentence, or by itself as a substantive penalty. If a monetary penalty is appropriate and the offender's means are limited, preference must be given to ordering compensation instead of a fine.

A[6.24]

Licensed premises. If the offence takes place on licensed premises an exclusion order may be made. See **B[32]**.

A[7]

Burglary

Charge

A[7.1]

Entering a building (or part of a building) as a trespasser with intent to steal therein (or with intent to do unlawful damage)

or

Having entered a building (or part of a building) as a trespasser stole (or attempted to steal)

Theft Act 1968, s 9(1)(a) and s 9(1)(b) respectively

Maximum penalty – Fine level 5 and 6 months (**12 months). Triable either way. Specified violent offence under Sch 15, Part 1, CJA 2003 if the offence is committed with intent to (i) inflict GBH on a person; or (ii) do unlawful damage to a building or anything in it.

Crown Court – 14 years' imprisonment or life following a third separate conviction (for burglaries involving a dwelling), 10 years (other premises) and unlimited fine.

Mode of trial

A[7.2]

Aggravated burglary is the commission of a burglary whilst armed with a firearm or other weapon of offence at the time of entry and is triable only at the Crown Court. Crime and Disorder Act 1998, s 51 applies.

A[7.3]

Burglary comprising the commission of, or an intention to commit, an offence of rape or grievous bodily harm may only be heard at the Crown Court. Crime and Disorder Act 1998, s 51 applies.

A[7.4]

If the building is a dwelling-house a magistrates' court can try the case unless it is alleged that the defendant used, or threatened, violence to someone in the dwelling-house in which case the Crime and Disorder Act 1998, s 51 applies (*R v McGrath* [2003] EWCA Crim 2062, 167 JP 554, [2004] Crim LR 142, [2003] All ER (D) 397 (Jun)).

A[7.4A]

Consult the legal adviser. Where the charge is burglary of a dwelling and the accused has two separate convictions for dwelling house burglaries, the charge may only be heard at the Crown Court (PCC(S) A 2000, s 111). See *R v Webster* [2003] EWCA Crim 3597, [2003] All ER (D) 313 (Nov) for an example of a third offence becoming indictable only.

A[7.5]

Where the offence is triable either way consider first the general notes at **I[4]**.

A[7.6]

Having considered these, then in general, **except** for the presence of one or more of the following factors, a burglary may be tried summarily:

Burglary in a dwelling-house

A[7.7]

(a) day time when the occupier is present;
(b) night time when the house is normally occupied (whether or not it is actually occupied);
(c) a series of similar offences;
(d) soiling, vandalism or ransacking;
(e) offence has professional hallmarks;
(f) unrecovered property of high value;
(g) offence is racially motivated.

Burglary (non-dwelling-house)

A[7.8]

(a) premises are a pharmacy or doctor's surgery;
(b) fear caused or violence offered to a person lawfully on the premises;
(c) offence has professional hallmarks;
(d) vandalism on a substantial scale;
(e) unrecovered property of high value;
(f) offence is racially motivated.

Legal notes and definitions

A[7.9]

Entering. Whether the defendant can properly be described as entering or having entered the building is a question of fact for the magistrates. They will have to decide whether the accused had made an effective entry into the building (*R v Brown* [1985] Crim LR 212, CA). An effective entry can be made by the burglar putting his hand through a broken shop window and stealing therefrom. It can be sufficient for only a part of the burglar's body to enter the premises.

A[7.10]–A[7.14]

Building. The offence is committed by one who is lawfully in part of a building but trespasses into another part.

A[7.15]

An inhabited vehicle (eg a caravan) or vessel is within the section notwithstanding that the occupant is absent at the time of the offence.

A[7.16]

Stealing is dishonestly appropriating another person's property with the intention of permanently depriving the other person of it. See **A[79]**.

A[7.17]

Trespass. Accidental trespass would not be an offence. The defendant must know, or be reckless as to whether, he is trespassing (*R v Collins* [1973] QB 100, [1972] 2 All ER 1105, CA). If there is doubt whether the defendant was trespassing, consult the legal adviser.

A[7.18]

Third conviction. Where magistrates have before them a defendant who appears to be facing a third time domestic burglary, the case must be committed for trial at Crown Court (see **A[7.4A]**). In all cases of burglary dwelling the court should announce in open court for the record that the defendant has been convicted of a qualifying offence.

Sentencing

A[7.19]

Structure of the sentencing decision. See **B[3.6]**.

Guideline: Are magistrates sentencing powers appropriate?

A[7.20]

Available sentences. See Table A at **B[4.1]**.

This is a serious offence especially when committed during the hours of darkness. Amongst the factors to be taken into account when fixing sentence are those referred to under mode of trial above.

A[7.21]

An overall survey of the cases shows:

1 Burglary of a dwelling-house, occupied or unoccupied, was not necessarily and in all cases an offence of such seriousness that a non-custodial sentence could not be justified.
2 The decision whether a custodial sentence was required, and if so the length of such sentence, was heavily dependent on the aggravating and mitigating features and usually, to a lesser extent, the personal circumstances of the offender.
3 The courts, particularly the higher courts, had generally reflected in their sentences the abhorrence with which the public regarded those who burgled the houses of others.

A[7.22]

Lord Bingham, CJ, made the following observations in *R v Brewster* [1998] 1 Cr App Rep 220, [1998] 1 Cr App Rep (S) 181, 94 LS Gaz R 22, CA, which has been updated from subsequent case law:

(a) Domestic burglary is, and always has been, regarded as a very serious offence. It may involve considerable loss to the victim. Many victims are uninsured; because they may have fewer possessions, they are the more seriously injured by the loss than those who have insurance.
(b) The loss of material possessions is, however, only part (and often a minor part) of the reason why domestic burglary is a serious offence. That an intruder should break in or enter, for his own dishonest purpose, leaves the victim with a sense of violation and insecurity.
(c) The seriousness of the offence can vary almost infinitely from case to case. It may involve an impulsive act involving an object of little value (reaching through a window to take a bottle of milk, or stealing a can of petrol from an outhouse). At the other end of the spectrum it may involve a professional, planned organisation, directed at objects of high value.
(d) The record of the offender is of more significance in the case of domestic burglary than in the case of some other crimes. There are some professional burglars whose records show that from an early age they have behaved as predators preying on their fellow citizens, returning to their trade almost as soon as each prison sentence has been served. Such defendants continue to receive substantial terms of imprisonment.
(e) It is common knowledge that many domestic burglars are drug addicts who burgle and steal in order to raise money to satisfy their craving for

drugs. This is often an expensive craving, and it is not uncommon to learn that addicts commit a burglary, or even several burglaries, each day, often preying on houses in less affluent areas of the country. Self induced addiction cannot be relied on as mitigation. The courts will not be easily persuaded that an addicted offender is genuinely determined and able to conquer his addiction. However the DTTO [Drug Rehabilitation Order] may be appropriate in attempting to break a cycle of offending.

(f) Generally speaking, domestic burglaries are the more serious if they are of occupied houses at night; if they are the result of professional planning, organisation or execution; if they are targeted at the elderly, the disabled and the sick; if there are repeated visits to the same premises; if they are committed by persistent offenders; if they are accompanied by vandalism or any wanton injury to the victim; if they are shown to have a seriously traumatic effect on the victim; if the offender operates as one of a group; if goods of high value (whether actual or sentimental) are targeted or taken; if force is used or threatened; if there is a pattern of repeat offending.

Mitigation

Where it is a first offence, there is nothing or only items of low value stolen, or the defendant only played a minor role the court may mitigate in his favour. It mitigates the seriousness of an offence if the offender pleads guilty, particularly if the plea is indicated at an early stage and there is hard evidence of genuine regret or remorse. *R v McInerney and Keating* [2002] EWCA Crim 3003, [2003] 1 All ER 1089, provides further guidance to the courts allowing for a reduced use of imprisonment by the appropriate use of such orders as the DTTO [Drug Rehabilitation Order] However, breach of such an order will still result in a substantial custodial sentence outside the scope of the magistrates' court. *R v Chute* [2003] EWCA Crim 177, [2003] 2 Cr App Rep (S) 445 points to the inability of a magistrates' court to commit a breach of community penalty to the Crown Court for sentence and questions whether magistrates' courts should accept jurisdiction where they might be considering a DTTO [Drug Rehabilitation Order].

A[7.23]

Burglary of commercial premises will often attract a custodial sentence where there is planning and the premises are targeted as containing durable or easily disposable goods.

A[7.24]

Custodial sentence. See **B[2]**.

A[7.25]–A[7.30]

Community sentences. See **B[3]**.

A[7.31]

Fines. See **B[33]**.

A[7.32]

Compensation. This may be ordered up to £5,000 either as part of a wider sentence or by itself as a substantive penalty. If the offender's means are limited and a monetary penalty is appropriate, preference must be given to ordering compensation instead of a fine. Compensation may also be ordered for similar offences taken into consideration.

A[7.33]

An order may be made depriving the defendant of any property used in the commission of the offence; this would include, for example, a motor vehicle used to carry away stolen property. Such an order may be made notwithstanding that the property concerned did not belong to the defendant, but in such cases the legal adviser should be consulted.

A[8]

Common assault and racially/ religiously aggravated assault

Charge

A[8.1]

Did assault [ ] [by beating]

Contrary to the Criminal Justice Act 1988, s 39.

Maximum penalty – Fine level 5 and 6 months (**51 weeks). Triable only by magistrates.

A[8.2]

Racially/religiously aggravated assault

Contrary to the Crime and Disorder Act 1998, s 29.

Maximum penalty - Fine level 5 and 6 months (**12 months). Triable either way. Specified violent offence under Sch 15, Part 1, CJA 2003.

Crown Court - 2 years' imprisonment and unlimited fine.

Legal notes and definitions

A[8.3]

The basic offence is triable only by magistrates but may be alleged as an alternative charge at a trial at the Crown Court if the prosecution chooses with a maximum penalty of £5,000 and 6 months (51 weeks). Racially or religiously aggravated assault is triable either way. The two offences may be tried together in the alternative (*R (CPS) v Blaydon Youth Court* [2004] EWHC 2296 (Admin), 168 JP 638).

A[8.4]

Intent. The defendant must intend to cause his victim to apprehend immediate and unlawful violence, or be reckless whether such apprehension be caused (*R v Venna* [1976] QB 421, [1975] 3 All ER 788, CA). 'Reckless' means that the accused foresaw the risk and went on to take it (*R v Cunningham* [1957] 2 QB 396, [1957] 2 All ER 412, CA).

A[8.5]

Assault. Does not require any contact between the two parties, a threatening gesture is enough. Words, however insulting, are probably not an assault but any attempt to commit a battery, even if the blow does not connect, can be an assault. It is not necessary that the other party should receive an actual injury, but there must have been a hostile intent. In modern usage the term assault will now include a battery, ie the actual application of force as opposed to its threatened use, and this is how it is used in most statutes. But if a charge alleges 'did assault and batter' then 'assault' will be taken to mean assault in its pure form and the charge will be as bad as being duplicitous. If anything other than 'did assault' is to be alleged it should be 'did assault by beating' (*DPP v Taylor and Little* (1991)). A reckless act which causes injury will suffice, for example a man who having fallen to the ground when struggling with the police lashed out wildly with his legs, striking the officer and fracturing a bone in his hand, was held to have been properly convicted. Just placing a hand on someone's shoulder to call his attention to something is not an assault. Throwing something at a person, even if it misses, may be an assault.

A[8.6]

If a man strikes at another but at such a distance that it would be quite impossible for it to connect then it is not an assault (although it might be an attempt). If the other person is actually touched then it is a battery which includes an assault. Equally a punch to a mother causing her to drop her baby is an assault on the baby (*Haystead v Chief Constable of Derbyshire* [2000] 3 All ER 890, [2000] 2 Cr App Rep 339).

A[8.7]

Racially or religiously aggravated. This means that at the time of committing the offence, or immediately before or after doing so, the offender demonstrates towards the victim of the assault, hostility based on the victim's membership (or presumed membership) of a racial/religious group, or the offence is motivated (wholly or partly) by hostility towards members of a racial/ religious group based on their membership of that group. It is immaterial whether or not the offender's hostility is also based on other factor not mentioned above. The prosecution can proceed on one or both limbs and will not need to specify which (*G v DPP; T v DPP* [2004] EWHC 183 (Admin), [2004] All ER (D) 278 (Jan)) (*DPP v Woods* [2002] EWHC 85 (Admin) [2002] All ER (D) 154 (Jan)) The victim's perception of the words used is irrelevant, as is the defendant's frame of mind at the time he uttered the words. This offence may also be aggravated by a motivation towards the victim's disability or sexual orientation but not as a separate offence.

A[8.8]

Misadventure. If a horse out of control strikes a person that is not an assault. In an old decision a soldier drilling in the ranks fired his gun as a man was passing unexpectedly and this was held not to be an assault.

A[8.9]

Accidental jostling. In a crowd there is not an assault as there is an implied consent to the physical contacts of ordinary life.

A[8.9A]

Hostile intent. See *Collins v Wilcock* [1984] 1 WLR 1172.

A[8.10]–A[8.15]

Consent. Consent of the victim is a defence but there are limits to this. The test is whether it is in the public interest to allow the activity complained of. In 1981 the Lord Chief Justice decided consent was irrelevant where two youths settled an argument in a public street by agreeing to have a fight. It was not in the public interest for people to cause each other actual bodily harm for no good reason. A similar principle has been applied by the House of Lords to assault which took place in the course of sado-masochistic activities (*R v Brown* [1992] QB 491, [1992] 2 All ER 552, CA; affd [1994] 1 AC 212, [1993] 2 All ER 75, HL). But see (*ADT v United Kingdom* [2000] 2 FLR 697, [2000] Fam Law 797, ECtHR) ECtHR for protection from prosecution for such genuinely 'private ' activities.

A[8.16]

Reasonable chastisement is a defence available to a parent accused of assaulting their child; however the chastisement must be reasonable and moderate. This is assessed by:

i) the nature and context of the defendant's behaviour
ii) the duration
iii) physical/ mental consequences to the child (injury will make it unlawful)
iv) age and characteristics of the child

Note that no battery of a child can be justified on the grounds that it constitutes reasonable punishment; Children Act 2004, s 58.

However consensual activity between husband and wife in the privacy of the matrimonial home was held not to be a proper matter for criminal investigation in *R v Wilson* [1997] QB 47, [1996] 3 WLR 125, CA. Lawful sport would be unimpeachable as being in the public interest and the exercise of a legal right.

A[8.17]

Defendants who maintained that they had been engaged in rough and undisciplined horseplay, had not intended any harm, and had thought that the victims were consenting to what had occurred, were entitled to have their defence considered by the court (*R v Muir* (1986) 83 Cr App Rep 375, CA).

A[8.18]

Lawful sport. Players in games which involve some risk of injury in play must be taken to accept that risk. So a player who injures another in a fair tackle would not be guilty of an offence. Even where the accused infringes the 'rules of the game' he might still not be acting unreasonably although it might be otherwise if he was guilty of serious and dangerous foul play which showed a reckless disregard for the victim's safety and fell far below the standards which might reasonably be expected in anyone pursuing the game. Where one player offers violence to another otherwise that in actual pursuit of the game this would be an assault (*R v Barnes* [2004] EWCA Crim 3246, [2005] 2 All ER 113).

A[8.19]

Self-defence. A person must not use force in attacking or retaliating, or revenging himself. It is permissible to use force not merely to counter an actual attack but to ward off an attack honestly believed to be imminent. The reasonableness or otherwise of the belief is only relevant in ascertaining whether he actually held the belief or not (*Beckford v R* [1988] AC 130, [1987] 3 All ER 425, PC).

A[8.20]

Proof that the accused tried to retreat or call off the fight might be a cast-iron method of rebutting the suggestion that he was an attacker or retaliator or trying to revenge himself. It is to be stressed, however, that this is not the only method of doing so and it depends on the circumstances of the particular case (*R v Bird* [1985] 2 All ER 513, [1985] 1 WLR 816, CA).

A[8.21]

A man who is attacked can defend himself but can only do what is reasonably necessary to effect such defence. The level of violence must be objectively reasonable in the circumstances as the defendant believes them to be (*DPP v Brown* (1998) 162 JP 333, [1998] 17 LS Gaz R 30). A man cannot rely on a belief of fact which was induced by voluntary intoxication (*R v O'Grady* [1987] QB 995, [1987] 3 All ER 420, CA).

A[8.22]

A trespasser should first be asked to leave the house or land. If he refuses, as much force as is reasonably necessary to remove him can be used. Similarly, such reasonable force can be used to protect one's property from actual or imminent damage which constituted an unlawful or criminal act (*DPP v Bayer* [2003] EWHC 2567 (Admin), [2003] All ER (D) 28 (Nov)).

A[8.23]

Onus of proof. Once the defendant raises the issue of self-defence the onus is on the prosecution to disprove the defence beyond reasonable doubt.

A[8.24]

Execution of legal process. An officer of justice acting on a court order can, if he is resisted, use whatever force is necessary to carry out the order of the court.

A[8.25]–A[8.30]

Justification or triviality. In a case of common assault where the information was preferred by or on behalf of the party aggrieved, if the court finds that an assault has been committed but that either it was justified or that it was so trifling as not to merit any punishment, they may dismiss the charge and issue a certificate of dismissal (see OPA 1861, s 44).

A[8.31]

Certificate of dismissal. If, after hearing such a case, the magistrates decide to dismiss the case the defendant can apply for a certificate of dismissal which will protect him from being subsequently prosecuted or sued for damages for the same assault. It is also worth noting that a defendant who has pleaded not guilty to an offence of an assault of actual bodily harm and the prosecution offer no evidence resulting in a dismissal cannot be then tried for common assault on the same facts (*R v G (Autrefois Acquit)* [2001] EWCA Crim 1215, [2001] 1 WLR 1727).

A[8.32]

Provocation. This is not a defence but may be put forward to mitigate the penalty.

Sentencing

A[8.33]

Structure of the sentencing decision. See **B[3.6]**.

Guideline: Is it serious enough for a community penalty?

Racially/religiously aggravated: Is it so serious that only custody is appropriate? The correct approach is for the sentencer to determine the sentence for the underlying offence and then uplift the sentence to reflect the element of racial aggravation (*R v Greenwood* [2003] EWCA Crim 1937, [2003] All ER (D) 305 (Jun)).

A[8.34]

Available sentences. See Table B at **B[4.2]**.

In addition to any penalty the court may decide to inflict, the magistrates have the power to bind over, with or without sureties for any reasonable period. See **B[10]**.

A[8.35]

Where a case of common assault involves injury or serious injury the court should take those injuries into account in sentencing (*R v Crown Court at Nottingham, ex p DPP* [1996] 1 Cr App Rep (S) 283, 160 JP 78, [1995] Crim LR 902). Lesser cases can often be adequately met by binding over the defendant but this must be in addition to the sentence. A prosecution witness may also be bound over but not before he has been warned that the court has this course in mind and has been given the opportunity to address the court. Caution should be exercised in such cases. Cases involving racial aggravation will often be committed [sent] either for trial or for sentence. In *Re Michael Foster* (2001) the approach for the sentencer was set out. Firstly consider the level of offending without the racial aggravation, then add to it for the racial element.

A[8.36]

Custodial sentence. See **B[2]**

A[8.37]

Community sentence. See **B[3]**.

A[8.38]

Fines. See **B[33]**.

A[8.39]

Compensation. This may be ordered up to £5,000, either as part of a wider sentence or by itself as a substantive penalty. If the offender's means are limited and a monetary penalty is appropriate, preference must be given to ordering compensation instead of a fine.

A[9]

Damage to Property

1 Criminal damage and racially/ religiously aggravated criminal damage

Charge

A[9.1]

Without lawful excuse destroyed (or damaged) property namely [ ] belonging to [ ] intending to destroy (or damage) it or being reckless as to whether such property would be destroyed or damaged

Criminal Damage Act 1971, s 1

A[9.2]

Maximum penalty and venue for trial – Where the damage or destruction is caused by fire (arson) the offence is triable either way without regard to the value of the damage caused and the maximum penalty is a fine on level 5 and 6 months' (**12 months') imprisonment. If it is alleged in the charge that the accused intended to endanger life, or was reckless as to whether life would be endangered, the offence is triable only on indictment and is punishable in the Crown Court with life imprisonment. Where the offence involves racial aggravation it will always be an either way offence (see below).

Offences of arson (s 1(3)) or where life is endangered (s 1(2)) are specified violent offences under Sch 15, Part 1, CJA 2003.

A[9.3]

The plea before venue procedure only applies to criminal damage allegations in excess of £5,000 (*R v Kelly* [2001] RTR 45, CA). If the value is ascertained as £5,000 or under the court must proceed to summary trial and the sentence will be restricted to a maximum of 3 months' imprisonment or 6 months for two offences (*R v Gwynn* [2002] EWCA Crim 2951, [2003] All ER (D) 318 (Dec)).

A[9.4]

Where the defendant does not indicate a guilty plea and it is unclear to the court whether the value of the damage is more than £5,000 or not the court must decide whether the value is more or less than that sum (it is not necessary to decide what the value is, simply whether it is above £5,000). If the court decides that the value of the damage exceeds £5,000 (and it may hear representations from the prosecution and defence to assist in arriving at a decision) then the offence is triable either way as in the preceding paragraph. Likewise if the court reaches a decision that the value of the damage does not exceed £5,000 the offence is triable summarily, as above. In those cases where the court is unable to decide whether the value is more or less than £5,000 the accused must be told that if he wishes he may consent to be tried summarily, and if he does he will be so tried and will be liable to a maximum penalty on level 4 and 3 months (** 51 weeks) (level 5 and 6 months (**12 months) in a case of aggravated vehicle taking). If the accused then consents, the trial will proceed summarily.

A[9.5]

If he does not consent, the court proceeds as for an ordinary either way offence, with the plea before venue and mode of trial procedure as is appropriate.

A[9.6]

Assessing the value of the damage. Unless the damage was caused by fire, or racial aggravation was involved, where property has been destroyed the mode of trial depends upon its value. This means what it would probably have cost to buy in the open market at the material time. See (*R (on application of DPP) v Prestatyn Magistrates' Courts* [2002] All ER (D) 421 (May)) for further guidance

A[9.7]

If the allegation is one of damage (excluding damage caused by fire) the mode of trial depends upon the value of the damage. If, immediately after the damage was caused, the property was capable of repair (eg a car windscreen) then the value of the damage is the lesser of: (a) what would probably have been the market price for the repair of the damage immediately after the damage was caused (this would, for example, not include the cost of repairing further deterioration since the offence); or (b) what the property would probably have cost to buy in the open market at the material time, whichever is the less. Thus, if it would cost more to repair the property than its probable market value, then the value of the damage for the purposes of deciding the venue of trial would be the probable market price. If, immediately after the damage was caused, the property was beyond repair (eg a shattered crystal decanter) then the value for trial purposes is its probable cost in the open market at the time of the offence.

A[9.8]

The use of the word 'probable' in the Act indicates that the court must make up its mind in the light of the available information.

A[9.9]

Multiple offences. Where an accused is charged with a series of offences of damage or destruction the offences are only triable either way if their aggregate value is in excess of £5,000.

A[9.10]–A[9.15]

Mode of trial considerations. See first the general notes at **I[4]**. In general, except for the presence of one or more of the following factors, criminal damage should be tried summarily:

(a) deliberate fire raising;
(b) offence committed by a group;
(c) damage of high value (ie in excess of £10,000);
(d) there was an element of racial motivation;
(e) a motivation against the victim's disability or sexual orientation.

Charge

A[9.16]

Racially/religiously aggravated criminal damage

Crime and Disorder Act 1998, s 30

Maximum penalty - level 5 and 6 months' (**12 months) imprisonment. Triable either way. **Crown Court** – 14 years' imprisonment and unlimited fine.

A[9.17]

Racially/religiously aggravated. This means that at the time of committing the offence, of immediately before or after doing so, the offender demonstrates towards the victim's property hostility based on the victim's membership (or presumed membership) of a racial or religious group (see *Parry v DPP* [2004] EWHC 3112 (Admin), [2004] All ER (D) 335 (Dec) for guidance on immediacy); or the offence is motivated (wholly or partly) by hostility towards members of a racial or religious group based on their membership of that group. In *DPP v M* [2004] EWHC 1453 (Admin), [2004] All ER (D) 358 (May) the term 'bloody foreigners' was held to be a group defined by nationality and was hostile. *DPP v M* was followed in *R v Rogers* [2005] EWCA Crim 2863, [2006] Crim LR 351.

A[9.18]

The victim's perceptions of the words used is irrelevant here, as is the fact that the defendant would have used those words to anyone with the victim's characteristics (*DPP v Woods* [2002] EWHC 85 (Admin) [2002] All ER (D) 154 (Jan)).

It is immaterial whether the offender's hostility is also based to any extent on any other factor not mentioned above.

Legal notes and definitions

A[9.19]

Without lawful excuse. It is a defence if the defendant proves he had a lawful excuse for destroying or damaging the property. He only has to establish that this defence is probably true, he does not have to establish it beyond reasonable doubt. Section 5(2) provides that, inter alia, the following can be lawful excuses:

(a) that at the time he destroyed or damaged the property he believed that a person or persons entitled to consent to the destruction or damage had given consent; or that person or persons would have consented if he or they had known of the destruction or damage and the circumstances; or
(b) that at the time he destroyed or damaged the property he believed that property belonging to himself or another was in immediate need of protection and that the adopted or proposed means of protection were reasonable in all the circumstances.

Provided that the defendant honestly held such a belief, it is immaterial whether the belief was justified or not (even if the defendant was drunk) (*Jaggard v Dickinson* [1981] QB 527, [1980] 3 All ER 716, [1981] 2 WLR 118, 72 Cr App Rep 33, [1980] Crim LR 717, 124 Sol Jo 847). See *R v Mitchell* [2003] EWCA Crim 2188, [2004] RTR 224, [2004] Crim LR 139, [2003] All ER (D) 99 (Aug) on possible defences to removing a wheel clamp.

Individuals facing charges for criminal damage and aggravated trespass arising out of their actions in protesting against the war in Iraq could not argue that they were using **reasonable force** to prevent the commission of a crime under s 3 of the Criminal Law Act 1977, nor that the activities of the activities of the Crown at military bases were unlawful (*R v Jones* [2006] UKHL 16).

A[9.20]

Destroy or damage. Where a defendant was initially unaware that he had done an act that in fact set in train events which, by the time he became aware of them, would make it obvious to anyone who troubled to give his mind to them that they presented a risk that property belonging to another would be damaged, he would be guilty if he did not try to prevent or reduce the damage because he gave no thought to the possibility of such a risk or having done so he decided not to prevent or reduce the risk. An example would be the man who, unawares, drops a lighted cigarette down a chair and later, on discovering the chair is smouldering, leaves the room not caring whether the chair catches light or not.

A[9.21]

Property is defined at length in s 10(1). It means property of a tangible nature and includes money. It also includes wild creatures which have been tamed or are ordinarily kept in captivity. It does not include mushrooms, fungus, flowers, fruit or foliage of a plant, shrub or tree which are growing wild on any land.

A[9.22]

Damage. Defendants who had painted graffiti on a pavement with a water-soluble whitewash in the expectation that the graffiti would be washed away by rainwater, were guilty especially since expense and inconvenience had been caused to the local authority which removed the marks before it rained. 'Damage' may be used in the sense of mischief to property. The 'temporary functional derangement' of a police officer's cap by the defendant's stamping on it constituted damage although it could be pushed back into shape. Accordingly the erasure of a computer program on a plastic circuit card was damage and although it could be restored, this necessitated time, labour and expense (*Cox v Riley* (1986) 83 Cr App Rep 54, [1986] Crim LR 460).

A[9.23]

Belonging to another person (s 10(2)). In addition to an ordinary owner this includes a person who had the custody or control of the property, or a proprietary right or interest in the property (except for an equitable interest arising only from an agreement to transfer or grant an interest), or who had a charge on the property.

A[9.24]

As far as trust property is concerned, it can be treated for the purposes of this offence as belonging to any person having the right to enforce the trust (s 10(3)).

A[9.25]–A[9.30]

Intending. The court must decide whether the defendant intended the damage by considering all the evidence and drawing from it such inferences as appear proper in the circumstances.

A[9.31]

Reckless. A person is reckless with respect to:

(a) a circumstance when he is aware of a risk, that it exists or will exist;
(b) a result, when he is aware of a risk that it will occur; and
(c) it is, in the circumstances known to him, unreasonable to take the risk (*R v G* [2003] UKHL 50, [2004] 1 AC 1034, [2003] 4 All ER 765, HL).

For a more recent example of the application of the test of recklessness see *Booth v Crown Prosecution Service* [2006] EWHC Admin 192; (2006) 170 JP 305, QBD.

Sentencing

A[9.32]

Structure of the sentencing decision. See **B[3.6]**.

Guideline: Is a discharge or fine appropriate?

Racially/religiously aggravated: Is it serious enough for a community penalty? See **A[8.33]**.

A[9.33]

Available sentences. For an offence triable either way see Table A at **B[4.1]**, for a purely summary offence see Table B at **B[4.2]**.

A[9.34]

Reference might usefully be made to the factors relevant to deciding mode of trial (see **I[4]**).

A[9.35]

Imprisonment can be ordered as well as a fine, and should be considered whenever the offence is serious or made so by its prevalence.

A[9.36]

Custodial sentence. See **B[2]**.

A[9.37]

Community sentence. See **B[3]**.

A[9.38]

Fines. See **B[33]**.

A[9.39]

Compensation. This may be ordered up to £5,000 either as part of a wider sentence or by itself as a substantive penalty. If the offender's means are limited and a monetary penalty is appropriate, preference must be given to ordering compensation instead of a fine.

A[10]–A[15]

2 Threatening to destroy or damage property

(Criminal Damage Act 1971, s 2(a))

Charge

A[10.1]

Without lawful excuse made to [ ] a threat to destroy (or damage) property belonging to that other person (or belonging to a third person), intending that the other person would fear it would be carried out

Maximum penalty – Fine level 5 and 6 months (**12 months). Triable either way.

The legal notes and definitions relating to the previous offence at **A[9]** also apply here, except for the reference to compensation and mode of trial. The threats can be spoken or in writing.

Crown Court – 10 years' imprisonment and unlimited fine.

A[16]

3 Possessing anything with intent to destroy or damage property

(Criminal Damage Act 1971, s 3(a))

Charge

A[16.1]

Had in his custody (or under his control) a [ ] intending without lawful excuse to use it to destroy (or damage) property belonging to another person

Maximum penalty – Fine level 5 and 6 months (**12 months). Triable either way.

The legal notes and definitions relating to offence no 1 at **A[9]** also apply here except for mode of trial.

Crown Court – 10 years' imprisonment and unlimited fine.

A[17]

Cruelty to animals

Charge

A[17.1]

Cruelly beating, kicking, ill-treating, overloading, torturing, infuriating, terrifying or causing by act or omission any unnecessary suffering to an animal or tethering any horse, ass or mule under such conditions as to cause that animal unnecessary suffering

Protection of Animals Act 1911, s 1, as amended

Maximum penalty – Fine level 5 and 6 months (**51 weeks) – triable only summarily.

Legal notes and definitions

A[17.2]

Each of the types of cruelty listed above is a separate offence and a charge should only allege one of them. The information should set out the act or omission alleged (*Nash v Birmingham Crown Court* [2005] EWHC 338 (Admin), 169 JP 157, sub nom Nash v Royal Society for the Prevention of Cruelty of Animals [2005] All ER (D) 285 (Feb)).

A[17.3]

Ill-treatment of a number of animals. If the defendant ill-treated a number of animals on the same occasion there may be one charge in respect of all the animals.

A[17.3A]

Unreasonably. The test to establish whether the defendant had acted unreasonably by permitting unnecessary suffering to be caused to an animal owned by him, was not to be confined so that it had to be applied objectively. It could include a subjective element. Therefore, although the suffering of an animal had to be judged objectively, it was for the court to decide whether any explanation given by the accused was or was not reasonable having regard to subjective considerations (*RSPCA v C*, March 21, 2006, DC).

A[17.4]

Abandonment. If the animal's owner or any person having charge or control of an animal abandons it permanently or temporarily, without reasonable cause or excuse in circumstances likely to cause unnecessary suffering, then an offence has been committed.

A[17.4A]

Omission. Justices were entitled to take account of the defendant's youth in determining the unreasonableness of an omission alleged to cause unnecessary suffering to an animal under s 1(a): *R (on the application of the RSPCA) v C* (2006) 170 JP 463.

A[17.5]

Necessary purpose. If pain is inflicted for a necessary purpose (e g branding) then no offence has been committed.

A[17.6]

Animal. Means any domestic or captive animal. Wild mammals are protected from any unnecessary suffering or ill-treatment under the Wild Mammals (Protection) Act 1996. Maximum penalty: fine level 5.

A[17.7]

Domestic animal. Means any horse, ass, mule, bull, sheep, pig, goat, dog, cat, fowl or any other animal of whatever kind or species whether a quadruped or not, which is tame or which has been tamed or is being sufficiently tamed to serve some purpose for the use of man.

A[17.8]

Captive animal. Means any animal (other than a domestic animal) of any kind or species, whether quadruped or not, and includes any bird, fish or reptile which is in captivity or confinement or which has been maimed, pinioned or subjected to any appliance or contrivance for the purpose of hindering or preventing its escape from captivity or confinement. However it does not include the maiming of wild animals whilst still in that state.

A[17.9]

Owner of an animal. It is an offence for the owner of an animal to permit any of the listed kinds of ill-treatment and an owner will be deemed guilty if he has failed to exercise reasonable care and supervision to protect the animal from ill-treatment. Where an owner is deemed guilty in this way he cannot be sent to prison without the option of a fine.

Sentencing

A[17.10]–A[17.15]

Structure of the sentencing decision. See **B[3.6]**.

Guideline: Is it serious enough for a community penalty?

A[17.16]

Available sentences. See Table B at **B[4.2]**.

The maximum penalty for this offence was doubled in 1987 to reflect concern at the gravity of some offences that had been committed and offences of this kind often arouse strong public feeling. Magistrates should therefore be careful to maintain some relationship with penalties for assaulting persons, lest a criticism may be sustained that a more serious view has been taken of cruelty to an animal than of cruelty to a human being.

A[17.17]

Custodial sentence. See **B[2]**.

A[17.18]

Community sentence. See **B[3]**.

A[17.19]

Fines. See **B[33]**.

A[17.19A]

Interim orders. An interim power exists under the Protection of Animals (Amendment) Act 1988, on the application of the prosecutor, to make a number of orders, variously authorising the care, sale, disposal or even slaughter of animals if it appears from veterinary evidence that such a course 'is necessary in the interests of the welfare of the animals in question' (*Cornwall County Council v Baker* [2003] EWHC 374 (Admin), [2003] 2 All ER 178).

A[17.20]

Deprivation of ownership. If the court comes to the conclusion that leaving the animal in the ownership of the defendant is likely to expose the animal to further cruelty either because of a previous conviction for this offence or because of evidence of the owner's character or otherwise, it can deprive the defendant of ownership and make such order for the animal's disposal as it thinks fit.

A[17.21]

Destruction of animal. After conviction the court, if satisfied that it would be cruel to keep the animal alive, can order the destruction of the animal and order the defendant to pay the costs involved.

A[17.22]

Disqualification. The court may disqualify the defendant for any period it thinks fit from having custody of an animal of the kind ill-treated or the disqualification may embrace all kinds of animals. The court may suspend the order pending an appeal or to allow time for arrangements to be made for the handing over of the animal to someone else. A disqualification may only be imposed in the defendant's absence if the case has been adjourned after conviction and the defendant given an opportunity to attend and make representations.

A[17.23]

After the disqualification has been in force for 12 months the defendant can apply for its removal and if refused can re-apply at intervals of 12 months.

A[17.24]

If the disqualification order is disobeyed the maximum penalty is a fine on level 3 or 3 months (**51 weeks).

A[18]

Cruelty to children

Charge

A[18.1]

Having responsibility for a child or young person under the age of 16 and wilfully assaulting, ill-treating, neglecting, abandoning, or exposing him in a manner likely to cause him unnecessary suffering or injury to health

Children and Young Persons Act 1933, s 1, as amended

Maximum penalty – Fine level 5 and 6 months (**12 months). Triable either way. Specified violent offence under Sch 15, Part 1, CJA 2003.

Crown Court – 10 years' imprisonment and unlimited fine.

Mode of trial

A[18.2]

Consider first the general notes at **I[4]**.

A[18.3]

In general, except for the presence of one or more of the following factors, offences of cruelty to children should be tried summarily:

(a) substantial injury caused;
(b) the neglect or assault repeated over a long period of time even if the harm is slight;
(c) deliberate sadistic injury.

Legal notes and definitions

A[18.4]

All or any of the types of cruelty listed in the charge above can be included in a single information but on conviction one penalty must cover the lot.

A[18.5]

The offence of cruelty can only be committed by a person over the age of 16.

A[18.6]

Exemptions. The Act expressly stipulates that a parent or teacher or other person having lawful control of a child or young person is not guilty of this offence if the child is punished by them moderately and reasonably.

A[18.7]

A child. Means someone under 14 years of age.

A[18.8]

A young person. Means for this offence someone aged 14 or 15 years.

A[18.9]

Wilfully. Means deliberately (as opposed to accidentally or by mistake or inadvertence) or because the defendant knew there was a risk or he was unaware of the risk because he did not care that the treatment of the child was likely to cause him unnecessary suffering etc. The legal adviser should be consulted on this concept and it appears that in a case of assault whether the force used was moderate and reasonable is to be decided by the magistrates. The prosecution only has to prove that the defendant intended to use *force*.

A[18.10]–A[18.15]

Assaulting. See under the charge of 'Common assault', at **A[8]**.

A[18.16]

Ill-treating. Actual assault or battery need not be proved: Bullying or frightening or any course of conduct calculated to cause unnecessary suffering or injury to health will suffice.

A[18.17]

Neglecting. Means omitting to take such steps as a reasonable parent would take and can include failing to apply for state benefits. Failure to obtain medical care can amount to neglect. It is a question of fact which the magistrates have to determine in each case.

A[18.18]

Abandoning. Means leaving the child to his fate. In one case a child was carefully packed in a hamper and sent by train to the father's address and although the child came to no harm it was held that the child had been abandoned.

A[18.19]

In another case a child had been left on his doorstep and the father knew he was there and permitted the child to remain there during an October night for six hours. It was held that he had abandoned the child.

A[18.20]

Leaving children at a youth court has been held not to be an offence under this section.

A[18.21]

Exposing. It is not necessary to prove that the defendant intended to cause suffering or injury to health. The requisite is that the defendant exposed the child or young person in a manner which was likely to cause unnecessary suffering or injury to health.

A[18.22]

In a manner likely to cause him unnecessary suffering or injury to health. This part of the offence must be proved in addition to wilfully assaulting, ill-treating, neglecting, abandoning or exposing as set out in the charge.

A[18.23]

Presumption of guilt. A parent or person legally liable to maintain a child or young person will be presumed to have neglected the child or young person in a manner likely to cause injury to health if he has failed to provide adequate food, clothing, medical aid or lodging. If the parent has been unable to provide any of these things he will still be presumed to have neglected him if he fails to apply for them under state benefits. (However the prosecution must still establish that this neglect was 'wilful'.)

A[18.24]

Dealing with the children. As the defendant is almost always over the age of 18, this offence is usually tried in the adult court.

A[18.25]–A[18.30]

Either before the charge is heard in the adult court or concurrently it is often the practice that the ill-treated child or young person is brought before the family proceedings court as in need of care and the family proceedings court can make a care order placing the child or young person in the care of a local authority.

A[18.31]

The court may direct that nothing may be published or broadcast which would identify any child concerned; the legal adviser should be consulted.

Sentencing

A[18.32]

Structure of the sentencing decision. See **B[3.6]**.

A[18.33]

Available sentences. See Table A at **B[4.1]**.

If two or more children are concerned in the same occasion then all of them can be included in one charge and if this is done then only one penalty can be imposed for the one collective charge and not a penalty for each child (s 14).

A[18.34]

If the prosecution has brought a separate charge for each child, then a separate penalty can be ordered for each charge.

A[18.35]

As mentioned above, if in the case of an individual child one information is laid alleging assault, ill-treatment, neglect, etc, only one penalty may be imposed.

A[18.36]

The court may usefully consider the factors referred to under 'Mode of trial' above.

A[18.37]

An isolated assault on a child caused perhaps by loss of temper will attract a less severe penalty than a course of conduct covering a period of time. Lord Roskill has drawn attention to the difficulties of sentencing in cases of assault on or ill-treatment of children:

> 'There are few cases which cause more difficulty to a court in assessing the appropriate sentence than cases of "child bashing". At one extreme they reveal utter brutality which must be dealt with very severely both as a punishment and as a deterrent and, up to a point, in order to assuage outraged public feeling. At the other extreme one gets cases of undoubted maltreatment, but where the explanation is to be found in social inadequacy or momentary loss of temper where a parent is utterly unable to control his feelings when he becomes angry.'

Leaving a child under three without food and water resulted in a suspended prison sentence in *R v L* [2003] All ER (D) 74 (Apr), CA, where the defendant had learning difficulties.

Where both parents are convicted, see *R v J and M* [2004] EWCA Crim 2002, [2005] 1 Cr App Rep (S) 284 for sentencing considerations.

A[18.38]

Custodial sentence. See **B[2]**.

A[18.39]

Community sentence. See **B[3]**.

A[18.40]–A[18.45]

Fines. See **B[33]**.

A[19]

Customs and excise duty

Charge

A[19.1]

Knowingly and with intent to defraud Her Majesty of the duty payable was concerned in carrying, removing, depositing, harbouring, keeping or concealing or dealing with goods, namely, which were chargeable with a duty which had not been paid

OR

Knowingly and with intent to defraud Her Majesty of the duty payable acquired possession of goods namely, which were chargeable with a duty which had not been paid

OR

Knowingly was concerned in a fraudulent evasion (or attempt at evasion) of any duty chargeable on certain goods, namely

Customs and Excise Management Act 1979, s 170

Maximum penalty – Three times the value of the goods or £5,000 fine whichever is the greater and 6 months (**12 months). Triable either way.

Crown Court – 7 years' imprisonment and unlimited fine.

A[19.2]

Drugs – Different penalties will apply in both the magistrates' court and the Crown Court if drugs are involved and in the Crown Court where there is the import or export of counterfeit money. The legal adviser should be consulted.

Mode of trial

A[19.3]

See general notes at **I[4]**.

Legal notes and definitions

A[19.4]

Knowing. If it is proved that dutiable goods were in the defendant's possession there is a presumption that he knew they were in his possession. Recklessness is not sufficient (*R v Panayi (No 2)* [1989] 1 WLR 187, 88 Cr App Rep 267, CA).

A[19.5]

Intent to defraud. The intention of defrauding the Crown of duty can be inferred from the circumstances of the case. It has been held that telling a lie to a customs officer can be evidence of an intention to defraud.

A[19.6]

The prosecution. Must be authorised by HM Revenue and Customs. Neither the police nor a private citizen can instigate proceedings on their own authority.

A[19.7]

Death of informant. If the informant (or person authorised by HM Revenue and Customs) dies, is dismissed or is absent then the Revenue and Customs can nominate another person to proceed with the case.

A[19.8]

Presumptions against the defendant. The Act is so worded that it gives to the prosecution a number of advantages in presuming certain points to be in the prosecution's favour.

A[19.9]

For example, if a defendant claims that the goods were lawfully imported or lawfully unloaded from a ship or aircraft the burden of proving these points rests on the defendant. However, the burden of proof is not to establish his defence beyond all reasonable doubt but to satisfy the magistrates that on the balance of probabilities his defence is true.

A[19.10]–A[19.15]

Mistake. If the customs officer makes a mistake and undercharges the duty, no offence is committed by a person who pays the duty realising the mistake, provided that he has not given false information or induced the error.

Sentencing

A[19.16]

Structure of the sentencing decision. See **B[3.6]**.

A[19.17]

Available sentences. See Table A at **B[4.1]**.

A[19.18]

The value of the goods, for the purpose of determining the penalty, shall be the price they might reasonably be expected to have fetched on the open market, after duty has been paid, at or about the time of the commission of the offence. See *R v Dosanjh* [1998] 3 All ER 618, [1999] 1 Cr App Rep 371, CA for aggravating features and the use of imprisonment and *R v Howlett* [1999] All ER (D) 777, CA which suggest that cases involving a loss of duty under £10,000 may be dealt with by sentences of under six months' imprisonment.

A[19.19]

Custodial sentence. Large volume, organised importation of goods such as cigarettes will usually attract an immediate prison sentence. See **B[2]**.

A[19.20]

Community sentence. See **B[3]**.

A[19.21]

Fines. See **B[33]**.

A[19.22]

Note that HM Revenue and Customs may appeal **any** decision of the court including sentence (*Customs and Excise Comrs v Brunt* (1998) 163 JP 161).

A[20]

Dangerous dogs

Offences under the Dangerous Dogs Act 1991

A[20.1]

Being the owner (person for the time being in charge) of a dog which on [ ] was dangerously out of control in a public place namely [ ] (and which injured a person)

Dangerous Dogs Act 1991, s 3(1)

Maximum penalty – Fine level 5 and 6 months' (**51 weeks) imprisonment . Triable only by magistrates.

Where it is alleged and proved that the dog injured a person (an 'aggravated offence') the offence is triable either way with a maximum penalty of level 5 fine and 6 months' (**12 months) imprisonment on summary conviction. The maximum penalty at the Crown Court is 2 years' imprisonment and an unlimited fine.

Legal notes and definitions

A[20.2]

Owner. Includes, where the dog is owned by a person who is less than 16 years old, the head of the household of which that person is a member. See *R v Huddart* [1999] Crim LR 568, CA, where the dog has been placed in the control of someone other than the owner.

A[20.3]

Dangerously out of control. Is defined to include any occasion on which there are grounds for reasonable apprehension that the dog will injure any person, whether or not it actually does so (exception is made, inter alia, for police dogs). The Act imposes strict liability on the owner (*R v Bezzina* [1994] 3 All ER 964, [1994] 1 WLR 1057, CA).

A[20.4]

The offence (under s 3(3)) of allowing the dog to enter a place, not being a public place, where it injures someone, can be committed by omission, ie where the dog escapes from an enclosed area (*Greener v DPP* (1996) Times, 15 February).

A[20.5]

Public place. Any street, road or other place (whether or not enclosed) to which the public have or are permitted to have access whether for payment or otherwise and includes the common parts of a building containing two or more separate dwellings. This will often be a question of fact based on the usage of the street (*R (on the application of the DPP) v Zhao* [2003] EWHC 1724 (Admin), 167 JP 521).

A[20.6]

It is an offence under s 3(3) to allow a dog to enter a place which is not a public place where it is not permitted to be and while there it injures a person or there are grounds for reasonable apprehension that it will do so.

A[20.7]

If this type of dog is in a car which is parked in a public place then the dog itself is in a public place (*Bates v DPP* (1993) 157 JP 1004). An inference can be drawn from the fact that a place is publicly owned (*Cummings v DPP* (1999) 143 Sol Jo LB 112, Times, 26 March).

Sentencing

A[20.8]

Structure of the sentencing decision. See **B[3.6]**.

A[20.9]

Available sentences. See Table B at **B[4.2]**; for aggravated offences see Table A at **B[4.1]**. In *R v Cox* (2004) Times, 20 February, CA a sentence of 3 months was upheld for an aggravated offence where a pack of dogs attacked a child resulting in hospitalisation.

A[20.10]–A[20.15]

Order for destruction. Where a person is convicted of an offence under s 3(1) or s 3(3) the court may order the destruction of the dog and must do so in the case of an aggravated offence, unless the court is satisfied the dog does not constitute a danger to public safety. A court should not make an order for destruction without giving the dog's owner an opportunity to be heard (*R v Ealing Magistrates' Court, ex p Fanneran* (1995) 160 JP 409, 8 Admin

LR 351). Any person having custody of the dog may be required to deliver it up to a person appointed by the court to undertake its destruction which will be suspended pending the determination of any appeal. Note that disobedience of a court order to deliver up for destruction is a criminal offence. The maximum penalty under these provisions is a level 5 fine.

A[20.16]

Additional powers. A person convicted under s 3(1) or (3) may be ordered to keep the dog under proper control or failing that the dog shall be destroyed. The court may also specify measures for keeping the dog under proper control such as muzzling, keeping on a lead or excluding the dog from entering specific places. The court may also order a male dog to be neutered.

A[20.17]

Disqualification. Whether or not there is an order for destruction of the dog the court may disqualify the person convicted (i e not necessarily the owner) for having custody of a dog for a period specified in the order. A person disqualified for having custody of a dog may apply to the court after one year to terminate the disqualification having regard to his character, conduct and any other circumstances (*R v Holland* [2002] All ER (D) 113 (Jun), CA). Where an application is refused, no further application can be considered for a further year. Costs may be awarded.

Note there is no power to make a disqualification order under s 4(1)(b) that would allow for a single dog to be kept, nor is there power to attach other conditions (*R v Haynes* [2004] EWCA Crim 390, (2004) Times, 27 February, [2004] All ER (D) 235 (Mar), CA).

A[20.18]

Having custody of a dog in contravention of a disqualification is an offence, maximum penalty a fine on level 5.

A[20.19]

Right to appeal to the Crown Court. A person convicted of an offence has an automatic right to appeal to the crown court against his conviction, sentence or any order made. In addition, where an order has been made for the destruction of a dog owned by a person other than the offender, then, unless the order was one which the court was required to make the owner may appeal to the Crown Court against the destruction order.

Other offences

A[20.20]

The Dangerous Dogs Act 1991 creates a number of offences in connection with 'fighting dogs' which are defined as pit bull terriers, Japanese Tosas and other dogs specified by the Secretary of State. It is unlawful to breed, sell, exchange, advertise for sale or to make a gift of such a dog. Accordingly, these dogs will decline in numbers with the effluxion of time. Those persons who already possess such dogs must obtain a certificate of exemption and comply with the stringent conditions attached thereto. It is an offence for an owner to have such a dog which is not registered, or to abandon it. The most common charge is for the owner or person for the time being in charge of such a dog to allow it to stray or to be in a public place without being muzzled and kept on a lead: maximum penalty 6 months' imprisonment (**51 weeks) and a level 5 fine – triable only by magistrates. It should be noted that a dog 'of the type known as a pit bull terrier' is not to be taken as being synonymous with the definition breed (*R v Crown Court at Knightsbridge, ex p Dunne* [1993] 4 All ER 491, [1994] 1 WLR 296). The provisions relating to destruction and disqualification apply as for 'aggravated offences' under s 3 of the 1991 Act. Except that where no destruction order is made in the case of a designated dog, the court must order that unless a certificate of exemption is obtained for the dog within two months of the date of the order the dog shall be destroyed. If a certificate is not obtained the court has a discretion to extend the two-month period.

Control or destruction order

(Dogs Act 1871, as amended)

A[20.21]

As an alternative to prosecution under the Dangerous Dogs Act 1991 the pre-existing civil remedy under the Dogs Act 1871 is still available and is not confined to public places nor where the dog has injured a person, but is determined by where the dog resides (*R (on the application of Shufflebottom) v Chief Constable of Greater Manchester Police* [2003] EWHC 246 (Admin), 167 JP 153). The introduction of a national jurisdiction under the Courts Act 2003 means that the case could be heard at any venue within England and Wales. In practice, jurisdiction will usually be exercised by reference to residence or where the cause of action arose.

Legal notes and definitions

A[20.22]

Application for dangerous dog to be kept under control or destroyed.

Application may be made to a magistrates' court for an order that the dog be destroyed or kept under proper control by the owner. The magistrates may in their discretion make a destruction order without the option of a control order. A dog is not allowed his 'one bite' although in most cases a control order is sufficient for the first transgression. Costs can be awarded by the court to the successful party.

A[20.23]

The proceedings must be in the form of a **complaint** and not as an **information** for an offence.

A[20.24]

The court must be satisfied (a) that the dog *is* dangerous and (b) that it *is* not kept under proper control. The dog need not be dangerous to mankind. It is sufficient if it is proved that the dog injured cattle or chased sheep. It need not be proved that the owner knew his dog was dangerous. Moreover the dog need not be dangerous by temperament if he is shown to have been dangerous on one occasion. Evidence of the temperament of the animal, however, is admissible if it shows the likelihood of its being dangerous on a particular occasion. The correct approach is for the justices to ask themselves whether on the facts the behaviour of the dog showed that it had a dangerous disposition (*Briscoe v Shattock* [1999] 1 WLR 432, 163 JP 201, [1999] Crim LR 396).

A[20.25]–A[20.30]

Change of ownership. If the owner of the dog establishes in court that he is no longer the owner of the dog but has made a bona fide transfer of the dog to some other person no order can be made against him for the dog's destruction or its proper control; but the order can be made against the new owner provided that a complaint is made against the new owner within six months from the date of the cause of the complaint.

A[20.31]

Procedure at the hearing. If the **complaint** is accompanied by an **information** alleging some additional offence (such as worrying livestock) then the **information** should be dealt with first and the **complaint** afterwards. The legal adviser should be consulted in such cases.

A[20.32]

Control order. The court may specify the measures to be taken for keeping the dog under proper control, whether by muzzling, keeping on a lead, excluding it from specified places, or otherwise. Where the dog is male, the court may order it to be neutered if thereby it would be less dangerous.

A[20.33]

Destruction order. Any person having custody of the dog may be required to deliver it up to a person appointed by the court to undertake its destruction which will be suspended pending the determination of any appeal.

A[20.34]

Disqualification. A court which makes a destruction order may disqualify the owner for having custody of a dog for a period specified in the order. Disqualification may also be imposed on conviction of an offence of failure to comply with a court order (either to keep the dog under proper control or deliver it up for destruction), maximum penalty a fine on level 3.

A[20.35]

A person disqualified for having custody of a dog may apply to the court after one year to terminate the disqualification having regard to his character, conduct and any other circumstances. Where an application is refused, no further application can be considered for a further year. Costs may be awarded.

A[20.36]

Disobedience of a court order for control or to deliver up for destruction is a criminal offence, maximum penalty a fine on level 3.

A[20.37]

Having custody of a dog in contravention of a disqualification is an offence, maximum penalty a fine on level 5.

A[20.38]

Right of appeal to the Crown Court. If an order is made for control or destruction, the owner can appeal to the Crown Court. Appeal against conviction and sentence for the criminal offences lie to the Crown Court in the normal way.

A[21]

Deception: obtaining by deception (a) pecuniary advantage, (b) services, (c) evasion of liability Making off without payment

Charges

A[21.1]

1 (a) Dishonestly obtaining for himself [or for ...] a pecuniary advantage, namely [ ], by a deception

Theft Act 1968, s 16

A[21.2]

(b) Dishonestly obtained services namely [ ] from [ ] by deception

Theft Act 1978, s 1

A[21.3]

(c) Dishonestly secured the remission of [part of] an existing liability to make a payment to [ ] by deception

Theft Act 1978, s 2(1)(a)

A[21.4]

(d) With intent to make permanent default in whole or part of an existing liability to make a payment dishonestly induced [ ] to wait for [or forgo] payment by deception

Theft Act 1978, s 2(1)(b)

A[21.5]

(e) Dishonestly obtained an exemption from [or abatement of] a liability to make a certain payment to [ ] by deception

Theft Act 1978, s 2(1)(c)

A[21.6]

2 Knowing that payment on the spot for certain goods supplied [or service done] was required or expected dishonestly made off without having paid as required or expected and with intent to avoid payment of the amount due

Theft Act 1978, s 3

A[21.7]

Maximum penalty – Fine level 5 and 6 months (**12 months). Triable either way.

Crown Court -

Charges 1 (a)-(e): 5 years and unlimited fine.

Charge 2: 2 years and unlimited fine.

Mode of trial

A[21.8]

Consider first the general notes at **I[4]**. In general, offences of deception should be tried summarily except for the presence of one or more of the following factors:

(a) breach of trust by a person in a position of substantial authority or in whom a high degree of trust has been placed;
(b) there has been sophisticated hiding or disguising of the offence;
(c) the offence has been committed by an organised gang;
(d) the victim was particularly vulnerable;
(e) there is unrecovered property of high value.

Legal notes and definitions

A[21.9]

Some dishonest activities may be caught by more than one current statutory provision and for this reason the offences shown above are included in one section in this book.

A[21.10]–A[21.15]

The basis of this offence is deception and dishonesty. Dishonesty can be inferred from the surrounding circumstances.

A[21.16]

It is an offence whether the advantage is obtained for the defendant or for someone else.

A[21.17]

Dishonesty. The test of dishonesty is (a) whether the accused's actions were dishonest according to the ordinary standards of reasonable and honest people and, if so, (b) whether the accused himself had realised that his actions were, according to those standards, dishonest (*R v Ghosh* [1982] QB 1053, [1982] 2 All ER 689, CA).

A[21.18]

Obtaining a pecuniary advantage. Includes the following:

(a) where a defendant is allowed to borrow by way of overdraft, or to take out an insurance policy or annuity contract, or has obtained improved terms for any of those arrangements; or
(b) where a defendant is given the opportunity to earn remuneration or greater remuneration in an office or employment, or to win money by betting.

A[21.19]

Deception means any deception (whether deliberate or reckless) by words or conduct as to a fact or as to a point of law. It also includes a deception as to the **present** intentions of the defendant or someone else.

A[21.20]

Obtaining services. This includes where another is induced to confer some benefit by doing an act, or causing or permitting an act to be done, on the understanding that the benefit has been or will be paid for. An example would be having a free roadside repair of one's car by the AA or RAC by dishonestly pretending to be a member.

A[21.21]

Liability means a legally enforceable liability.

A[21.22]

Payment by cheque. A person induced to accept a cheque or other security (eg a credit card) by way of conditional satisfaction of a pre-existing liability is to be treated as being induced to wait for payment, and not as having been paid.

A[21.23]

Obtains includes obtaining for a third party and enabling a third party to obtain.

A[21.24]

Payment on the spot includes payment at the time of collecting goods on which work has been done, or in respect of which a service has been provided, eg collecting one's car from a garage after repair.

A[21.25]–A[21.30]

With intent to avoid payment of the amount due. This means with intent *never* to pay the sum due. An intent merely to defer or delay payment is not enough for a 'making off' offence (*R v Allen* [1985] 1 All ER 148, [1985] 1 WLR 50, CA; affd [1985] AC 1029, [1985] 2 All ER 641, HL).

Sentencing

A[21.31]

Structure of the sentencing decision. See **B[3.6]**.

Guideline: Is it serious enough for a community penalty? *R v Mills* [2002] EWCA Crim 26 [2002] 2 Cr App Rep (S) 51 gives guidance on appropriate non-custodial sentences for first-time offenders and female defendants with children.

A[21.32]

Available sentences. See Table A at **B[4.1]**.

A[21.33]

Reference might usefully be made to the factors relevant to deciding mode of trial.

A[21.34]

Custodial sentence. See **B[2]**.

A[21.35]

Community sentence. See **B[3]**.

A[21.36]

Fines. See **B[33]**.

A[21.37]

Compensation. This may be ordered up to £5,000 either as part of a wider sentence or by itself as a substantive penalty. If the offender's means are limited and a monetary penalty is appropriate, preference must be given to ordering compensation instead of a fine.

A[21.38]

Compensation should be awarded only when it can easily be assessed. Otherwise it might be better to leave it to the county court to deal with it as a civil matter. If in doubt consult the legal adviser.

A[21.39]

If compensation is to be awarded in respect of offences taken into consideration, consult the clerk as to the maximum amount.

A[22]

Deception: obtaining property

Charge

A[22.1]

Dishonestly obtaining from [ ] property, namely [ ], with the intention of permanently depriving the said [ ] of it by deception

Theft Act 1968, s 15

Dishonestly obtaining a money transfer by deception

Theft Act 1968, s 15A

Maximum penalty – Fine level 5 and 6 months (**12 months). Triable either way.

Crown Court – 10 years' imprisonment and unlimited fine.

Mode of trial

A[22.2]

Consider first the general notes at **I[4]**. In general, offences of deception should be tried summarily except for the presence of one or more of the following factors:

(a) breach of trust by a person in a position of substantial authority or in whom a high degree of trust has been placed;
(b) there has been sophisticated hiding or disguising of the offence;
(c) the offence has been committed by an organised gang;
(d) the victim was particularly vulnerable;
(e) there is unrecovered property of high value.

Legal notes and definitions

A[22.3]

The defendant must have acted dishonestly. Dishonesty may be inferred from the surrounding circumstances.

A[22.4]

It is an offence whether the property is obtained for himself or someone else. The offence also includes the case of enabling another person to obtain or retain the property.

A[22.5]

Dishonesty. The test of dishonesty is: (a) whether the accused's actions were dishonest according to the ordinary standards of reasonable and honest people and, if so, (b) whether the accused himself had realised that his actions were, according to those standards, dishonest (*R v Ghosh* [1982] QB 1053, [1982] 2 All ER 689, CA).

A[22.6]

Obtaining property. The defendant need only obtain possession or control of the property. It is not essential that he obtained ownership.

A[22.7]

Deception. Means every deception (whether deliberate or reckless) by words or conduct as to a fact or as to a point of law. It also includes a deception as to the present intentions of the defendant or someone else. The prosecution must establish that the deception induced the person deceived to part with the property.

A[22.8]

With the intention of permanently depriving the other person of it. The court must be satisfied that the defendant had this intention, or that he intended treating the property as his own regardless of the owner's rights. The court must decide the defendant's intention by considering all the evidence and drawing from it such inferences as appear proper in the circumstances.

A[22.9]

Borrowing or lending. Obviously ordinary borrowing or lending are not offences, but borrowing or lending can amount to intending to deprive the other person permanently if the borrowing or lending were for a period and the circumstances show that the borrowing or lending were equivalent to an outright taking or disposal of the property.

A[22.10]–A[22.15]

Fraudulent letters from abroad. In a decided case the defendant posted fraudulent letters from abroad addressed to football pool promoters in England. The Court of Appeal upheld his conviction for attempting to commit this offence even though the letters were posted from abroad.

Sentencing

A[22.16]

See the notes under this heading at **A[21.31]–A[21.39]**.

For benefit fraud see *R v Graham, R v Whatley* [2004] EWCA Crim 2755, [2005] 1 Cr App Rep (S) 640, [2004] All ER (D) 320 (Nov).

A[23]

Disorderly conduct (Harassment, alarm or distress) Racially/religiously aggravated disorderly conduct (Harassment, alarm or distress)

Charges

A[23.1]

Using threatening, abusive or insulting words or behaviour or disorderly behaviour (or displaying any writing, sign or other visible representation which is threatening, abusive or insulting) within the hearing or sight of a person likely to be caused harassment, alarm or distress thereby

Public Order Act 1986, s 5

Maximum penalty – Fine level 3. Triable only by magistrates.

A[23.2]

Racially or religiously aggravated threats, abuse or insulting or disorderly behaviour

Crime and Disorder Act 1998, s 31

Maximum penalty - Fine level 4. Triable only by magistrates.

Legal notes and definitions

A[23.3]

This offence is designed to deal with such cases as groups of youths persistently shouting abuse and obscenities, rowdy behaviour in the street late at night, hooligans causing disturbances in the common parts of flats, banging on doors, knocking over dustbins and throwing items downstairs.

A[23.4]

The charge. Only one offence is created. However, the racially/religiously aggravated offence can be heard at the same time as alternative offences (*R (CPS) v Blaydon Youth Court* (2004)).

A[23.5]

Threatening; abusive; insulting; ECHR. See **A[80] and A[80.5].**

A[23.6]

Racially/religiously aggravated. This means that at the time of committing the offence, or immediately before or after doing so, the offender demonstrates towards the victim of the offence, hostility based on the victim's membership (or presumed membership) of a racial or religious group, or the offence is motivated (wholly or partly) by hostility towards members of a racial or religious group based on their membership of that group.

A[23.7]

It is immaterial whether or not the offender's hostility is also based, to any extent, on any other factor not mentioned above, nor is the victim's perception nor the defendant's usual usage of the words uttered relevant (*DPP v Woods* [2002] EWHC 85 (Admin), [2002] All ER (D) 154 (Jan)).

A[23.8]

Another person. The defendant's behaviour must be within the hearing or sight of a person likely to be caused harassment etc. The prosecution must identify the person who was likely to have been alarmed etc though he need not be called as a witness. In *Chambers and Edwards v DPP* [1995] Crim LR 896 demonstrators made it difficult for a surveyor to carry out his work. Although the surveyor was in no fear for his safety, his annoyance and inconvenience were sufficient to meet the requirements of the section.

A[23.9]

Vigon v DPP (1997) 162 JP 115, [1998] Crim LR 289 – A concealed camera in a changing cubicle is capable of being disorderly and insulting behaviour.

A[23.10]

Intent. The accused must intend his words or behaviour etc to be, or be aware that his words etc may be threatening, abusive or insulting, or intend his behaviour to be or is aware that it may be disorderly.

A[23.11]-A[23.15]

Visible Representation. *R v Norwood* [2002] Crim LR 888 set out the four elements that need to be proved in such a case.

A[23.16]

Intoxication. See under the offence of violent disorder, at **A[83]**. Disorderly conduct may be committed in a public or private place. For offences committed in dwelling-houses see under the offence of threatening behaviour below, at **A[80]**.

A[23.17]

Defences. Where the accused proves

(a) that he had no reason to believe that there was any person within hearing or sight who was likely to be caused harassment, alarm or distress, or
(b) that he was inside a dwelling and had no reason to believe that the words or behaviour used, or the writing, sign or other visible representation displayed, would be heard or seen by a person outside that or any other dwelling, or
(c) that his conduct was reasonable,

he must be acquitted. He does not have to establish his defence beyond a reasonable doubt, but only on the balance of probabilities.

A[23.18]

Power of arrest. Police powers of arrest under what was s 5 of the Public Order Act 1986 are now governed by s 24 of the Police and Criminal Evidence Act 1984 as substituted by Part 3, s 110 of the Serious Organised Crime and Police Act 2005.

Sentencing

A[23.19]

Guideline: Is a fine or discharge appropriate?

Racially/religiously aggravated: Is it serious enough for a community penalty?

Available sentences. See Table C at **B[4.3]**.

These offences are is not imprisonable and therefore sentences such as detention in a young offender institution are *not* available.

A[23.20]

Fines. See **B[33]**.

A[24]

Dog worrying livestock

Charge

A[24.1]

Being the owner of (or being in charge of) a dog worrying livestock namely [ ] on agricultural land situated at [ ]

Dogs (Protection of Livestock) Act 1953, s 1, as amended

Maximum penalty – Fine level 3.

Legal notes and definitions

A[24.2]

A dog's owner or the person in charge of a dog commits an offence if the dog worries livestock on agricultural land. A prosecution for livestock worrying can only be brought by or with the consent of the chief officer of the police, or by the occupier of the agricultural land or the owner of the livestock.

A[24.3]

Worrying livestock means:

(a) attacking livestock; or
(b) chasing livestock in such a way as may reasonably be expected to cause injury or suffering to the livestock, or abortion or loss or diminution in their produce; or
(c) being at large in a field where there are sheep except a dog owned by or in the charge of the occupier or the owner of the sheep or a person authorised by them or a police dog, guide-dog, trained sheep dog, working gun dog or pack of hounds.

Livestock is extensively defined by s 3 of the Act and means cattle, sheep, goats, swine, horses or poultry.

A[24.4]

Possible lines of defence

(a) That the livestock were trespassing and the dog in question was owned by or in the charge of the occupier of the land on which the livestock were trespassing or the dog was in the charge of a person authorised by the occupier of the land. This defence is not available if the dog was deliberately set on the livestock.
(b) The owner of the dog is not liable if at the time of the attack on the livestock the dog was in the custody of a person whom the owner considered to be a fit and proper person to have charge of the dog.
(c) That the worrying took place on land that was not agricultural land. A street or a private garden is not therefore agricultural land and some moors and heaths are excluded from the definitions of agricultural land.
(d) That the Ministry of Agriculture, Fisheries and Food has directed that this offence shall not apply to the land in question.

A[24.5]

Compensation. This may be ordered up to a maximum of £5,000 on each charge, eg for the loss of livestock, either as part of a wider sentence or by itself as a substantive penalty. If the offender's means are limited and a monetary penalty is appropriate, preference must be given to ordering compensation instead of a fine.

A[25]

Drugs

A[25.1]

The misuse of drugs is made unlawful by the Misuse of Drugs Act 1971, which introduced the term 'controlled drugs' (ie drugs, the use of which is controlled by the Act). The second schedule of the Act allocates controlled drugs to Classes A, B or C and maximum penalties vary according to the class to which a controlled drug belongs.

A[25.2]

The second schedule can be varied by an order in council. Magistrates will be able to ascertain full details from their legal adviser; the following table sets out the class of some of the commoner controlled drugs.

A[25.3]

The sections mentioned below are sections of the Act.

A[25.4]

Class A

Cocaine, heroin, LSD, morphine, opium, ecstasy (MDMA), remifentanil and dihydroetrophine.

A[25.5]

Class B

Amphetamines, codeine, dexedrine, methadrine, some derivatives of morphine, preludin.

A[25.6]

Class C

Lucofen, mandrax and villescon, Gammahydroxy-butyrate (GHB), zolpidem, cannabis and cannabis resin.

The text below concerns two drug offences which seem likely to be among the most frequently committed offences created by the Act. These are the offences created by the Misuse of Drugs Act 1971, ss 5(2) and 5(3).

A[26]

I Fail to attend for drug assessment

(Police and Criminal Evidence Act 1984, s 63B as amended)

A[26.1]

A person guilty of an offence under s 63B is liable on summary conviction to a punishment not exceeding 3 months (**51 weeks) or to a level 4 fine or both.

A[27]–A[30]

2 Fail to give drug sample

(Police and Criminal Evidence Act 1984, s 63B as amended)

A[27.1]

A person guilty of an offence under s 63B is liable on summary conviction to a punishment not exceeding 3 months (**51 weeks) or to a level 4 fine or both.

A[31]

I Possessing a controlled drug

(Misuse of Drugs Act 1971, s 5(2))

Charge

A[31.1]

Having a quantity of a controlled drug, namely [ ], in his possession

Maximum penalty

Class A	level 5 and 6 months (**12 months)
Class B	£2,500 and 3 months (**12months)
Class C	£1,000 and 3 months (**12 months)

Court can order forfeiture but see 'Forfeiture' below.

Crown Court -

Class A	7 years and fine
Class B	5 years and fine
Class C	2 years and fine

Triable either way in respect of any class of drug although see **A[31.3]** below.

Mode of trial

A[31.2]

See the general notes at **I[4]**.

A[31.3]

Possession or supply of Class A drugs should go to the Crown Court unless the offence is possession and the amount small and consistent with personal use. See *R v Cox* [1993] 2 All ER 19, [1993] 1 WLR 188, CA – possession of 16 ecstasy tablets and 1.5 grammes of crack cocaine, sentence reduced to 3 months' imprisonment by the Court of Appeal.

It should be noted that the Powers of Criminal Courts (Sentencing) Act 2000, s 110 makes provision for the imposition of a minimum seven-year custodial sentence on 18-year-olds and above who have been convicted of a third Class A drug trafficking offence.

A[31.4]

Supply of Class B drugs should go to the Crown Court unless the supply was of small scale and not for payment; possession should only be committed when the amount involved is substantial.

Legal notes and definitions

A[31.5]

Quantity. The charge should state the quantity involved. If it is a diminutive quantity consult the legal adviser. Scrapings from a pocket can be enough. A few droplets in a tube only discernible microscopically are not enough; the court must be satisfied that there is sufficient there to amount to something. If the quantity is very small it may be relevant to the question of the accused's knowledge that it was in his possession.

A[31.6]

Expert examination. The court should be satisfied that an expert has confirmed that the substance is the controlled drug alleged. In a contested case this would have to be proved by the prosecution or admitted by the defendant.

A[31.7]

Possession. In many cases this may be established by proving that the defendant had the drug in his custody. Possession can also be established by showing that the drug was in someone else's custody, but subject to the defendant's control (Misuse of Drugs Act 1971, s 37(3)). A drug which has changed its nature by digestion would not be a drug for the purposes of prosecution but evidence of digestion might go towards proving possession prior to consumption.

A[31.8]

Defences. Each of the following defences is expressly provided by the Act, but a defendant is also entitled to rely on other common law defences (see **A[31.8A]** below).

(a) Authorised by regulation (s 7). After consulting the Advisory Council on the Misuse of Drugs, the Home Secretary is empowered to introduce regulations exempting certain persons (e g doctors, dentists, veterinary surgeons, pharmacists) and controlled drugs (in certain circumstances) from the scope of this offence.

or

(b) Knowing or suspecting it was a controlled drug, the defendant took possession of it to prevent another person from committing or continuing to commit an offence with it; and further that as soon as possible after taking possession of it he took all reasonable steps to destroy it or to deliver it to a person lawfully entitled to take it (s 5(4)(a)).

or

(c) Knowing or suspecting it was a controlled drug, the defendant took possession of it to deliver it to a person lawfully entitled to it and as soon as possible he took all reasonable steps to deliver it to that person (s 5(4)(b)).

or

(d) The defendant neither knew nor suspected, nor had reason to suspect, the existence of any fact (except whether the article was a controlled drug, see (e) below) which the prosecution must prove if the defendant is to be convicted (s 28(2)); eg he did not know he possessed anything (this is where quantity might be relevant). Possession is not dependent on the accused's *recollection* that he has it. Where a man had knowingly placed some cannabis in his wallet and had later forgotten it was there, he was still in possession of it. Of course it would be otherwise if a third party had slipped it in his pocket unawares so that he never knew it was there (*R v Martindale* [1986] 3 All ER 25, [1986] 1 WLR 1042, CA). [Where the defendant knew he possessed something but denies he knew it was a controlled drug the next defence ((e) below) is appropriate.]

or

(e) In cases where the prosecution must prove that the substance or product was the controlled drug alleged in the charge and has done so, the defendant shall not be acquitted by reason only of proving that he neither knew or suspected that the substance was the particular drug alleged but shall be acquitted if he proves either:
   (i) that he neither believed nor suspected nor had reason to suspect that the substance or product was *any kind* of controlled drug, ie not just that it was not the controlled drug referred to in the charge; or
   (ii) that he believed it to be a controlled drug and that he also believed the circumstances were such that he would not be committing any offence (s 28(3)).

A[31.8A]

Common law defence of necessity. In *R v Quayle and other appeals; Attorney General's Reference (No 2 of 2004)* [2005] EWCA Crim 1415, [2006] 1 All ER 988, the Court of Appeal held that the common law defence of necessity was not available for individuals who contended that they genuinely and reasonably believed that the cultivation, production, importation and possession of cannabis had been necessary to avoid them suffering serious pain or injury by reason of their medical condition.

A[31.9]

Burden of proof upon the defendant. A defendant relying upon one of the above defences does not have to establish it beyond reasonable doubt. He need only establish it was more probable than not (see **ECHR (A[31]10)** below)

A[31.10]

ECHR. In the light of *R v Lambert* [2001] UKHL 37, [2002] 2 AC 545, it appears that the imposition of a legal burden of proof on the accused may be disproportionate to a fair trial as required by art 6 (2) ECHR. Accordingly, the MDA 1971 should be read as imposing an evidential burden on the accused ie the accused only bears the burden of raising the defence. Once raised it is for the prosecution to negative the defence beyond a reasonable doubt.

A[31.11]–A[31.15]

Cannabis. Means the whole or any part of the plant except cannabis resin or the separated mature stalk, fibre produced from the mature stalk or the seed.

Sentencing

A[31.16]

Structure of the sentencing decision. See **B[3.6]**.

Guide-line:	Possession:	Class A Is it serious enough for a community penalty?
		Class B Is a fine or discharge appropriate?
	Supply Class A or B: Are the magistrates sentencing powers appropriate?	

A[31.17]

Available sentences (Class A, B and C drugs). See Table A at **B[4.1]**.

A[31.18]

The gravity of this offence will be appreciated from the maximum penalties which may be inflicted. A difference may properly be made between 'hard' and 'soft' drugs and between possession of a large quantity of drugs for distribution (which would normally attract a custodial sentence) and a small quantity for private consumption. Heroin will almost always attract a custodial sentence.

A[31.19]

Possession of cannabis. Where only small amounts are involved for personal use a fine is often appropriate. Larger amounts will indicate a community penalty (*R v Hughes* [1999] 2 Cr App Rep (S) 329, CA). Imprisonment may become necessary for a persistent flouting of the law (*R v Aramah* (1982) 76 Cr App Rep 190, 4 Cr App Rep (S) 407, CA). The different maxima in the Crown Court should be noted and magistrates should be careful in deciding whether to deal summarily with cases involving Class A drugs and the supply of drugs on a large scale because offences of that kind will attract substantial periods of imprisonment at the Crown Court. Cultivation of large amounts of cannabis may still lead to a custodial sentence (*R v Hare* [2002] All ER (D) 98 (May), CA). Many of those who commit sexual offences, assaults, robberies and burglaries do so when they are under the influence of drugs or alcohol, and many offences of dishonesty are committed by those desperate to obtain money to buy drugs. Possession in the context of a university night club of 32 Ecstasy tablets resulted in 10 months' imprisonment (*R v Orrin* [2005] EWCA Crim 88, [2005] All ER (D) 08 (Jan)).

A[31.20]

Custodial sentence. See **B[2]**.

A[31.21]

Community sentence. See **B[3]**.

A[31.22]

Forfeiture (s 27). The court can order the controlled drugs, or anything proved to relate to the offence, to be forfeited and either destroyed or otherwise dealt with as the court may order.

A[31.23]

However, if a person claims to be owner of the drug or item to be forfeited, or to be otherwise interested in it, he must first be given an opportunity to show cause why a forfeiture order should not be made.

A[32]

2 Possessing a controlled drug with intent to supply it to another

(Misuse of Drugs Act 1971, s 5(3))

Charge

A[32.1]

Having in his possession a quantity of [ ] a controlled drug of Class [ ] with intent to supply it to another person

Maximum penalty -

Class A	£5,000 and 6 months (**12 months)
Class B	£5,000 and 6 months (**12 months)
Class C	£2,500 and 3 months (*12 months)

Court can order forfeiture, but see 'Forfeiture' above.

Crown Court -

Class A	Life imprisonment and fine
Class B	14 years and fine
Class C	14 years and fine

Triable either way in respect of any class of drug but see A[31.3]

Mode of trial

A[32.2]

See general notes at **I[4]**.

Legal notes and definitions

A[32.3]

The notes in respect of the previous offence at **A[25]** and **A[31]** also apply here except that the defences numbered (b) and (c) in para **A[31.8]** are not applicable.

A[32.4]

Intent to supply to another person. In deciding whether or not the defendant had this intention, the court must consider all the evidence drawing such inferences from it as appear proper in the circumstances. An involuntary keeper of drugs can be guilty of supply (*R v Panton* [2001] 19 LS Gaz R 36, CA).

A[32.4A]

Aggravation of offence of supply of controlled drug. A new s 4A was added to the Misuse of Drugs Act 1971 by the Drugs Act 2005, s 1. This section applies if –

(a) a court is considering the seriousness of an offence under s 4 (3) of the 1971 Act, and
(b) at the time the offence was committed the offender had attained the age of 18 years.

If **either** of the following conditions is met the court must treat the fact that the condition is met as an aggravating factor ie a factor that increases the seriousness of the offence and when giving its reasons in open court must state that the offence is so aggravated. The conditions are:

(a) the offence was committed on or in the vicinity of school premises at the relevant time;
(b) in connection with the commission of the offence the offender used a courier who, at the time the offence was committed, was under the age of 18 years.

Defence and ECHR See **A[31.9]** and (*R v Lambert* [2001] 1 All ER 1014, [2001] 2 WLR 211, CA; affd sub nom R v Lambert [2001] UKHL 37, [2002] 2 AC 545, [2001] 3 All ER 577) and Misuse of Drugs Act 1971, s 28.

Sentencing

A[32.5]

Structure of the sentencing decision. See **B[3.6]**.

Guideline: Are magistrates sentencing powers appropriate? Selling cannabis with a value of £3000-£6000 resulted in a 2½-year prison sentence in *R v Wright* [2001] EWCA Crim 1072 [2001] All ER (D) 190 (Apr).

A[32.6]

Available sentences (Class A, B and C drugs). See Table A at **B[4.1]**.

A[32.7]

The notes in respect of the previous offence at **A[31.18]** also apply here.

A[32.8]

The gravity of this offence will be appreciated from the penalties which can be inflicted. Normally prison will be considered for the supply of heroin, cocaine and ecstasy (*R v Warren* [1996] 1 Cr App Rep 120, [1996] 1 Cr App Rep (S) 233 CA). 2 years' imprisonment upheld respectively for a limited supply of ecstasy (*R v Kenyon* [2003] EWCA Crim 3446, [2003] All ER (D) 161 (Nov) and *R v Robinson* [2004] EWCA Crim 215, [2004] All ER (D) 12 (Feb) - supplying drugs to a prisoner).

A[32.9]

Supplying cannabis. The only cases likely to be heard in the magistrates' court are those of supplying small amounts gratis to a friend. Where there is a commercial motive (for example, where cannabis is supplied at a party) the offence may well be serious enough to justify a custodial sentence (*R v Aramah* (1982) 76 Cr App Rep 190, 4 Cr App Rep (S) 407, CA). Those who have supplied on a regular basis have generally received custodial sentences. Supply to a prisoner may indicate a sentence outside the magistrates' powers (*R v Alger* [2004] EWCA Crim 1868, [2005] 1 Cr App Rep (S) 347, [2004] All ER (D) 154 (Jul)).

A[32.10]–A[32.11]

Custodial sentence. See **B[2]**.

A[32.12]–A[32.15]

"Crack Houses" – Closure orders – S 2 Anti-Social Behaviour Act 2003

Closure orders. Within 48 hours of the serving of a closure notice an application must be made to a magistrates' court. If satisfied that:

(a) the premises have been used for the production or supply of a class 'A' drug;
(b) that use is associated with disorder or serious public nuisance; and
(c) the order is necessary to prevent reoccurrence,

the court can order closure of the premises for a period no longer than 3 months. Closure order applications are civil proceedings. Although closure order applications should be dealt with as a matter of urgency in *R (on the application of Turner v Highbury Corner Magistrates' Court and Commissioner of the Metropolis (Interested Party)* [2005] EWHC Admin 2568, [2006] 1 WLR 220, it was decided that the general power of a magistrates' court to grant an adjournment co-existed with the limited and specific power granted under s 2(6) of the Anti-Social Behaviour Act 2003. Accordingly, an adjournment of more than 14 days could be granted where the court was satisfied that there was a need for such an adjournment consonant with the interests of justice (*Metropolitan Police Comr v Hooper* [2005] EWHC 340 (Admin) explained).

The standard of proof applicable to making an order under s 2(3)(a) and (b) of the 2003 Act was the civil standard of proof, namely on a balance of probabilities (*Chief Constable of Merseyside v Harrison* [2006] EWHC 1106 (Admin), [2006] 3 WLR 171).

For general guidance on disclosure of evidence in s 2 applications and observations on the admissibility of and weight to be accorded to hearsay evidence see *R (on the application of Cleary) v Highbury Corner Magistrates' Court and the Comr of Police of the Metropolis and the Secretary of State for the Home Department* [2006] EWHC 1869 (Admin), (2006) Times, 12 September.

An offence in contravention of the order is punishable summarily by 6 months' (**51 weeks) imprisonment or a level 5 fine (ss 2 and 4 Anti-Social Behaviour Act 2003).

For the closure of **"noisy premises"** see s 40 of the 2003 Act.

A[32.16]

Community sentence. See **B[3]**.

A[32.17]

Forfeiture. See **A[31.22]–A[31.23]**.

A[32.18]

Drug trafficking. For the power of the Crown Court to make a confiscation order in respect of the proceeds of drug trafficking offences, see **B[19]**.

A[33]

Drunkenness

Charges

A[33.1]

1 Being found drunk in any highway, public place, or on licensed premises

Licensing Act 1872, s 12

Maximum penalty – Fine level 2.

A[33.2]

2 In a public place namely [ ] was guilty while drunk of disorderly behaviour

Criminal Justice Act 1967, s 91

Maximum penalty – Fine level 3.

Legal notes and definitions

A[33.3]

Found. Means 'ascertained to be', not 'discovered'.

A[33.4]

Drunk. Typical evidence of drunkenness is strong smell of drink, falling over, swaying, stumbling, showing evidence of a lack of co-ordination, slurred thick speech, rapid pulse, redness in the face, glazed expression, drowsiness or semi-coma and no evidence of any other cause for these symptoms. A person exhibiting these symptoms as a result of 'glue sniffing' is not drunk for the purposes of this offence or the offence of being drunk and disorderly.

A[33.5]

The offence is constituted by the state of drunkenness. The inability of the defendant to take care of himself may permit a constable to arrest the defendant. On a charge of being drunk and disorderly it is the disorderly behaviour that normally provides the trigger for an arrest without warrant (*H v DPP* [2005] EWHC 2459 (Admin), 170 JP 4.

A[33.6]

Public place. Includes buildings and any place to which the public has access whether on payment or otherwise, as well as buses or taxis. The entrance hall of a block of flats where admission was controlled by an intercom and a security lock was not a public place (*Williams v DPP* [1992] Crim LR 503).

A[33.7]

Licensed premises. This not only includes normally licensed premises for the sale of liquor but also premises given an occasional licence and includes any part of licensed premises hired out to a private party. This definition must now be read in the light of the **Licensing Act 2003**.

Sentencing

A[33.8]

Guideline: Is a fine or discharge appropriate?

A[34]

Excessive noise

(Prosecution)

A[34.1]

Problems caused by noise amounting to a nuisance, eg caused by noisy neighbours, are dealt with by proceedings for a nuisance order, see **A[61]**.

Night time charge

A[34.2]

Operating a loudspeaker in a street between 9 p.m. and 8 a.m.

Control of Pollution Act 1974, s 62

Maximum penalty – Fine level 5 (and a further fine not exceeding £50 for each day on which the offence continues after the conviction). The notes which follow only apply to proceedings brought under the Control of Pollution Act 1974, s 62 and magistrates should confirm with their legal adviser that the proceedings are in fact being brought under that Act.

Legal notes and definitions

A[34.3]

In certain circumstances loudspeakers are exempt from prosecutions as follows:

(a) those used by the police, fire, ambulance, water authority or local authority;
(b) those used for communicating with a vessel to direct it or any other vessel;
(c) those forming part of the public telephone system;
(d) those fitted to vehicles solely for the entertainment of persons in the vehicle or for communicating with persons in the vehicle or for giving warning to other vehicles if the loudspeaker forms part of the vehicle's horns or warning system but all such loudspeakers fitted to vehicles

must not operate so loudly that they give reasonable cause for annoyance to persons in the vicinity or the exemption is forfeited;
(e) transport undertakings may use loudspeakers off the highways to make announcements to passengers, prospective passengers and staff;
(f) a travelling showman may use a loudspeaker on his fairground;
(g) loudspeakers may be used in an emergency.

Except for the above exemptions there is a complete ban on the use of loudspeakers in a street between 9 p.m. and 8 a.m.

A[34.4]

Loudspeaker. Includes a megaphone and any other device for amplifying sound.

A[34.5]

Street. Means any highway, road, footway, square or court which is for the time being open to the public.

Day time charge

A[34.6]

Operating a loudspeaker in a street between 8 a.m. and 9 p.m. for the purpose of advertising an entertainment, a trade or a business

Control of Pollution Act 1974, s 62

Maximum penalty – Fine level 5 (and a further fine not exceeding £50 for each day on which the offence continues after the conviction).

Legal notes and definitions

A[34.7]

See under this heading at **A[34.3]**.

A[34.8]

Defences. It is permissible to use a loudspeaker in a street between the hours of 8 a.m. and 9 p.m. except as outlined above for advertising. However, there is an exception to this ban on advertising in the following circumstances. Where the loudspeaker is:

(a) fixed to a vehicle conveying a perishable commodity for human consumption; and
(b) is used solely to inform the public (otherwise than by words) that the commodity is on sale from the vehicle; and

(c) is so operated as not to give reasonable cause for annoyance to persons in the vicinity,

it may be operated between the hours of noon and 7 p.m. on the same day. This is the provision, for example, under which ice cream vans are allowed to use chimes to advertise their wares.

Sentencing

A[34.9]

Noise amounting to a statutory nuisance. If a noise is persistent and seriously affects persons in an area then the local authority may serve a noise abatement notice or the person affected can lay a complaint alleging that the noise or vibration amounts to a statutory nuisance. See **A[61]**.

A[35]

False trade description

Charge

A[35.1]

In the course of a trade or business applying a false trade description, namely [ ], to goods, namely [ ]

OR

A[35.2]

In the course of a trade or business supplying (or offering to supply) to [ ] goods, to which a false trade description is applied; namely [ ]

Trade Descriptions Act 1968, s 1(1)(a) and (b) respectively

Maximum penalty – Fine level 5 (individual). Triable either way.

Crown Court – Unlimited fine and 2 years' imprisonment.

Mode of trial

A[35.3]

See general notes at **I[4]**.

Legal notes and definitions

A[35.4]

Applying a false trade description, supplying and offering to supply are three separate offences and only one of them should be alleged in one charge. They are strict liability offences and the prosecution do not have to prove dishonesty.

A[35.5]

The defendant must have acted in the course of a trade or business, ie for instance, he was not merely indulging in a hobby.

A[35.6]

Applying (s 1(1)(a)). This includes affixing the description to the goods, or marking it on the goods themselves or on, in or with anything with which the goods are supplied. It is also enough if the defendant used the description in any manner likely to be taken as referring to the goods. An oral trade description is sufficient. In *Formula One Autocentres Ltd v Birmingham City Council* [1999] RTR 195, 163 JP 234 it was said that an inaccurate invoice for the service of a vehicle 'applied' a false trade description and the return of the vehicle was a 'supply' – see below.

It is not open to a person charged with an offence of applying a false trade description to rely on any disclaimer (see **A[35.10]** below).

A[35.7]

Offering to supply (s 1(1)(b)). This includes exposing goods for supply as well as having goods in one's possession for supply.

A[35.8]

Section 1(1)(a) offences usually deal with the dishonest trader and s 1(1)(b) with the careless trader, although that would not always be the case (*R v Southwood* [1987] 3 All ER 556, [1987] 1 WLR 1361, CA).

A[35.9]

Trade description. This too is widely defined and includes an indication as to quantity, size, composition, strength, performance, accuracy, results of any testing, place or date of manufacture, person by whom manufactured, history of the goods including previous ownership and use etc.

A[35.10]

Disclaimer. Where a false trade description has been applied or goods supplied to which a false trade description has been applied certain defences may be open to the accused (see below). However the defendant may deny that there is a false trade description at all. For example, the odometer (or mileometer) of a motor vehicle is a trade description. A dealer charged with an offence under s 1(1)(b) (supplying) may rely on a suitable and effective disclaimer (such 'disclaimers' often take the form of a label glued over the mileometer reading).

A[35.11]–A[35.15]

False trade description. This means a trade description which is false or misleading to a material degree. 'Showroom condition throughout' has been held to be a false trade description when the vehicle had mechanical defects. In that case a judge commented that even if the word 'throughout' had been omitted the remaining words would be taken to refer to the exterior, interior and mechanical condition of the vehicle. The test set in *Northampton City*

Council v Purity Soft Drinks (2004) Times, 14 December is 'what could a reasonable consumer think' of the description.

A[35.16]

Advertisements. If an advertisement contains a false trade description, it can be treated as having referred to all goods of the class mentioned in the advertisement. This can also be the position even though the goods did not exist at the time when the advertisement was published.

A[35.17]

If the person whose business it is to publish or to arrange for the publication of advertisements is prosecuted, he may be able to rely upon the defence of innocent publication.

A[35.18]

Where a case turns on the meaning which is to be attributed to an advertisement, consult the legal adviser for rules of interpretation.

A[35.19]

Partners. A partner of a firm may be convicted of selling goods for which a false trade description has been attached even though the sale was affected without his knowledge by another partner. The legal adviser should be consulted if this situation arises.

A[35.20]

Defences of mistake or accident. As far as any of the above three offences are concerned, it is a defence for the defendant to prove that:

(a) the commission of the offence was due to a mistake or to reliance on information supplied to him or to the act or default of another person, an accident or some other cause beyond his control. 'Another person' can be an employee. Whether or not one of the defence points mentioned in this paragraph applies appears to be a question of fact for the court to decide in each case; *and*

(b) the defendant took all reasonable precautions and exercised all due diligence to avoid the commission of the offence by himself or any person under his control. Again this appears to be a question of fact for the court to decide in each case. The House of Lords has ruled that a large company had fulfilled the requirements of this paragraph by instructing superior employees to supervise inferior employees whose acts might otherwise lead to the commission of an offence. Where this defence takes the form of attributing fault to an employee, it will succeed only if the defendant proves on the balance of probabilities that he had done all that could reasonably be expected to discover who was the person responsible. It is not enough to show that one of several persons must have been at fault.

A defendant relying on the defence of a third person's default should at least seven clear days before the hearing serve a notice on the prosecution giving certain prescribed information; if the defendant has not done this he must obtain the court's leave to dispense with the notice. If the court refuses leave, he cannot rely upon the above defences.

A[35.21]

If the offence alleged is supplying or offering to supply goods it is also a defence for the defendant to prove that he did not know, and could not with reasonable diligence have ascertained, that the goods did not conform to the description or that the description had been applied to the goods.

A[35.22]

Degree of proof required from the defendant. The defendant does not have to prove one of the above defences beyond reasonable doubt. It is enough for him to prove that one of those defences is probably right.

A[35.23]

Offences by buyers. An offence can be committed by one who buys in the course of trade, eg a car dealer, antique dealer, etc. A car dealer was convicted when, after persuading a seller that a car was dangerous beyond repair and good only for scrap, he repaired it and offered it for sale.

A[35.24]

Offence by a private individual. Where an offence committed by a trader under s 1 is due to the fault of another person, even an individual not acting in the course of trade of business, that other person commits the same offence by virtue of the Trade Descriptions Act 1968, s 23. For example, an individual knowingly selling a car with a false odometer reading to a dealer who sells it in the course of his trade (*Olgeirsson v Kitching* [1986] 1 All ER 746, [1986] 1 WLR 304).

Sentencing

A[35.25]–A[35.30]

Unlike most either way offences, trade description offences do not carry imprisonment on summary conviction. Therefore, community penalties are not generally considered appropriate because the offence or offences are not "serious enough" to warrant such a disposal. See *R v Docklands Estates Ltd* (2000) 164 JP 505, [2000] 3 EGLR 17, [2000] 45 EG 175, CA for fines levels and *R v Richards* [2004] EWCA Crim 192, [2004] All ER (D) 15 (Mar) for elements likely to take the case over the custody threshold in the Crown Court. In *R v Bore* [2004] EWCA Crim 1452, [2005] All ER (D) 12 (Feb) a conditional discharge was imposed on appeal for selling 27 falsely autographed photographs and costs of £1,000 quashed as wholly excessive.

A[35.31]

Compensation. This may be ordered up to £5,000 either as part of a wider sentence or by itself as a substantive penalty. If the offender's means are limited and a monetary penalty is appropriate, preference must be given to ordering compensation instead of a fine.

A[35.32]

Crown Court. Prison is appropriate only where there has been a deliberate dishonesty. Prison has been upheld in cases involving dishonest dealers eg traders who deliberately "clock" motor vehicles.

A[36]

Firearm or air gun or loaded shotgun in a public place

Charge

A[36.1]

Without lawful authority or reasonable excuse having in a public place (a loaded shotgun), (a firearm loaded or not and ammunition suitable for use in the said firearm) (an air weapon loaded or not) or (an imitation firearm)

Firearms Act 1968, s 19

Maximum penalty -

Firearm: Fine level 5 and 6 months (**12 months) and forfeiture. Triable either way.

Air weapon: Fine level 5 and 6 months (**51 weeks) and forfeiture. Triable only by magistrates.

Crown Court – 7 years' imprisonment and unlimited fine.

Mode of trial

A[36.2]

See general notes at **I[4]**.

Legal notes and definitions

A[36.3]

Public place. Means any highway, premises or place to which the public at the material time has access whether on payment or otherwise. This did not include a causeway linking an island to the mainland with notices declaring it was a private road (*Planton v DPP* [2001] EWHC Admin 450 (2001) 166 JP 324).

A[36.4]

Without lawful authority or reasonable excuse. The Firearms Act 1968 expressly places on the defendant the burden of proving that he had lawful authority or reasonable excuse. He only has to prove that on the balance of probabilities he had lawful authority or reasonable excuse. He does not have to prove this beyond all reasonable doubt.

(a) A certificate for a firearm was not in itself lawful authority under the Firearms Act 1968, s 19, for the holder of the certificate to have the firearm and ammunition for it in a public place.
(b) The mistaken belief by the holder of an invalid firearm certificate that it was valid and that it was lawful authority under the Firearms Act 1968, s 19 was not capable of being a reasonable excuse and therefore a defence under that section

(*R v Jones* [1995] QB 235, [1995] 3 All ER 139, CA).

A[36.4A]

ECHR. Having regard to the legitimate aims of the legislation, it is suggested that the shifting of the legal burden of proof to the accused is necessary and proportionate in ECHR terms.

A[36.5]

Shotgun. Although the firearm need not be loaded a shotgun must be loaded to establish this offence. A shotgun is a smooth bore gun whose barrel is 24 inches or longer with a bore not exceeding two inches and which is not a revolver nor has an illegal magazine, not being an air gun.

A[36.6]

Air weapon. An air weapon may be loaded or not to establish this offence. An air weapon is an air gun, air rifle or an air pistol of a type which has not been declared by the Home Office to be specially dangerous (see **A[37.7]**).

A[36.7]

Firearm. Means any lethal barrelled weapon of any description from which any shot, bullet or other missile can be discharged but for this offence excludes shotguns and air weapons as described above. A lethal weapon includes one capable of inflicting injury although not designed to do so, eg a signal pistol. An imitation firearm which is so constructed or adapted as to be readily converted into a firearm is to be treated as a firearm even though it has not been so converted (*Castle v DPP* (1998) Times, 3 April).

A[36.8]

A starting pistol which could be adapted to fire bullets if the barrel was drilled was held to be a firearm (*R v Freeman* [1970] 2 All ER 413, [1970] 1 WLR 788, CA).

A[36.9]

An offence is committed whether the firearm is loaded or not but the defendant must have with him ammunition suitable for use in that firearm.

Sentencing

A[36.10]–A[36.15]

Structure of the sentencing decision. See **B[3.6]**.

A[36.16]

Available sentences. See Table A at **B[4.1]** (firearms) and Table B at **B[4.2]** (air weapons).

A[36.17]

Custodial sentence. The more serious offences will include those committed by a former prisoner debarred from possessing a firearm. See **B[2]**.

A[36.18]

Community sentence. See **B[3]**.

A[36.19]

Fines. See **B[33]**.

A[36.20]

Forfeiture. The court can order the firearm (imitation, or shotgun or air weapon) to be forfeited to the police or to be disposed of as the court thinks fit. The court can also cancel any firearm or shotgun certificate held by the defendant.

A[37]

Firearm (purchasing etc without certificate)

Charge

A[37.1]

Purchasing or acquiring or possessing a firearm (or ammunition) without certificate

Firearms Act 1968, s 1

For shotguns see **A[70]**.

Maximum penalty – Fine level 5 and 6 months (**12 months) and forfeiture. Triable either way.

Crown Court – 5 years' imprisonment and unlimited fine.

Mode of trial

A[37.2]

See general notes at **I[4]**.

Legal notes and definitions

A[37.3]

Purchasing, acquiring and wrongly possessing. These are three separate offences and the charge should only include one of these allegations. Possession can include where a person has a firearm in his custody for another for the purpose of cleaning it, and is not restricted to physical possession but includes proprietary control (*R v Pawlicki and Swindells* [1992] 3 All ER 902, [1992] 1 WLR 827, CA). More than one person can control a firearm at the same time (*R v Hall-Chung* [2002] EWCA Crim 3088, [2003] All ER (D) 113 (Feb)).

A[37.4]

Excessive ammunition. It is also an offence to have in one's possession more ammunition than the quantity authorised by a firearms certificate.

A[37.5]

Certificate. This is granted by the police. It may specify conditions. Failure to observe such conditions is an offence. The certificate may bear a photograph of the holder and, unless revoked or cancelled, remains in force for the period specified which may be up to three years.

A[37.6]

Firearm. This means any lethal barrelled weapon of any kind from which any shot, bullet or missile can be discharged. A lethal weapon includes one capable of inflicting injury although not designed to do so, eg a signal pistol. An imitation firearm which is so constructed or adapted as to be readily converted into a firearm is to be treated as a firearm even though it has not been so converted. Two fingers inside the defendant's pocket cannot constitute possession of an imitation firearm under s 17(2) of the Act (*R v Bentham* [2005] UKHL 18, [2005] 2 All ER 65, HL)).

A[37.7]

A smooth bore shotgun with a barrel of 24 inches or more with a bore not exceeding two inches and which is not a revolver nor has an illegal magazine is not a firearm as far as this offence is concerned; nor normally are air guns, air rifles or air pistols unless the Home Secretary declares them to be of a specially dangerous type. This now includes high powered air weapons (Brococks) and all disguised weapons including those designed for use only when submerged in water (HOC 1/2004). However, an air weapon may be found to be a 'lethal' barrelled weapon capable of killing vermin etc, for the purposes of s 21(2) Firearms Act 1968 (possession of a firearm within five years of release from prison). The Court of Appeal has ruled that a starting pistol which could be adapted to fire bullets if the barrel was drilled was a firearm. In this case the barrel was partly drilled (*R v Freeman* [1970] 2 All ER 413, [1970] 1 WLR 788, CA).

A[37.8]

Ammunition. Means ammunition for any firearm as defined above. It also means grenades, bombs and other similar missiles. It also includes ammunition containing or adapted to contain any noxious liquid, gas or other noxious thing.

A[37.9]

Exemptions. If a defence is raised that a weapon or ammunition is not covered by the Act the legal adviser should be consulted.

A[37.10]–A[37.15]

Certain persons and organisations are exempted from having to hold firearms certificates such as the following:

(a) A registered dealer and his staff, an auctioneer, carrier or warehouseman in the course of his business, a licensed slaughterer in respect of his slaughtering instruments, ships and aircraft (Firearms Act 1968, ss 8–10 and 13).
(b) A person may carry a firearm or ammunition for another person who does hold a firearms certificate if he is acting under that other person's instructions and if that other person is to use the firearm or ammunition for sporting purposes only. Sporting purposes does not include the shooting of rats (Firearms Act 1968, s 11(1)).
(c) Members of rifle clubs, miniature rifle clubs and cadet corps in possession of Home Office approval do not require certificates for club or corps activities such as drilling or target practice (Firearms Act 1968, s 11(3) and Firearms (Amendment) Act 1988, s 15).
(d) A certificate is not necessary for weapons at a miniature rifle range if the miniature rifles do not exceed 0.23 calibre or if the weapons are air guns, air rifles or air pistols which have not been declared as dangerous by the Home Office (Firearms Act 1968, s 11(4)).
(e) Persons participating in a theatrical performance or rehearsal or in producing a film may have a firearm without a certificate (Firearms Act 1968, s 12).
(f) Starters at athletic meetings may have a firearm without a certificate (Firearms Act 1968, s 11(2)).
(g) A person who has obtained a permit from the police may have a firearm and ammunition, as authorised by that permit without holding a firearms certificate. The permit will usually be for short periods such as one month to allow, for example, the next of kin of the holder of a firearms certificate time to sell the weapons and ammunition after the holder has died (Firearms Act 1968, s 7).
(h) A person may borrow a shotgun or, if over 17 years, a rifle from the occupier of private premises (which includes land) and use it on those premises in the occupier's presence (Firearms Act 1968, s 11(5) and Firearms (Amendment) Act 1988, s 16).
(i) A person visiting Great Britain may have in his possession a firearm or shotgun without a certificate where he has been granted a visitor's permit. Such permits are granted by the police and may continue in force for up to 12 months (Firearms (Amendment) Act 1988, s 17).
(j) A person temporarily in Great Britain purchasing weapons for export (Firearms (Amendment) Act 1988, s 18).
(k) Museums granted a licence by the Secretary of State (Schedule to the Firearms (Amendment) Act 1988, para.1).

A[37.16]

Degree of proof. A defendant wishing to establish one of the above exemptions does not have to satisfy the court beyond reasonable doubt; he need only satisfy the court that on the balance of probabilities his defence is true. Having regard to the legitimate aims of the above legislation, the shifting of the legal burden to the accused is necessary and proportionate in ECHR terms.

A[37.17]

Antique firearms. The legislation does not apply to an antique firearm sold, transferred, purchased, acquired or possessed as a curiosity or ornament (Firearms Act 1968, s 58(2)). See *Bennett v Brown* (1980) 71 Cr App Rep 109.

Sentencing

A[37.18]

Structure of the sentencing decision. See **B[3.6]**.

Should the case be committed for sentence? (*R v Gent* [2002] EWCA Crim 943 [2002] All ER (D) 46 (Apr)) 2 years' imprisonment for possession of a sawn-off shotgun.

A[37.19]

Available sentences. See Table A at **B[4.1]**.

R v Charles [2004] EWCA Crim 1977, [2005] 1 Cr App Rep (S) 253 – 5 years when coupled with a siege and threats to the police.

A[37.20]

Custodial sentence. See **B[2]**. See *R v Clarke* [1997] 1 Cr App Rep (S) 323, CA on the use of imprisonment.

A[37.21]

Community sentence. See **B[3]**.

A[37.22]

Fines. See **B[33]**.

A[37.23]

Forfeiture. The court can order the firearm and ammunition to be forfeited to the police or disposed of as it thinks fit.

A[37.24]

The court can cancel any firearm or shotgun certificate held by the defendant.

A[38]

Firearm (trespassing in a building and on land)

Charges

A[38.1]

1 Whilst having a firearm or imitation firearm with him, entering or being in any building or part of a building, as a trespasser and without reasonable excuse

Firearms Act 1968, s 20(1)

Maximum penalty -

Firearm: Fine level 5 and 6 months (**12 months) and forfeiture. Triable either way.

Air weapon or imitation firearm: Fine level 5 and 6 months (**51 weeks) and forfeiture. Triable only by magistrates.

Crown Court – 7 years' imprisonment and unlimited fine.

A[38.2]

2 Whilst having a firearm or imitation firearm with him entering or being on any land as a trespasser and without reasonable excuse

Firearms Act 1968, s 20(2)

Maximum penalty – Fine level 4 and 3 months (**51 weeks) and forfeiture.

Mode of trial

A[38.3]

See general notes at **I[4]**.

Legal notes and definitions

A[38.4]

Trespasser. The court must be satisfied that the defendant was a trespasser which means that the defendant was personally within the domain of another person without his consent.

A[38.5]

Land. The Act provides that 'land' includes 'land covered by water'.

A[38.6]

With him. The prosecution must establish more than mere possession, namely, a close physical link and immediate control over the firearm, but not necessarily that he had been carrying it (*R v Kelt* [1977] 3 All ER 1099, [1977] 1 WLR 1365, CA). In the context of an offence under s 18 of the Act a defendant was said not to have a firearm with him when it was 2 or 3 miles away (*R v Bradish* [2004] EWCA Crim 1340, 148 Sol Jo LB 474, [2004] All ER (D) 40 (Apr), CA).

A[38.7]

Reasonable excuse. The onus of establishing reasonable excuse for his presence, when a trespasser, in a building and in possession of a firearm rests on the defendant. He does not have to prove reasonable excuse beyond all reasonable doubt. He has only to prove that on the balance of probabilities he had reasonable excuse. For ECHR, see **A[37.16]** above.

A[38.8]

Firearm. Means any lethal barrelled weapon of any description from which any shot, bullet or other missile can be discharged. A lethal weapon includes one capable of inflicting injury although not designed to do so, e g a signal pistol. An imitation firearm which is so constructed or adapted as to be readily converted into a firearm is to be treated as a firearm even though it has not been so converted. The Court of Appeal has ruled that a starting pistol which could be adapted to fire bullets if the barrel was drilled was a firearm. In this case the barrel was partly drilled.

A[38.9]

Shotguns and air weapons count as firearms for the purpose of this offence. An air weapon is an air rifle, air gun or air pistol of a type which has not been declared by the Home Office to be specially dangerous.

Sentencing

A[38.10]–A[38.15]

Structure of the sentencing decision. See **B[3.6]**.

A[38.16]

Available sentences. See Table A at **B[4.1]** (firearms) and Table B at **B[4.2]** (air weapons and trespass on land).

A[38.17]

Custodial sentence. See **B[2]**. In practice charge 2 is generally not so serious as the offence of trespassing in a building.

A[38.18]

Community sentence. See **B[3]**.

A[38.19]

Fines. See **B[33]**.

A[38.20]

Forfeiture. The court can order the weapon and ammunition to be forfeited to the police or disposed of as the court thinks fit.

A[38.21]

The court can also cancel any firearm or shotgun certificate held by the defendant.

A[39]

Football spectators

Charges

A[39.1]

1 Being a person at a regulated football match and throwing anything at or towards (the playing area, or any area adjacent to the playing area to which spectators are not generally admitted) (any area in which spectators or other persons are or may be present) without lawful authority or lawful excuse

Football (Offences) Act 1991, s 2

A[39.2]

2 Taking part at a regulated football match in chanting of an indecent or racialist nature

Football (Offences) Act 1991, s 3

A[39.3]

3 At a regulated football match going onto the playing area, or any area adjacent to the playing area to which spectators are not generally admitted, without lawful authority or lawful excuse

Football (Offences) Act 1991, s 4

Maximum penalty (for each offence) – Fine level 3.

Legal notes and definitions

A[39.4]

The creation of these offences follows the recommendations of the Taylor report into the Hillsborough Disaster. They can be committed only in respect of matches in England and Wales.

A[39.5]

Regulated football match. Means any association football match, designated, or of a description designated where one of the participating clubs is a member (full or associate) of the Football League or Premier League; it also includes international matches, and those which involve a team representing a club in a country outside England and Wales, and matches in a competition organised by UEFA.

A[39.6]

In addition, the match must take place on a ground occupied by a Football (or Premier) League Club or which is designated under the Safety of Sports Grounds Act 1975.

A[39.7]

Being or taking part at. The offence may be committed in a period beginning two hours before the start of the match or, if earlier, two hours before the time it is advertised to start and ending one hour after the end of the match. Where a match is postponed or cancelled, the period includes the two hours before and one hour after the advertised starting time.

A[39.8]

Without lawful authority or lawful excuse. The defendant must establish this but he only has to establish that his defence is probably true, he does not have to establish it beyond reasonable doubt.

A[39.9]

Charge 1: Throwing an object. The prosecution only has to prove that the object was thrown, not that a particular person was aimed at or caused alarm or distress thereby.

A[39.10]–A[39.15]

Charge 2: Indecent or racialist chanting. 'Chanting' means the repeated uttering of any words or sounds alone or with one or more others. 'Racialist nature' means consisting of or including matter which is threatening, abusive or insulting to a person by reason of his colour, race, nationality (including citizenship) or ethnic or national origins, whether alone or in concert with one or more others. In *DPP v Stoke on Trent Magistrates' Court* [2003] EWHC 1593 (Admin), [2003] 3 All ER 1086, for example, 'Paki' was racially offensive.

Sentencing

A[39.16]

Available sentences. See Table C at **B[4.3]**.

A[39.17]

None of these offences carry imprisonment and therefore a community order can only be imposed where the offence is "serious enough" to warrant such a disposal..

However, in addition to any sentence it may impose, the court will normally make a **football banning order** (at **B[40]**). These orders prevent the defendant from attending football matches in England and Wales or outside England and Wales under s 10 of the Act, if the court is satisfied, on conviction of a relevant offence, that there are reasonable grounds for believing that such an order will help prevent disorder at football matches (*R (on the application of Brown) v Crown Court at Inner London* [2003] EWHC 3194 (Admin), [2003] All ER (D) 256 (Dec)). If the court is not so satisfied, it must state that fact in open court and give its reasons. Those reasons will be recorded in the court register.

A[40]–[45]

Forgery

Charge

A[40.1]

1 Unlawfully making a false instrument with the intention that he (or another) should use it to induce somebody to accept it as genuine, and, by reason of so accepting it to do, or not to do, some act to that person's or some other person's prejudice

Forgery and Counterfeiting Act 1981, s 1

A[40.2]

2 Unlawfully using a false instrument, which is and which he knows or believes to be false, with the intention of inducing somebody to accept it as genuine, as above

Forgery and Counterfeiting Act 1981, s 3

A[40.3]

3 Unlawfully using a copy of a false instrument, which is and which he knows or believes to be false, as above

Forgery and Counterfeiting Act 1981, s 4

Maximum penalty – Fine level 5 and 6 months (**12 months). Triable either way.

Crown Court – 10 years' imprisonment and unlimited fine.

Mode of trial

A[40.4]

Consider first the general guidelines at **I[4]**. In general, forgery offences should be tried summarily except for the presence of one or more of the following factors:

(a) breach of trust by a person in a position of substantial authority or in whom a high degree of trust has been placed;
(b) there has been a sophisticated hiding or disguising of the offence;
(c) the offence has been committed by an organised gang;
(d) the victim was particularly vulnerable;
(e) there is unrecovered property of high value.

Legal notes and definitions

A[40.5]

Instrument. Means any document whether of a formal or informal character, any stamp issued or sold by the Post Office, any Inland Revenue stamp and any disk, tape, soundtrack or other device on or in which information is recorded, or is stored by mechanical, electronic or other means.

A[40.6]

False. This is extensively defined in the Forgery and Counterfeiting Act 1981. The essence of falsity in this connection is that the document should tell a lie about itself.

A[40.7]

Make. A person makes a false instrument if he alters it so as to make it false in any respect, whether or not it is false in some other respect apart from that alteration. There is no further element of dishonesty required.

A[40.8]

Intention. In *R v Tobierre* [1986] 1 All ER 346, [1986] 1 WLR 125, CA for an offence under s 3, it was held that the prosecution must prove both that the accused intended to induce somebody to accept the forgery as genuine *and* intended that by so doing he should act, or not act, to that person's or some other person's prejudice.

A[40.9]

Prejudice. An act or omission intended to be induced is to be regarded as being to a person's prejudice only if it is one which *will* result (and not merely which has the *potential* to result (*R v Garcia* (1987) 87 Cr App Rep 175, [1988] Crim LR 115, CA):

(a) in his temporary or permanent loss of property;
(b) in his being deprived of the opportunity to earn remuneration, or greater remuneration;
(c) in his being deprived of an opportunity to gain a financial advantage otherwise than by way of remuneration; or would result in someone being given an opportunity;
(d) to earn remuneration, or greater remuneration from him; or

(e) to gain a financial advantage from him otherwise than by way of remuneration; or
(f) would be the result of his having accepted a false instrument as genuine, or a copy of a false instrument as a copy of a genuine one, in connection with the performance of a duty.

In deciding whether to deal summarily with an offence of forgery the court will have regard, amongst other things, to the harm intended to be caused, or which potentially would be caused by the offence and will compare the very different levels of maximum penalty available at the Crown Court.

Sentencing

A[40.10]–A[40.15]

Structure of the sentencing decision. See **B[3.6]**.

A[40.16]

Available sentences. See Table A at **B[4.1]**.

A[40.17]

Reference might usefully be made to the factors relevant to deciding mode of trial on assessing seriousness.

A[40.18]

Custodial sentence. See **B[2]**

A[40.19]

Community sentence. See **B[3]**.

A[40.20]

Fines. See **B[33]**.

A[40.21]

Compensation. This may be ordered up to £5,000 either as part of a wider sentence or by itself as a substantive penalty. If the offender's means are limited and a monetary penalty is appropriate, preference must be given to ordering compensation instead of a fine.

A[46]

Found on enclosed premises

Charge

A[46.1]

Being found in or upon any dwelling-house, warehouse, outhouse, or in any enclosed yard, garden or area for an unlawful purpose

Vagrancy Act 1824, s 4

Maximum penalty – For a first offence fine level 3 or 3 months. For a subsequent offence the accused may sometimes be committed to the Crown Court as an incorrigible rogue for sentence.

**For an offence committed from a date to be appointed, the power to impose imprisonment will be repealed by the CJA 2003, Sch 25. In addition the power to commit the offender as an incorrigible rogue to the Crown Court will be repealed by the CJA 2003, Sch 37, Part 9.

Legal notes and definitions

A[46.2]

Found. The defendant must have been found there although his arrest happened elsewhere.

A[46.3]

Enclosed. The yard may still rate as being enclosed even if there is access through spaces in surrounding buildings, an archway, open gate, etc but does not include a room within a building (*Talbot v DPP* [2000] 1 WLR 1102, 164 JP 169, sub nom Talbot v Oxford City Magistrates' Court [2000] 2 Cr App Rep 60).

A[46.4]

Yard. Would not include a very large area, such as a shipyard or railway sidings, the essential feature of a yard is that it should be a relatively small area ancillary to a building.

A[46.5]

Unlawful purpose. Means that the defendant was there for the purpose of committing a criminal offence. In deciding whether the defendant had such a purpose, the court must consider all the evidence drawing such inferences from it as appear proper in the circumstances.

Sentencing

A[46.6]

Structure of the sentencing decision. See **B[3.6]**.

A[46.7]

Available sentences. See Table B at **B[4.2]**.

A[46.8]

Custodial sentence. See **A[46.1] and B[2]**.

A[46.9]

Community sentence. See **A46.1 and B[3]**.

A[46.10]–A[46.15]

Fine. See **B[33]**.

A[46.16]

Committal for sentence. For a subsequent offence, as long as the previous offence was **not** dealt with by absolute or conditional discharge the court may commit the defendant to the Crown Court for sentence on bail or in custody as an incorrigible rogue. The Crown Court can impose imprisonment for up to one year. **For offences committed on or after a date to be appointed the power to imprison or commit for sentence has been repealed.

A[46.17]

Even if there is no previous conviction for a similar offence but there is evidence of previous convictions under the Vagrancy Act 1824, then this procedure may still be available to the magistrates. **See **A[46.16]** above.

A[47]

Going equipped for stealing

Charge

A[47.1]

Having, when not at his place of abode, an article, namely a [ ], for use in the course of burglary, theft or cheat

Theft Act 1968, s 25

Maximum penalty – Fine level 5 and 6 months (**12 months). Triable either way.

Crown Court – 3 years' imprisonment and unlimited fine.

Motor vehicles. If the defendant intended to steal or take a motor vehicle the offence is not endorsable nor are penalty points applicable but disqualification may be ordered.

Mode of trial

A[47.2]

See general notes at **I[4]**.

Legal notes and definitions

A[47.3]

Theft includes taking a conveyance without the owner's consent.

A[47.4]

Cheat means an offence of obtaining by deception.

A[47.5]

If the article was made or adapted for use in committing a burglary, theft or obtaining property by deception, the court can treat that as evidence that the defendant had the article with him for such use.

A[47.6]

The offence can be committed by day or night. The offence cannot take place at the defendant's place of abode. It must be proved that he had the articles with him for the purpose of using them in connection with burglary, theft or obtaining property by deception though it is not necessary for the prosecution to prove that the defendant intended to use them himself. An intention to use the item if the opportunity arose would be sufficient to convict the accused, but it would not be sufficient where he had not actually decided whether to use the item if the opportunity presented itself.

A[47.7]

More than one article may be specified in the charge without offending the rule against duplicity.

Sentencing

A[47.8]

Structure of the sentencing decision. See **B[3.6]**.

Guideline: Is it serious enough for a community penalty?

A[47.9]

Available sentences. See Table A at **B[4.1]**.

A[47.10]–A[47.15]

The relative gravity of this offence will vary with the circumstances in each case but by convicting the defendant of this offence the court is saying that it believes the defendant had placed himself in a position to commit a serious offence. Absolute or conditional discharge therefore would not usually be appropriate.

A[47.16]

Custodial sentence. See **B[2]**.

A[47.17]

Community sentence. See **B[3]**.

A[47.18]

Fines. See **B[33]**.

A[47.19]

Forfeiture. The court may deprive the defendant of any property in his possession which was, or was intended to be, used for committing a crime, see Forfeiture order, at **B[34]**.

A[48]

Grievous bodily harm, malicious wounding and racially/religiously aggravated grievous bodily harm and malicious wounding

(Offences Against the Person Act 1861, s 20)

Charges

A[48.1]

Unlawfully and maliciously inflicting grievous bodily harm

A[48.2]

Unlawfully and maliciously wounding

Offences against the Person Act 1861, s 20

Maximum penalty – Fine level 5 and 6 months (**12 months). Triable either way. Specified violent offence under Sch 15, Part 1, CJA 2003.

Crown Court - 5 years and unlimited fine.

Racially/religiously aggravated offences.

Maximum penalty - Fine level 5 and 6 months (**12 months). Triable either way. Specified violent offence under Sch 15, Part 1, CJA 2003.

Crown Court - 7 years and unlimited fine.

Mode of trial

A[48.3]

In general, cases should be tried summarily unless the court considers that one or more of the features below is present in the case and that its sentencing powers are insufficient:

(a) the use of a weapon likely to cause serious injury;
(b) a weapon is used and serious injury is caused;

(c) more than minor injury is caused by kicking, headbutting or similar forms of assault;
(d) serious violence is caused to those whose work has to be done in contact with the public, eg police officers, bus drivers, taxi drivers, publicans and shopkeepers;
(e) violence to vulnerable people, eg the elderly and infirm;
(f) the offence has clear racial motivation.

The same considerations apply to cases of domestic violence.

A[48.4]

For guidance on mode of trial see notes at **I[4]**.

Legal notes and definitions

A[48.5]

Intent. 'Maliciously' means intentionally or recklessly (*R v Mowatt* [1968] 1 QB 421, [1967] 3 All ER 47, CA) and 'recklessly' means that the accused foresaw the particular risk and yet went on to take it (*R v Cunningham* [1957] 2 QB 396, [1957] 2 All ER 412, CCA). In offences under the Offences Against The Person Act 1861, s 20 what must be intended or foreseen is that some physical harm might occur, not necessarily amounting to grievous bodily harm or wounding. An intention to frighten is not enough. (*DPP v A* [2000] All ER (D) 1247). In *Re Dica* (5 May 2004, unreported), CA it was held that where a person, knowing he suffers from a serious sexual disease, infects another through consensual sex (but not deliberately intending to pass on the disease) he will be guilty of the offence, so long as the victim did not consent to the risk of infection. An honest belief in an informed consent will amount to a defence (*R v Konzani* [2005] EWCA Crim 706, [2005] All ER (D) 292 (Mar)).

A[48.6]

Grievous bodily harm. Means really serious bodily harm. The injuries caused do not have to be permanent or dangerous, but they have to be more severe than actual bodily harm. (See **A[1]**.)

A[48.7]

Provocation is no defence, but can be taken into account when sentencing.

[48.8]

Racial/religious aggravation (See **A[8.7]**.)

A[48.9]

Misadventure (See **A[8.8]**.)

A[48.10]–A[48.15]

Consent (See **A[8.10]–A[8.17]**.)

A[48.16]

Lawful sport (See **A[8.18]**.)

A[48.17]

Trespasser on property (See **A[22]**.)

A[48.18]

Execution of legal process (See **A[8.24]**.)

A[48.19]

Reduction of charge/alternative verdict. The court cannot reduce this charge to a less serious one (eg actual bodily harm or common assault); but if a separate charge for a lesser offence has been preferred there could be a conviction for that. Consult a legal adviser and **A[8.31]** on the effect of a dismissal for common assault.

Sentencing

A[48.20]

Structure of the sentencing decision. See **B[3.6]**.

Guideline: For either offence, are the magistrates' sentencing powers appropriate?

A[48.21]

Available sentences. See Table A at **B[4.1]**.

A[48.22]

Although the maximum penalty for these offences is the same as that for 'Actual bodily harm' (at **A[1]**), offences under s 20 are regarded as more serious. The factors set out under 'Sentencing' at **A[1.31]** will be relevant here. Guidelines on the mode of trial decision encourage magistrates to accept jurisdiction in more serious cases. However, where aggravating features such as a gang attack or the use of a weapon exist the magistrates must be prepared to use the full range of their powers which include up to 6 (**12) months' imprisonment or, in appropriate cases, committal for sentence. [NB: Committal for sentence can only follow an indication of a plea of guilty on the mode of trial or, following conviction, on the grounds that the offender is dangerous.]

A[48.23]

Decided cases in the Court of Appeal have been mainly concerned with sentences for offences too serious to be heard by magistrates, but occasionally in cases which might now be within the jurisdiction of justices, sentences of up to 6 (**12) months' immediate custody have been imposed. This is even truer in a case of racially aggravated wounding. In *A-G v Charlton* (2004) 148 Sol Jo LB 539, CA a 3 year sentence of imprisonment was imposed for stabbing a black youth in the neck.

A[48.24]

Compensation. This may be ordered up to £5,000 either as part of a wider sentence or by itself as a substantive penalty. If the offender's means are limited and a monetary penalty is appropriate, preference must be given to ordering compensation instead of a fine.

A[48.25]–A[48.30]

The court may deprive the defendant of any property in his possession which was used or intended to be used to commit the offence.

A[48.31]

Custodial sentence. See **B[2]**.

A[48.32]

Community sentence. See **B[3]**.

A[48.33]

Fines. See **B[33]**.

A[48.34]

Husband and wife. See the notes at **A[1.39]–A[1.40]** under this heading.

A[48.35]

Licensed premises. If the offence took place on licensed premises an exclusion order may be made. See **B[32]**.

A[49]

Handling stolen goods

Charge

A[49.1]

Handled stolen goods, namely [ ], knowing or believing them to have been stolen

Theft Act 1968, s 22

Maximum penalty – Fine level 5 and 6 months (**12 months). Triable either way.

Crown Court – 14 years' imprisonment and unlimited fine.

Mode of trial

A[49.2]

Consider first the general guidelines at **I[4]**. In general, handling offences should be tried summarily except for the presence of one or more of the following factors:

(a) the handler commissioned the offence;
(b) the offence has professional hallmarks;
(c) the property is of high value (ie more than £10,000).

Legal notes and definitions

A[49.3]

The prosecution must prove that the goods were:

(a) stolen; or
(b) obtained by deception; or
(c) obtained by blackmail.

Also that the defendant knew or believed the goods had been obtained by one of those methods (see below).

A[49.4]

Handling. Any of the following actions can constitute handling:

(a) dishonestly receiving the goods; or
(b) dishonestly undertaking in the retention, removal, disposal or realisation of the goods by or for the benefit of another; or
(c) dishonestly assisting in the retention, removal, disposal or realisation of the goods by or for the benefit of another; or
(d) arranging to do (a) or (b) or (c).

Thus a defendant who has not himself personally handled goods can be convicted for this offence.

A[49.5]

As far as (c) is concerned failure to reveal stolen goods during a police search does not amount to 'dishonestly assisting in the retention of stolen goods'. 'Assisting' means helping or encouraging, amongst other things. It would be otherwise where deliberate lies were told to the police.

A[49.6]

If the only evidence against the defendant is that of the thief, it may be unsafe to convict and the legal adviser should be consulted.

A[49.7]

Goods. Includes money and every kind of property except land. The term also includes things severed from land by stealing.

A[49.8]

Knowledge or belief. Mere suspicion which does not amount to knowledge or belief is not sufficient to justify conviction. The state of the defendant's mind must be judged subjectively, ie what did *this* defendant know, or believe, not what did he suspect.

A[49.9]

The word 'believe' has its ordinary meaning of holding something to be true.

A[49.10]–A[49.15]

In a case decided in 1985 (*R v Hall*), the Lord Chief Justice presided in a court which gave some examples of what might amount to knowledge and what might amount to belief. A man might be said to *know* that goods were stolen when he was told by someone with first-hand knowledge, such as the thief, that such was the case. *Belief* was something short of knowledge. It might be said to be the state of mind of a person who said to himself: 'I cannot say I know for certain that those goods are stolen, but there can be no other reasonable conclusion in the light of all the circumstances of all I have heard and seen.' It was enough for belief even if the person said to himself: 'Despite all that I have seen and heard, I refuse to believe what my brain tells me is obvious.'

A[49.16]

What was insufficient was a mere suspicion: 'I suspect that these goods may be stolen but on the other hand they may not be stolen.' That state of mind does not fall within the words 'knowing or believing'. Contrast the intention under s 22 with an offence under say, s 329 of the Proceeds of Crime Act 2002 (acquisition, use and possession of criminal property).

Sentencing

A[49.17]

Structure of the sentencing decision. See **B[3.6]**.

Guideline: Is it serious enough for a community penalty?

A[49.18]

Available sentences. See Table A at **B[4.1]**.

A[49.19]

The gravity of this offence varies with the circumstances but it should be regarded at least as seriously as theft. If the property was of low monetary value and acquired for the receiver's own use, then a moderate fine or, in some cases, especially if a fine could not be paid by the defendant, a discharge is appropriate, for example for someone of previous good character handling low value domestic goods for his own use, low value being some figure under four figures.

A[49.20]

On the other hand, irrespective of value, the presence of any of the aggravating factors above is likely to result in a community sentence, not a fine or a discharge, for example, where property of value below four figures was acquired for resale by a handler, or where more valuable goods were acquired for the handler's own use. Such a sentence might be appropriate for a young offender with little criminal experience, playing a peripheral role.

A[49.21]

Custody threshold. Offenders with a significant record of dishonesty, or who engaged in sophisticated law breaking, would attract a custodial sentence. The aggravating and mitigating features above would have a bearing on length (*R v Webbe* [2001] EWCA Crim 1217 [2002] 1 Cr App Rep (S) 82).

A[49.22]

Custodial sentence. See **B[2]**.

A[49.23]

Community sentence. See **B[3]**.

A[49.24]

Fines. See **B[33]**.

A[49.25]–A[49.30]

Compensation. This may be ordered up to £5,000 either as part of a wider sentence or by itself as a substantive penalty. If the offender's means are limited and a monetary penalty is appropriate, preference must be given to ordering compensation instead of a fine. The defendant may be deprived of any property in his possession which was used or intended for use in the commission of the offence.

A[50]

Harassment and racially/ religiously aggravated harassment

Charges

A[50.1]

1 Did pursue a course of conduct amounting to harassment of another which he knew or ought to have known amounted to harassment

Protection from Harassment Act 1997, s 2

Maximum penalty – Fine level 5 and 6 months (**51 weeks) summary only.

A[50.2]

2 Did pursue a course of conduct on two or more occasions, causing another to fear that violence would be used against him, which he knew or ought to have known would cause that other person to fear violence would be used against him

Protection from Harassment Act 1997, s 4

Maximum penalty – Fine level 5 and 6 months (**12 months). Triable either way. Specified violent offence under Sch 15, Part 1, CJA 2003.

Crown Court – 5 years' imprisonment and unlimited fine.

A[50.3]

3 Racially/religiously aggravated conduct amounting to harassment of another etc

Crime and Disorder Act 1998, s 32

Maximum penalty - Fine level 5 and 6 months (**12 months). Triable either way.

Crown Court - 2 years' imprisonment and unlimited fine.

A[50.4]

4 Racially/religiously aggravated course of conduct on two or more occasions causing fear of violence etc

Crime and Disorder Act 1998, s 32

Maximum penalty - Fine level 5 and 6 months (**12 months). Triable either way. Sch 15, Part 1, CJA 2003 does not identify this offence as a "specified violent offence". This would appear to be a drafting error given the classification of the basic offence under s 4 PHA 1997 above.

Crown Court - 7 years' imprisonment and unlimited fine.

In response to animal rights protests and the like the Serious Organised Crime and Police Act 2005 amends the Protection from Harassment Act to make it an offence to harass two or more persons with the intention of persuading them not to do something they are required or entitled to do, or to do something they are not required to do. A course of conduct may involve conduct on just one occasion for each victim if there is more than one.

Section 126 of the Act adds s 42A to the Criminal Justice and Police Act 2001 and creates an offence of harassment of a person in his home. Punishable with fine level 4 and 4 months (**the maximum term of imprisonment may be subject to alteration under s 280(2) CJA 2003). Triable only by magistrates.

Mode of trial

A[50.5]

Consider first the general guidelines at **I[4]**. In general trial before the magistrates will be appropriate except for the presence of one or more of the following factors:

(a) the victim was particularly vulnerable;
(b) there was a racial motivation;
(c) the course of conduct complained of took place over a long period of time.

Note that the Crown Court can bring in an alternative verdict under the Protection from Harassment Act 1997, s 2 but the magistrates cannot.

Legal notes and definitions

A[50.6]

Course of conduct denotes actions taking place on at least two occasions. In the case of a s 4 offence the victim must have been put in fear that violence would have been used against him on at least two of those occasions (*Caurti v DPP* [2002] Crim LR 131). The fewer the incidents and the wider apart they are spread, the less likely it is that a finding of harassment can reasonably be made (*Lau v DPP* [2000] 1 FLR 799, [2000] Fam Law 610). In *Pratt v DPP* [2001] EWHC Admin 483 (2001) 165 JP 800 incidents three months apart were said to be borderline, while in *Kelly v DPP* [2002] All ER (D) 177 (Jun) nine telephone calls all within five minutes amounted to a course of conduct even though the victim listened to them as recorded messages at the same time. A threat to harm a person's dog may be inferred to be a threat directed at them (*R v DPP* [2001] EWHC Admin 17 (2001) 165 JP 349).

At least one of the incidents relied on by the prosecution must have occurred within the 6 months limitation period for summary proceedings (*DPP v Baker* (2004) 169 JP 140, [2004] All ER (D) 28 (Nov), DC).

A[50.7]

Knows or ought to have known. In the case of the defendant this means that he will be presumed to have that knowledge if a reasonable person in possession of the same information would think the course of conduct would amount to harassment or cause the other person to fear violence would be used against him.

A[50.8]

Racial aggravation. See **A[1.16]** and **A[23]**.

May be heard together with a harassment charge as an alternative (*R (CPS) v Blaydon Youth Court* [2004] EWHC 2296 (Admin), [2004] All ER (D) 45 (Oct)).

A[50.9]

Defences. The Protection from Harassment Act 1997 gives three possible defences if the defendant can show:

(a) his course of conduct was pursued for the purposes of preventing or detecting crime;
(b) that it was pursued under an enactment or rule of law;
(c) that in the particular circumstances the course of conduct was reasonable and in the case of a s 4 offence that it was reasonable for the protection of himself or another or his or another's property.

A[50.9A]

ECHR. Under the ECHR if would appear that it is sufficient for the defendant to raise one or other of the above defences. Once raised, it is for the prosecution to negative that defence(s) beyond a reasonable doubt.

Sentencing

A[50.10]–A[50.15]

Structure of the sentencing decision. See **B[3.6]**.

Guideline: Is it so serious that only custody is appropriate?

Racially/religiously aggravated: Are the magistrates' sentencing powers appropriate?

A[50.16]

Available sentences. See Table A at **B[4.1]**.

A[50.17]

The relative gravity of this offence will vary with the circumstances in each case, but by convicting the defendant of this offence the court is saying that it believes the defendant had harassed or put another in fear of violence and consequently it should always be treated seriously. A history of previous breaches of court orders or a second conviction will normally indicate a committal to the Crown Court for sentence (*R v Liddle* [1999] 3 All ER 816, [2000] 1 Cr App Rep (S) 131, CA).

A[50.18]

Restraining orders. On conviction under the Protection from Harassment Act 1997, s 2 or s 4 the court can (in addition to any other sentencing disposal) make a restraining order to protect the victim or any named person from further conduct which would amount to harassment or which would cause the fear of violence. The order can be made for a determinate or indeterminate period of time. (From a date to be appointed, under s 5A the same power arises on acquittal if the court is satisfied a person needs to be protected from harassment by the defendant). In the case of a prison sentence a copy of the order should be sent to the prison. Any order should be specific and name parties protected by it (*R v Mann* (2000) 144 Sol Jo LB 150, CA).

In *R v Debnath* (2 December 2005, unreported), the Court of Appeal stated that when considering whether or not to make a restraining order the following principles applied: (i) the purpose of a restraining order was to prohibit particular conduct with a view to protecting the complainant from further offences; (ii) the order had to be clear and in precise terms so that there could be no doubt as to what the defendant was prohibited from doing; (iii) the order had to be practical in its terms; (iv) when considering the terms, or the extent of an order, the court had to have regard to the issue of proportionality; and (v) the power to vary or discharge an order was an important safeguard and the Court of Appeal would be unlikely to interfere with the order where an application could be made to the court that made the order for its variation or discharge.

Breach of restraining order. This is an offence punishable at the Crown Court with 5 years' imprisonment or a fine and by the magistrates with 6 (**12) months' imprisonment or a fine level 5. Deliberate breach of an order is likely to result in custody (*R v Goble* [2003] EWCA Crim 3171, [2004] 2 Cr App Rep (S) 12, [2003] All ER (D) 450 (Oct)).

In *McCaskill v DPP* [2005] EWHC 3208 (Admin), 170 JP 301, the defendant was charged with sending letters between January and November 2004 in contravention of a restraining order imposed by the Crown Court. It was held that the breach was not duplicitous and therefore complied with the legal requirements of s 5(5) and (6) PHA 1997.

Variation of restraining order. Where a restraining order has been made for a specified period of time, on a true construction of s 5(4), a court had power to vary a restraining order by extending the expiry date of the order (*DPP v Kevin Hall* [2005] EWHC 2612 (Admin), [2006] 3 All ER 170).

A[50.19]

Custodial sentence. A sentence of 12 months' imprisonment was upheld in *R v Hill* [2000] 1 Cr App Rep (S) 8, CA for an offence involving threat of rape to a girl aged 14. See **B[2]**.

A[50.20]

Community sentence. See **B[3]**.

A[50.21]

Fines. See **B[33]**.

A[50.22]

Compensation. This may be ordered for terror or distress caused (*Bond v Chief Constable of Kent* [1983] 1 All ER 456, [1983] 1 WLR 40): see **B[18]**.

A[51]

Health and safety at work

Charges

A[51.1]

Did fail to comply with an improvement or prohibition notice (specified)

Health and Safety at Work Act 1974, s 33(2A)

A[51.2]

Did fail to comply with an order of the court to remedy (specified)

Health and Safety at Work Act 1974, s 33(2A)

Maximum penalty - Fine £20,000 and 6 months (**12 months). Triable either way.

Crown Court - 2 years' imprisonment and unlimited fine.

A[51.3]

Did fail to comply with a duty specified in the Health and Safety at Work Act 1974, ss 2–6 (for example), under s 3(1) did fail to conduct an undertaking in such a way as to ensure, so far as is reasonably practicable, that persons not in your employment, who may be affected thereby, were not exposed to risks to their health and safety.

Health and Safety at Work Act 1974, s 33(1A)

Maximum penalty - Fine £20,000. Triable either way.

Crown Court - Unlimited fine.

A[51.4]

Other breaches of the Act or Regulations

Triable summarily only - Fine level 5.

Mode of trial

A[51.5]

See general notes at **I[4]**.

A[51.6]

Offences having an impact on the public at large and breaches of licensing requirements (for example in relation to asbestos, explosives or nuclear plant) may indicate trial on indictment.

Legal notes and definitions

A[51.7]

The Health and Safety at Work Act 1974 imposes general duties on employers towards their employees, self-employed persons, persons connected with premises other than employees and articles and substances for use at work in ss 2–6. Most prosecutions are now brought under these sections.

A[51.8]

Specific offences are detailed in the Health and Safety at Work Act 1974, s 33.

A[51.9]

Offences by bodies corporate. Where an offence committed by a body corporate is proved to have been committed with the consent or connivance of or attributable to neglect by a director, manager, secretary or other officer of the company, he as well as the company shall be guilty of that offence and may be proceeded against.

A[51.10]–A[51.15]

Prosecution by inspectors. An inspector if authorised by the enforcement authority may prosecute before a magistrates' court.

A[51.16]

Power to order remedial action. Where it appears to the court that the defendant can remedy matters they may in addition to or instead of a punishment order him within a given time to remedy the matters complained of (s 42).

A[51.17]

Work means work as an employee, or self-employed person. Regulations may extend the meaning of work to include at work.

A[51.18]

Article for use at work, means any plant designed for use or operation by persons at work and any article designed for use as a component in any such plant.

Defences

A[51.19]

Typical prosecutions involve breaches of duty to safeguard health and safety so far as **is reasonably practicable as well as specific requirements under regulations.** It is therefore a common defence that an employer has safe systems of work and has done all that was reasonably practicable to avoid a breach of duty.

ECHR. This is a legal rather than an evidential burden on the defendant and the reverse burden of proof is compatible with the presumption of innocence under the ECHR (*R v Davies* [2002] EWCA Crim 2949, [2002] All ER (D) 275 (Dec), sub nom Davies v Health and Safety Executive [2003] IRLR 170, 147 Sol Jo LB 29).

Sentencing

A[51.20]

Aggravating and mitigating factors. Factors which may aggravate an offence are:

- a deliberate or reckless breach of the law rather than carelessness;
- action or lack of action prompted by financial motives-profit or cost saving;
- disregarding warnings from a regulatory authority or the workforce;
- an awareness of the specific risks likely to arise from action taken;
- lack of co-operation with a regulatory authority;
- serious extent of damage resulting from offence (but lack of actual damage does not render the offence merely technical; it is still serious if there is risk);
- previous offences of a similar nature;
- death or serious injury or ill health of humans has been a consequence of the offence;
- animal health or flora affected.

Factors in mitigation may include:

- the offender's minor role with little personal responsibility;
- genuine lack of awareness or understanding of specific regulations;
- an isolated lapse.

There may be some offender mitigation:

- prompt reporting;
- ready co-operation with regulatory authority;
- good previous record;
- timely guilty plea.

Costs

A[51.21]

The prosecution will normally claim the costs of investigation and presentation. These may be substantial and can incorporate time and activity expended on containing and making the area safe.

A[51.22]

Very high fines are often imposed on companies and individuals for serious breaches of health and safety legislation: *R v Keltbray Ltd* [2000] All ER (D) 705, [2001] 1 Cr App Rep (S) 132, CA. Fines on companies need to be large enough to bring the message to managers and shareholders alike. Where the court is of the opinion that the offence or the combination of the offence and other offences associated with it was so serious that greater punishment should be inflicted for it than the court has power to impose, the defendant, whether an individual or a company, may be committed to the Crown Court for sentence: **see however **B[16]** and the changes to the powers of magistrates' courts to commit for sentence as a result of the CJA 2003.

A deliberate breach with a view to profit will be viewed seriously as will a failure to heed warnings or comply with notices. The penalty should 'reflect' public disquiet at the unnecessary loss of life (*R v F Howe & Son (Engineers) Ltd* [1999] 2 All ER 249, [1999] 2 Cr App Rep (S) 37, CA). Such cases are suitable for sentence at the Crown Court (*R v Yorkshire Sheeting and Insulation Ltd* [2003] EWCA Crim 458, [2003] 2 Cr App Rep (S) 548, [2003] All ER (D) 369 (Feb); *R v P & O Ferries (Irish Sea) Ltd* [2004] EWCA Crim 3236, [2005] 2 Cr App Rep (S) 113, [2004] All ER (D) 380 (Nov)).

A[51.23]

Those whose work brings with it a familiarity with machinery notoriously become indifferent to safety precautions and will sometimes take the most appalling risks. It may be appropriate to take into account any contribution a worker may have made to his own misfortune in accident cases, but employers must be expected to know the nature of their workers and take and maintain measures to protect workers not only from dangerous machines but from themselves.

A[52]

Immigration offences

Charges

A[52.1]

1 Illegal entry and similar offences by a person who is not a British citizen

Immigration Act 1971, s 24

Maximum penalty – Triable summary only. Fine level 5 or 6 months' (**51 weeks) imprisonment

A[52.2]

2 Assisting unlawful entry to a member state, assisting an asylum seeker to enter the UK and entry to the UK in breach of an exclusion or deportation order.

Immigration Act 1971, s 25, 25A, 25B

Maximum penalty – Fine level 5 and 6 months (**12 months). Triable either way.

Crown Court – Unlimited fine and/or 14 years' imprisonment.

A[52.3]

3 Possession of false passports, work permits, registration cards etc and other offences in connection with the administration of the Act.

Immigration Act 1971, s 26, 26A

Maximum penalty – Triable summary only. Level 5 and 6 months (**51 weeks).

NB. The Nationality, Immigration and Asylum Act 2002 created a large number of related offences under the Act with effect from 10 February 2003. If charged under s 26A they are punishable with a maximum of ten years' imprisonment and a fine unless they only involve possession without reasonable excuse when the maximum penalty is two years' imprisonment and a fine. Both offences are triable either way carrying on summary conviction a fine level 5 and 6 months (**12 months) imprisonment.

Mode of trial

A[52.4]

See general notes at **I[4]** and sentencing below for further guidance, although many cases will be most appropriately dealt with at Crown Court (*R v Uluc* [2001] EWCA Crim 2991 [2001] All ER (D) 273 (Dec)).

Legal notes and definitions

A[52.5]

No asylum seeker can be convicted for using false documents without consideration of whether he is protected by Article 31 of the United Nations Convention Relating to the Status of Refugees, this provides for a defence to any individual who has come to the United Kingdom directly from a country where his life or freedom was threatened **and**;

1. presented himself to the authorities in the United Kingdom without delay;
2. showed good cause for his illegal entry or presence; and
3. made a claim for asylum as soon, as was reasonably practicable after his arrival in the United Kingdom (*R v Uxbridge Magistrates' Court, ex p Adimi* [2001] QB 667, [1999] 4 All ER 520).

A person commits an offence of knowingly remaining beyond the time limit of a limited leave to stay on the day when he first knows that the time limit of his leave has expired. He continues to commit the offence (Immigration Act 1971, s 24(1)(b)(i)) throughout any period he is in the United Kingdom thereafter.

A[52.6]

Extended time limits for prosecution. The normal time limit for laying an information for a summary offence is 6 months. However in cases charged under s 28 (1)(a) (knowingly entering the United Kingdom in breach of a deportation order), s 28(1)(c)(having lawfully entered the United Kingdom remains without leave beyond the time allowed), s 26(1)(c) (making a false representation to an immigration officer) or 26(1)(d) (altering any relevant certificate, work permit or passport) an information relating to the offence may in England and Wales be tried by a magistrates' court if it is laid within six months after the commission of the offence, or if it is laid within three years after the commission of the offence and not more than two months after the date certified by a police officer above the rank of chief superintendent to be the date on which evidence sufficient to justify proceedings came to the notice of the police.

A[52.7]

Search warrants. In the case of offences of illegal entry (s 24(1)(a)), obtaining leave to enter or remain by deception (s 24(1)(aa)) and remaining beyond a time-limited leave or failing to observe conditions of leave (s 24(1)(b)) may all be the subject of an arrest without warrant by a constable or immigration officer with reasonable grounds to suspect an offence has been committed. A justice of the peace may grant a warrant of entry of search to premises if satisfied by written information on oath that a person suspected of one of the above offences is to be found on those premises.

Immigration and Asylum Act 1999, s 7

A[52.8]

An immigration officer is a person appointed by the Secretary of State or may be employed as a revenue and customs officer.

Facilitating entry is not an offence if it is done otherwise than for gain or by a bona fide organisation whose purpose is assisting asylum claimants.

Illegal entrant is not confined to persons who have actually entered the country but includes those seeking to enter (*R v Eyck* [2000] 3 All ER 569, [2000] 1 WLR 1389, CA).

Sentencing

A[52.9]

Structure of the sentencing decision. See **B[3.6]**.

A[52.10]–A[52.15]

Available sentences. See Table A at **B[4.1]** (either way offences) and Table B at **B[4.2]** (summary offences).

A[52.16]

Custodial sentence. See **B[2]**.

A[52.17]

Community sentence. See **B[3]**.

A[52.18]

Fines. See **B[33]**.

A[52.19]

Immigration offences are generally considered seriously by the courts and may lead to custodial sentences, often after committal for sentence. See for example *R v Anthoni Angel* [1998] 1 Cr App Rep (S) 347, CA. A man of good character acting out of humanitarian motives sentenced to 15 months' imprisonment for facilitating the illegal entry of another (*R v Daljit Singh* [1999] 1 Cr App Rep (S) 490, [1999] Crim LR 236, CA). Knowingly using a false passport merited a deterrent sentence of between 6 and 9 months' imprisonment despite a guilty plea and previous good character. See *R v Kolawole* [2004] EWCA Crim 3047, [2005] 2 Cr App Rep (S) 71, [2004] All ER (D) 439 (Nov).

A[52.20]

Bail See **J[1]**.

It may be the case that some asylum seekers face charges before the criminal courts. In these circumstances, the courts have no powers under immigration and asylum legislation to bail or detain them. Where the criminal proceedings have to be adjourned for any reason, magistrates are advised that defendants who are also asylum seekers should have their applications for bail under the Bail Act 1976 considered by the courts in the same way as any other defendant. Where the case proceeds to sentence, the courts have no additional powers to exercise in relation to the offender's immigration status, save for making a recommendation for deportation under the Immigration Act 1971, s 3(6), where this is appropriate. Before considering or making a recommendation for deportation consult the legal adviser.

A[53]–[58]

Indecent photographs

Charges

A[53.1]

Did take or make an indecent photograph of a child or

Distribute or show such photographs or

Possess such photographs with a view to distribution or

Publish an advertisement conveying that the advertiser distributes or shows such photographs.

Protection of Children Act 1978, s.1

Maximum penalty – Fine level 5 and 6 months' (**12 months) imprisonment. Triable either way. Specified sexual offence under Sch 15, Part 2, CJA 2003.

Crown Court –10 years' imprisonment (3 years if committed before 11/01/2001) and unlimited fine.

Mode of Trial

A[53.2]

Consider general notes at **I[4]**. Possession of indecent photographs of children may be tried in the magistrates' court but the court must have regard to an ascending level of seriousness.

1 Erotic posing with no sexual activity
2. Sexual activity between children, or solo masturbation by a child
3. Non penetrative sexual activity between adults and children
4. Penetrative activity between children and adults
5. Sadism or bestiality

In particular one or more of the following aggravating features may indicate trial on indictment:

a) images shown or distributed to a child
b) a large number of images

c) the age of the children involved
d) the offender is responsible for the original production of the images
e) images are posted on a public area of the internet.

Where there are significant numbers of images, see *R v Thomson* (2004) Independent, 31 March, CA, CA for guidance on their presentation to the court.

Legal Notes and definition

A[53.3]

Photographs. The section makes it an offence to make a photograph, pseudo photograph, copy, negative or data stored on a computer disc. A person who downloads indecent images of children from an internet site and prints or saves them is also making an indecent photograph (*R v Smith, R v Jayson* [2002] EWCA Crim 683, [2003] 1 Cr App Rep 212, CA).

A[53.4]

Evidence. It is for the court to decide on the evidence as a whole whether a child in a photograph was under age at the material time (*R v Land* [1999] QB 65, [1998] 1 All ER 403, CA).

Child includes 16 and 17 year olds: Sexual Offences Act 2003, s 45.

A[53.5]

Distribution. A person distributes an indecent photograph if he parts with possession of it, or exposes or offers it to another person.

A[53.6]

Defences. It is a defence for a person to prove that he had a legitimate reason for possessing, distributing or showing the showing the photographs.

It is also a defence that he had not himself seen the photographs and did not know or have cause to suspect them to be indecent.

In respect of 16 and 17 year olds specific defences are provided that the defendant can show

a) the child was 16 or over or they were married or in an enduring family relationship
b) there was consent or a reasonable belief the child consented
c) the photograph is not of the child and another person other than the defendant

There is also a defence for those involved in law enforcement activities.

Sentencing

A[53.7]

Structure of the decision. See **B[3.6]**.

Available sentences. See Table A at **B[4.1]**.

Guidelines. See (*R v Oliver* [2002] EWCA Crim 2766, [2003] 1 Cr App Rep 463) and (*R v Sears* [2003] EWCA Crim 367, [2003] All ER (D) 115 (Feb), CA).

The Court of Appeal has given the following sentencing guidance:

> 'First, sentencing up to (the) statutory maximum should be imposed where there is a contested case and there is evidence of commercial or large scale exploitation, and the amount of the material is significant, especially if the offender has previous convictions.
>
> Second, non-custodial disposals should normally be reserved for isolated offences where the amount of material is very small, and it is for personal use, or use within a very restricted circle, as for example by passing it on to one other recipient, where there is no commercial element and the defendant has pleaded guilty and is a first offender.
>
> Third, where between those two extremes a particular case falls, will depend on the circumstances, and in particular on, first of all, the quality and nature of the material and the quantity thereof. Secondly whether there is any element of exploitation or commercial gain …
>
> … whether the offence is simply one of making, that is to say in most cases downloading and saving, or also involves distribution, and if so to what extent there has been distribution, whether it has been by e-mail to a single specified recipient, or whether the distribution has been significantly more widespread.
>
> Fourth, the character of the defendant is an important factor, and also the effect of the conviction on the individual.
>
> Finally, it is of great importance to consider whether there has been a plea of guilty coupled with co-operation from the outset of the investigation.'

In *R v Bekus* [2004] EWCA Crim 600, [2004] All ER (D) 355 (Mar) a sentence of imprisonment was reduced to 6 months for the possession of small number of images, three of which were higher level, with 3 months concurrent for possession of lower level images. In *R v Shearer* [2005] EWCA Crim 2431, [2005] All ER (D) 141 (Sep), 4,626 indecent images were discovered – one image was at level five and involved a very young child. The judge's starting point of 27 months before a discount and in view of the guilty plea and full co-operation was found to be too long. The CA quashed an 18 month prison sentence and an extended sentence substituting 12 months' imprisonment.

Community Sentence. See **B[3]**.

Fines. See **B[33]**.

Custodial Sentence. See **B[2]**.

Notification requirements. See **A[68.23]**.

Requirements apply even on the making of a conditional discharge (*R v Longworth* [2004] All ER (D) 439 (Jul), CA).

A[59]

Kerb crawling and soliciting women for prostitution

Charges

A[59.1]

Being a man, soliciting a woman (or different women) for the purpose of prostitution

(a) from a motor vehicle while it is in a street or public place or
(b) in a street or public place while in the immediate vicinity of a motor vehicle that the accused has just got out of or off

persistently (or in such a manner or in such circumstances as to be likely to cause annoyance to the woman (or any of the women) solicited, or nuisance to other persons in the neighbourhood)

Sexual Offences Act 1985, s 1(1)

A[59.2]

Being a man in a street or public place persistently soliciting a woman (or different women) for the purpose of prostitution

Sexual Offences Act 1985, s 2(1)

Maximum penalty - (for either offence) Fine level 3. Triable only by magistrates.

Legal notes and definitions

A[59.3]

The words in brackets in the Sexual Offences Act 1985, s 1 enable proceedings to be taken where the soliciting was likely to cause annoyance etc to the woman or nuisance to other persons in the neighbourhood, eg to local residents who are annoyed at their district becoming a 'red light' area.

A[59.4]

Soliciting a woman for the purpose of prostitution means soliciting her for the purpose of obtaining her services as a prostitute. The accused must have given some indication, by act or word, to the woman that he required her services as a prostitute (*Darroch v DPP* (1990) 90 Cr App Rep 378, 154 JP 844).

A[59.5]

Woman includes girl. These offences can only be committed by a man and for this act 'man' includes 'boy'.

A[59.6]

Street includes any bridge, road, lane, footway, subway, square, court, alley or passage, whether a thoroughfare or not, which is for the time being open to the public; and the doorways and entrances of premises abutting on a street and any ground adjoining and open to a street are to be treated as forming part of the street.

A[59.7]

Persistently means a degree of repetition, of either more than one invitation to one person or a series of invitations to different people.

A[59.8]

Likely to cause annoyance. No persons need be present witnessing the incident for the offence to be made out; it is sufficient if there is a likelihood of nuisance to other persons in the neighbourhood. Justices may use their local knowledge that an area is a frequent haunt of prostitutes with a constant procession of cars there (*Paul v DPP* (1989) 90 Cr App Rep 173, [1989] Crim LR 660, sub nom Paul v Luton Justices, ex p Crown Prosecution Service 153 JP 512).

Sentencing

A[59.9]

Child prostitutes should be treated as victims rather than offenders and will rarely be put before the court.

A[59.10]

Since neither of these offences is punishable with imprisonment, a fine will be the usual penalty. The court might consider the amount of distress caused to the victim. When a prosecution is brought on the basis of annoyance to a neighbourhood, an element of deterrent sentencing may be necessary.

A[59.11]

Fines. See **B[33]**.

A[59.12]–A[59.15]

Anti-Social Behaviour Orders. ASBOs have been made for this offence as an ancillary order. See **B[8.8]**.

Binding-over orders

A[59.16]

Complaints for bind over are sometimes included by the prosecution or brought as an alternative remedy to the above charges. Magistrates may use their common law powers to bind over the offender where a future breach of the peace is anticipated (see **B[10]**).

A[60]

Litter (including dumping articles and car dumping)

A[60.1]

Under the general term of **litter** there are three different offences: car dumping, dumping objects other than vehicles, and depositing general litter.

Charge 1

A[60.2]

Without lawful authority abandoning on land in the open air or on land forming part of a highway a motor vehicle

Refuse Disposal (Amenity) Act 1978, s 2(1)(a)

Maximum penalty – Fine level 4 and 3 months' (**51 weeks) imprisonment. May be dealt with by a fixed penalty notice.

A removal charge can also be imposed if the local authority applies.

Legal notes and definitions

A[60.3]

It is also an offence to abandon on such land a part of a motor vehicle if the vehicle was brought to that land and there dismantled and some part of the vehicle abandoned there.

A[60.4]

Motor vehicle. This is defined in the Act as a mechanically propelled vehicle intended or adapted for use on roads whether or not it is in a fit state for such use. It includes a trailer, a chassis or body with or without wheels appearing to have formed part of a motor vehicle or trailer and anything attached to a motor vehicle or trailer.

A[60.5]

Burden of proof. If the vehicle (or part of a vehicle) was left on the land in such circumstances or for such a period that it may be reasonably assumed that the defendant had abandoned it then he shall be deemed to have abandoned the vehicle (or part of a vehicle) unless he can prove the contrary. The degree of proof required of the defendant is not such as is necessary to establish this point beyond all reasonable doubt but only such as establishes that on the balance of probabilities it is true. Give the stated aims of the legislation and the fact that the reason for leaving [abandoning] the vehicle may peculiarly be within the knowledge of the accused, it is suggested that the shifting of the legal burden of proof to the accused is both necessary and proportionate and therefore ECHR compliant.

A[60.6]

Land. The land must be land in the open air or land which forms part of the highway.

Sentencing

A[60.7]

Prison will rarely be appropriate but a fine will in most cases need to be such as to reflect the seriousness of the offence.

A[60.8]

On application by police or local authority, a removal charge can also be imposed.

A[60.8A]

Disqualification from driving. See **C[5.45]**.

Charge 2

A[60.9]

Without lawful authority abandoning on land in the open air (or on land forming part of the highway) property namely [ ] which he brought to the land for the purpose of abandoning it there

Refuse Disposal (Amenity) Act 1978, s 2(1)(b)

Maximum penalty – Fine level 4 and 3 months' (**51 weeks) imprisonment.

Legal notes and definitions

A[60.10]–A[60.15]

Although this offence does not apply to motor vehicles it does apply to a part of a motor vehicle which was dismantled elsewhere and then brought and abandoned. If the motor vehicle was dismantled on the land then the charge should have been the previous one on at **A[60.3]**.

A[60.16]

Land. Means land in the open air or land forming part of a highway.

Sentencing

A[60.17]

The position is the same as for the previous charge at **A[60.7]** except that ordering a removal charge is limited to removing motor vehicles.

A[60.17A]

Disqualification from driving. See **C[5.45]**.

Charge 3

A[60.18]

Throwing down (or dropping or depositing) [in a public open place] [in a place to which this section applies] and there leaving certain articles namely [ ] in such circumstances as to tend to lead to defacement by litter

Environmental Protection Act 1990, s 87

Maximum penalty – Fine level 4.

Legal notes and definitions

A[60.19]

The charge should allege one or other of the following:

A[60.20]

Throwing down; dropping; depositing. If two or more of these words are included in the charge then it may be defective.

A[60.21]

Public open place. Means a place in the open air to which the public are entitled or permitted to have access without payment. Any covered place open to the air on at least one side and available for public use is to be treated as a public open place. An enclosed telephone kiosk is not an open space (*Felix v DPP* [1998] Crim LR 657).

A[60.22]

Place to which the section applies. Includes publicly maintained highways and motorways, local authority open spaces, certain Crown lands and land belonging to certain designated statutory undertakers and educational establishments. Also included is land designated by a local authority as a 'litter control area', e g a shopping mall.

A[60.23]

Time limit. Proceedings must be commenced within six months of the litter being thrown down or dropped or deposited. If litter is left for a considerable period then the time limit of six months still commences from the time the litter was deposited.

A[60.24]

Leaving. No offence is committed if the litter is not left; thus prompt clearing up can be a defence.

A[60.25]–A[60.30]

Consent of the owner. If the owner, occupier or person having control of the place consented to the depositing of the litter then no offence is committed.

Sentencing

A[60.31]

Aggravating factors to which the court may have regard may include the defacement by litter, but also the nature of the litter and any resulting risk of injury to persons or animals or of damage to property.

A[60.32]

Whatever the circumstances the fine will usually need to be such as to reflect the prevalence of the offence in an area.

A[60.33]

Fines. See **B[33]**.

A[60.34]

Disqualification from driving. See **C[5.45]**.

A[61]

Nuisance

A[61.1]

In addition to the remedies which the law affords in respect of nuisances in civil proceedings before the county court and the High Court, local authorities and private persons may bring proceedings for the abatement or restriction of a statutory nuisance before the magistrates' court. Further see **A[32.12]**.

Statutory nuisance

(Environmental Protection Act 1990, s 79)

A[61.2]

The following matters constitute statutory nuisances where they are such as to be prejudicial to health or a nuisance:

(a) the state of any premises;
(b) the emission of smoke from premises;
(c) the emission of fumes or gases from private dwellings;
(d) any dust, steam, smell or other effluvia arising on industrial, trade or business premises;
(e) any accumulation or deposit;
(f) the manner or keeping in such a place of any animal;
(g) noise emitted from premises;

and also

(h) any other matter declared by any enactment to be a statutory nuisance.

Note however that a steep staircase cannot in itself constitute a statutory nuisance (*R v Bristol City Council, ex p Everett* [1999] 2 All ER 193, [1999] 1 WLR 1170, CA).

A[61.3]

Prejudicial to health. Means injurious, or likely to cause injury to health.

A[61.4]

Noise. Includes vibration.

A[61.5]

Exceptions are made to the definitions of a statutory nuisance given above. These include activities of the armed forces, smoke emissions covered by the Clean Air Acts (excluding bonfires), dark smoke from trade or industrial premises, smoke and steam from steam locomotives and noise from aircraft.

A[61.6]

Premises. Includes land and any vessel (except one powered by steam reciprocating engines).

Proceedings by the local authority

(Environmental Protection Act 1990, s 82)

A[61.7]

The local authority must from time to time cause its area to be inspected to detect the existence of any statutory nuisance and, where a complaint has been made, take such steps as are reasonably practicable to investigate the complaint (s 79).

They may also require premises subject to a premises licence on a temporary event notice to close for up to 24 hours if they believe noise from the premises is causing a public nuisance. Contravention is punishable by 3 months' (**51 weeks) imprisonment and/or a £20,000 fine (Anti Social Behaviour Act 2003, s 40).

A[61.8]

Abatement notice. Where the local authority are satisfied that a statutory nuisance exists or is likely to occur or reoccur, the local authority must serve a notice requiring abatement or prohibiting or restricting its occurrence and if the means of abatement are required by the local authority the description of any steps necessary for this purpose and any times within which the required action is to be taken (*R v Falmouth and Truro Port Health Authority, ex p South West Water Services* [2001] QB 445, [2000] 3 All ER 306, [2000] All ER (D) 429, CA).

A[61.9]

Appeal. The person served with the notice may appeal within 21 days to the magistrates' court. These are civil proceedings by way of complaint and the court is unable to impose a criminal penalty (*Hounslow London Borough Council v Thames Water Utilities Ltd* [2004] All ER (D) 94 (Feb)).

A[61.10]–A[61.15]

Offence. Contravention of or failure to comply with the terms of a notice without reasonable excuse is an offence triable only by magistrates. The maximum penalty is a fine of £5,000 and £500 per day for each day the offence continues after conviction. For an offence on industrial, trade or business premises the fine is £20,000.

A[61.16]

Defence. It is a defence for the defendant to prove that the best practicable means were used to prevent, or to counteract the effects of, the nuisance. This defence is not available:

(a) in paras (a), (d), (e), (f) and (g) at **A[61.2]** except where the nuisance arose on trade, industrial or business premises;
(b) in para (b) except where the smoke is emitted from a chimney.

Certain other defences are available where it is alleged that the activity is in conformity with consents or notices under control of pollution legislation.

A[61.17]

If the defendant raises the defence of reasonable excuse under s 80(4) and (6) then it is for the prosecution to satisfy the court beyond reasonable doubt that the excuse was not reasonable (*Polychronakis v Richards and Jerrom Ltd* [1998] JPL 588, [1998] Env LR 347).

A[61.18]

Appeal. A person convicted of an offence may appeal against conviction and sentence to the Crown Court in the usual way.

Complaint by person aggrieved by a statutory nuisance

(Environmental Protection Act 1990, s 82)

A[61.19]

A private individual may complain to the local authority about an alleged statutory nuisance and it will be the duty of the authority to take such steps as are reasonably practicable to investigate the complaint and if they consider it appropriate to serve an abatement notice as described above (Environmental Protection Act 1990, s 79).

A[61.20]

However, a person may also lay a complaint before the magistrates on the ground that he is aggrieved by the existence of a statutory nuisance.

Proceedings are normally brought against the person responsible for the nuisance; where he cannot be found it will be the owner or occupier of the premises.

A[61.21]

Notice of intention to bring proceedings and the matters complained of should be served not less than 3 days before, in respect of noise, and 21 days before, in respect of any other allegation.

A[61.22]

Magistrates' order. If the court is satisfied that the alleged nuisance exists or that, although abated, it is likely to reoccur, the court must make either one or both of the following orders:

(a) to abate the nuisance, within a time specified in the order, and to execute any works necessary for that purpose;
(b) prohibiting a recurrence of the nuisance, and requiring the defendant, within a time specified in the order, to execute any works necessary to prevent the recurrence.

The court may also impose a fine not exceeding £5,000 (level 5).

A[61.23]

Where the nuisance renders premises unfit for human habitation, the order may prohibit their use for this purpose until the court is satisfied they are fit for such use.

A[61.24]

Offence. See **A[61.10]** for private premises.

A[61.25]–A[61.30]

Defence. See **A[61.16]–A[61.17]**. The 'best practicable means' defence is not available for a nuisance which is such as to render the premises unfit for human habitation.

A[61.31]

Costs. Where the alleged nuisance is proved to have existed at the making of the complaint then, whether or not at the date of the hearing it still exists or is likely to recur, the court shall order the defendant to pay the complainant's proper costs. Such costs should include costs incurred in establishing that a statutory nuisance existed (*Hollis v Dudley Metropolitan Borough Council* [1998] 1 All ER 759, [1999] 1 WLR 642).

A[61.32]

Local authority. Where a person has been convicted of failing to comply with an order the court, after allowing the local authority an opportunity to be heard, may direct the authority to do anything which the person convicted was required to do by the order. Similarly, where the defendant cannot be found the court may direct the local authority to do that which it would have ordered him to do.

Noise Act 1996

A[61.33]

If a warning notice has been served under this Act, in respect of noise emitted from a dwelling, any person who is responsible for such a breach is liable to a fine not exceeding **level 3**.

A[61.34]

Defence. It is open to the defendant to show he has reasonable excuse.

A[61.35]

Forfeiture. Magistrates may direct the forfeiture of any equipment related to a noise conviction.

A[61.36]

Before doing so the court must have regard:

(a) to the value of the equipment; and
(b) to the likely financial and other effects on the offender of the making of the order.

A[62]

Obstructing or resisting a constable in the execution of his duty
Obstructing a court security officer in the execution of his duty

Charges

A[62.1]

1Resisting a constable in the execution of his duty

A[62.2]

2Resisting a person assisting a constable in the execution of his duty

A[62.3]

3Wilfully obstructing a constable in the execution of his duty

A[62.4]

4Wilfully obstructing a person assisting a constable in the execution of his duty

Police Act 1996, s 89(2)

Maximum penalty – Fine level 3 and one month (**51 weeks).

A[62.5]

5Wilfully obstructing a court security officer in the execution of his duty

Criminal Justice Act 1991, s 78(2) [from 1 April 2005 contrary to Courts Act 2003, s 57]

Maximum penalty - Fine level 3.

Legal notes and definitions

A[62.6]

The offences of resisting and wilfully obstructing will usually involve some other activity than an assault on the police or a court security officer (which would constitute a different charge). A person exercising their right to silence does not commit the offence of obstructing a police officer.

A[62.7]

Resisting. Means striving against, opposing or trying to impede. For the intention which the defendant must have to commit the offence see **A[6]** (police assault).

A[62.8]

Wilfully means that there must be an intention to bring about a state of affairs whereby, judged objectively, the constable is obstructed in the sense of making it more difficult for him to carry out his duty. The accused need not be hostile to the police; motives are irrelevant. Two examples may make this clear:

(a) The defendant sees the constable trying to arrest a robber. With the intention of helping the officer, the defendant intervenes but he is so clumsy that the villain escapes. He is not guilty of obstruction because the state of affairs that he *intended* to bring about was that the officer would be helped to effect the arrest.
(b) The defendant sees the constable about to arrest what he considers to be the wrong man. He intervenes to stop the arrest. The arrest was in fact lawful. He is guilty because, objectively, the officer has been obstructed in his duty and this was the intention of the accused. It is irrelevant that his motives for doing so were good (otherwise the police would be in peril of all sorts of interruptions whilst exercising their duty).

Unlike a charge of assaulting a police officer, it may be that the defendant must know that the person he is obstructing is a police officer. A defendant who honestly believes the complainant is *not* a police officer, is not guilty of the offence.

A[62.9]

Obstructing. Deliberately causing a physical obstruction is an offence and so is shouting a warning to a person committing an offence or about to commit an offence. It is not a wilful obstruction if a person refuses to answer questions which he is not legally obliged to answer. However, where the police were lawfully investigating a criminal offence (shoplifting), had identified themselves to three suspects, and notified them they wished to question them in relation to an offence of shoplifting, the offenders' actions in running away could amount to an obstruction within the terms of the Act (*Sekfali v DPP* [2006] EWHC 894 (Admin).

A[62.10]–A[62.15]

Constable. A constable includes a special constable and member of the police force of any rank however high. Offences against designated and accredited persons acting in the execution of their duty ie community support officer, investigating officer, detention officer and escort officer are catered for by the Police Reform Act 2002, s 46. Wilful obstruction carries on conviction imprisonment of one month (**51 weeks) or a level 3 fine.

A[62.16]

In the execution of his duty. If as a finding of fact/law the constable was not acting in the course of his duty then the charge must be dismissed. See **A[6.5]**.

A[62.17]

This type of defence sometimes raises difficult questions of law as to whether, for example, a constable had a right to be on private premises when not in possession of a search warrant, or whether a constable had a right to detain a person without there being in force a warrant for arrest. See *James and Chorley v DPP* (1997) 161 JP 89, [1997] Crim LR 831 where a defendant had ceased driving thus ending a constable's right to arrest for driving whilst disqualified. His friend did not obstruct the constable by preventing an arrest as the arrest was not lawful.

A[62.18]

The burden of proof that the constable was acting in the execution of his duty rests on the prosecution (*Redmond-Bate v DPP* (1999) 163 JP 789, [1999] Crim LR 998).

A[62.19]

See **A[6]**.

A[62.20]

Court security officer. See **A[6.4]** for definitions.

Sentencing

A[62.21]

Guideline: Is a fine or discharge appropriate?

A[62.22]

Structure of the sentencing decision. See **B[3.6]**.

A[62.23]

Available sentences. See Table B at **B[4.2]**.

A[62.24]

Custodial sentence. See **B[2]**.

A[62.25]

Community sentence. See **B[3]**.

A[62.26]–A[62.30]

Fines. See **B[33]**.

A[63]

Obstructing the highway

Charge

A[63.1]

Without lawful authority or excuse wilfully obstructing the free passage along a highway

Highways Act 1980, s 137

Maximum penalty – Fine level 3.

Legal notes and definitions

A[63.2]

This offence can be committed in a number of different ways apart from leaving a motor vehicle. It should not be confused with the offence of causing an unnecessary obstruction on a road with a motor vehicle or with a breach of parking regulations. See **C[36]**.

A[63.3]

The correct approach for magistrates dealing with an offence of obstruction is as follows:

(a) Was there an obstruction? Unless within the *de minimis* rule, any stopping on the highway is prima facie an obstruction.
(b) Was it wilful, ie deliberate?
(c) Have the prosecution proved that the obstruction was without lawful authority or excuse? Lawful authority includes permits and licences granted under statutory provision; lawful excuse embraces activities otherwise lawful in themselves which may or may not be reasonable in all the circumstances, including the length of time the obstruction continues, the place where it occurs, the purpose for which it is done and whether it does in fact cause an actual obstruction as opposed to a potential obstruction (*Hirst and Agu v Chief Constable of West Yorkshire* (1986) 85 Cr App Rep 143, 151 JP 304).

A[63.4]

Highway. A highway means the whole or part of a highway. Only a part of a highway needs to be obstructed to commit this offence and the highway, available to the general public, may be a wide road or a narrow passageway, only suitable for pedestrians. Bridges and tunnels used by the public are also highways.

A[64]

Offensive weapon

Charge

A[64.1]

Having, without lawful authority or reasonable excuse, an offensive weapon in any public place

Prevention of Crime Act 1953, s 1

Maximum penalty – Fine level 5 and 6 months (**12 months). Triable either way.

Crown Court – 4 years' imprisonment and unlimited fine.

Mode of trial

A[64.2]

See general notes at **I[4]**.

Legal notes and definitions

A[64.3]

General. The possession of offensive weapons is also controlled by several other statutes. The Crossbows Act 1987 regulates the sale or hire of crossbows to persons under 17 years, and the purchase or possession of crossbows by such persons. The Firearms Act 1968 controls the possession and use of airguns, shotguns and firearms and the possession of articles with blades or sharp points is governed by the Criminal Justice Act 1988 (see **A[5]**).

A[64.4]

Controls are also imposed on the manufacturers of and dealers in or persons who lend or give 'flick-knives' by the Restriction of Offensive Weapons Act 1959 and the Criminal Justice Act 1988 extends such controls to offensive weapons specified by the Home Office such as weapons used in martial arts, stun guns and so-called stealth knives. Selling a knife to a person under the age of 16 is an offence by virtue of amendments brought into force in January 1997. The maximum penalty for contravention of such regulations is a fine on level 5 and 6 months' (**51 weeks) imprisonment.

A[64.5]

Offensive weapon. A police constable may arrest without warrant anyone carrying or suspected of carrying an offensive weapon in a public place. In order to convict the prosecution must first prove that the defendant was in possession of an offensive weapon. An offensive weapon means any article either:

(a) made or adapted for use for causing injury to the person; or
(b) intended by the person having it with him for such use by him or by some other person.

Articles in category (a), such as knuckle dusters and flick-knives and disguised knives, are always offensive weapons. An article in category (b), such as for example a milk bottle, only becomes an offensive weapon when the person carrying it has the intention of using it to cause injury to the person. The prosecution must prove this intention.

A[64.6]

Have with him. The prosecution must prove that the defendant knowingly was "carrying" the offensive weapon with him. 'Carrying' would not include the situation where the accused seized a clasp knife, which he had not been carrying, for instant use on his victim.

A[64.7]

Knowledge of possession. The accused must have acquired the weapon knowingly (eg it was not slipped into his pocket unawares) (*R v Cugullere* [1961] 2 All ER 343, [1961] 1 WLR 858, 45, CCA). He still has it if he subsequently forgets it is there (*R v McCalla* (1988) 87 Cr App Rep 372, 152 JP 481, CA; *Bayliss v DPP* [2003] All ER (D) 71 (Feb)) until he or another does something to rid him of it. A person who has forgotten that he has an offensive weapon is unlikely to have a 'reasonable excuse' (see below) for having it with him, but it might be otherwise where the original possession was lawful, eg picking up a policeman's truncheon intending to take it to the police station and then forgetting to do so (*R v McCalla* (1988) 87 Cr App Rep 372, 152 JP 481, CA).

A[64.8]

In a public place. This includes any highway and any other premises or place to which at the material time the public have or are permitted to have access, whether on payment or otherwise. In *Harriot v DPP* [2005] EWHC 965 (Admin), (2005) 170 JP 494, the Divisional Court held that a "public place" is not a term of legal art and that the statutory definition under the Prevention of Crime Act 1953 was illustrative not exhaustive. Accordingly, the open area between a bail hostel building and a road, was, on the face or it, private premises.

A[64.9]

Without lawful authority or reasonable excuse. If the prosecution has established that an offensive weapon was carried in a public place then the onus shifts to the defendant to prove that lawful authority or reasonable excuse existed. The degree of proof is not to establish this beyond all reasonable doubt but that on the balance of probabilities it is true. The common excuse put forward is that the article was carried for use in self-defence. As the authority or excuse relates to the reason for carrying the offensive weapon, not to a use for which it is subsequently employed, one has to look at the situation when the defendant was carrying it. Accordingly, fear of being attacked, arising from the experience of friends and general violence in the neighbourhood, has been held not to be a reasonable excuse for carrying a metal ball and chain for self-protection. Self-protection from an actual or imminent attack might provide a 'reasonable excuse'. There would be no excuse or authority for a bouncer at a dance carrying an offensive weapon.

ECHR. In the light of *R v Matthews* [2003] EWCA Crim 813, [2004] QB 690, it is submitted that the imposition of a reverse legal burden on the accused is proportionate in accordance with art 6(2) of the ECHR. See **A[5.8]**.

A[64.10]–A[64.15]

A claim by the accused that he did not know that the article in question was an offensive weapon cannot amount to a defence of reasonable excuse (*R v Densu* [1998] 1 Cr App Rep 400, [1998] Crim LR 345, CA). However, forgetfulness that one has unintended possession of an offensive weapon may be a reasonable excuse: *R v Glidewell* (1999) 163 JP 557, CA.

The burden on the defendant to show a reasonable excuse was a heavy one where the weapon (a butterfly knife) was offensive per se, but the court still has a wide discretion on the facts (*DPP v Patterson* [2004] All ER (D) 239 (Oct), DC).

Sentencing

Guideline: Is it so serious that only custody is appropriate? See *R v Poulton, R v Celaire* [2002] EWCA Crim 2487, [2003] 4 All ER 869, [2002] All ER (D) 365 (Oct). The Court of Appeal sets out guidelines indicating a custodial sentence where the offence is aggravated by threats, racial hostility or the defendant was under the influence of drink or drugs. Other aggravating features include carrying the weapon at vulnerable premises such as a school, doctor's surgery or a social security office.

A community penalty may still be appropriate where there are no threats or aggravating features, but see *R v Brooks and MacIntosh* [2003] EWCA Crim 2291, [2004] 1 Cr App Rep (S) 315, (2003) Times, 29 July – immediate custody for possession of a disguised knife in a pub.

A[64.16]

Structure of the sentencing decision. See **B[3.6]**.

A[64.17]

Available sentences. See Table A at **B[4.1]**.

A[64.18]

Custodial sentence. See **B[2]**.

A[64.19]

Community sentence. See **B[3]**.

A[64.20]

Fines. See **B[33]**.

A[64.21]

Forfeiture. The court may order the weapon to be forfeited.

A[65]

Poaching

I Day time offence

A[65.1]

Trespassing by entering or being in the day time upon any land in search or pursuit of game, or woodcocks, snipes or conies

Game Act 1831, s 30, as amended

Maximum penalty – Fine level 3. Triable only by magistrates.

Note – Where it is alleged that there were five or more persons together trespassing in pursuit of game the maximum penalty is a fine set at level 5 for each defendant.

For hunting wild mammals with dogs and hare coursing see ss 1–5 of the Hunting Act 2004.

Legal notes and definitions

A[65.2]

A prosecution must be commenced within three calendar months after the commission of the offence (Game Act 1831, s 41). The charge creates only one offence, that of trespass, and the summons may refer to pursuit of more than one species.

A[65.3]

Claim of right. The magistrates' jurisdiction is ousted if the accused contends that he had a right to act as he did. However, this claim must be bona fide and made on reasonable grounds. The magistrates may decide on the reasonableness and sufficiency of the evidence to support it.

A[65.4]

Trespassing is a complicated concept. However, for this offence the accused must himself have been personally entering on the land and 'constructive' trespass, eg sending a dog into the land, would not be sufficient.

A[65.5]

Day time commences at the beginning of the last hour before sunrise and concludes at the expiration of the first hour after sunset (s 34).

A[65.6]

Game means hares, pheasants, partridges, grouse, heath or moor game, and black game (s 2).

A[65.7]

Game licence. A conviction of this offence renders a licence to kill game void (Game Licences Act 1860, s 11).

A[65.8]

Hunting. This offence does not apply to hunting or coursing in fresh pursuit of deer, hare, or fox (Game Act 1831, s 35). NB: By virtue of the Hunting Act 2004, Sch 3, the words, "to any person hunting or coursing upon any land with hounds or greyhounds, and being in pursuit of any deer, hare or fox already started upon any other land, nor" have been repealed.

A[65.8A]

Disqualification from driving. See **C[5.45]**.

2Night time offences

A[65.9]

(a) Unlawfully taking or destroying any game or rabbits by night in any land, open or enclosed or by night unlawfully entering or being on any land, whether open or enclosed, with any gun, net, engine, or other instrument for the purpose of taking or destroying game

Night Poaching Act 1828, s 1, as amended

Maximum penalty – Fine level 3 (offence under s 2 where violence is offered to gamekeepers etc with the weapons described in charge (b) the maximum is a fine on level 4 and 6 months (**51 weeks)). Triable only by magistrates.

A[65.10]–A[65.15]

(b) Three or more persons together by night unlawfully entering or being on any land, whether open or enclosed, for the purpose of taking or destroying game or rabbits, any of such persons being armed with gun, cross bow, firearms, bludgeon or any other offensive weapon

Night Poaching Act 1828, s 9, as amended

Maximum penalty – Fine level 4 and 6 months (**51 weeks). Triable only by magistrates.

Legal notes and definitions

A[65.16]

Claim of right. See above at **A[65.3]**.

A[65.17]

Game includes hares, pheasants, partridges, grouse, heath or moor game, black game and bustards (Night Poaching Act 1828, s 13).

A[65.18]

Land includes public roads, highways, or paths, or the sides thereof or at the opening, outlets, or gates, from any such land into any such road, highway or path.

A[65.19]

Charge. Section 1 creates two offences and any information must allege only one offence.

A[65.20]

Unlawfully entering or being. (See above.) This offence does not relate to the taking or destroying of rabbits.

A[65.21]

Night time commences at the expiration of the first hour after sunset and concludes at the beginning of the last hour before sunrise.

A[65.22]

Three or more together. It is not necessary for all the persons actually to enter provided they are associated together on a common purpose, some entering while others remain near enough to assist.

A[65.23A]

Disqualification from driving. See **C[5.45]**.

3Pursuing game without a licence

A[65.23]

Taking, killing, pursuing, or using any dog, gun, net or other engine for the purpose of taking, killing, or pursuing any game, or any woodcock, snipe or any coney, or deer, without a proper licence

Game Licences Act 1860, s 4, as amended

Maximum penalty – Fine level 2. Triable only by magistrates.

Legal notes and definitions

A[65.24]

Game licences are granted by local authorities.

A[65.25]–A[65.30]

Exceptions. Include taking woodcocks and snipe with nets or springs; taking or destroying conies by proprietors or tenants of lands; pursuing and killing of hares by coursing with greyhounds or hunting with beagles or other hounds; a person assisting a licence holder in his company or presence; a person authorised under the Hares Act 1848 to kill hares without a game certificate.

Sentencing

A[65.31]

Where the police have arrested a person for an offence under the Night Poaching Act 1828 or Game Act 1831 they may search him and may seize and detain any game or rabbits, or any gun or cartridges or other ammunition, or any nets, traps, snares or other devices of a kind used for the killing or taking of game or rabbits, which are found in his possession.

A[65.32]

If convicted the court may order any of these items to be forfeited (whether or not the offence of which he was convicted concerned that game, rabbit etc) (Game Laws Amendment Act 1960, s 4).

A[65.32A]

Disqualification from driving. See **C[5.45]**.

A[66]

Police (Property) Act 1897

A[66.1]

Application for an order for the delivery of property in possession of the police in connection with their investigation of a suspected offence under s 1 of the Act.

Legal notes and definitions

A[66.2]

While this proceeding is a civil case of a kind that is more usually dealt with at a county court, nevertheless it can be dealt with at a magistrates' court. Clearly it will be cheaper and more expeditious if a magistrates' court deals with the matter fairly soon after the hearing of a criminal charge, thus saving a hearing in the county court or High Court. Sufficient notice of the date of hearing should be given to each claimant of the property to enable him to prepare for the hearing before the magistrates.

A[66.3]

When applicable. This procedure applies when the police have in their possession property which has come into their hands during investigation into a suspected offence. It is not necessary that the person has been charged with any offence.

A[66.4]

Often there is no such difficulty as stolen property can be restored direct to the rightful owner. In other cases where the defendant has been convicted for several offences eg theft, at the end of the case the police may be in possession of a large sum of money taken from the defendant. The various losers may each claim part or all of this money as being stolen from them or arising from the sale by the thief of the stolen property.

A[66.5]

The police, any claimant or even the defendant can lay a complaint or make an application asking the magistrates to decide the ownership of property and/or to whom the property should be delivered.

A[66.6]

At the hearing the police or a claimant has the right to call witnesses, cross-examine the other party's witnesses and to address the magistrates. The hearing can be expedited by the filing of written evidence which can include hearsay evidence.

A[66.7]

Powers of the magistrates. Having heard all the parties the magistrates may make an order for delivery of the property to the person who appears to the court to be the owner or if he cannot be ascertained they may make such order as they think fit (see **A[66.17]**).

A[66.8]

This gives the magistrates wide powers of discretion. If, for instance, the magistrates are not impressed by any of the claims then they can order the money or the monies the police obtain from selling the stolen property (e g a stolen motor vehicle) to be paid to the Police Property Act Fund which is administered by the Police Authority. The money is invested and the income is used (a) to defray the expenses in handling and storing such property; (b) for compensating the persons who deliver such property to the police; (c) for charitable purposes.

A[66.9]

If there are several claimants, magistrates might find in favour of one claimant and order his claim to be paid and find against the other claimants and then order the balance of the money to be delivered to the fund.

A[66.10]–A[66.16]

Deliver. It is to be noted that the word used in disposing of the property is 'delivered'. This means that an unsuccessful claimant can sue in the county court the authority or person to whom the magistrates order delivery, but must do so within six months from the date of the hearing, or his/her right ceases.

A[66.17]

Case unsuitable for magistrates' courts. The High Court has ruled that magistrates should hesitate to deal with a claim of a similar kind if the value of the property is substantial or if difficult matters of law are likely to arise. For example, a motor car which was stolen whilst subject to a hire-purchase agreement led to there being several claimants. See *Gough v Chief Constable of West Midlands* [2004] EWCA Civ 206, [2004] All ER (D) 45 (Mar) for the interaction with civil proceedings.

A[66.18]

If the magistrates decide that if either of the above points arise the best course is to adjourn the hearing *sine die* and to invite the claimant or claimants to commence proceedings in the county court or the High Court. Alternatively, the magistrates can decline to exercise their jurisdiction. A magistrates' court is not obliged to make an order.

A[66.19]

Criminal Damage Act 1971. The above provisions also apply if the police have possession of property following the execution of a search warrant granted under the Criminal Damage Act 1971, s 6.

A[66.20]

Costs. Proceedings should be commenced by way of complaint because in magistrates' courts there is no power to award costs where proceedings have been commenced by way of "application" (see for example, *R v Salisbury and Tisbury and Mere Combined Juvenile Court, ex p Ball* (1985) 149 JP 346. Where proceedings have begun by way of a complaint it is inappropriate to order costs against the police where they do not object to the order sought (*R v Uxbridge Justices, ex p Metropolitan Police Comr* [1981] 1 All ER 940, [1981] 1 WLR 112; affd [1981] QB 829, [1981] 3 All ER 129, CA).

A[67]

Railway offences

Charge 1

A[67.1]

Failure to give name and address following a failure to produce a valid ticket

Regulation of Railways Act 1889, s 5 (1)

Maximum penalty – Fine level 2 (Railway Company or London Transport)

Charge 2

A[67.2]

Travelling on a railway without having previously paid the fare with the intention of avoiding payment

OR

Having paid a fare knowingly and wilfully travelling beyond the distance paid for without previously paying for an additional distance with the intention of avoiding additional fare

OR

Giving a false name and address following a failure to pay

Regulation of the Railways Act 1889, s 5(3)(a), (b), and (c) respectively

Maximum penalty – Fine level 3 or 3 months (**51 weeks) (Railway Company or London Transport).

Legal notes and definitions

A[67.3]

A fare must be paid to the railway authority or one of its employees.

A[67.4]

The prosecution must satisfy the magistrates that the defendant intended to avoid paying the fare or additional fare (if he paid for part of the journey). If the magistrates believe that the defendant genuinely forgot to pay his fare then the case must be dismissed. It is sufficient for a conviction if the defendant's intention was to avoid paying until payment was demanded; there is no need to prove an intention permanently to avoid payment.

A[67.5]

The prosecution has only to establish the intention to avoid paying the fare, not the intention to defraud.

A[67.6]

It has been held that the offence of 'without having previously paid the fare with the intention of avoiding the fare' has been committed if the defendant uses the return half of a ticket issued to another person. It is not necessary to show that the offender knew that the ticket was non-transferable.

A[67.7]

Travelling. This includes the time between leaving the railway carriage and proceeding to the exit barrier. Thus an offence is committed if a passenger decides to avoid the fare at that stage of the journey.

A[67.8]

Wilfully. This means deliberately.

Sentencing

A[67.9]

See Table B at **B[4.2]** for available sentences.

A[67.10]

Byelaws. All railway operators and Railtrack have adopted the Framework Railway Byelaws. Penalty for a breach of a byelaw is a level 3 fine.

Legal notes and definitions

A[67.11]–A[67.15]

The request for a traveller's name and address must be made by an officer of the railway operator.

Sentencing

A[67.16]

The position is the same as for the previous offence.

A[68]

Sexual activity with a child

Charge

A[68.1]

(1) Intentionally touching a child under 13 in a sexual manner

Sexual Offences Act 2003, s 7

Maximum penalty - Fine level 5 and 6 months (**12 months). Triable either way. Specified sexual offence under Sch 15, Part 2, CJA 2003.

Crown Court - 14 years' imprisonment and unlimited fine.

(2) Being over 18 years did intentionally engage in sexual touching with a child under 16

Sexual Offences Act 2003, s 9

Maximum penalty – As (1) above unless penetration is involved when triable on indictment only – life imprisonment.

Mode of trial

A[68.2]

See general notes at **I[4]**.

Legal notes and definitions

A[68.3]

Sexual activity. An activity is sexual if a reasonable person would conclude:

(a) whatever the circumstances or purpose, it is because of its nature sexual; or
(b) because of its nature it may be sexual and because of the circumstances and or purpose it is sexual (s 77).

A[68.4]

Consent is agreement by choice. A child under 13 does not have legal capacity to consent nor is consent material in the case of a child under 16 other than to absolve the defendant of a more serious offence

A[68.5]

Age. It is a defence that the defendant did not reasonably know or was mistaken about the age of the child (*B v DPP* [2000] 2 AC 428, [2000] 1 All ER 833, HL) in the case of a s 9 offence and the burden of proving the absence of reasonable belief rests on the prosecution. In the case of a s 7 offence this defence is not available.

A[68.6]

Evidence of children. The evidence of children (ie those persons under 14 years) must be given unsworn (Youth Justice & Criminal Evidence Act 1999, s 55). Such evidence need not be corroborated only because it is unsworn (*R v Hampshire* [1996] QB 1, [1995] 2 All ER 1019, CA).

A[68.7]

A court may not refuse to admit the evidence of a child complainant by reason of age only. The court should assess whether the child is capable of giving intelligible testimony either by watching a video of the child or by questioning the complainant themselves (*DPP v M* [1998] QB 913, [1997] 2 All ER 749).

A[68.8]

Proceedings involving child witnesses. In cases of assault, cruelty or neglect and sexual offences, the legal presumption is that a video recording of a child witness' evidence will be admitted albeit the leave of the court is required. A 'child witness' is one who is, under 17 years at the time of the hearing.. A defendant may not cross-examine a child witness in person; this must be done by his solicitor or counsel – see **A[68.10]** below.

A[68.9]

Adult magistrates' courts may consider such a video even though the child is not called to give evidence. In trials before magistrates a screen may be used so that the witness may not feel intimidated by the presence of the accused (*R v X* (1989) 91 Cr App Rep 36, [1990] Crim LR 515, CA).

A[68.10]

Special measures. A witness under 17 years is eligible for assistance by a special measures direction if the quality of his evidence (ie completeness, coherence or accuracy) is likely to be diminished by reason of fear or distress (Youth Justice and Criminal Evidence Act 1999, ss 16–19). In magistrates' courts, special measures are screens, TV links and video-recorded evidence. For child witnesses in cases involving sexual offences, violence (including threats) and cruelty who are defined as witnesses in need of special protection, the provision of special measures is near to mandatory (*R v Camberwell Green Youth Court* [2005] UKHL 4, [2005] 1 All ER 999, [2005] All ER (D) 259 (Jan)). This is intended to provide protection for children in cases involving assaults, muggings and domestic violence and to bring the adult magistrates' court into line with the provision in the Youth Court. The provisions apply to defence and prosecution witnesses but not to the defendant (*R (on application of S) v Waltham Forest Youth Court* [2004] EWHC 715 (Admin), [2004] All ER (D) 590 (Mar)).

Special measures may be applied for in proceedings for an anti-social behaviour order.

A[68.11]–A[68.15]

Privacy: clearing the court. The magistrates can order the court to be cleared (except for those directly concerned with the case and the press) whilst the child or young person is testifying (Children and Young Persons Act 1933, s 37 as amended).

A[68.16]

Anonymity of victim. The general prohibition on the revealing of the identity of the victim of a sexual offence applies (see **A[69.11]**). In the case of persons under 18 the existing power under s.39 of the Children and Young Persons Act 1933 (as amended) is preserved. The court may direct that any press, radio or television report of the case must not reveal the name, address, school or identity of any child or young person concerned in the proceedings including the defendant. However, such an order must be clear as to precisely what is prohibited (*Briffet v DPP* [2001] EWHC Admin 841 (2001) 166 JP 66, sub nom Briffett and Bradshaw v Crown Prosecution Service [2002] EMLR 203) and should be in writing (*Re BBC Litigation Department* [2002] All ER (D) 69 (Apr), CA). (Children and Young Persons Act 1933, s 39).

A[68.17]

Corroboration. The evidence of a complainant in sexual cases is no longer required.

Sentencing

A[68.18]

Structure of the sentencing decision. See **I[4]**.

A[68.19]

Available sentences. See Table A at **B[4.1]**.

A[68.20]

Custodial sentence. See **B[2]**.

A[68.21]

Community sentence. See **B[3]**.

A[68.22]

Fines. See **B[33]**.

A[68.23]

Sexual Offences Act 2003 (Part II). On conviction the court must require the defendant to:

(a) **notify the police** within the next three days (or if in custody or otherwise detained, within three days of release) of his name, any other names he uses, his date of birth and his home address;
(b) **notify the police** of any change of name or home address within 14 days of any change;
(c) **notify the police** of any address where he resides or stays for 14 days or longer. This means either 14 days at a time, or a total of 14 days in any 12-month period;
(d) **notify the police** of an intention to leave the UK for a period of 24 hours or longer, at least 24 hours prior to departure of the particulars of the journey;
(e) **notify the police** of his national insurance number.

In *R v Longworth*, January 26, 2006, the House of Lords held that for persons convicted before May 1, 2004, the notification requirements under the Sex Offenders Act 1997 do not arise if an order of **absolute** or **conditional discharge** is made. In some cases this means that a notification requirement will arise on conviction but where sentencing is adjourned, will cease on the imposition of an absolute or conditional discharge. Persons conditionally discharged after May 1, 2004 are subject to the notification requirements of the 2003 legislation.

A[68.24]

Sexual offences prevention order may be applied for separately under Part II of the Sexual Offences Act 2003 The application is a civil matter (*B v Chief Constable of Avon and Somerset Constabulary* [2001] 1 All ER 562, [2001] 1 WLR 340) or made on conviction. See **A[69.34]**. The police may also apply independently for a **Risk of Sexual Harm Order**.

A[69]

Sexual assault

Charge

A[69.1]

Sexual assault

Sexual Offences Act 2003, s 3

OR

A[69.2]

Causing a person to engage in sexual activity without consent

Sexual Offences Act 2003, s 4

Maximum penalty – Fine level 5 and 6 months (**12 months). Triable either way. Specified sexual offence under Sch 15, Part 2, CJA 2003.

Crown Court – 10 years' imprisonment and unlimited fine.

Mode of trial

A[69.3]

Consider first the general notes at **I[4]**. In general, except for the presence of one or more of the following factors, offences of indecent assault should be tried summarily if:

(a) there is a substantial disparity in age and the assault was not trivial;
(b) the assault was accompanied by violence or threats;
(c) there was trust between victim and offender;
(d) there were several offences and they were not trivial;
(e) the assault was of a serious nature;
(f) the victim was particularly vulnerable.

Legal notes and definitions

A[69.4]

Sexual assault. The accused must intentionally touch the victim. The touching and the circumstances accompanying it, must be capable of being considered by reasonable persons as sexual taken together with the intentions of the accused

A[69.5]

An accused's explanation for the assault, whether or not it reveals a sexual motive, is admissible to support or negative that the touching was sexual and was so intended by the accused (*R v Court* [1989] AC 28, [1988] 2 All ER 221, HL; grabbing a girl's tracksuit bottoms coupled with the request 'Do you fancy a shag?' (*R v H* [2005] EWCA Crim 732, [2005] 2 All ER 859, [2005] All ER (D) 16 (Feb)).

A[69.6]

Defences. Consent of the alleged victim is a defence except if obtained by force or fraud. A reasonable belief that the person consents is a defence, as would be non-intentional touching. The following two categories of persons cannot give consent, or in the case of a mental disorder consent may be impeded.

A[69.7]

Persons under 16. A person under the age of 16 years is incapable in law of consent in these circumstances and therefore it is no defence that a person under 16 consented. It is for the prosecution to prove that the defendant did not honestly believe that the girl was aged 16 or over. The defendant's belief must be honest and genuine but the more unreasonable the belief, the less likely it was to be accepted as genuine (*R v K* [2001] 1 Cr App Rep 493, [2001] Crim LR 134, CA; revsd sub nom R v K [2001] UKHL 41 [2002] 1 AC 462, [2001] 3 All ER 897). Offences involving children will normally be charged under ss 9–15 of the Sexual Offences Act 2003 and where the child is under 13 the defendant is not entitled to raise any issues about mistaken belief in age.

A[69.8]

Mental disorder. If the person subject to sexual activity has a mental disorder he or she is deemed not to have freely given consent; the defendant can only be convicted if he knew or had reason to suspect that the person has a mental disorder and because of that was likely to be unable to refuse.

A[69.9]

Sexual activity with children. If a child under the age of 13 is involved in sexual activity a number of offences arise under ss 5–15 of the Sexual Offences Act 2003. See **A[68]**.

A[69.10]

Evidence of children. See under this heading on at **A[68.6]**.

A[69.11]–A[69.15]

Anonymity of victim. Where an allegation has been made or a person is accused of this offence neither the name or address nor any moving or still picture of the victim shall be published or broadcast during his lifetime if it is likely to lead members of the public to identify him as the victim of the offence (Sexual Offences (Amendment) Act 1992). Before the trial a magistrate may direct that the prohibition does not apply where he is satisfied the direction is necessary to induce witnesses to come forward, or the applicant's defence is otherwise likely to be substantially prejudiced. The restriction may also be lifted during the trial to such an extent as is necessary in the public interest.

A[69.16]

The existing power under s 39 of the Children and Young Persons Act 1933, in respect of persons under 18, to direct that any press, radio or television report of the case must not reveal his name, address, school or identity is preserved. See **A[68.16]**.

A[69.17]

The magistrates can order the court to be cleared (except for those directly concerned with the case and the press) whilst the child or young person is testifying (Children and Young Persons Act 1933, s 37).

A[69.18]

Corroboration. The Criminal Justice and Public Order Act 1994 removed any requirement for corroboration in sexual offences.

Sentencing

A[69.19]

Structure of the sentencing decision. See **B[3.6]**

Guideline: Is it so serious that only custody is appropriate?

A[69.20]

Available sentences. See Table A at **B[4.1]**.

A[69.21–22]

See *R v Corran* [2005] EWCA Crim 192, [2005] All ER (D) 40 (Feb) for general guidance from the Court of Appeal.

A 28-day immediate prison sentence was held to be wrong in the case of a 42-year-old man of previous good character who indecently assaulted a young woman on an underground train. The indecent assault consisted of rubbing himself up against the victim. The Court of Appeal was of the view that such cases could be dealt with by a fine. The Court substituted on appeal a fine of £300 and a compensation order of £250 was left unchanged (*R v Neem* (1992) 14 Cr App Rep (S) 18, CA). *R v Neem* has not been followed by subsequent decisions of the Court of Appeal. See *R v Townsend* (1994) 16 Cr App Rep (S.) 553 and *R v Diallo* [2000] 1 Cr App R (S) 426.

A[69.23]

In the youth court. It should be noted that sexual assault may be treated as a grave crime in the youth court and where appropriate committed to the Crown Court for trial. See **E[3.18]– E[3.19]**.

A[69.24]

Custodial sentence. See **B[2]**.

R v Brimonte [2004] EWCA Crim 2655, [2005] All ER (D) 03 (Feb) – 3 months' custody for a person of good character who grabbed the victim's crotch by putting his hands up her skirt. In *R v Isa* [2005] EWCA Crim 3330, [2006] Crim LR 356, 12 months' imprisonment was upheld in the case of a sexual assault by the appellant on a young girl. The appellant had four previous convictions for indecent assaults on girls and women.

A[69.25]–A[69.30]

Community sentence. See **B[3]**.

A[69.31]

Fines. See **B[33]**.

A[69.32]

Compensation. This may be ordered up to £5,000 either as part of a wider sentence or by itself as a substantive penalty. If the offender's means are limited and a monetary penalty is appropriate, preference must be given to ordering compensation instead of a fine.

A[69.33]

Sexual Offences Act 2003 (Sch 3) Depending upon the nature of the conviction, on conviction, including a conditional discharge, the court must require the defendant to:

(a) **notify the police** within the next three days (or if in custody or otherwise detained, within three days of release) of his name, any other names he uses, his date of birth and his home address;

(b) **notify the police** of any change of name or home address within 14 days of any change;
(c) **notify the police** of any address where he resides or stays for 14 days or longer. This means either 14 days at a time, or a total of 14 days in any 12-month period;
(d) **notify the police** of an intention to leave the UK for a period of 24 hours or longer, at least 24 hours prior to departure of the particulars of the journey;
(e) **notify the police** of his national insurance number.

In the case of a conviction under s 3 or s 13 (sexual assault or sexual assault of a child under 13) notification is mandatory for any custodial sentence of at least 12 months or where the victim is under 18. Otherwise any custodial sentence or community sentence of 12 months or a mental health detention will trigger notification in the case of an adult offender.

Juvenile offenders. Where the offender is under 18 years these provisions will apply to a person identified as having parental responsibility.

Order for absolute or conditional discharge. See **A[68.23]** and *R v Longworth*, January 26, 2006, HL.

A[69.34]

Sexual Offences prevention order may be applied for separately under Part II of the Sexual Offences Act 2003. The application is a civil matter (*B v Chief Constable of Avon and Somerset Constabulary* [2001] 1 All ER 562, [2001] 1 WLR 340). Alternatively where on conviction the court is satisfied it is necessary to protect the public from serious sexual harm from the defendant an order may be made prohibiting the defendant prescribed activities for a period not less than 5 years. Similar to anti-social behaviour orders, given the fact that breach of an order is punishable by a sentence of up to five years, there was a need for the terms of the order to be clear and precise (*R v H* [2006] EWCA Crim 1470, [2006] All ER (D) 87 (Jun)).

The police may also apply independently for a **risk of sexual harm order**.

A[70]–A[75]

Shotgun (purchasing etc without shotgun certificate)

Charge

A[70.1]

Possessing, or purchasing or acquiring a shotgun without holding a shotgun certificate

Firearms Act 1968, s 2(1)

Maximum penalty – Fine level 5 and 6 months (**12 months). Triable either way.

Crown Court – 5 years' imprisonment and unlimited fine.

Mode of trial

A[70.2]

See general notes at **I[4]**.

Legal notes and definitions

A[70.3]

Purchasing, possessing, acquiring. These are three separate offences and the charge should only allege one of these.

A[70.4]

Shotgun. Means a smooth bore gun with a barrel of 24 inches or longer with a bore not exceeding two inches and which is not a revolver nor has an illegal magazine, which is not an air gun.

A[70.5]

Certificate. This is granted by the police and it may contain conditions. Failure to observe the conditions is an offence which is also punishable with a fine of level 5 and 6 months' (**51 weeks) imprisonment (Firearms Act 1968, s 2(2)) and is only triable before magistrates. The police can revoke the certificate if they are satisfied that it entails danger to public safety or peace.

A[70.6]

Exemptions. These include visitors to Great Britain who are holders of a visitor's shotgun permit; persons using shotguns on occasions and at places approved by the police; a person who borrows a shotgun and uses it on the lender's private premises, in the presence of the lender; persons holding a Northern Ireland firearm certificate which authorises holders to possess shotguns. See also **A[37]**.

A[70.7]

ECHR. The degree of proof required from the defendant is to establish that on the balance of probabilities he was exempt. He does not have to establish this beyond reasonable doubt. Having regard to the legitimate aims of the legislation it is suggested that the imposition of a legal burden on the accused is necessary and proportionate so as to accord with art 6 (2) of the ECHR.

Sentencing

A[70.8]

Structure of the sentencing decision. See **B[3.6]**.

A[70.9]

Available sentences. See Table A at **B[4.1]**.

A[70.10]–A[70.15]

Custodial sentence. See **B[2]**.

A[70.16]

Community sentence. See **B[3]**.

A[70.17]

Fines. See **B[33]**.

A[70.18]

Forfeiture. The court can order the shotgun to be forfeited to the police or disposed of as it thinks fit.

A[70.19]

The court can also cancel any firearm or shotgun certificate held by the defendant.

A[76]

Sporting events (control of alcohol etc)

Charges

A[76.1]

1(a) Being the operator (or hirer) (or his servant or agent) knowingly causing or permitting intoxicating liquor to be carried on a public service vehicle which was being used for the principal purpose of carrying passengers for the whole or part of a journey to or from a designated sporting event

OR

(b) Possessing intoxicating liquor whilst on such a vehicle

OR

(c) Being drunk on such a vehicle

Sporting Events (Control of Alcohol etc) Act 1985, 1(2), 1(3) and 1(4)

A[76.2]

2(a) Possessing intoxicating liquor (or an article specified by the Act namely [ ]) at a time during the period of a designated sporting event when in an area of a designated sports ground from which the event might have been directly viewed (or while entering or trying to enter such an event)

OR

(b) Being drunk in a designated sports ground at a time during the period of a designated sporting event (or, being drunk while entering or trying to enter such an event)

Sporting Events (Control of Alcohol etc) Act 1985, 2(1) and 2(2)

Maximum penalties -

Offences under	s 1(2) – Fine level 4
	ss 1(3) and 2(1) – Fine level 3 and 3 months (**51 weeks)
	ss 1(4) and 2(2) – Fine level 2.

Legal notes and definitions

A[76.3]

These offences were created in an attempt to deal with rowdy behaviour at football matches primarily where teams belonging to the Football (or Premier) League are involved (including their reserve and youth teams) but generally not at games exclusively concerning 'non-league' or amateur clubs. In addition, the Act provides for a total ban on the sale of alcohol at such matches although there is the opportunity for the club to apply to the relevant local authority for an order modifying this prohibition (see Section F).

A[76.4]

Public service vehicle means a motor vehicle adapted to carry more than eight passengers for hire or reward. (For this and the definition of 'operator' see the Public Passenger Vehicles Act 1981, s 181.) This offence also applies to a person who knowingly causes or permits intoxicating liquor to be carried in these circumstances on a railway passenger vehicle which he has hired. The Sporting Events (Control of Alcohol etc) Act 1985, s 1A makes provision for offences similar to those under s 1(a), (b) and (c) for drivers and keepers of a minibus, ie not a public service vehicle, but one which is adapted to carry more than eight passengers, and is being used for the principal purpose of carrying two or more passengers for the whole or part of a journey to or from a designated sporting event.

A[76.5]

Designated sporting event means any association football match where one of the participating clubs is a member (full or associate) of the Football (or Premier) League. It also includes all international association football matches and matches in competition for the European Champion Clubs Cup, European Cup Winner's Cup or UEFA Cup (whether or not either of the teams concerned is a member of the Football (or Premier) League e g where a final is played in England between two foreign teams). Also included are events in Scotland designated under the equivalent Scottish legislation (all Scottish League Clubs are designated as well as rugby internationals at Murrayfield). A match is also designated if it takes place outside Great Britain where either the team represents the Football Association or is a Football (or Premier) League Club or where a Football Association Club (not necessarily being a 'league' club) participates in one of the three European competitions. Accordingly, persons on a journey to Scotland or to Europe for a designated event are subject to the provisions of the Sporting Events (Control of Alcohol etc) Act 1985 whilst they are in England.

A[76.6]

Period of the event. The prohibitions apply to a period beginning two hours before the start of the event or, if earlier, two hours before the time it is advertised to start and ends one hour after the end of the event. Where a match is postponed or cancelled, the period includes the two hours before and one hour after the advertised start of the event. A shorter restricted period starting 15 minutes before and ending 15 minutes after the event applies to private boxes overlooking the ground.

A[76.7]

Exceptions. Apart from those clubs or matches not covered by the designation, eg games exclusively concerning 'non-league' clubs, the Sporting Events (Control of Alcohol etc) Act 1985 does not apply to matches where all competitors take part without reward *and* all spectators are admitted free of charge.

A[76.8]

Prohibited articles. As well as intoxicating liquor this includes any article capable of causing injury to a person struck by it being a bottle, can or other portable container (including such a container when crushed or broken) which is for holding *any* drink and which when empty is of a kind normally discarded or returned to the supplier, or part of such a container eg a beer glass. Thus a vacuum flask containing tea would be exempt. Also exempted are containers for holding medicinal products.

A[76.9]

Prohibited articles also include under s 2A any article or substance whose main purpose is the emission of a flare for purposes of illuminating or signalling (as opposed to igniting or heating) or the emission of smoke or visible gas, eg distress flares, fog signals, pellets for fumigating, but not matches, lighters, or heaters; fireworks are also prohibited. It is a defence if the accused proves that he was in possession of an article under s 2A with lawful authority.

A[76.10]–A[76.15]

Designated sports ground. These are the home grounds of all Football Association clubs (ie not necessarily just those clubs in the Football (or Premier) League) including any ground used occasionally or temporarily by such a club, Wembley Stadium and any ground used for any international association match. However, it should be noted that all the restrictions apply only to a designated sporting event and so where, for example, a boxing match is held on a Football League ground the provisions of the Act do not apply.

Sentencing

A[76.16]

For the non-imprisonable offences see Table C at **B[4.3]** and for the offences contrary to ss 1(3) and 2(1) see Table B at **B[4.2]**.

A[76.17]

For the power to make banning orders on persons convicted of certain offences in relation to football matches see **B[41]**.

For offences committed on licensed premises see **B[32].**

A[76.18]

Fines. See **B[33]**.

A[77]

Taking motor vehicle (or other conveyance)

Charge

A[77.1]

Without the owner's consent or other lawful authority taking a conveyance, namely a [ ] for his own use (or for another person's use)

Theft Act 1968, s 12(1)

Note – It is also an offence to drive a conveyance, or allow oneself to be carried in or on it, if one knows the conveyance has been taken without such authority; the penalty for such offences is the same as for the offence of unauthorised taking.

Maximum penalty – Fine level 5 and 6 months (**51 weeks). Triable only by magistrates.

Motor vehicles. The defendant may be disqualified but no endorsement or penalty points are applicable.

Legal notes and definitions

A[77.2]

Pedal cycles. The Theft Act 1968, s 12(5) applies a special provision if the conveyance is a pedal cycle. The maximum penalty is a fine up to level 3.

A[77.3]

If the circumstances amounted to theft and theft is alleged, the notes at **A[79.3]** will apply.

A[77.4]

Taking. An offence is committed if the conveyance is taken. 'Driving away' does not have to be proved but there must be evidence of some movement and that the vehicle was used as a conveyance. Accordingly, the moving of a motor car round the corner as a practical joke to lead the owner to believe it had been stolen was not an offence as it was not established that anyone rode inside it (*R v Stokes* [1983] RTR 59, [1982] Crim LR 695, CA). But where a defendant allowed a vehicle to roll down a hill by climbing in it and releasing the handbrake, he was guilty of the offence (*R v Bow* [1977] RTR 6, 64 Cr App Rep 54, CA). It would be otherwise if he did not get inside the vehicle. It is not a defence that the conveyance was stolen, as opposed to being taken. Nor is it a defence that the vehicle had been previously taken (*DPP v Spriggs* [1994] RTR 1, 157 JP 1143, [1993] Crim LR 622).

A[77.5]

Conveyance. Means a conveyance constructed or adapted for carrying one or more persons by land, water or air. It does not include a conveyance which can only be controlled by a person not carried in or on it.

A[77.6]

Motor vehicle. A motor vehicle is a mechanically propelled vehicle intended or adapted for use on a road.

A[77.7]

Owner. Includes a person in possession of the conveyance under a hiring or hire-purchase agreement.

A[77.8]

Owner's consent. Where the owner is induced by fraud to part with possession of his vehicle, no offence under this section has been committed (*Whittaker v Campbell* [1984] QB 318, [1983] 3 All ER 582). The owner has in fact consented even though in the civil law he may have a remedy against the fraudster.

A[77.9]

No offence was committed where consent was obtained by a false pretence as to the destination and purpose of the journey (*R v Peart* [1970] 2 QB 672, [1970] 2 All ER 823, CA). Nor where consent of an owner to allow a vehicle to be hired was obtained by the fraudulent misrepresentation of the hirer as to his identity and the holding of a full driving licence.

A[77.10]

Reduction of charge from theft of conveyance. If a defendant is tried in a magistrates' court for stealing a conveyance, the court cannot reduce the charge to this offence of taking the conveyance.

A[77.11]–A[77.15]

Time Limits. Like many summary road traffic offences, proceedings may be commenced within six months of the day the prosecution had knowledge of the offence subject to an overall time limit of three years from the commission of the offence.

A[77.16]

Successful defence. If the court is satisfied the defendant acted in the belief that he had lawful authority, or that the owner would have consented if the owner knew the circumstances, then he must be acquitted. The defendant only has to raise the defence. The absence of lawful authority or the owner's consent is an essential ingredient of the offence and it remains the prosecutor's duty to prove the allegation beyond a reasonable doubt.

A[77.17]

Aggravated vehicle-taking. See **A[3]**.

Sentencing

A[77.18]

Structure of the sentencing decision. See **B[3.6]**.

Guideline: Is it serious enough for a community penalty?

A[77.19]

Available sentences. See Table B at **B[4.2]**.

A[77.20]

Custodial sentence. See **B[2]**.

A[77.21]

Community sentence. See **B[3]**.

A[77.22]

Fines. See **B[33]**.

A[77.23]

Disqualification may be ordered in the case of a motor vehicle.

A[77.24]

Compensation. This may be ordered up to £5,000 either as part of a wider sentence or by itself as a substantive penalty. If the offender's means are limited and a monetary penalty is appropriate, preference must be given to ordering compensation instead of a fine.

A[78]

Television licence

Charge

A[78.1]

Using (or installing) apparatus for wireless telegraphy, namely a television receiver without a licence

Wireless Telegraphy Act 1949, s 1

Maximum penalty – Fine level 3.

Legal notes and definitions

A[78.2]

The charge should allege either that the apparatus was used or was installed.

A[78.3]

Using should be given its natural and ordinary meaning. This might create problems for enforcing authorities. They would if necessary have to persuade the court to draw the inference that the apparatus in question had been used by the defendant during the relevant period. If, for example, a television set in working order was found in the sitting-room of a house occupied by the defendant, it would not be difficult for a court to draw the necessary inference in the absence of some credible explanation by the defendant to the effect that it was not being used (*Rudd v Secretary of State for Trade and Industry* [1987] 2 All ER 553, [1987] 1 WLR 786, HL) and (*Whiley v DPP* [1995] Crim LR 39) in respect of a radio scanner.

A[78.4]

A user does not have to be an owner or hirer. Therefore where a set belonged to a husband but the wife switched it on, she was convicted of using it (*Monks v Pilgrim* [1979] Crim LR 595).

A[78.5]

Licence. Applies to the person named on the licence, his family and domestic staff living with him on the premises. The prosecution does not have to prove that the defendant did not have a valid licence (see s 101 MCA 1980).

A[78.6]

Applies to the premises named on the licence. Also covers members of family living away as full-time students at educational establishments using a portable television set (black and white or colour as described in the licence) in any other place provided:

(a) they normally reside at the licence holder's address; and
(b) the equipment is powered by internal batteries; and
(c) is not permanently installed.

There are concessions for touring caravans.

A[78.7]

Duration. Normally one year. If the licence is paid for by a subsequently dishonoured cheque, it continues in force until it is properly revoked. It may be short-dated if it is not renewed immediately on the expiry of the previous licence.

A[78.8]

Wireless telegraphy. This technical expression is defined in the Wireless Telegraphy Act 1949.

A[78.9]

A licence is required where a television set is used to receive BBC, ITV, satellite or cable television programmes, whether or not it is used for other purposes such as a home computer. No licence is required for closed circuit television or a set which reproduces a signal only from a recorder.

A[78.10]–A[78.14]

Concessions and exemptions are made under regulations for particular categories of persons. The number of sets that may be used on the same or different premises is also regulated by secondary legislation.

Sentencing

A[78.15]

Guideline: Is a discharge or fine appropriate?

A[78.16]

Although a conditional or absolute discharge may occasionally be appropriate the most usual penalty is a fine but the court cannot order 'arrears' of the licence fee. Ordering forfeiture of the television set is not provided for under this legislation and would be disproportionate to the overall penalty if ordered under s 143 Powers of Criminal Courts (Sentencing) Act 2000. See **B[34]**.

A[78.17]

Any fine will be fixed in accordance with the seriousness of the offence, ie duration of unlicensed use and the means of the offender (see **B[33]**).

A[79]

Theft

Charge

A[79.1]

Stealing

Theft Act 1968, s 1(1)

Maximum penalty – Fine level 5 and 6 months (**51 weeks). Triable either way.

Crown Court – 7 years' imprisonment and unlimited fine.

Motor vehicles. See **A[77]**.

Mode of trial

A[79.2]

Consider first the general notes at **I[4]**. In general, offences of theft should be tried summarily except for the presence of one or more of the following factors:

(a) breach of trust by a person in a position of substantial authority or in whom a high degree of trust has been placed;
(b) there has been sophisticated hiding or disguising of the offence;
(c) the offence has been committed by an organised gang;
(d) the victim was particularly vulnerable;
(e) there is unrecovered property of high value.

Legal notes and definitions

A[79.3]

Theft or **stealing** means dishonestly appropriating property belonging to another person with the intention of permanently depriving the other person of it. It does not matter whether the purpose of the theft was gain or not. Nor does it matter if the theft was for the benefit of the defendant or another person.

A[79.4]

The prosecution does not have to prove that the property was appropriated without the owner's consent. However, if the defendant believed he had the owner's consent that could be relevant in deciding whether the defendant acted dishonestly.

1 Dishonestly

A[79.5]

The appropriation can be dishonest even though the defendant was willing to pay for the property.

A[79.6]

The general test of dishonesty is: first, whether the accused's actions were dishonest according to the ordinary standards of reasonable and honest people and second, if so, whether the accused himself had realised that his actions were, according to those standards, dishonest. Thus a genuine belief by the accused that he was morally justified in acting as he did is no defence if he knew that ordinary people would consider such conduct to be dishonest (*R v Ghosh* [1982] QB 1053, [1982] 2 All ER 689, CA).

A[79.7]

The Theft Act 1968 provides that appropriation in the following circumstances is not 'dishonest':

(a) if the defendant believed he had the legal right to deprive the other of the property, either for himself or a third party; or
(b) if the defendant believed the other person would have consented had the other person known of the appropriation and the circumstances of the appropriation; or
(c) if the defendant believed the person to whom the property belonged could not be discovered by taking reasonable steps (but this defence is not available if the property came to the defendant as a trustee or a personal representative).

A[79.8]

2 Appropriates

Any assumption of the rights of an owner amounts to appropriation. If the defendant came by the property (innocently or otherwise) without stealing it and later assumed a right to it by keeping it or dealing with it as an owner, he has appropriated it. An appropriation may occur even though the owner has consented to the property being taken (*R v Hinks* [2001] 2 AC 241, [2000] 4 All ER 833, HL).

A[79.9]

The following are examples of dishonest appropriation:

(a) a parent whose child has brought home someone else's property and who retains the property; or
(b) a person who has found property (but see (1)(c) above); or
(c) a person who has acquired property through another person's mistake and has taken advantage of the error; or
(d) a person who switches price labels in a supermarket in order to obtain the goods at a price lower than the original marked price.

A[79.10]–A[79.15]

Repentance. It is important in some cases to appreciate the moment when the offence is complete. Sometimes, for example, the shoplifter decides either to put the goods back or to pay for them. Once the offence is completed such action is evidence of repentance only and may affect the sentence, but it does not establish innocence.

A[79.16]

Acquiring in good faith. If the defendant in good faith gave value for the property and later found that the vendor (or other person from whom he acquired the property) had no right to the goods, then the defendant is not guilty of theft in the event of his keeping or disposing of the property.

3 Property

A[79.17]

Includes money, stocks and shares, bills of exchange, insurance policies and all kinds of goods and property.

A[79.18]

Land. Land or anything forming part of land cannot be stolen except in the following circumstances:

(a) dishonest appropriation by trustees, personal representatives, liquidators of companies, persons holding a power of attorney and certain similar persons; or
(b) dishonest appropriation of something forming part of land by a person not in possession of the land (eg removing soil); or
(c) dishonest appropriation by tenants of fixtures let to be used with land.

A[79.19]

Attempting the impossible. A person may be guilty of an attempt to steal even though the facts are such that the commission of the offence of theft is impossible, for example by placing one's hand into an empty pocket.

A[79.20]

Things growing wild. If mushrooms, flowers, fruit or foliage from a plant which is growing wild are picked, that only amounts to theft if it is done for reward, or for sale or any other commercial purpose.

A[79.21]

Wild creatures. Appropriating a wild creature can only amount to theft if it has been reduced into the possession of someone else who has not lost or abandoned such possession of the creature; or if someone else is in the course of reducing it into his possession.

4 Belonging to another

A[79.22]

The property must be treated as belonging to anyone having possession or control of it or having any proprietary right or interest in it. Petrol ceases to belong to another when it is put in a vehicle's petrol tank at a self-service filling station (this accounts for the offence under s.3 of the Theft Act 1978 – see **A[21]**). When goods in a supermarket are for convenience or hygiene bagged, weighed and priced by an assistant they remain the property of the supermarket until paid for, and may therefore be the subject of the theft.

A[79.23]

Trust property. Must be treated as belonging to anyone having a right to enforce the trust. An intention to defeat the trust shall be treated as an intention to deprive the person entitled to enforce the trust of the property.

A[79.24]

Being entrusted with property. If a defendant (eg the treasurer of a holiday fund or Christmas club) has received property and is under an obligation to retain it or deal with it in a particular way, the property shall be treated as belonging to the beneficiary and not to the defendant.

A[79.25]–A[79.30]

Getting property by mistake. If the defendant obtained property by a mistake on the part of another person, and is under a legal (as opposed to a moral or social) obligation to restore it, then the property must be treated as belonging to the other person.

A[79.31]

If the court considers the defendant formed an intention not to restore the property, he must be deemed to have intended to deprive the other person of the property.

5 With the intention of permanently depriving

A[79.32]

The court must be satisfied that the defendant had this intention; or alternatively that he intended treating the property as his own to dispose of regardless of the owner's rights. The court must decide the defendant's intention by considering all the evidence and drawing from it such inferences as appear proper in the circumstances.

A[79.33]

Borrowing or lending. Can be used to establish that the defendant had the intention of permanently depriving the owner if, and only if, the borrowing or lending were for a period and the circumstances of the case make it equivalent to an outright taking or disposal. Ordinary borrowing or lending would not have this effect.

A[79.34]

Reduction of the charge (motor vehicles). If the property is a motor vehicle a magistrates' court cannot reduce the charge of theft to one of 'taking a conveyance', see **A[77]**.

A[79.35]

Proof of stealing one article enough. If the charge alleges the theft of several articles, the court can convict of theft if it decides that only one of the articles was stolen. The announcement of decision and court register should make the decision clear.

A[79.36]

Partnership property. A partner can be convicted of stealing property which he and another or other partners own.

Sentencing

A[79.37]

Structure of the sentencing decision. See **B[3.6]**.

Guideline: Is it serious enough for a community penalty?

See *R v Page* [2004] EWCA Crim 3358, [2004] All ER (D) 108 (Dec) for guidance on shop theft. Custody is a last resort.

A[79.38]

Available sentences. See Table A at **B[4.1]**.

A[79.39]

Custodial sentence. See **B[2]**.

A[79.40]–A[79.45]

Community sentence. See **B[3]**.

A[79.46]

Fine. See **B[33]**.

A[79.47]

Compensation. This may be ordered up to £5,000 either as part of a wider sentence or by itself as a substantive penalty. The court may deprive the defendant of any property in his possession when arrested if it was used, or intended for use, in the commission of a crime.

A[79.48]

Motor vehicles. If the property was a motor vehicle (defined as a mechanically propelled vehicle intended or adapted for use on a road) the court may disqualify but there is no endorsement or penalty points.

A[80]

Threatening behaviour or intentional harassment, alarm or distress and racially/religiously aggravated threatening behaviour or intentional harassment

Charge 1

A[80.1]

Using towards another threatening, abusive or insulting words or behaviour (or distributing or displaying to another person any writing, sign or other visible representation being threatening, abusive or insulting) intending to cause that other person to believe that immediate unlawful violence would be used against him or another by any person, or to provoke the immediate use of unlawful violence by that person or another or whereby that other person was likely to believe that such violence would be used or it was likely that such violence would be provoked

Public Order Act 1986, s 4(1)

Maximum penalty – Fine level 5 and 6 months (**51 weeks). Triable only by magistrates.

Charge 2

A[80.2]

A person is guilty of an offence if with intent to cause a person harassment, alarm and distress, he

(a) uses threatening, abusive or insulting words or behaviour, or
(b) displays any writing, sign or visible representation which is threatening, abusive or insulting,

thereby causing that or another person harassment, alarm or distress

Public Order Act 1986, s 4A

Maximum penalty – Fine level 4 and 6 months (**51 weeks). Triable only by magistrates.

Charge 3

A[80.3]

Using towards another threatening, abusive or insulting words or behaviour etc which was racially or religiously aggravated.

Maximum penalty – see Charge 4 below.

Charge 4

A[80.4]

Intentional harassment alarm or distress etc which is racially or religiously aggravated.

Crime and Disorder Act 1998, s 31

Maximum penalty - Fine level 5 and 6 months' imprisonment (**12 months). Triable either way. Specified violent offence under Sch 15, Part 1, CJA 2003.

Crown Court - 2 years' imprisonment and unlimited fine.

Legal notes and definitions

A[80.5]

Threatening; abusive; insulting. (The following comments are based on repealed legislation but still seem applicable.) The High Court has described these as being 'all very strong words'. If the evidence shows that the words or behaviour used fell short of being abusive, insulting or threatening but merely annoying then the case should be dismissed. The words 'f … off' shouted at a police officer who was trying to prevent a breach of the peace have been held to be 'insulting'. Shouting encouragement to a gang throwing stones at another gang is sufficient for a conviction under this section. See *Hammond v DPP* [2004] EWHC 69 (Admin), [2004] All ER (D) 50 (Jan) and *Percy v DPP* [2001] EWHC Admin 1125, 166 JP 93, [2002] Crim LR 835, [2001] All ER (D) 387 (Dec). Insulting words or an insulting sign should cause harassment, alarm or distress to another not just strong disagreement.

A[80.5A]

ECHR. In *Dehal v DPP*, [2005] WHC 2154 (Admin), [2005] All ER (D) 152 (Sep), the defendant had entered a Sikh Temple and affixed a notice to a notice board which, inter alia, described the president of the Temple as a hypocrite. The Administrative Court held that in order to justify the interference with a right to freedom of expression as set out in art 10 of the ECHR, the prosecution had to demonstrate that the prosecution was being brought in pursuance of a legitimate aim and that the prosecution was the minimum necessary response to that aim. Accordingly, the prosecution of the defendant had not been a proportionate response to his conduct.

A[80.6]

Violence does not include violence justified by law (eg self-defence or prevention of crime). The violence apprehended must be immediate which does not mean 'instantaneous' but connotes proximity in time and causation (*R v Horseferry Road Metropolitan Stipendiary Magistrate, ex p Siadatan* [1991] 1 QB 260, [1991] 1 All ER 324). For what is included see under the offence of violent disorder see **A[83]**.

A[80.7]

Intent. The accused must *intend* his words or behaviour etc to be, or be aware that his words etc may be, threatening, abusive or insulting and intend the apprehension of unlawful violence etc. In order to ensure that an arrest is lawful the defendant must be warned first about his conduct. This warning is not however part of the offence and so a case can still be determined where the arrest was not lawful (*DPP v Chippendale* [2004] EWHC 464 (Admin), [2004] All ER (D) 308 (Jan)).

A[80.8]

Intoxication. See under the offence of violent disorder at **A[83]**.

A[80.9]

Threatening etc behaviour may be committed in a public or private place. If the threatening etc words or behaviour are used inside a dwelling-house, the offence can only be committed if the other person is not inside that or another dwelling-house, but parts of a dwelling not occupied as a person's house or living accommodation do not count as a dwelling for this purpose, eg the shop underneath the owner's flat. A tent, caravan, vehicle, vessel or other temporary or movable structure may be a dwelling for this purpose where it is occupied as a person's house or as other living accommodation.

A[80.10]–A[80.15]

Racial/religious aggravation. See **A[23]**. Words such as 'jungle bunny', 'black bastard' and 'wog' will be a racial aggravation regardless of the fact that the defendant may have some other reason to abuse the victim (*DPP v McFarlane* [2002] EWHC 485 (Admin) [2002] All ER (D) 78 (Mar)). May often be sent to Crown Court for sentence and will usually result in a custodial sentence (*R v Miller* [1999] 2 Cr App Rep (S) 392, [1999] Crim LR 590, CA and *R v White* [2001] EWCA Crim 216 [2001] 1 WLR 1352, [2001] Crim LR 576).

Police officers are also entitled to the protection of the courts. See *Re Emma Lisa Jacobs* (2001) where a sentence of 3 months' imprisonment was upheld.

Sentencing

A[80.16]

Structure of the sentencing decision. See **B[3.6]**.

Guideline: Is it serious enough for a community penalty?

The correct approach is for the sentencer to determine the sentence for the underlying offence and then use a multiplier for the racial aggravation (*R v Greenwood* [2003] EWCA Crim 1937, [2003] All ER (D) 305 (Jun)).

Racially/religiously aggravated: Is it so serious that only custody is appropriate?

Even where no violence is used, serious verbal abuse in public may indicate sentence at the Crown Court (*R v Clark* [2004] 2 Cr App R (S.) 1, CA).

A[80.17]

Available sentences. See Table B at **B[4.2]**.

A[80.18]

Custodial sentence. See **B[2]**.

A[80.19]

Community sentence. See **B[3]**.

A[80.20]

Fines. See **B[33]**.

A[80.21]

Bind over. The court can bind over the defendant, with or without sureties. Prosecution witnesses may also be bound over if they are first warned and given the chance to address the court; the legal adviser should be consulted in such cases. Any bind over should be to keep the peace and be made for a specified period of time in a sum of money.

A[81]

Threats or intimidation of witnesses

Charge 1

A[81.1]

Did intimidate [ ] knowing or believing [ ] is assisting an investigation/is a witness or potential witness in proceedings with the intention that the investigation/course of justice would be interfered/perverted/obstructed

Criminal Justice and Public Order Act 1994, s 51(1)

See Charge 2 for penalty.

Charge 2

A[81.2]

Did threaten [ ] with harm intending to harm him knowing or believing that [ ] has assisted in an investigation or has given evidence in proceedings for an offence because he believes/ knows that assistance or evidence was given

Criminal Justice and Public Order Act 1994, s 51(2)

Maximum penalty – Fine level 5 and 6 months (**12 months). Triable either way.

Crown Court – maximum 5 years' imprisonment.

Note that similar offences carrying the same maximum penalty may now be charged under the Criminal Justice and Police Act 2001, ss 39 and 40. These offences are specifically aimed at incidents not covered by CJPOA 1994, s 51 and cover both civil and criminal proceedings.

Legal notes and definitions

A[81.3]

A person does an act to another person with the intention of intimidating/ harming not only when it is done directly but also when it is done to a third party with the same intention. The threat may be at a distance, eg over the telephone (*DPP v Mills* [1997] QB 300, [1996] 3 WLR 1093). An act might amount to intimidation under the section even though the victim is sufficiently steadfast not to be intimidated (*R v Petrascu* (2004)).

A[81.4]

Harm may be financial/physical to a person or property.

A[81.5]

Intention. The intention or motive required for the two charges need not be the only or predominant motive or intention with which the act is done or threatened. A threat to harm a witness relayed via a third party constitutes an offence under this section. If a threat to harm a witness takes place within one year after the trial the prosecution do not have to prove a connection between the threat and the trial: *A-G's Reference* (*No 1 of 1999*). If the prosecution can prove the act/threat and the defendant's knowledge/belief in the circumstances then the resultant motive/intention shall be presumed unless the contrary is proven.

A[81.5A]

Knowingly and ECHR. Section 51(7) of the CJPOA 1994 provides that if the defendant knowingly commits an act of intimidation it will be presumed that the defendant intended to interfere with the course of justice unless otherwise proven. The fact that the legislation imposes a reverse burden of proof on the defence is both justiciable and proportionate in ECHR terms having regard to the stated aims of the legislation and *Attorney General's Reference (No 1 of 2004)* [2004] EWCA Crim 1025, [2004] 1 WLR 2111.

A[81.6]

Witness includes jurors or potential jurors in the Crown Court.

A[81.7]

Investigation into an offence means an investigation by police or such other person charged with the duty of investigating offences or charging offenders.

A[81.8]

Offence includes an alleged or suspected offence.

Sentencing

A[81.9]

Generally this will be considered a serious offence and if committed in respect of a juror at the Crown Court will normally be dealt with by that court. Eighteen months' custody approved for intimidation of a 12-year-old witness by an 18-year-old defendant (*R v Rogers* [2001] EWCA Crim 1528 [2002] 1 Cr App Rep (S) 272). In *R v McDonnell* [2002] EWCA Crim 3201, [2003] 2 Cr App Rep (S) 117, eight months' imprisonment was upheld for threats to kill coupled with a slap to the face.

A[81.10]–A[81.15]

Structure of the sentencing decision. See **B[3.6]**.

A[81.16]

Available sentences. See Table B at **B[4.2]**.

A[81.17]

Custodial sentences. See **B[2]**.

A[81.18]

Community sentences. See **B[3]**.

A[81.19]

Fines. See **B[33]**.

A[82]

Vehicle interference

Charge

A[82.1]

Interfered with a motor vehicle or anything carried in or on the same with the intention that an offence of theft of the said motor vehicle or part of it or of anything carried in or on the said motor vehicle or an offence of taking and driving it away without consent should be committed

Criminal Attempts Act 1981, s 9(1)

Maximum penalty – Fine level 4 and 3 months (**51 weeks).

Legal notes and definitions

A[82.2]

This offence applies to trailers. A trailer means a vehicle drawn by a motor vehicle.

A[82.3]

Interfere. It will be for the court to decide whether a particular activity amounts to interference; simply keeping a vehicle under observation in the hope that an opportunity will arise to commit an offence would not be interference. In many cases the alleged activity would support a charge of attempting to steal which, unlike this offence is triable either way but this offence may be easier to prove because of the provision regarding 'intent'.

A[82.4]

Intent. There must be evidence of an intention to commit theft of the vehicle, trailer, any parts of them or anything carried in or on them, or to commit the offence of unauthorised taking of the vehicle or trailer. The prosecution does not have to prove precisely which of these offences the accused intended. In some cases, for example, the prosecution would be unable to prove whether the intention was to take the vehicle, steal it, or steal goods from inside it.

A[82.5]

Motor vehicle. Means a mechanically propelled vehicle intended or adapted for use on the road.

Sentencing

Guideline: Is it serious enough for a community penalty?

A[82.6]

See Table B at **B[4.2]** for available sentences.

A[83]

Violent disorder

Charge

A[83.1]

Being one of three or more persons present together and using or threatening unlawful violence so that the conduct taken together is such as would cause a person of reasonable firmness present at the scene to fear for his personal safety

Public Order Act 1986, s 2(1)

Maximum penalty - Fine level 5 and 6 months (**51 weeks). Triable either way. Specified violent offence under Sch 15, Part 1, CJA 2003.

Crown Court – 5 years' imprisonment and unlimited fine.

Mode of trial

A[83.2]

Cases of violent disorder should generally be considered for trial on indictment and see general notes at **I[4]**.

Legal notes and definitions

A[83.3]

The charge. Only one offence is created.

A[83.4]

Three or more persons. The defendants need not be using or threatening violence simultaneously.

A[83.5]

Violence does not include violence justified by law (eg self-defence or prevention of crime) but apart from that includes violent conduct towards property or persons and is not restricted to conduct causing or intended to cause injury or damage but includes any other violent conduct (for example, throwing at or towards a person a missile of a kind capable of causing injury which does not hit or falls short).

A[83.6]

Person of reasonable firmness need not actually be or be likely to be, present at the scene. See **A[2.7]**.

A[83.7]

Intent. A person may be guilty only if he intends to use or threaten violence, or is aware that his conduct may be violent or threaten violence.

A[83.8]

Intoxication. A person whose awareness is impaired by intoxication shall be taken to be aware of that of which he would be aware if not intoxicated, unless he shows that his intoxication was not self-induced, or that it was caused solely by the taking of a substance in the course of medical treatment. 'Intoxication' may be caused by drink, drugs or other means.

A[83.9]

Violent disorder may be committed in a public or private place.

Sentencing

A[83.10]–A[83.15]

Are magistrates' powers sufficient? (See *R v M* [2001] All ER (D) 403) where 18 months' detention and training order for a 17-year-old was upheld.)

Structure of the sentencing decision. See **B[3.6]**.

A[83.16]

Available sentences. See Table A at **B[4.1]**.

A[83.17]

Custodial sentence. See **B[2]**.

A[83.18]

Community sentence. See **B[3]**.

A[83.19]

Fines. See **B[33]**.

A[83.20]

Compensation. See **B[18]**.

Section B

Sentencing

Index to sentencing

(Indicates changes introduced by virtue of the CJA 2003 from a date to be appointed)**

B[1]

Remission to another court

B[1.1]

If the following conditions are met a magistrates' court may remit an offender to another magistrates' court (Powers of Criminal Courts (Sentencing) Act 2000, s 10). The conditions are:

(a) The court proposing to remit has convicted the offender of an offence which is punishable by either imprisonment or disqualification.
(b) The offender has attained 18 years of age.
(c) The court to which the convicting court proposes to remit has convicted the offender of another such offence but has not sentenced him nor committed him to the crown court to be dealt with.
(d) The receiving court consents to the remission.

B[1.2]

The offender may be remitted on bail or in custody. He is not required to consent to the remission nor has he any right of appeal against it.

B[1.3]

Juveniles. A magistrates' court which has found a juvenile offender (under 18) guilty of an offence must remit the juvenile to a youth court unless satisfied that it is undesirable to do so (Powers of Criminal Courts (Sentencing) Act 2000, s 8) and must exercise that power unless it is of the opinion that the case is one which can properly be dealt with by means of:

(a) an absolute or conditional discharge;
(b) a fine.

B[1.4]

The court to which he is remitted will normally be the youth court for the area in which he resides. If the court finding the juvenile guilty is itself a youth court it may remit to another youth court or deal with him as it thinks fit.

Remittal to an adult court.

B[1.5]

If a juvenile attains the age of 18 before trial in the youth court or after conviction but before sentence the youth court may remit for trial or sentence to the adult court in the same petty sessions area. The remittal may be on bail or in custody.

B[1A]

Transfer of Criminal Proceedings

B[1A.1]

Where a person appears or is brought before a magistrates' court –

(a) to be tried by the court for an offence, or
(b) for the court to inquire into the offence as examining justices,

the court may transfer the matter to another magistrates' court (MCA 1980, s 27A as inserted by Courts Act 2003, s 46).

The court may transfer the matter before of after beginning the trial or inquiry. If the magistrates' court transfers before hearing all of the evidence and the parties the court to whom the case has been transferred must, in effect, hear the evidence and the parties again. The power to transfer must be exercised in accordance with any directions given under Courts Act 2003, s 30(3).

B[1A.2]

It would appear that the consent of the magistrates' court to which the proceedings are to be transferred is not a legal requirement. Good practice suggests that the court to whom the case has been transferred should be contacted prior to transfer.

B[1A.3]

The reference to "examining justices" will become otiose on or after a date to be appointed by virtue of the CJA 2003 (allocation proceedings).

B[2]

Custodial sentences

B[2.1]

There are three main forms of custodial sentence: imprisonment, detention in a young offender institution and detention and training orders. By virtue of the CJA 2003, sentences of custody plus and intermittent custody will be available nationally from a date to be appointed. Assuming the provisions of the CJA 2003 are implemented, the new sentencing disposals will only apply to offences committed on or after the operative date.

B[2.2]

Imprisonment (at **B[37]**) is confined to defendants over the age of 21 years (**18 years). The minimum period is 5 days (**14 days) and the maximum is that fixed by statute. There is one other form of imprisonment – the suspended sentence.

B[2.3]

Detention in a young offender institution (at **B[25]**) is the equivalent of imprisonment for those under 21. The minimum age is 18 years for both males and females. (**From a date to be appointed sentences of detention in a YOI will be replaced by imprisonment for offences committed on or after the operative date.)

B[2.4]

The general minimum for 18–21 year old offenders is 21 days. In the case of detention in a young offender institution imposed for breach of a supervision order made on release from such an institution a term not exceeding 30 days may be imposed. (****B[2.2]** will apply to offences committed on or after the appointed date.)

B[2.5]

The maximum term is generally the maximum term that an adult could receive for the offence. The maximum is 12 months for two indictable offences. (**From an appointed date, the maximum sentence prescribed for summary offences will be 51 weeks. For indictable offences the maximum sentence will be 12 months imprisonment for a single offence and 65 weeks maximum for two or more indictable offences.)

B[2.6]

Detention and training orders. Available for 12 to 17 year old offenders inclusive. The court may order a period of 4, 6, 8, 10, 12, 18 or 24 months, half of which will be detention in a training centre and half of which will be supervised in the community.

B[2.7]

Presence of the accused. Imprisonment (or its equivalent) cannot be imposed in the absence of the accused.

B[2.8]

Legal representation. A person shall not be sentenced to a custodial sentence of any form (whether suspended or not) unless he is legally represented. There are two exceptions:

(i) where he has either been granted the right to representation funded by the Legal Services Commission and had it withdrawn because of his conduct or has been informed of his right to apply for representation and he failed to apply for it;
(ii) (as from October 2, 2006) his means have been assessed as such that he is required to make a contribution to his legal costs and he declines or fails to make the appropriate contributions in accordance with regulations made under the Criminal Defence Service Act 2006.

B[2.9]

Restrictions on imposing custodial sentences. A court may not pass a custodial sentence in any form on an offender of any age unless it is satisfied that:

(a) the offence, or the combination of the offence and one or more offences associated with it, was so serious that neither a fine alone nor a community sentence can be justified for the offence; or
(b) the offender fails to express a required willingness to comply with a requirement in a community order; or
(c) the offender fails to comply with an order for pre-sentence drug testing (CJA 2003, s 161(2)).

B[2.10]–B[2.15]

In forming such an opinion a court must take into account all such information about the circumstances of the offence (including any associated offences and any aggravating or mitigating factors) as is available to it, which will almost invariably include information in a pre-sentence report (see below). A court may also take into account any information about the offender which is before it. The court may take into account previous convictions and previous failures to respond to sentences when assessing the seriousness of current offending.

B[2.16]

Exceptionally ((b) above) the court may impose a custodial sentence where the defendant refuses to give his consent to a requirement in a community order proposed by the court which requires his consent.

B[2.17]

Apart from the exceptional case, the court must state in open court that it is of the opinion that either one or other of the criteria (a), (b) or (c) apply and why it is of that opinion. In any case, the court must explain to the offender in ordinary language why it is imposing a custodial sentence on him.

Even where the custody threshold is reached the court should ask if custody is unavoidable and, if so,

(a) can it can be suspended and, failing that:
(b) can the custodial sentence be served intermittently.

Any immediate sentence of custody should be for the shortest term, taking into account the aims or objectives of imposing a sentence (CJA 2003, ss.152 & 153). The fact that prisons were overcrowded might, for that reason, be a relevant factor where the sentencer's choice between custody and a community order was, so to speak, on the cusp (*A-G's Reference (No 11 of 2006); R v Scarth* [2006] EWCA 856, (2006) Times, 28 March.

Length of custodial sentences

B[2.18]

A custodial sentence passed by a court shall be for such term (not exceeding the permitted maximum) as in the opinion of the court is commensurate with the seriousness of the offence, or a combination of the offence and other offences associated with it.

B[2.19]

In determining sentence the court must have regard to the guidelines set by the Sentencing Guidelines Council and, if it departs from those guidelines, the court must state its opinion and reasons in open court and give an explanation to the offender in ordinary language.

B[2.20]

In forming an opinion on the appropriate length of sentence the court must take into account all such information about the circumstances of the offence (including any associated offences and any aggravating or mitigating factors) as is available to it (such as a pre-sentence report). In passing a sentence of imprisonment, subject to the exceptions contained in CJA 2003, s 240(4), the court must direct that the number of days for which the offender was remanded in custody in connection with an offence or a related offence shall count as time served by the offender as part of the sentence imposed (CJA 2003, s 240(3)). For concurrent or consecutive sentences imposed on the same occasion or on subsequent occasions the drafting of the legislation is far from clear (see *R v Barber* [2006] EWCA Crim 162, [2006] 2 Cr App Rep (S) 539). Justices should consult their legal adviser.

In passing a detention and training order on a juvenile offender the [youth] court must also take into account any time spent on secure remand when fixing the length of sentence, and time spent on remand must be calculated and announced at time of sentence in cases of imprisonment.

Pre-sentence report

B[2.21]

This means a report in writing which is made by a probation officer (or social worker) with a view to assisting the court in determining the most suitable method of dealing with an offender and contains such information as to such matters as may be prescribed by the Secretary of State.

B[2.22]

Before forming an opinion on the necessity for, and appropriate length of, a custodial sentence the court should obtain a pre-sentence report. Although a custodial sentence is not invalidated by the court's failure to obtain such a report, magistrates will no doubt continue to wish to meet the statutory requirement in all cases where an offender is in jeopardy of losing his liberty despite the 'let out' clause 'unless the court is of the opinion that it is unnecessary to obtain a pre-sentence report'.

Mentally disordered offenders

B[2.23]

Where the offender is, or appears to be, mentally disordered, the court must, unless in the circumstances of the case it appears unnecessary to do so, obtain a medical report made orally or in writing by a doctor approved under the Mental Health Act 1983 as having special experience in the diagnosis or treatment of mental disorder.

B[2.24]

Where a court is considering a custodial sentence in such circumstances it must consider:

(a) any information before it which relates to his mental condition (whether given in a medical report, a pre-sentence report or otherwise); and

(b) the likely effect of such a sentence on that condition and on any treatment which may be available for it.

B[3]

Community sentences

B[3.1]

The Criminal Justice Act 2003 introduced the concept of a 'community order', ie a sentence which consists of or includes one or more requirements: see **B[17.35]**. This generic community order only applies to defendants over 18 years, with community rehabilitation, community punishment, drug treatment and testing and curfew orders being preserved for 16 and 17 year olds at least until April 2007.

B[3.2]

A court may not impose a community sentence unless:

(a) it is of the opinion that the offence was serious enough to warrant such a sentence taking into account all such information about the circumstances of the offence (including any associated offences or any aggravating or mitigating factors) as is available to it;
(b) the particular order or orders comprising or forming part of the sentence are such as in the opinion of the court is, or taken together are, the most suitable for the offender taking into account any information about the offender which is before it (such as a pre-sentence report, see below);
(c) the restrictions on liberty imposed by the order or orders are such as in the opinion of the court are commensurate with the seriousness of the offence, or the combination of the offence and other offences associated with it, taking into account information about the circumstances etc as in (a) above.

Note that there will still be cases where the community threshold has been passed but a fine or discharge is still an appropriate penalty.

B[3.3]

When considering seriousness of the current offence or offences previous convictions and previous failures to respond to court orders may be taken into account.

B[3.4]

In the case of a 16 or 17 year old a community sentence shall not consist of or include both a community rehabilitation order and a community punishment order (but may, of course, consist of a, community punishment and rehabilitation order described at **B[11]**).

Pre-sentence report

B[3.5]

Before forming an opinion as to the suitability for an offender of one or more of the above orders, the court should obtain and consider a pre-sentence report unless it is of the opinion that it is unnecessary to obtain one.

B[3.6]

An adult community order must specify a date of not more than 3 years after commencement when all requirements must be completed. Individual requirements may be specified to be completed in a shorter period than that of the overall order.

The sentencing decision

B[3.7]

SENTENCING FORM FOR PSR

A: PRE-SENTENCE ASSESSMENT STAGE

DATE: ☐ 1a) **DEFENDANT**: ☐

b) **D.O.B**: ☐ c) **ADDRESS**: ☐

2. **CUSTODY**: ☐ **BAIL**: ☐

3. **CHARGES**: ☐

4. **GUIDELINE SENTENCE**: Fine/discharge ☐ Community ☐ Custody ☐ Commit for Sentence ☐

5. **OFFENCE FACTORS INFLUENCING ASSESSMENT**

a) Aggravating factors: ☐

b) Mitigating factors: ☐

c) Culpability

intentional	☐	reckless	☐
knew likely outcome	☐	negligent	☐

d) Harm caused/risked: ☐

6. **OFFENDER FACTORS INFLUENCING ASSESSMENT**

☐

7. **SERIOUSNESS** (sentencing range justified by offence and offending factors)

			L	M	H
Fine/discharge (no **PSR**)	☐	Community (serious enough)	☐	☐	☐
Custody (so serious)	☐	Commit to Crown Court (too serious)	☐		

8. **MAIN (1) AND SECONDARY (2) PURPOSE(S) OF SENTENCE**

Punishment	☐	Rehabilitation	☐	Reduction in crime/ deterrence	☐
Protection of public	☐	Reparation	☐		

9. **REPORT TYPE**: Fast ☐ Standard ☐ Due: ☐

B: SENTENCING STAGES

10. **FACTORS ARISING FROM REPORT**
Including, if appropriate, a) why you have reached a different conclusion from the indications of seriousness and purpose already given, or b) why you are departing from the proposals in the report.

11. **SENTENCE TO BE IMPOSED** (referring to reasons)

12. **CREDIT FOR GUILTY PLEA**
Record a) the extent of credit given and reasons for it, or b) what the sentence would have been if a timely guilty plea had been entered. (NB: Do not double count credit)

13. **ANCILLARY ORDERS**
Details of compensation (or reasons for not awarding it), plus other ancillary orders.

14. **REASONS FOR DEPARTING FROM SENTENCING COUNCIL GUIDELINES**

15. **EXPLAIN SENTENCE USING APPROPRIATE PRONOUNCEMENTS**

B[4.1]

TABLE A

■ Available sentences for either way offences punishable with imprisonment on summary conviction
See Index to sentencing for paragraph references

Age	10	11	12	13	14	15	16	17	18	19	20	21 and over	Notes
Imprisonment												■	
Suspended with requirements												■	Restrictions on custodial sentences: offence 'so serious' etc, pre-sentence report, legal representation
Detention in young									■	■	■		
offenders inst													
Detention Training Order*			■	■	■	■	■	■					**Under 15-year-old: court must specify the offender is persistent
Detention (One Day)												■	
Community order with requirements							■	■	■	■	■	■	
Community punishment							■	■	■	■	■	■	Community Orders offence 'serious enough' pre-sentence report
Community rehabilitation							■	■	■	■	■	■	
CP & CR Order							■	■	■	■	■	■	
Supervision	■	■	■	■	■	■	■	■					
Attendance Centre	■	■	■	■	■	■	■	■	■	■	■		
Curfew Order**	■	■	■	■	■	■	■	■	■	■	■	■	** Max 3 months for u-16s
Drug Treatment and Testing							■	■	■	■	■	■	
Action Plan Order[1]	■	■	■	■	■	■	■	■					
Fine	■	■	■	■	■	■	■	■	■	■	■	■	u-14 max £250, 14–17 £1,000
Compensation/Deprivation	■	■	■	■	■	■	■	■	■	■	■	■	see **B[18]** and **B[34]**
Order													
Discharge (Abs/Cond)	■	■	■	■	■	■	■	■	■	■	■	■	
Hospital Order	■	■	■	■	■	■	■	■	■	■	■	■	Medical recommendation
Guardianship Order	■	■	■	■	■	■	■	■	■	■	■	■	
Committal for Sentence									■	■	■	■	
PCC(S)A 2000, s 4													
Deferred Sentence with requirements	■	■	■	■	■	■	■	■	■	■	■	■	Court to give reasons
Reparation Order	■	■	■	■	■	■	■	■					

Notes

1 May not make if similar order in force or court proposes to make a community penalty or pass a custodial sentence.

2 Will change to requirements within a community sentence post April 2005.

B[4.2]

TABLE B

■ Available sentences for purely summary offences punishable with imprisonment
See Index to sentencing for paragraph references

Age	10	11	12	13	14	15	16	17	18	19	20	21 and over	Notes
Imprisonment												■	
Suspended with requirements												■	Restrictions on custodial sentences: offence 'so serious' etc, pre-sentence report, legal representation
Detention in young									■	■	■		
offenders inst													
Detention Training Order*			■	■	■	■	■	■					**Under 15-year-old: court must specify the offender is persistent
Detention (One Day)												■	
Community order with requirements							■	■	■	■	■	■	
Community punishment							■	■	■	■	■	■	
Community rehabilitation							■	■	■	■	■	■	Community Orders offence 'serious enough' pre-sentence report
CP & CR Order							■	■	■	■	■	■	
Supervision	■	■	■	■	■	■	■	■					
Attendance Centre	■	■	■	■	■	■	■	■	■	■	■		
Curfew Order**	■	■	■	■	■	■	■	■	■	■	■	■	** Max 3 months for u-16s
Drug Treatment and Testing							■	■	■	■	■	■	
Action Plan Order[1]	■	■	■	■	■	■	■	■					
Fine	■	■	■	■	■	■	■	■	■	■	■	■	u-14 max £250, 14–17 £1,000
Compensation/Deprivation	■	■	■	■	■	■	■	■	■	■	■	■	see **B[18]** and **B[34]**
Order													
Discharge (Abs/Cond)	■	■	■	■	■	■	■	■	■	■	■	■	
Hospital Order	■	■	■	■	■	■	■	■	■	■	■	■	Medical recommendation
Guardianship Order	■	■	■	■	■	■	■	■	■	■	■	■	
Committal for Sentence													
PCC(S)A 2000, s 4													
Deferred Sentence with requirements	■	■	■	■	■	■	■	■	■	■	■	■	Court to give reasons
Reparation Order	■	■	■	■	■	■	■	■					

Notes

1 May not make if similar order in force or court proposes to make a community penalty or pass a custodial sentence.

2 Will change to requirements within a community sentence post April 2005.

B[4.3]

TABLE C

■ Available sentences for purely summary offences not carrying imprisonment
See Index to sentencing for paragraph references

Age	10	11	12	13	14	15	16	17	18	19	20	21 and over	Notes
Imprisonment													
Suspended with requirements													
Detention in young offenders inst													
Detention (One Day)													
Detention and Training Order													
Community order with requirements									■	■	■	■	
Community punishment													Community Orders offence 'serious enough' pre-sentence report
Community rehabilitation							■	■					
CP & CR Order													
Supervision	■	■	■	■	■	■	■	■					
Attendance Centre													
Curfew Order**	■	■	■	■	■	■	■	■	■	■	■	■	** Max 3 months for u-16s
Drug Treatment and Testing							■	■	■	■	■	■	
Action Plan Order[1]	■	■	■	■	■	■	■	■					
Fine	■	■	■	■	■	■	■	■	■	■	■	■	u-14 max £250, 14–17 £1,000
Compensation/Deprivation Order	■	■	■	■	■	■	■	■	■	■	■	■	see **B[18]** and **B[34]**
Discharge (Abs/Cond)	■	■	■	■	■	■	■	■	■	■	■	■	
Hospital Order													
Guardianship Order													
Committal for Sentence													
Deferred Sentence with requirements	■	■	■	■	■	■	■	■	■	■	■	■	Court to give reasons
Reparation Order	■	■	■	■	■	■	■	■					

Notes

1 May not make if similar order in force or court proposes to make a community penalty or pass a custodial sentence.
2 Will change to requirements within a community sentence post April 2005.

B[4.4]

TABLE D

■ Available sentences according to age of offender
For full details refer to pages following on sentencing

Age	10	11	12	13	14	15	16	17	18	19	20	21 and over	Notes
Imprisonment												■	
Suspended with requirements												■	Restrictions on custodial sentences: offence 'so serious' etc, pre-sentence report, legal representation
Detention in young offenders inst[1,2]									■	■	■		
Detention Training Order[1,2]*			■	■	■	■	■	■					**Under 15-year-old: court must specify the offender is persistent
Detention (One Day)[1]												■	
Community order with requirements									■	■	■	■	
Community punishment[1,2]							■	■					
Community rehabilitation[2]							■	■					Community Orders offence 'serious enough' pre-sentence report
CP & CR Order[1,2]							■	■					
Supervision[2]	■	■	■	■	■	■	■	■				+	
Attendance Centre[1,2]	■	■	■	■	■	■	■	■					
Curfew Order**	■	■	■	■	■	■	■	■					** Max 3 months for u-16s
Drug Treatment and Testing							■	■					
Action Plan Order	■	■	■	■	■	■	■	■					
Fine	■	■	■	■	■	■	■	■	■	■	■	■	u-14 max £250, 14–17 £1,000
Compensation/Deprivation Order[3]	■	■	■	■	■	■	■	■	■	■	■	■	
Discharge (Abs/Cond)	■	■	■	■	■	■	■	■	■	■	■	■	
Hospital Order[1,2]	■	■	■	■	■	■	■	■	■	■	■	■	Medical recommendation
Guardianship Order[1,2]	■	■	■	■	■	■	■	■	■	■	■	■	
Committal for Sentence PCC(S)A 2000, s 4									■	■	■	■	Either way offences Court to give reasons
Deferred Sentence with requirements	■	■	■	■	■	■	■	■	■	■	■	■	
Reparation Order[2]	■	■	■	■	■	■	■	■					

(a) Sentences marked with [1] can only be imposed if the offence is punishable with imprisonment when committed by an adult over 21 years.
(b) As far as defendants aged under 18 are concerned, a magistrates' court (as opposed to a youth court) cannot impose any of the penalties marked with a [2]. The magistrates' court must remit such juveniles on bail or in care to a youth court which will usually be the youth court for the area in which he lives
(c) [3] Under PCCA 2000, s 143: see **B[34]**
\+ Avaiable up to the age of 25 in cases of default in payment of money where the court would have the power to commit to prison

B[5]

The process of sentencing

Introduction

B[5.1]

Sentencing is not and never will be an exact science; only rarely could a group of sentencers agree that a particular sentence was exactly right and, even if they did, they would probably be agreeing only that it was right to show a particular level of leniency. The prerogative of saying what is 'right' in terms of sentencing levels belongs to the Sentencing Guidelines Council who aim to promote consistency in sentencing and guidance in respect of offences or offenders in a particular category.

B[5.2]

However, a degree of vagueness might be thought to be inevitable when there are so many variables to be considered before a sentencing decision is reached. Not only should this fact not discourage a proper study of the subject of sentencing, but it should positively encourage it and the area of study most profitable to the lay magistrate is that of the process of sentencing, the route to be followed in order to reach a sentence which, if it cannot be said to be exactly right, at least is unlikely to be disturbed on appeal if the offender's circumstances remain the same. The framework for a structured sentencing decision is given at **B[3.7]**. This is amplified and explained in paragraphs 1–8 which follow. Determination of guilt and the factual basis for the sentencing decision is dealt with in Section I court procedure.

1 The offence

B[5.3]

An important principle of sentencing is that a sentence should not be more severe than is warranted by the seriousness of the offence and other offences associated with it. When considering the seriousness of the current offence or offences, previous convictions and failures to respond to previous sentences may be taken into account where relevant. Custodial sentences are reserved primarily for offenders who have committed an offence 'so serious' that only a custodial sentence can be justified for it, and community sentences are only available where the offence is 'serious enough' to warrant such a sentence.

The Purposes of Sentencing

B[5.4]

In respect of adults, the Criminal Justice Act 2003 sets out the objectives of sentencing as punishment, the reduction of crime (including deterrence), reforms and rehabilitation, protection of the public and reparation.

B[5.5]

A custodial sentence may also be imposed where the offender has refused to consent to a drug testing order or certain conditions requiring consent (see **B[2.9]**).

B[5.6]

Otherwise any sentence imposed will generally be commensurate with the seriousness of the offence, although the court, having considered all the mitigation, may take this into account in mitigating an offender's sentence.

Determining seriousness

B[5.7]

The facts. The court must be satisfied that the facts of the offence or offences for which sentence is to be passed have been proved or agreed.

B[5.8]

In determining the seriousness of an offence the court must take into account all information about the circumstances of the offence, any aggravating or mitigating factors as are available to it, and information in a pre-sentence report. The court must consider the offender's culpability and any harm or potential harm caused by the offence.

B[5.9]

Associated offence. In considering whether an offence is 'serious enough' to warrant a community sentence, or 'so serious' that only a custodial sentence can be justified, the court may consider the combination of the offence and other offences associated with it. An 'associated offence' is in essence another offence for which the offender is to be sentenced at that time or is to be taken into consideration.

B[5.10]–B[5.15]

Guidance on the seriousness of offences and aggravating and mitigating features is given by decisions of the Court of Appeal, the National Mode of Trial guidelines (**from a date to be appointed the National Allocation guidelines) and National Sentencing guidelines, published by the Sentencing Guidelines Council.

B[5.16]

Parliament also gives broad guidance to the courts by prescribing the maximum penalties available. For example, many minor offences are punishable only by a fine on level 1 (max £200) and level 5 (max £5,000). Other, more serious, offences are also punishable with imprisonment of up to 6 (**12) months.

2 Mitigation

B[5.17]

There are two particular objectives of mitigation: to draw to the attention of the court any factors relevant to mitigating the seriousness of the offence, and to highlight mitigation personal to the offender.

B[5.18]

The first consideration for the court in determining sentence is the seriousness of the offence. The seriousness of the offence will generally determine whether the court must impose a custodial sentence or if the offence warrants the making of a community sentence, a fine or discharge.

B[5.19]

In addressing the seriousness of the offence, the circumstances of the offence should be examined to see whether they disclose any mitigating circumstances. Guidance on what may amount to a mitigating (or aggravating) feature of an offence is given by the Court of Appeal, the National Mode of Trial Guidelines (**National Allocation guidelines) and guidelines issued by the Sentencing Guidelines Council (see http://www.sentencing-guidelines.gov.uk). Such guidance is noted where appropriate in the articles on particular offences in Sections A and C of this work. An example would be an offence of assault. The court would be concerned to know whether a weapon was used, whether the victim was subjected to kicks, and if the offender was provoked. An offence committed under considerable provocation will obviously be treated differently from one for which elaborate plans were made in advance. Considerations in an offence of theft might include the value of the property stolen, whether any or all of the property was recovered and whether the offender was in a position of trust? An offence committed whilst on bail must be treated as an aggravating circumstance.

Racial aggravation, religious aggravation and aggravation related to sexual orientation or disability, together with offences committed whilst on bail, are all statutory aggravating factors which will also make an offence more serious.

B[5.20]

The seriousness of the offence including culpability and harm considerations will broadly determine which range of sentencing options is open to the court: custody, community, financial or a discharge. Where the court is concerned with a violent or sexual offence and is considering a custodial sentence to protect the public, the personal circumstances and history will become relevant. However, personal mitigation is usually more relevant at the second stage when the general level of seriousness has been determined, where mitigation will affect the final choice of sentence and the impact it will have on the offender. While no sentence may be more severe than is justified by the defendant's offence, personal mitigation may serve to reduce the punishment or suggest that a more individualised approach may be appropriate. In forming an opinion, whether a particular community order or orders comprising a community sentence is or are the most suitable for the offender, the court may take into account any information about the offender which is before it. Mitigating factors which have commonly been considered by the courts are referred to under 'Consideration of sentences' at **B[5.36]–B[5.48]**.

3 Availability of sentences

B[5.21]

Available sentences are determined by the maximum penalties prescribed by Parliament and by the court's assessment of the gravity of the offence.

As mentioned above the maximum penalty for an offence is fixed by statute as being a fine, or a fine and custody. Some sentences and orders of the court are available only where an offence is punishable in the case of an adult with imprisonment (the defendant himself does not need to be liable to imprisonment). A comparison of Tables A and C at **B[4.1]** and **B[4.3]** will make this apparent. Furthermore some sentences are only available to offenders of a certain age – see **B[1.5]**.

B[5.22]

By a systematic process of noting whether an offence is punishable with imprisonment and the age of the offender, the sentencing options available to the court can be narrowed progressively.

B[5.23]

Criminal Justice Act 2003. This further categorises sentences and orders into four broad divisions: discharges (instead of sentencing), financial, community and custodial. In addition there are orders providing for the medical treatment of mentally disturbed offenders.

B[5.24]

Discharges (absolute/conditional). These are available to all offenders and for all offences where the court is satisfied that having regard to the circumstances of the offence and the offender it is inexpedient to inflict punishment. See **B[31]**.

B[5.25]–B[5.30]

Financial penalties. These include fines (**B[33]**), compensation (**B[18]**) and deprivation of property (**B[34]**) and are available to all offenders and for all offences.

B[5.31]

Community orders for 16 and 17 year olds (see **B[3]**). These are:

community rehabilitation order (**B[38]**);
community punishment order (**B[17]**);
community punishment and rehabilitation order (**B[11]**);
curfew order (**B[21]**);
supervision order (juveniles only) (**B[47]**);
attendance centre (**B[9]**);
action plan order (juveniles only) (**B[7A]**);
drug rehabilitation requirement (formerly drug treatment and testing order) (over 16 years old) (**B[31A]**).

B[5.32]

Community orders (adults). The court may only impose a community sentence which consists of one or more requirements where it considers the offence, or a combination of the offence and other 'associated offences' to be 'serious enough' to warrant such a sentence. The fact that an offence is 'serious enough' does not mean that the court must pass a community sentence, only that it may do so (see **B[17.35]** onwards).

B[5.33]

Custodial sentences (see **B[2]**). The custodial sentences available to the magistrates are imprisonment and for offenders under 21, detention in a young offender institution (**to be replaced by a sentence of imprisonment from a date to be appointed by virtue of the CJA 2003) and detention and training orders for offenders aged 12 to 17 inclusive. They are only available where statute defines an offence as being punishable with imprisonment and for adult offenders only **where the offence carries a custodial sentence of

28 weeks or more. (**It is anticipated Custody plus and intermittent custody will be available nationally from a date to be appointed but consult the legal adviser.)

B[5.34]

A custodial sentence may generally only be imposed where the offence or a combination of the offence and 'associated offences' is 'so serious' that only such a sentence can be justified for it. The court will usually find it helpful to consider the nature and extent of the defendant's criminal culpability and the nature and extent of any injury or damage caused to the victim (*R v Howells* [1999] 1 All ER 50, [1999] 1 WLR 307, CA). However, although this criterion may be satisfied the court may nevertheless, in the case of a mentally ill defendant, make a hospital or guardianship order.

B[5.35]

Exceptionally a custodial sentence may be imposed where the offender has refused to consent to a drug testing order and certain conditions in a community order requiring consent ie a willingness to comply with the requirements.

4 Consideration of sentences

B[5.36]

When the court has ascertained the range of sentences appropriate for the seriousness of the offence, it must then proceed to select the particular sentence appropriate for the case. In this task it will be assisted by its appreciation of the seriousness of the offence but also by mitigation personal to the offender, any pre- sentence report and the court's objective in sentencing.

B[5.37]

Mitigation. Nothing shall prevent a court from mitigating an offender's sentence by taking into account any such matters as, in the opinion of the court, are relevant in mitigation of sentence. Mitigating factors which have commonly been considered by courts include the following.

B[5.38]

1 Youth of the offender. This may operate as mitigation and will usually indicate a lower level of sentence (eg a smaller fine or shorter period of custody) than would be appropriate otherwise. The mitigating effect of youth, however, may be cancelled out by other factors, such as a record of previous convictions which is serious having regard to the offender's age, or which shows a proclivity for crime beyond what one would expect for his age.

B[5.39]

2 Older offenders who have not previously offended would receive credit for a previously blameless life especially when receiving a more serious penalty such as a community sentence or custody.

B[5.40]–B[5.45]

3 Effect of previous convictions. Previous convictions must be taken into account and may make an offence more serious although this will depend upon the nature of the offence and the time elapsed since conviction. Within the range of sentences appropriate to the seriousness of the offence good character is almost always strong mitigation and the worse an offender's previous record is, the less 'discount' he can expect for good character. Occasionally, the record of previous convictions may show a significant gap since the last conviction and might be taken as evidence of a genuine effort to keep out of trouble. The record may also show that the present offence is out of character, for example, when a man with a long record of petty theft appears on a charge of indecent assault.

B[5.46]

4 Plea of guilty. A plea of guilty will nearly always give a sentencing discount of between 10% and 33% depending upon the stage of proceedings and the circumstances that the indication of plea was given. Remorse or contrition will mitigate the sentence particularly when there is real evidence of it. A ready admission of guilt, a willingness to assist the police, and voluntary efforts to make compensation can all be interpreted as evidence of contrition. Particularly in cases involving sexual offences a plea of guilty will spare witnesses, especially young persons, from the ordeal of giving evidence, even though the law now provides more sympathetic means for the reception of such evidence. Where the court does reduce or does not reduce the sentence because of the circumstances and stage at which the guilty plea is entered it must state in open court the reasons for its decision.

B[5.47]

5 Loss of employment etc. An offender must generally be taken to have foreseen the normal consequences of conviction and so factors such as distress to his family, loss of job, pension, good character, etc will usually have little mitigating value. Where consequences follow which could not reasonably have been foreseen, for example, where the offence was unconnected with the offender's employment but he nevertheless finds himself dismissed, or where the offence was committed on the spur of the moment under provocation with no opportunity to consider the consequences, some allowance may be made if those consequences turn out to be disastrous. The person who is especially vulnerable must be expected to take special care. So, for example, the person whose employment depends upon his having a driving licence must be expected to take particular care not to commit endorsable offences. People such as doctors, nurses and solicitors, from whom a high ethical standard is expected, must expect the consequences of conviction for an offence which amounts to a breach of those standards and cannot claim professional disciplinary action in mitigation.

B[5.48]

Unrepresented defendant. The court has a duty itself to seek out mitigating factors before finally arriving at a sentence. It should be especially careful not to assume that there are none in the case of the inarticulate unrepresented defendant.

5 The totality of sentencing

B[5.49]

It has already been seen that the choice of available sentences is limited by the seriousness of the offence(s). In some cases where the offence(s) is (are) 'so serious', a custodial sentence is the only option. For community sentences the offences must be 'serious enough'. There is accordingly a link between the sentences for an offence and its seriousness. The general principle is that the term of a custodial sentence, the restriction of liberty imposed by a community sentence or the amount of a fine must be commensurate with the offence or associated offences, ie all the offences for which the defendant is being sentenced. This is referred to as the 'totality' principle of sentencing. An important consequence with that principle is that the sentence may not, with the exception of custodial sentences for dangerous offenders, exceed that which is proportionate to the offence(s) committed.

6 Choice of sentence

B[5.50]

The deliberations of the court will have brought into focus more than one form of sentence. For example, it may be that the offence is 'serious enough' to warrant a community sentence. The pre-sentence report may have considered a range of community orders. The probation officer will have considered the seriousness of the offence and have proposed a sentence which is commensurate with the seriousness of the offence and takes into account the circumstances of the offender. The court will need to be clear that the sentence adequately reflects the seriousness of the offence while (in the case of a community penalty) also being the most suitable for the offender. It does not mean that if an offence is serious enough to warrant a community sentence that is the only sentence which may be imposed. If there is mitigation which allows the court to impose a fine then the fine must reflect the seriousness of the offence and the financial circumstances of the offender.

B[5.51]

The advice of the legal adviser will be essential to ensure that all the statutory criteria which must be satisfied before sentence can be passed and the correct ancillary orders made.

B[5.52]

The good chairman will have noted during the hearing such matters as applications for costs, or forfeiture of drugs. Liability for endorsement and disqualification will also have occupied attention and after the substantive sentence has been agreed by (at least) a majority of the justices, the chairman will deal with each of these matters in turn. Save in the simplest cases, the chairman will make a written note of the total decision so that no error or omission is made.

7 Statement accompanying the sentence

B[5.53]

The Criminal Justice Act 2003, s 174 requires a court to give reasons for and explain the effect of its sentence

The requirement of Article 6 of the European Convention on Human Rights means that reasons should be given. Indeed the effect, not to say the benefit, of a sound sentencing decision can sometimes be lost because the defendant does not understand the reasoning behind it, or because the public do not.

B[5.54]

When a particular sentence falls within the Sentencing Guidelines Council guidance for the kind of offence and offender – when it is the sort of sentence the defendant probably expected to receive – there will seldom be justification for garnishing the reasons. However, when the court imposes a sentence which might be unexpected the reasons for this departure from normal sentencing habits might be fuller. Likewise, when different types of sentence are imposed on co-accused whose circumstances may appear to be similar. The needs of the public as well as those of the defendant and any victim of his offence should be borne in mind. A structured approach to the sentencing decision, consultation with the clerk and a careful note will assist the chairman when giving reasons

Victim Impact Statement

B[5.55]–B[5.60]

Victim impact statements read by the prosecution give victims a formal method to say how the crime has affected them. It may identify a need for protection or support and can be taken into account when sentencing (*Practice Direction* (2001)).

B[5.61]

It is worth noting the pre ECHR law which requires reasons to be given. Before announcing the court's reasons the chairman should consult the legal adviser:

(a) When sentencing an offender to imprisonment [**for offences committed before a date to be appointed under the CJA 2003 – detention in a young offender institution] (except where he has refused to consent to a community sentence);
(b) when not requiring the subject of a suspended sentence to serve that sentence after committing a further offence;
(c) when declining to endorse or disqualify for special reasons;
(d) when not disqualifying for the minimum period where 12 penalty points have accumulated;
(e) when deferring sentence an indication should be given to the offender as to what is expected of him during the period of deferment, i e the reason for the deferment;
(f) in the youth court it is desirable that the court should indicate in advance what sentence or disposal it has in mind to order;
(g) when refusing bail or in certain circumstances granting bail for murder, manslaughter or rape;
(h) when deciding not to award compensation when otherwise empowered to do so;
(i) when refusing to grant an appeal it is good practice for the court to give its reasons;
(j) where an offence is treated more seriously because the court finds that it was statutorily aggravated that fact should be stated in open court.

B[5.62]

It is generally inadvisable to deliver a lecture or homily or offer any other words of worldly wisdom to a defendant who is being sentenced. Research has shown that most prisoners cannot remember even a short time after sentence much of what the judge said and even whether he said anything at all.

8 Pronouncement of sentence

B[5.63]

The chairman should announce the sentence(s) in a way which leaves no one in court in any doubt as to the court's decision. In the following pages each possible sentence is considered and a form of words is provided as a guide to the way in which the sentence may be announced. It is not suggested that the chairman should read the sentence from this book but that a glance at the wording suggested here will assist in ensuring that all the necessary legal points have been covered. Where an offender is to be sentenced for more than one offence it is advised that each sentence is related to each offence by description. It is bad practice to sentence in such terms as, 'For the first offence you will be fined £50. For the second offence you will be fined £100 and your licence endorsed. For the third offence etc.' Bear in mind that the offender has no idea of the order in which offences appear on the list and therefore has no way of relating the penalties to the offences if they are announced in this fashion. The better practice is exemplified as follows: 'For the burglary and theft at Jackson's, the butchers, you will go to prison for 20 days; for using the credit card to obtain a camera from Browns, you will go to prison for 15 days which will be in addition to the first sentence, which means you will go to prison for a total of 35 days.' Whenever there are several sentences to be announced, the chairman should totalise the effect of them, that is, the total amount of a monetary penalty, the total period of imprisonment or of disqualification should be stated. Words such as concurrent or consecutive need not be used if other words are used which make it clear what the total effect of the sentence is, as in the example above.

B[5.64]

When offences have been taken into consideration in arriving at a sentence that fact should be stated as a preamble to the sentence.

B[5.65]

Where relevant the chairman should announce by how much the sentence has been reduced by virtue of the defendant's guilty plea.

B[6]

Multiplicity of charges

B[6.1]

Sometimes a defendant faces more than one charge stemming from the same circumstances and while this is generally unobjectionable there are occasions when the court feels that the prosecution is having two bites at the cherry. Some courts impose the appropriate penalty on one charge and mark the other 'No separate penalty'. Another practice is to decide the appropriate penalty and divide it between the two offences but this may result in penalties which appear inadequately low.

B[7]

Power to review decisions (MCA 1980, s 142)

B[7.1]

It occasionally happens that information reaches a court after a case is disposed of which, if it had been known earlier, might have affected the court's decision. Sometimes, for example, it is simply the realisation by a clerk that one of his staff failed to advise the justices that they had no power to make a particular decision. Or it may be that for some compelling reason, where the defendant was convicted after a not guilty plea, the verdict should be reconsidered (e g after a conviction for driving without insurance, a valid insurance certificate is discovered). The test as to whether a court should reopen a case is whether it would be in the interests of justice to do so (*R v Ealing Magistrates' Court, ex p Sahota* (1997) 161 JP 73, [1997] 45 LS Gaz R 29).

B[7.2]

The court has power to vary or rescind a sentence or order and may substitute some other sentence or order (*R v Sheffield City Justices, ex p Foster* (1999) Times, 2 November. If, however, the decision has already been subject to an appeal to a higher court, the power to reopen no longer applies.

B[7.3]

The provisions may operate against a defendant, for example where the court has omitted to impose penalty points or an endorsable road traffic offence. Note, however, the power does not extend to overturning an acquittal (*R v Gravesend Justices, ex p Dexter* [1977] Crim LR 298).

B[7.4]

When the court alters a sentence or order under this procedure, and substitutes another, that other sentence or order will take effect from the date of the first sentence or order, unless the court otherwise directs. Note the power under the Magistrates Courts Act 1980, s 142 does not extend to civil proceedings (*R (on the application of Mathialagam) v Southwark London Borough Council* [2004] EWCA Civ 1689, [2004] All ER (D) 179 (Dec)).

B[7A]

Action plan orders (PCC(S) Act 2000, ss 69–72 as amended)

Limitations

B[7A.1]

May only be made by the Youth Court.

Reasons

B[7A.2]

The court must be satisfied that it is desirable to make an action plan order in the interests of securing the offender's rehabilitation or preventing the commission of further offences.

B[7A.3]

An action plan order may not be made if an action plan order is already in force, or if the court proposes to pass a custodial sentence, or make a community rehabilitation order, a community punishment order and a combination of these two orders, a supervision order or an attendance centre order. An action plan order may not be made where the court makes a referral order.

Reports

B[7A.4]

Before making an action plan order, the court must obtain and consider a written report. (This is not a full pre-sentence report.)

Consent

B[7A.5]

The consent of the offender is not required.

How to announce

B[7A.6]

This court makes an action plan order. You will be supervised for the next three months. During that time you will be required to comply with the following. [*Added requirement should be explained in ordinary language***]**

B[7A.7]

The order requires the offender be under supervision for three months and to comply with any of the following requirements:

(a) to participate in specified activities;
(b) to present himself to a specified person(s) at a specified place or places and at a specified time;
(c) to attend at an attendance centre for a specified number of hours;
(d) to stay away from a specified place or places;
(e) to comply with any specified arrangements for his education;
(f) to make specified reparation to a person or persons or to the community at large;
(g) to attend any hearing fixed by the court. The court may fix a further hearing not more than 21 days after the order is made allowing the responsible officer to review progress and any unforeseen problems; and
(h) ("drug treatment requirement") to submit to treatment by or under the direction of a specified person having the necessary qualifications and experience with a view to the reduction or elimination of the offender's dependency on or a propensity to misuse drugs.

Restrictions

B[7A.8]

An offender may be required to attend at an attendance centre only if the offence is punishable with imprisonment, and reparation requirements may be made in respect of a specified individual only if that individual has been identified as the victim of the offence and consents to the reparation requirement being made.

In the case of a drug treatment requirement (**B[7A.7]** above), the treatment period must be specified in the order. The court must consult with the relevant youth offending team prior to making the requirement and it is also advisable for justices to seek the advice of their legal adviser.

B[8]

Anti-social behaviour orders (ASBOs)

(Crime and Disorder Act 1998, ss 1–4)

Limitations

B[8.1]

Civil Applications – Can only be applied for by either:

(i) the relevant local authority;

(ii) the police;

(iii) the British Transport Police; or

(iv) a recognised housing association or action trust.

B[8.2]

Age limits – May be made for a person aged 10 years or over.

B[8.3]

Maximum/minimum period – An order must be for a minimum period of 2 years, but it is inappropriate to make an order for an indefinite period (*R v Vittles* [2004] EWCA Crim 1089, [2004] All ER (D) 334 (May)).

B[8.4]

The Application – The application is to a magistrates' court by way of complaint. If the respondent is under 18 years of age the justices constituting the court should normally be qualified to sit in the youth court. There are dispensations for interim orders or if it is not practicable to constitute a bench contributing to a delay in hearing the case (*Practice Direction (Magistrates' Courts: Anti-Social Behaviour Orders: Composition of Benches)* 24 February 2006, BLD 2702060704). A separate application must be made in respect of each named individual. The defendant will receive a summons with a copy of the written application. Due to the severe sanction for breach a criminal standard of proof is required (*R v Manchester Crown Court, ex p McCann* [2001] 1 WLR 358, sub nom R v Crown Court at Manchester, ex p McCann 165 JP 225, [2001] 02 LS Gaz R 40, 144 Sol Jo

LB 287; affd sub nom R (on the application of McCann) v Crown Court at Manchester [2001] EWCA Civ 281 [2001] 4 All ER 264, [2001] 1 WLR 1084, 165 JP 545). Even though the proceedings are civil in nature, the court may rely upon facts which previously formed the basis of criminal prosecutions (*S v Poole Borough Council* [2002] EWHC 244 (Admin) [2002] All ER (D) 143 (Feb)); *R (on the application of the Chief Constable of Mercia Constabulary) v Boorman* [2005] EWHC Admin 2559).

B[8.5]

The order and its terms – may be made against a person who it has been proved has acted in an anti-social manner (that is in a manner that caused or was likely to cause harassment, alarm or distress, to one or more persons not in the same household as himself) and an order is necessary to prevent further anti-social acts. It may prohibit further anti-social acts described in the order, necessary to protect relevant persons. The terms of the ASBO must be clear and commensurate with the risk they seek to guard against (*R v McGrath* [2005] EWCA Crim 353, [2005] All ER (D) 81 (May)). A curfew may be a legitimate condition so long as it was preventive and protective (*R (on the application of Lonergan) v Lewes Crown Court and Secretary of State for the Home Department (interested party)* [2005] EWHC 457 (Admin), [2005] All ER (D) 382 (Mar)).

Judicial Guidance – In *R v Boness, R v Bebbington* [2005] EWCA Crim 2395, [2006] 1 Cr App Rep (S) 690, the Court of Appeal ruled as follows:

(1) An ASBO had to be precise and capable of being understood by the offender. It followed that the court should ask itself, before making an order, whether the terms of the order were clear so that the defendant would know precisely what it was that he was prohibited from doing.

(2) There must be evidence of anti-social behaviour (see *R (on the application of Mills) v Birmingham Magistrates' Court* [2005] EWHC 2732 (Admin), (2005) 170 JP 237). Following a finding that the defendant had acted in an anti-social manner (whether or not the act constituted a criminal offence), the test for making an order that prohibited the offender from doing something was one of necessity (see *R v W; R v F* [2006] EWCA Crim 686).

(3) Each separate order prohibiting a person from doing a specified thing had to be necessary to protect persons from further anti-social acts by him. Accordingly, any order had to be tailor-made for the individual defendant, not designed on a word processor for use in every case.

(4) The purpose of an order was preventative, not to punish. The use of an ASBO to punish a defendant was unlawful.

(5) Where the ASBO was being sought as ancillary to a criminal sentence or disposal, the court should not allow itself to be diverted by a defendant's representative at the sentencing stage in the hope that the court might make such an order as an alternative to prison or other sanction. It might be better for the court to decide the substantive sentence and then move on to consider whether an ASBO should be made or not after sentence has been pronounced, albeit at the same hearing [subject to the

power of the court to adjourn consideration of an ASBO to a later date (Crime and Disorder Act 1998, s 1C as amended)].

(6) The court should not impose an order which prohibited a defendant from committing a specified criminal offence, if the sentence which could be passed following conviction for the offence should be a sufficient deterrent. It followed that an ASBO should not be used merely to increase the sentence of imprisonment which a defendant was liable to receive. Whilst different considerations might apply where the maximum sentence was a fine, the court had still to go through all the steps to ensure that the order was necessary.

(7) The corollary to (6) above was that a court should be reluctant to impose an order which prohibited a defendant from committing a specified criminal offence. The aim of an ASBO was to prevent anti-social behaviour, by enabling action to be taken before the anti-social behaviour it was designed to prevent was to take place.

(8) The terms of the order had to be proportionate in the sense that they had to be commensurate with the risk to be guarded against. That was particularly important where an order might interfere with a defendant's right under the European Convention of Human Rights.

B[8.6]

Statutory defence – to an application is available namely that the behaviour complained of was reasonable in the particular circumstances.

B[8.7]

Interim Orders – For guidance on ex parte applications *see R (on the application of Manchester City Council) v Manchester Magistrates' Court* (2005) Times, 8 March, [2005] All ER (D) 103 (Feb). Interim orders may be made pending the determination of an order if the court considers it just. An application may be made without notice if the justices are satisfied that it is necessary. The court itself may direct that notice be served on the defendant and refuse to make an order without notice (*R (Kenny) v Leeds Magistrates* [2003] EWHC 2963 (Admin), [2004] 1 All ER 1333, [2003] All ER (D) 104 (Dec); affd sub nom R (on the application of M) v Secretary of State for Constitutional Affairs and Lord Chancellor [2004] EWCA Civ 312, [2004] All ER (D) 345 (Mar)). See also *R (on the application of M) v Secretary of State for Constitutional Affairs and Lord Chancellor* [2004] EWCA Civ 312, [2004] All ER (D) 345 (Mar), CA.

There is no presumption that an order against publicity will be made on an interim order against a juvenile but age is an important consideration (*R (on the application of K) v Knowsley Metropolitan Borough Council* [2004] EWHC 1933 (Admin), 168 JP 461, sub nom Keating v Knowsley Metropolitan Borough Council [2004] All ER (D) 383 (Jul)).

B[8.8]

Criminal Proceedings – An ASBO may also be made as an ancillary order following a conviction for a criminal offence committed after 2 December 2002 if:

a) the offender has acted at any time since 1 April 1999 in an anti-social manner (causing or likely to cause harassment, alarm or distress to a person not in the same household) and
b) the order is necessary to protect persons in England and Wales from further anti-social behaviour.

Guidance was given in *R v Parkin* [2004] EWCA Crim 287, [2004] All ER (D) 32 (Feb) on the principles to be followed. This must be read in the light of *R v Boness, R v Bebbington* and others at ***B[8.5]*** above.

The order must be necessary, precise, recorded, explained to the defendant and reduced to writing. The order may be at the invitation of the prosecution or in the court's discretion. The court may hear evidence not admissible in criminal proceedings (CDA 1998, s 1C). The court may adjourn proceedings in respect of an ASBO after conviction even after sentencing the defendant. If it does so, it may make an interim order and may issue a warrant if the defendant does not reappear.

It is not inappropriate to make an ASBO in motoring offences if their regularity and type constitutes anti-social behaviour. It is not appropriate to make an order just to increase the penalty for breach of it (*R v Hall* [2004] EWCA Crim 2671, [2004] All ER (D) 377 (Nov)).

B[8.9]

The Order – May be for any term not less than 2 years and may require the defendant to refrain from any specified activities. In the case of a juvenile under 16 the court must make a parenting order unless it is able to justify its reasons for not doing so. It must also consider whether the individual support conditions are satisfied. If fulfilled the court must make an individual support order. If the court is not satisfied that the conditions are fulfilled it must state its reasons and cause those to be recorded in the court register: Crime and Disorder Act 1998, s 1A as amended by CJA 2003, s 322.

B[8.10]

Restrictions – The order may not be made following an order of absolute discharge or no separate penalty.

B[8.11]

An order may be suspended while the defendant remains in custody.

B[8.12]

Variation or discharge – of a civil order may only be done within the first two years with the consent of both parties. There is no provision for discharge of a criminal order before the two year period without the consent of the DPP or the offender. Notice to vary or discharge must be served by either party on the other.

B[8.13]

Breach of an order – will result in the commission of a criminal offence triable either way. The order commences when announced in court and not when reduced in writing (*Walkling v DPP* (2004) Independent, 26 January). Repeated and deliberate breaches will indicate committal to Crown Court for sentence (*R v Braxton* [2004] EWCA Crim 1374, [2005] 1 Cr App Rep (S) 167).

Breach – Collateral Attack on validity of the order or its terms: In *W v DPP* [2005] EWCA Civ 1333, it was decided that an ASBO was to be treated as a valid order unless and until it was varied or declared invalid. The Court of Appeal said it was open to a magistrates' court considering an allegation of a breach of an order to determine whether the original order was ultra vires and therefore not a valid order. In *DPP v T* [2006] EWHC 728 (Admin), [2006] 3 All ER 471; sub nom *CPS v T* (2006) 170 JP 470, the Divisional Court reached a slightly different conclusion. The Divisional Court made reference to the normal rule that an order of the court was to be obeyed unless and until it was set aside. The Court noted that the person against whom an ASBO was made had had a full opportunity to challenge that order on appeal or to apply to vary it. The policy consideration that a magistrates' court had jurisdiction to determine issues of the validity of a byelaw or an administrative decision was wholly absent when the issue was the validity of an order of the court. It was open to a magistrates' court to consider whether the provision lacked sufficient clarity to warrant a finding that the defendant's conduct did not amount to a breach of the order; or that the lack of clarity provided him with a reasonable excuse; or whether, assuming a breach was established, it was appropriate in the circumstances not to impose any penalty for the breach.

Breach – Reasonable excuse – In the context of an ASBO, ignorance, forgetfulness or misunderstanding, whether arising from an error as to the terms of the order or lack of knowledge of where the defendant was at the material time, might be capable of constituting a defence of reasonable excuse (*R v Nicholson* [2006] EWCA Crim 1518, 170 JP 573)).

B[8.14]

Maximum penalty – On summary conviction 6 months (**12 months) and/or level 5. On indictment 5 years or an unlimited fine.

B[8.15]–B[8.16]

The court may not impose a conditional discharge following a breach.

Reporting restrictions – see **E[2.4]**.

B[9]

Attendance centre orders

(Powers of Criminal Courts (Sentencing) Act 2000, s 60; Criminal Justice Act 2003, s 177)

B[9.1]

Jurisdiction - Offence must be punishable with imprisonment (even though the individual offender may not be).

B[9.2]

Age limits – 10 to under 25 years (25 years old also when used as a fine default power).

B[9.3]

Maximum period - 12 hours unless the court thinks that would be inadequate in which event the maximum periods are:

offender under 16: 24 hours
offender aged 16 to under 25: 36 hours

Note - A further order may be made during the currency of a previous one, in which case the period of the later order may be determined as above without regard to the unexpired part of the previous order.

B[9.4]

Minimum period – If defendant is under 14 the normal minimum of 12 hours does not apply if the court is of the opinion that 12 hours would be excessive. If the defendant is 14 or older, the minimum period is 12 hours.

B[9.5]

Availability. Court must have been notified of the availability of a centre for persons of the offender's age and sex.

B[9.6]

Regard must be paid to the accessibility of the centre to the offender.

B[9.7]

Juveniles. A magistrates' court may not make this order against a juvenile but must remit him to a youth court.

May be made as part of an action plan order in the youth court.

B[9.8]

Community sentences. Note the restrictions on imposing a community sentence, see **B[3]**.

Ancillary orders

B[9.9]

Compensation at **B[18]**

Costs at **B[20]**

Disqualification at **C[5]**

Endorsement at **C[5]**

Deprivation of property and forfeiture at **B[34]**

Legal aid contribution order at **I[7]**

Restitution at **B[39]**

How to announce

B[9.10]–B[9.15]

We shall order you to attend the attendance centre at [ ] for a total of [ ] hours starting on [ ]. You will be given a copy of the order which will show the date and time of your first attendance. After that you will attend as directed by the officer in charge. You will make up the period of [ ] hours by attending on Saturday afternoons (or as the case may be) for two (or three, as the case may be) hours at a time. If you arrive late the officer in charge may not count that day's attendance. If you fail to attend without a very good excuse, or if you fail to carry out the officer's instructions properly, he will bring you back here and we shall deal with you. Do you understand?

General considerations

B[9.16]

The aims of the attendance centre have been described by the Home Office as follows:

(a) to vindicate the law by imposing loss of leisure, a punishment that is generally understood by children and young persons;
(b) to bring the offender for a period under the influence of representatives of the authority of the state; and
(c) to teach him the constructive use of leisure and to guide him, on leaving, towards organisations or activities where he may use what he has learned. Centres usually require attendance for two-hour (juveniles) or three-hour (young offenders) periods on alternate Saturday afternoons. Only one period of attendance may be required in any one day. The court must take into account the availability of suitable transport and the journey time from home to the centre. A distance of 10 miles or a journey time of 45 minutes is roughly the limit for boys up to 14, but for boys of that age or above, 15 miles or a 90-minutes journey would be the limit.

B[9.17]

The court must announce for how many hours the defendant must attend. The court should also tell the defendant the date, time and place of the first attendance.

B[10]

Binding over

Limitations

B[10.1]

None.

B[10.2]

Age limits – None. However, a refusal to enter a recognisance (see below) will result in imprisonment and as those under 21 [**18] may not be imprisoned the court would be powerless to enforce an order to enter into a recognisance.

B[10.3]

Maximum period – None, but consistent with community orders generally no more than three years.

B[10.4]

Minimum period – None, but consistent with community orders generally not less than six months.

Ancillary orders

B[10.5]

Costs at **B[20]**. It would appear that there is no power to award costs where a defendant is bound over under the court's inherent powers where the substantive charge is withdrawn or dismissed.

How to announce

B[10.6]

We are going to order you to enter a recognisance – that is a binding promise – that you will keep the peace for the next [*period*]. The amount of that

recognisance will be [*amount*] and that means that if you repeat the kind of behaviour we have heard about today, during the next [*period*] we will order you to pay that amount. Do you understand? Do you agree to making that promise and to guaranteeing to pay the [*amount*] if you break that promise?

General considerations

B[10.7]

One or more sureties may also be required if the court thinks fit. This order is commonly and conveniently referred to as a bind over order but this tends to disguise its real form. The court orders the defendant to enter a recognisance in terms chosen by the court as to the duration and amount. The defendant or his legal representative must be given an opportunity to address the court in order not to breach Article 6 rights (*Hooper v UK* (2004) Times, 19 November, [2004] All ER (D) 254 (Nov), ECtHR). If the defendant so agrees, he is said to be bound over to keep the peace. If he refuses to enter the recognisance the only course left to the court is to send him to prison from which he will be released after a term fixed by the court of up to six months (**51 weeks) or when he enters the recognisance, whichever is the sooner. Great care should therefore be exercised before making such an order especially if there is any possibility of refusal to comply with it. An order to be of good behaviour should be avoided as it is imprecise and may breach the ECHR (*Hashman and Harrup v United Kingdom* (1999) 30 EHRR 241, [2000] Crim LR 185, 8 BHRC 104, ECtHR).

NB: The defendant's consent is not required if the binding over order is made as an ancillary penalty to a criminal sentence (*R v Crown Court at Lincoln, ex p Jude* [1997] 3 All ER 737.

B[10.8]

Before a court has any power to order a person to enter a recognisance to keep the peace, it must have grounds for believing that there is a possibility of a future breach of the peace.

B[10.9]

Sometimes the court is asked to make this order by an applicant who has taken out a summons for that purpose. In addition to this, the court may on its own initiative consider the need to make the order when dealing with an offender. Moreover, a witness or complainant may also be ordered to enter a recognisance. Whenever the court takes the initiative it should explain to the person concerned what it has in mind to do and offer an opportunity to address the court before it is decided whether to make the order or not.

B[10.10]–B[10.15]

The procedure for binding over a complainant or witness must be followed punctiliously, and if this is in contemplation, the advice of the legal adviser should be followed.

B[10.16]

There is no power generally to impose any conditions, but an order may be made in terms 'to keep the peace towards all Her Majesty's subjects, and especially towards A.B'. Also it appears that there may be a condition not to possess, carry or use firearms or as part of a community order (Firearms Act 1968, s 21(3)).

B[10.17]

Breach of the order will be dealt with by forfeiting the recognisance, or any part of it. The defendant may be given time to pay and in default, after a means inquiry, he may be committed to prison, as if he owed a fine.

Binding over a parent

B[10.18]

Either a magistrates' court or a youth court may require the parent of a young person (or an 18-year-old who was 17 when the proceedings commenced) who has been found guilty of an offence to enter a recognisance to take proper care of him and to exercise proper control over him. The court must exercise these powers where the juvenile has not attained 16 years if it is satisfied, having regard to the circumstances of the case, that it would be desirable in the interests of preventing the juvenile from committing further offences. If the court does not exercise the powers it must say so and give its reasons in open court. The court's duty to bind over the parent is replaced by a power where the juvenile has attained 16 years. In such a case the maximum amount of the recognisance is £1,000 and the maximum period is three years or until a young person attains 18, whichever is the shorter.

B[10.19]

The parent must consent to the order. An unreasonable refusal is punishable by a fine of up to £1,000. A parent may appeal to the Crown Court against the bind over.

B[11]–B[15]

Community punishment and rehabilitation order

Powers of the Criminal Courts (Sentencing) Act 2000, s 51)

B[11.1]

Made as an order in the Youth Court (16 and 17 year olds)

Although a community sentence (see **B[3]**) may be composed of one or more community orders, the Criminal Justice Act 1991 only permits the combining of community punishment and community rehabilitation orders under this provision. This places a limit on the court's powers in that the period of supervision is restricted to a minimum period of one year and a maximum of three years and the number of hours of community punishment to a range of 40 to 100 hours in aggregate. Subject to these limitations the two elements of the order are treated as if they were a community punishment and community rehabilitation order respectively. During a pilot scheme the requirements of the order may be secured by electronic monitoring but only if the defendant lives in Hampshire, Nottinghamshire or West Yorkshire.

Note that the 100 hours is a maximum and additional hours on another offence made to run consecutively will breach the maximum (*Gibson v DPP* [2005] EWHC 1282 (Admin), [2005] All ER (D) 204 (Feb)).

Breach of the order: See ***B[17.25]***.

B[16]

Committal to Crown Court for sentence

(Powers of the Criminal Courts (Sentencing) Act 2000, ss 3 and 4**)

(Note – There are a few circumstances in which a person may be committed to the Crown Court which are mentioned at the end of this section. The following notes are intended to refer to committal for sentence after conviction for an either way or related offence.)

Limitations

B[16.1]

A magistrates' court when dealing with an either way offence (excluding criminal damage where the value makes the offence triable only by magistrates) may commit on bail or in custody an offender aged at least 18 to be sentenced by the judge with all the powers available to the Crown Court (*R v Warley Magistrates' Court, ex p DPP* [1999] 1 All ER 251, [1999] 1 WLR 216). However where a previous bench had indicated that the defendant has a legitimate expectation that he will be dealt with in the magistrates' court, the option to commit is no longer open (*R v Norwich Magistrates' Court, ex p Elliott* [2000] 1 Cr App Rep (S) 152). For this reason the 'all options open' form of words when requesting a pre-sentence report does not preserve the option of committal (*R v Feltham Justices, ex p Rees* [2001] 2 Cr App Rep (S) 1, [2001] Crim LR 47) but will be adequate where committal takes place immediately after conviction on disclosure of the defendant's record (*R v McHoul* [2002] EWCA Crim 1918, [2003] 1 Cr App Rep (S) 382). Where a court departs form a non-custodial recommendation in a pre-sentence report in favour of a committal, they should state their reasons in open court (*R v Law* [2002] All ER (D) 40 (Jan), CA).

B[16.2]

The court must be satisfied that the offence (or combination of the offence and any associated offences of which he is convicted) was so serious that the magistrates' powers of sentence are inadequate. The power under the Magistrates' Courts Act 1980, s 38A can be used to commit an offence or offences to the crown court which are related to other offences which are to be dealt with in the Crown Court for trial. The court may use this power to commit a company for sentence (although there will be no question of bail or custody).

B[16.3]

Alternatively, the court may use the same powers in the case of an offender who has committed an offence of violence or a sexual offence, where the court considers it is necessary that a sentence longer than it has power to impose is necessary to protect the public from serious harm by him.

Ancillary orders

B[16.4]

Disqualification pending sentence, but this would be unusual since committal for sentence is almost always in custody. It may be, however, that the reason for the committal is that the offence calls for a larger fine than the magistrates have power to impose.

Dangerous offenders

B[16.5]

The Criminal Justice Act 2003, ss 224–236 make provision for the sentencing of dangerous offenders. To qualify the offender must be convicted of a specified violent or sexual offence in Sch 15 of the Act.

Magistrates do not have power to impose the necessary extended or life sentences and must send dangerous offenders to Crown Court under the provisions of the Powers of the Criminal Courts (Sentencing) Act 2000, s 3A for sentence and s 51A for trial in the case of young offenders.

General considerations

B[16.6]

The power to commit for sentence is used where a custodial sentence is likely to be imposed which would exceed the maximum available to the magistrates' court. The maximum period of custody which a magistrates' court may impose for an offence triable either way is six months**. If an offender is convicted of more than one such offence, the maximum custodial sentence is 12 months. Magistrates may acquaint themselves with the sentences imposed in their local crown court either by sitting there, or through the liaison judge.

B[16.7]

Generally where a defendant appears on bail before the magistrates he may be committed to the Crown Court for sentence on bail. The provisions of the Bail Act 1976 do not apply.

B[16.8]

An offender committed for sentence under the procedure described here may be dealt with by the Crown Court in any manner as if he had been convicted on indictment at the Crown Court, so long as the committal is clearly under PCC(S)A 2000, s 3(2) (*R v Sallis* [2003] EWCA Crim 233, [2003] All ER (D) 275 (Jan)).

B[16.9]

The legal adviser should always be consulted if a committal to the Crown Court is contemplated.

B[16.10]–B[16.19]

An offender committed for sentence under the procedure described here may also be committed to be dealt with in respect of another offence of which he has been convicted by the committing court and which that court could have dealt with (Powers of the Criminal Courts (Sentencing) Act 2000, s 6). The Powers of the Criminal Courts (Sentencing) Act 2000, s 4 is used to commit offences where a guilty plea has been indicated but those offences are related to matters which are to be dealt with at Crown Court for trial.

*Committals for sentence under other provisions***

B[16.20]

Other circumstances in which an offender may be committed to the Crown Court to be dealt with:

(a) where the offender has failed to surrender to bail (Bail Act 1976, s 6);
(b) where the offender is in breach of an order or sentence of the Crown Court, e g community rehabilitation, suspended sentence (Criminal Justice Act 1991, Sch 6 and Powers of Criminal Courts (Sentencing) Act 2000);
(c) where a prisoner subject to early release commits an imprisonable offence during the original period of a custodial sentence and is liable to be returned to prison to serve more than six months (Powers of the Criminal Courts (Sentencing) Act 2000, s 116);
(d) where the offender has been convicted of an offence under the Vagrancy Act 1824 which renders him liable to be sentenced as an incorrigible rogue (Vagrancy Act 1824, s 5).

B[17]

Community punishment order

(Powers of Criminal Courts (Sentencing) Act 2000, s 46)

Limitations

B[17.1]

This order is only available in the Youth Court (16 and 17 year olds)

Offender must have been convicted of an offence which is punishable with imprisonment (even if the offender is not personally liable to imprisonment).

B[17.2]

Effect of the order must be explained to the offender. He must keep in touch with the relevant officer in accordance with instructions he may be given and must also notify any change of address to the officer in charge of him. He must perform the allotted work in accordance with the instructions he receives. During a pilot scheme (commencing 2 July 2001) the requirements of the order may be secured by electronic monitoring but only where the defendant lives in Hampshire, Nottinghamshire or West Yorkshire.

B[17.3]

Court must be satisfied after considering a pre-sentence report or a specific sentence report in the case of an order under 100 hours by a probation officer (or social worker), that the offender is a suitable person to perform unpaid work under a community punishment order.

B[17.4]

Age limits – Offender must be 16 or over.

B[17.5]

Maximum period – 240 hours.

B[17.6]

Minimum period – 40 hours. The hours of work specified must normally be completed within 12 months.

B[17.7]

Community sentence. For the restrictions on imposing a community sentence see **B[3]**.

Ancillary orders

B[17.8]

Compensation at **B[18]**

Costs at **B[20]**

Disqualification at **C[5]**

Endorsement at **C[5]**

Deprivation of property and forfeiture at **B[34]**

Legal aid contribution order at **I[7]**

Restitution at **B[39]**

General considerations

B[17.9]–B[17.17]

The choice of work and the environment in which it is performed is that of the community service officer and not the court. Even if an indication is given to the court of the type of work available for the offender the community service officer is not bound to allocate the offender to that work, or to require him to perform it for the full period of the order.

B[17.18]

Community punishment is a community sentence and is subject to the restriction on imposing community sentences that the offence etc is 'serious enough' to warrant such a sentence. It is a sentence in its own right and is not an 'alternative to imprisonment'. Community punishment is generally regarded as an onerous punishment which imposes a considerable restriction on the offender's liberty.

B[17.19]

In determining the number of hours to be imposed magistrates might consider sentences of community punishment as 'short' (40–80 hours),'medium' (80–120 hours) and 'long' (120–180 hours), although it must be stressed that these are merely the suggestions of the editor and magistrates should seek the advice of their legal adviser.

B[17.20]

The permitted number of hours represent broadly, a minimum of one working week (40 hours) and a maximum of six working weeks. The offender, whether in employment or not, is unlikely to be allowed to meet his obligations under the order in quite this way, but is more likely to be required to do several hours' work each week. The weekly numbers of hours will depend on the nature of the work to be done and whether the offender is in gainful employment. Every precaution is taken by the community service officer to ensure that the offender is not put to temptation, or the beneficiaries of the work put at risk when considering whether suitable work is available. Where appropriate the approval of relevant trade unions will have been obtained before any work is included in the scheme so there is little risk that the offender is putting or keeping out of work an honest man by his community punishment.

B[17.21]

Where the offender is convicted of more than one offence, consecutive community punishment orders may be made provided that the total does not exceed 240 hours.

B[17.22]

Where the offender is liable to more than one sentence at the same time, a suspended prison sentence should not be imposed at the same time as a community punishment order (*R v Starie* (1979) 69 Cr App Rep 239, 1 Cr App Rep (S) 179, CA).

B[17.23]

The Court of Appeal has approved the use of community punishment for some quite serious offences, e g burglary, where the trial judge imposed custodial sentences. It has done so, however, only when there has been real evidence of remorse and circumstances indicating a significant hope that the offender will not offend again, such as a marriage or similar relationship which is proving to be supportive.

B[17.24]

When varying a custodial sentence to one of community punishment, the Court of Appeal has frequently reduced the number of hours to reflect the period already spent in custody. Therefore it would be right in principle, if magistrates were to make some small reduction when an offender has been on remand in custody.

Breach of requirements of order

B[17.25]–B[17.30]

An offender who fails without reasonable excuse to comply with the requirements of a community punishment order, if it was made by a magistrates' court, may be either fined up to £1,000 or made subject to further community punishment up to 60 hours (or a total liability of 240 hours whichever is the less), when the order remains in force, or be dealt with for the original offence. If the order was made by the Crown Court a magistrates' court may commit him on bail or in custody to the Crown Court to be dealt with. Note that the Crown Court may reserve to itself any breach or revocation application. Such proceedings will be heard directly in the Crown Court.

B[17.31]

Unacceptable and violent behaviour towards a Community Service Officer can amount to a failure, without reasonable excuse, to comply with the requirements of the order (*Caton v Community Service Office* (1995) 159 JP 444, [1995] COD 264).

B[17.32]

In so far as a court deals with an offender by substituting a different sentence for the original offence, this would not affect any order for endorsement, disqualification or compensation which may have been made at the same time as the community punishment order. The court should have information concerning the circumstances of the original offence before substituting a sentence and should take account also of the extent to which the offender has complied with the community punishment order and compensation order if there was one. However, it is not necessary for the court sentencing for the original offence for which the community punishment order was made to have a fresh pre-sentence report (*R v Meredith* (1993) 15 Cr App Rep (S) 528, 158 JP 322, [1994] Crim LR 142, CA). Best practice suggests the court obtain the original pre-sentence report which can be considered in the light of the breach report and any relevant mitigation put forward on behalf of the offender.

B[17.33]

An offender who has wilfully and persistently failed to comply with the requirements of the order may be subject to a revocation of the order and the court may then substitute a custodial sentence (see **B[2]**). In the event of the defendant being re-sentenced to a custodial sentence it should be reduced to reflect both time spent on remand and the proportion of the order completed (*R v McCleod* (27 November 1998, unreported), CA).

B[17.34]

An alleged breach may be dealt with by the magistrates notwithstanding that the defendant has lodged a notice of appeal, if it is right to do so in all the circumstances (*Greater Manchester Probation Committee v Bent* (1996) 160 JP 297).

Community Orders

B[17.35]

Sections 147–150 Criminal Justice Act 2003 define community orders and the restrictions that apply to them. Any requirements imposed must be the most suitable for the offender and must be commensurate and proportionate with the seriousness of the offending. The court may take account of time spent on remand before sentence.

Community Orders

B[17.36]

The court must set a date for completion of all requirements (not later that three years from sentence), but may set different dates for different requirements. If a supervision requirement is included it must be for the full length of the order. The court must impose an electronic monitoring requirement with a curfew or exclusion requirement and may do so for various requirements.

Permissible requirements

(*1*) ***Unpaid work requirement***

B[17.37]

This is a requirement that the offender must perform unpaid work in accordance for the number of hours specified in the order such work at such times as he may be instructed by the responsible officer. Unless revoked, a community order imposing an unpaid work requirement remains in force until the offender has worked under it for the number of hours specified in it. The work required to be performed under an unpaid work requirement of a community order or a suspended sentence order must be performed during a period of twelve months.

The number of hours which a person may be required to work under an unpaid work requirement must be specified in the relevant order and must be in the aggregate-

(a) not less than 40, and
(b) not more than 300.

The court may not impose an unpaid work requirement in respect of an offender unless after hearing (if the court thinks necessary) an appropriate officer, the court is satisfied that the offender is a suitable person to perform work under such a requirement.

Where the court makes orders in respect of two or more offences of which the offender has been convicted on the same occasion and includes unpaid work requirements in each of them, the court may direct that the hours of work specified in any of those requirements is to be concurrent or consecutive. However the total number of hours must not exceed the maximum of 300 hours.

(2) *Activity requirement*

B[17.38]

An activity requirement means a requirement that the offender must do either or both of the following-

(a) present himself to a person or persons specified in the relevant order at a place or places so specified on such number of days as may be so specified and comply with instructions given by, or under the authority of, the person in charge of that place.
(b) participate in activities specified in the order on such number of days as may be so specified.

The specified activities may consist of or include reparation, for example contact between the offender and victims affected by their offences.

A court may not include an activity requirement in a relevant order unless it has consulted either an officer of a local probation board or a member of a youth offending team, and it is satisfied that it is feasible to secure compliance with the requirement.

A court may not include an activity requirement in a relevant order if compliance with that requirement would involve the co-operation of a person other than the offender and the offender's responsible officer, unless that other person consents to its inclusion.

The aggregate of the number of days specified must not exceed 60.

A place specified in a requirement for the offender's attendance must be either,

(a) a community rehabilitation centre, or
(b) a place that has been approved by the local probation board for the area in which the premises are situated as providing facilities suitable for persons subject to activity requirements.

A requirement to participate in activities operates to require the offender,

(a) to participate in activities on the number of days specified in the order in accordance with instructions given by his responsible officer, and

(b) while participating, to comply with instructions given by, or under the authority of, the person in charge of the activities.

(3) *Programme requirement*

B[17.39]

This requirement involves the offender in participation in an accredited programme specified in the order at a place approved by the local probation board and on such number of days as may be so specified.

The activities in programme, will be accredited by an accreditation body designated for that purpose by the Secretary of State.

The court may not include a programme requirement in a relevant order unless-

(a) the accredited programme which the court proposes to specify in the order has been recommended to the court as being suitable for the offender by an officer of a local probation board or by a member of a youth offending team, and
(b) the court is satisfied that the programme is available at the place proposed to be specified.

A court may not include a programme requirement in a relevant order if compliance with that requirement would involve the co-operation of a person other than the offender and the offender's responsible officer, unless that other person consents to its inclusion.

A requirement to attend an accredited programme operates to require the offender,

(a) in accordance with instructions given by the responsible officer, to participate in the accredited programme at the place specified in the order on the number of days specified in the order, and
(b) while at that place, to comply with instructions given by, or under the authority of, the person in charge of the programme.

(4) *Prohibited activity requirement*

B[17.40]

This means a requirement that the offender must refrain from participating in activities specified in the order-

(a) on a day or days so specified, or
(b) during a period so specified.

A court may not include a prohibited activity requirement in a relevant order unless it has consulted, either an officer of a local probation board or a member of a youth offending team.

The statute provides that the requirements that may be included in a relevant order include a requirement that the offender does not possess, use or carry a firearm within the meaning of the Firearms Act 1968.

(5) *Curfew requirement*

B[17.41]

A curfew requirement is a requirement that the offender must remain, for periods specified in the relevant order, at a place so specified. It may specify different places or different periods for different days, but may not specify periods which amount to less than two hours or more than twelve hours in any one day.

The order may not exceed a period of six months beginning with the day on which it is made. For youths and curfew orders see **B[21]**.

Before making a relevant order imposing a curfew requirement, the court must obtain and consider information about the place proposed to be specified in the order (including information as to the attitude of persons likely to be affected by the enforced presence there of the offender). An electronic monitoring requirement must be made unless it requires the co-operation of a third party which is not forthcoming.

(6) *Exclusion requirement*

B[17.42]

An exclusion requirement, is a provision prohibiting the offender from entering a place named in the order for a specified period of not more than two years.

An exclusion requirement,

(a) may provide for the prohibition to operate only during the periods specified in the order, and
(b) may specify different places or areas for different periods or days.

(7) *Residence requirement*

B[17.43]

This is a requirement that, during a period specified in the relevant order, the offender must reside at a place specified in the order.

If the order makes provision, a residence requirement does not prohibit the offender from residing, with the prior approval of the responsible officer, at a place other than that specified in the order.

Before making a community order containing a residence requirement, the court must consider the home surroundings of the offender.

A court may not specify a hostel or other institution as the place where an offender must reside, except on the recommendation of an officer of a local probation board.

(8) *Mental health treatment requirement*

B[17.44]

This requires the offender to submit, during periods specified in the order, to treatment by or under the direction of a registered medical practitioner or a chartered psychologist (or both, for different periods) with a view to the improvement of the offender's mental condition.

The treatment required must be one of the following kinds of treatment as may be specified in the relevant order:

(a) treatment as a resident patient in an independent hospital or care home within the meaning of the Care Standards Act 2000 or a hospital within the meaning of the Mental Health Act 1983, but not in hospital premises where high security psychiatric services within the meaning of that Act are provided;
(b) treatment as a non-resident patient at such institution or place as may be specified in the order;
(c) treatment by or under the direction of such registered medical practitioner or chartered psychologist (or both) as may be so specified;

The nature of the treatment may not be specified in the order except as mentioned in (a), (b) or (c) above.

A court may not by virtue of this section include a mental health treatment requirement in an order unless-

(a) the court is satisfied, on the evidence of a registered medical practitioner approved for the purposes of s 12 of the Mental Health Act 1983, that the mental condition of the offender-
    (i) is such as requires and may be susceptible to treatment, but
    (ii) is not such as to warrant the making of a hospital order or guardianship order within the meaning of that Act;

(b) the court is also satisfied that arrangements have been or can be made for the treatment intended to be specified in the order (including arrangements for the reception of the offender where he is to be required to submit to treatment as a resident patient); and
(c) the offender has expressed his willingness to comply with such a requirement.

While the offender is under treatment as a resident patient in pursuance of a mental health requirement, his responsible officer shall carry out the supervision of the offender to such extent only as may be necessary for the purpose of the revocation or amendment of the order.

Note that sub-ss (2) and (3) of s 54 of the Mental Health Act 1983 have effect with respect to proof for the purposes of sub-s (3)(a) of an offender's mental condition as they have effect with respect to proof of an offender's mental condition for the purposes of s 37(2)(a) of that Act.

(9) Mental health treatment at place other than that specified in order

B[17.45]

Where the medical practitioner or chartered psychologist, treating the offender in pursuance of a mental health treatment requirement, is of the opinion that part of the treatment can be better or more conveniently given in or at an institution or place which-

(a) is not specified in the relevant order, and
(b) is one in or at which the treatment of the offender will be given by or under the direction of a registered medical practitioner or chartered psychologist,

he may, with the consent of the offender, make arrangements for him to be treated accordingly.

These arrangements as are mentioned may provide for the offender to receive part of his treatment as a resident patient in an institution or place notwithstanding that the institution or place is not one which could have been specified for that purpose in the relevant order.

> (3) Where any such arrangements are made for the treatment of an offender the medical practitioner or chartered psychologist by whom the arrangements are made shall give notice in writing to the offender's responsible officer giving details of the place and the treatment provided.

(10) Drug rehabilitation requirement

B[17.46]

A drug rehabilitation requirement means a requirement that during a period specified in the order the offender must submit to treatment by or under the direction of a specified person having the necessary qualifications or experience with a view to the reduction or elimination of the offender's dependency on or propensity to misuse drugs.

During that period he must provide samples for the purpose of ascertaining whether he has any drug in his body.

A court may not impose a drug rehabilitation requirement unless-

(a) it is satisfied-
    (i) that the offender is dependent on, or has a propensity to misuse, drugs, and

(ii) that his dependency or propensity is such as requires and may be susceptible to treatment,

(b) it is also satisfied that arrangements have been or can be made for the treatment intended to be specified in the order (including arrangements for the reception of the offender where he is to be required to submit to treatment as a resident),
(c) the requirement has been recommended to the court as being suitable for the offender either by an officer of a local probation board or by a member of a youth offending team, and
(d) the offender expresses his willingness to comply with the requirement.

The treatment and testing period must be not less than six months or more than three years and must be treatment as a resident in such institution or place as may be specified in the order, or treatment as a non-resident place, as may be so specified.

The nature of the treatment may not be specified in the order except as mentioned in paragraph (a) or (b) above.

A community order imposing a drug rehabilitation requirement must provide that the results of tests carried out on any samples provided by the offender in pursuance of the requirement to a person other than the responsible officer are to be communicated to the responsible officer.

(10A) Drug rehabilitation requirement: provision for review by court

B[17.47]

A community order imposing a drug rehabilitation requirement may (and must if the treatment and testing period is more than 12 months),

(a) provide for the requirement to be reviewed periodically at intervals of not less than one month,
(b) provide for each review of the requirement to be made, at a hearing held for the purpose by the court responsible for the order (a "review hearing"),
(c) require the offender to attend each review hearing,
(d) provide for the responsible officer to make to the court responsible for the order, before each review, a report in writing on the offender's progress under the requirement, and
(e) provide for each such report to include the test results communicated to the responsible officer and the views of the treatment provider as to the treatment and testing of the offender.

References to the court responsible for a community order or suspended sentence order imposing a drug rehabilitation requirement are:-

(a) where a court is specified in the order, to that court;
(b) in any other case, to the court by which the order is made.

Where the area specified in a community order is not the area for which the court acts, the court may, if it thinks fit, include in the order provision specifying a magistrates' court which acts for the area specified in the order.

(*10B*) *Periodic review of drug rehabilitation requirement*

B[17.48]

At a review hearing the court may, after considering the responsible officer's report, amend the community order, so far as it relates to the drug rehabilitation requirement but only if the offender expresses his willingness to comply with the requirement as amended.

The court may not amend any provision of the order so as to reduce the period for which the drug rehabilitation requirement has effect below the minimum period of 6 months.

Nor may the court amend any requirement or provision of the order while an appeal against the order is pending, except with the consent of the offender.

If the offender fails to express his willingness to comply with the drug rehabilitation requirement as proposed to be amended by the court, the court may, revoke the community order and deal with him, for the offence in respect of which the order was made. If the court decides to re-sentence it must take into account the extent to which the offender has complied with the requirements of the order, and may impose a custodial sentence (where the order was made in respect of an offence punishable with such a sentence) notwithstanding anything in section CJA 2003 s 152(2). In the case of a juvenile who has attained the age of 18 the court's powers are to do either or both of the following,

(a) to impose a fine not exceeding £5,000 for the offence in respect of which the order was made;
(b) to deal with the offender for that offence in any way in which the court could deal with him if it had just convicted him of an offence punishable with imprisonment for a term not exceeding twelve months.

If at a review hearing the court, after considering the responsible officer's report, is of the opinion that the offender's progress under the requirement is satisfactory, the court may so amend the order as to provide for each subsequent review to be made by the court without a hearing.

If at a review without a hearing the court, after considering the responsible officer's report, is of the opinion that the offender's progress under the requirement is no longer satisfactory, the court may require the offender to attend a hearing of the court at a specified time and place.

At that hearing the court, after considering that report, may:-

(a) exercise the powers conferred by this section as if the hearing were a review hearing, and

(b) so amend the order as to provide for each subsequent review to be made at a review hearing.

(*11*) *Alcohol treatment requirement*

B[17.49]

This is a requirement that the offender submits during a specified period (of not less than 6 months) to treatment by or under the direction of a specified person having the necessary qualifications or experience with a view to the reduction or elimination of the offender's dependency on alcohol.

The court may not impose an alcohol treatment requirement in respect of an offender unless it is satisfied that he is dependent on alcohol, and his dependency is such as requires and may be susceptible to treatment. Arrangements must be made for the treatment intended to be specified in the order (including arrangements for the reception of the offender where he is to be required to submit to treatment as a resident).

A court may not impose an alcohol treatment requirement unless the offender expresses his willingness to comply with its requirements.

The treatment required by an alcohol treatment requirement for any particular period must be,

(a) treatment as a resident in such institution or place as may be specified in the order,
(b) treatment as a non-resident in or at such institution or place, and at such intervals, as may be so specified, or
(c) treatment by or under the direction of such person having the necessary qualification or experience as may be so specified;

but the nature of the treatment shall not be specified in the order except as mentioned in paragraph (a), (b) or (c) above.

(*12*) *Supervision requirement* (*includes 16 & 17 year olds*)

B[17.50]

A supervision requirement is a requirement that, during the relevant period, the offender must attend appointments with the responsible officer or another person determined by the responsible officer, at such time and place as may be determined by the officer.

The purpose for which a supervision requirement may be imposed is that of promoting the offender's rehabilitation.

For these purposes the relevant period means the period for which the community order remains in force.

B[17.51]

Breach of a requirement

Under national standards an offender will be given one warning and then returned to court following a subsequent breach. The court's powers are contained in Sch 8 Criminal Justice Act 2003. On breach of a requirement the court may impose more onerous requirements with the aim being completion of the order, or deal with the original offence as if he had just been convicted. In the latter case the court must make the original order. Crown Court orders may contain a direction that breaches are dealt with in the magistrates' court or reserved to itself.

B[17.52]

Revocation

The offender or responsible officer may apply to revoke the order and the court if satisfied it is in the interests of justice may revoke and or deal with the original offence, giving credit for any part of the order already completed.

It would be wrong in principle to resentence the offender where the revocation was on the grounds of ill health (*R v Bishop* [2004] EWCA Crim 2956, [2004] All ER (D) 116 (Dec)).

B[18]

Compensation order

(Powers of Criminal Courts (Sentencing) Act 2000, ss 130–138)

B[18.1]

Compensation order. Either as a sentence in its own right or in addition to another sentence, the court may order the defendant to pay compensation to a person who has suffered as a consequence of the defendant's crime. Compensation orders are intended to be used in simple, straightforward cases where no great amount is at stake. A compensation order can only be made when sentence is being passed and, therefore, cannot be made when committing for sentence or deferring sentence. The court shall give its reasons, on passing sentence, if it does not make a compensation order where it is empowered to do so. Examples of such reasons will be the defendant's lack of means, or that the loss is difficult to quantify (see below).

B[18.2]

For what may compensation be ordered? For any personal injury, loss or damage (or to make payments for funeral expenses or bereavement in respect of a death resulting from any such offence, other than a death due to an accident arising out of the presence of a motor vehicle on a road – (i e the only such situation likely to arise in a magistrates' court, death arising from careless driving, not being covered)) resulting from the offence or any offences taken into consideration. Personal injury need not be physical injury, compensation may be ordered for terror or distress caused by the offence (*Bond v Chief Constable of Kent* [1983] 1 All ER 456, [1983] 1 WLR 40).

B[18.3]

In the case of an offence under the Theft Act 1968, if the property is recovered but is damaged, a compensation order may be made against the defendant no matter how the damage was caused provided it was caused while the property was out of the owner's possession.

Exceptions

B[18.4]

(a) Loss caused to the dependants of a victim who has died (except funeral expenses etc in the circumstances referred to above).
(b) Injury, loss or damage due to an accident arising out of the presence of a motor vehicle on a road except compensation may be awarded:
  (i) for damage caused to a motor vehicle stolen or taken without the owner's consent but not damage caused by the vehicle, e g to another car on the road; and
  (ii) in cases where the defendant's use of the vehicle was uninsured and no compensation is payable under the Motor Insurers' Bureau scheme (see **C[33.18]–C[33.22]**).

The amounts ordered under (i) and (ii) may include payment to cover loss of a 'no claims' bonus.

B[18.5]

Proof of loss. As a result of amendments made to the law in 1982 it was considered that the approach to establishing the amount of the loss was not so strict as it was formerly. However, in 1985 the judges of the Divisional Court reaffirmed that (unless the amount was admitted by the accused at the outset) it was the duty of the prosecution to establish the loss and its amount, and make it clear to the defendant by means of evidence. If, after this, there was any real dispute as to the loss suffered by the victim, a compensation order should not be made and the victim should be left to resort to civil remedies to obtain compensation (*R v Horsham Justices, ex p Richards* [1985] 2 All ER 1114, [1985] 1 WLR 986). However where the exact loss cannot be ascertained but finding the minimum loss was a simple task that latter sum may be ordered (*R v Brazil* [2004] EWCA Crim 1975, [2004] All ER (D) 348 (Jun)).

Fixing the amount

B[18.6]

(a) The amount of the loss should be established after proof or agreement.
(b) Where the loss is not determined the court cannot fix an arbitrary amount at a figure below that which is in dispute. Either the lowest amount admitted should be adopted or no order made at all.
(c) Compensation for personal injury may be ascertained having regard to guidelines issued by the Criminal Injuries Compensation Board (see **B[18.19]**).
(d) The maximum compensation that may be awarded is £5,000 for each offence against each defendant. For the maximum where offences are to be taken into consideration the legal adviser should be consulted.

(e) Having ascertained what the loss is, and what the maximum amount is that can be ordered, the court must have regard to the defendant's ability to pay. He may be allowed to pay by instalments but generally such instalments should not extend beyond two years (*R v Olliver and Olliver* (1989) 11 Cr App Rep (S) 10, 153 JP 369, [1989] Crim LR 387, CA), a case in the Crown Court where a large sum was to be paid) although in the magistrates' courts simple straightforward orders will probably be paid within a shorter period. Judicial guidance suggests that magistrates' court orders should be paid within a short period of time, preferably 13 weeks and 52 weeks should be regarded as the maximum period for repayment. Where the defendant is of limited means and would be unable to pay both compensation and a fine, preference must be given to the award of compensation.

(f) If the defendant cannot afford to pay for the whole amount of the loss, then this lower amount, which he can afford, must be ordered.

(g) The circumstances in which a court may subsequently vary a compensation order are limited. Accordingly, an unrealistically high order for compensation may result in the defendant being committed to prison for default; this is wrong in principle (see **B[18.17]–B[18.18]** 'appeal and review').

B[18.7]

Making an order. When deliberating whether to make an order, the court should bear in mind that the wealthy offender should never be allowed to buy his way out of prison by offering compensation. Also, the court should be wary of an accused mitigating for a suspended sentence on the basis of extravagant promises to pay compensation.

B[18.8]

On the other hand, when a custodial sentence is imposed, compensation should be ordered only if the offender has the means to pay immediately or out of existing resources. He should not have to face the payment of compensation upon his discharge from a custodial sentence unless it is clear that he will then have the means to pay, e g he has savings or by being able to return to gainful employment immediately.

B[18.9]

The court should announce the amount of compensation for each offence and against each defendant. Where there are competing claims for compensation, the court may make an order for one compensatee in preference to another, e g a private individual in preference to a financial institution (*R v Amey* [1983] 1 All ER 865, [1983] 1 WLR 345, CA).

B[18.10]–B[18.15]

In all cases where a compensation order is contemplated, the legal adviser should be consulted.

B[18.16]

Compensation and deprivation orders. Where a court makes a deprivation order (see **B[34]**) in a case where a person has suffered personal injury, loss or damage, but a compensation order for the full loss cannot be made because of the offender's inadequate means, it may direct that the proceeds arising from the disposal of the forfeited goods be paid to the victim to make good the deficiency. The amount to be paid is a sum not exceeding the amount of compensation that the court would have ordered were it not for the offender's lack of means. See also **B[19]** for confiscation orders.

Appeal and review

B[18.17]

The entitlement of the victim is suspended for 21 days to allow the defendant time to appeal if he wishes, or until after the appeal is heard. But the enforcement of the order against the offender is not suspended; the obligation to pay arises immediately. Accordingly, where an appeal is successful, the court will have to repay to the appellant any monies that he has already paid.

B[18.18]

At any time before the order has been fully complied with, the court may discharge or reduce the order:

(a) if a civil court determines an amount of damage or loss less than that stated in the order; or
(b) if the property or part of it is subsequently recovered; or
(c) where the defendant's means are insufficient to satisfy in full the compensation order and a confiscation order made in the same proceedings; or
(d) where the defendant has suffered a substantial reduction in his means which was unexpected at the time the compensation order was made, and his means seem unlikely to increase for a considerable period.

The permission of the Crown Court is required where it made the original order, if the magistrates' court contemplates the action at (c) or (d).

Guidelines for compensation for personal injury

B[18.19]

Guidelines were to be found originally in Home Office circular 53/1993 for the assistance of magistrates. They were prepared by the Criminal Injuries Compensation Board (now renamed the Criminal Injuries Compensation Authority) and reflect the level of damages which would be awarded in the civil courts for the injuries described. The Criminal Injuries Compensation Authority has no power to compensate for injuries attracting compensation under £1,000 and therefore guidelines for some of the more minor injuries commonly encountered in the magistrates' court are reproduced at **B[18.21]–B[18.23]**.

B[18.20]

In each example the victim is assumed to be in the age bracket 20–35 years but the age of the victim may materially affect the assessment, cf for example, the psychological effect of an assault on an elderly victim as opposed to a youth. Scarring is particularly problematical and reference should be made to the full circular for this and other injuries not referred to in the list below. Before making an award magistrates must also take into account the defendant's ability to pay any order made.

Type of injury

B[18.21]

Less serious injury		*Suggested award*
including:		
Graze	depending on size	up to £50
Bruise	depending on size	up to £75
Black eye		£100
Cut (without permanent scarring)	depending on size and whether stitched	£75-£500
Sprain	depending on loss of mobility	£100-£1,000
Loss of a tooth (not a front tooth)	depending on position of tooth and age of victim	£250-£500
Minor injury	causing reasonable absence from work of about 3 weeks	£550-£850

B[18.22]

More serious injury		
Loss of a front tooth		£1,000
Nasal	undisplaced fracture of the nasal bone (see note)	£750

More serious injury		
Nasal	displaced fracture of the bone requiring manipulation under general anaesthetic (see note)	£1,000
Nasal	not causing fracture but displaced septum requiring a sub-mucous resection (see note)	£1,750

B[18.23]

NB: Assuming that after the appropriate treatment there is no visible deformity of the nose and no breathing problem. If either of these factors is present, an increased award is appropriate and the amount of the increase will depend on the severity of the remaining problems. It is not uncommon for a fractured nasal bone to be manipulated and for the patient thereafter to have breathing problems which after some months require a sub-mucous resection – in this situation the suggested award would be £2,000 assuming full recovery after a second operation.

B[19]

Confiscation orders

Part VI of the CJA 1988 is repealed by the Proceeds of Crime Act 2002. See **M[3.2]**.

The prosecutor may ask the magistrates' court to commit the offender to the Crown Court so that a confiscation order may be made. The court must comply with such a request and may also commit any other offence for which he stands to be sentenced (PCA 2002, s 10).

B[20]

Costs

B[20.1]

The award of costs is the exercise of a judicial discretion and any decision must always be made after taking each case on its merits, hearing each party and taking proper account of the law. As a general rule, the successful party in any proceedings can expect to be reimbursed for the costs he has incurred in conducting the proceedings. In civil proceedings, a successful party can receive his costs from the other party. Under the Litigants in Person (Costs and Expenses, Magistrates' Courts) Order 2001 an individual who has been successful in civil proceedings may also benefit from an order for costs to cover work done by him in connection with the case and any resultant expenses or losses. In criminal proceedings, according to the circumstances of the particular case, it may be possible for costs to be awarded either against the unsuccessful party or from central funds, which are monies provided by Parliament to defray the costs of criminal proceedings.

Criminal proceedings

(Prosecution of Offences Act 1985, ss 16–19)

B[20.2]

In a criminal case, the court's duty is firstly to consider what is the appropriate sentence. If that is a fine, the offender's means so far as they are known to the court must be taken into account. It is wrong in principle to reduce a fine in order to accommodate an order for costs. Costs should never be awarded as a disguised penalty and the offender's means should be taken into account as above (*R v Nottingham Magistrates' Court, ex p Fohmann* (1986) 84 Cr App Rep 316, 151 JP 49). The costs awarded should be proportionate to the level of any fine (*Nedic v South Staffordshire Council* [2005] EWHC 1481 (Admin), [2005] All ER (D) 182 (Jun)).

Prosecution costs

B[20.3]

Central funds. Almost all criminal prosecutions are conducted by the Crown Prosecution Service or a public authority such as the Trading Standards

Department of a local authority. The funding for these prosecutions is provided by national or local revenues, and so there is no power to award the costs of the prosecution to these authorities out of central funds, even where the prosecution is successful. This avoids the wasteful practice of transferring moneys from one public fund to another.

B[20.4]

Private prosecutors. The court may, in a case where an indictable offence is concerned, order the costs of the prosecutor to be paid out of central funds whether the prosecution is successful or not. An indictable offence includes an offence triable either way and also offences of criminal damage where the damage is under £5,000 and is therefore triable only summarily. This provision does not apply to public authorities such as the CPS and local authorities (POA 1985, s 17(2)).

B[20.5]

There is no power to order costs from central funds to a prosecutor for purely summary offences. The costs to be awarded would normally be such amounts as the court considers reasonably sufficient to compensate the prosecutor for any expenses properly incurred by him and can include the costs of compensating a witness for the expense, trouble or loss of time properly incurred in his attendance at court. The amount payable to witnesses in respect of travelling expenses and loss of earnings is fixed by regulations and witnesses' expenses are dealt with in the clerk's office. A witness may be reimbursed even if he did not actually give evidence, if he was properly called to do so. Witnesses may be called, for example, in anticipation of a trial only to find that there is a last minute guilty plea. The cost of investigating offences is not included.

B[20.6]

Making an order for the costs of a private prosecutor. The court may fix the amount to be paid to the prosecutor out of central funds at the hearing where the prosecutor is in agreement, or in any other case the amount of the costs can be assessed afterwards by the justices' clerk.

B[20.7]

Reducing the amount of the prosecutor's order. Where the court is prepared to order the prosecutor's costs out of central funds but is of the opinion that there are circumstances that make it inappropriate to order the full amount of costs, eg where the defendant is convicted of some offences and acquitted of others, the court can assess what in its opinion would be just and reasonable, and specify that amount.

B[20.8]

Ordering the accused to pay the prosecution costs. Where a person has been convicted of an either way or purely summary offence, the court can order the accused to pay to the prosecutor (the Crown Prosecution Service, a public authority or a private prosecutor) such costs as it considers just and reasonable. The amount of the costs is specified by the court at the hearing and cannot be left to be assessed later. In general the principle applied to fines imposition (**B[33.16]**) should be applied and should be in keeping with the level of the fine (*R v Northallerton Magistrates' Court, ex p Dove* [2000] 1 Cr App Rep (S) 136, 163 JP 657, [1999] Crim LR 760).

B[20.9]

Monetary penalty not exceeding £5. Where, on conviction of an offence, the court orders payment of any sum as a fine, penalty, forfeiture or compensation not exceeding £5, the court shall not order the accused to pay the prosecution costs unless in the particular circumstances of the case it considers it right to do so.

B[20.10]–B[20.15]

Juveniles. Where a person under 17 years of age is convicted of an offence before a magistrates' (or youth) court and he is ordered to pay the costs, the amount that is ordered shall not exceed the amount of any fine that is properly imposed on him. This restriction does not apply if a parent is made responsible for paying the fine etc (see **B[33.95]**).

Defence costs

B[20.16]

Where an accused is acquitted, or where the information is not proceeded with, i e withdrawn or discontinued, or where the defendant is discharged in committal proceedings, the court may order the defendant's costs to be paid out of central funds. This applies whether the charge is triable purely summarily or is an indictable offence. Apart from exceptional circumstances, a prosecutor cannot be ordered to pay an acquitted defendant's costs. The amount of the order will be such amount as the court considers reasonably sufficient to compensate him for any costs incurred in the proceedings and includes the expense of compensating any witness for the expense, trouble or loss of time properly incurred or incidental to his attendance, in a similar manner to that for prosecution witnesses. *R (on the application of Hale) v North Sefton Justices* [2002] EWHC 257 (Admin) [2002] All ER (D) 10 (Jan) gives guidance on the appropriate taxation of such costs. A defendant cannot claim any loss of earnings or income foregone by himself personally. He can claim defence witness expenses even where convicted.

B[20.17]

A publicly aided defendant can only claim those costs which cannot be covered by the representation order, e g his travelling expenses to court.

B[20.18]

Reducing the amount of the defendant's order. A court should not deny a defendant his costs order where it would undermine the presumption of innocence in the Human Rights Convention (*R v South West Surrey Magistrates, ex p James* [2000] All ER (D) 564, [2000] Crim LR 690). An order will normally be made unless there are positive reasons for not making such an order, eg where the defendant's own conduct has brought suspicion on himself and has misled the prosecution into thinking that the case against him is stronger than it is. In these circumstances the court may make no order or a reduced order for costs. It would appear that where a defendant is convicted of an offence of 'due care' when charged with reckless driving he is not entitled to costs, as the information is not dismissed. However where he always intended to plead guilty to the lesser charge a partial order for costs may be appropriate (*Practice Direction (Costs: Criminal Proceedings)* (2004)).

Costs unnecessarily or improperly incurred

B[20.19]

Where the court is satisfied that one party to criminal proceedings has incurred costs as a result of an unnecessary or improper act or omission, it may order the party responsible to pay the additional costs thereby incurred whatever the final result of the case. This includes the whole of the defence costs where a private prosecutor instituted proceedings knowing an identical prosecution brought by CPS on the same ground had been dismissed without challenge (*Oddy v Bug Bugs Ltd* [2003] All ER (D) 156 (Nov)). This enables the court to mark its displeasure at the unreasonable behaviour of a party, eg where one party has put the other to unnecessary expense by requiring an adjournment when they should have been ready to proceed. Before making such an order both parties should be invited to make representations to the court and the court should determine the sum to be paid.

B[20.20]

Costs against legal representatives. The magistrates may disallow or order a legal representative to meet the whole or any part of any costs incurred by a party as a result of any improper, unreasonable or negligent act or omission of the representative or, where the conduct occurred after the incurring of the costs, the court considers it is unreasonable for the party to pay. Such orders are not common and the court must follow a detailed procedure before ordering costs against a legal representative. If such an order is contemplated, the legal adviser must be consulted.

B[20.20A]

Costs against third parties. Section 19B of the Prosecution of Offences Act 1985 (inserted by s 98 of the Courts Act 2003) empowers a criminal court to make costs orders against a third party where it has been guilty of serious misconduct. If such an order is contemplated, the legal adviser must be consulted.

Miscellaneous provisions

B[20.21]

Medical reports. In criminal proceedings, where the court has required a medical practitioner to make a report to the court orally or in writing, for the purpose inter alia of determining the most suitable method of dealing with the offender, his costs may be ordered to be paid from central funds.

B[20.22]

Interpreters. In any criminal proceedings provision is made for the payment of interpreters from central funds.

B[20.23]

Proceedings for breach or revocation of community orders including youth community orders etc. The editor is unable to identify a provision which empowers magistrates in summary breach proceedings to make an award of costs against the offender.

Civil proceedings

(Magistrates' Courts Act 1980, s 64)

B[20.24]

On hearing a complaint (eg concerning a dangerous dog), the court may order the defendant to pay to the successful complainant such costs as it thinks just and reasonable and, where the complaint is dismissed, the complainant may similarly be ordered to pay the defendant's costs (see the case law and principles discussed in detail in section **F[16.1]**). However, where the complaint is for the revocation, revival, variation or enforcement of an order for the paying of maintenance, a court can order either party to pay the others costs whatever order is made. In proceedings under the Children Act 1989 the court may at any time during the proceedings order that a party pay the whole or any part of the costs of any other party.

B[20.25]–B[20.30]

In civil cases, it is not usual to order one party to pay or contribute towards the other's costs if both are publicly funded, but there is no reason why an order for costs should not be paid against a party who is not publicly funded where the successful party is so aided, so that the legal aid fund will receive the benefit of the order.

B[20.31]

Applications. There is no power to award costs where proceedings are begun by way of an application (eg an application under the Police (Property) Act 1897) except in family proceedings (see above and *R v Salisbury and Tisbury and Mere Juvenile Court, ex p Ball* (1985) 149 JP 346).

B[21]

Curfew order

(Powers of Criminal Courts (Sentencing) Act 2000, ss 37 and 38)

B[21.1]

Available only in the Youth Court (for adults see B[17.41])

The Criminal Justice Act 1991 introduced the 'curfew order' whereby the court may require an offender who has been convicted of an offence to remain at a specified place during specified periods.

B[21.2]

As this is a 'community sentence' the criteria for imposing such a sentence must be satisfied and the court must obtain and consider information about the place proposed to be specified in the order and as to the attitude of the persons likely to be affected by the offender's enforced presence with them. Before making a curfew order in respect of an offender under 16, the court must obtain and consider information about his family circumstances and the likely effect of such an order. The probation officer of the youth offending team will usually provide the court with this information.

B[21.3]

The court must explain to him in ordinary language the effects of the order, the consequences of any breach of its requirements and the power to review the order.

B[21.4]

The curfew must be for a period of at least 2 hours and not more than 12 hours in any one day and any curfew requirements may only have effect during a period of six months from the making of the order (or three months in the case of an offender under the age of 16). As far as practicable the curfew should not conflict with the offender's religious beliefs, work or attendance at school.

B[21.5]

The court may require the electronic monitoring of the offender's whereabouts during the curfew periods.

B[21.6]

However a court shall not make an order unless it has been notified by the Secretary of State that arrangements for monitoring the offender's whereabouts are available in the area.

B[21.7]

National implementation was effective from 1 December 1999 and 1 February 2001 for electronically monitored curfews for 10–15-year-olds.

B[22]

Deferment of sentence

(Powers of Criminal Courts (Sentencing) Act 2000, ss 1A-1F)

Limitations

B[22.1]

The offender must consent, and undertake to comply with any requirements the court considers appropriate to impose during the period of deferment.

B[22.2]

Deferment may be used only once in respect of any one offence.

B[22.3]

The court must be satisfied that it is in the interests of justice to defer sentence, having regard to the nature of the offence and the character and circumstances of the offender.

B[22.4]

There are no limitations as to age or the nature of the offence. The court may have regard to the defendant's conduct after conviction (including if appropriate any reparation made by him) and any change in his circumstances. The court may impose requirements as to the offender's conduct during the deferment and appoint an appropriate supervisor with their consent.

Ancillary orders

B[22.5]

None, because this is not a final disposal of the case, except that a restitution order may be made.

How to announce

B[22.6]

We feel that it is not in the interests of justice that we impose a sentence on you today and we are considering deferring our decision for [*state period, and give the reason*] during that period you will comply with the following requirements *[state what is expected from the offender during the period of deferment]*. **Do you understand? We cannot defer sentence without your consent. Do you consent? [*If answered affirmatively*] Then you must attend court here on [*date*] when we shall consider what sentence to impose after hearing how you have progressed in the meantime.**

B[22.7]

Note - The essential ingredients of this announcement are the request for consent and the date when the case will be heard again. Consent must be obtained before the order is formally made and, as with any consent, has no value unless the offender understands exactly to what he is consenting. Accordingly the words above may be varied according to the circumstances and in the light of the general considerations below.

General considerations

B[22.8]

This power of the court might be less confusing if it were referred to as deferment of sentencing. There is no question, contrary to what is sometimes believed, that the court decides upon a sentence but postpones announcing it in case it changes its mind.

B[22.9]

Only exceptionally may a custodial sentence be imposed after deferment; it is advised that where an offender is liable to be ordered to serve a suspended sentence it will rarely be appropriate to defer sentencing him for the offence which he has committed during the operational period.

B[22.10]–B[22.15]

Deferment is appropriate when some event may occur in the near future which, according to whether it occurred or not, would influence the court when imposing a sentence. It may be, for example, that the offender has an uncertain chance of employment upon which voluntary compensation depends. There should always be some reason for deferment which can be stated so that the offender knows what is expected of him and may, as he thinks fit, take steps to improve his situation from a sentencing point of view. Great care should be exercised, however, not to use this power as a threat or coercion or to give an offender an opportunity to buy his way out of prison by making compensation (especially if he may do so by resorting to further offences).

B[22.16]

The concern of a victim of the offence should be borne in mind when considering deferment; one effect of deferment, for example, may be to postpone the day when compensation is ordered.

B[22.17]

The maximum period for which sentencing may be deferred is six months. The defendant cannot be remanded. A summons or warrant may be issued if he fails to appear on the date for sentencing specified by the court.

B[22.18]

Magistrates should never fall into the trap of deferring sentencing because they are unable to make up their minds as to the appropriate sentence. The court will obviously wish to be informed at the end of the period of deferment whether the offender has done what it was hoped he would do, or whether the event has taken place which was the reason for the deferment. In many cases it will be convenient to ask the supervising officer to report, but in some cases only the offender or a third party will be able to satisfy the court. It is advised that the court when deferring sentence makes clear arrangements at that time as to how such information is to be provided.

B[22.19]

The court might consider that a conditional discharge for six months but imposed immediately would achieve the court's objectives. It is not necessary, but may be desirable, that the same magistrates should impose the sentence as those who deferred sentence. Provided the requirement and reasons for deferment are explicitly stated, the legal adviser will note them and bring them to the attention of the sentencing court.

B[22.20]

The offender can be returned to court if the supervisor has reported to the court that the offender has failed to comply with one or more requirements in respect of which an offender gave an undertaking (s 1B(2)(c)). The can issue a summons or warrant for the offender to appear before it (s 1B (3)).

B[22.21]

If the offender commits an offence during the period of deferment, the court convicting him of that offence may deal with the deferred case even though the period of deferment has not expired. Section 1C sets out the powers of the Crown Court and magistrates' courts in these cases. If the original sentence was deferred by a Crown Court, it must be a Crown Court that passes sentence for both offences. The power to commit to the Crown Court for sentence under s 3 PCC(S)A 2000 is retained by s 1D(2)(b) PCC(S)A 2000**.

B[23]

Deportation

B[23.1]

> '... a person who is not a British citizen shall be ... liable to deportation from the United Kingdom if, after he has attained the age of seventeen, he is convicted of an offence for which he is punishable with imprisonment and on his conviction is recommended for deportation by a court'

Immigration Act 1971, s 3(6)

B[23.2]

Recommendation. A magistrates' court cannot order deportation, but it can make a recommendation to the Home Secretary for the deportation of the convicted person. In sentencing the offender the court does not have to take into account what might happen in the offender's own country if he is returned (*R v Ukoh* [2004] EWCA Crim 3270, [2005] All ER (D) 58 (Jan)).

B[23.3]

Not a British citizen. The following categories of citizens cannot be deported:

(a) British citizens;
(b) Commonwealth citizens having a right of abode in the United Kingdom;
(c) Commonwealth citizens not included in (b) and citizens of the Republic of Ireland provided in either case they were such citizens at the time of the coming into force of the Immigration Act 1971 and were ordinarily resident in the United Kingdom and at the time of conviction had been ordinarily resident in the United Kingdom and Islands for the last five years.

B[23.4]

The following may be deported:

(d) Commonwealth citizens not included in (b) or (c) above;
(e) aliens;
(f) aliens being citizens of countries which are members of the European Community.

B[23.5]

Age of seventeen. A person shall be deemed to have obtained the age of 17 at the time of his conviction, if on consideration of any available evidence he appears to have done so to the court.

B[23.6]

Convicted. Means found to have committed the offence.

B[23.7]

Punishable with imprisonment. This means punishable with imprisonment in the case of a person over 21 years even though the defendant himself may not be liable to imprisonment.

Criteria for making a recommendation

General considerations

B[23.8]

The court. In deciding whether to make a recommendation for deportation the court may consider:

(a) Would the offender's continued presence in the United Kingdom be detrimental. In considering this the court might take account of:
  (i) the seriousness of the crime, eg a simple offence of shoplifting would not merit such a recommendation;
  (ii) the length of the defendant's criminal record.

(b) The effect of a deportation order on innocent persons such as the offender's family.

The court should not consider:

(c) The consequences to the offender of his being returned to his own country, eg persecution. This is generally a matter for the Home Secretary (*R v Jelk* [2002] EWCA Crim 184 [2002] All ER (D) 200 (Jan)).
(d) The fact that the offender is in receipt of social security.

See generally *R v Bouchereau* 30/77 [1978] QB 732, [1981] 2 All ER 924n, ECJ.

B[23.9]–B[23.15]

Home Secretary's considerations. In considering a recommendation the Home Secretary takes into account:

(a) the nature of the offence;
(b) the length of time the offender has spent in this country;
(c) the offender's criminal record;

(d) the strength of his connections with this country, his personal history and domestic circumstances (eg if the offender's wife or children are citizens of this country and resident here, it might be a great hardship to them to order deportation of the offender);
(e) any compassionate feature that may be present;
(f) any representation made by the offender.

B[23.16]

The Home Secretary will not normally deport an offender sentenced to borstal training (now abolished and replaced by youth custody), or detention, or a first offender unless the offence was very grave or other offences were taken into consideration.

Citizens of EC countries

B[23.17]

Before recommending the deportation of a national of a country in the EC the court must have regard to Community laws. Article 48 of the Treaty makes the following relevant provisions:

> '1 Freedom of movement for workers shall be secured within the Community by the end of the transitional period at the latest.
>
> 2 Such freedom of movement shall entail the abolition of any discrimination based on nationality between workers of the member states as regards employment, remuneration and other conditions of work and employment.
>
> 3 It shall entail the right, subject to limitations justified on grounds of public policy, public security or public health:
> (a) to accept offers of employment actually made;
> (b) to move freely within the territories of member states for this purpose;
> (c) to stay in the member state for the purpose of employment in accordance with the provisions governing the employment of nationals of that said state laid down by law, regulation or administrative action;
> (d) to remain in the territory of a member state after having been employed in that state subject to conditions which shall be embodied in implementing regulations which shall be drawn up by the Commission.
>
> 4 The provisions of this Article shall not apply to employment in the public service.'

B[23.18]

With regard to the references in paragraph 3 above to public policy or security, a directive has been issued (no. 64/221) which states:

'(1) Measures taken on grounds of public policy or public security shall be based exclusively on the conduct of the individual concerned.

(2) Previous criminal convictions shall not themselves constitute grounds for the taking of such measures.'

B[23.19]

The European Court of Justice has ruled:

(a) that any action affecting the rights of persons covered by article 48 to enter and reside freely in a member state under the same conditions as nationals of that state constituted a 'measure' for the purposes of the directive quoted above;
(b) that a recommendation for deportation by a court of a member state according to its national law was such an action (ie the 'action' referred to in (a) above);
(c) that the directive must be interpreted to mean that previous convictions are relevant only in so far as the circumstances which gave rise to them are evidence of personal conduct constituting a present threat to the requirements of public policy;
(d) that the justification for restricting free movement provided in article 48 (above) presupposed the existence of a genuine and sufficiently serious threat affecting one of the fundamental interests of society additional to the disturbance of order which any infringement of the law involved.

See guidance handed down in *R v Secretary of State for the Home Department, ex p Santillo* [1981] 2 All ER 897.

B[23.20]

It should be noted that not all EC nationals come within the ambit of the directive. In practice it covers those who come to the United Kingdom to take or seek work, to set up in business or in a self-employed capacity or to receive services for money, e g medical, educational or business.

Procedure

B[23.21]

There should be a full inquiry into the case before a recommendation is made. A person who is likely to be the subject of an order must be given seven clear days' notice of what may happen to him. The defendant should have legal representation. Solicitors should be asked to address the court specifically on the possibility of a recommendation for deportation being made. In the case of an **EU National** the court must give reasons for making a recommendation as to deportation (*R v Secretary of State for the Home Department, ex p Dannenburg* [1984] 2 All ER 481, (1984) 148 JP 321).

B[23.22]

What should not be done is to add a sentence as if by an afterthought at the end of observations about any sentence of imprisonment.

EC national within the scope of article 48

B[23.23]

The recommendation can only be based on the grounds of public policy, public security or public health. The offender must be informed of the grounds on which the recommendation is based. A short statement in writing should be given to the offender and also attached to the written recommendation (see **B[23.21]** above). It should include some indication of the extent to which the current and previous criminal convictions of the defendant have been taken into account and the light which such conviction or convictions threw on the likely nature of the defendant's personal conduct in the future. Of particular importance will be the court's assessment of the gravity of the conduct and the likelihood of reoffending.

EC national to which article 48 does not apply

B[23.24]

It is desirable that the same procedure be followed.

Aliens (see generally *R v Nazari* [1988] QB 631, [1988] 2 WLR 1005, sub nom R v Kuxhaus [1988] 2 All ER 705, 56 P & CR 229, CA).

B[23.25]–B[23.30]

Similarly reasons, not necessarily in writing, should be given.

B[23.31]

The effect of a recommendation. Where the court makes a recommendation and the defendant is not sentenced to imprisonment or is not liable to be detained in any other way he will be detained under the Immigration Act 1971 until he is deported. The court may, however, order his release subject to such restrictions as to residence and/ or to reporting to the police as it may direct.

B[24]

Detention for one day at the court or at a police station

(Magistrates' Courts Act 1980, s 135)

B[24.1]

Magistrates may order the detention of a defendant aged 18 years or more in the precincts of the court house or at a police station for any period until 8 p.m. on the day of the hearing; but the offence must be punishable with imprisonment or alternatively the detention must be an alternative to payment of a fine. The magistrates should announce at what time the defendant can be released, taking into account that the defendant should be given the opportunity of returning home that day.

B[25]

Detention and training orders

(Powers of the Criminal Courts (Sentencing) Act 2000, s 100)

B[25.1]

Detention and training orders (DTO) are the sole custodial sentence available to the courts which may be imposed on a young person aged under 18. Age is generally determined at the time of conviction rather than at sentence. The order is available in the youth court only and not the adult court. The DTO is a rehabilitative order and not simply a young offender's prison.

B[25.2]

Where a DTO is a likely sentence the Youth Offending Team (YOT) will make contact with the Youth Justice Board before the court hearing to establish if accommodation is available.

B[25.3]

All the restrictions outlined at **B[37]** and contained in s 152 CJA 2003 apply to the detention and training order because it is defined as a custodial sentence.

B[25.4]

Before making an order the court must be satisfied that the following additional circumstances pertain:

(a) the offender is not less than 12 years of age when the offence for which he is to be dealt with is found proved;
(b) where the offender is under the age of 15 years at the time of conviction the courts must be of the opinion that he is a persistent young offender. Note this is 15 years old at the time of conviction (*R v Thomas* (2004) although *R v LM* [2002] EWCA Crim 3047, [2002] All ER (D) 35 (Dec) suggests that a non-persistent offender who is under the age of 15 when a non-grave offence is committed cannot receive a DTO even when 15 at date of conviction.

This is not the same definition as a persistent offender for the purposes of monitoring speed of case throughput (*R v Charlton* (2000) 164 JP 685, CA). Where there has been a series of offences on separate occasions the offender may be persistent (*R v Smith* (2000) 164 JP 681, [2000] Crim LR 613, CA). However, such offending should be of a similar character (*R v JD* (2000) 165 JP 1, CA).

B[25.5]

Where the court passes a detention and training order it must state in open court that it is of the opinion that the above conditions are satisfied.

B[25.6]

Length of the order. The term of a detention and training order (DTO) may only be made up of terms of 4, 6, 8, 10, 12, 18 or 24 months. However the court may not exceed the maximum term the Crown Court could impose for the offence on an offender aged 21. This means that the youth court must be careful when dealing with a case of summary criminal damage (maximum three months' imprisonment) making the DTO unavailable and cases involving other summary offences where the maximum sentence for an adult offender will generally be less than six months [**28 weeks]. Another exception to this is an offence under the Bail Act where the maximum penalty is currently three months. [**At the time of writing there are residual plans to alter the penalty linked to the alteration of custodial sentences under the CJA 2003. This means that in the magistrates' court or a youth court it will be possible to impose a custodial sentence for an offence of absconding under s 6 of the Bail Act 1976. Such sentence will be served first and then the sentence for the substantive offence thereafter.]

B[25.7]

In assessing the length of sentence the court must give credit for a timely guilty plea. The level of credit will generally depend on the time the plea of guilty is entered. **Sentencing Guideline Council** guidance suggests up to a third for a timely guilty plea, reducing to roughly 10% for a plea entered on the date set for trial. In rare circumstances credit for plea can be withheld altogether. Magistrates should consult their legal adviser before determining to withhold any credit for a plea of guilty (see *R v Barber* [2006] EWCA Crim 162, [2006] 2 Cr App Rep (S) 539).

The court must also take into account in deciding the overall the length of the DTO any time spent on remand in custody (*R v B* [2000] Crim LR 870).

B[25.8]

Consecutive orders may be made provided that the overall term does not exceed 24 months. Note that an aggregate term of more than the statutory maximum** may be imposed on the same occasion for summary only offences (*C v DPP* [2001] EWHC Admin 453 [2002] 1 Cr App Rep (S) 189, [2001] Crim LR 671). For indictable and either way offences each offence must be one of the specified terms above, although when aggregated it may come to an unspecified term of, for example, 6+ 8+ 10 = 24 months.

B[25.9]

Half the order will be served in a secure establishment and half will be the subject of supervision under a member of the Young Offender Team.

B[25.10]

Breach of supervision. Supervision takes place throughout the order, but if a supervision order is breached the offender may be detained for at least three months or the whole of the remaining term of the DTO, or may be fined up to the maximum of level 3. Offenders brought before the court for further offending during the period of supervision may be dealt with for the new offence as well as the remainder of the existing order.

B[25.11]

See *R v Ganley* [2000] All ER (D) 594, [2001] 1 Cr App Rep (S) 60, CA for general guidance on the use of the order.

B[26]–B[30]

Detention in a young offender institution

(Powers of the Criminal Courts (Sentencing) Act 2000, s 96)

B[26.0]

Section 96 will be repealed by the Criminal Justice and Courts Services Act 2000, Sch 7 from a date to be appointed. Section 96 will, in effect, be replaced by the provisions to be found in Chapter 3 (ss 181–195 inclusive) of the CJA 2003. This will make available prison sentences, intermittent custody and suspended sentences for offenders aged 18 years or more at the date of conviction (not sentence). It is likely the new regime will only apply to offences committed on or after the operative date ie from a date to be appointed. See **B[37] onwards.

There are currently transitory provisions making suspended sentence available for offenders aged 18–20 years inclusive. However, see *R v Campbell* [2006] EWCA Crim 726, [2006] All ER (D) 137 (Mar).

General

B[26.1]

Imprisonment is not available for offenders under the age of 21 years. The main custodial provision for these offenders is detention in a young offender institution. This is subject to the criteria restricting the use of custodial sentences imposed by the Powers of the Criminal Courts (Sentencing) Act 2000.

B[26.2]

As with all custodial sentences the court must explain:

(a) how long the defendant will spend in custody;
(b) how long after release he will be liable to recall; and
(c) how long after release he will be subject to supervision.

Limitations

B[26.3]

Imprisonable offence. The offence of which the offender is found guilty must be punishable with imprisonment in the case of a person aged 21 or over.

B[26.4]

Age of offender. The minimum age for male and female offenders is 18 years. In either case the offender must be under 21 years.

B[26.5]

Criteria for imposing a custodial sentence. The court must be of the opinion:

(a) that the offence, or the combination of the offence and any other offences associated with it, was so serious that only such a sentence can be justified for the offence;
(b) where the offence is a violent or sexual offence, that only such a sentence would be adequate to protect the public from serious harm from the offender.

B[26.6]

Other circumstances in which custody may be imposed. Nothing in paragraphs (a) and (b) above prevents the court imposing a custodial sentence on an offender who refuses to consent to a community sentence proposed by the court which requires his willingness to comply with a proposed requirement. A court may also impose custody for a wilful and persistent breach of a community order.

B[26.7]

So serious. See **B[37.6]**. The court must take account of all the information about the circumstances of the offence including any aggravating or mitigating factors as are available to it.

B[26.8]

Associated offence. An offence of which the offender has been convicted in the same proceedings or for which he is sentenced at the same time, or an offence taken into consideration.

B[26.9]

Violent offence. An offence which leads, or is intended or likely to lead, to a person's death or to physical injury to a person, and includes an offence which is required to be charged as arson.

B[26.10]–B[26.15]

Sexual offence under the Sexual Offences Act 2003. It does not include offences relating to prostitution. Nor does it include offences in public lavatories.

B[26.16]

Protection from serious harm. This refers to protecting members of the public from death or serious personal injury, whether physical or psychological, occasioned by further such offences committed by the offender.

B[26.17]

Pre-sentence report. Except where the court considers it unnecessary to do so, the court must obtain and consider a pre-sentence report before forming an opinion on:

(a) whether the offence etc was so serious;
(b) (violent or sexual offence) only custody would be adequate to protect the public etc;
(c) the length of term commensurate with the offence;
(d) (violent or sexual offence) the length of term necessary to protect the public etc.

B[26.18]

In all cases where a court is contemplating sentencing a defendant to custody for the first time a report should be obtained: *R v Gillette* (1999) Times, 3 December, CA.

B[26.19]

Failure to obtain pre-sentence report. Does not invalidate the sentence but the appeal court must obtain and consider such a report if the court below was not justified in forming an opinion that a report was unnecessary.

B[26.20]

Mentally disordered offender. Where an offender is or appears to be mentally disordered, ie suffering from a mental disorder within the meaning of the Mental Health Act 1983, the court must additionally obtain and consider a medical report before passing a custodial sentence unless the court considers it unnecessary to do so. The court must take any such information into account and consider the likely effect of any custodial sentence on his condition and any treatment for it. Failure to obtain a medical report does not invalidate any sentence but one must be obtained and considered by an appeal court.

B[26.21]

Legal representation. The offender must first be given the opportunity to be legally represented unless he has failed to take up the offer of legal representation or has been refused legal representation based on financial grounds. Note that the requirement is not that he should be represented, but that he should have an opportunity to be.

B[26.22]

Offenders under 18 years. A magistrates' court (as opposed to a youth court) cannot commit defendants aged under 18 years to custody. Such juveniles must be remitted on bail or in local authority accommodation to a youth court which will usually be the youth court for the area in which they reside.

Passing sentence

B[26.23]-B[26.24]

Maximum length of sentence. Twelve months or the maximum term of imprisonment available for the offence, whichever is the lesser term, six months if suspended.

B[26.25]–B[26.30]

Minimum length of sentence. 21 days over 18 years of age, 14 days if suspended except for detention imposed where an offender has breached a supervision order made on his release. See **B[26.39]**.

B[26.31]

Consecutive terms. Detention in a young offender institution may be ordered to be consecutive to an existing period of detention or, if more than one period of detention is imposed on the same occasion, one period of detention may be ordered to be consecutive to another so, however, that the offender will not be liable to a period of more than 12 months in total. If a longer period is ordered the excess period will be treated as remitted.

B[26.32]

Length of custodial sentence. Shall be for a term which is commensurate with the seriousness of the offence or the combination of the offence and other offences associated with it or, in the case of a violent or sexual offence, for such longer term as is necessary to protect the public from serious harm from the offender. The court may suspend the sentence for an operational period of 2 years maximum, see **B[37.60]**.

B[26.33]

Committal to Crown Court. The longest term of detention available to a magistrates' court in respect of an offender for a single indictable or either way offence is six months. However, in certain circumstances a magistrates' court may commit offenders aged 18 years to the Crown Court for sentence under s 3 Powers of Criminal Courts (Sentencing) Act 2000** (see **B[16]**).

Reasons for decisions

B[26.34]

It is the duty of the court to state in open court:

(a) that it is of the opinion that either or both of paragraphs (a) and (b) at **B[26.35]** apply:
(b) that it is of the opinion that in the case of a violent or sexual offence it is necessary to pass a longer term than is commensurate with the seriousness of the offence to protect the public from serious harm from the offender;
(c) why it is of that opinion;

and in all cases to explain to the offender in open court and in ordinary language why it is passing a custodial sentence on him or such longer term.

How to announce

B[26.35]

We have decided to pass a sentence of detention in a young offender institution on the defendant and we are of the opinion that:

(a) the offence (or the combination of the offence and other associated offence(s) namely [ ]) was so serious that only such a sentence can be justified for the offence; and/or
(b) this is a violent/sexual offence and only such a sentence would be adequate to protect the public from serious harm from him

because [*then explain why either or both of the paragraphs apply***]. (Violent/ sexual offence): We are also passing a sentence of detention for a term longer than is commensurate with the seriousness of the offence as this is necessary to protect the public from serious harm from him because [***give reasons***].**

Accordingly [*addressing the defendant***] you will be sent to a young offender institution for [***state period***]. On release you will be subject to supervision for [***state how long***] and you will be subject to recall to detention for the next [***state time***] and this is because [***explain in ordinary language why he is receiving a custodial sentence and, where applicable, why he is receiving a term longer than is commensurate with the seriousness of the offence***].**

Note – If there is more than one offence it should be clearly stated what the total period of detention is to be.

Ancillary orders

B[26.36]

Compensation at **B[18]**

Costs at **B[20]**

Disqualification at **C[5]**

Endorsement at **C[5]**

Deprivation of property and forfeiture at **B[34]**

Restitution order at **B[39]**

Early release

B[26.37]

An offender subject to a term of detention in a young offender institution for 12 months or less will be automatically released after he has served one half of the term. In determining the period that has been served, time spent on remand in custody or secure accommodation is to be taken into account. However, additional days may be imposed under the prison rules where the offender has been guilty of disciplinary offences.

B[26.38]

Supervision following release. An offender who is released and is under 22 years will be under the supervision of a probation officer or social worker for a period of three months or until he attains the age of 22 years, whichever is the shorter period.

B[26.39]–B[26.45]

Failure to comply with requirements as to supervision is punishable by custody of up to 30 days or a fine of up to £1,000.

B[26.46]

Further offences. Where an offender commits an imprisonable offence before he would (but for his release) have served his sentence in full, the court which deals with him for the later offence may return him to custody for the whole or part of the period which begins with the making of the order of return and is equal in length to the period between the date of commission of the new offence and the date of expiry of the original term.

B[31]

Discharge (absolute or conditional)

(Powers of Criminal Courts (Sentencing) Act 2000, s 12)

Limitations

B[31.1]

Absolute	-	none.
Conditional	-	minimum period, none,
	-	maximum period, three years.

B[31.2]

Special consideration. Before making either of these orders the court must be of opinion, having regard to the circumstances including the nature of the offence and the character of the offender, that it is inexpedient to inflict punishment.

Unless there are exceptional circumstances a magistrates' court (which includes a youth court), may not make an order for conditional discharge in respect of an offence committed within two years of a final warning (CDA 1998, s 66(4)).

B[31.3]

Before making an order for conditional discharge the court must explain to the offender in ordinary language that if he commits another offence during the period of discharge he will be liable to be sentenced for the offence for which the conditional discharge is given. This is the court's duty and only in the most exceptional circumstances may it be delegated to another person, e g the accused's lawyer.

Ancillary orders

B[31.4]–B[31.6]

Compensation at **B[18]**

Costs at **B[20]**

Disqualification at **C[5]**

Endorsement at **C[5]**

Deprivation of property and forfeiture at **B[34]**

Restitution at **B[39]**

Legal note

B[31.7]

A defendant who is convicted of an offence while subject to a Crown Court conditional discharge may be committed to the Crown Court to be sentenced for the offence for which the conditional discharge was originally ordered, under the Powers of Criminal Courts (Sentencing) Act 2000, s 13(5). He may also be committed to be dealt with for the new offence, under Powers of Criminal Courts (Sentencing) Act 2000, s 6 (*R v Penfold* (1995) 16 Cr App Rep (S) 1016, [1995] Crim LR 666, CA).

General considerations

B[31.8]

It is most important to note that only after the court has decided that it is inexpedient to inflict punishment because of all the circumstances may it make an order for discharge. But magistrates are specifically empowered to make a deprivation order or order for costs and compensation where appropriate: Power of Criminal Courts (Sentencing) Act 2000, s 12 (7) as amended. Disqualification and endorsement may be ordered where appropriate.

B[31.9]

This is not a conviction for the purposes of the Sex Offenders Act 1997 (see **A[69.33]**).

B[31.10]–B[31.15]

No conditions or requirements may be added to either of these orders.

B[31.16]

Period of conditional discharge. This must always commence on the pronouncement of sentence. There is no provision to make this period consecutive to any other period.

B[31A]

Drug treatment and testing orders

(Powers of Criminal Courts (Sentencing) Act 2000, s 52)

General

B[31A.1]

Applicable in the Youth Court only (16 and 17 year olds)

The drug treatment and testing order is a community penalty directed at reducing the amount of crime directly attributable to drug misuse by reducing or eliminating the offenders misuse of drugs. The order anticipates compliance with a testing regime run by the probation service with review hearings during the course of the order to act as an opportunity to receive a written report detailing test results and the views of the treatment provider on the defendant's response to treatment. Sentencers should not forget the criminality of the offender (*A-G's Reference No 28* (2001)) but large scale acquisitive crime could attract a DTTO if there was a chance of breaking the habit (*R v Kelly* [2002] All ER (D) 434).

Limitations

B[31A.2]

The order is available for all offenders 16 and 17 years at the date of conviction. The court must be satisfied that the offender is dependent on or has a propensity to misuse drugs and that his dependency or propensity is such as requires and may be susceptible to treatment.

Community sentence

B[31A.3]

The order is a community penalty and the general requirements relating to community orders must be satisfied before the order may be made. The order must include both a treatment requirement, although the nature of the treatment is not specified in the order, and a testing requirement that the offender provides samples during the period of the order at such times and in such circumstances as are determined by the treatment provider. The order will also provide that the defendant shall be under supervision (of a probation officer) during the treatment and testing period.

Period

B[31A.4]

The court may make an order for treatment and testing for a minimum period of six months and a maximum of three years. The order must also provide for periodic reviews at intervals of not less than one month. These hearings will be at court and the offender must attend the review. If at a review hearing the court is satisfied that the offender is making good progress the order may be amended to allow for subsequent reviews to be heard without a formal hearing.

Consent

B[31A.5]

The court may not make an order unless the offender has expressed a willingness to comply with the requirements of the order including requirements for treatment testing and review. The drug treatment and testing order is seen as a high level intervention. Following the case of *R (on the application of Inner London Probation Service) v Tower Bridge Magistrates' Court* [2001] EWHC 401 (Admin), [2001] All ER (D) 262 (May), where the court does not have the support of the probation service in making a drug treatment and testing order, the only community option available to the court which could make specific reference to the offender's drug misuse would be a community rehabilitation order with specified activities.

How to announce

B[31A.6]

We believe your offending is so serious (or serious enough), that you are dependent on drugs and that dependency may be treatable. We are therefore placing you on a drug treatment and testing order for [specify] months. You will be placed under supervision of a probation officer for that period. During that period you must submit to treatment under the order at [*name of institution*] at [*specify*] intervals. This means that you will be tested [*specify number*] times over the next [*specify*] months and random tests as deemed appropriate.

The court will review the order at [*state number*] monthly intervals when you must attend. The probation officer will make a written report to the court before each hearing which will tell us the results of tests samples and your response to treatment.

If you breach any requirement of the order you will be brought back to court and may be punished or be dealt with in a different way for the offence we have considered today. If your offend again during the order you will be punished separately for the offence.

Do you understand? Do you consent to the making of the drug treatment and testing order?

The general considerations

B[31A.7]

Guidelines for use are set out in *R v Harrison* [2003] EWCA Crim 3514, [2003] All ER (D) 288 (Nov) including the prerequisite that the defendant has made an effort to become free of drugs, and the offences are acquisitive in nature rather than violent.

The drug treatment and testing order is a community penalty aimed at defendants, convicted of crimes committed to fund their drug habit, who show a willingness to co-operate with treatment. The order may be made together with another community penalty but courts should be aware that unless it is made in respect of a particular series of events problems can arise if the order is breached. Note also that there is no power for the youth court to commit a breach to the Crown Court for sentence (*R v Chute* [2003] EWCA Crim 177, [2003] 2 Cr App Rep (S) 445, [2003] Crim LR 295).

B[31A.8]

A pre-sentence report, although not obligatory, will almost always be required. The report should satisfy the court as to the offender's motivation that a place on a scheme is available either as in or out patient and should set out the proposed plan of treatment, and specify testing and reviews. The court also needs to be satisfied that the offender is susceptible to treatment and that he is a dependent drug user.

B[31A.9]

The treatment provider must administer the minimum number of tests required by the court and submit results to the supervising probation officer although additional random tests may also be taken. The offender must report to a probation officer as required by him and notify him of any change of address during the course of the order.

B[31A.10]

Review hearings must take place no more frequently than monthly and a written report including the results of drug tests will be submitted by the probation officer to the court. If the court is happy with progress it may allow subsequent reviews to be held without a hearing. The court may subsequently reinstate review hearings if it is not happy with the offender's progress. The court may amend the order at a review hearing, with the offender's consent. If the offender does not consent, it may revoke the order and re-sentence the offender.

B[31A.11]

The order must be explained fully but in ordinary language to the offender and his consent must be obtained before the order is made.

B[31A.12]

The option for the youth court in the case of a breach was reviewed in *R v Robinson* (2002) CLR 425.

B[32]

Exclusion orders

Licensed Premises (Exclusion of Certain Persons) Act 1980

B[32.1]

When a person is convicted of an offence (of whatever nature) which was committed on licensed premises and the court which convicts him is satisfied that when he committed the offence he resorted to violence, or offered or threatened violence, the court may make an exclusion order prohibiting him from entering those licensed premises or any other licensed premises which the court may specify in the order. Such an order is made in addition to any sentence imposed, including a discharge.

"Licensed premises" for this purpose means those in respect of which a premises licence under the Licensing Act 2003 has been granted by the relevant local authority authorising the supply of alcohol (within the meaning of s 14 of that Act) for consumption on the premises.

The court must state the period during which the defendant is to be excluded; the minimum period is three months and the maximum is two years. Any person who is subject to such an order and is in the specified premises otherwise than with the express consent of the licensee or one of his staff is guilty of an offence punishable with a fine on level 4 and one months' imprisonment (**from a date to be appointed, 51 weeks).

Thus, a person convicted of breach of an exclusion order who is also the subject of a suspended sentence (which might be imposed for the offence which gave rise to the exclusion order) will be in jeopardy of having to serve that additional sentence. Courts would probably want to make this point to the defendant both in fairness to him and also perhaps the better to enforce the order. At the time of convicting a person for breach of an exclusion order the court may also determine whether to revoke the order or vary it by deleting the name of any specified premises.

B[32.2]

The licensee or his staff may expel from his premises any person whom he reasonably suspects of having entered in breach of an exclusion order and a constable shall at the request of the licensee or his staff, help to expel any person whom the constable reasonably suspects of being present in breach of such an order.

B[33]

Fines

Limitations

B[33.1]

Offences. The court may fine for any criminal offence.

B[33.2]

Maximum fine. The power of magistrates' courts (unlike that of the Crown Court) to impose a fine is entirely controlled by statute. Therefore the maximum fine for the offence may not be exceeded.

B[33.3]

The maximum fine for the vast majority of offences which are only triable by magistrates is expressed as being on one of five levels, each level representing a monetary limit. (The maximum for most offences triable either way is expressed as the 'statutory maximum' or 'prescribed sum'.)

Level 1: maximum fine is £200
Level 2: maximum fine is £500
Level 3: maximum fine is £1,000
Level 4: maximum fine is £2,500
Level 5: maximum fine is £5,000

(Either way offences: prescribed sum is £5,000.)

B[33.4]

This is known as the standard scale of fines and it has been devised as an attempt to rationalise the maximum amounts of fines and to provide a simple means of increasing them in inflationary times.

Juveniles

B[33.5]

Offender under 14 (a child). Maximum fine is the amount in the statute creating the offence or £250, whichever is less.

B[33.6]

Offender 14 to under 18 (young person). Maximum fine is the amount in the statute creating the offence or £1,000, whichever is less.

Parental responsibility for payment

B[33.7]

In the case of a person under 16 the court must order the parent or guardian to pay unless either he cannot be found or the court is satisfied that it would be unreasonable to order the parent to pay having regard to the circumstances of the case. Provided the parent has been given the opportunity to attend court, an order for payment may be made against him in his absence. If he is present, he must be given the opportunity of making representations about whether he should be ordered to pay.

B[33.8]

Before exercising its power to make an order that a parent should pay a financial order in respect of an offence committed by a child the court must be satisfied that it is reasonable to do so. Before making an order a parent or guardian should be given the opportunity of being heard (PCC(S)A 2000, s 137(4)).

B[33.9]

Where the offender is aged 16 or 17, and it would not be unreasonable to do so, the court has a power to make the parent responsible for the financial order.

B[33.10]–B[33.15]

Where a local authority has parental responsibility (see **D[3.1]–D[3.7]**) for a child in their care or accommodated by them, the local authority is responsible for payment, unless it has done everything reasonably and properly expected of it to protect the public from the young offender (*D v DPP* (1995)).

Determining the amount of any fine

B[33.16]

In accordance with the sentencing principles of the Criminal Justice Act 1991 and what are now ss 162–164 CJA 2003, the court must ensure that any penalty is commensurate with the seriousness of the offence for which it is imposed. The court therefore must assess carefully the gravity of the offence having regard to the circumstances and to any mitigation. The court's assessment of the seriousness of the offence should then be reflected in the fine imposed. However, in fixing the amount of any fine the court must also inquire into the offender's financial circumstances and ability to pay before setting the level of the fine (*R v Ingram* (2004) Telegraph, 27 May, CA). This requirement to take the offender's financial circumstances into account in setting the amount of a fine also applies to compensation orders and to the financial circumstances of a parent or guardian who is ordered to pay the fine of a young offender. The defendant must provide the court with a statement of means and before conviction where an offender has pleaded guilty by post. Failure to furnish a statement of means is punished by a level 3 fine (CJA 2003, s 162(5)).

The court is entitled to take into account joint family income where someone who was not the main breadwinner is before the court (*R v Enger* [2004] EWCA Crim 994, [2004] All ER (D) 117 (Apr)). The court has the power to make such determination as it thinks fit of the financial circumstances of an offender where he has been convicted in his absence, or where the offender (or a parent or guardian who has been ordered to pay the fine of a young offender) has failed to comply with an order to give a statement of financial circumstances, or has in any other way failed to comply with the court's inquiry into his financial circumstances. Where the court has made a determination of the offender's financial circumstances in the absence of sufficient information it may, on subsequently inquiring into means, remit the whole or part of the fine, if it is of the opinion as a result of that inquiry that the original fine was too high. In making its determination of the offender's financial circumstances the court may take into consideration income, capital and outgoings and the fine may be increased as well as reduced to reflect the financial circumstances of the offender.

Means Information

Under s 95 of the Courts Act 2003 (which amends s 20A of the Criminal Justice Act 1991) it is an offence for a defendant to fail to provide means information to the court when charged. The best way for the court to receive that information is on the standard *Means Form* which should be issued to all defendants so that if they are found guilty the court can impose a fine appropriate to the offender's means and ability to pay. If the defendant declines to complete a form or the case is dealt with in the absence of the defendant, the court may draw such inferences as it considers appropriate regarding the means of the defendant and his ability to pay. The level of the fine can be reviewed at a later hearing if the means of the offender are made known to the court.

B[33.16A]

Fines are meant to be a punishment and to cause some hardship to the offender to act as a deterrent to future offending. However, in fixing the level of the fine, where payment is to be by way of instalments, magistrates' courts should regard 13 weeks as the normal starting point although in cases such as compensation this period can be extended for up to 52 weeks (see *R v Stockport Justices, ex p Conlon* (1997) 161 JP 81). As a good rule of thumb 52 weeks should be regarded as the maximum period of repayment. Longer periods of repayment can be made by the Crown Court in unusual cases and in exceptional cases three years has been upheld (*R v Olliver and Olliver* (1989) 11 Cr App Rep (S) 10, 153 JP 369).

B[33.17]

Courts using the National Sentencing Guidelines have a grid system showing both levels of seriousness and levels of disposable income, thus providing a starting point for fines imposition to meet most circumstances.

B[33.18]

So, for example, if two offenders have committed the same offence for which they should receive the same punishment and are to be fined, the court will determine the same seriousness for each offender. However, the financial consequences for each may be widely differing because the monetary value of the unit will be assessed according to each offender's financial circumstances.

Announcing the fine and time to pay

B[33.19]

We have taken into account the seriousness of this/these offence(s) and your financial circumstances and have decided to impose a fine of £'X'. Can this be paid now?

B[33.20]

Time to pay. When a fine is announced, unless payment can be made forthwith, in the case of an adult offender the court should normally make a collection order. The same applies in the youth court where a parent or guardian has been made responsible for the payment of the fine. In those cases where the juvenile is made responsible it is recommended that fixing time for payment should be deferred by the youth court and responsibility delegated to the fines officer.

B[33.21]

An immediate committal to prison in default of payment can only be ordered in the four types of cases mentioned below. In other cases the court must announce (and cause to be entered in the register) the time allowed for payment. This may be a fixed period, e g 14 days, or it may be an order that the defendant pays by instalments.

B[33.22]

The court, when imposing a fine, should establish if the defendant is an existing defaulter. If he/she is in default of an existing order the court is normally obliged to make either a deductions of earnings order (if working) or a deductions from benefits order (if claiming benefits). If the offender is not in default of an existing order the court may make these orders with the defendant's consent. In either case the court should make a reserve payment order in case the order fails ie payment in full within 10 working days. In the case of a **compensation order** see **B[33.2]** below.

B[33.23]

Costs and compensation. Costs against a defendant in criminal cases and compensation are normally enforceable in the same way as a fine. However, on imposition it is now **mandatory** that an attachment/deduction order should be considered where the offender is liable to pay compensation as part of the financial imposition. If the attachment/deduction order is subsequently made it should be applied to the whole sum adjudged to be paid.

B[33.24]

Limited companies. In law a company is a person. Therefore a fine imposed against a company can only be enforceable against the company and not against any of its officials. For non-payment of a fine a distress warrant can be issued against the company and its property seized and sold to meet the fine and any costs involved in conducting the sale.

B[33.25]–B[33.30]

Payment of the fine can sometimes be enforced in the High Court or county court. Consult the legal adviser. In certain circumstances the appropriate officer (the collecting officer, in this case the Area Director) may apply to the High Court to have a company wound up under the Insolvency Act 1986.

B[33.31]

Partnership firm. The conviction will have been against the partners personally and fines can be enforced against them personally in the usual way.

B[33.32]

Searching. The court may order the defendant to be searched and any money found used to pay the fine, compensation and costs. If there is a balance this must be returned to the defendant.

B[33.33]

Such money must not be taken if the court is satisfied that the money does not belong to the defendant or if the loss of money would be more injurious to his family than his detention.

B[33.34]

Fine supervision order. Instead of the court fixing the time to pay or ordering fixed instalments, it may decide that the defendant is so incompetent or feckless that he will not put aside the money to meet the fine. In such circumstances the court can make a supervision order placing the defendant under the care of some person (often a probation officer) whose duty is not to collect the fine or decide the rate of payments, but to persuade the offender to pay so as to keep out of prison. When making such an order the rate of payment should be fixed by the court.

B[33.35]

Imposing a fine and suspended imprisonment. If an offence is punishable both by a fine and imprisonment, a fine and a suspended prison sentence can be imposed.

B[33.36]

Fine and immediate imprisonment. This combination is appropriate where the defendant has made a substantial profit from the offence. Generally, however, a fine should be imposed with an immediate custodial sentence only when the defendant has resources from which to pay the fine despite his imprisonment. The situation should be avoided which saddles a discharged prisoner with a fine. Generally offenders who profit from crimes are subject to the Proceeds of Crime Act 2002 confiscation provisions.

Procedure for enforcing fines

B[33.37]

Enforcement of a fine. See **B[33.16A]**. This should begin the moment it is imposed with a fines collection order. The chairman of the court should never invite an application for time to pay. The court should always inquire how much can be paid immediately (if the defendant cannot pay in full) and should consider requiring even a small sum to be paid forthwith. It is usually better to fix any reserve payment order by reference to the offender's pay day rather than seven days from the date of his conviction. On a first default the fines officer must make an attachment of earnings order or apply for an attachment of benefit unless it is impracticable or inappropriate. Thereafter once a fines collection order has been made the fines officer has a wide range of powers but the court still has a role to play in many cases (see Courts Act 2003, Sch 5).

On default the fines officer can impose the following steps:

- Clamping of the offender's car
- Registration of the fine with the Register of Fines and Judgments
- Distress warrant
- Attachment of Earnings
- Deductions from Benefit
- Transfer the case to the civil courts for enforcement where it is cost effective to do so

If the fines officer clamps a car and wants to sell the vehicle he will have to first seek the permission of the court. The fines officer will have to have the case listed and go before the court to seek permission.

There is a new power for the fines officer to transfer cases for enforcement without referring them back to the court. This can be used where the court receives new information on the whereabouts of the offender and it is necessary to transfer for enforcement purposes.

If the fines officer considers that the above disposals are insufficient to recover payment he will refer the matter back to court, for example, to increase the fine or to impose imprisonment in default.

Immediate enforcement

B[33.38]

When a fine is imposed the court can use the following methods to enforce immediate payment, if there is a good reason not to make a collection order.

B[33.39]

1 Search. The court can order the defendant to be searched for money to meet the fine. See above.

B[33.40]–B[33.45]

2 Immediate committal to prison. In the circumstances listed below the court may order imprisonment forthwith for a period determined in accordance with the following scale:

An amount not exceeding £200	7 days
An amount exceeding £200 but not exceeding £500	14 days
An amount exceeding £500 but not exceeding £1,000	28 days
An amount exceeding £1,000 but not exceeding £2,500	45 days
An amount exceeding £2,500 but not exceeding £5,000	3 months
An amount exceeding £5,000 but not exceeding £10,000	6 months
An amount exceeding £10,000	12 months

B[33.46]

It must be borne in mind that these are the maximum periods applicable, the court is not obliged to impose the maximum period in default. In other words, the number of days in default should be proportionate to the sum outstanding e g if the sum imposed was £520 and nothing has been paid, pro rata 15 days (rather than 28 days) should be ordered to be served in default of payment.

B[33.47]

If part payments have been made then the period of imprisonment is calculated by taking the period of imprisonment considered appropriate for the whole sum and reducing that period by the proportion which the part payment bears to the original sum due. For example, if a defendant is fined £600 and over a period pays £400, the maximum period of imprisonment for that balance is one-third of 28 days in band 4. Where a defendant is fined at one time for several offences, each fine must be calculated separately and the periods of imprisonment may be made consecutive. However, it is not appropriate to fix consecutive terms of imprisonment in respect of fines imposed for several offences arising out of the same incident. In every case where several fines are outstanding the court must look realistically at the total situation.

NB: Where several fines are ordered to run consecutive to each other the total number of days in default should not exceed the statutory maximum. For example, if four separate fines of £240 are ordered to run consecutive to each other the total number of days in default should not exceed the statutory maximum outlined in **B[33.40]** above ie 28 days.

B[33.48]

The above table applies to monetary penalties (ie fines, costs and compensation) and not to civil orders eg arrears of maintenance for which the maximum period is six weeks. Nor does it apply to the community charge for which the maximum period is three months. (It may be convenient to mention here that periods of imprisonment for more than one amount of unpaid community charge may not be made consecutive.)

B[33.49]

An immediate committal to prison can only be ordered in the following cases:

(a) if the offence is punishable with imprisonment and the defendant appears to the court to have sufficient means to pay immediately; or
(b) if it appears to the court that the defendant is unlikely to remain at an address in the United Kingdom long enough for the fine to be enforced by other methods; or
(c) if the defendant is already serving a prison or detention sentence; or
(d) if the defendant is being sent to prison or detention on the same or another charge.

B[33.50]

The court should announce its reasons (that is, (a), (b), (c) or (d) above) for making an immediate committal to prison and these reasons should be entered in the court register and on the committal warrant. Failure to comply may result in a challenge to the decision by judicial review (*R v Oldham Justices, ex p Cawley* [1997] QB 1, [1996] 1 All ER 464). If the defendant has second thoughts about paying and tenders payment to the court staff, the police or the prison officials he is entitled to be released. If only part of the fine is paid then he is entitled to a proportionate remission of the prison sentence. This applies even if he offers part payment after he has served a part of the prison sentence. A committal order, forthwith or suspended, will be inappropriate for a single mother with very little income, trying her best to balance her financial obligations (*R (on the application of Stokes) v Gwent Magistrates' Court* [2001] EWHC Admin 569 [2001] All ER (D) 125 (Jul)). A defaulter's human rights may be breached if he is not offered legal representation (*Best v UK* (2005) Times, 10 March).

B[33.51]

The period of imprisonment for non-payment can be concurrent with or consecutive to another sentence already being served; or if more than one fine is being enforced, the periods of imprisonment for non-payment can be consecutive to each other subject to the overall restrictions on the aggregate length of sentences. Consult the legal adviser.

B[33.52]

3 Suspended committal order. The court can order a committal to prison under the scale at **B[33.40]** to be suspended for a definite period of time during which the defendant has to find the money for the fine or it may suspend the prison sentence whilst he pays instalments at a rate decided by the court (usually weekly, fortnightly or monthly). Such a suspended committal order can only be ordered if the case falls into one of the categories listed at **B[33.49]** as (a), (b), (c), or (d). If more than one fine is being enforced in this way, the periods of imprisonment for non-payment can be concurrent with or consecutive to each other subject to the overall restrictions on the aggregate length of sentence (at **B[33.40]**). The defendant may apply subsequently to the court to vary the terms of the postponement. Where the defendant subsequently defaults in payment of the order, the court must give him notice that the warrant of commitment falls to be issued. Magistrates should adjourn hearing a warrant for committal case if they know that the defendant has not been served with proceedings (*R v Doncaster Justices, ex p Hannan* (1998) 163 JP 182, [1998] 32 LS Gaz R 30). He then has an opportunity to make representations orally or in writing as to why the warrant should not issue. Consult the legal adviser.

B[33.53]

4 Detention for one day or overnight at a police station. The court can order the defendant to be detained for the remainder of the day within the precincts of the court or police station but must be released at a time which will allow him to get home the same day or at the latest by 8 p.m. The release time should be announced by the court. Similarly, overnight detention authorises the police to arrest the defendant and keep him until 8 a.m. on the morning following his arrest or if he is arrested between midnight and 8 o'clock in the morning, until 8 o'clock in the morning of the day on which he is arrested. The effect of this is to wipe out the fine.

B[33.54]

5 Distress warrant. The magistrates can issue a distress warrant which orders the seizure of the defendant's property to meet the unpaid fine. Such an order may be suspended on terms that the defaulter pays as ordered by the court.

B[33.55]–B[33.60]

6 Supervision order. This means placing the defendant under supervision, usually of the probation officer, see **B[33.34]**.

B[33.61]

7 Fixing a means inquiry. When imposing a fine etc the court may fix a date on which the offender must appear in court for a means inquiry if at that time any part of the monetary penalty remains unpaid.

Enforcement as a result of a referral by the fines officer

B[33.62]

If the defendant fails to pay the fine or other enforcement has failed, the fines officer will arrange for the issuing of a summons or warrant to bring the defendant back before the court who will conduct a means inquiry to investigate the defendant's ability to pay the fine and may demand that the defendant produce documentary evidence of his financial resources, eg pay slips, account books, post office savings book, bank statements etc. The defendant must produce a statement of means either before the inquiry or during the inquiry by a specified date and failure to produce such a statement is punishable with a fine up to level 3 if directed by the court and level 2 if directed by the fines officer.

Additionally the court may discharge a fines collection order and revert to its standard powers following an appeal against a decision of the fines officer to vary terms or take action by the use of alternative sanctions (including wheel clamping).

B[33.63]

Power to remit whole or part of the fine. Magistrates are empowered to remit the whole or part of a fine having regard to any change of circumstances since the defendant's conviction. Arrears of national insurance cannot be remitted. The court may also remit or reduce the fine where the court fixed the fine in the absence of adequate information about the offender's means either because he was convicted in absence or failed to comply with an order to furnish a statement of means and the result was that the original fine was set too high.

B[33.64]

For compensation see **B[18]**.

B[33.65]

If the fine was imposed by a higher court, magistrates can only remit the whole or part of the fine if the higher court consents.

B[33.66]

At a means inquiry magistrates can enforce payment by the following methods:

B[33.67]

1 Attachment orders. If the magistrates are satisfied that the defendant is being paid earnings they may make an attachment order directing that the employer make deductions from the defendant's wages and remit them to the court. If the magistrates have this course in mind they should first consult the legal adviser and/or direct that the defendant completes a means form as the court must obtain certain details about the defendant and his employment.

B[33.68]

2 Distress warrants. See above.

B[33.69]

3 Search. See **B[33.32]**.

B[33.70]–B[33.75]

4 Immediate committal to prison. The magistrates can order an immediate committal to prison for a specified period according to the scale set out at **B[33.40]**. For calculation of the term in default see **B[33.47]**. Immediate committal to prison can only be ordered if:

(a) the offence for which he has been fined is also punishable with imprisonment and the defendant appears to the court to have the means to pay immediately; or
(b) the court is satisfied that the default is due to the offender's wilful refusal or culpable neglect and the court has considered or tried all other methods of enforcement and it appears to the court that they are inappropriate or unsuccessful.

Culpable neglect cannot be found where a defaulter has no capital or income to pay a fine. Nor should the assumption be made that someone else will pay the fine (*R (on the application of McDonough) v Wigan Magistrates Court* [2004] EWHC 3272 (Admin), [2005] All ER (D) 304 (Feb)).

B[33.76]

The other methods referred to are distress warrants, application to the High Court or county court for enforcement, supervision, attachment of earnings and, if under 21, attendance centre.

B[33.77]

5 Detention for one day or overnight at a police station. See **B[33.53]**.

B[33.78]

6 Suspended committal to prison. The court can order a suspended committal to prison for a period in accordance with the scale on at **B[33.40]**. This imprisonment can then be suspended for a definite period of time during which the defendant must pay the fine or alternatively the court may direct that the defendant shall pay at so much per week or month. Such a suspended committal can only be ordered if the offence for which the defendant was fined is punishable with imprisonment and the defendant appears to have sufficient means to pay; or the court is satisfied that the default is due to the offender's wilful refusal or culpable neglect and the court has considered all the other methods of enforcement and it appears that they are inappropriate or unsuccessful. See above.

B[33.79]

7 Supervision order. See **B[33.34]**.

B[33.80]

8 Deduction from benefit. After a means inquiry has been made the court may request the Department of Works and Pensions to make payments towards a fine or compensation direct from the offender's benefit, subject to any right of review or appeal he may have.

B[33.81]

9 Transfer to High Court or county court. If the defendant is a holder of shares or has certain kinds of assets, enforcement can sometimes be transferred to the High Court or county court. Consult the legal adviser.

B[33.82]

Defendant already in prison. If a defendant, who has not paid part or the whole of a fine, is serving a sentence of imprisonment or is confined in a detention centre a committal warrant can be issued without any means inquiry taking place. The clerk will give notice to the debtor who may appear or make written representations.

B[33.83]

Fines Payment work. If, on a means inquiry, it is clear that the offender has very few, and is unlikely to acquire sufficient means, to pay a fine in the foreseeable future, the payment terms may be in the form of fines payment work, at he rate of £6 per hour. The court will make the order but the offender must see the fines officer to make arrangements for the fines payment work to take place. The scheme has been piloted in five areas namely Cambridgeshire, Cheshire, Cumbria, Devon and Cornwall and South Yorkshire. The pilot scheme will continue until March 2007 and then evaluated. The Home Office has produced guidance on fines payment work.

Fines imposed by Central Criminal Court and Crown Court

B[33.84]

These fines are payable to and enforceable by magistrates' courts.

B[33.85]

The whole fine or part of it can be remitted only with the consent of the higher court.

Defendants aged 18 to 21

B[33.86]–B[33.90]

The above provisions can also be employed in respect of defendants in this age group except that an order of detention in default of payment should only be ordered if a supervision order has already been tried or the court is satisfied that a supervision order is either undesirable or impracticable. These considerations must be noted on any commitment warrant (*R v Oldham Justices, ex p Cawley* [1997] QB 1, [1996] 1 All ER 464 and *R v Stockport Justices, ex p Conlon* [1997] 2 All ER 204, 161 JP 81).

B[33.91]

If the court has available to it an attendance centre for defaulters to the age of 25, the court can send the defendant for up to 36 hours in all in default of payment.

B[33.92]

The clerk should be consulted as to the exact number of hours that the defendant should attend at the attendance centre.

Defendants aged 10 to 17

B[33.93]

Maximum fine. Children under 14, £250; young persons, 14 or over, £1,000, or, in either case the lesser sum applicable in the case of an adult (Powers of the Criminal Courts (Sentencing) Act 2000, s 135).

B[33.94]

Costs. The costs ordered must not exceed the amount of the fines unless a parent or guardian is ordered to pay.

B[33.95]

Parental liability to pay. The child's parent or guardian must be ordered to pay the fine and costs unless he cannot be found or the court considers it would be unreasonable to order him to pay. In the case of a young person the court has a power to order the parent to pay. If the parent or guardian does not pay, enforcement takes place in the adult court as described at **B[33.7]–B[33.10]**.

Enforcement

B[33.96]

The power to make a fines supervision order or an attachment of earnings order is available in the case of juveniles. In addition, where the court is satisfied that the juvenile has had the money to pay but has refused or neglected to pay it may make an order requiring:

(a) the parent to enter a recognisance to ensure that the defaulter pays the fine or balance; or
(b) the court may transfer the debt to the parent in which case further enforcement, if necessary, would be taken as if the fine has been imposed on that parent.

B[33.97]

The parent must, according to the statute, consent before an order may be made for him to enter into a recognisance. The parent's consent is not required for the responsibility for the fine to be transferred to him provided the court is satisfied in all the circumstances that it is reasonable to make the order.

B[33.98]

If an attendance centre is available for persons of the debtor's class or description, he may be ordered to attend, up to the age of 25 years.

B[33.99]

The powers mentioned under this heading must be exercised after a means inquiry. An order transferring the debt to the parent may be made in his absence provided he has been given adequate notice of the proceedings; if he is present, he must be given the opportunity of speaking to the court before such an order is made.

B[34]

Deprivation of property and forfeiture

(Powers of Criminal Courts (Sentencing) Act 2000, s 143)

B[34.1]

Any court which has convicted a person of an offence and

(a) is satisfied
  (i) that any property
  (ii) which has been lawfully seized from him or was in his possession or under his control at the time when he was apprehended for the offence or when a summons in respect of it was issued
  (iii) has been used for the purposes of committing, or facilitating the commission of any offence or was intended to be used for that purpose

or

(b) the offence (or an offence taken into consideration) consists of unlawful possession of property in the circumstances of (ii) above

may make an order to deprive him of that property.

B[34.2]

Property. Does not include land. For applications under the Proceeds of Crime Act 2002 see **M[3.2]**.

B[34.3]

Possession. Usually means physical possession but can include a legal right to possession. If there is any dispute the legal adviser should be consulted.

B[34.4]

Facilitating. This includes the taking of any steps after the offence has been committed to dispose of property which is the subject of the crime or to avoid apprehension or detection. The property need not have been used personally by the defendant provided he intended it be used for criminal purposes, even by another.

B[34.5]

The effect of an order. The accused is deprived of his rights in the property which passes into the possession of the police. The provisions of the Police Property Act 1897 (at **A[66]**) apply and a person may claim the property provided that he satisfies the court that either:

(a) he had not consented to the offender having possession; or
(b) he did not know, and had no reason to suspect, that the property was likely to be used for the purpose of committing an offence.

B[34.6]

If no successful claim is made the property will be sold and the proceeds disposed of in the same way as described at **A[66]**.

B[34.7]

Sentencing. The court may make an order under this section in respect of the property whether or not it also deals with the offender in respect of the offence in any other way, and may combine the making of the order with an absolute or conditional discharge.

B[34.8]

Under previous legislation it was stated that an order depriving a defendant of property should not be made for the purpose of realising assets to pay fines or compensation (*R v Kingston-upon-Hull Stipendiary Magistrates, ex p Hartung* [1981] RTR 262, 72 Cr App Rep 26).

B[34.9]

In considering whether to make a deprivation order the court shall have regard:

(a) to the value of the property; and
(b) to the likely financial and other effects on the offender of the making of the order (together with any other order the court is contemplating);
(c) any representations of the parties (*R v Ball* [2002] EWCA Crim 2777, [2003] 2 Cr App Rep (S) 92).

B[34.10]–B[34.15]

But where the offence has resulted in a person suffering personal injury, loss or damage and the court has not been able to make a compensation order because of the defendant's lack of means, the proceeds of sale resulting from a deprivation order may be used for compensation.

B[34.16]

This order only takes effect after a period of six months in order to allow a person to make a claim under the Police Property Act 1897.

B[34.17]

Motor vehicles. Where a person has committed an offence under the Road Traffic Act 1988 which is imprisonable, eg driving with excess alcohol or whilst disqualified, the Road Traffic Act 1991 provides that the vehicle concerned is to be regarded as used for the purpose of committing the offence. Accordingly, the offender runs the risk of the court, after considering all relevant factors, depriving him of his vehicle.

B[34.18]

Disqualification for any offence: See **C[5.45]**.

B[34.19]

Other provisions for forfeiture. Formerly the provisions described here were confined to offences punishable with at least 2 years' imprisonment, but now they are available without regard to maximum penalty and so will overlap with some existing forfeiture powers, eg forfeiture of controlled drugs and firearms and the Customs and Excise Management Act 1979. See for example *Customs and Excise Comrs v Newbury* [2003] EWHC 702 (Admin), [2003] 2 All ER 964.

B[35]

Guardianship order

(Mental Health Act 1983, s 37)

Limitations

B[35.1]

Offence must be punishable in the case of an adult with imprisonment, even though the offender may be immune from imprisonment.

B[35.2]

Two medical reports must be received indicating that the offender is suffering from one of four specified illnesses.

B[35.3]

The minimum age for a guardianship order is ten.

B[35.4]

Court must be of opinion (which it will usually form from the contents of the medical reports and a consideration of the circumstances of the offence) that a guardianship order is the most suitable method of dealing with the offender.

B[35.5]

Court must also be satisfied that arrangements have been made for a guardian to take care of the patient.

Ancillary orders

B[35.6]

Compensation at **B[18]**

Costs at **B[20]**

Disqualification at **C[5]**

Endorsement at **C[5]**

Deprivation of property and forfeiture at **B[34]**

Restitution at **B[39]**

B[35.7]

Period of order. This is an indeterminate order but the patient's condition is reviewed periodically by the medical authorities.

General considerations

B[35.8]

Medical evidence. The evidence can be two written reports by the doctors who made the examination, but the defendant has the right to insist that the doctors be present in court so that he can cross-examine them, and if the written reports only are before the court, then the defendant must be asked if he is agreeable to the court acting on those written reports.

B[35.9]

Copies of the doctors' reports must be given to the defendant's advocate. If the defendant is not represented the substance of the reports should be explained to the defendant.

B[35.10]–B[35.15]

The defendant has the right to call his own medical evidence to rebut all or any part of the two reports.

B[35.16]

The court can require the personal appearance of the doctors.

B[35.17]

Effect of guardianship order. Once the guardianship order has been made the defendant is in effect handed over as a mental patient to the mental health authorities and the court has no more powers over the defendant and cannot stipulate what happens later. Thus, there can be no restriction order, and the court cannot stipulate the length of the guardianship order. The guardian will be a social worker or person approved by the local authority.

B[35.18]

Normally it will lapse after six months, but the mental specialists can recommend an extension when it will be extended for a further six months. After that the order can be extended for one-year periods or until the mental health authorities consider it safe to grant the defendant a discharge.

B[35.19]

As the defendant has now become a patient and not a prisoner his discharge from guardianship can be made on the advice of the mental specialist in charge of his case.

B[35.20]

The defendant need not wait for the mental specialist to act, but can apply for his discharge at any time during the first six months of the guardianship order or on any occasion when the order is renewed.

B[35.21]

The defendant's nearest relative can make application once a year to the Mental Health Review Tribunal for his release.

B[36]

Hospital order

(Mental Health Act 1983, s 37)

Criteria

B[36.1]

These are as follows:

(a) defendant must have been convicted of an imprisonable offence, or (in certain circumstances) is proved to have committed an act which would amount to such an offence in the case of a normal person; see *R (on the application of Bartram) v Southend Magistrates' Court* [2004] All ER (D) 326 (Oct), DC for some of the procedural difficulties on fitness to plead

(b) court must be satisfied on written or oral evidence of two registered doctors that the defendant suffers from:
   (i) mental illness;
   (ii) psychopathic disorder;
   (iii) severe mental impairment; or
   (iv) mental impairment;

(c) the mental disorder is of a nature or degree that makes it appropriate for him to be detained in a hospital;

(d) (pyschopathic disorder or mental impairment) such treatment is likely to alleviate or prevent a deterioration of his condition;

(e) the court is of the opinion having regard to all the circumstances including the nature of the offence and the character and antecedents of the offender and other available methods of dealing with him, that a hospital order is the most suitable means of dealing with him;

(f) justices have no jurisdiction to make a hospital order in respect of a defendant charged with an offence triable only on indictment (*R v Chippenham Magistrates' Court, ex p Thompson* (1995) 160 JP 207).

General considerations

B[36.2]

Legal representation should be offered to the defendant, or he should be recommended to consult a solicitor if the court is considering a hospital order.

B[36.3]

Medical reports. The court must obtain reports from two doctors, one of whom must be an approved mental specialist, certifying that the defendant is suffering from some form of mental disorder which warrants detention in hospital for mental treatment. The court can, with the consent of the defendant, act on the two written mental reports. The defendant has the right to insist that the doctors attend court so that they can be cross-examined, and he is also entitled to bring his own medical evidence to rebut the reports. The court can also require that the doctors attend in person.

B[36.4]

If written reports are used copies must be given to the defendant's advocate. If the defendant is not represented then the court should explain to the defendant the substance of the reports.

B[36.5]

Before announcing that a hospital order is being made the court should ensure that a vacancy in a mental hospital has definitely been arranged; if it has not, consult the clerk. An adjournment may be necessary. Alternatively a hospital order may be possible with the defendant's date of admission deferred for up to 28 days.

B[36.6]

Effect of a hospital order. The court does not fix the period that the defendant has to stay in hospital. The date of his release will be decided by the hospital authorities.

B[36.7]

Normally the hospital order lapses after six months but it can be renewed for a further six months on the recommendation of the mental specialist in charge of the case, and thereafter the order can be renewed for one-yearly periods. The procedure is that the responsible mental specialist examines the patient and sends a report to the mental health authorities, which can be the hospital managers, who may then act on the recommendation to retain or discharge the patient. Thus the patient can be discharged at any time without reference back to the sentencing court.

B[36.8]

The defendant, once a mental patient, can apply for his discharge at any time after the first six months of the order or whenever it is proposed to extend the order. For these reasons the order is in the discretion of the court and custody may still be dictated by public policy considerations (*R v Nafel* (2004)).

B[36.9]

The defendant's nearest relative can apply for his discharge once a year to the Mental Health Review Tribunal.

B[36.10]–B[36.15]

Including a restriction clause in a hospital order (Mental Health Act 1983, s 41). If the defendant is 14 or more and was convicted (as opposed to having 'done the act'), and the magistrates consider a court restriction should be imposed on his release, he can be committed to the Crown Court for sentence pursuant to PCC(S)A 2000, s 3. [**It would appear that this power will no longer be available on or after a date to be appointed unless the committal for sentence is made immediately after the entering of a plea or the offence is a specified offence and the defendant is committed for sentence on the basis that he is a dangerous offender: see **B[16]**).

B[36.16]

The Crown Court can make a hospital order, and include in it a restriction upon the date of release either for a specified period of time or indefinitely.

B[36.17]

The magistrates can commit the defendant to prison pending his appearance at the Crown Court or, if satisfied that a vacancy is available at a mental hospital, can order him to be detained there pending his appearance at the Crown Court.

B[36.18]

If the Crown Court includes a restriction clause the defendant cannot be discharged by the mental specialist or allowed out of the specified hospital without the consent of the Home Secretary.

B[36.19]

The Home Secretary may at any time refer the case to a Mental Health Review Tribunal for their advice, but does not have to accept the advice if he considers that discharge of the patient is not in the public interest.

B[36.20]

If the Home Secretary does decide that the patient should be discharged from the mental hospital, he has powers to impose conditions for the discharge such as the place of residence, a scheme of supervision and the liability to recall if a lapse occurs.

B[36.21]

Remand for report on accused's mental condition (s 35). Where a doctor satisfies the court that there is reason to suspect that the accused suffers from one or other of several mental disorders and

(a) the accused has been convicted of an offence punishable on summary conviction with imprisonment or 'did the act' or has consented to this course of action; and
(b) it is otherwise impracticable to obtain medical reports; and
(c) arrangements have been made for his reception into a hospital;

the court may remand the accused in a hospital for up to 28 days. There may be further such remands for a total period of up to 12 weeks.

Interim hospital order (s 38)

B[36.22]

Where:

(a) an accused has been convicted of an offence punishable with imprisonment; and
(b) the court is satisfied on the evidence (written or oral) of two doctors that he is suffering from one of several mental disorders and it may be appropriate to make a hospital order; and
(c) arrangements have been made for his reception into a hospital;

the court may make an interim hospital order for up to 12 weeks initially before finally passing sentence. An interim hospital order may be further renewed for up to 28 days at a time subject to a total period of six months before sentence is imposed.

B[37]

Imprisonment

(Powers of Criminal Courts (Sentencing) Act 2000, s 78**)

Limitations

B[37.1]

(**a**) **Imprisonable offence.**

B[37.2]

(**b**) **Presence of offender**. Imprisonment may only be imposed in the presence of the defendant.

B[37.3]

(**c**) **Age limit**. Defendant must be 21 or over**. For offenders under 21 the appropriate custodial sentence would be detention in a young offender institution**.

B[37.4]

Criteria for imposing a custodial sentence. The court must be of the opinion

(a) that the offence, or the combination of the offence and other offences associated with it was so serious that neither a fine nor a community sentence can be justified; or

B[37.5]

Other circumstances in which custody may be imposed. Nothing in paragraph (a) above prevents the court imposing a custodial sentence on an offender who refuses to consent to a community sentence proposed by the court which requires his consent. A court may also impose custody for a wilful and persistent breach of a community order.

B[37.6]

So serious. Courts should always bear in mind that criminal sentences were in almost every case intended to protect the public whether by punishing the offender or reforming him, or deterring him and others, or all of those things. The sentence imposed should be no longer than is commensurate with the seriousness of the offence (Criminal Justice Act 2003, s 153). The court must take account of all the information about the circumstances of the offence including any aggravating or mitigating factors as is available to it.

In *R v Mills* [2002] EWCA Crim 26 [2002] 2 Cr App Rep (S) 51, the Lord Chief Justice said that imprisonment was often unnecessary for non-violent crimes of dishonesty committed by mothers caring for young families. In *R v Kefford* [2002] EWCA Crim 519, [2002] Crim LR 432 this principle is extended to those persons with no previous convictions convicted of economic crimes.

B[37.7]-B[37.15]

Associated offence. An offence of which the offender has been convicted in the same proceedings or for which he is sentenced at the same time, or an offence taken into consideration.

B[37.16]

Pre-sentence report. A magistrates' court, unless it considers it unnecessary to do so, must obtain and consider a pre-sentence report before forming an opinion on:

(a) whether the offence etc was so serious;
(b) the length of term commensurate with the offence.

In all cases where a court is contemplating sentencing a defendant to prison for the first time, other than a very short period, it should be the inevitable practice that a pre-sentence report is obtained (*R v Gillette* (1999) Times, 3 December, CA).

B[37.17]

Failure to obtain pre-sentence report. Does not invalidate the sentence but the appeal court must obtain and consider such a report if the court below was not justified in forming the opinion that a report was not necessary (Criminal Justice Act 2003, s 156).

B[37.18]

Mentally disordered offender. Where an offender is or appears to be mentally disordered, ie suffering from a mental disorder within the meaning of the Mental Health Act 1983, the court must additionally obtain and consider a medical report before passing a custodial sentence unless the court considers it unnecessary to do so. The court must take any such information into account and consider the likely effect of any custodial sentence on his condition and any treatment for it. Failure to obtain a medical report does not invalidate any sentence but one must be obtained and considered by an appeal court (Criminal Justice Act 2003, s 157).

B[37.19]

Legal representation. The offender, who has not previously been imprisoned, must first be given the opportunity to be legally represented unless he has been refused legal aid for financial reasons. Note the requirement is not that he should be represented but that he should have the opportunity to be.

Reasons for decisions

B[37.20]

It is the duty of the court to state in open court that it is of the opinion that either or both of paragraph **B[37.4]** and **B[37.2]** above apply and why it is of that opinion and in all cases (including where a custodial sentence has been imposed following the offender's refusal to comply with a proposed requirement in a community sentence) explain to the offender in open court and in ordinary language why it is passing a custodial sentence on him or, if applicable, why imprisonment is for a longer term than would normally be commensurate with the seriousness of the offence.

B[37.21]

Suspended sentences. All these limitations apply equally to suspended sentences.

General considerations

B[37.22]

Consecutive sentences. If the defendant is sentenced to immediate or suspended imprisonment on each of two or more offences the terms will run concurrently unless the court orders they are to run consecutively. Consecutively means that one term of imprisonment follows another.

B[37.23]

When a magistrates' court sentences an offender for two or more offences it may order that one sentence runs consecutively to the other. In addition (when sentencing for one or more offences) the court may order that a term of imprisonment shall be consecutive to a term already being served by the defendant. In such a case the term imposed should be stated to be consecutive to the total period to which the defendant is subject.

B[37.24]

The total period of two or more consecutive sentences imposed on the same occasion by a magistrates' court must not exceed 6 months, unless either two or more of the offences are triable either way, when the total period may not exceed 12 months. If the defendant is convicted of two offences, the former being an offence triable either way and the latter which is purely summary, the maximum total remains as 6 months. If the court orders a suspended prison sentence to take effect, it can order that sentence to take effect consecutively to a period of imprisonment for the later offence, even though the total period will exceed the above limits. When a previously suspended sentence is ordered to be served it should normally be made consecutive to a sentence imposed for the later offence. Minimum sentence is 14 days if the sentence is suspended.

B[37.25]–B[37.30]

Where several offences arise out of one incident consecutive sentences should not be imposed but the incident should be looked at as a whole and one appropriate period fixed. The same principle would apply to a series of offences committed against the same person over a relatively short period, eg an employee who falsifies a weekly claim for expenses.

B[37.31]

Consecutive sentences are appropriate where, although there is a single incident, there is more than one offence but they do not arise as a matter of course from the principle offence. For example, the burglar who attacks a householder who discovers him, or an assault on a police officer effecting an arrest for another offence. Offences committed on bail should normally attract a consecutive sentence where imprisonment is appropriate as offending on bail is an aggravating factor.

B[37.32]

When consecutive sentences are imposed the court should pay particular regard to the total period and reduce it if it is excessive; this is especially the rule to follow with young offenders and those receiving a first custodial sentence. One method of adjusting the total period in such cases is to consider concurrent rather than consecutive sentences.

B[37.33]

Multiple offences. When sentencing a defendant for several offences it is best to refer to the nature of each offence and the sentence and to state the total time to be served. To say 'For the first offence you will go to prison for two months, for the second two months consecutive, for the third two months concurrent …' can be quite meaningless. Some chairmen prefer to begin with what is perhaps the most important aspect of the sentence first: 'You will go to prison for a total of 6 months. That is made up of two months for stealing the watch, a further two months for stealing the camera … etc.'

B[37.34]

When consecutive sentences are being considered the total period should be reviewed and reduced if it is excessive.

B[37.35]

Period of imprisonment. Great care must be exercised in determining the period of imprisonment, especially if it is to be suspended. The length of a custodial sentence must not exceed a term justified by the seriousness of the offence(s) and where there is appropriate mitigation, may be shorter.

B[37.36]

Magistrates' courts tend to consider sentences in units of months and the commonest terms are 3, 6 (and where appropriate) 9 and 12 months. It should be remembered that there is a complete discretion within the range available for a particular offence. It may be that for some offenders receiving a custodial sentence for the first time, a sentence of 7 or 14 days would be a salutary lesson, but with no other sentencing objective.

B[37.37]

Magistrates should reserve the maximum period available for an offence for those cases which are the worst type of case they would deal with.

B[37.38]

Offences of attempt will not usually attract the same period as would the completed offence.

B[37.39]

Time spent in custody on remand will be deducted from the sentence by the court, announced in open court and recorded on the warrant and in the register.

B[37.40]–B[37.45]

Suspended sentences (Criminal Justice Act 2003, s 189). In any case where the court has power to impose imprisonment or Young Offenders' Institution it has a discretion to suspend that sentence, that is, to postpone the time when the sentence must be served on condition that the defendant is not convicted of another offence and complies with the requirements imposed by the court during the operational period. Such requirements under the Criminal Justice Act 2003, s 190 are the same as outlined at **B[17.34]** for a community sentence. This power must not be exercised unless the court would have imposed an immediate sentence of imprisonment if the power to suspend did not exist. The court must also be satisfied that the exercise of the power to suspend can be justified by the exceptional circumstances of the case. The court must also consider whether the additional imposition of a fine or compensation is warranted.

B[37.46]

The Court of Appeal has stated that it is not possible to lay down a definition of 'exceptional circumstances'. It would depend on the facts of each individual case.

B[37.47]

The court is not required to find exceptional circumstances before suspending. The following passages from the old provisions may still provide some guidance to sentences.

Although exceptional circumstances are not limited to the offence taken on their own or in combination, good character, youth and an early plea are not exceptional circumstances justifying a suspended sentence. They are common features of many cases (*R v Lowery* (1992) 14 Cr App Rep (S) 485, [1993] Crim LR 225, CA). They can amount to mitigation sufficient to persuade the court that a custodial sentence should not be passed or to reduce its length (*R v Okinikan* [1993] 2 All ER 5, [1993] 1 WLR 173, CA).

B[37.48]

Nor in a case of breach of trust are treatment for depression and financial difficulties likely to be exceptional circumstances (*R v Bradley* (1993) 15 Cr App Rep (S) 597, [1994] Crim LR 381, CA). However in *R v L* [2002] EWCA Crim 628 a confession to indecent assault 10 years after the event, together with the fact the assault had stopped of the defendant's own volition was held to be exceptional.

B[37.49]

The operational period during which the liability to serve the sentence if reconvicted must be stated in court and cannot exceed two years. The court must explain the sentence clearly to the defendant. The supervision period must not be for less than 6 months but not more than 2 years.

B[37.50]

In passing a suspended sentence the court must be careful to avoid the following dangers:

(a) imposing a suspended sentence where custody is not merited by the seriousness of the offence(s);
(b) imposing a term of imprisonment which, although suspended, is longer than is commensurate with the seriousness of the offence(s).

B[37.51]

A suspended sentence should not be passed in respect of one offence on the occasion when either immediate imprisonment or a community sentence is ordered in respect of another (*R v Starie* (1979) 69 Cr App Rep 239, 1 Cr App Rep (S) 179, CA; see Criminal Justice Act 2003, s 189).

B[37.52]

When determining a sentence for an offence committed during the operational period of a suspended sentence the sentence appropriate to that offence must be imposed.

B[37.53]

Suspended sentence and fine. For many offences it is possible to impose a fine as well as a suspended term of imprisonment. Courts must consider a fine but care should be taken in deciding such matters. If the defendant pays the monetary part of the penalty and then after a further offence is ordered to serve the prison sentence he may feel that he has been sentenced twice for his offence. On the other hand, if he is given a suspended sentence and avoids conviction during the operational period he may feel he has got away with it. Some would argue that the court ordering the suspended sentence to take effect would reduce the period because the monetary penalty had been paid, but this is neither a logically nor legally attractive argument. A careful explanation from the chairman emphasising the dual obligations of a single sentence is recommended. If the defendant defaults on the monetary part of his penalty he will be liable to imprisonment in accordance with the scale at **B[33.40]**, not to the sentence which has been suspended. In any event compensation will not take precedence in the court's thinking.

Powers of court to deal with suspended sentence or conviction of further offence or breach of requirements

B[37.54]

A defendant is in jeopardy for a further offence or breach of requirement (Criminal Justice Act 2003, Sch 12). If a defendant subject to a suspended sentence imposed by a magistrates' court is dealt with for a subsequent offence by the making of an absolute or conditional discharge, he is not in breach of the suspended sentence since these orders are not convictions for these purposes (*R v Moore* [1995] QB 353, [1995] 4 All ER 843, CA).

B[37.55]–B[37.60]

1 If the suspended sentence was imposed by the Crown Court and during the operational period the defendant commits a further offence punishable by imprisonment for which he is convicted by a magistrates' court, the magistrates have two courses open to them, if the order includes a direction allowing the magistrates' court to act:

(a) the defendant can be committed on bail or in custody back to the Crown Court. The higher court will then decide whether the suspended sentence shall take effect. The magistrates can also commit for sentence to the higher court in respect of the new offence at the same time; or
(b) the magistrates' court can sentence the defendant for the further offence and their clerk will notify the Crown Court of the decision leaving it to

the higher court to take what action it thinks fit. However if the magistrates' court deals with the subsequent offence by way of an absolute or conditional discharge these do not rank as a conviction for the purpose of proceedings in the crown court. It is wrong, however, to order discharge, when they are inappropriate, as a device to avoid the implementation of a suspended sentence and it is better to commit the defendant for sentence (*R v Tarry* [1970] 2 QB 560, [1970] 2 All ER 185, CA).

B[37.61]-B[37.62]

2 If the original suspended sentence was ordered by a magistrates' court any other magistrates' court before which the defendant appears has four courses open to it:

(a) It can order that the suspended sentence takes effect unaltered. This must be ordered unless the magistrates are of the opinion that it would be unjust to do so in view of all the circumstances. One example where it could be unjust is when the subsequent offence is fairly trivial. The Court of Appeal has stated that the fact that the subsequent offence was of a different character or committed in anger was not sufficient to permit the court not to activate the sentence in full (*R v Clitheroe* (1987) 9 Cr App Rep (S) 159, [1987] Crim LR 583, CA). This sentence should be ordered to be served consecutively to any other sentence for the new offence unless there are special circumstances. (If the magistrates do not order the suspended sentence to be carried out in full they must state their reason which should be inserted in the court register); or
(b) the magistrates can order that the suspended sentence be put into effect but for a specified shorter period than originally ordered and this sentence can be concurrent or consecutive to any other sentence passed by the same court or any other court. The court may also take account of the extent to which the offender has complied with the community requirements; or
(c) the magistrates can decide not to put the suspended sentence into effect but order that the operational period originally fixed with the suspended sentence shall be varied. The new operational period runs from the date of variation and can be for up to two years; or
(d) the magistrates may amend the order by imposing more onerous community requirements or extend the supervision period.

PARAGRAPH (a) MUST BE FOLLOWED UNLESS THE MAGISTRATES ARE OF THE OPINION IT WOULD BE UNJUST TO DO SO IN VIEW OF ALL THE CIRCUMSTANCES.

B[37.63]

Where a fresh offence has been committed, the court should first consider the appropriate sentence for the current offence and should not consider it to be more serious only because it has been committed during the operational period (ie the period of suspension) of a suspended sentence. The court must then apply its mind to the suspended sentence as explained above. If the suspended sentence is to be brought into operation it should be ordered to be served after the expiry of any custodial sentence for the current offence unless there is some very good reason to the contrary. Likewise, it must be for the original period unless such an order would be unjust, as explained above. Breach of the requirements may also trigger imprisonment but will depend on the severity, repetition and time left on the order amongst other things.

B[37.64]

Note – If there is more than one offence it should be clearly stated what the total period of imprisonment is to be.

Ancillary orders

B[37.65]

Compensation at **B[18]**

Costs at **B[20]**

Disqualification at **C[5]**

Endorsement at **C[5]**

Deprivation of property and forfeiture at **B[34]**

Restitution order at **B[39]**

*Early release***

B[37.66]

A person subject to a term of imprisonment for less than 12 months will automatically be released after he has served one half of the term. In determining the period that has been served, time spent on remand in custody is to be taken into account. A person serving a term of 12 months and under 4 years is released on licence after serving one half of the original term and is unconditionally released after three-quarters of the sentence.

B[37.67]

Further offences (Powers of the Criminal Courts (Sentencing) Act 2000, s 116). Where the offender commits an imprisonable offence before he would (but for his release) have served his sentence in full, the court which deals with him for the later offence may return him to custody for the whole or part of the period which begins with the making of the order of return, and is equal in length to the period between the date of commission of the new offence and the date of expiry of the original term. As a matter of good practice, the court should have precise information about the unexpired term of the offender's sentence before ordering a return to custody (*R v Divers* [1999] 2 Cr App Rep (S) 421, [1999] Crim LR 843, CA).

B[37.68]

When sentencing for the new offence, the court can take into account the fact that it was committed in breach of a home detention curfew as an aggravating factor. In *R v Teasdale* [2003] Crim LR 657, CA it is made clear that if a defendant commits an offence while on licence form prison and it is dealt with under s 116 of the PCC(S)A, the court should take into account any period of custody served following an administrative recall and deduct it from the maximum available under s 116. If the defendant is a short term prisoner, a double period could be deducted as the defendant would be entitled to release half way through the term.

Section 116 of the Powers of the Criminal courts (Sentencing) Act 2000 continues to apply to sentences of less than 12 months or more than 12 months if committed before 4 April 2005. It does not apply to sentences of 12 months or more committed on or after 4 April 2005 leaving the court to sentence on the new offence alone.

B[37A]

Parenting order

(Crime and Disorder Act 1998, s 8 **as amended by CJA 2003, Sch 34)

Limitations

B[37A.1]

A parenting order is an order made against the parent or guardian of a child or young person:

- where the juvenile has been convicted of an offence, or
- where a court makes a child safety order, or
- where a court makes an anti-social behaviour order in respect of the juvenile, or
- where a court makes a sex offender order in respect of the juvenile, or
- where a conviction is recorded for failure to ensure regular school attendance or comply with a school attendance order.
- in the case where the court intends to make a referral order and a parenting order it must first obtain a report as to why such an order is necessary. Parenting orders may also be made on complaints in respect of parents whose children have been excluded from school or have been referred to a Youth Offending Team because of anti social behaviour (Anti-Social Behaviour Act 2003, ss 20 and 26).

Reasons

B[37A.2]

A court must make a parenting order in respect of a child or young person under the age of 16 who is convicted of an offence, or state in open court that a parenting order would not be desirable in the interests of preventing the commission of any further offence by the child or young person, and the reasons why.

Consent

B[37A.3]

Consent of the parent/guardian is not required although many courts recognise the importance of a willing participation.

How to announce

B[37A.4]

We are satisfied that you need help and support in stopping [*child's name*] offending/anti-social behaviour. We are therefore making an order that you attend counselling and guidance sessions for [*a period not exceeding three months*]. The parenting order itself will last for [*a period not exceeding 12 months*] and during that time you must ensure that [*child's name*] [*insert requirements as appropriate*]. If you fail to comply with the order without reasonable excuse you may be guilty of an offence and fined up to £1,000.

General considerations

B[37A.5]

The order must require the parent or guardian to comply for a period not exceeding 12 months, with requirements that the court considers desirable in the interests of preventing the commission of further offences. The order must include a requirement to attend for a period, not exceeding three months, counselling or guidance sessions, unless the parent has previously been the subject of a parenting order. An order may include attendance at a residential course.

B[37A.6]

In the case of a juvenile under 16 years the court must make an order unless it can state reasons as to why it would not be desirable in the interests of preventing further offending by the juvenile.

Requirements

B[37A.7]

Additional requirements may be imposed to ensure or encourage the parent in preventing undesirable behaviour or offending such as:

(a) making sure the juvenile does not have contact with co-defendants,
(b) ensuring the juvenile is indoors between certain hours,
(c) ensuring the juvenile is accompanied to school,
(d) preventing the juvenile from visiting certain clubs or shopping centres.

Breach, variation and appeals

B[37A.8]

Breach is punishable by a fine not exceeding level 3

Variation and discharge are by way of complaint and governed by the Magistrates' Courts (Parenting Orders) Rules 2004

Appeals are governed by CDA 1998, s 10.

B[38]

Community rehabilitation order

(Powers of Criminal Courts (Sentencing) Act 2000, s 41)

Limitations

B[38.1]

This order is only available in the Youth Courts (16 and 17 year olds only)

The court must be of opinion that the supervision of the offender by a probation officer is desirable in the interests of securing the rehabilitation of the offender or protecting the public from harm from him or preventing the commission by him of further offences.

B[38.2]

The court must first explain in ordinary language the effect of the order, including any additional requirements therein. It must also explain that if he fails to comply with the order he may be dealt with in some other way for the offence for which the order is made, and that the court may review the order on the application of either the offender or the supervising officer.

B[38.3]

The offender, after having had the effect of the order explained as above, must express his willingness to comply with its requirements, if they include stipulations that the offender must undergo treatment for a mental condition or for drug or alcohol dependency.

B[38.4]

Community sentence. The offence must be 'serious enough' to warrant the application of a community sentence. See **B[3]**.

B[38.5]

Age limits - Offender must be 16 or 17.

B[38.6]

Maximum period – 3 years.

B[38.7]

Minimum period – 6 months.

Ancillary orders

B[38.8]

Compensation at **B[18]**

Costs at **B[20]**

Disqualification at **C[5]**

Endorsement at **C[5]**

Deprivation of property and forfeiture at **B[34]**

Restitution at **B[39]**

General considerations

B[38.9]–B[38.17]

The purpose of the order is the ultimate re-establishment of the defendant in the community. It is intended to protect society and also to assist the defendant in becoming a more responsible person.

B[38.18]

Provided the law has not fixed the sentence on conviction an order may be ordered for any defendant aged 16 or 17 and for any offence.

B[38.19]

If a defendant appears before the court on two or more offences and a suspended prison sentence is imposed for one offence, an order cannot be made on any of the other offences.

B[38.20]

The period of rehabilitation must be at least 6 months and not more than 3 years.

B[38.21]

Before announcing a community rehabilitation order, the court must explain the requirements of the order (see below) and ask the defendant if he is willing to comply with them if they include mental, or alcohol treatment. If he refuses an alternative sentence must be imposed.

B[38.22]

Later the defendant will be served with a copy of the order specifying the requirements imposed on him. These requirements may vary from one court to another. The requirements which must be included in all orders are that the defendant shall notify any change of address to the probation officer and that he shall keep in touch with the probation officer in accordance with such directions as he may be given. A curfew may be inserted into the order, but only where the offender lives in Hampshire, Nottinghamshire or West Yorkshire.

B[38.23]

The court may decide to include a requirement relating to the offender's place of residence, after reviewing the circumstances of his home surroundings. Residence may be required at an approved probation hostel, or at some other place.

B[38.24]

The name and address of the hostel or place of residence must be announced in court and entered in the register as well as recorded in the order.

B[38.25]–B[38.30]

Where residence is to be at an approved probation hostel or any other institution, the period of residence shall be specified in the order.

B[38.31]

The Secretary of State has made regulations concerning the regulation, management and inspection of approved probation hostels.

B[38.32]

Where there are convictions for several offences, if rehabilitation is ordered in respect of one a custodial sentence, even if suspended, may not be ordered in respect of another.

Order requiring mental treatment

B[38.33]

A requirement that the offender receives mental treatment may be made after the court has received written or oral evidence from an approved mental specialist that the defendant would benefit from such mental treatment, but that his condition is not such as to warrant his detention under a hospital or guardianship order.

B[38.34]

If a written mental report is accepted in court a copy of it must be shown to the defendant's advocate. If the defendant is not represented the substance of the report must be explained to him.

B[38.35]

Both the court and the defendant may insist on the personal appearance of the mental specialist who submitted the mental report, and the court has a duty to tell the defendant that he has this right to have the personal appearance of the doctor. Alternatively the defendant must be asked if he consents to the court acting on the written report.

B[38.36]

Types of treatment: The defendant or his advocate may call evidence to rebut the mental report. The following are the types of treatment that the court may order:

B[38.37]

Treatment as a resident patient means admission by consent to a mental hospital within the meaning of the Mental Health Act 1983, or a mental nursing home, not being a 'special hospital' under the National Health Service Act 1977.

B[38.38]

Treatment as a non-residential patient usually means attending a mental specialist at a psychiatric clinic.

B[38.39]

Treatment by a medical practitioner named in the community rehabilitation order. In effect this usually means one of the local consultant psychiatrists.

B[38.40]–B[38.45]

The court must announce the type of treatment ordered and record it in the register and insert it on the order.

B[38.46]

Before announcing its decision the court should be satisfied that the necessary arrangements have been made with the hospital or psychiatrist. The defendant must consent to the arrangements.

Treatment for drug or alcohol dependency

B[38.47]

Where the court is satisfied:

(a) the offender is dependent on drugs or alcohol;
(b) his dependency caused or contributed to the offence;
(c) his dependency requires and is susceptible to treatment,

it may include a condition of treatment by or under the direction of a person with the necessary qualifications or experience. Treatment may be as a resident or non-resident, in an institution, or under the direction of a specified person. The nature of the treatment may not be specified.

Additional requirements

B[38.48]

The court when making a rehabilitation order may include requirements specifying where or with whom the offender must reside. Any requirement may be included which the court considers to be necessary for securing the good conduct of the offender, protecting the public from harm from him or for preventing a repetition by him of a similar offence or other offences. Care should be taken in devising such requirements; they must be clear, enforceable and compatible with the nature of a community rehabilitation order (a requirement to leave the country, for example, would not be compatible with the order).

B[38.49]

Requirements may be included in the order that the offender shall:

(a) present himself to a specified person; and/or
(b) present himself at a place (or places) specified in the order; and/or
(c) participate, or refrain from participating in activities which must be specified, and to do so either:
  (i) on the specified day or days; or
  (ii) during the whole of the period of the order; or
  (iii) during a specified part of the order.

B[38.50]

An offender who is subject to any such requirement will be in breach of his order not only if he fails to present himself or participate etc but also if he fails to carry out the instructions of the officer or person in charge of the place or activity in which he must take part. He shall not be required to comply with such requirements for a longer total period than 60 days (or, in the case of sex offenders, such number of days as the court may specify).

B[38.51]

No such requirement may be included in an order unless:

(a) the offender consents in a case of mental, alcohol treatment conditions (when he is asked whether he consents to the requirements of the order, all the requirements must be carefully explained);
(b) the consent has been obtained of any third person who will be involved (e g the person to whom the offender must present himself, if it is not the supervising probation officer);
(c) the court has consulted the probation officer (this consultation will generally be initiated by the probation officer in his pre-sentence report). The subject matter of this consultation is to be the offender's circumstances and the feasibility of securing compliance with the requirement.

B[38.52]

Probation centres. The comments above apply mutatis mutandis to a requirement that the offender shall attend a probation centre. A probation centre is a non-residential establishment provided by the probation service for use in connection with the rehabilitation of offenders. The effect of such a requirement includes an obligation on the part of the probationer not only to attend the probation centre, but to attend also any other place at which the activities or any of them of the centre are carried out.

Breach of community rehabilitation order made by a magistrates' court (Powers of Criminal Courts (Sentencing) Act 2000, Sch 3)

B[38.53]

If an offender is alleged to have failed to comply with a requirement of his order, the hearing must take place in the magistrates' court which made the order, or in the supervising magistrates' court.

B[38.54]

If the failure is proved the court may deal with the offender as if he had just been convicted of the offence for which the community rehabilitation order was made. This means that any other appropriate sentence may be imposed, but where compensation was ordered at the time the order was made that compensation order must stand. If the court decides to substitute another sentence for the original order it should have information regarding the circumstances of the original offence.

B[38.55]–B[38.60]

If the court decides not to revoke the order and to deal with the original offence it may order a fine of up to £1,000, impose a community punishment order of up to 60 hours or an attendance centre order for the breach and allow the community rehabilitation order to continue.

Orders made by the Crown Court

B[38.61]

When a higher court has made a community rehabilitation order it is usually supervised by the magistrates' court of the area in which the offender resides.

B[38.62]

In the event of a breach of the order the magistrates' court has the power to commit the offender in custody or on bail to the Crown Court for sentence until he appears or is brought before that court. Alternatively, it may punish the breach by a fine, a community punishment order or an attendance centre order in the case of an offender under the age of 21 and allow the order to continue. Note, however, that the Crown Court may reserve any breach or revocation application to itself. Such proceedings will be heard directly in the Crown Court.

When the case is dealt with in the Crown Court it has the same powers to deal with the offender as have been mentioned above in connection with the magistrates' court.

B[38.63]

A magistrates' court may not revoke the order if it was made by the crown court, but may commit the defendant to custody or release him on bail until he is brought or appears before the crown court.

Revocation of orders (*Powers of Criminal Courts* (*Sentencing*) *Act 2000, Sch 3*)

[38.64]

Before the end of the period, the probation officer or the offender can apply to a magistrates' court to revoke the order on the ground, for example, of good progress or to deal with the offender in some other way.

B[38.65]

After hearing the application the magistrates' court can:

(a) refuse the application, thus leaving the order in force; or
(b) adjourn the application, eg to obtain further information or to see if the offender maintains good progress; or
(c) revoke the community rehabilitation order completely; or
(d) revoke the order and deal with the offender in some other way for the offence. In the case of (d) the court must take into account such matters as the extent to which the offender complied with the requirements of the relevant order.

Crown Court orders cannot generally be revoked by a magistrates' court. Either the offender must have been committed to the Crown Court for sentence or the application to revoke must be made direct to the Crown Court.

B[38.66]

Substitution of a conditional discharge for a community rehabilitation order. If the probation officer or offender can satisfy the court that an order has ceased to be appropriate, he can apply to the court to substitute a conditional discharge for the remainder of the rehabilitation period. A formal application must be laid and heard in open court.

Checklist for an order

B[38.67]

1 Offence – sentence not fixed by law.
2 Age – 16 or 17 years.
3 Supervision desirable to:
   (a) secure rehabilitation;
   (b) protect public;
   (c) prevent further offences.

4 Offence(s) 'serious enough'.
5 Order suitable for offender.
6 Restriction on liberty commensurate with offence(s).
7 Explain:
   (a) effect of order;
   (b) consequence of breach;
   (c) review.

8 Consent of offender where a treatment requirement for mental or drug/alcohol problems is imposed.

B[38A]

Reparation order

(Powers of Criminal Courts (Sentencing) Act 2000, s 73)

Limitations

B[38A.1]

May only be made in the Youth Court. The offence involved need not be serious enough to merit a community penalty.

B[38A.2]

A reparation order may not be made if the court proposes to pass a custodial sentence or to make ****a community punishment order, a community punishment and community rehabilitation order**, an action plan order, a referral order or a supervision order, which includes requirements under ss 12–12C of the Children and Young Persons Act 1969.

[**When Sch 32, para.106 of the CJA 2003 is brought into force from a date to be appointed, for the highlighted words substitute "a community order made under s 177 CJA 2003".]

Maximum periods

B[38A.3]

A reparation order may not require the offender to work for more than 24 hours in all, or to make reparation to any person without the consent of that person.

B[38A.4]

The reparation must be made within three months of the making of the order.

Reports

B[38A.5]

The order does not require a full pre-sentence report (PSR) but before making a reparation order the court must obtain and consider a report indicating:

(a) the type of work that is suitable for the offender; and
(b) the attitude of the victim or victims to the requirements proposed to be included in the order.

General consideration

B[38A.6]–B[38A.7]

A reparation order should be considered in less serious cases where the court wishes to

- take into account the feelings and wishes of the victims of crime; and
- prevent the young offender from committing further offences by confronting him with the consequences of his criminal behaviour, and allowing him to make some amends.

B[38A.8]

Reparation can be in the form of direct or indirect reparation. The court will require a report setting out the reparation activities appropriate, such as writing a letter of apology or meeting the victim in person to apologise, repairing criminal damage for which the young person has been responsible, cleaning graffiti, and working on an environmental or other community project.

B[38A.9]-B[38A.15]

Reparation carried out under a reparation order should be reparation in kind rather than financial reparation. Courts are already able to make a compensation order if they believe that financial reparation is appropriate.

Reasons

B[38A.16]

The court must give reasons if it does not make an order where it has power to do so.

Breach of the order

B[38A.17]

The responsible officer will instigate breach proceedings.

B[38A.18]

The powers available to the court are:

(a) fine up to level 3 or,
(b) impose an attendance centre order or,
(c) a curfew order (whether or not order varied or discharged), or
(d) revoke and re-sentence for the original offence; or
(e) in the case of an order made by the Crown Court the magistrates can commit the offender on bail or in custody until he can be brought up or appear before the Crown Court.

B[39]–B[40]

Restitution order

(Powers of Criminal Courts (Sentencing) Act 2000, s 148)

B[39.1]

Where goods have been stolen and a person is convicted of any offence with reference to the theft (whether or not the stealing is the gist of his offence) or such an offence is taken into consideration the court may make a restitution order.

B[39.2]

Stolen includes obtaining by deception or blackmail.

B[39.3]

Restitution. The court:

(a) may simply order the defendant to restore the goods to the person entitled to them whether or not any application is made for restitution; or
(b) (where an application has been made) order the delivery over of any goods directly or indirectly representing the proceeds of the stolen goods; or
(c) where money was taken from the possession of the accused on his apprehension, order its payment to the aggrieved,

but the beneficiary of the restitution must not receive more than the value of the original goods, a matter particularly to note when a combination of orders under (b) and (c) is made.

B[39.4]

Innocent purchasers. Sometimes the thief has sold the goods to an innocent purchaser. The goods will be restored to the owner but the court may also order the defendant to pay out of any monies in his possession when apprehended a sum to the innocent third party up to the amount he paid for the goods.

B[39.5]

Making a restitution order. Can be made on conviction of the offender whether or not sentencing is otherwise deferred.

B[39.6]

Evidence. In the opinion of the court the relevant facts must sufficiently appear from the evidence at the trial, or available documents (ie witness statements, depositions or other documents which were made for use and would have been admissible as evidence in the proceedings) together with any other admissions made.

B[41]

Football banning orders

(Football Spectators Act 1989, ss 14 and 22 and Football (Disorder) Act 2000)

Criminal orders

B[41.1]

Where a person has been convicted of a relevant offence the court shall make a restriction order which requires him to report at a police station at the time that a designated football match is being played outside England and Wales, i e the order prohibits football hooligans from attending certain football matches played abroad.

B[41.2]

A Regulated football match is an association football match in which one or both of the participating teams represents a club which is for the time being a member (whether a full or associate member) of the Football League, the Football Association Premier League, the Football Conference or the League of Wales, or represents a country or territory.

An association football match (outside England and Wales) described below is also a regulated football match for the purposes of Part II of the 1989 Act.

A regulated match is an association football match involving-

(a) a national team appointed by the Football Association to represent England or the Football Association of Wales to represent Wales; or
(b) a team representing a club which is, at the time the match is played, a member (whether a full or associate member) of the Football League, the Football Association Premier League, the Football Conference or the League of Wales.

B[41.3]

Failure to comply with a banning order is a criminal offence triable only by magistrates with a maximum penalty on level 5 and six months' [**51 weeks] imprisonment.

B[41.4]

Relevant offence means:

(1)An offence in the Football Spectators Act 1989, Sch 1 which includes:

(a) an offence under the Sporting Events (Control of Alcohol etc) Act 1985, s 2;
(b) offences under the Public Order Act 1986, s 5 and Part III (racial hatred);
(c) an offence involving the threat or use of violence to a person or property: this includes an offence under Public Order Act 1986, s 4(1)(a) (*R v O' Keefe* (2004))
(d) offences under the Football (Offences) Act 1991.

See Football Spectators Act 1989, Sch 1 (as amended) for an exhaustive list.

B[41.5]

Offences (b) – (d) must be committed during a period relevant to a designated football match at any premises while the accused was at, or was entering or leaving or trying to enter or leave, the premises. Therefore a defendant convicted of a public order offence on a train travelling away from a match he had been refused entry to was on a factual basis not related to a football match (*R v Smith* [2002] EWCA Crim 683, [2003] 1 Cr App Rep 212).

There is, however, no need to prove in a criminal case the civil requirements that the defendants caused or contributed to violence or disorder: s 14B (*R (on the application of Brown) v Inner London Crown Court* [2003] EWHC 3194 (Admin), [2003] All ER (D) 256 (Dec)).

B[41.6]

Relevant period. A period beginning 24 hours before the start of the match or, if earlier, 24 hours before the time it is advertised to start or the time at which spectators are first admitted to the premises, and ends 24 hours after the end of the match. Where a match is postponed or cancelled, the period includes the 24 hours before and 24 hours after the advertised start of the event. Regulated football match' for the purposes of these offences and those described below (e)-(h) is described above.

B[41.7]

(2) The following offences committed on a journey to or from a designated football match where the court makes a declaration that the offence related to football matches:

(e) offences under (b) and (c) above;
(f) drunkenness;
(g) an offence under the Sporting Events (Control of Alcohol etc) Act 1985, s 1;

(h) driving whilst unfit or over the prescribed limit of alcohol: Road Traffic Act 1988, ss 4 and 5.

B[41.8]

The prosecution must normally give five days' notice of its intention to seek a declaration that the offence related to football matches.

B[41.9]

(3) Offences under paras (e) and (g) committed on journeys to designated matches played outside England and Wales.

B[41.10]–B[41.15]

(4) 'Corresponding offences' committed in countries designated from time to time by the Secretary of State.

B[41.16]

Therefore an order can be made in respect of a relevant offence whether committed in England and Wales or abroad, and the restriction order will apply to designated matches both domestically and internationally.

B[41.17]

Offences committed abroad. Where the relevant offence was committed abroad the court may, on information being laid, issue a summons or warrant to bring the offender before the court to consider whether to make a restriction order.

B[41.18]

Criterion. The court must make a football banning order in relation to the offender if satisfied that there are reasonable grounds to believe that it would help to prevent violence or disorder at or in connection with regulated football matches. If it does not make an order the court must state in open court its reasons for not being satisfied an order was required.

B[41.19]

Procedure. May only be made in addition to a sentence (which includes a community rehabilitation order and an order for conditional or absolute discharge) imposed in respect of the offence of which the accused was convicted. The court must:

(a) certify that the offence is a relevant offence where appropriate;
(b) specify the police station in England and Wales at which the person must report initially;
(c) explain to the person the effect of the order in ordinary language;

(d) give a copy of the order to the defendant, and send copies to the Football Banning Orders Authority, the specified police station and, if appropriate, the relevant prison governor.

B[41.20]

The court must also impose conditions in the order including the surrender of the defendant's passport not more than five days before the date of each designated football match in respect of which the defendant is required to report unless there are exceptional circumstances for not doing so.

B[41.21]

Duration. Where the person receives an immediate prison sentence but not other forms of detention the mandatory period is a maximum of 10 years and a minimum of 6 years. In any other football case the maximum is 5 years and the minimum three years. In a non-football-related offence, the period is between two and three years.

B[41.22]

Effect. The person is under a duty to report initially to the police station specified in the order within five days of the making of the order and thereafter to report to a police station specified when notified by the Banning Orders Authority. Note a banning order is not a punishment for the purposes of ECHR Art 7 (*Gough v Chief Constable of Derbyshire* [2001] EWHC Admin 554 Admin, [2002] QB 459; affd sub nom Gough v Chief Constable of Derbyshire Constabulary [2002] EWCA Civ 351, [2002] 2 All ER 985).

B[41.23]

Exemption may be granted from reporting in respect of a particular match either an application to the Banning Orders Authority or in cases of urgency to the police. Exemption might be granted, for example, to cover a stay in hospital or the funeral of a close relative.

B[41.24]

Application to terminate. The person subject to the order may apply to the court to terminate the order after two-thirds of the period determined has expired.

B[41.25]–B[41.30]

The court will have regard to the person's character, his conduct since the order was made, the nature of the offence which led to it and any other circumstances of the case.

B[41.31]

Further application may not be made within six months of a refusal.

B[41.32]

Appeal is to the Crown Court against the making of a banning order or a refusal to award compensation (see below).

B[41.33]

Civil applications In addition to its imposition as a result of a football-related conviction, a banning order may be imposed by a magistrates' court in accordance with a civil procedure, following a complaint by the police. The court must be satisfied that the person who is the subject of the complaint has at any time caused or contributed to any violence or disorder in the United Kingdom or elsewhere, and that there are reasonable grounds to believe that making a banning order would help to prevent violence or disorder at or in connection with any regulated football matches. This is a civil order and not a sentence (*Gough v Chief Constable of Derbyshire* [2001] EWHC 554 (Admin), [2002] QB 459; affd sub nom Gough v Chief Constable of Derbyshire Constabulary [2002] EWCA Civ 351, [2002] 2 All ER 985).

B[41.34]

If, during a control period when international bans are activated, a police officer has reasonable grounds for suspecting that a person before him or her has caused or contributed to any violence or disorder in the United Kingdom or elsewhere, and for believing that imposing a banning order on that person would help to prevent violence or disorder at or in connection with any regulated football matches, the officer may, with the authorisation of an inspector of police, give the person a notice in writing requiring him or her to appear before a magistrates' court within 24 hours and in the meantime not to leave England and Wales. The magistrates' court will then treat the notice as an application for a banning order under the new civil procedure. The Act also gives the police the power to detain a person for up to four hours (or six hours if authorised by an inspector) while deciding whether to issue a notice.

B[41.35]

Compensation Where a notice has been issued by a police officer under these powers and a court subsequently refuses to impose a banning order, the court may order compensation up to £5000 to be paid to that person out of central funds if it is satisfied that the notice should not have been given in the first place, that the person has suffered loss as a result of the notice, and that it is appropriate to order the payment of compensation in respect of that loss. There is no statutory definition of the word refuse and so presumably if the police seek to withdraw the proceedings the right to compensation is lost although the right to apply for legal costs remains.

B[41.36]

Length of order The minimum civil order will last for two years and the maximum three years.

B[42]-B[46]

Referrals to youth offender panels

(Powers of Criminal Courts (Sentencing) Act 2000, s 16 **as amended by CJA 2003, Sch 34)

B[42.1]

This procedure is in force throughout England and Wales. In general every young offender who pleads guilty and who has never previously been convicted, or bound over for an offence, must be referred by the Youth Court to a youth offender panel. The exceptions to this compulsory referral include cases where a custodial sentence is appropriate or at the other end of the scale where the court imposes an absolute discharge. Neither is the court precluded from ordering hospital admission in respect of a mentally ill juvenile.

B[42.2]

A discretionary referral may be made where a juvenile pleads guilty to one or more offences and not guilty to other offences of which he is convicted.

Compulsory orders only apply to imprisonable offences, discretionary orders may be made for non-imprisonable offences. If there are imprisonable and non-imprisonable offences and the defendant pleads guilty to everything the compulsory order applies.

B[42.3]

Length of order The Youth Court must specify the length of the order during which time the offender will have contact with the panel. This must be between 3 and 12 months and will be assessed on the basis of the seriousness of the offence. The order must also include an appointment with the Youth Offending Team in the offender's home area and a requirement that the offender must attend each meeting of the panel as directed.

B[42.4]

Ancillary orders. A referral order is not an additional sentence and may be accompanied by ancillary orders such as costs, compensation and forfeiture. The court may also bind over the parent or guardian under PCC(S)A 2000, s 150. If the court wishes to make a referral order and make the parent subject to a parenting order, it must first obtain a report as to why such an order would be desirable and how it would operate.

B[42.5]–B[42.10]

Breach If the juvenile is referred back to the court by the panel, because he is in breach of his contract, or he has committed a further offence while subject to the referral the court may revoke the original order and re-sentence. Any fresh sentence (other than an absolute discharge) has the effect of revoking the referral order. There is also power to extend the period of the referral order for offences committed before and during the currency of the order. This may be done once only and must not extend the order beyond the 12 month maximum.

B[42.11]

Youth Offender Panels. The role of youth offender panels is outside the scope of this work but, following a referral, they will meet with the offender and devise programmes, participation and reparation in an attempt to address offending behaviour. The imposition of intensive or intrusive programmes by the youth offender panels has the potential to lead to an increased number of not guilty pleas in the Youth Court in the hope of securing a financial penalty or less intensive order in the event of a finding of guilt.

B[42.12]

Problems. Non-recordable offences are previous convictions but by definition may not be available before the court. In such circumstances, if the prosecution suggest the defendant has no previous convictions, a referral order will follow.

Both the court and the referral panel have power to make a compensation order but the court has a duty to make one and must give its reasons in open court for not doing so.

B[42.13]

Breach. The young offender may be referred back to the court for a revocation of the order if he fails to attend the panel, fails to agree a contract or fails to comply with the terms of the contract.

On receiving a report of a breach the court must summons or issue a warrant for the appearance of the juvenile.

On his appearance they must consider if the panel was right to refer the breach back. If they decide it was not then the order continues.

If a breach is proved the court has power to extend the period for compliance with the order or to revoke it and deal with the original offence in any way it could have done other than the making of a referral order.

B[47]

Supervision order (Criminal Proceedings)

(Powers of Criminal Courts (Sentencing) Act 2000, s 63)

Limitations

B[47.1]

May be made only by a youth court.

B[47.2]

Age limits – Person in respect of whom the order is made must be under 18.

B[47.3]

Maximum period – 3 years.

B[47.4]

Minimum period – None.

B[47.5]

Consent - Consent of offender not required except for medical treatment or 'supervised activities'.

B[47.6]–B[47.15]

If any requirements are to be added they should be explained in ordinary language and the offender should be asked whether he fully understands the obligations to be imposed upon him.

Ancillary orders

B[47.16]

Compensation at **B[18]**

Costs at **B[20]**

Disqualification at **C[5]**

Endorsement at **C[5]**

Deprivation of property and forfeiture at **B[34]**

Restitution at **B[39]**

General considerations

B[47.17]

A magistrates' court (as opposed to a youth court) cannot make a supervision order, but must remit the juvenile on bail or in local authority accommodation to a youth court which will usually be the youth court of the area in which the juvenile resides.

B[47.18]

When a youth court makes a supervision order the effect is to place the juvenile under the supervision of a local authority or probation officer for up to three years. The youth court should announce as to whether the supervisor will be the local authority or the probation officer. The duty of the supervising officer is to advise, assist and befriend the juvenile.

B[47.19]

The youth court should also announce the length of the order which can be made for up to three years.

Additional requirements

B[47.20]

1 Residence. A supervision order may contain a requirement that the juvenile resides with a specified person who consents to such arrangement. Such a requirement shall be subject to any of the requirements detailed below and the effect of this order of priority is that, for example, a general requirement to reside with John Smith will not be broken by complying with a further requirement which involves residence elsewhere for a short period.

B[47.21]

2 Requirements A requirement may be included in a supervision order that the juvenile shall comply with directions given to him by his supervising officer. The initiative for giving directions then lies with that officer, not with the court, but the law describes the forms that those directions may take. Once the court includes the general requirement to comply with the supervising officer's directions then that officer may give directions requiring the juvenile to do any or all of the following things:

(a) To live at a place or at places specified by the officer for a period or periods so specified. This might be used, for example, in connection with a series of weekend residential courses and, as explained above, it would take precedence over a general requirement as to residence.
(b) To present himself to a specified person at specified times and places.
(c) To take part in specified activities on specified occasions. This and the preceding requirement might be used together to ensure the attendance of the juvenile, for example, on a day training course.

B[47.22]

The total number of days upon which a juvenile may be required to comply with directions may not exceed **90 or such lower number as the court specifies. The inclusion of a requirement to comply with directions will almost always be the result of the supervisor's initiative, either at the time of making the order or later on an application to vary it by including such a requirement. Although in theory the court gives the supervisor a fairly blank cheque, in practice the supervisor will have set out for the court the kind of directions he intends to give. Having secured the inclusion of the requirement in the order, however, the supervisor is under no obligation to give any directions, or to give the same, or all of the directions which he may have previously indicated to the court. Some may see this as a derogation of the power of the youth court, but it is suggested that the better view is that it provides the supervisor with a useful element of flexibility in his handling of the case.

[**Substitute 180 when, from a date to be appointed, the Anti-Social Behaviour Act 2003, Sch 2, is brought into force.]

B[47.23]

3 Mental treatment. Where the court is satisfied by the report of a medical practitioner specialising in mental health that a juvenile is suffering from mental ill-health which may be susceptible to treatment, the court may include in a supervision order a requirement to undergo treatment for a specified period. That treatment must take one of the following forms and the requirement in the order will be framed accordingly:

(a) treatment by or under the direction of a registered medical practitioner specified in the order; or
(b) treatment as a non-resident patient in a place specified in the order; or
(c) treatment as a resident patient in a hospital or mental nursing home.

B[47.24]

A juvenile aged 14 or more must consent before a requirement for mental treatment may be included and the court must be satisfied that arrangements have been made for the carrying out of the requirement.

B[47.25]

4 Additional requirements in criminal proceedings. Requirements analogous to those discussed above may be included in a supervision order made in family proceedings (see Section D, below). When dealing with a juvenile who has been found guilty of an offence there are further powers which the court can exercise. These requirements cannot be combined with an order for intermediate treatment under para 2 at **B[47.21]–B[47.22]** above.

B[47.26]

(**a**) **Supervised activities**. The court may order the juvenile to do anything which a supervisor could require under para 2 (intermediate treatment) at **B[47.21]–B[47.22]**. On the face of it this looks like a duplication of para 2 but in fact there are two important differences. First, it is the court which spells out the requirements rather than leaving them to the discretion of the supervisor. Second, as these requirements are restricted to criminal proceedings, local authorities and the probation service have prepared schemes which are more rigorous than those for intermediate treatment. Although it is the court which specifies the requirements, in fact the reporting officer will set out his proposals in the social inquiry report for the court to incorporate in its order if it considers them to be suitable.

B[47.27]

(**b**) **Night restriction order**. A requirement may be included which is called a night restriction and which is in the nature of a curfew. The period of restriction must not exceed 10 hours which must be between 6 p.m. and 6 a.m. The nature of the restriction is that the supervised person must during the specified hours remain at the place, or one of several places, specified in the order. The supervised person may not be required to suffer this restriction for more than 30 nights nor for any period beyond 3 months from the date of the order. Notwithstanding the restriction the supervised person may leave the specified place if when he does so he is accompanied by his parent, his supervising officer or any other person who is specified in the order. If only one place to which he is restricted is specified then that place must be the place where he lives; if more than one place is specified, the place where he lives must be one of those places.

B[47.28]

(**c**) **Non-participation**. The court may also include a requirement that the juvenile shall refrain from participating in activities specified in the order either on specified days (e g every Saturday) or for the whole or part of the period of supervision.

B[47.29]

The night restriction and the requirement to refrain from taking part in activities may not be included unless the court has consulted the supervisor as to the offender's circumstances and as to the feasibility of securing compliance with the requirement. The court must also be of opinion that the inclusion of such requirement is necessary to secure the good conduct of the juvenile or for the prevention of future offences by him. If the juvenile is under 16 the court must obtain and consider information about the family circumstances and the likely effect of the requirements on those circumstances before imposing the order.

B[47.30]

(d) **Residence in local authority accommodation**. A juvenile who has been found guilty of an offence committed whilst he was the subject of a supervision order with a residence requirement, intermediate treatment or specified activities, or fails to comply with a requirement may be made the subject of a requirement to live in local authority accommodation for a period of up to six months. The requirement may also stipulate that he is not to live with a named person.

B[47.31]

The court must consult the authority concerned. The object of the requirement is not punitive but to remove the offender from undesirable surroundings so that the court must be satisfied that the offending behaviour was due to a significant extent to the circumstances in which he was living. The juvenile must be given an opportunity to be legally represented.

B[47.32]

(e) **Education**. The court may add a requirement to a supervision order made in respect of a person of compulsory school age that he comply with arrangements made for his education. The court must:

(i) have consulted the supervisor as to the offender's circumstances; and
(ii) consider the requirement necessary to secure his good conduct or to prevent his further offending.

B[47.33]

Intensive Supervision and Surveillance Programmes (ISSPs). These are not orders in themselves but can be attached to supervision and community rehabilitation orders, bail and detention and training orders.

ISSPs are available nationally in all youth courts.

B[47.34]

The order may be use for juveniles who have:

(i) been charged or warned for an imprisonable offence on four or more occasions within the past 12 months;
(ii) received at least one custodial or community penalty in the past;
(iii) been charged with an imprisonable offence; and

(iv) committed an offence which is so serious that a custodial sentence or custodial remand is under consideration.

B[47.35]–B[47.37]

All ISSPs will contain provision for education and training, a restorative element and work on changing behaviour, together with family support, community surveillance which will involve electric monitoring if available.

Variation and discharge

B[47.38]

The powers to vary a supervision order are complex. They may be summarised as follows:

Supervised persons under 18 years

B[47.39]

Applications to vary and discharge supervision orders are made to the youth court, which may discharge the order or vary it by cancelling any requirement or insert certain other requirements.

B[47.40]–B[47.45]

Breach of requirements. In addition to the powers described above, for breach of requirements, except those relating to mental treatment, the court may impose a fine of up to £1,000, a curfew order or an attendance centre order either in addition to or instead of varying the supervision order; the court may also discharge the supervision order and re-sentence for the original offence, or where the original order was made by the Crown Court, the youth court may commit the offender to the Crown Court on bail or in custody and the Crown Court may deal with the original offence.

B[47.46]

Where the breach is of Crown Court imposed supervision order, the magistrates' court [youth court] must provide written details of the breach and other relevant information to the Crown Court.

Section C

Road traffic offences

C[1]

Index and penalties for road traffic offences

Maximum fines and the standard scale

C[1.1]

MCA 1980, s 32(9); Interpretation Act 1978, s 32, Sch 1	The **statutory maximum** fine on summary conviction of an offence triable either way, being the prescribed sum under the Magistrates' Court Act 1980,	£5,000
CJA 1982,	**The standard scale** giving maximum fines on an adult on conviction for a summary offence: s 37(2)	
	level 1	£200
	level 2	£500
	level 3	£1,000
	level 4	£2,500
	level 5	£5,000

C[1.2]

The following table contains an alphabetical list of the road traffic offences dealt with in this book, together with some others included to provide the maximum penalty. Readers will wish to note the penalties recommended in the Magistrates' Association National Sentencing Guidelines.

C[1.3]

Speed/distance chart. See **C[2]**

C[1.4]

Stopping distances. See **C[3]**

C[1.5]

Endorsement codes. See **C[6]**

C[1.6]

Offences and endorsement code	Standard scale	*Licence and penalty points*	para
Abandoning a motor vehicle	level 4+ 3 months [**51 weeks]		
Accident, failing to give particulars AC 20	level 5 +6 months [**51 weeks]	E 5–10	**C[32]**
report AC 20	level 5 +6 months [**51 weeks]	E 5–10	**C[32]**
stop after AC 10	level 5 +6 months [**51 weeks]	E 5–10	**C[31]**
Bicycle			
defective brakes riding	level 3		
careless	level 3		
dangerous	level 4		
inconsiderate	level 3		
two persons on	level 1		
when unfit through drink	level 3		
Brakes, defective			
on private vehicle CU 10 §	level 4	E*3	**C[9]**
on goods vehicle CU 10 §	level 5	E*3	**C[9]**
on bicycle	level 3		
Breath test, refusing DR 70	level 3	E 3–11	**C[24]**
Car door, opening to cause			
injury or danger §	level 3		**C[37]**
Car dumping	level 4 +	104	**A[60]**
	3 months [**51 weeks]		
Careless driving CD 10	level 4	E 3–9	**C[25]**
Common land, driving on §	level 3		

Offences and endorsement code	Standard scale	*Licence and penalty points*	para
Dangerous condition			
using private vehicle in CU 20 §	level 4	E*3	**C[10]**
using goods vehicle in CU 20 §	level 5	E*3	**C[10]**
Dangerous load			
on private vehicle CU 50 §	level 4	E*3	
on goods vehicle CU 50 §	level 5	E*3	
Dangerous position, leaving			
motor vehicle in MS 10 §	level 3	E 3	
Date of birth, failing to give	level 3		
Defective tyre			
private vehicle CU 30 §	level 4	E*3	**C[53]**
goods vehicle CU 30 §	level 5	E*3	**C[53]**
Driver, failing to give particulars of date of birth	level 3		
Driving			
careless CD 10	level 4 [level 5 under the Road Safety Act 2006]	E 3–9	**C[25]**
dangerous†DD 40	level 5+ 6 months [**51 weeks]	D 3–11	**C[16]**
disqualified BA 10	level 5+ 6 months [**51 weeks]	E 6	**C[19]**
drink, under influence of DR 20	level 5+ 6 months [**51 weeks]	D 3–11	**C[20]**
excess alcohol DR 10	level 5+ 6 months [**51 weeks]	D 3–11	**C[22]**
excessive periods on footpath, common land, etc	level 4		
(RT Act) §	level 3		
without			

Offences and endorsement code	Standard scale	*Licence and penalty points*	para
due care and attention CD 10	level 4 [level 5 under the Road Safety Act 2006]	E 3–9	**C[25]**
insurance IN 10 §	level 5	E 6–8	**C[33]**
licence (excise)	£1,000 or 5 times duty		**C[47]**
reasonable consideration CD 20	level 4 [level 5 under the Road Safety Act 2006]	E 3–9	**C[46]**
test certificate			
(private)	level 3		**C[51]**
(goods)	level 4		**C[51]**
Drunk in charge DR 50	level 4+ 3 months [**51 weeks]	E 10	**C[21]**
Excess alcohol			
driving DR 10	level 5+ 6 months [**51 weeks]	D 3–11	**C[20]**
in charge DR 40	level 5+ 3 months [**51 weeks]	E 10	**C[21]**
Excise licence			
failing to display §	level 1		
making false statement to obtain	level 5		
using/keeping vehicle without	level 3 or 5 times duty		**C[47]**
Eyesight, driving with defective	level 3	E 3	
MS 70			
Failing to comply with traffic sign §	level 3	+ 3	**C[52]**
(constable or traffic warden on traffic duty) TS 40 §	level 3	E 3	
give			
name and address to	level 5	E 5–10	**C[31]**

Offences and endorsement code	Standard scale	*Licence and penalty points*	para
police AC 20	+6 months [**51 weeks]		
particulars after accident AC 20	level 5	E 5–10	**C[31]**
	+6 months [**51 weeks]		
specimen of			
breath DR 70	level 3	E 4	**C[24]**
blood/urine/breath			
driving or attempting DR 30	level 5 + 6 months [**51 weeks]	D 3–11	**C[24]**
in charge DR 60	level 4 + 3 months [**51 weeks]	E 10	**C[24]**
statement by owner	level 3		
produce			
driving licence	level 3		**C[17]**
insurance certificate	level 3		**C[17]**
test certificate	level 3		**C[17]**
wear seat belt (front §)	level 2		**C[48]**
(rear §)	level 1		
report accident AC 20	level 5 +6 months [**51 weeks]	E 5–10	**C[31]**
sign driving licence	level 3		
stop			
after accident AC 10	level 5 +6 months [**51 weeks]	E 5–10	**C[31]**
at school crossing TS 60	level 3	E 3	
False declaration to obtain excise licence †	level 5		
False statement to obtain			
driving licence	level 4		
insurance	level 4		

Offences and endorsement code	Standard scale	*Licence and penalty points*	para
Footpath, driving on			
(Highways Act 1835, s 72)	level 2		
Forging, etc			
driving licence, excise licence †	level 5		
insurance certificate	level 5		
test certificate †	level 5		
Front seat, carrying child in §	level 3		**C[48]**
Getting on to vehicle to	level 1		
be carried			
Heavy goods vehicle			
driving without LGV licence	level 3		
overloading §	level 5		**C[38]**
parking on verge, etc §	level 3		
using without plating certificate	level 3		
using without test certificate	level 4		
Holding on to vehicle to be towed or carried	level 1		
Hours, driving for excessive number	level 4		
Insecure load			
private vehicle CU 50 §	level 4	E*3	
goods vehicle CU 50 §	level 5	E*3	
Insurance			
using without, causing or			
permitting IN 10 §	level 5	E 6–8	**C[33]**
failing to produce certificate	level 3		**C[17]**
false statement to obtain	level 4		
Jay walking	level 3		
Licence			
driving otherwise than in accordance with LC 10 §	level 3	E 3–6	**C[18]**

Offences and endorsement code	Standard scale	*Licence and penalty points*	para
excise, keeping/using vehicle without	level 3 or 5 times duty		**C[47]**
failing to produce for endorsement	level 3		
failing to produce to constable	level 3		**C[17]**
LGV, driving otherwise than in accordance with	10 units		**C[19]**
obtaining while disqualified	level 3		
Lights, driving or parking			
without §	level 4 (goods vehicle etc)		**C[34]**
	level 3 (other)		
Mobile Telephone	level 3	E 3 (when the Road Safety Act 2006 is brought into force)	
Motor cyclists not wearing helmet §	level 2		**C[35]**
Neglecting policeman's directions			
driver TS 40 §	level 3	E 3	
pedestrian	level 3		
Obstruction, causing			
unnecessary §	level 4 (goods vehicle etc)		**C[36]**
	level 3 (other)		
Opening door to cause danger or			
injury §	level 4 (goods vehicle)		**C[37]**
	level 3 (other)		

Offences and endorsement code	Standard scale	*Licence and penalty points*	para
One way street, driving in wrong direction §	level 3	E 3	**C[52]**
Overloading §	level 5		**C[38]**
Owner failing to identify driver	level 3	E 3 [6 under the Road Safety Act 2006]	
Parking			
heavy vehicle on footpath,	level 3		
on offside at night §	level 4 (goods vehicle etc)		
on yellow lines §	level 3		
breach of regulations for			
on street parking places §	level 2		
(abuse of parking for the disabled) §	level 3		
off street parking places	level 2		
(abuse of parking for the disabled)	level 3		
failure to pay initial or excess charge	level 2 + amount unpaid		
interfering with meter with intent to defraud	level 3		
Pedal cycle, *see* Bicycle			
Pedestrian			
failing to comply with direction of constable on traffic duty	level 3		
Pedestrian crossing			
not giving precedence PC 20 §	level 3	E 3	**C[39]**
overtaking within limits PC 20 §	level 3	E 3	**C[39.10]**
stopping within limits PC 30 §	level 3	E 3	**C[40]**
Provisional licence holder			

Offences and endorsement code	Standard scale	*Licence and penalty points*	para
(See driving otherwise than in accordance with licence)			
Reasonable consideration			
driving without CD 20	level 4 [level 5 under the Road Safety Act 2006]	E 3–9	**C[46]**
Record of hours, failing to keep	level 4		
Refusing blood/urine/breath			
specimen			
in charge DR 60	level 4+ 3 months [**51 weeks]	E 10	**C[23]**
driving DR 30	level 5+ 6 months [**51 weeks]	D 3–11	**C[23]**
Riding bicycle, *see* Bicycle			
Road fund licence			
keeping/using without	level 3 or 5 times duty		**C[47]**
fail to display §	level 1		
false statement to obtain †	level 5		
Seat belt, failure to wear (front §)	level 2		**C[48]**
(rear §)	level 1		
School crossing, fail to stop			
at TS 60	level 3	E 3	
Silencer, defective §	level 4 (goods vehicle etc)		
	level 3 (other)		
Speeding SP 30 §	level 3	E 3–6(FP3) [2–6 under the Road Safety Act 2006]	**C[49]**

Offences and endorsement code	Standard scale	*Licence and penalty points*	para
motorway SP 50 §	level 4	E 3–6(FP3)	**C[49]**
Stealing (or attempt) vehicle †			
NE 99	level 5 + 6 months [**12 months]	D (discretionary)	
Steering, defective			
private vehicle CU 40 §	level 4	E*3	**C[50]**
goods vehicle CU 40 §	level 5	E*3	
Taking motor vehicle			
without consent			
NE 99	level 5	D (discretionary)	**A[77]**
(Theft Act 1968, s 12) Aggravated Vehicle Taking UT 50 (Theft Act 1968, s 12A)	6 months [**51 weeks] Level 5 6 months [**12 months]	D	**A[3]**
Tampering with motor vehicle	level 3 +		**A[82]**
	3 months [**51 weeks]		
Test certificate §			
using etc vehicle without	level 3		**C[51]**
using goods vehicle without	level 4		**C[51]**
failing to produce	level 3		**C[17]**
Traffic sign, non compliance			
with §	level 3	E 3	**C[52]**
Tyre, defective			
private vehicle CU 30 §	level 4	E*3	**C[53]**
goods vehicle CU 30 §	level 5	E*3	**C[53]**
Waiting on yellow lines §	level 3		

D means that the offence attracts an obligatory disqualification.

E means that the offence attracts an obligatory endorsement; in all such cases disqualification is discretionary.

- * The defendant in cases thus marked is not liable to an endorsement if he satisfies the court that he did not know of the defect and had no reasonable cause to suspect that it was present.
- \+ Endorsable only if the sign is a traffic light (TS 10), double white lines (TS 20), Stop (TS 30), no entry sign or failure to comply with a green arrow traffic sign, abnormal load failing to observe procedure at railway crossing (TS 50), or vehicle contravening height restriction (TS 50).
- † Triable either way.
- § The prosecution may offer a fixed penalty instead of prosecuting in the normal way. See **C[8]**.
- ** Denotes changes to the sentencing powers of magistrates under the Criminal Justice Act 2003 earmarked to be brought into force from a date to be appointed.

C[2]

Speed and distance chart

C[2.1]

An approximate guide to the distance covered by a vehicle moving at a constant speed is that half the number of miles per hour is roughly the number of yards per second, e g 30 mph = 15 yds per second. The following table is more accurate than that and the distances are expressed in feet. But it must be borne in mind that the distance given will be covered only by a vehicle travelling at the speed given for the whole of the distance, i e at a constant speed. The table cannot therefore be used in the case of a vehicle slowing down or accelerating.

Miles per hour	*Feet per second*
20	29
30	44
40	59
50	73
60	88
70	103
80	117
90	132
100	146

C[3]

Braking distances

(Taken, with permission, from the Highway Code)

C[3.1]

The following braking table appears in the Highway Code. It must be taken as a guide only since no information is given with it as to whether a vehicle with disc or servo assisted brakes, or any particular tyres could improve upon these figures. It is submitted that the court can take judicial notice of the table and may form part of the cross-examination of a witness including the defendant. Moreover, the table, like any other part of the Highway Code, is embraced by the Road Traffic Act 1988, s 38(7) which states:

> 'A failure on the part of a person to observe a provision of the Highway Code shall not of itself render that person liable to criminal proceedings of any kind, but any such failure may in any proceedings (whether civil or criminal and including proceedings under the Traffic Acts …) be relied upon by any party to the proceedings as tending to establish or negative any liability which is in question in those proceedings.'

C[4]

Shortest stopping distances – in feet

C[4.1]

'On a dry road, a good car with good brakes and tyres and an alert driver will stop in the distances shown. Remember these are shortest stopping distances. Stopping distances increase greatly with wet and slippery roads, poor brakes and tyres and tired drivers.'

Mph	*Thinking distance*		*Braking distance*		*Overall stopping distance*	
	m	ft	m	ft	m	ft
20	6	20	6	20	12	40
30	9	30	14	45	23	75
40	12	40	24	80	36	120
50	15	50	38	125	53	175
60	18	60	55	180	73	240
70	21	70	75	245	96	315

C[5]

Endorsement and disqualification

C[5.1]

The Traffic Acts impose on the courts an obligation to endorse the licence of any person convicted of certain offences. In the case of a convicted person who does not hold a driving licence this acts as an order to endorse any licence which he may obtain during the period when the endorsement is effective. An endorsement means that particulars of the offence and sentence will be recorded in code (as to which see **C[6]**) on the defendant's licence, unless it is a foreign licence. In the case of a foreign licence, the order for endorsement should be made (subject to there being special reasons for not making it, see below) and the clerk will notify the DVLA. The court must order endorsement unless it decides after hearing sworn evidence (which may be no more than the evidence given during the trial of the offence) that there are special reasons for not doing so.

C[5.2]

Special reasons. This has become a term of art; it has a significance which is determined by law rather than by the ordinary meaning of the words. In order to avoid endorsement or compulsory disqualification the defendant must give to the court at least one specific reason why he should not be penalised by endorsement (or disqualification in cases where that is mandatory) and that reason must meet all of the following criteria:

(a) it must be a mitigating or extenuating circumstance;
(b) it must not amount to a legal defence to the charge;
(c) it must be directly connected with the circumstances in which the offence was committed, and not relate solely to the circumstances of the offender;
(d) it should be a factor which the court ought properly to take into consideration when deciding the sentence (*R v Wickins* (1958) 42 Cr App Rep 236, 122 JP 518, CCA).

C[5.3]

Case law has provided very many examples of circumstances under (c) above which may, and other circumstances which may not, be accepted as special reasons and some circumstances (eg the distance driven by the defendant) may be accepted or rejected according to the offence with which he is charged. For this reason examples are not set out here since they may confuse rather than clarify the position. Magistrates are recommended always to consult the legal adviser before reaching any final decision on this question.

C[5.4]

Disqualification. Disqualification is mandatory for certain offences. In every case where the court can order an endorsement it has the discretion also to disqualify. Thus it can be seen how important it may be for a defendant to persuade the court that there are special reasons for not endorsing, because if he is successful and the court does not order endorsement, it may not disqualify. In cases where disqualification is mandatory, eg dangerous driving and drinking and driving offences, the defendant may submit special reasons for not disqualifying while conceding the endorsement.

C[5.5]

For offences of theft of vehicles, going equipped to steal vehicles and taking vehicles without consent, the court may disqualify even though there is no power to impose penalty points. Disqualification may also be imposed for offences of assault involving a motor vehicle and, indeed, where following a motoring incident one driver follows another and assaults him the power to disqualify will arise (*R v Rajesh Patel* (1994) 16 Cr App Rep (S) 756, [1995] Crim LR 440, CA). A discretionary disqualification may not be imposed where the defendant is also liable to be disqualified under the penalty points provisions (see below).

There is a discretionary power to disqualify for any offence under PCC(S) Act 2000, s 146. See **C[5.45]**.

C[5.6]

Length of disqualification. A minimum period of disqualification must, in the absence of special reasons, be imposed in the following cases:

driving with excess alcohol/whilst	one year; three years
unfit	where second offence
refusing to supply a specimen	within ten years
dangerous driving	*one year *two years where there has been two or more bans of 56 days or more, 3 years immediately preceding the commission of the latest offence (s 34(4) RTOA 1988).

Dangerous driving also carries a mandatory disqualification until a test is passed.

C[5.7]

There is a tendency for magistrates to think of disqualification in units of say, 6, 12, 18 and 24 months. Research has shown that the longer the period of disqualification the more it is likely to be disobeyed. Moreover, the driver who is disqualified, say for two years, will probably decide within a few weeks that he will ignore the ban. There is, therefore, a strong case for short-term disqualifications especially, for example, for bad cases of careless driving and young men charged with driving licence offences (see below for disqualification under the penalty points system).

C[5.8]

Disqualification starts on the day on which the order is made and that day counts as one full day of the disqualification.

C[5.9]

Disqualification for life. Such a disqualification will be rare. Only where there are exceptional circumstances should a disqualification for life be imposed (*R v Rivano* (1993) 14 Cr App Rep (S) 578, 158 JP 288, CA), for example, where there is psychiatric evidence that the driver would indefinitely be a danger to the public if allowed to drive (*R v King* [1993] RTR 245, 13 Cr App Rep (S) 668, CA) or evidence of many previous convictions which indicated the same possibility (*R v Buckley* (1994) 15 Cr App Rep (S) 695, [1994] Crim LR 387, CA).

The penalty points system

C[5.10]–C[5.15]

Persons convicted of certain offences must be disqualified from driving, eg for driving with excess alcohol. A court has a discretion to disqualify any person who has been convicted of an endorsable offence and will do so where the particular offence with which it is dealing is serious. The person who persistently commits minor endorsable offences may therefore escape these mandatory or discretionary disqualifications but will be caught by the disqualification imposed under the penalty points system. This provides in essence that where a person accumulates 12 or more penalty points over a three-year period, he must generally be disqualified for a minimum period.

C[5.16]

Penalty points. Every endorsable offence attracts a number of penalty points varying from 2 to 11. Some offences (including careless driving, uninsured use of a vehicle and failing to stop or report after an accident) give the court a discretion to attach a number of penalty points within a range, so indicating the court's view of the relative gravity of the offence. The choice of the number of penalty points in these cases will on occasion determine whether a disqualification must be imposed. For example, Brian A Driver has already accumulated 8 penalty points and is convicted of careless driving for which anything from 3 to 9 penalty points may be awarded. If the court imposes 3 points, Driver escapes disqualification because he does not reach a total of 12; but if the court imposes more than 3 then he must be disqualified, subject to his proving mitigating circumstances amounting to exceptional hardship.

C[5.17]

When a driver is convicted of a single endorsable offence his licence will be endorsed with the number of penalty points appropriate to that offence, or with a number within the appropriate range. However, where he is convicted of a number of offences committed on the same occasion (which is not the same as saying on the same day) the number of points to be endorsed will usually be the number for the offence attracting the highest number. For example, if in addition to his careless driving conviction (3–9 penalty points) Brian A Driver is also convicted of driving whilst disqualified (6 penalty points) and driving in a play street (2 penalty points) then his endorsement will show at least 6 penalty points, that being the highest figure. If the court decides to endorse 8 penalty points for the careless driving (that being a number within the range for that offence) then the endorsement would show 8 penalty points. It is these 8 penalty points which count towards disqualification, not the total number for the three offences.

C[5.18]

Two things will be evident from this in the normal situation:

(a) although every endorsable offence has a penalty points value, the endorsement relating to that offence may show a higher number; and
(b) when a conviction relates to a number of offences committed on the same occasion the number of penalty points which count towards disqualification is the number relating to the offence with the highest number of penalty points.

C[5.19]

However, the court may if it thinks fit decide to accumulate the points for offences committed on the same occasion. If it does so it must state its reasons in open court and enter them in the register.

Note that the court should not order penalty points to be endorsed if it orders the offender to be disqualified in respect of any offence of which he has been convicted on that occasion (*Martin v DPP* [2000] RTR 188, [2000] 2 Cr App Rep (S) 18, 164 JP 405, [2000] Crim LR 320).

Penalty points to be taken into account

C[5.20]

There is a general misunderstanding as to the law and practice following the decision in *Jones v Chief Constable of West Mercia Police Authority* (2000)

165 JP 6. A totting ban is usually for not less than 6, 12 or 24 months which is substantially longer than the majority of discretionary bans. Accordingly, the starting point is to calculate the number of points to be taken into account and to determine whether the offender tots. As the court in *Jones* indicated the usual practice is to impose a totting ban without reference to the seriousness or triviality of the offence (as provided for by s 35 of the Offenders Act). Only in an exceptional case will the court first consider if it wishes to impose a discretionary disqualification bearing in mind the seriousness of the offence and previous offences. If a discretionary disqualification is imposed any existing points remain on the licence. If discretionary disqualification is not appropriate the court imposes points and goes on to consider the totting-up procedure.

Subject to there being grounds for mitigation, disqualification is incurred when the number of penalty points to be taken into account reaches or exceeds 12. The following penalty points are to be taken into account at the time of conviction:

(a) those endorsed at the time of that conviction. Where a person is made the subject of a mandatory or discretionary disqualification no penalty points for the offence for which he was disqualified will be taken into account, for the purpose of imposing an additional disqualification under the penalty points provisions;
(b) those endorsed previously in respect of any offence committed within three years of the present offence, except where a disqualification under the penalty points provisions has been ordered, in which case the court is only concerned with the penalty points incurred since that disqualification.

C[5.21]

Therefore, only a disqualification under the penalty points provisions will have the effect of 'wiping clean' any points previously incurred.

Period of disqualification

C[5.22]

Once a defendant becomes liable for disqualification under this scheme he may be disqualified for any period at the court's discretion, but this discretion is limited by the fixing of minimum periods. These minimum periods are as follows:

(a) six months if no previous disqualification is to be taken into account;
(b) one year if one previous disqualification is to be taken into account; and
(c) two years if there is more than one such disqualification.

C[5.23]

For a prior disqualification to be taken into account it must have been imposed within three years of the latest offence which has brought the offender's total of penalty points up to 12. Such disqualification may have been imposed:

(a) for an offence for which it was obligatory (eg driving with excess alcohol); or
(b) for an offence for which it was optional (eg a bad case of careless driving); or
(c) for 12 or more penalty points;

and must have been for a period of 56 days or more and was not imposed for stealing a motor vehicle, taking without consent or going equipped for theft.

Mitigating grounds

C[5.24]

When a defendant becomes liable to disqualification under this procedure he may claim that there are grounds for mitigating the normal consequences of conviction and if the court finds such grounds it may reduce the minimum period to which the offender is liable or it may decide not to disqualify. In either event it must state its reasons which will be recorded. The court's discretion, however, is limited. It may not take into account:

(a) any circumstances which are alleged to make the offence (or any of them) not a serious offence;
(b) the fact that disqualification would cause hardship (but it may take account of exceptional hardship);
(c) any circumstances which have been taken into account during the previous three years so as to avoid or reduce disqualification.

The case of *Miller v DPP* [2004] EWHC 595 (Admin), [2004] 17 LS Gaz R 30, [2004] All ER (D) 477 (Mar) suggests that where there has been excessive delay (over 2 years) in sentencing the defendant this is a proper ground for reducing the length of a disqualification under RTOA 1988, s 35(1).

C[5.25]–C[5.30]

So, for example, Mr Zimmer is liable to disqualification but successfully avoids it by pleading that being disabled a disqualification would cause exceptional hardship because his specially adapted vehicle is his only means of getting to work. If he is convicted and attracts a totting disqualification again within three years he is unable to put forward that ground for avoiding disqualification but once three years have passed, that ground is resurrected and may be used again.

C[5.31]

Under the penalty points scheme only one disqualification is imposed irrespective of the number of offences. In the event of an appeal against any one or more of the offences, the disqualification will be treated as having been imposed on each offence and in any event the Crown Court has the power to alter sentences imposed by the magistrates' court for several offences even if there is only an appeal against the sentence on one offence.

C[5.32]

Summary. Upon conviction of certain offences the court must order endorsement unless either there are special reasons (although the Road Traffic Offenders Act 1988 uses the plural it has always been treated as the singular) for not doing so, or in the case of some offences under the Road Vehicles (Construction and Use) Regulations 1986, the defendant did not know of and had no reason to suspect the condition of the vehicle. These offences are noted in the table at **C[1.6]**.

C[5.33]

No disqualification may be ordered unless it is for an endorsable offence (except for offences of theft, going equipped to steal vehicles and taking vehicles without consent). Some few offences carry a compulsory order for disqualification and this must be imposed by the court unless there are special reasons for not doing so.

C[5.34]

The term 'special reasons' has a very narrow meaning, in particular, hardship to the defendant is excluded from consideration.

C[5.35]

A period of disqualification takes effect immediately. This includes disqualification for 12 or more penalty points. Only one period of disqualification is ordered under the penalty points scheme irrespective of the number of offences. The three year period during which penalty points are to be counted runs between dates of offence, not conviction. The three year period during which, the circumstances once used as mitigating grounds for not disqualifying under the penalty points system may not be used again, is measured between dates of their original use and the present conviction.

C[5.36]

Where appeal against sentence is lodged, the court may suspend the effect of disqualification until the appeal is *heard*. This should not be done automatically but only after careful consideration.

Disqualification until passes a test

C[5.37]

The court *must* disqualify an offender until he passes an extended driving test where:

(a) he is convicted of an offence of dangerous driving; or

(b) in the Crown Court, the offences of manslaughter, causing death by dangerous driving or causing death by careless driving whilst under the influence of drink or drugs; or
(c) the court orders him to be disqualified until a test of competence is passed, having convicted him of an offence involving obligatory disqualification under s 34 or he is disqualified under s 35 of the RTOA 1988.

C[5.38]

The court has a *discretion* to disqualify until an ordinary test of competence is passed where the offender has been convicted of any offence involving obligatory endorsement. The defendant is entitled to drive but must display L plates and be supervised. In cases where the court is exercising its discretion it must have regard to the safety of road users and an order is inappropriate as a punishment, but is suitable for the following cases:

(a) for people who are growing aged or infirm, or show some incompetence in the offence which needs looking into. In addition a licence may be revoked by the Secretary of State on medical grounds and a provisional licence issued for the sole purpose of a road reassessment;
(b) where the defendant is disqualified for a long period for the offence and there is doubt about his ability to drive at the expiry of the disqualification period;
(c) where the manner of the defendant's driving suggests a threat to the safety of other road users (*R v Miller* (1993) 15 Cr App Rep (S) 505, [1994] Crim LR 231, CA). See the Road Traffic Offenders Act 1988, s 36;
(d) it is not usually appropriate in the cases of passengers in vehicles taken without the owner's consent (*R v Wiggins* [2001] RTR 37, CA).

The onus is on the defendant charged with driving whilst disqualified when not having completed a retest to show he held a provisional licence and was complying with the conditions of that licence (*DPP v Barker* (2004) 168 JP 617, [2004] All ER (D) 246 (Oct), DC).

Interim disqualification

C[5.39]

A magistrates' court may impose an interim disqualification on a person where:

(a) it commits him to the Crown Court for sentence or remits his case to another magistrates' court; or
(b) it defers or adjourns his case before passing sentence (including a transfer to another magistrates' court post conviction). An interim order of disqualification may continue until the defendant is finally dealt with

subject to a limit of six months and any subsequent order of disqualification will be reduced by the period of the interim order.

Disqualification by the Crown Court

C[5.40]–C[5.44]

Where the Crown Court either convicts or sentences a person who was convicted by a magistrates' court of an offence punishable with at least two years' imprisonment it may disqualify the defendant for an unlimited period if it is satisfied that a motor vehicle was used (whether by him or by an accomplice) to commit or to facilitate the commission of the offence.

C[5.45]

Disqualification for any offence. This is a power to disqualify a person from driving instead of or as an addition to dealing with him in any other way and it applies to any criminal offence (PCC(S)A 2000, s 146). Certain non endorsable offences recommend themselves for such a penalty including kerb crawling, unlawful tipping and driving off road unlawfully. See *R v Doick* [2004] EWCA Crim 139, [2004] 2 Cr App Rep (S) 203 for guidance when coupled with custody. The power should not be used arbitrarily but could be used where a vehicle was driven to an affray (*R v Clift* [2004] EWCA 3139 (Crim), [2005] RTR 147, [2004] All ER (D) 400 (Nov)) or when used in connection with the fraudulent evasion of duty on cigarettes (*R v Skitt* [2004] EWCA 3141 (Crim), [2004] All ER (D) 401 (Nov)).

The effect of endorsement on new drivers

C[5.46]

Drivers within the first two years of first passing a driving test are in a probationary period. If, during that period, such a driver accumulates 6 or more penalty points on his licence the DVLA will automatically revoke his driving licence when it is sent to them or they are notified by the court.

C[5.47]

This is not a disqualification but the new driver will only be entitled to hold a provisional licence until he passes a retest, which will restore his previous entitlements. Revocation will occur whether the penalty points are added following a conviction by a court or following a fixed penalty.

C[5.48]

Points accumulated before the test was taken will count, unless they were committed more than three years before the current offence (*R (on the application of Adebowale) v Secretary of State for Transport* [2004] EWHC

1741 (Admin), [2004] All ER (D) 335 (Jun)). Points accumulated after the test is passed will count if the *offence* is within two years of the date on which the test was passed. In *R v Damien Joseph Edmunds* [2000] 2 Cr App Rep (S) 62, CA the Court of Appeal reduced the points imposed from 6 to 5 to avoid the defendant from losing his full licence on the grounds that he lived in a rural area without public transport. It is submitted that the Court's basis for so doing was not what Parliament intended when introducing changes to the law on endorsement for new drivers.

C[5.49]

If in any proceedings for an offence committed in respect of a motor vehicle it appears to the court that the accused may be suffering from any relevant disability or prospective disability (within the meaning of Part III of the Road Traffic Act 1988), the court **must** notify the Secretary of State.

There must be sufficient material before the court, even if only by way of something said in mitigation, suggesting that the defendant is suffering from a relevant disability or a prospective disability, before the court can properly refer the matter to the Secretary of State. A good example is alcoholism or epilepsy (see *R v Chichester JJ, ex p Crouch* (1981) 146 JP 26). Note that the court has no discretion in the matter. It is advisable to consult the legal adviser.

C[6]

Driving licence codes

C[6.1]

Offences and the sentences imposed therefor are recorded on driving licences in code. The codes are reproduced below by permission of the Department of the Environment.

Endorsement code

C[6.2]

Causing or permitting

Offences as coded below, but with zero changed to 4, eg IN 10 becomes IN 14.

Inciting

Offences as coded below, but with zero changed to 6, eg DD 30 becomes DD 36.

Periods of time

Periods of time are signified as follows: D = days; M = months; Y = years.

Code	Accident offences
AC 10	Failing to stop after an accident.
AC 20	Failing to give particulars or to report an accident within 24 hours.
AC 30	Undefined accident offence.
	Disqualified driver
BA 10	Driving whilst disqualified by order of court.
BA 20	Driving whilst disqualified by reason of age (obsolete).
BA 30	Attempting to drive whilst disqualified by order of court.
	Careless driving
CD 10	Driving without due care and attention.

Code	Accident offences
CD 20	Driving without reasonable consideration for other road users.
CD 30	Driving without due care and attention or without reasonable consideration for other road users (primarily for use by Scottish courts).
CD 40	Causing death by careless driving when unfit through drink.
CD 50	Causing death by careless driving when unfit through drugs.
CD 60	Causing death by careless driving with alcohol level above the limit.
CD 70	Causing death by careless driving, then failing to supply specimen for analysis.
	Construction and use offences
CU 10	Using a vehicle with defective brakes.
CU 20	Causing or likely to cause danger by reason of use of unsuitable vehicle or using a vehicle with parts or accessories (excluding brakes, steering or tyres) in a dangerous condition.
CU 30	Using a vehicle with defective tyres.
CU 40	Using a vehicle with defective steering.
CU 50	Causing or likely to cause danger by reason of load or passengers.
CU 60	Undefined failure to comply with Road Vehicles (Construction and Use) Regulations 1986.
	Reckless driving
DD 30	Reckless driving (obsolete).
DD 40	Dangerous driving.
DD 60	Manslaughter or culpable homicide while driving a vehicle.
DD 70	Causing death by reckless driving (obsolete).
DD 80	Causing death by dangerous driving.
	Drink or drugs
DR 10	Driving or attempting to drive with alcohol concentration above limit.
DR 20	Driving or attempting to drive while unfit through drink.
DR 30	Driving or attempting to drive then refusing to supply a specimen for laboratory testing.

Code	Accident offences
DR 40	In charge of a vehicle with alcohol concentration above limit.
DR 50	In charge of a vehicle when unfit through drink.
DR 60	In charge of a vehicle then refusing to supply a specimen for laboratory testing.
DR 70	Failing to provide specimen for breath test (roadside).
DR 80	Driving or attempting to drive when unfit through drugs.
DR 90	In charge of a vehicle when unfit through drugs.
	Insurance offences
IN 10	Using a vehicle uninsured against third party risks.
	Licence offences
LC 10	Driving without a licence (obsolete).
LC 20	Driving otherwise than in accordance with a licence.
LC 30	Driving after making a false declaration about fitness when applying for a licence.
LC 40	Driving a vehicle having failed to notify a disability.
LC 50	Driving after a licence has been revoked or refused on medical grounds.
	Miscellaneous offences
MS 10	Leaving a vehicle in a dangerous position.
MS 20	Unlawful pillion riding.
MS 30	Playstreet offences.
MS 40	Driving with uncorrected defective eyesight or refusing to submit to a test. (Obsolete code, see now MS 70 and MS 80.)
MS 50	Motor racing on the highway.
MS 60	Offences not covered by other codes.
MS 70	Driving with uncorrected defective eyesight.
MS 80	Refusing to submit to eyesight test.
MS 90	Failure to give information as to identity of driver in certain cases.
	Motorway offences
MW 10	Contravention of Special Road Regulations (excluding speed limits). Road Traffic Regulation Act 1984
	Non-endorsable offences
NE 98	Disqualification under Powers of Criminal Courts (Sentencing) Act 2000, s 146

Code	Accident offences
NE 99	Disqualification under Criminal Justice Act 1972, s 24 and Powers of Criminal Courts (Sentencing) Act 2000, s 147 (and for offences of unauthorised taking see **A[77]**).
	Pedestrian crossings
PC 10	Undefined contravention of Zebra, Pelican and Puffin Pedestrian Crossing Regulations and General Directions 1997 (primarily for use by Scottish courts).
PC 20	Contravention of Zebra, Pelican and Puffin Pedestrian Crossing Regulations and General Directions 1997 with moving vehicle.
PC 30	Contravention of Zebra, Pelican and Puffin Pedestrian Crossing Regulations and General Directions 1997 with stationary vehicle.
	Provisional licence offences (obsolete, see now LC 20)
PL 10	Driving without 'L' plates.
PL 20	Not accompanied by a qualified person.
PL 30	Carrying a person not qualified.
PL 40	Drawing an unauthorised trailer.
PL 50	Undefined failure to comply with conditions of a provisional licence.
	Speed limits
SP 10	Exceeding goods vehicle speed limit.
SP 20	Exceeding speed limit for type of vehicle (excluding goods or passenger vehicles).
SP 30	Exceeding statutory speed limit on a public road.
SP 40	Exceeding passenger vehicle speed limit.
SP 50	Exceeding speed limit on a motorway.
SP 60	Undefined speed limit offence.
	Traffic directions and signs
TS 10	Failing to comply with traffic light signals.
TS 20	Failing to comply with double white lines.
TS 30	Failing to comply with a 'stop' sign.
TS 40	Failing to comply with directions of a constable or traffic warden.
TS 50	Failing to comply with a traffic sign (excluding 'stop' signs, traffic lights or double white lines).
TS 60	Failing to comply with a school crossing patrol sign.
TS 70	Undefined failure to comply with a traffic direction or sign.

Code	Accident offences
	Theft or unauthorised taking (obsolete (except UT 50), see now NE 99)
UT 10	Taking and driving away a vehicle without consent or an attempt thereat (primarily for use by Scottish courts).
UT 20	Stealing or attempting to steal a vehicle.
UT 30	Going equipped for stealing or taking a vehicle.
UT 40	Taking or attempting to take a vehicle without consent; driving or attempting to drive a vehicle knowing it to have been taken without consent, allowing oneself to be carried in or on a vehicle knowing it to have been taken without consent.
UT 50	Aggravated taking of a vehicle.
	Special codes
TT 99	Disqualification for accumulating 12 or more penalty points.
NSP	(No separate penalty.) Where court does not impose penalty points for minor offences committed at the same time as a more serious one.

C[7]

Sentence code

C[7.1]

The sentence is represented by four characters, eg G 02 Y (community rehabilitation order two years). The first letter indicates the nature of the sentence, the middle two numbers (0 always precedes what would otherwise be a single figure) and the final letter indicate the period of the sentence, if any, as hours (H), days (D), months (M), or years (Y). Apart from the special code TT 99 which indicates a disqualification under the penalty points procedure there is no code to represent disqualification because this appears in a special column on the licence. In the case of an absolute discharge there is no period so the code J 000 is used.

C[7.2]

The first letter of the code indicates the sentence as follows:

A imprisonment

B detention in a place approved by the Secretary of State

C suspended sentence of imprisonment

E conditional discharge

F bound over

G community rehabilitation

H supervision order (youth court)

I no separate penalty

J absolute discharge

K attendance centre

M community punishment order

P young offender institution

S compensation

T hospital or guardianship order

W care order

C[8]

Fixed penalties

C[8.1]

For some time it has been possible to avoid the expense of court proceedings for some criminal and motoring offences by the expedient of the prosecution offering the defendant a 'fixed penalty ticket'. If he accepts the offer he pays the required sum and the matter is settled, otherwise he is summoned to court and the matter proceeds in the usual way.

C[8.2]

In the interests of relieving the burden on the courts of having to deal with many minor motoring cases, the fixed penalty system (formerly almost exclusively confined to motoring offences) has been greatly extended to cover a wide range of offences. These are noted in the index at **C[1.6]** and include a number of offences which carry an endorsement.

C[8.3]

A summary of the procedure is as follows:

Offering the fixed penalty

C[8.4]

When a constable observes that a 'fixed penalty' offence has been committed, he must decide whether it is endorsable or not.

C[8.5]

Non-endorsable offences. He may give the fixed penalty ticket to the driver or affix it to the vehicle if the driver is not present. In the case of criminal offences the offender must be present and at least 18 years old.

C[8.6]

Endorsable offences. The driver must be present and the officer will require him to produce his driving licence for examination. If the driver is not liable to disqualification because he will not have accumulated 12 or more penalty points, the officer may offer him the option of a fixed penalty and invite him to surrender his licence in exchange for a receipt which he may use as evidence that he is a licence holder. It is then for the driver to decide whether to accept the offer of a fixed penalty.

C[8.7]

If the driver does not have his driving licence with him, the procedure is modified in that he may be required to produce his driving licence within seven days at a chosen police station where it will be inspected and, if appropriate, a fixed penalty offered.

C[8.8]

Note - There are no fixed penalties for endorsable offences when the driver is not present (but see 'Conditional offer of fixed penalty', below), nor where he is present but declines the offer. Also the police have a discretion whether to offer a fixed penalty so that, for example, a constable might decline to offer it for an isolated offence which is serious in nature.

Paying the fixed penalty

C[8.9]

The defendant has to pay the fixed penalty within 21 days (or such longer period as is allowed by the ticket) to the court responsible for fixed penalties.

Offences	*Fixed penalty*
A fixed penalty offence under s 143 of the RTA 1988 (no insurance)	£200
A fixed penalty offence under s 172 of the RTA 1988 (failure to supply name and address of driver)	£120
Any other fixed penalty offence involving obligatory endorsement	£60
A fixed penalty parking offence committed in Greater London on a red route)	£60
Other fixed penalty parking offence committed in Greater London	£40
A fixed penalty offence under s 47 of the RTA 1988 (no test certificate)	£60
A fixed penalty offence under s 33 of the Vehicle Excise and Registration Act 1994 (failure to display a VEL)	£60
Any other fixed penalty offence	£30

C[8.10]–C[8.15]

For the purpose of the higher parking penalties, London is regarded as the Metropolitan Police District. The licence that was surrendered to the police is sent to the fixed penalty clerk who places the endorsement on it and returns it to the defendant when the penalty has been paid.

Instituting proceedings

C[8.16]

In any case where a fixed penalty has been offered the defendant can at any time before the time for payment has expired, request a hearing before the magistrates and plead guilty or not guilty as he thinks fit.

Where the fixed penalty is not paid

C[8.17]

In the case of an endorsable offence, the defendant's licence will already be in the possession of the police who will have forwarded it to the clerk responsible for fixed penalties. If the penalty is unpaid at the end of the required period, the police will register the penalty at the court for the area in which the defendant lives and the clerk who already holds the licence will endorse it and return it to the defendant. Unfortunately for him the penalty is registered as a fine 50% above the fixed penalty. Similar provisions apply to non-endorsable offences where the ticket is given to the driver.

C[8.18]

Where the offence is non-endorsable and the ticket was affixed to the vehicle, the police send a notice to the person they believe to be the owner requesting him either to pay the penalty or to inform them who is the actual owner. If he fails to co-operate by not replying at all, he will have the enhanced penalty registered against him. He is similarly liable if he replies and admits he was the owner unless either (a) he pays the penalty, or (b) persuades the actual driver to pay it for him, or (c) he returns a form signed by the person who was actually driving and who requests a court hearing.

Enforcement of payment

C[8.19]

Once a penalty has been registered, it is regarded as a fine. Non-payment of the registered penalty will result in enforcement proceedings being taken in the manner described at **B[33.96]**.

Penalty points

C[8.20]

If the accused has committed several endorsable offences on the *same occasion*, and one is dealt with under the fixed penalty procedure and his licence is to be endorsed, the penalty points for those offences dealt with at a court hearing are to be treated as being reduced by those points to be endorsed under the fixed penalty procedure.

Conditional offer of fixed penalty

C[8.21]

The Road Traffic Act 1988, s172 provides for the police to issue a notice to the keeper of the vehicle requiring information as to the identity of the driver. If the keeper fails to give the information he will be guilty of an endorsable offence deemed to have taken place in the place to where the reply ought to have been sent (*Kennet District Council v Young* [1999] RTR 235, 163 JP 622). Any reply must be in writing and signed (*DPP v Broomfield* [2002] EWHC 1962 (Admin), [2003] RTR 108). A telephone call will not be sufficient compliance with the section but a letter accompanying the form and disclosing the required information will be (*Jones v DPP* [2004] EWHC 236 (Admin), [2004] All ER (D) 319 (Jan)) but not if it is left unsigned (*Francis v DPP* [2004] EWHC 591 (Admin), [2004] All ER (D) 443 (Mar)). In *R (on the application of Flegg) v Southampton and New Forest Justices* [2006] EWHC 396 (Admin), 170 JP 373 the defendant returned a section 172 request with a covering note stating that he could not say who the driver was. The conviction was upheld on the basis that the information given was both misleading and inaccurate. The defendant as the owner or keeper of the vehicle has a duty to name potential drivers not just actual drivers.

Where the driver is identified, a conditional offer of a fixed penalty is sent to him and if he wishes to accept the offer he will send his driving licence and payment to the fixed penalty office within 28 days of the issue of the offer. The fixed penalty will be accepted unless the details of the licence disclose that the offender is liable to be disqualified under the penalty points provisions. In this case the police will be notified and a summons issued in the normal way.

In *DPP v Holden* [2006] All ER (D) 363 (Feb), the notice sent to the defendant stated that the response to the police had to be returned within 28 days but failed to specify the period during which a speeding offence could be commenced (see s 75(7)(c) RTOA 1988). In the absence of bad faith this was not a matter which directly affected the fairness of the trial; further, the delay in instituting proceedings was not so exceptional as to warrant a stay of proceedings on the ground of delay.

C[8.22]

This procedure would not appear to breach the protection against self-incrimination contained in Art 6 of the ECHR: see *Tora Tolinos v Spain* (No 23816/94) (17 May 1995, unreported), ECtHR, *Brown v Stott* [2001] 2 All ER 97, [2001] 2 WLR 817, PC and *Hayes v DPP* [2004] EWHC 277 (Admin), [2004] All ER (D) 55 (Feb).

The prosecution should annex to s 9 statements proving service, a notice of intended prosecution and the requirement to provide details. If the defence fail to raise the issue, that the requirement was not lawfully made, before the end of the prosecution case the court should permit the prosecution to re open their case to prove the point (*Mohindra v DPP* [2004] EWHC 490 (Admin), [2004] All ER (D) 269 (Mar)).

C[9]

Brakes

Charge

C[9.1]

Using, causing or permitting to be used on a road a motor vehicle or trailer with defective brakes

Road Vehicles (Construction and Use) Regulations 1986, reg 18; Road Traffic Act 1988, s 41A(b)

Maximum penalty – For goods vehicles fine level 5. Other motor vehicles or trailers fine level 4 (for fines see para **B[33]**). For endorsement and disqualification – see below, and under 'Sentencing'.

'Goods vehicles' for this purpose includes vehicles adapted to carry more than eight passengers; as to whether this includes the driver, consult the clerk.

If the defendant can satisfy the court that he did not know and had no reasonable cause to suspect the deficiency of the brakes then disqualification and endorsement cannot be ordered. The defendant does not have to establish this point beyond reasonable doubt but merely that it is true on the balance of probabilities.

Penalty points – 3.

Fixed penalty – £60.

Legal notes and definitions

C[9.2]

Goods vehicle. Means a motor vehicle or trailer constructed or adapted for the carrying or hauling of goods or burden.

C[9.3]

The law requires that every part of every braking system and of the means of operating the braking system must be maintained in good and efficient working order and must be properly adjusted. The offence is an absolute one and the vehicle must have proper brakes at all times. If the charge is using the prosecution need not prove that the defendant knew of the defect. If the vehicle had no brakes at all then he will be charged under a different regulation.

C[9.4]

Using. This does not mean only driving along a road; mere presence on a road, even in a useless condition, may constitute using (*Pumbien v Vines* [1996] RTR 37, [1996] Crim LR 124). The term means 'to have the use of the vehicle on the road'. The test to be applied is whether or not such steps had been taken as would make it impossible for anyone to use the car. 'Use' involves an element of control, management or operation as a vehicle. Therefore, an accused who was in the driving seat of a 'vehicle' where the steering was locked, there was no ignition key, the brakes were seized on and the engine could not be started was not 'using' it when it was being towed along the road. It was an inanimate hunk of metal. It would be different if there was a possibility of control, ie its steering could be operated and its brakes were working, even if its engine were not working. In doubtful cases the legal adviser should be consulted. A person, limited company or corporate body which owns a vehicle that is being driven in the course of the owner's business is using the vehicle (*West Yorkshire Trading Standards Service v Lex Vehicle Leasing* Ltd [1996] RTR 70). Knowledge of the facts which constitute the offence is not necessary. For a recent judgment where the High Court were unable to agree on whether knowledge on the part of the employer company was required (s 5 RTRA 1984) see *Cambridgeshire County Council v Associated Lead Mills Ltd* [2005] EWHC 1627 (Admin), [2006] RTR 82.

A passenger in a car knowing the driver to be uninsured and allowing himself to be carried in it in pursuance of a joint enterprise is a person using the vehicle for insurance purposes (*Stinton v Stinton* [1995] RTR 167, [1995] 01 LS Gaz R 37, sub nom Stinton v Motor Insurers Bureau 159 JP 656, [1999] Lloyd's Rep IR 305, CA).

C[9.5]

Causing. This implies some express or positive mandate from the person causing the vehicle to be used or some authority from him and knowledge of the *fact* which constitutes the offence (but there need be no *intention* to commit an offence). Acquiescence could amount to permission (see below) but falls short of a positive mandate (*Redhead Freight Ltd v Shulman* [1989] RTR 1, [1988] Crim LR 696).

C[9.6]

Permitting. This includes express permission and also circumstances in which permission may be inferred. If the defendant is a limited company or corporate body it must be proved that some person for whose criminal act the company is responsible permitted the offence. A defendant charged with permitting must be shown to have known that the vehicle was being used or it must be shown that he shut his eyes to something that made it obvious to him that the vehicle was being used on a road (*Roper v Taylor's Central Garages Ltd* [1951] 2 TLR 284). In other road traffic offences permitting in the case of an employer may mean failing to take reasonable steps to prevent a contravention of the transport regulations (*Vehicle Inspectorate v Nuttall (t/a Redline Coaches)* [1999] 3 All ER 833, [1999] 1 WLR 629, HL).

C[9.7]

Motor vehicle. Means a mechanically propelled vehicle intended or adapted for use on roads. 'Intended' does not mean intended by the user of the vehicle either at the moment of the alleged offence or for the future nor the intention of the manufacturer or the wholesaler or the retailer. The test is whether a reasonable person looking at the vehicle would say that one of its users would be a road user. If a reasonable man applying the test would say 'Yes, this vehicle might well be used on a road' then the vehicle was intended or adapted for such use. For example a Go-Ped requires both a driving licence and insurance (*DPP v Saddington* [2001] RTR 227, sub nom Chief Constable of North Yorkshire Police v Saddington (2001) 165 JP 122, [2001] Crim LR 41). If that were the case then it is nothing to the point if the individual defendant says that he normally used the vehicle for scrambling and was only pushing it home on this occasion because there was no other means of taking it home, or something of that sort (*Chief Constable of Avon and Somerset v Fleming* [1987] 1 All ER 318, [1987] RTR 378, 84 Cr App Rep 345).

C[9.8]

For 'mechanically propelled' see the note at **C[47.9]**.

C[9.9]

A trailer. Means any vehicle being drawn by a motor vehicle.

C[9.10]–C[9.15]

A road. Means any highway (including footpaths and bridleways) and any other road to which the public has access and includes bridges but not a car park the purpose of which is to enable cars to stand and wait rather than move along it to a destination (*Cutter v Eagle Star Insurance Co Ltd* [1998] 4 All ER 417, [1998] 1 WLR 1647, HL).

Sentencing

C[9.16]

If the defendant proves that he did not know, and had no reasonable cause to suspect, that the brakes were deficient, endorsement and disqualification cannot be ordered. The defendant only has to prove that it is more probable than not that this was the case. Otherwise he can be disqualified and the licence **must** be endorsed unless there are 'special reasons'; see **C[5.2]**.

C[9.17]

It may sometimes be appropriate to grant a conditional or absolute discharge but if this course is adopted then a disqualification can still be imposed. Endorsement must still be ordered unless 'special reasons' exist.

C[9.18]

If it appears to the court that the accused suffers from some disease or physical disability likely to cause his driving to be a source of danger to the public then the court shall notify the licensing authority (see **C[5.49]**).

C[9.19]

When the vehicle concerned is a goods vehicle the fine will reflect the potential danger to the public and to the driver of the vehicle, and the gross weight and nature of the load may well be relevant.

C[9.20]

For fines see **B[33]**.

C[10]–C[15]

Dangerous condition

Charge

C[10.1]

Using, causing or permitting to be used a motor vehicle or trailer on a road when

[the condition of the motor vehicle or trailer, or of its accessories or equipment]
[the purpose for which it is used]
[the number of passengers carried by it, or the manner in which they are carried]
[the weight, position or distribution of its load, or the manner in which it is secured]

is such that the use of the motor vehicle or trailer involves a danger of injury to another person

Road Traffic Act 1988, s 40A

Maximum penalty – For goods vehicle or vehicle adapted to carry more than eight passengers fine level 5. For other vehicles or trailers fine level 4 (for fines see **B[33]**).

Licence must be endorsed unless special reasons exist. May be disqualified for any period and/or until he passes a driving test. Endorsement and disqualification cannot be ordered if defendant can satisfy the court that he did not know of, and he had no reasonable cause to suspect, the dangerous condition.

The defendant does not have to prove this beyond reasonable doubt. He need only prove that on the balance of probabilities it is true.

Penalty points – 3.

Fixed penalty – £60.

Legal notes and definitions

C[10.2]

Goods vehicle. Means a motor vehicle or trailer constructed or adapted for the carriage of goods or burden. The clerk should be consulted if there is a question whether a vehicle is a goods vehicle.

C[10.3]

Using, causing, permitting. See the notes under these headings for the offence of defective brakes at **C[9.4]–C[9.6]**.

C[10.4]

Road. Means any highway (including footpaths and bridleways) and any other road to which the public has access and includes bridges.

Motor vehicle. See **C[9.7]**.

C[10.5]

The offence is an absolute one. It is no defence that the defect was latent, and only became apparent during the journey. The section requires that the vehicle (or trailer) and all its parts and accessories are both in good repair and efficient working order.

C[10.6]

The wording of the summons or charge should specify the exact part or accessory which is said to be dangerous. The court can allow the prosecution to amend the wording to remedy such an omission and to offer the defence an adjournment if it needs further time to prepare its case.

Sentencing

C[10.7]

If the defendant can establish that he did not know and he had no reason to suspect the dangerous condition, in this case endorsement and disqualification cannot be ordered. The defendant does not have to prove this beyond reasonable doubt. He need only prove that on the balance of probabilities it is true.

C[10.8]

If it appears to the court that the accused suffers from some disease or physical disability likely to cause his driving to be a source of danger to the public then the court shall notify the licensing authority (see **C[5.49]**).

C[10.9]

For fines see **B[33]**.

C[16]

Dangerous driving

Charge

C[16.1]

Driving a mechanically propelled vehicle dangerously on a road or other public place

Road Traffic Act 1988, s 2 (as substituted by the Road Traffic Act 1991)

Maximum penalty - Fine level 5 and 6 months [**12 months] (for fines see **B[33]**). Must disqualify for at least one year unless special reasons. The disqualification may be for any period exceeding a year. If disqualified he *must* also be ordered to pass an extended driving test. Must endorse licence unless special reasons exist.

Crown Court – 2 years' imprisonment and unlimited fine.

Penalty points – 3–11.

Mode of trial

C[16.2]

Consider first the guidance notes at **I[4]**. In general, offences of dangerous driving should be tried summarily except for the presence of one or more of the aggravating factors (a)-(e), outlined under 'Sentencing' at **C[16.18]**.

Legal notes and definitions

C[16.3]

Driving. See the note under the offence of no driving licence at **C[18.8]**.

C[16.4]

Mechanically propelled vehicle. See **C[47.9]**.

C[16.5]

Dangerously. Means that the defendant's driving falls far below what would be expected of a competent and careful driver *and* it would be obvious to a competent and careful driver that driving in that way would be dangerous.

A person is also to be regarded as driving dangerously if it would be obvious to a competent and careful driver that driving the vehicle in its current state would be dangerous. The unintentional pressing of the wrong pedal is not a defence to dangerous driving (*A-G's Reference* (*No 4 of 2000*) (2001)).

C[16.6]

Aid and Abet. In *R v Webster* [2006] EWCA Crim 415, (2005) Times, 15 March, the defendant allowed a friend to drive his vehicle while drunk. It was held that whilst the condition of the driver could be relevant to the manner in which the vehicle was driven on the facts this had not been established by the Crown. In this case there was no evidence that the defendant had been given the opportunity to intervene once he became aware the defendant was driving in a dangerous manner.

C[16.7]

Dangerous refers to danger either of injury to any person or of serious damage to property.

C[16.8]

In determining what would be expected of, or obvious to, a competent and careful driver in a particular case, regard shall be had not only to the circumstances of which he could be expected to be aware but also to any circumstances shown to have been within the knowledge of the accused.

C[16.9]

In determining the state of the vehicle regard may be had to anything attached to or carried on or in it and to the manner in which it is attached or carried.

C[16.10]–C[16.14]

Road. See **C[10.4]** and **C[22.5]**.

C[16.15]

Public place. See **C[20.7]–C[20.8]**.

C[16.16]

Warning of proceedings. If the defence claim that notice should have been given within 14 days of intention to prosecute, consult the legal adviser.

Sentencing

C[16.17]

Guideline: Are magistrates' sentencing powers appropriate?

C[16.18]

See Table A at **B[4.1]** for available sentences.

C[16.19]

If the prosecution have not brought an alternative charge of careless driving and the court finds the defendant not guilty of dangerous driving but the allegations amount to an offence of careless driving or inconsiderate driving, he may be convicted of one of these offences. For the procedure see *R v Gloucester Magistrates' Court, ex p Chung* (1989) 153 JP 75.

C[16.20]

If convicted of dangerous driving the defendant's licence must be endorsed and he must be disqualified from holding a licence for at least one year (two years if the defendant has had two or more disqualifications of 56 days or more imposed three years immediately preceding the commission of the latest offence). If special reasons are found (at **C[5.2]**) he may avoid endorsement or a disqualification. If he is not disqualified the court must determine the number of penalty points to be recorded on any endorsement.

C[16.21]

In June 1984 the Lord Chief Justice expressed his concern at the leniency of sentences for reckless driving (now dangerous driving) imposed by the Crown Court. His remarks have to be treated with care by magistrates for two reasons. First, the Court of Appeal was mainly concerned, though not exclusively, with offences of causing death by reckless driving – a matter which cannot be tried by magistrates. Second, the crown court would normally be dealing with cases of reckless (dangerous) driving where magistrates had themselves decided that the offence was too serious to be tried summarily.

C[16.22]

In the light of the above it is clear that magistrates should treat offences of dangerous driving as serious.

C[16.23]

The Lord Chief Justice gave guidelines for considering the gravity of these cases (with modifications to make them appropriate for magistrates' courts). Aggravating features include:

(a) consumption of alcohol or drugs;

(b) racing at a grossly excessive speed, showing off;
(c) disregarding warnings from passengers;
(d) prolonged, persistent and deliberate course of very bad driving;
(e) previous convictions, particularly for bad driving or driving with excess alcohol.

C[16.24]

Mitigating factors include:

(a) a 'one off' piece of reckless driving, a momentary reckless error of judgment, briefly dozing at the wheel or failing to notice a pedestrian at a crossing;
(b) good driving record;
(c) good character generally;
(d) a plea of guilty would always be taken into account in favour of the defendant;
(e) sometimes the effect on the defendant, if he was genuinely remorseful or shocked.

C[16.25]–C[16.30]

Forfeiture of vehicle. See **B[34]**.

C[17]

Failing to produce driving licence, insurance certificate or test certificate

Charge

C[17.1]

1 Being the driver of a motor vehicle on a road,

OR

C[17.2]

2 Being a person whom a police constable reasonably believed to have driven a motor vehicle when an accident occurred owing to its presence on a road, or other public place.

OR

C[17.3]

3 Being a person whom a police constable reasonably believed had committed an offence in relation to the use on a road or other public place of a motor vehicle, failed on being so required by a police constable to produce (his driving licence) (the relevant certificate of insurance) (the relevant test certificate) for examination.

Road Traffic Act 1988, s 164 (driving licence); s 165 (insurance and test certificates)

Maximum penalty – Fine level 3 (for fines see **B[33]**). No power to disqualify or endorse.

Legal notes and definitions

C[17.4]

Right to demand production. Before the police officer is entitled to require the defendant to produce his driving licence or certificate of insurance the defendant must:

(a) be driving a motor vehicle on a road or other public place; or
(b) have been reasonably believed by the police to be the driver of a motor vehicle which was on a road or other public place and involved in an accident; or
(c) have been reasonably believed by the police to have committed a motor vehicle offence on a road or other public place;

in addition, where a requirement is made to produce a test certificate, the vehicle must require a test certificate.

C[17.5]

Purpose of production. In the case of a driving licence, to enable the constable to ascertain inter alia the holder's name and address; in the case of test and insurance certificates the person must give his name and address and those of the owner where required. Additionally, if a driver fails to produce his insurance/licence when required and the constable has reasonable grounds to believe that he doesn't have a licence/insurance, or he fails to stop for long enough for enquiries to be made, and the constable believes that he has no licence or insurance, the constable may seize and remove the vehicle, and may enter premises by force to do so (but not a private dwelling). The constable must first warn the driver unless it is impracticable to do so.

C[17.6]

Driver. See the notes under the heading 'driving' for the offence of driving without a licence **C[18.8]**.

C[17.7]

Person supervising a learner driver. In the circumstances (a)-(c) outlined above the supervisor may be required to produce his driving licence.

C[17.8]

Motor vehicle. See **C[9.7]**.

C[17.9]

Road. Means any highway (including footpaths and bridleways) and any other road to which the public has access and includes bridges.

Other public place. Will exclude private property but will normally include such places as car parks.

C[17.10]–C[17.15]

Constable. Includes a police constable of any rank. Traffic wardens also have power to require production of a driving licence and the giving of a name and address in certain, very limited, circumstances. Certain vehicle examiners may also require production of documents.

C[17.16]

Insurance certificate. The law requires that the insurance certificate be produced and not the policy or a premium receipt, unless the vehicle is covered by a certificate of security instead of a conventional insurance policy. Instead of an insurance policy the compulsory insurance of a motor vehicle can be covered by depositing £500,000 with the Accountant-General of the Supreme Court and a duplicate copy of this certificate will suffice instead of an insurance certificate. It will also be acceptable to produce a certificate in the prescribed form signed by the vehicle's owner (or by an agent on his behalf) stating that he has £500,000 on deposit with the Accountant-General of the Supreme Court.

C[17.17]

If the vehicle is subject to a hire-purchase agreement either party to that agreement can be the 'owner'.

C[17.18]

If the motor vehicle is owned by a local authority or a police authority then that authority may issue a 'Certificate of Ownership' in a prescribed form which makes an insurance certificate unnecessary.

Defences

C[17.19]

(a) If the defendant is unable to produce his documents at the time, he can elect to produce them at some police station of his own choosing within seven days. Although it is not compulsory, the constable will issue the defendant with a special form (HORT1) requiring him to produce the documents. A driving licence has to be produced in *person*; insurance and test certificates merely have to be *produced*.

(b) If the documents were not produced within the seven days it is a defence if they were produced (in person for a driving licence) at the specified police station as soon as was reasonably practicable.

Or

(c) It is also a defence if it was not reasonably practicable for the documents to be produced in the required manner before the day on which the proceedings for non-production were commenced by the laying of an information. A defendant may instead produce a *current* receipt for a licence surrendered for a fixed penalty.

C[17.20]

The burden of proof to establish any of these defences rests with the defendant, however he does not have to prove his point beyond reasonable doubt but only on the balance of probabilities.

Sentencing

C[17.21]

The generosity of the available defences leaves the defendant with little excuse. Failure to produce involves the police in a good deal of work, often including visiting the defendant to interview him.

C[17.22]

For fines see **B[33]**.

C[18]

Driving licence offences

Charges

C[18.1]

Driving on a road a motor vehicle otherwise than in accordance with a licence to drive a vehicle of that class

Road Traffic Act 1988, s 87

Maximum penalty – Fine level 3. May disqualify for any period and must endorse, unless special reasons exist (except where the driving of the accused was in accordance with any licence that could have been granted to him).

Penalty points – 3–6 (fixed penalty 3).

Fixed penalty – £60.

Legal notes and definitions

C[18.2]

On an appropriate application the Secretary of State may grant a provisional licence with a view to the applicant passing a test of competence to drive. A provisional licence is subject to conditions and restrictions such as to class of vehicle which may be driven, or, in the case of motor cycles, the power of the engine. Breach of any of these conditions or restrictions is an offence (Road Traffic Act 1988, s 87 and the Motor Vehicles (Driving Licences) Regulations 1987).

C[18.3]

For driving a motor car a provisional licence holder must comply with the following conditions:

(a) *Learner plates.* He must clearly display front and rear in a conspicuous position a red letter 'L' of regulation size (102mm x 89mm x 38mm) on a white background (178mm x 178mm; the corners may be rounded off).
(b) *Supervision.* He must be supervised by a qualified driver. This offence applies to three-wheeled cars.

C[18.4]

From July 1999 all driving licence applications are in the form of the new photocard type licence.

C[18.5]

Supervised. Means that the supervisor must have been in a suitable part of the vehicle for supervising. For example, if the supervisor was in a rear seat from which it was difficult to supervise, the court may decide the defendant was not supervised. If a supervised driver is convicted of an offence, eg driving without due care, the supervisor can be convicted of aiding and abetting.

C[18.6]

Qualified driver. Means that the supervisor must have held a full licence to drive the same type of vehicle for at least three years and be at least 21 years of age (exemption is provided for the military).

C[18.7]

Motor cyclists who are learners must not drive or ride a motorcycle to which a sidecar is not attached and carry a passenger. A motor cycle which has a bare chassis or framework attached to its side does not have a side car.

C[18.8]

Driving. A person steering a car whilst another person pushes the vehicle is driving. A person who walks alongside his car, pushing it and steering it with one hand is not driving it. A motor cyclist sitting on his machine and propelling it along with his feet is driving but he is not driving it if he walks beside it pushing it [but he may be "riding" the vehicle] (*Gunnell v DPP* [1993] Crim LR 619). A person sitting in the driver's seat of a car, stationary but with the engine running, was found to be driving. (*Planton v DPP* [2001] EWHC 450 (Admin), (2001) 166 JP 324). In *DPP v Alderton* [2003] EWHC 2917 (Admin), [2003] All ER (D) 360 (Nov) the defendant was driving even though the car was stationary on the verge as the wheels were spinning and he was exercising control over the vehicle by use of the handbrake. In *R (on the application of Traves) v DPP* [2005] EWHC 1482 (Admin), 169 JP 421, applying the brakes to a vehicle being towed was held to be "driving".

C[18.9]

A person pushed a motor cycle along a road, its lights were on and he had used the brakes. At some point he had turned the ignition on for long enough to warm up the exhaust pipe. When apprehended he was astride the machine and was wearing a crash helmet. It was held to be within the magistrates' discretion to find that he was driving (*McKoen v Ellis* [1987] RTR 26, 151 JP 60, [1987] Crim LR 54). A person is driving who steers and brakes a vehicle being towed by a rope or chain. The position with regard to a vehicle drawn by a rigid tow bar has not been authoritatively decided but a case decided in 1985 implies that a person in the driving seat of the towed vehicle in such a case is not driving. The nature of the force used to put or keep a vehicle in motion is irrelevant in determining whether a person is driving. The essence of driving is the use of the driver's controls in order to direct the movement, however that movement is produced (*Traves v DPP* [2005] EWHC 1482 (Admin), 169 JP 421, sub nom Traves v DPP [2005] All ER (D) 381 (Jun)). An important test in deciding whether a person is driving is whether he was in a substantial sense controlling the movement and direction of the vehicle. If he is, then the question has to be answered whether his actions fall within the ordinary meaning of the word 'driving'. It is also helpful to consider whether the defendant himself deliberately set the vehicle in motion and also the length of time that he was handling the controls. A person who knelt on the driving seat of a vehicle, released the handbrake and thereafter attempted to reapply the handbrake to stop the movement of the vehicle was held to be driving the vehicle. However a momentary seizing of the steering wheel causing the vehicle to swerve cannot properly be said to be driving (*DPP v Hastings* [1993] RTR 205, 158 JP 118). In *Cawthorn v DPP* [2000] RTR 45, sub nom Cawthorn v Newcastle upon Tyne Crown Court (1994) 164 JP 527 a man who had left his vehicle briefly to post a letter, leaving the hazard warning lights on, was held to be the driver responsible for reporting an accident when the vehicle rolled down a hill and into a wall.

C[18.10]–C[18.15]

Motor vehicle. See **C[9.7]**.

C[18.16]

A road. Is any highway (including footpaths and bridleways) and any other road to which the public has access and includes bridges. However it will not normally include a car park (*Clarke v Kato* [1998] 4 All ER 417, [1998] 1 WLR 1647, sub nom Clarke v General Accident Fire and Life Assurance Corpn plc [1999] RTR 153, 163 JP 502, HL).

C[18.17]

Burden of proof. Proof that the driver held the appropriate driving licence rests with the defendant. The prosecution does not have to prove that the defendant did not hold a licence. As with all document offences there is not statutory requirement that the prosecution issue the defendant with a production notice; it is sufficient that they show he drove the vehicle on a road (*DPP v Hay* [2005] EWHC 1395 (Admin), [2005] All ER (D) 90 (Jun)).

C[18.18]

The driver does not have to prove this beyond reasonable doubt. He need only prove that on the balance of probabilities he did hold a licence.

C[18.19]

Employers. No employer shall let an employee drive unless the employee holds the appropriate driving licence, and it is his responsibility to make the necessary check that the employee has such a licence. Thus the employer is liable for permitting unless he can prove that his employee was licensed. Being misled by the employee is probably not a defence though the court might consider it a mitigating circumstance.

C[18.20]

A partner is not the employee nor employer of another partner in the same firm.

Sentencing

C[18.21]

If it appears to the court that the accused suffers from some disease or physical disability likely to cause his driving to be a source of danger to the public, then the court shall notify the licensing authority. Even if the accused has never obtained a licence, the court may consider it appropriate to bring the disease or disability to the attention of the licensing authority in case the accused should apply for a licence at some future date (see **C[5.49]**).

C[18.22]

A defendant will generally not have a licence because he has not passed a test. Therefore, the case is serious and may attract a high fine and compulsory endorsement.

C[18.23]

For fines see **B[33]**.

Large goods vehicles

C[18.24]

It is an offence to drive a large goods vehicle (or to employ a person to do so) unless the driver holds a large goods vehicle driving licence authorising him to drive large goods vehicles of that class. The LGV licence is an additional entitlement to the ordinary licence.

C[18.25]–C[18.30]

Penalty. Same as for an ordinary licence. For definition of large goods vehicle consult the legal adviser.

C[18.31]

Under the provisions of the Road Traffic (Driver Licensing and Information Systems) Act 1989 existing Heavy Goods Vehicle Licences will be phased out. Instead a driver who passes an appropriate test of competency and who satisfies the Secretary of State that he is a fit person may be granted a 'large goods vehicle licence' which is in effect an ordinary driving licence which authorises the holder to drive vehicles of the classes formerly covered by a Heavy Goods Vehicle Licence. The penalty for driving without a licence is the same as for an ordinary licence.

C[18.32]

The new style licences were issued from 1 October 1990 for licences commencing on or after 1 January 1991 and as existing HGV licences become due for renewal.

C[19]

Driving whilst disqualified

Charge

C[19.1]

Driving a motor vehicle on a road when disqualified for holding or obtaining a driving licence

Road Traffic Act 1988, s 103

Maximum penalty – Fine level 5 and 6 months' imprisonment [**51 weeks] (for fines see **B[33]**). May disqualify for any period and/or until a driving test has been passed. Must endorse unless special reasons. Triable only by magistrates.

Penalty points – 6.

Legal notes and definitions

C[19.2]

Time limit. Subject to overall maximum of three years, proceedings may be brought within six months from when, in the prosecutor's opinion, he had sufficient evidence to warrant proceedings. A certificate signed by or on behalf of the prosecutor, as to when that date was, is conclusive evidence on that point.

C[19.3]

Driving. See the notes under the offence of driving without a licence at **C[18.8]–C[18.9]**. Once it is established that a person was driving, he may continue to be the driver of a vehicle although his conduct has changed and he no longer fulfils the test mentioned on that page.

C[19.4]

Motor vehicle. See **C[9.7]**.

C[19.5]

Road. Means any highway (including footpaths and bridleways) and any other road to which the public has access and includes bridges.

C[19.6]

Disqualified. The prosecution must prove the defendant was driving and that the record of disqualification relates to that defendant, although there are a number of ways in which this can be done (*R v Derwentside Magistrates' Court, ex p Swift* [1997] RTR 89, 160 JP 468). It is the prosecution's task to prove all the elements of the offence and it is therefore not for the court to consult its own records to show that the defendant was in fact a disqualified driver (*Kingsnorth v DPP* [2003] All ER (D) 235 (Mar)). In *R (on the application of Howe) v South Durham Justices* [2004] EWHC 362 (Admin), 168 JP 424, [2004] All ER (D) 226 (Feb) a court permitted the defendant's solicitor to be a witness summoned for the purposes of identifying the disqualified person. A defendant disqualified in his absence and subsequently arrested for driving whilst disqualified may make a statutory declaration to the effect that he did not know of the proceedings. However this will make the earlier proceedings void but not void ab initio leaving the disqualification as valid at the time he was driving (*Singh v DPP* [1999] RTR 424, 164 JP 82, [1999] Crim LR 914).

In *Pattison v DPP* [2005] EWHC 2938 (Admin), [2006] 2 All ER 317, it was held that evidence of identity could be proved by admission (formal or otherwise), fingerprints, a witness who was present in court, or a match between the personal details of the accused and a certificate of conviction. Even where the personal details were not uncommon e g the name, address and date of birth of the accused, that might be sufficient to found a prima facie case.

C[19.7]

Knowledge. It is not necessary to prove that the defendant knew he was disqualified, nor that he knew he was on a road. When disqualified until a test is passed the onus is on the defendant to show that he held a provisional licence and was complying with the conditions of that licence at the time he was driving (*DPP v Baker* (2004) 168 JP 140, [2004] All ER (D) 28 (Nov), DC).

Sentencing

C[19.8]

Guideline: Is it so serious that only custody is appropriate?

C[19.9]

See Table B at **B[4.2]** for available sentences.

C[19.10]

If it appears to the magistrates that the accused suffers from a disease or physical disability likely to cause his driving to be a source of danger to the public, they must notify the licensing authority in case the accused applies for a licence at some future date (see **C[5.49]**).

C[19.11]–C[19.15]

The gravity of this offence lies largely in the flouting of a penalty imposed by the court – often for the protection of the public. The offence often attracts a custodial sentence.

C[19.16]

Research sponsored by the Home Office in 1990 indicated that there are approximately 257,000 drivers in Britain who have been disqualified of whom 17% have been caught driving whilst disqualified and 36% of disqualified drivers who responded to a survey admitted having driven whilst disqualified.

C[19.17]

The offence does not apply to offenders who are driving under age. They are guilty of driving otherwise than in accordance with a licence, see **C[18]**.

C[20]

'Drunken' driving

Charge

C[20.1]

Driving or attempting to drive a mechanically propelled vehicle on a road (or public place) when unfit through drink or drugs

Road Traffic Act 1988, s 4(1), as amended

Maximum penalty – Fine level 5 and 6 months' imprisonment [**51 weeks] (for fines see **B[33]**). Must disqualify for at least one year unless special reasons. The disqualification may be for any period exceeding a year. He may also be ordered to pass a driving test. Must endorse licence unless special reasons exist.

Previous convictions – Where there is a previous conviction during the ten years preceding the current offence, the compulsory disqualification must be for at least three years unless special reasons exist.

A previous conviction for driving (or attempting to drive) a motor vehicle with alcohol over the prescribed limit or a previous conviction for refusing a blood etc specimen in such circumstances counts as a previous conviction for this offence.

Penalty points – 3–11.

Legal notes and definitions

C[20.2]

The charge may allege either driving or attempting to drive. It must not allege both.

C[20.3]

The court must be satisfied that the defendant drove (or attempted to drive) a mechanically propelled vehicle on a road or public place when his ability to drive properly was impaired by drink or drugs. The offence is one of strict liability and therefore the defence of insanity is not available (*DPP v H* [1997] 1 WLR 1406, [1998] RTR 200, sub nom DPP v Harper (1997) 161 JP 697).

C[20.4]

Driving. See the notes under this heading for the offence of driving without a licence at **C[18.9]**.

C[20.5]

Mechanically propelled vehicle. See **C[47.9]**.

C[20.6]

Road. Means any highway (including footpaths and bridleways) and any other road to which the public has access and includes bridges.

C[20.7]

Public place. Need not be a road. A field or enclosure at the rear of licensed premises for parking cars has been held to be a public place. In *Lewis v DPP* [2004] EWHC 3081 (Admin), [2005] All ER (D) 66 (Jan), it was decided that magistrates were entitled to infer that a public house car park was a public place and that the prosecution did not need to adduce evidence of public utilisation. See also *May v DPP* [2005] EWHC 1280 (Admin), [2005] All ER (D) 182 (Apr).

C[20.8]

Whether the scene of the charge is a road or public place is a question of fact for the court to decide (such as a car park in (*R v Spence* [1999] RTR 353, 163 JP 754, [1999] Crim LR 975, CA).

C[20.9]

Unfit. A person is taken to be unfit to drive if his ability to drive properly is for the time being impaired. It need not be proved that the defendant was *incapable* of driving.

C[20.10]

The court may take note of such evidence as, for example, where there is evidence of drink or drugs:

(a) driving erratically;
(b) colliding with a stationary object for no apparent reason;
(c) the defendant's condition – slurred speech, staggering, mental confusion. Also account may be taken of evidence of an analyst's certificate where the accused has given a sample of blood/breath/urine.

C[20.11]–C[20.15]

Even where the defendant has taken a drink subsequent to the incident the certificate may be evidence of the amount of alcohol consumed at the time of the incident unless the accused proves on the balance of probabilities that had he not consumed the subsequent drink his ability to drive would not have been impaired.

C[20.16]

A witness who is not an expert can give his impressions as to whether an accused had taken drink but he may not give evidence whether the accused was fit to drive.

C[20.17]

Drink or drugs. Drink means an alcoholic drink. Drugs can refer to medicine, ie something given to cure, alleviate or assist an ailing body, or it can be something which, when consumed, affected the control of the body. Accordingly, 'glue sniffing' would come within the ambit of this offence.

C[20.18]

Alternative verdict. If the allegation is 'driving' the court may convict on the basis of attempting to drive. Where the defendant is found not guilty of an offence under s 4(1) but the allegations amount to or include an offence under the Road Traffic Act 1988, s 4(2) (being in charge when unfit to drive through drink or drugs) the court may convict him of that offence (Road Traffic Offenders Act 1988, s 24 as substituted by the Road Traffic Act 1991, s 24).

Sentencing

C[20.19]

See Table B at **B[4.2]** for available sentences and the notes to the offence of 'Alcohol over the prescribed limit' at **C[22.2]** and **C[22.56]** for rehabilitation courses and their effect upon disqualifications.

C[21]

Drunk in charge

Charge

C[21.1]

Being in charge of a mechanically propelled vehicle on a road (or public place) when unfit through drink or drugs

Road Traffic Act 1988, s 4(2), as amended

Maximum penalty – Fine level 4 and 3 months' imprisonment [**51 weeks] (for fines see **B[33]**). May disqualify for any period and/or until a driving test has been passed. Must endorse unless there are special reasons.

Penalty points – 10.

Legal notes and definitions

C[21.2]

See the notes for the offence of 'drunken driving' at **C[20.2]**.

C[21.3]

In charge. This is a potentially wide concept. There must be proof of some connection, which can be less than attempting to drive, between the defendant and a motor vehicle on a road or public place. The owner or a person who had recently driven the vehicle would be 'in charge' unless he put the vehicle in someone else's charge or unless there was no realistic possibility of his resuming actual control, eg where he was at home in bed or a great distance from the car (*DPP v Watkins* [1989] QB 821, [1989] 1 All ER 1126 where there is further guidance in respect of defendants who are not the owner or have not recently driven the vehicle). A qualified driver supervising a provisional licence holder is 'in charge'.

C[21.4]

A person is deemed not to be in charge if he can demonstrate from the evidence that at the material time the circumstances were such that there was no likelihood of his driving the vehicle so long as he remained unfit to drive through drink or drugs but in determining whether there was such a likelihood the court may disregard any injury to him and any damage to the vehicle. A supervisor of a learner driver is in charge and may need to take over at any time (*DPP v Janman* [2004] EWHC 101 (Admin), [2004] Crim LR 478, [2004] All ER (D) 171 (Jan)).

C[21.4A]

ECHR. The House of Lords held that this was a reasonable and legitimate burden on the defendant (*Sheldrake v DPP* [2003] EWHC 273 (Admin), [2004] QB 487; revsd [2004] UKHL 43, [2004] 3 WLR 976).

Sentencing

C[21.5]

See Table B at **B[4.2]** for available sentences and the notes to the offence of 'Alcohol over the prescribed limit' at **C[22.2]**.

C[22]

Alcohol over prescribed limit offences

Charge 1

C[22.1]

Driving (or attempting to drive) a motor vehicle on a road (or public place) with alcohol above the prescribed limit

Road Traffic Act 1988, s 5(1)(a)

Maximum penalty – Fine level 5 and 6 months' imprisonment [**51 weeks] (for fines see **B[33]**). Must disqualify for at least one year unless special reasons. The disqualification may be for any period exceeding a year. The defendant may also be ordered to take a test again. Must endorse licence unless special reasons.

It is not a special reason that the defendant's driving was not impaired.

Previous convictions – Where there is a previous conviction during the ten years preceding the current offence, the compulsory disqualification must be for at least three years unless special reasons.

A previous conviction for driving (or attempting to drive) a motor vehicle when unfit through drink or a previous conviction for refusing a blood or urine specimen in such circumstances counts as a previous conviction for this offence.

Penalty points – 3–11.

Legal notes and definitions

C[22.2]

The charge may allege either driving or attempting to drive. It is important to note that it must not allege both. The prosecution need not prove that the defendant's ability to drive was impaired.

C[22.3]

Driving. See the notes under the offence of no driving licence at **C[18.2]**.

C[22.4]

Motor vehicle. See **C[9.7]**.

C[22.5]

Road. Means any highway (including footpaths and bridleways) and any other road to which the public has access and includes bridges. The information may read 'road or other public place', but if it does not the specific allegation must be proved (*Plunkett v DPP* [2004] EWHC 1937 (Admin), [2004] All ER (D) 82 (Jul)).

C[22.6]

Public place. Need not be a road. A field or enclosure at the rear of licensed premises for parking cars has been held to be a public place (see **C[20.7]**).

C[22.7]

Whether the scene of the charge is a road or public place is a question of fact for the court to decide. It is basically a question of whether at the relevant time the public enjoyed access to the place where the offence was committed.

C[22.8]

Prescribed limit. If a blood specimen was provided by the defendant the prescribed limit is 80 mg of alcohol in 100 ml of blood; if a urine specimen, 107 mg of alcohol in 100 ml of urine; if breath, 35 µg of alcohol in 100 ml of breath. Comparison of these levels is achieved by multiplying a breath/alcohol level by 2.3 and rounding up to convert to blood alcohol. The following conversion table relates blood, urine and breath levels.

C[22.9]

Blood	*Urine*	*Breath*	*Blood*	*Urine*	*Breath*
80	107	35	110	147	48
83	110	36	113	150	49
85	113	37	115	153	50
87	116	38	117	156	51
90	119	39	120	159	52
92	122	40	122	162	53
94	125	41	124	165	54
97	129	42	126	168	55
99	132	43	129	171	56
101	135	44	131	174	57
103	138	45	133	177	58

Blood	*Urine*	*Breath*	*Blood*	*Urine*	*Breath*
106	141	46	136	181	59
108	144	47	138	184	60
140	187	61	163	217	71
143	190	62	166	220	72
145	193	63	168	223	73
147	196	64	170	226	74
147	199	65	172	230	75
152	154	205	175	233	76
154	205	67	178	236	77
156	208	68	180	239	78
159	211	69	182	242	79
161	214	70	184	245	80

C[22.10]–C[22.15]

Breath tests. A constable in uniform may require a person to submit to a breath test if the constable reasonably suspects him to have alcohol in his body or to have committed a traffic offence while the vehicle was in motion. The test may also be required in these circumstances after a person has ceased to be a driver. If the test indicates the presence of alcohol the driver need not, but may be, arrested and taken to a police station where he will be required to offer a specimen of blood, urine or breath at the choice of the police. The roadside breath test may be taken by blowing into a bag or into a machine, but these devices are a preliminary test and the sample of breath used in these tests is not the one which is analysed to determine its alcohol content.

Once a negative breath test has been given, the police lose the power of arrest under the Road Traffic Act 1988, s 6, but may in appropriate circumstances arrest under s 4 of the Act (*DPP v Robertson* [2002] 15 LS Gaz R 33).

Breath is not confined to deep lung air but includes all that is exhaled (*Zofar v DPP* (2004) Times, 1 November).

C[22.16]

If the police require a breath sample for analysis it will be analysed in a machine approved by the Secretary of State such as a Lion Intoxilyzer 6000 UK. It works by, analysing the level of alcohol in the breath by the absorption of infra red radiation and giving a printed record of the result of two samples of breath given within a short time. The lower reading is the one which will be used to determine whether a prosecution will follow. Each machine works with a simulator, a device enabling the machine to check itself for accuracy. If for any reason the police decide not to use the machine they may ask for a sample of blood or urine.

C[22.17]

The form of print-out from the machine will give the subject's name and the time and date of the test. They will show the results of each of two samples given by the subject and the results of each of two checks which the machine carries out to prove its accuracy. These calibration checks must show a reading within a range of 32–38 µg; figures outside this range on either check will render the test void.

C[22.18]

The print-out will be signed by the operator and by the subject and a machine-produced copy will be handed to the driver, the other copy being retained by the police. It is unlikely that a prosecution will follow if the lowest reading is less than 40, but if it is 50 or less the driver is entitled to ask for an analysis of a sample of blood or urine. In the absence of any suggestion that the machine was not used properly and providing the calibration checks show readings within the parameters mentioned above, the print-out from the machine is evidence of the level of alcohol in the breath without further proof provided that a print-out was handed to the accused at the time it was produced, or served on him more than seven days before the hearing, either personally or by registered or recorded post.

C[22.19]

Evidence by certificate. A certificate signed by an authorised analyst stating the proportion of alcohol in the specimen is admissible without the analyst being called as a witness: the same applies to a certificate signed by a doctor who took a blood specimen from the defendant.

C[22.20]

The defendant is entitled to insist on the attendance at court of the analyst or doctor. As the police were bound to provide the defendant with specimens of blood or urine taken at the same time, it is possible that sometimes a defendant may call his own analyst to give evidence as to the proportion of alcohol.

C[22.21]

If difficulty arises about the provision of a specimen to a defendant, or about the admissibility of a certificate, the legal adviser should be consulted. The police are entitled to divide the specimen into three parts and not two.

C[22.22]

The High Court has quashed a conviction because a pathologist declared the blood specimen handed to the defendant to be inadequate for examination.

C[22.23]

The defendant is entitled to be acquitted if he can raise a reasonable doubt about the accuracy of the machine. However the prosecution do not have to prove a specific alcohol content, but that the alcohol content exceeded the prescribed limit so that where an accused called expert evidence to show that the variation in readings on the breath machine was unacceptable but where it was conceded that the readings must have been 5 microgrammes above the limit, he was convicted. In some circumstances it may not be necessary for the defendant to call expert evidence in order to rebut the presumption that the machine is reliable (*DPP v Spurrier* [2000] RTR 60, sub nom R v Crown Prosecution Service, ex p Spurrier 164 JP 369), but such evidence should relate to a particular fault relevant to the issues in the case (*DPP v Teixeira* (2002) 166 JP 1). For further case law on the statutory presumption and reliability of breath testing equipment see *DPP v Memory* (2003) 167 JP 238; *Skinner v DPP* [2004] EWHC 2914 (Admin).

C[22.24]

Special reasons. It is not a defence to the charge that unknown to him the defendant's drink had been laced. If this is put forward as a reason for not disqualifying the question must be answered whether the extra drink by itself is what took the level of alcohol in the blood over the limit and the defendant, if there is any doubt, should be invited to call expert evidence. Note that even if special reasons are proved this only gives the justices a discretion not to disqualify. They may still do so depending on the circumstances of the case (*R v Crown Court at St Albans, ex p O'Donovan* [2000] 1 Cr App Rep (S) 344).

A motorist drove 350 metres to his home address fearing the loss of valuable work tools in his van. Held, not special reasons: *DPP v Oram* [2005] EWHC 964 (Admin), [2005] All ER (D) 57 (May).

C[22.25]–C[22.30]

Driving in an emergency may amount to a special reason not to disqualify, but only where a sober, reasonable and responsible friend of the defendant present at the time, but unable to drive, would have advised the defendant to drive (*DPP v Bristow* [1998] RTR 100, 161 JP 35). Shortness of distance driven may be a special reason but not where the defendant's intention was to drive a longer distance than he in fact managed (*DPP v Humphries* [2000] RTR 52, sub nom Crown Prosecution Service v Humphries [2000] 2 Cr App Rep (S) 1, 164 JP 502). No specific reasons could be argued by a defendant who assumed without enquiry that a drink he consumed contained no alcohol (*Lloyd Robinson v DPP* [2003] EWHC 2718 (Admin), (2004) 168 JP 522, [2004] Crim LR 670, [2003] All ER (D) 05 (Nov)); nor where the defendant drove to the scene of an accident involving his son, having failed to wake his wife who could have legally driven (*Khan v DPP* [2004] EWHC 2505 (Admin), sub nom Khan v DPP [2004] All ER (D) 134 (Oct)).

C[22.31]

Drinking after driving. If the accused claims that the alcohol level was increased because he had taken drink after ceasing to drive then he must prove on the balance of probabilities that the post-driving drink took him over the limit and that he was not over the limit while he was driving. This is because the law requires the court to assume that the alcohol level at the time of the driving was not less than that at the time of the test (*Griffiths v DPP* [2002] EWHC 792 (Admin), 166 JP 629, [2002] All ER (D) 132 (Apr)). If an accused wishes to raise this defence he will almost certainly have to call medical or scientific evidence.

C[22.32]

Alternative verdict. If the allegation is 'driving' the court may convict him on the basis of attempting to drive. Where the defendant is found not guilty of an offence under the Road Traffic Act 1988, s 5(1) (a) but the allegations amount to or include an offence under s 5(1) (b) (being in charge of a vehicle with excess alcohol in breath, blood or urine) the court may convict him of that offence (RTOA 1988, s 24).

Sentencing

C[22.33]

Structure of the sentencing decision. See **B[3.7]**.

C[22.34]

Available sentences. See Table B at **B[4.2]**.

C[22.35]–C[22.40]

Custodial sentence. See **B[2]**.

C[22.41]

Community sentence. See **B[3]**.

C[22.42]

Fine. See **B[33]**.

C[22.43]

Forfeiture of vehicle. See **B[34]**.

C[22.44]

Disqualification. See **C[5]**.

C[22.45]

High risk offenders. Drivers who are convicted of the following offences are regarded as high risk offenders (for endorsement codes see **C[6]**):

(a) one disqualification for drinking and driving with alcohol two and a half or more times the legal limit (DR 10 and DR 50);
(b) two disqualifications for drinking and driving within 10 years (DR 10, DR 20, DR 40 and DR 50);
(c) one disqualification for refusal to provide a specimen for analysis (DR 30 and DR 60).

C[22.46]

The DVLA will write to a high risk offender and explain that the disqualification is considered to be an indication of a drink problem. Shortly before the expiry of the disqualification, a further letter will be sent explaining what must be done to apply for the return of the licence. The applicant will have to submit to a medical examination and pay an administration fee and medical fees to the examining doctor.

C[22.47]

If it appears to the court that the accused suffers from a disease or physical disability likely to cause his driving to be a source of danger to the public, it must notify the licensing authority (see **C[5.49]**).

C[22.48]

The fact that the amount of alcohol is only slightly over the statutory limit is **not** a special reason for avoiding imposing disqualification and endorsement.

C[22.49]

The 12 months' mandatory disqualification is to be regarded as a minimum and not as a tariff and should be increased in appropriate cases. The national sentencing guidelines suggest an increased disqualification for cases between 56mg and 70mg.

C[22.50]–C[22.55]

If the defendant submits as a special reason for not disqualifying him that he was obliged to drive by some sudden crisis or emergency he must show that he acted responsibly and that the crisis or emergency was not one which arose through his own irresponsibility or lack of reasonable foresight. The driving must have been only to the extent occasioned by the emergency.

C[22.56]

Reduced disqualification for attendance on course (Road Traffic Offenders Act 1988, s 34A). The court may reduce the period of disqualification where a person completes an approved course by a date specified in the order.

C[22.57]

This power applies where there is a conviction for driving (or being in charge) under the influence of drink or drugs; driving etc with excess alcohol (**C[22]**and **C[20]**); or failing to provide a specimen (**C[23]**).

C[22.58]

The court must have made an order for disqualification for not less than 12 months.

C[22.59]

The reduction specified must be not less than three months and not more than one quarter of the original period (ie 9 months' disqualification must remain where the original unreduced period was 12 months). The reduction should be announced in open court.

[22.60]

Criteria. The court should decide whether or not to offer the offender an opportunity to participate. It must then check that:

(a) a place on the course is available;
(b) the offender is aged 17 years or more;
(c) the court has explained the effect of the order in ordinary language, the amount of fees payable and that they must be paid before beginning the course;
(d) the offender consents.

The course must be completed at least two months before the end of the reduced period of disqualification. The scheme is voluntary after referral. There is no additional penalty if the offender fails to attend the course but the full period of disqualification applies.

C[22.61]

On completion, the organiser of the course will give the offender a certificate for presentation to the court.

Charge 2

C[22.62]

Being in charge of a motor vehicle on a road (or public place) having consumed alcohol over the prescribed limit

Road Traffic Act 1988, s 5(1)(b)

Maximum penalty – Fine on level 4 and 3 months' imprisonment [**51 weeks] (for fines see **B[33]**). May disqualify for any period and/or until a driving test has been passed. Must endorse unless there are special reasons.

Penalty points – 10.

Legal notes and definitions

C[22.63]

In charge. See notes at **C[21.3]**.

C[22.64]

ECHR. The defendant is entitled to be acquitted if he can establish from the evidence that there was no likelihood of his driving whilst he probably had an excessive proportion of alcohol in his blood. He only has to prove this on the balance of probabilities and the House of Lords held that the burden on the defendant was both reasonable and legitimate (*Sheldrake v DPP* [2003] EWHC 273 (Admin), [2004] QB 487; revsd [2004] UKHL 43, [2004] 3 WLR 976). Note that a passenger supervising a learner driver who has been drinking may be in charge for the purposes of this section (*DPP v Janman* [2004] EWHC 101 (Admin), [2004] All ER (D) 171 (Jan)).

See also the legal and sentencing notes for the previous offence, at **C[21.2]**.

Sentencing

C[22.65]–C[22.71]

See Table B at **B[4.2]** for available sentences and the notes for the previous offence. See *R v Shoult* [1996] RTR 298, [1996] 2 Cr App Rep (S) 234, CA on the use of imprisonment.

C[23]

Refusing specimen of blood, urine or breath

Charge

C[23.1]

Failing, without reasonable excuse, to provide a specimen of blood, urine or breath for analysis

Road Traffic Act 1988, s 7 (6) and s 7A

Maximum penalty – This varies according to whether it is alleged the defendant was driving or in charge. Accordingly the summons should make clear which of the alternative offences at **C[21]** and **C[22]**, is alleged.

(a) If the defendant drove or attempted to drive a motor vehicle on a road or public place fine on level 5 and 6 months' imprisonment. Must disqualify for at least one year (the guideline penalty is **two years**) unless special reasons. The disqualification may be for any period exceeding a year. The defendant may also be ordered to take a test again. Must endorse licence unless special reasons.

For a subsequent offence committed within ten years of a previous conviction must disqualify for at least three years and must endorse unless special reasons. The minimum ban is two years if the defendant has been disqualified for more than 56 days on at least two occasions, three years immediately preceding the commission of the current offence (s 34(4) RTOA 1988).

A previous conviction for driving (or attempting to drive) a motor vehicle when unfit through drink (see **C[20]**) or a previous conviction for driving (or attempting to drive) with alcohol over prescribed limit (see **C[21]**) count as a previous conviction for this offence.

Penalty points - 3–11.

(b) If the defendant was in charge of a motor vehicle on a road or a public place fine level 4 and 3 months' imprisonment (**51 weeks). May disqualify for any period and/or until a driving test has been passed. Must endorse unless there are special reasons.

Penalty points – 10.

Legal notes and definitions

C[23.2]

A constable, in the course of an investigation into whether a person has committed an offence under the Road Traffic Act 1988, s 3A (causing death by careless driving where under the influence of drink or drugs) the Road Traffic Act 1988, s 4 or s 5, may require him to provide two specimens of breath or a specimen of blood or urine for analysis.

C[23.3]

If the case concerns a refusal to provide a blood specimen, an offence is committed if the defendant would only allow blood to be taken from an inappropriate part of the body (toe, penis, etc). In one case a woman refused to provide a blood or urine specimen and claimed embarrassment, there being no doctor or policewoman present. The High Court ruled this amounted to refusal. An agreement to provide a specimen which is conditional will generally be treated as a refusal. In the case of a sample of breath being required for analysis it must be provided in such a way as to make that analysis possible, that is, the required quantity at the required pressure. If a driver has a phobia/medical condition he must inform the police officer so that the police officer can require an alternative specimen (*Martiner v DPP* [2004] EWHC 2484 (Admin), [2004] All ER (D) 122 (Oct)).

C[23.4]

Reasonable excuse. The Court of Appeal has said: 'In our judgment no excuse can be adjudged a reasonable one unless the person from whom the specimen is required is physically or mentally unable to provide it, or the provision of the specimen would entail a substantial risk to health.' The fact that a driver has not consumed alcohol at all, or that he has consumed alcohol since being involved in an accident, does not amount to a reasonable excuse for not providing a specimen. Nor can he demand to see a law book before complying (*DPP v Noe* [2000] RTR 351, [2000] 20 LS Gaz R 43), or refuse to take a test until legal advice has been received (*Kirkup v DPP* [2003] EWHC 2354 (Admin), [2003] All ER (D) 53 (Oct)).

Defendant must have been warned of consequences of refusing a specimen

C[23.5]

The Act expressly directs a policeman requesting a specimen to warn the defendant that a failure to provide such a specimen may make the defendant liable to prosecution. If this warning has not been given, the magistrates can dismiss the charge. If the driver is incapable of understanding the warning (for example, because he does not understand English sufficiently) he may not be convicted if he refuses to provide a sample. Separate procedures apply under s 7A where the defendant is unable to give consent due to a medical condition following an accident. In such circumstances the police surgeon may take a sample of blood. The defendant must be told that the sample has been taken when he is conscious and his permission for a lab test has been obtained. Failure to give consent is an offence with the same penalties as failure to supply a sample.

C[23.6]

There are three possible ways of providing a specimen: breath, blood or urine. The current law places the choice entirely in the hands of the police who will use the breath-analysis machine, only offering the defendant blood or urine if the machine is broken or unavailable, or where there are medical reasons for not requiring a sample of breath. Where the police require a specimen of blood for analysis they are not required to offer the motorist a preference but must ask whether there are any reasons why a specimen cannot or should not be taken by a medical practitioner (*DPP v Warren* [1993] AC 319, [1992] 4 All ER 865, HL). The officer must act reasonably in his choice and not ignore for example a defendant's assertions that he could not give blood due to religious reasons (*Joseph v DPP* [2003] EWHC 3078 (Admin), [2003] All ER (D) 326 (Nov)).

Sentencing

C[23.7]

Where either the defendant was driving or attempting to drive or where he was in charge see Table B at **B[4.2]** and see the notes to the offence of 'Alcohol over the prescribed limit' at **C[22]**.

C[23.8]

See **C[22.56]** for rehabilitation courses and the effect on disqualification.

C[24]

Refusing to take breathalyser test

Charge

C[24.1]

Failing, without reasonable excuse, to provide a specimen of breath for a breath test when required to do so by a policeman in uniform

Road Traffic Act 1988, s 6(4)

Maximum penalty – Fine of level 3. Must endorse unless special reasons. Disqualification discretionary.

Penalty points – 4.

Legal notes and definitions

C[24.2]

The policeman must have been in uniform at the time he requested the defendant to take a breath test and used a Home Office approved breathalyser.

C[24.3]

A defendant can only be required to take this test by a constable in uniform who has reasonable cause for suspecting:

(a) the defendant *is* driving or attempting to drive a motor vehicle on a road or other public place and has alcohol in his body or has committed a traffic offence whilst the vehicle was in motion; or
(b) he *has been* driving or attempting to drive on a road or other public place with alcohol in his body and he still has alcohol in his body; or
(c) he *has been* driving or attempting to drive a motor vehicle on a road or other public place and has committed a traffic offence whilst the vehicle was in motion.

For these purposes 'driving' includes being 'in charge'.

C[24.4]

In addition, where there has been an accident, a constable (whether in uniform or not) may require any person who he has reasonable cause to believe was driving or attempting to drive or in charge of the vehicle at the time of the accident to provide a breath test.

C[24.5]

The instructions on the breath test device need not be strictly observed. If the constable had no reason to suspect that the motorist had drunk alcohol in the previous 20 minutes he can be required to take the test immediately.

C[24.6]

Motorist in hospital. If a motorist is in a hospital as a patient, he can still be required to take a breath test, provided that the doctor in immediate charge of him is notified and does not object.

C[24.7]

Reasonable excuse. If the defendant satisfies the magistrates that he had a reasonable excuse for failing to take a breath test he is entitled to be acquitted. Such a defendant will probably be rare. One example may be that the defendant was hurrying to get a doctor to deal with an emergency. The degree of proof required of the defendant is to prove that this point is probably true. He does not have to establish it beyond reasonable doubt.

C[24.8]

The legal adviser should be consulted if the defence raise this point.

Sentencing

C[24.9]

Since 'reasonable excuse' is a defence (see above) conviction implies that the defendant had no excuse and therefore this is not a trivial offence and carries an endorsement.

C[25]–C[30]

Due care

Charge

C[25.1]

Driving a mechanically propelled vehicle on a road or other public place without due care and attention

Road Traffic Act 1988, s 3, as amended

Maximum penalty – Fine level 4 [level 5 under the Road Safety Act 2006] (for fines see **B[33]**). May disqualify for any period and/or until a driving test has been passed. Must endorse unless special reasons.

Penalty points – 3–9.

Legal notes and definitions

C[25.2]

Mechanically propelled vehicle. See **C[47.9]**.

C[25.3]

Road. See **C[22.5]**.

C[25.4]

Public place. See **C[20.7]–C[20.8]**. The car park of a dealership has been found to be a public place (*May v DPP* [2005] EWHC 1280 (Admin), [2005] All ER (D) 182 (Apr)).

C[25.5]

Due care and attention. The standard of driving expected by the law is that of the degree of care and attention to be exercised by a reasonable and prudent driver in the circumstances. The standard of careful driving expected in law from a motorist is the same for all, even the holder of a provisional licence.

C[25.6]

A skid may or may not be due to lack of care, but being overcome by sleep is not a defence.

C[25.7]

Where a motorist is confronted by an emergency during the course of driving, he should be judged by the test of whether it was reasonable for him to have acted as he did and not according to the standard of perfection yielded by hindsight.

C[25.8]

If the driving complained of was due to a mechanical defect in the vehicle, that is a defence unless the defendant knew of the defect, or he could have discovered it by exercising prudence; but the burden of proof remains on the prosecution to establish beyond reasonable doubt a lack of due care and attention.

C[25.9]

Observance or non-observance of the Highway Code can be used to establish or disprove guilt. General impressions formed by a witness as to the speed of a vehicle may be admitted (*Blake v DPP* [2002] EWHC 2014 (Admin), [2002] All ER (D) 125 (Sep)).

C[25.10]

Warning of proceedings. If the defence claim that notice should have been given within 14 days of intention to prosecute, consult the clerk.

Evidence will not be excluded because of the failure of a police officer to issue a caution before asking a driver if he was driving a particular vehicle involved in an accident (*Kemsley v DPP* [2005] 169 JP 148).

C[25.11]–C[25.15]

Death. As a matter of practice justices should not proceed with a summary trial until the inquest has been held (*Smith v DPP* [2000] RTR 36, 164 JP 96).

C[25.16]

Careless or inconsiderate driving (Road Traffic Act 1988, s 3) and dangerous driving (s 2). Where the magistrates see fit, they may allow information for an offence under s 3 and s 2 to be heard together. In this event, if the defendant is convicted of one offence, the second information may be adjourned *sine die* or the justices may make "*no adjudication*". Should the driver successfully appeal against conviction, he can later be tried on the second information.

C[25.17]

Alternatively, where there is a single information alleging dangerous driving and the magistrates do not find this proved, they may convict of careless driving in the alternative (s 24 RTOA 1988).

C[25.18]

Emergency vehicles. The same standard of care and attention is required of the drivers of fire engines, ambulances, coastguard and police vehicles as of any other driver. That standard is that the driver takes 'due' care and pays 'due' attention.

C[25.19]

Driving. See the note under the offence of no driving licence at **C[18.2]**.

Sentencing

C[25.20]

Endorsement must be ordered unless special reasons exist.

C[25.21]

If it appears to the court that the offender suffers from a disease or physical disability likely to cause his driving to be a source of danger to the public, then the court shall notify the licensing authority who may take steps to withdraw the driving licence (see **C[5.49]**).

C[25.22]

The unforeseen and unexpected results following an accident are not generally relevant to the penalty. The primary consideration is the quality of the driving, the extent to which the motorist on the particular occasion fell below the standard of the reasonably competent driver, in other words, the degree of carelessness and culpability. The death of a victim is something however that the court is entitled to take into account in its sentence (*R v Simmonds* [1999] RTR 257, [1999] 2 Cr App Rep 18, CA) and is part of the sentencing considerations of the court as it weighs culpability against the harm caused. Where death results from careless driving and the driver was unfit through drink or drugs or had consumed alcohol in excess of the prescribed limit, he may commit an offence under the Road Traffic Act 1988, s 3A which is triable only at the Crown Court, and is punishable with up to 14 years' imprisonment and an unlimited fine.

C[25.23]

However, the unforeseen consequences might be relevant to culpability, eg that the defendant had not seen the pedestrian until it was too late; it was clearly not a case of momentary inattention as the defendant was not keeping a proper lookout throughout the sequence of the traffic lights.

C[25.24]

Disqualification is optional but should be seriously considered for a second offence. The court may disqualify until a test is passed; a useful provision for the very elderly driver.

C[31]

Failing to stop and give details after accident

Charge

C[31.1]

As a driver of a mechanically propelled vehicle, owing to the presence of which on a road or other public place, an accident occurred whereby injury was caused to another person (or damage caused to another vehicle or to roadside property or injury to an animal)

[failed to stop]

[upon being reasonably required to give his name and address, the name and address of the owner of the vehicle and the number of the vehicle, failing to do so]

Road Traffic Act 1988, s 170 (4), as amended

Maximum penalty – Fine level 5 and 6 months' imprisonment [**51 weeks]. May disqualify for any period and/or until a driving test has been passed. Must endorse unless there are special reasons.

Penalty points – 5–10.

Legal notes and definitions

C[31.2]

Charge. The one charge may include both factual situations without offending the rule against duplicity (*DPP v Bennett* [1993] RTR 175, 157 JP 493).

C[31.3]

Relationship between the offences of failing to stop and give details and failing to report an accident. Where an accident has occurred in the circumstances described above, there is an obligation on the driver to stop at the scene of the accident. If he does not do so immediately and as soon as he could safely and conveniently, he commits the offence described here (*Hallinan v DPP* [1998] Crim LR 754). Having stopped at the scene of the accident, he has a duty to give his name and address, the name and address of the owner of the vehicle and the identification marks of the vehicle to any person having reasonable grounds for such a request. If he fails to do so, he has also committed the offence described here. Unless he has actually given his particulars to such other person, he must report the accident at a police station or to a police constable *as soon as reasonably practicable*, and in any case within 24 hours of the accident, otherwise he commits the offence at **C[32.18]**.

C[31.4]

Mechanically propelled vehicle. See **C[47.9]**.

C[31.5]

A road or other public place. See **C[22.5]**.

C[31.6]

An animal. Means any horse, cattle, ass, mule, sheep, pig, goat or dog.

C[31.7]

Roadside property. Means any property constructed on, fixed to, growing in or otherwise forming part of the land on which the road in question is situated, or land adjacent thereto.

C[31.8]

The law requires the driver to give the appropriate particulars upon being reasonably required to do so. It is acceptable to give a business address or a lawyer's office where one can be contacted *(DPP v McCarthy* [1999] RTR 323, 163 JP 585). It is not sufficient to report the incident to the police within 24 hours. Where the defendant was the driver of the vehicle involved in the accident, there is a rebuttable presumption that the defendant knew that he had been involved in the accident. If the defendant can satisfy the court that he was unaware of any accident he must be acquitted (*Selby v Chief Constable of Avon and Somerset* [1988] RTR 216).

C[31.9]

The degree of proof required of the defendant is to satisfy the court that this was probably true; he does not have to prove this beyond reasonable doubt.

C[31.10]–C[31.15]

Driver. The notes under the heading 'driving' for the offence of driving without a licence at **C[18.2]** may be of assistance. A person may continue to be the driver of a motor vehicle if having fulfilled the requirements mentioned on that page he ceases to do so by reason of a change of activity.

C[31.16]

Accidents involving personal injury (to a person other than the driver). The driver must at the time produce his certificate of insurance to a constable or other person having reasonable cause to require it. If he does not do so, he must report the accident as described above and produce his insurance certificate. Otherwise he commits an offence under the Road Traffic Act 1988, s 170(7) – maximum penalty a fine of up to level 3. There is a defence if the certificate is produced within seven days of the accident at a police station specified by him at the time when the accident was reported. This provision does not apply to the driver of an invalid carriage.

Sentencing

C[31.17]

If it appears to the court that the accused suffers from a disease or physical disability likely to cause his driving to be a source of danger to the public, then the court shall notify the licensing authority who may take steps to withdraw the driving licence (see **C[5.49]**).

C[31.18]

The gravity of this offence is lessened if the defendant subsequently reports the accident.

C[31.19]

The number of penalty points must be fixed to reflect the gravity of the circumstances of the offence.

C[31.20]

For fines see **B[33]**.

C[32]

Failing to report after accident

Charge

C[32.1]

As a driver of a mechanically propelled vehicle, owing to the presence of which on a road or other public place an accident occurred whereby injury was caused to another person (or damage caused to another vehicle or to roadside property or to an animal), not giving his name and address to any person having reasonable grounds for requiring this information, failing to report to the police as soon as reasonably practicable and in any case within 24 hours

Road Traffic Act 1988, s 170(4), as amended

Maximum penalty – Fine level 5 and 6 months' imprisonment [**51 weeks]. May disqualify for any period and/or until a driving test has been passed. Must endorse unless there are special reasons.

Penalty points – 5–10.

Legal notes and definitions

C[32.2]

Relationship between the offences of failing to stop and give details and failing to report an accident. See **C[31]**.

C[32.3]

Mechanically propelled vehicle. See **C[47.9]**.

C[32.4]

A road or other public place. See **C[22.5]**.

C[32.5]

An animal. Means any horse, cattle, ass, mule, sheep, pig, goat or dog.

C[32.6]

Report. Means approaching the police oneself as soon as reasonably practicable, even if no one else was present at the scene of the accident and therefore there was nobody present to ask for the driver's particulars.

C[32.7]

If the defendant were approached by a police officer within 24 hours of the accident, that would not constitute reporting the accident.

C[32.8]

If the defendant can satisfy the court that he was unaware that an accident had occurred, he must be acquitted of this charge.

C[32.9]

The degree of proof is to satisfy the court that this was probably true. The defendant need not prove this beyond reasonable doubt.

C[32.10]–C[32.15]

If the defendant gave his name and address to the other party he need not report the accident to the police.

C[32.16]

Roadside property. Means any property constructed on, fixed to, growing in or otherwise forming part of the land on which the road in question is situated or land adjacent thereto.

C[32.17]

Driver. See note under the offence of no driving licence at **C[18.8]**. A person does not necessarily cease to be a driver if having met the requirements mentioned on that page, he ceased to do so by reason of a change of activity.

C[32.18]

Reasonably practicable. A driver is not saved from conviction because he reported the accident within 24 hours if he could reasonably have reported it sooner. If, for example, he continued his journey after the accident and drove past a police station he would need a very strong reason for not reporting at that station. It appears that he is not obliged to go in search of a public telephone in order to telephone the police. It is for the court to decide what is 'reasonably practicable' in the particular circumstances of each case and the test is not 'Is it reasonable for the defendant to have reported the accident earlier?' but 'Did he report it as soon as practicable?'

In *DPP v Hay* [2005] EWHC 1395 (Admin), (2005) Times, 13 July, it was decided that, after discharging himself from hospital, a driver was still under an obligation to report an accident despite the fact that the police had seen the motorist at the hospital and despite the fact that the police did not issue the driver with an HORT 1 notice to produce the relevant documents such as insurance within 7 days.

Sentencing

C[32.19]

See sentencing notes to previous offence at **C[31.7]**.

C[33]

No insurance (using, causing, or permitting)

Charge

C[33.1]

Using (or causing or permitting to be used) a motor vehicle on a road or other public place when there is not in force a policy of insurance or security against third party risks

Road Traffic Act 1988, s 143

Maximum penalty – Fine level 5. May disqualify for any period and/or until defendant has passed a driving test. Must endorse unless special reasons.

Penalty points – 6–8.

Fixed penalty – £200/6 points

Legal notes and definitions

C[33.2]

Motor vehicle. See **C[9.7]**.

Other public place. Not private property but can include such places as car parks.

C[33.3]

A road. Means any highway (including footpaths and bridleways) and any other road to which the public has access and includes bridges.

C[33.4]

Security in respect of third party risks. The requirement to have insurance or a security does not apply to a vehicle owned by a person who has deposited with the Accountant General of the Supreme Court the sum of £500,000, at a time when the vehicle is being driven under the owner's control. Nor does it apply to vehicles owned by bodies such as local authorities or the police.

Certain other undertakings may have instead of insurance a security given by an insurer that the undertaking will meet any liability it may incur.

C[33.5]

Time limit. Subject to an overall maximum of three years, proceedings may be brought within 6 months from when, in the prosecutor's opinion, he had sufficient evidence to warrant proceedings. A certificate signed by or on behalf of the prosecutor as to when that date was constitutes conclusive evidence on that point.

C[33.6]

Burden of proof. If the prosecution prove that the defendant used a motor vehicle on a road or other public place, the burden of proof shifts to the defendant to establish that he was insured. The defendant does not have to prove beyond reasonable doubt; he need only prove that he was probably insured.

C[33.7]

Insurance certificate. This is in law the main item of proof of insurance and until it has been delivered to the insured he is held not to be insured. Mere proof that he has paid the premium or holds an actual policy is not sufficient.

C[33.8]

Using on a road or other public place. This expression does not in law only mean driving the vehicle along the road; its mere presence on a road, jacked up and without a battery, may constitute using on a road (*Pumbien v Vines* [1996] RTR 37, [1996] Crim LR 124). A vehicle which is being towed is being used. In any given case where doubt exists consult the legal adviser. See also at **C[9]** (Brakes).

C[33.9]

A person, limited company or body corporate which owns a vehicle that is being driven in the course of the owner's business is using the vehicle.

C[33.10]–C[33.15]

Causing involves an express or positive mandate from the defendant to the driver.

C[33.16]

Permitting. Permission must be given by someone able to permit or withhold permissions but may be express or inferred. See further the note under this heading at **C[9.6]** in the section on Brakes.

C[33.17]

Defence open to employed drivers. An employed driver cannot be convicted if he can prove that:

(a) the vehicle did not belong to him; and
(b) it was not in his possession under a hiring contract or on loan to him; and
(c) he was using it in the course of his employment; and
(d) he did not know and had no reason to believe he was not insured. The degree of proof required from the defendant is to prove that this defence is probably true; he does not have to prove beyond reasonable doubt.

C[33.18]

The Motor Insurers' Bureau is a company funded by insurers transacting compulsory motor insurance. Under an agreement with the Secretary of State for Transport the Bureau, subject to certain limitations and exceptions, will compensate the victims of uninsured motorists. A brief outline of the scheme is given here (for the full details see the text of the agreement which is published by HMSO).

C[33.19]

To obtain compensation the victim must obtain judgment in a civil court against the uninsured driver, having given the MIB notice within seven days of starting the proceedings. If the judgment is not met within seven days the victim will be entitled to be compensated by the MIB.

C[33.20]

Compensation is payable for personal injury or for damage to property (except for the first £300 of the claim in respect of property damage and this figure will be the relevant limit of a compensation order made against an uninsured driver in the magistrates' court).

C[33.21]

There are exceptions to claims against the MIB such as claims in relation to Crown vehicles but more particularly where damage is to the claimant's own vehicle which he himself has failed to insure as required by the Road Traffic Act or where the claimant is the passenger in a vehicle which he knew had been stolen or unlawfully taken or was being used without insurance.

C[33.22]

A separate agreement covers the case of victims of untraced drivers.

Sentencing

C[33.23]

Endorsement must be ordered unless special reasons exist. A short distance driven can amount to a sepcial reason. In *DPP v Heritage* [2002] EWHC 2139 (Admin), 166 JP 772 a car was pushed onto the road to be cleaned and a vehicle collided with it.

C[33.24]

If it appears to the court that the accused suffers from some disease or physical disability likely to cause his driving to be a source of danger to the public, then the court shall notify the licensing authority who may take steps to withdraw the driving licence (see **C[5.49]**).

C[33.25]–C[33.30]

Clearly a lower level of fine may be appropriate for the vehicle sitting unused outside the owner's house, whereas deliberate driving around without insurance cover aggravates the seriousness considerably.

C[33.31]

Although using a vehicle without insurance is a serious offence which merits a stiff fine, there may be occasions when it is inappropriate to impose the usual penalty, for example, where the defendant is charged with driving whilst disqualified, a matter which is invariably accompanied by a summons for using the vehicle without insurance. It is submitted that the defendant is being punished twice over if the sentence for each offence is the same as it would be for the individual offences, as one of the attributes of a driving whilst disqualified offence is that there is generally no insurance in force.

C[33.32]

For fines see **B[33]**.

C[34]

Lights

Charge

C[34.1]

1 Using or causing or permitting to be used on a road a vehicle without every front position lamp, rear position lamp, headlamp, rear registration plate lamp, side marker lamp, end-outline marker lamp, rear fog lamp, retro reflector and rear marking with which it is required to be fitted by the Regulations, and every stop lamp and direction indicator, running lamp, dim- dip device, headlamp levelling device and hazard warning signal device with which it is fitted in good working order and, in the case of a lamp, clean

C[34.2]

2 Using, causing or permitting to be used on a road any vehicle with a headlamp, front fog lamp, or rear fog lamp so as to cause undue dazzle or discomfort to other persons using the road

C[34.3]

3 Using or causing or permitting to be used on a road a vehicle which is in motion between sunset and sunrise (or between sunrise and sunset in seriously reduced visibility), (or allowing to remain at rest, or causing or permitting to be allowed to remain at rest, on a road any vehicle between sunset and sunrise) unless every front position lamp, rear position lamp, rear registration plate lamp, side marker lamp and end-outline marker lamp with which the vehicle is required by the Regulations to be fitted is kept lit and unobscured

C[34.4]

4 Using, or causing or permitting to be used on a road a vehicle which is fitted with obligatory dipped beam headlamps without such lamps being lit during the hours of darkness (or in seriously reduced visibility)

Road Vehicles Lighting Regulations 1989, reg 23(1) (charge 1); reg 27 (charge 2); reg 24(1) (charge 3); reg 25(1) (charge 4);

Road Traffic Act 1988, s 42

Maximum penalty – Fine level 4 (goods vehicles etc), level 3 (private vehicles) (for fines see **B[33]**). No power to disqualify or endorse.

Fixed penalty – £30.

Legal note and definitions

C[34.5]

Using, causing or permitting. The charge should allege only one of these. For 'using', 'causing' and 'permitting' see **C[9.4]–C[9.6]**.

C[34.6]

The obligatory minimum requirements for an ordinary motor car are two front position lights, two headlights (with a dipped beam facility), direction indicators, hazard warning lights, two rear position lamps, one rear fog lamp (vehicles first used after 1 April 1980), two stop lamps, a rear registration plate lamp and two rear reflex reflectors.

C[34.7]

These requirements vary according to the category of vehicle concerned. If the matter is in dispute the legal adviser will be able to provide a list of the requirements.

C[34.8]

Vehicle. Means a vehicle of any description and includes a machine or implement of any kind drawn or propelled along roads whether by animal or mechanical power.

C[34.9]

Road. Means any road or highway to which the public has access and includes bridges and footways.

C[34.10]–C[34.15]

Front position lamp. Means a lamp used to indicate the presence and width of a vehicle when viewed from the front.

C[34.16]

Hours of darkness. Means the time between half an hour after sunset and half an hour before sunrise. An almanac can be produced to establish this period if it is in dispute.

C[34.17]

Exempted vehicles include

(a) Pedal cycles and hand drawn vehicles are not required to be fitted with lamps between sunrise and sunset.

(b) Vehicles temporarily imported or proceeding to port for export provided they comply with international Conventions.
(c) Military vehicles which comply with certain requirements.
(d) Vehicles drawn or propelled by hand which have an overall width (including load) not exceeding 800 millimetres are not required to be fitted with lamps and reflectors except when they are used on a carriageway between sunset and sunrise (unless they are close to the near side or are crossing the road).

Possible defences include

C[34.18]

Offence 1 where a defective lamp or reflector is fitted to the vehicle which is in use between sunrise and sunset if the lamp etc becomes defective during the journey or if arrangements have been made to remedy the defect with all reasonable expedition.

C[34.19]

Offence 3 where the vehicle is a car or does not exceed 1,525 kilograms and is parked on a road with a speed limit of 30 miles per hour or less in force and the vehicle is parked in a designated parking place or lay-by or is parked parallel to the kerb, close to it and facing the direction of traffic and is not less than 10 metres from a junction.

C[34.20]

Offence 4. Except where there is seriously reduced visibility, the car is on a road restricted to 30 miles per hour by virtue of a system of street lighting which is lit at the time of the alleged offence.

Sentence

C[34.21]

Although this offence lends itself to a fairly fixed rate, that rate should vary according to:

(a) whether the vehicle was moving or stationary; and
(b) whether the road was lit or unlit.

C[34.22]

For fines see **B[33]**.

C[35]

Motor cyclist not wearing helmet

Charge

C[35.1]

Being a person driving (or riding on) a motor cycle on a road, did not wear protective headgear

Motor Cycles (Protective Helmets) Regulations 1980, reg 4; Road Traffic Act 1988, s 16(4)

Maximum penalty – Fine level 3 (for fines see **B[33]**). There is no power to endorse or disqualify.

Fixed penalty – £30.

Legal notes and definitions

C[35.2]

Where the person actually in breach of the regulations by not wearing a helmet is over 16, there can be no prosecution of another person for aiding and abetting. However, aiders and abettors of defendants under 16 can be prosecuted.

C[35.3]

Riding on. This includes a pillion rider but not a passenger in a side-car.

C[35.4]

Protective headgear is defined in the regulations as being that which complies with a certain British Standard. Headgear manufactured for use by persons on motorcycles which appears to afford the same or a greater degree of protection than laid down by the Standard is also included. But before any helmet satisfies the definition it must also be securely fastened to the head of the wearer by the straps or fastenings provided on the helmet. An unfastened helmet, therefore, would not suffice.

C[35.5]

Driving. See the notes under this heading for the offence of driving without a licence at **C[18.8]–C[18.9]** but bear in mind the exemption mentioned at (b) below.

C[35.6]

Exemptions. There is no requirement to wear a helmet:

(a) if the motor cycle is a mowing machine;
(b) if the motor cycle is being propelled by a person on foot;
(c) if the driver is a Sikh and is wearing a turban.

Sentencing

C[35.7]

The wearing of a helmet contributes greatly to the rider's safety. A small fine will meet most cases.

C[35.8]

For fines see **B[33]**.

C[36]

Obstruction

Charge 1

C[36.1]

Causing unnecessary obstruction of a road by a person in charge of a motor vehicle or trailer

Road Vehicles (Construction and Use) Regulations 1986, reg 103; Road Traffic Act 1988, s 42

Maximum penalty – Fine level 4 (goods vehicle etc), level 3 (otherwise) (for fines see **B[33]**). No power to disqualify or endorse.

Fixed penalty – £30.

Charge 2

C[36.1A]

Did without lawful authority or excuse wilfully obstruct the free passage along a highway.

Highways Act 1980, s 137

Maximum penalty – Fine level 3

Legal notes and definitions

C[36.2]

Unnecessary obstruction. There need be no notice or sign displayed as is the case where a driver is charged in parking offences. This offence can be committed on a road to which local parking regulations are applicable.

Wilful. If anyone does something by exercise of their free will which causes an obstruction the offence is usually made out (*Arrowsmith v Jenkins* [1963] 2 QB 561, [1963] 2 All ER 210).

C[36.3]

If the vehicle is parked in a lawfully designated parking place then there can be no charge of obstruction.

C[36.4]

The High Court has ruled that a motorist who left his car on a road 24 ft wide for 75 minutes did not commit this offence (*Evans v Barker* [1971] RTR 453). An obstruction was not committed by a reasonable protest taking up 2 ft of an 11ft-wide path (*Westminster City Council v Haw* [2002] All ER (D) 59 (Oct)).

C[36.5]

A taxi-driver was held by the High Court to have committed this offence in waiting in the road to turn right, thereby holding up heavy traffic.

C[36.6]

The question is one for the justices to decide on the facts of each case. An obstruction caused by a doctor answering an emergency call may, for example, be necessary.

C[36.7]

A road. Means any highway (including footpaths and bridleways) and any other road to which the public has access and includes bridges. A road is provided as a means of transit from one place to another and not as a place to park motor vehicles.

C[36.8]

Trailer. Means any vehicle drawn by a motor vehicle.

C[36.9]

A motor vehicle. See **C[9.7]**. If left on a road for an unreasonable time may constitute an unnecessary obstruction.

Power to order the removal of the obstruction rests with the magistrates when recording a conviction under the Highways Act 1980, s 137. Failure to comply with the order without reasonable excuse is an offence punishable by a fine not exceeding level 5 and a daily fine thereafter.

Sentencing

C[36.10]–C[36.15]

An average case will not usually attract more than a small fine; where there is a complete disregard for the convenience or safety of others (e g access of fire appliances or ambulances) a heavier fine is called for.

C[36.16]

For fines see **B[33]**.

C[37]

Opening door

Charge

C[37.1]

Opening a door of a motor vehicle or trailer on a road so as to cause injury or danger

Road Vehicles (Construction and Use) Regulations 1986, reg 105; Road Traffic Act 1988, s 42

Maximum penalty – Fine level 4 (goods vehicle etc), level 3 (otherwise) (for fines see **B[33]**). No power to disqualify or endorse.

Fixed penalty – £30.

Legal notes and definitions

C[37.2]

Motor vehicle. See **C[9.7]**.

C[37.3]

Trailer. Means any vehicle drawn by a motor vehicle.

C[37.4]

Road. Means any highway (including footpaths and bridleways) and any other road to which the public has access and includes bridges.

C[37.5]

The offence. Consists of opening or causing or permitting a door to be opened so as to cause injury or danger to any person. The offence can be committed by a passenger as well as the driver. If a child opened the door and his parent was present and knew the child was about to open the door, then the parent could be charged with permitting. If the child opened the door on the instructions of a parent then the latter could be guilty of causing the offence. Door opening, permitting or causing are all identical offences for the purpose of the penalties that may be inflicted. Only one of the offences should be alleged.

C[37.6]

The prosecution does not have to prove carelessness; nor that someone was actually struck or injured. It is enough if the act caused danger.

Sentencing

C[37.7]

If it appears to the court that a driver suffers from some disease or physical disability likely to cause his driving to be a source of danger to the public, then the court shall notify the licensing authority who may take steps to withdraw his driving licence (see **C[5.49]**).

C[37.8]

The amount of the fine will vary according to the circumstances. It will rarely be appropriate to impose a fine less than the fixed penalty. When the offence is very dangerous, e g where it causes a motor cyclist to swerve to the offside of a busy main road, this will aggravate the seriousness. Where actual injury is caused a similar level of penalty should apply.

C[37.9]

For fines see **B[33]**.

C[38]

Overloading

Charge

C[38.1]

Using, causing or permitting to be used on a road a vehicle which exceeds the maximum (gross weight) (train weight) (weight for specified axle) shown on the (plating certificate) (manufacturer's plate fitted to the vehicle)

Road Vehicles (Construction and Use) Regulations 1986, reg 80; Road Traffic Act 1988, s 41B

Maximum penalty – Fine level 5 (for fines see **B[33]**). Not endorsable.

Fixed penalty – £60.

Legal notes and definitions

C[38.2]

Certain vehicles specified in the Road Vehicles (Construction and Use) Regulations 1986, reg 66 must be fitted with a plate which contains information prescribed in Sch 8 or the relevant EC Directives. In particular the plate must show the maximum gross weight, train weight and weight for each axle. The weights may be specified by the manufacturer and are the limits at or below which the vehicle is considered fit for use, having regard to its design, construction and equipment and the stresses to which it is likely to be subjected in use. Further, the weights must also be specified at which the use of the vehicle will be legal in the UK having regard, inter alia, to the maximum weights set out in regs 75–79. This is a 'manufacturer's plate'.

C[38.3]

In addition, goods vehicles are now covered by the compulsory 'type approval' system whereby the Secretary of State issues a certificate that a type of vehicle conforms with the appropriate requirements and the manufacturer issues a Certificate of Conformity that the vehicle conforms with the approved type. This certificate is *treated* as a 'plating certificate' and a plate (which is in fact a piece of paper) is affixed to the vehicle, which is *deemed* to be a 'ministry plate' (for this and 'plating certificate' see below).

C[38.4]

After one year and annually thereafter goods vehicles must be submitted for a goods vehicle test and at the *first* test the vehicle will also be examined for the purpose of issuing a 'plating certificate'. The examiner will issue a certificate containing information similar to that on the plate previously affixed to the vehicle. If the vehicle passes its goods vehicle test the ministry plate will remain affixed in a conspicuous and readily accessible position on the vehicle and in the cab. Only one plating certificate is issued, but it will be amended where there has been a 'notifiable alteration' to the vehicle.

C[38.5]

Using; causing; permitting. See **C[9.4]–C[9.6]**.

C[38.6]

Road. See **C[9.10]**.

C[38.7]

Vehicle. The provisions concerning manufacturers' plates cover such vehicles as non-agricultural tractors of various weights which do not carry loads, buses and various trailers. This article is concerned with offences committed by goods vehicles, being the most commonly encountered in the magistrates' court.

C[38.8]

Maximum gross weight. The sum of the weights to be transmitted to the road surface by all the wheels of the motor vehicle (including any load imposed by a trailer on the vehicle).

C[38.9]

Maximum train weight. The maximum gross weight and the weight transmitted to the road surface by any trailer drawn.

C[38.10]–C[38.15]

Maximum axle weight. The sum of the weights to be transmitted to the road surface by all the wheels of that axle.

C[38.16]

Multiple charges. Under the former regulations 'gross', 'train' or 'axle' weight were the subject of separate charges and not combined into one. It was not oppressive for there to be a charge in respect of each axle that was overweight and for exceeding the gross weight. The new regulations are worded slightly differently but it is still permissible to prefer several charges where appropriate (*Travel-Gas (Midlands) Ltd v Reynolds* [1989] RTR 75).

C[38.17]

Evidence. Unless proved to the contrary the weight indicated on a ministry plate is presumed to be the weight recorded on the relevant plating certificate.

C[38.18]

Defences. In the case of a goods vehicle it is a defence for the accused to prove:

(a) that at the time when the vehicle was being used on the road it was proceeding to a weighbridge which was the nearest available one to the place where the loading of the vehicle was completed for the purpose of being weighed, or was proceeding from a weighbridge after being weighed to the nearest point at which it was reasonably practicable to reduce the weight to the relevant limit without causing an obstruction on any road; or
(b) in a case where the limit of that weight was not exceeded by more than 5%, that limit was not exceeded at the time the loading of the vehicle was originally completed and that since that time no person has made any addition to the load (eg a load which becomes wet owing to falling rain).

C[38.18A]

"**Nearest available weighbridge**" means the nearest available weighbridge that was actually available as a matter of objective fact regardless of the knowledge of the driver (*Vehicle and Operator Services Agency v F & S Gibbs Transport Services Ltd* [2006] EWHC 1109 (Admin), 170 JP 586.

C[38.19]

The degree of proof required from the defendant is to prove that the defence is probably true; he does not have to prove beyond reasonable doubt.

Sentencing

C[38.20]

Overloading a goods vehicle is potentially a very serious offence. The steering and braking capabilities of the vehicle may be adversely affected. Excess axle weights are particularly liable to damage road surfaces and the drains beneath. In addition there may be substantial commercial advantages to an operator. The fines imposed should reflect this. HGV drivers are often treated more seriously than non-HGV drivers and separate penalties are often appropriate for each offence summoned. Penalties may be doubled in the case of the owner of an HGV. In deciding the culpability it may be useful to consider the percentage of the overload rather than simply the number of kilograms in excess.

See *Norbert Dentressangle Continental Ltd v Wing* (1998, unreported) for a useful review of sentencing considerations.

C[38.21]

For fines see **B[33]**.

C[39]

Pedestrian crossing (failing to accord precedence)

Charge

C[39.1]

Failure of a driver of any vehicle to accord precedence to a pedestrian within the limits of an uncontrolled pedestrian crossing

'Zebra' Pedestrian Crossings Regulations 1971, reg 8 (or 'Pelican' Pedestrian Crossings Regulations 1987, reg 17); Road Traffic Regulation Act 1984, s 25(5)

Maximum penalty – Fine of level 3 (for fines see **B[33]**). If the offence was committed in a motor vehicle, the court may disqualify for any period and/or until a driving test has been passed. Must endorse unless special reasons exist.

Penalty points – 3.

Fixed penalty – £60 (3PP)

Legal notes and definitions

C[39.2]

Vehicle. A bicycle is a vehicle (but not in the case of offences of stopping in an area *adjacent* to a zebra crossing, see **C[40.7]–C[40.9]**).

C[39.3]

Zebra crossing. A driver should approach such a crossing in a manner that enables him to stop before reaching it, unless he can see there is no pedestrian on the crossing.

C[39.4]

The law imposes a very strict duty on the driver and the prosecution has the advantage of not having to prove any negligence or want of care. It would, however, be a sufficient defence to satisfy the magistrates that the failure to accord precedence was due to circumstances over which the defendant had no control (e g being attacked by a swarm of bees, or a sudden brake failure).

C[39.5]

The High Court in Scotland has held that where a woman was pushing her child in a pram and the pram was on the crossing but she herself had not actually stepped on to the crossing, the mother had the right of way.

C[39.6]

The limits of the crossing are marked by studs bordering the striped lines. The broken white line along the striped crossing is to indicate where vehicles should give way.

C[39.7]

The sections of pedestrian crossings on each side of a dual carriageway, central street refuge or reservation are considered to be two separate crossings.

C[39.8]

A crossing may still legally remain a crossing even if one or more of its stripes are missing, discoloured or imperfect, or if a globe or one of its lights is missing, or even if some of the studs have disappeared. The magistrates should consult the legal adviser if a submission is made on any of these matters.

C[39.9]

The regulations require pedestrians to cross 'with reasonable dispatch'.

C[39.10]–C[39.15]

On each side of crossings are zigzag lines parallel to the carriageway. These indicate the 'area controlled by the crossing'. On the approach side of the crossing it is an offence for a vehicle to overtake another vehicle in that area if that vehicle is either the only other vehicle in the area or is the nearest vehicle of several to the crossing. 'Overtaking' includes allowing part of the rearmost vehicle to pass the front of the overtaken vehicle, a complete passing is not necessary. The prohibition on overtaking does not apply if the overtaken vehicle is stationary otherwise than to allow pedestrians to cross (e g if it is waiting to turn left or right) or if the crossing is for the time being controlled by a policeman or traffic warden, but it applies where a vehicle has stopped to wait for pedestrians to step on to the crossing, for example as a courtesy. It also applies when the pedestrians have passed the stationary vehicle which is overtaken.

C[39.16]

Pelican crossings. Similar provisions apply. A vehicle approaching such a crossing shall proceed with due regard to the safety of other users of the road. When a red light shows the vehicle must stop, similarly where a constant amber light shows, a vehicle must stop except where the vehicle cannot safely be stopped in line with the signal. Where there is a flashing amber light, a vehicle must accord precedence to pedestrians already on the crossing. Failure to comply with any of the regulations is an offence with a maximum penalty of a fine on level 3.

C[39.17]

Pedestrian. A person walking and pushing a bicycle is a pedestrian. He ceases to be a pedestrian if he uses the bicycle to carry him, for example, by placing one foot on a pedal and pushing himself along with the other.

C[39.18]

Precedence means allowing the pedestrian to go before the vehicle. Once the pedestrian has safely passed the vehicle's line of travel the vehicle may proceed even though the pedestrian is still on the crossing.

Sentencing

C[39.19]

If it appears to the court that the defendant driver of a motor vehicle suffers from some disease or physical disability likely to cause his driving to be a source of danger to the public, then the court shall notify the licensing authority who may take steps to withdraw the driving licence (see **C[5.49]**).

C[39.20]

A fine will generally be considered. For fines see **B[33]**.

C[40]–[45]

Stopping on pedestrian crossing

Charge

C[40.1]

That a driver of a vehicle caused it or any part of it to stop within the limits of zebra crossing

'Zebra' Pedestrian Crossings Regulations 1971, reg 9; Road Traffic Regulation Act 1984, s 25(5)

Maximum penalty – Fine level 3 (for fines see **B[33]**). If the offence was committed in a motor vehicle, the court may disqualify for any period and/or until the defendant has passed a driving test. Must endorse unless special reasons exist.

Penalty points – 3.

Fixed penalty – £60 (3PP).

Legal notes and definitions

C[40.2]

The defendant must be acquitted if he establishes any of the following:

(a) that circumstances beyond his control compelled him to stop;
(b) that he had to stop to avoid an accident (see **C[40.9]**).

C[40.3]

The degree of proof required from the defendant is to prove that one of these is probably true; he does not have to prove one of them beyond reasonable doubt.

C[40.4]

The term 'vehicle' includes a pedal cycle.

C[40.5]

This charge does not apply to a push-button controlled crossing which is subject to special regulations.

C[40.6]

A crossing may still legally remain a crossing even if one or more stripes are missing, discoloured or imperfect, or if a globe or its light is missing or even if some of the studs have disappeared. Consult the legal adviser.

C[40.7]

Stopping in area adjacent to zebra crossing. It is also an offence to stop in a zebra-controlled area, ie the part of a road indicated by zig-zag lines at either side of the crossing ('Zebra' Pedestrian Crossings Regulations 1971, reg 12).

C[40.8]

For the purposes of this regulation 'vehicle' does *not* include a pedal cycle.

C[40.9]

Defences are:

(a) that circumstances beyond his control compelled him to stop;
(b) that he had to stop to avoid an accident;
(c) that the stopping was for the purpose of allowing free passage to pedestrians on the crossing;
(d) that he had to stop for fire brigade, ambulance or police purposes, because of demolitions, repairs to road, gas, water, electricity services etc;
(e) that he stopped for the purpose of making a left or right turn;
(f) a stage carriage or express carriage vehicle (not on a trip or excursion) in the controlled area beyond the zebra crossing for the purposes of picking up or setting down passengers.

Sentencing

C[40.10]–C[40.15]

If it appears to the court that the defendant driver of a motor vehicle suffers from some disease or physical disability likely to cause his driving to be a source of danger to the public, then the court shall notify the licensing authority who may take steps to withdraw the driving licence (see **C[5.49]**).

C[40.16]

A fine is usually appropriate in most cases.

C[40.17]

For fines see **B[33]**.

C[46]

Reasonable consideration

Charge

C[46.1]

Driving a mechanically propelled vehicle on a road or other public place without reasonable consideration for other persons using the road or place

Road Traffic Act 1988, s 3, as amended

Maximum penalty – Fine level 4 [level 5 under the Road Safety Act 2006] (for fines see **B[33]**). May disqualify for any period and/or until a driving test has been passed. Must endorse unless special reasons exist.

Penalty points – 3–9.

Legal notes and definitions

C[46.2]

At the time of the offence there must have been other people also using the road. They could be passengers in the defendant's vehicle. Another example of this offence is driving the vehicle through a muddy puddle and splashing pedestrians.

C[46.3]

If no other person but the driver is using the road then this charge fails.

C[46.4]

Observance or non-observance of the Highway Code can be used to establish or disprove liability.

C[46.5]

The driver alleged to have committed this offence must give his name and address on request to any person having reasonable grounds for requiring it, otherwise he commits an offence under the Road Traffic Act 1988, s 168, maximum penalty fine on level 3.

C[46.6]

Mechanically propelled vehicle. See **C[47.9]**.

C[46.7]

Road. See **C[22.5]**.

C[46.8]

Public place. See **C[20.7]–C[20.8]**.

C[46.9]

Warning of prosecution. If the defence claim that notice should have been given within 14 days of intention to prosecute, consult the legal adviser.

C[46.10]–C[46.15]

Other persons using the road. May include passengers in the defendant's vehicle. There must be evidence that another road user was inconvenienced by the manner of driving adopted by the accused.

C[46.16]

Careless or inconsiderate driving (Road Traffic Act 1988, s 3) and dangerous driving (s 2). Where the magistrates see fit, they may allow informations for an offence under s 3 and s 2 to be heard together. In this event, if the defendant is convicted of one offence, the second information can either be adjourned *sine die* or the justices may make *"no adjudication"*. Should the driver successfully appeal against conviction for dangerous driving, he can later be tried on the second information.

C[46.17]

Alternatively, where there is a single information alleging dangerous driving and the magistrates do not find this proved, they may convict of driving without reasonable consideration in the alternative (s 24 RTOA 1988).

C[46.18]

Driving. See the note under the offence of no driving licence at **C[18.8]–C[18.9]**.

Sentencing

C[46.19]

In rare cases it may be appropriate to grant an absolute discharge; if this course is adopted disqualification can be imposed but this would be an unusual course to take. Endorsement must be ordered unless special reasons exist.

C[46.20]

If it appears to the court that the accused suffers from some disease or physical disability likely to cause his driving to be a source of danger to the public then the court shall notify the licensing authority who may take steps to withdraw the driving licence (see **C[5.49]**).

C[46.21]

It is the lack of consideration rather than the consequences of it which normally determines the punishment.

C[46.22]

Most cases would attract a fine in the mid-region of the range.

C[46.23]

For fines see **B[33]**.

C[47]

Road fund or excise licence

Charge 1

C[47.1]

Using or keeping on a public road a mechanically propelled vehicle when no excise licence is in force and doing so when a SORN is in force

Vehicle Excise and Registration Act 1994, s 29 and s 29(3A)

C[47.2]

Maximum penalty – A fine of level 3 (s 29(3)) or level 4 (s 29(3A)) or 5 times the value of the licence, whichever is the greater. No power to disqualify or endorse.

Charge 2

Keeping an unlicensed vehicle while the registered keeper

Vehicle Excise and Registration Act 1994, s 31A

Maximum penalty –A fine of level 3 or 5 times the annual duty. Additional penalty of a least £1,000 if the vehicle remains unlicensed from the date of offence to the start of proceedings.

C[47.3]

In addition to a fine the court is compelled, in certain cases, to order the defendant to pay loss of duty. See **C[47.18]** under 'Sentencing'.

Legal notes and definitions

C[47.4]

The charge must stipulate whether the defendant is being charged with using or keeping. One charge cannot allege both.

C[47.5]

Prosecutor and time limit. Only the Secretary of State, the police acting with his approval, or a person or authority authorised by that Secretary of State can conduct the prosecution. Proceedings must start within 6 months of their receiving sufficient evidence to warrant proceedings; subject to an overall limit of three years from the offence.

C[47.6]

Using. In law means not only driving the vehicle but can also include the vehicle's mere presence on the road. The owner is not liable to be charged with using the vehicle if he allowed some other person to have the vehicle and who used it outside the scope of the authority given by the owner.

C[47.7]

Keeping. Means causing the vehicle to be on a public road for any period, however short, when the vehicle is not in use. See *Secretary of State for the Environment, Transport and the Regions v Holt* [2000] RTR 309, where the High Court ruled that proof that the defendant was the registered keeper together with the adverse inference drawn from his failure to give information as to the identity of the driver was sufficient to prove he was the keeper on the day in question.

C[47.8]

Public road. Refers to a road repairable at the public expense. This is different from the more usual definition of a road which means any highway (including footpaths and bridleways) and any other road to which the public has access and includes bridges.

C[47.9]

Mechanically propelled vehicle. Means a vehicle with some form of engine; thus even a motor assisted pedal cycle comes within the legal definition even if the rider is just pedalling the machine without the use of the engine. A car does not cease to be a mechanically propelled vehicle after removal of its engine, nor if there is some temporary defect which prevents the engine working. If the condition of the vehicle is such that there is no reasonable prospect of it ever being made mobile again, then it ceases to be a mechanically propelled vehicle.

C[47.10]–C[47.15]

Employees, drivers, chauffeurs. It has been decided that it is oppressive to prosecute an employee who was not responsible for licensing the vehicle.

C[47.16]

A dishonoured cheque. If offered in payment of the licensing fee renders the licence void. The licensing authority will send a notice requiring the excise licence to be delivered up within seven days of the posting of the notice. Failure to comply is an offence punishable with a maximum fine of level 3 or 5 times the annual rate of duty applicable (Customs and Excise Management Act 1979, s 102). For liability for back duty see below.

C[47.17]

Exempted vehicles. Certain vehicles are exempt from duty and the clerk can supply a list: ambulances, fire engines, military vehicles, some agricultural vehicles; vehicles going for a *pre-arranged* test and some vehicles acquired by overseas residents, vehicles more than 25 years old, calculated from the 31 December of the year of first registration. This latter class of vehicles must still be licensed annually and display a VED disc. See Sch 2 of the 1994 Act. A vehicle kept off the public road may be subject to a Statutory Off-Road Notification (SORN). A SORN declaration is valid for 12 months. Failure to make or renew a SORN may be subject to a level 3 fine.

Sentencing

C[47.18]

The fine and the arrears of duty should be announced as separate items; we do not commend the practice of some courts of announcing a single sum and stipulating that it includes the back duty.

Liability for back duty

C[47.19]

If the defendant was the person who *kept* the vehicle at the time of the offence the court must order him to pay an amount to cover the loss of duty. Such order is in addition to a fine and the chairman of the court must announce two amounts, namely the amount of the fine and the amount of the lost duty.

C[47.20]

If the court decides not to impose a fine but to grant an absolute or conditional discharge the court must still order the payment of the lost duty as well and this must be announced. It must be stressed that this provision applies only if the defendant is the person who *kept* the vehicle at the time of the offence. Thus this provision would not apply to an employed lorry driver but would apply to a private motorist who kept and used his own vehicle. It would also apply to a company which kept and used its own vehicles.

C[47.21]

Dishonoured cheques. In relation to licences taken out on or after 27 July 1989 the court must, in addition to any penalty it may impose under the Customs and Excise Management Act 1979, s 102, order the defendant to pay an amount to cover the loss of duty incurred for the period for which he had the benefit of the licence.

C[47.22]

Calculating back duty. This period will usually commence with the date of the expiry of the expired licence, or when the defendant notified his acquisition of the vehicle to the appropriate authority. It will terminate with the date of offence. If there is doubt about the length of the 'relevant period' consult the legal adviser. Back duty is calculated for each month or part thereof. Use on one day in a month will render him liable for back duty for the whole month.

C[47.23]

Previous convictions. If the defendant has a previous conviction in respect of the same vehicle for a similar offence for which the court made an order for lost revenue then in the present proceedings the relevant period will commence with the day after the date of the previous offence.

C[47.24]

Costs can be ordered as well as a fine and back duty.

C[47.25]–C[47.30]

Defence against back duty. If the defendant can prove any one of the following in respect of any part of the relevant period back duty cannot be ordered against him for that part of the relevant period:

(a) the vehicle was not kept by him; or
(b) he paid duty in respect of the vehicle for any month or part of a month (where relevant) whether or not on a licence. The defendant does not have to establish this beyond reasonable doubt but only that his contention is probably true.

Defences for a registered keeper (s 31B). The burden is on the defendant to show either:

(i) he is no longer the keeper and has complied with the requirements under the Act;
(ii) the vehicle was not kept on a public road and the requirements have been complied with;
(iii) the vehicle was stolen and not recovered and the notification requirements complied with.

Note that it is an offence to use a vehicle in public if it is not properly registered; defence of no reasonable opportunity or reasonable grounds for believing that registration details were correct – level 3 fine (fixed penalty offence). A constable or authorised person may require production of vehicle registration certificate – level 2 fine for failure to do so.

C[47.31]

A person is liable for all the periods when he kept a vehicle without a current tax whether it was on a public road or not. It is not obligatory for a person to tax a car that is kept off the road for the whole of that period. However since 31 January 1998 keepers of vehicles which become unlicensed and are to be kept off the public road are required to provide a declaration to the DVLA. If he ventures onto the road without tax he may find himself with a liability extending back over the time when it was not taxed or to the date when he notified his acquisition of the vehicle.

Charge 3

C[47.32]

Fraudulently using a vehicle excise licence

Vehicle Exercise and Registration Act 1994, s 44

Maximum penalty – Fine level 5 (for fines see **B[33]**). No power to disqualify or endorse.

Crown Court – Unlimited fine and 2 years' imprisonment. Triable either way.

Legal notes and definitions

C[47.33]

Other offences. The offence can also be committed by forging or fraudulently altering, lending or allowing to be used by another a licence or registration document under the Act. It is also an offence fraudulently to use etc a numberplate. Exhibiting an altered vehicle excise licence on a car parked on private land does not amount to fraudulent use within the meaning of the Act (*R v Johnson* [1995] RTR 15, 158 JP 788, CA).

C[47.34]

Fraudulently. Does not merely cover economic loss by the evasion of excise duty but also includes the case where the defendant intends by deceit to cause a public official such as a police officer to act, or refrain from acting, in a way in which he otherwise would not have done. See *R v Terry* [1984] AC 374, [1984] 1 All ER 65, HL and *R v Macrae* (1993) 159 JP 359, [1994] Crim LR 363, CA on forgery of a licence.

Sentencing

C[47.35]

The majority of cases are dealt with in the magistrates' court where a fine in the lower range may often be appropriate. The fine will normally be increased to reflect a period of unlicensed use over six months. Back duty is always payable in addition to a fine. It should be noted that unlike most either way offences this offence is not punishable with imprisonment by a magistrates' court, accordingly sentences such as a community order are not generally available.

C[47.36]

For fines see **B[33]**.

C[48]

Seat belts

Charge

C[48.1]

Unlawfully did drive or ride in a motor vehicle of a class specified in the Motor Vehicles (Wearing of Seat Belts) Regulations 1993 otherwise than in accordance with the provisions of those Regulations

Road Traffic Act 1988, s 14

Maximum penalty – Fine level 2 (for fines see **B[33]**). No power to endorse or disqualify.

C[48.2]

Unlawfully did drive a motor vehicle with a child in the front seat not wearing a seat belt

OR

C[48.3]

Unlawfully did drive a motor vehicle with a child in the rear seat not wearing a seat belt

Motor Vehicles (Wearing of Seat Belts by Children in Front Seats) Regulations 1993

Road Traffic Act, s 15

Maximum penalty - (Front seat) level 2
- (Rear seat) level 1

No endorsement or disqualification.

Fixed penalty – £30.

Legal notes and definitions

C[48.4]

Criminal liability. Only the person actually committing the contravention can be prosecuted. There are no provisions for another person to be prosecuted for aiding and abetting etc and causing or permitting.

C[48.5]

Specified passenger's seat is the front seat alongside the driver's seat, or, if there is more than one such seat, the one furthest from the driver's seat. If there is no seat alongside the driver's seat, then the specified passenger's seat is the foremost forward facing seat furthest from the driver's seat, unless there is a fixed partition separating it from the space in front of it and alongside the driver's seat as, for example, in a London type taxi cab.

C[48.6]

Class of vehicle. Every motor car registered on or after 1 January 1965, every three-wheeled vehicle not weighing more than 225 kg manufactured on or after 1 March 1970 and first used on or after 1 September 1970 and heavy motor cars first used on or after 1 October 1988, e g goods vehicles and minibuses.

C[48.7]

Seat belt. The seat belt must comply with the requirements of the relevant regulations, about which the legal adviser will clarify.

C[48.8]

Exemptions. Every driver and every person occupying the specified passenger's seat, as defined above, must wear a seat belt when in the vehicle, even when the vehicle is stationary, except a person who is:

(a) using a vehicle constructed or adapted for the delivery or collection of goods or mail to consumers or addressees, as the case may be, whilst engaged in making local rounds of deliveries or collections;
(b) driving the vehicle while performing a manoeuvre which includes reversing;
(c) a qualified driver, and is supervising a provisional licence holder while that person is performing a manoeuvre which includes reversing;
(d) the holder of a valid certificate in a form supplied by the Secretary of State, containing the information required by it, and signed by a registered medical practitioner to the effect that it is inadvisable on medical grounds for him to wear a seat belt;
(e) a constable protecting or escorting another person;
(f) not a constable, but is protecting or escorting another person by virtue of powers the same as or similar to those of a constable for that person;
(g) in the service of a fire brigade and is donning operational clothing or equipment;
(h) the driver of:
   (i) a taxi which is being used for seeking hire, or answering a call for hire, or carrying a passenger for hire; or
   (ii) a private hire vehicle which is being so used to carry a passenger for hire;

(i) a person by whom a test of competence to drive is being conducted and his wearing a seat belt would endanger himself or any other person;

(j) occupying a seat for which the seat belt either:
   (i) does not comply with the relevant standards; or
   (ii) has an inertia reel mechanism which is locked as a result of the vehicle being, or having been, on a steep incline;

(k) riding in a vehicle being used under a trade licence, for the purpose of investigating or remedying a mechanical fault in the vehicle.

C[48.9]

Children under 14 years. The above regulations do not apply but it is an offence under the Road Traffic Act 1988, s 15(2) punishable with a maximum fine on level 2 for a person without reasonable excuse to drive on a road with a child under 14 years in the front of a motor vehicle who is not wearing a seat belt.

C[48.10]–C[48.15]

The seat belt must conform with the Motor Vehicles (Wearing of Seat Belts by Children in Front Seats) Regulations 1993 which provide for the use of special child restraining devices, or, according to age, adult seat belts for use in the front passenger seat.

C[48.16]

Exemptions similar to those at (d) and (j) apply. Generally it is now unlawful to drive a vehicle with a small child in the front unless he is wearing a suitable restraint.

C[48.17]

Rear seat belts. It is also compulsory for both adults and children in the rear seats of a vehicle fitted with seat belts to wear them. If a child (ie a person under 14 years) on the rear seat is not wearing a seat belt (with a booster cushion where necessary, or a child restraint), the driver of the vehicle will incur liability (maximum penalty a fine on level 1). In the case of a passenger aged 14 years or more, only he will be liable (maximum penalty a fine on level 2), there are no provisions for the driver to be guilty of aiding and abetting the offence. There is no liability where all available seat belts are in use.

C[48.18]

The following table summarises the main legal requirements for wearing seat belts.

	Front seat	*Rear seat*	*Whose responsibility*
Driver	Must be worn if fitted	—	Driver

	Front seat	*Rear seat*	*Whose responsibility*
CHILD under 3 YEARS OF AGE	Appropriate child restraint must be worn	Appropriate child restraint must be worn	Driver
CHILD AGED 3–11 and under 1.5 metres (about 5 feet) in height	Appropriate child restraint must be worn if available. If not an adult seat belt must be worn	Appropriate child restraint must be worn if available. If not an adult seat belt must be worn	Driver
CHILD AGED 12 or 13 or younger 1.5 metres or more in height	Adult seat belt must be worn if available	Adult seat belt must be worn if available	Driver
ADULT PASSENGERS	must be worn if available	must be worn if available	Passenger

C[49]

Speeding

Charge

C[49.1]

Driving a motor vehicle on a road at a speed exceeding a statutory limit

Road Traffic Regulation Act 1984, ss 81 (84 or 86) and 89

Maximum penalty – Fine level 3 (for fines see **B[33]**). May disqualify for any period and/or until a driving test has been passed. Must endorse unless there are special reasons.

Note – Speeding on a motorway may be charged under the Road Traffic Regulation Act 1984, s 17 in which case the maximum penalty is a fine on level 4.

Penalty points – 3–6. [2–6 under the Road Safety Act 2006] (Fixed penalty – 3.)

Fixed penalty – £60

Legal notes and definitions

C[49.2]

Speeding can be considered under five main headings:

(A) Speeding on restricted roads (Road Traffic Regulation Act 1984, s 81).
(B) Speeding on motorways (s 17).
(C) Breaking the speed limit imposed by the Secretary of State for the Environment or highway authorities on roads other than restricted roads (s 84).
(D) Driving a vehicle at a speed in excess of that permitted for that class of vehicle (s 86).
(E) Breaking a temporary or experimental speed limit imposed by the Secretary of State for the Environment on certain specified roads (s 88).
These classes of speeding are dealt with in the above order on the following pages.

C[49.3]

Warning of prosecution must have been given to the defendant except in circumstances prescribed in the Road Traffic Offenders Act 1988, s 2, as amended (eg following an accident).

C[49.4]

Evidence. The Road Traffic Offenders Act 1988, s 20 (as substituted by the Road Traffic Act 1991) provides that it will be sufficient for evidence of an offence of speeding or contravening a red traffic light to be obtained by approved devices, such as a Gatso camera, which also records speeds and times as appropriate. The record must be signed by the police and the defendant given seven days notice of its intended use. The accused may require the attendance of the person who signed the document not less than three days before the trial.

In *DPP v Thornley* [2006] EWHC 312 (Admin), [2006] 09 LS Gaz R 32, it was held that s 20(8) of the RTOA 1988 was permissive in its terms and therefore the prosecution were entitled to admit the record of speeding as a species of "real evidence".

See 'Conditional offer of fixed penalty' at **C[8.21]–C[8.22]**.

C[49.5]

If the evidence merely consists of one witness's opinion that the defendant was exceeding the speed limit there cannot be a conviction. If the single witness is supported by a speedometer, stop watch, radar meter or Vascar, then there can be a conviction.

C[49.6]

The evidence of two witnesses estimating the speed at the same time can result in a conviction, but if their estimates refer to speeds at different parts of the road then that will not suffice.

C[49.7]

If a vehicle was being used for the purpose of the fire brigade, the police, or the ambulance services, and the driver can establish that observing the speed limit would have hindered him in the execution of his official duties, then that could be accepted as a successful line of defence by the court. It is for the court to decide this issue as there is no inherent right for all such vehicles to exceed the speed limit, for instance an empty ambulance merely returning to its garage or a fire engine out on routine test carry no exemption from a speed limit. A police officer using a vehicle to "hone" his skills may be guilty of speeding (see **C[16]** and *DPP v Milton* [2006] EWHC 242 (Admin), (2006) 170 JP 319).

C[49.8]

The defendant merely has to prove that this defence is probably true; he need not prove it beyond reasonable doubt.

C[49.9]

Although the driver must be identified, the fact that he was driving when stopped is prima facie evidence that he drove over the whole distance for which he was timed.

C[49.10]–C[49.15]

Speed limit signs. If the defendant submits that the speed sign was unlawful because of its size, composition, character or colour, etc, the legal adviser should be consulted.

Category A – speeding on restricted roads (Road Traffic Regulation Act 1984, s 81)
Legal notes and definitions

C[49.16]

Restricted road. A road becomes a restricted road in one of two ways:

(a) it has a system of street lamps placed not more than two hundred yards apart, in which case the speed limit is 30 miles per hour; or
(b) it is directed by the relevant authority that it becomes a restricted road, in which case the speed limit is again 30 miles per hour.

A road restricted by (a) above need not display 'repeater' signs but a road in category (b) does have to display the repeater '30' signs.

C[49.17]

The relevant authority may direct that an (a) category road may be derestricted. 'Restricted road' is a term of art referring to a road having a 30 mile per hour limit because of the above provisions. Confusingly, restricted road is commonly, but erroneously, used to refer to any road having a speed limit less than the overall maxima of 70 miles per hour for motorways and dual carriageways and 60 miles per hour for single carriageways.

C[49.18]

The limit on a restricted road of 30 mph can be altered by the Secretary of State for the Environment and the Home Secretary acting jointly.

C[49.19]

A vehicle which is limited to a lower speed than the limit for the road must always conform to its own scheduled speed limit, for example, a lorry drawing more than one trailer is limited to 20 mph and must keep to that limit even on a restricted road where a 30 mph limit is in force.

Category B – speeding on motorways (Road Traffic Regulation Act 1984, s 17)

C[49.20]

Motorway. The legal adviser can provide a detailed definition if it should be necessary. The motorway includes the hard shoulder and access and exit roads.

C[49.21]

The general speed limit on a motorway is 70 miles per hour although there are lower speed limits on certain stretches of motorway.

C[49.22]

Contraventions of certain temporary restrictions on motorways (eg for roadworks) are offences under s 16 and also carry an endorsement.

Category C – driving a motor vehicle at a speed in excess of a limit imposed on a road, other than a restricted road, by the highway authority (Road Traffic Regulation Act 1984, s 84)
Legal notes and definitions

C[49.23]

For the purposes of this offence the appropriate highway authority for trunk roads is the Secretary of State for the Environment. For non-trunk roads the appropriate authority is either the Secretary of State for the Environment or the local authority (for instance a county council or, in London, the relevant London borough) but the local authority has to have his consent.

C[49.24]

These speed limits can be ordered to be in general use or merely during specified periods.

C[49.25]–C[49.30]

This is the provision which enables a 40 or 50 (or whatever) miles per hour limit to be imposed on a specified road. If the road would otherwise be a 'restricted' (ie having a limit of 30 miles per hour) road, eg because of having lamp posts not more than 200 yards apart, it ceases to be a 'restricted' road when an order is made imposing a limit under this provision.

Category D – driving a motor vehicle at a speed exceeding the limit prescribed for that class of vehicle (Road Traffic Regulation Act 1984, s 86)
Legal notes and definitions

C[49.31]

Permitted speed limits for restricted classes of vehicles include:

	Motor-way	*Dual carriage-way*	*Other road*
Coach or motor caravan having an unladen weight exceeding 3.05 tonnes or adapted to carry more than 8 passengers			
(a) if not exceeding 12 metres in overall length	70	60	50
(b) if exceeding 12 metres in overall length	60	60	50
Car, motor caravan, car-derived van drawing one trailer, e g a caravan	60	60	50
Goods vehicle maximum laden weight not exceeding 7.5 tonnes (except car-derived van and articulated vehicles)	70	60	50
Goods vehicle maximum laden weight exceeding 7.5 tonnes	60	50	40
Articulated goods vehicles			
(a) maximum laden weight not exceeding 7.5 tonnes	60	50	50
(b) maximum laden weight exceeding 7.5 tonnes	60	50	40

Category E – where temporary or experimental speed limits have been imposed by the Ministry of Transport (Road Traffic Regulation Act 1984, s 88)
Legal notes and definitions

C[49.32]

The Secretary of State for the Environment may, for a period of up to 18 months, impose a speed limit on all roads or on certain specified roads in the interests of safety or traffic flow. The limit may be general or apply only at specified times.

C[49.33]

Unless such an order directs otherwise, it will not interfere with existing speed limits on restricted roads or roads which are already the subject of an order. It is an order under this provision which has imposed a general speed limit of 70 miles per hour on dual carriageways and 60 miles per hour on single carriageways. Originally of a temporary nature, the order has now been made indefinite.

C[49.34]

A speed limit may be imposed on a stretch of road for a temporary period to prevent danger from works on or near the highway.

C[49.35]

These provisions do not apply to motorways.

Sentencing

C[49.36]

If it appears to the court that the accused suffers from some disease or physical disability likely to cause his driving to be a source of danger to the public, then the court shall notify the licensing authority who may take steps to withdraw the driving licence (see **C[5.49]**).

C[49.37]

Courts will use the national sentencing guidelines to establish a starting point for a fine. The following factors should be considered in assessing seriousness:

(a) the type of vehicle;
(b) the nature of the road;
(c) whether the offence was committed during the hours of darkness and if so whether on lit or unlit road;

(d) weather conditions;
(e) time of day and use of road at the time.

C[50]

Defective steering

Charge

C[50.1]

Using, causing or permitting to be used on a road a motor vehicle with defective steering

Road Vehicles (Construction and Use) Regulations 1986, reg 29; Road Traffic Act 1988, s 41A(b)

Maximum penalty – For a goods vehicle, fine on level 5, otherwise level 4 (for fines see **B[33]**).

Penalty points – 3.

Fixed penalty – £60 (3PP).

Legal notes and definitions

C[50.2]

All the details as to maximum penalty, legal notes, exemption from endorsement and disqualification, and definitions and sentencing set out at **C[9]** for defective brakes apply to this charge of defective steering.

C[50.3]

As with brakes, the law demands that the steering fitted to a motor vehicle on a road shall at all times be maintained in good and efficient working order and properly adjusted.

C[51]

No test certificate

Charge

C[51.1]

Using, causing or permitting a motor vehicle to be on the road first registered 3 or more years previously without having a test certificate in force

Road Traffic Act 1988, s 47(1)

Maximum penalty – Fine level 3. Vehicles adapted to carry more than eight passengers, level 4 (for fines see **B[33]**). No power to endorse or disqualify.

Fixed penalty – £60

Legal notes and definitions

C[51.2]

Passenger vehicles carrying more than eight passengers. These vehicles and some taxis and ambulances must be tested after one year.

C[51.3]

Motor vehicle. See **C[9.7]**.

C[51.4]

Road. Means any highway (including footpaths and bridleways) and any other road to which the public has access and includes bridges.

C[51.5]

Using. This does not in law only mean driving a vehicle along a road; its mere presence on a road, even in a useless condition may constitute using (*Pumbien v Vines* [1996] RTR 37, [1996] Crim LR 124). The test is whether steps had been taken to make it impossible for a driver to drive the vehicle. Where doubt exists consult the legal adviser. A person, limited company, a corporate body which owns a vehicle that is driven in the course of the owner's business is using the vehicle. See **C[9.4]**.

C[51.6]

Causing. This implies some express or positive mandate from the person causing the vehicle to be used; or some authority from him and knowledge of the facts which constitute the offence.

C[51.7]

Permitting. This includes express permission and also circumstances in which permission may be inferred.

C[51.8]

If the defendant is a limited company, it must be proved that some person for whose criminal act the company is responsible permitted the offence. A defendant charged with permitting must be shown to have known the vehicle was being used or that he shut his eyes to something that would have made the use obvious to him.

C[51.9]

Examples of exempted vehicles include:

Goods vehicles the design gross weight of which exceeds 3,500 kg.

Motor tractors.

Articulated vehicles, and their several parts.

Works trucks.

Pedestrian-controlled vehicles.

Invalid vehicles.

Some taxis.

Certain vehicles from abroad and Northern Ireland only here temporarily.

Vehicles en route for export.

Agricultural motor vehicles.

C[51.10]–C[51.15]

Examples of exempted uses include:

(a) that by a previous arrangement the vehicle was being used for the purpose of taking it for a test or for bringing it back from a test (*Williams v Richards* (1997) Times, 29 July);
(b) that the examiner or a person under his personal direction was using the vehicle in the course of or in connection with a test;
(c) that following an unsuccessful test the vehicle was being used by being towed to a place where it could be broken up; or

(d) that by a previous arrangement the vehicle was being taken to or from a place where it was to be or had been taken to remedy defects on the ground of which a test certificate had been refused.

C[51.16]

The defendant need not prove either kind of exemption (ie exempted vehicle or exempted use) beyond reasonable doubt; he need only prove this defence is probably true.

C[51.17]

Renewal of certificate. A certificate lasts for one year. Within one month from the expiry of the certificate, the vehicle may be retested and a further certificate issued to commence on the expiry of the existing certificate.

Sentencing

C[51.18]

This offence is more serious if it is committed with a vehicle that would not pass the test, or would pass only if money is spent bringing it up to standard. In such cases, other offences are usually associated with it. In other cases a small fine is usual. The fine might be increased according to the length of time the vehicle has been untested.

C[52]

Traffic signs

Charge

C[52.1]

Failing to comply with the indication given by a traffic sign

Road Traffic Act 1988, s 36

Maximum penalty – Fine level 3 (for fines see **B[33]**). Endorsement and disqualification can only be ordered if the vehicle was a motor vehicle and the traffic sign was one of the following: **Stop, Traffic Lights** (including portable traffic lights and green filter arrows), **No Entry Sign** or **Double White Lines.** For these signs disqualification can be for any period or until the accused has passed a driving test. Must endorse for these signs unless there are special reasons.

Endorsement and disqualification also apply to drivers of 'abnormal loads' at railway level crossings who fail to phone the signalman before crossing and to drivers of vehicles which contravene relevant height restrictions.

Penalty points – 3 (only for endorsable offences).

Fixed penalty – £60 (endorsable offences); £30 (otherwise).

Legal notes and definitions

C[52.2]

It is not a defence that the sign was not seen.

C[52.3]

The defendant can only be convicted if at the time of the offence he was warned of possible prosecution, or a summons or a notice of intended prosecution was served within 14 days upon the registered owner of the vehicle. It will be presumed that this requirement was complied with unless the contrary is proved by the defendant on the balance of probabilities.

C[52.4]

The offence applies to all vehicles including pedal cycles and is not limited to mechanically propelled vehicles.

C[52.5]

Even wheeling a pedal cycle in contravention of the sign is an offence.

C[52.6]

A traffic sign. This is presumed to be of correct size, colour and type unless proved to the contrary by the defence.

C[52.7]

Automatic traffic lights are presumed to be in proper working order unless the contrary is proved by the defence.

C[52.8]

Traffic lights. It is an offence if any part of the vehicle crosses the 'stop' line when the light is red, for example, if the front part of the vehicle is already over the line and the light turns red an offence is committed if the rear part of the vehicle then crosses the line with the light still at red.

C[52.9]

Double white lines. It is an offence to overtake or park in contravention of double white lines in the middle of the road. There are certain exceptions, however, such as passing a slow moving road sweeper or a taxi stopping to allow a passenger to alight or board. Ask the legal adviser for details.

C[52.10]–C[52.15]

A road. Means any highway (including footpaths and bridleways) and any other road to which the public has access and includes bridges.

C[52.16]

Signs to which the offence applies. These include:

Emergency traffic signs placed by a constable on the instructions of a chief officer of police.

[1] Stop at major road ahead.

Give way at major road ahead.

Stop one way working.

[1] No entry.

Arrow indicating direction to be followed.

Arrow indicating keep left or right.

[1] Red light including portable light signals and at automatic level crossings.

[1]Double white lines.

Keep left dual carriageway.

Turn left at dual carriageway.

[1] Drivers of 'abnormal loads' at railway level crossings.

[1] Prohibition on vehicles exceeding specified height.

[1] Green arrow traffic signals.

No 'U' turn.

Mini roundabout sign.

[1] Only these offences qualify for endorsement and disqualification. See reg 10 of the Traffic Signs Regulations and General Directions 2002.

Sentencing

C[52.17]

Endorsement and disqualification can only be ordered if the vehicle was a motor vehicle and the traffic sign was one of those mentioned under 'Maximum penalty'.

C[52.18]

If it appears to the court that the accused suffers from some disease or physical disability likely to cause his driving to be a source of danger to the public, then the court shall notify the licensing authority who may take steps to withdraw the driving licence (see **C[5.49]**).

C[52.19]

The fine will depend to some extent on the sign ignored.

C[52.20]

For the endorsable offences a moderate fine may be considered.

C[53]

Defective tyres

Charge

C[53.1]

Using, causing or permitting to be used on a road a motor vehicle or trailer with defective tyres

Road Vehicles (Construction and Use) Regulations 1986, reg 27; Road Traffic Act 1988, s 41A(b)

Maximum penalty – For a goods vehicle, fine level 5, otherwise level 4 (for fines see **B[33]**). May disqualify for any period and/or until a driving test has been passed. Must endorse unless special reasons exist.

For 'special reasons', see **C[5.2]**.

Penalty points – 3.

Fixed penalty – £60 (3PP).

Legal notes and definitions

C[53.2]

All the details as to legal notes, exemption from endorsement and disqualification, definitions and sentencing set out on at **C[9]** for defective brakes also apply to these charges.

C[53.3]

It is an offence for a tyre on a car or light van (gross weight not exceeding 3,500 kg) and their trailers to be in any of the following conditions:

(a) tyre being unsuitable having regard to the use to which the vehicle is put;
(b) tyre being unsuitable having regard to types of tyres on other wheels;
(c) tyre not so inflated as to make it fit for use to which vehicle is being put;
(d) break in fabric of tyre;
(e) ply or cord structure exposed;

(f) the grooves of the tread pattern of the tyre do not have a depth of at least 1 millimetre throughout a continuous band comprising the central three-quarters of the breadth of the tread and round the entire outer circumference of the tyre;
(g) tyre must be free from any defect which might damage the road surface or cause danger to persons in the vehicle or on the road.

Consult the legal adviser for the complete list.

C[53.4]

The law requires all tyres of a motor vehicle or trailer on a road to be free from any defect which might in any way cause damage to the road surface or cause danger to persons in or on a vehicle or to other persons using the road.

C[53.5]

If no tyre is fitted at all the offence will be brought under a different regulation.

C[53.6]

Two or more defective tyres. If a vehicle has two or more defective tyres, a separate charge should be alleged for each.

Sentencing

C[53.7]

As for 'brakes' see **C[9.16]**. A vehicle with two defective tyres is much more dangerous than a vehicle with only one defective tyre. Where the means of the offender permit the penalty should usually ensure that it is cheaper to keep the vehicle in good condition than to risk a fine. A short disqualification can also be considered.

C[53.8]

The penalty should also reflect the potential danger not only to the driver and passengers in the offending vehicle, but to other road users.

Section D

Family proceedings

Index to family proceedings

D[1]

Family proceedings

D[1.1]

Magistrates' courts have an extensive jurisdiction in family proceedings which for this purpose are defined to include proceedings under the Children Act 1989, applications for maintenance of a spouse under the Domestic Proceedings and Magistrates' Courts Act 1978, applications for consent to marry (Marriage Act 1949, s 3), adoption (Magistrates' Courts Act 1980, s 65) and domestic violence applications (Family Law Act 1996).

D[1.2]

The Children Act 1989 has created a largely concurrent jurisdiction between the three courts which deal with the welfare of children – the High Court, county court and magistrates' court – and as far as practicable the procedures in the three courts have been assimilated. All these courts also have jurisdiction in adoption proceedings and this coming together of the separate jurisdictions will lay the foundations for one unified family court.

D[1.3]

In using the term 'family proceedings' it should be noted that the term is also used in a different and more restricted sense when referring to the power of the courts to make orders in family proceedings under the Children Act, see **D[4]**.

The family proceedings court

D[1.4]

Jurisdiction in the magistrates' court resides in the 'Family Proceedings Court'. Parties to a private dispute (ie one not involving a local authority) are able, subject to practical and financial limitations, to choose whether the High Court, county court or magistrates' court is to hear their case, whereas all public law proceedings (which include most matters formerly heard in wardship) will commence in the family proceedings court. In the case of public law proceedings the justices' clerk will allocate such cases to the more appropriate court, eg lengthy or complex matters to the county court where they will be heard there or transferred on to the High Court.

Family proceedings panel

D[1.5]

Only those justices who have been appointed to the Family Proceedings Panel may adjudicate in the family proceedings court. Justices were appointed by the bench at its meeting in October 1991 and served until 31 December 1993 and for periods of three years at a time thereafter. [It is anticipated that different arrangements will be made for the election of family panel members under rules to be made under the Courts Act 2003. These arrangements will be known colloquially as "ticketing" and will replace the current system. A date has yet to be fixed for when the new rules will come into force.]

D[1.6]

Each court, except in unforeseen circumstances, will be presided over by a panel member specially trained as a chairman and must so far as is practicable comprise both a man and woman.

Privacy

D[1.7]

The courtroom. So far as is consistent with the due dispatch of business, family proceedings should be heard separately from the hearing of other business (MCA 1980, s 69).

D[1.8]

Persons present during the hearing. Only the following are allowed to be present:

(a) officers of the court;
(b) parties to the case before the court, their solicitors and counsel, and witnesses and other persons directly concerned with that case;
(c) representatives of newspapers or news agencies;
(d) persons permitted by the court to be present, but permission shall not be withheld from a person who appears to the court to have adequate grounds for attendance (MCA 1980, s 69).

D[1.9]

More stringent requirements apply to adoption proceedings, when persons included in paragraphs (a) and (b) only may be in court.

D[1.10]–D[1.15]

Restrictions on reporting. The press may not report particulars of the proceedings other than:

(a) the names, addresses and occupations of the parties and witnesses;
(b) the grounds of the application and a concise statement of the charges, defences and counter-charges in support of which evidence has been given;
(c) submissions on points of law and the court's decision on them;
(d) the decision of the court and any observations of the court on making it (Magistrates' Courts Act 1980, s 71(1)).

D[1.16]

In adoption proceedings the press may also not report matters at (a) and (b) and must not identify the child in any way (MCA 1980, s 71).

Evidence

D[1.17]

In any family proceedings in a magistrates' court, hearsay evidence given in connection with the upbringing, maintenance or welfare of a child is admissible.

Reasons for decision

D[1.18]

The reasons for any decision of the family proceedings court must be announced and recorded at the time the decision is made and a copy of that record will be available on demand from the legal adviser to any person who is considering an appeal. The reasons must be drawn up in consultation with the legal adviser but they will be the justices' reasons (or the reasons of a majority of them) and not those of the legal adviser. It is advised that the justices retire with the legal adviser and after making their decision they formulate their reasons and ask the legal adviser to write them down before returning to court to announce the decisions. The availability of technology allows legal advisers to record the reasons on a PC rather than writing them in conventional form.

(a) Guidance to the courts on the giving of reasons is contained in *Re B (Procedure in Family Proceedings Courts)* [1992] 2 FCR 631, [1993] Fam Law 209, CA.
(b) Reasons may not be amplified later when an appeal is lodged (*Hillingdon London Borough Council v H* [1993] Fam 43, [1993] 1 All ER 198).

(c) Reasons must be formulated before making an order (*Hertfordshire County Council v W* [1992] 2 FCR 885, [1992] 39 LS Gaz R 33, sub nom W v Hertfordshire County Council [1993] 1 FLR 118, [1993] Fam Law 75).

(d) Reasons must be given for all decisions including interim orders, granting or refusing leave or on the refusal of an application to adjourn (*T v W* (contact: reasons for refusing leave) [1997] 1 FCR 118, [1996] 2 FLR 473).

(e) If the recommendations of a guardian ad litem or welfare officer are not followed reasons for that should be given (*S v Oxfordshire County Council* [1993] 2 FCR 676, [1993] 1 FLR 452).

(f) Magistrates must comply with rule 21(6) by stating their reasons and findings of fact but in doing so orally they are able to summarise their written reasons (*Oxfordshire County Council v S* (2005) FLR 426).

D[2]

The welfare of the child (Children Act 1989)

The welfare principle

D[2.1]

'When a court determines any question with respect to:

(a) the upbringing of a child; or
(b) the administration of a child's property or the application of any income arising from it,

the child's welfare shall be the court's paramount consideration' (Children Act 1989, s 1(1)).

D[2.2]

The test is amplified by two more provisions:

(i)Delay

D[2.3]

> 'the court shall have regard to the general principle that any delay in determining the question is likely to prejudice the welfare of the child' (s 1(2)).

September 2003 saw the launch of a national protocol and standard directions forms. The objective is to reduce delay in public law care cases and thereby produce better outcomes for children. Children should have to spend less time in temporary care arrangements. The period of instability which impacts on their personal and educational development should be reduced. The principle of making high quality decisions about their welfare must however be retained (at the time of writing a national protocol is being drawn up for private law family proceedings)

(ii) Welfare checklist

D[2.4]

Where a court is considering an *opposed* application to make, vary or discharge a 'section 8' order (see **D[4.3]**), or is considering making, varying or discharging a care or supervision order it must have regard in particular to a 'checklist' of factors:

(a) the ascertainable wishes and feelings of the child concerned (considered in the light of his age and understanding);
(b) his physical, emotional and educational needs;
(c) the likely effect on him of any change in his circumstances;
(d) his age, sex, background and any characteristics of his which the court considers relevant;
(e) any harm which he has suffered or is at risk of suffering;
(f) how capable each of his parents, and any other person in relation to whom the court considers the question to be relevant, is of meeting his needs;
(g) the range of powers available to the court under this Act in the proceedings in question (s 1(3)).

D[2.5]

It should be noted that the wishes and feelings of the child will normally be communicated to the court through the children's guardian or the children and family reporter. Only in rare or exceptional cases should justices see children in private for this purpose (*Re M (a minor)* [1993] 2 FCR 721, [1993] 2 FLR 706).

D[2.6]

Presumption of no order. The court should only make an order if it is in the child's best interests (Children Act 1989, s 1(5)).

D[3]

Parental responsibility

D[3.1]

The primary responsibility for the upbringing and care of children resides with their parents. Accordingly the Children Act 1989 refers to parental 'responsibilities' rather than parental 'rights'. Under the former law the obligations of parents to their children were not articulated as clearly as they might have been. In practice most disputes between parents concern residence and contact. The law now seeks consciously to emphasise that in reality both parents have an enduring responsibility for their children which continues whether or not the child is living with them unless and until the child reaches 18 years of age or, in certain circumstances is adopted.

D[3.2]

Accordingly it is necessary to determine who has parental responsibility for a child.

Persons having parental responsibility for a child

D[3.3]

(a) (where they were married to each other at the time of the child's birth) the mother and the father (Children Act 1989, s 2(1)) ('married etc' includes where the parents married subsequent to the birth);

(b) (where the parents were not so married) the mother alone, unless:
   (i) the parents make an agreement to share parental responsibility; or
   (ii) the father makes a successful application to the court for an order granting him parental responsibility which is then shared equally with the mother (s 4);

(c) anyone who acquires a residence order under s 8 acquires parental responsibility for as long as the order is in force;

(d) by the father being registered as the child's father under any of the Births and Deaths legislation applicable to England, Wales, Scotland or Northern Ireland.

D[3.4]

Once parental responsibility is acquired under para (a) above it can never be lost unless the child is adopted or reaches 18 years of age. Parental responsibility acquired under para (b) may be brought to an end by an order of the court.

D[3.5]

The court may also make orders in **family proceedings** which grant parental responsibility to other persons *in addition* to the parents, in which case parental responsibility is shared.

D[3.6]

Definition. Parental responsibility means 'all the rights, duties, powers, responsibilities and authority which by law a parent has in relation to the child and his property' (s 3(1)).

D[3.7]

A desire to exercise parental responsibility is something the courts should encourage (*Re S (a minor)* [1995] 3 FCR 225, [1995] 2 FLR 648, CA); an order may be made in favour of a father if the court is satisfied of:

(a) the degree of commitment he has shown to the child;
(b) the degree of attachment which exists between him and the child;
(c) the reasons for his applying for the order. (*Re G (a minor)* [1994] 2 FCR 1037, [1994] 1 FLR 504, CA)

Acquisition of parental responsibility by father (Children Act 1989, s 4)

D[3.8]

The Family Law Reform Act 1987 provides that as a general principle in legislation passed after the Act came into force and in certain other statutes in the relationship between two people no regard is to be paid to whether any of their parents or forebears have been married. The legislation refers to a child whose parents have not been married. Where a child is born to such parents the father will have parental responsibility if he is named on the birth certificate. If he is not so named, he may apply to the court under the Children Act 1989, s 4 for an order that he shall have parental responsibility for the child and if given this he will share it equally with the mother. Such an order may subsequently be discharged on a further application made by the father or mother.

If a mother agrees to the father's name being registered on the birth certificate he will obtain parental responsibility (PR) without the need for a court order. Step-parents may acquire PR by agreement or by order of the court.

D[3.9]

Proof of parentage. There is a rebuttable presumption that a child born to parents who are married is the child of both of them. Where parentage is in dispute various methods of proof are available.

D[3.10]–D[3.15]

1 Evidence of the father. As these are civil proceedings, he may be compelled to give evidence on behalf of the mother. His evidence on oath may provide the corroboration for her testimony.

D[3.16]

2 Scientific tests. The Family Law Reform Act 1969, Part III and the Family Law Act 1986 empowers the court to give a direction for the use of scientific tests (on application of either party) to be made on the mother, child and defendant. The rules are complicated so that when a court has scientific tests in mind, it should first consult its legal adviser.

D[3.17]–D[3.18]

No person can be compelled to submit to a scientific test, even though a direction has been given. The court has jurisdiction to order that a sample be taken from a child under 16 where it would be in his interests, even though the person with care and control of the child does not consent.

D[3.19]

Magistrates may direct scientific tests on an application for a declaration of parentage under s 55A of the Family Law Act 1986. This is a single mechanism for all applicants including the Child Support Agency. A refusal to comply with an order for blood tests may result in an adverse inference being drawn sufficient to rebut the presumption of legitimacy (*F v Child Support Agency* [1999] 2 FCR 385, [1999] 2 FLR 244). Although in *Re H and A (paternity: blood tests)* [2002] EWCA Civ 383, [2002] 2 FCR 469 it was said that the interests of justice are best served by the truth and the court should have the best scientific evidence rather than rely on inference.

D[3.20]

While blood tests cannot determine who is the actual father of a child, in about 80% of cases these tests can establish that a man cannot possibly be the father of a child and thus he can only be excluded from paternity.

It is now possible to employ DNA genetic fingerprinting which is not merely an 'exclusionary' test but can prove parentage with almost complete certainty.

D[3.21]–D[3.23]

3 Evidence of a conviction or a finding of adultery in previous matrimonial proceedings. If the complainant wishes to use the Civil Evidence Act 1968, s 11 or s 12 by proving that the defendant was convicted of an offence of having unlawful sexual intercourse with the complainant at the material time or if she wishes to rely on a finding of adultery in previous matrimonial proceedings, she may do so but the legal adviser should be consulted.

Appointment of guardian (Children Act 1989, s 5)

D[3.24]

Where a child has no parent with parental responsibility for him or a parent or guardian in whose favour a residence order has been made has died while the order was in force, any person may apply to the court to be appointed as the child's guardian and thereby acquire parental responsibility.

D[4]

Orders with respect to the upbringing of children

Private law proceedings

D[4.1]

Although parents have parental responsibility for their children, it will be necessary on occasion for the court to intervene either, for example, to resolve a dispute between parents as to how their responsibility should be exercised, or where individuals such as foster parents wish to acquire parental responsibility. It may also be appropriate to provide specifically for the upbringing of children involved in other family proceedings such as adoption, domestic violence and for maintenance of a spouse and in family proceedings under the Children Act 1989 itself: applications to acquire parental responsibility by unmarried fathers (s 4); appointment of guardians (s 5); applications for financial relief (Sch 1); are all normally referred to as **private law proceedings**. In all these private law proceedings the court may make one or more of the following orders.

Public law proceedings are dealt with at **D[6]**.

(References are all to the Children Act 1989.)

Welfare reports (Children Act 1989, s 7)

D[4.2]

A court considering any question with respect to a child under this Act may ask an officer of CAFCASS (the Children and Family Court Advisory and Support Service) or local authority social worker to report to the court on matters relating to the welfare of that child (s 7(1)). See CAFCASS Practice Note (2001). Information contained in such reports will be supplied to the parties in the proceedings. The officer may not give assurances of confidentiality and the court will only withhold information contained in reports in the most exceptional circumstances where real harm would be caused to the child by disclosure (*Re G (minors)* [1994] 1 FCR 37, [1993] 2 FLR 293, CA).

Section 8 orders

D[4.3]

The court may make one or more of the following orders under the Children Act 1989, s 8.

D[4.4]

Contact order requiring the person with whom the child lives to allow the child to visit or stay with or otherwise have contact with the person named in the order. The court should regard contact with both parents to be a right of the child which should not be denied due to earlier difficulties suffered after the parent separation (*Re H (minors)* [1992] 1 FCR 70, [1992] 1 FLR 148, CA). An application for contact and parental responsibility are to be treated separately. A refusal to grant contact does not mean parental responsibility should also be refused (*Re C and V (minors)* [1998] 1 FCR 52, [1998] 1 FLR 392, CA). See also *Glaser v United Kingdom* [2000] 3 FCR 193, [2001] 1 FLR 153, ECtHR on the human rights issues surrounding the court's obligations to enforce contact. The court may make an order for reasonable contact and should encourage parties to reach agreement but when faced with an issue the court must make a determination (*Re P (Parental Dispute: Judicial Determination)* [2002] EWCA Civ 1627, [2002] All ER (D) 80 (Oct)). Where repeated orders for contact have failed due to the actions of one parent a transfer of residence to the other parent may be used if it is in the best interests of the children and ensures a normal relationship with both parents (*V v V (children) (intractable contact dispute)* [2004] EWHC 1215 (Fam), [2004] All ER (D) 304 (May)).

D[4.5]

Prohibited steps order that no step which a person with parental responsibility might take, shall be taken without the consent of the court.

D[4.6]

Residence order settling the arrangements to be made as to with whom a child is to live.

D[4.7]

Specific issue order giving directions to determine a specific question in connection with any aspect of parental responsibility for a child.

D[4.8]

Availability. A s 8 order may be made:

(a) in the course of any family proceedings:
  (i) on the application of a person entitled to apply or who has obtained the leave of the court to apply;

(ii) where the court considers that the order should be made even though no application has been made; and
(iii) at any time during proceedings even though the court is not in a position finally to dispose of these proceedings.

D[4.9]–D[4.15]

A court will not normally hold a detailed hearing of a case to determine an application for leave to apply but may in a disputed case hear the main parties to form a broad view of the merits of the application (the Children Act 1989, s 10(a) and *Re F and R (s 8 Order Grandparents application)* [1998] Crim LR 657).

D[5]

Persons who may apply for a s 8 order

D[5.1]

	Contact	*Prohibited steps*	*Residence*	*Specific issue*
Parent/Guardian	✓	✓	✓	✓
Person with residence order	✓	✓	✓	✓
Party to marriage re child of family	✓	*	✓	*
Person with whom child has lived for 1 year	✓	*	✓	*
Persons with consent of:				
(1) persons with residence order	✓	*	✓	*
(2) (child in care) local authority	✓	*	✓	*
(3) those with PR	✓	*	✓	*
Other applicants	*	*	*	*
Local authority	-	*	-	*

Notes

* Leave of the court required.

- A residence order grants parental responsibility to the person in whose favour it is made.
- A specific issue or prohibited steps order shall not be made with a view to achieving a result which could be achieved by making a residence or contact order.
- No court may make a s 8 order other than a residence order in respect of a child in the care of a local authority.

- Local authority foster parents need consent of the authority unless they are relatives or the child has lived with them for at one year or more.

D[5.2]

The making of a residence order will give the person in whose favour the order is made parental responsibility for the child (subject to some limitations – eg there is no power to consent to adoption) whilst the order is in force (s 12). Certain persons who do not have parental responsibility may not apply for prohibited steps or specific issue orders as these would be an unwarranted interference in the exercise of the parental responsibility of others.

Only in exceptional circumstances should the court attach a condition restricting movement within the UK (*Re H (children: relocation)* (2001) Times, 29 August, CA)

D[5.3]

Children in care and applications by local authorities (Children Act 1989, ss 9 and 10). No s 8 order, except a residence order (which has the effect of discharging a care order), may be made with respect to a child in the care of a local authority. Conversely a local authority may not apply for a residence or contact order in respect of a child not in their care; those matters are more appropriately dealt with in care proceedings where 'threshold' criteria have to be fulfilled. Specific limitations are placed on applications by local authority foster parents.

D[5.4]

Welfare criterion and welfare checklist. See **D[2]**.

D[5.5]

Welfare reports. See **D[4.2]**.

D[5.6]

Delay and court timetable. In order to avoid delay rules of court provide for the court to draw up a timetable with a view to determining the issue without delay (s 11(1)). The importance of the court taking a proactive role at the directions hearing is emphasised *(Re G, S and M (care proceedings)* (1999)).

D[5.7]

Is a court order necessary? A court shall not make an order under the Children Act 1989 unless it considers that doing so would be better for the child than making no order at all (s 1(5)).

D[5.8]

Duration of orders. A s 8 order cannot be made in respect of a child who has attained 16 years, or extend beyond that age unless there are exceptional circumstances (s 9).

D[5.9]

Transfer of proceedings. Provision is made for a case under the Children Act 1989 to be transferred from one court to another either horizontally to another family proceedings court or vertically to the county court.

D[5.10]–D[5.15]

The overall test is whether the interests of the child demand that the proceedings be transferred. The legal adviser will advise on factors likely to affect this finding, such as complexity or consolidation of proceedings. Difficult evidential issues surrounding sexual abuse are best transferred to the county court (*Re W (a child) (sexual abuse)* [2002] All ER (D) 34 (Jan)).

D[5.16]

Supplementary provisions. A s 8 order may contain directions about how it is to be carried into effect, impose conditions which must be complied with by any person named in the order and make such incidental, supplemental or consequential provision as the court thinks fit (s 11(8)).

D[5.17]

Investigation by the local authority (s 37). Where it appears to the court that it may be appropriate to make a care or supervision order it may direct the local authority to undertake an investigation of the child's circumstances. If the court is considering making an interim care order then the proceedings become specified and a children's guardian may be appointed: see **D[6.17]–D[6.19]**.Where the authority decides not to apply for such an order it must report to the court generally within eight weeks giving its reasons, details of any services or assistance the authority will provide and any other action it proposes to take, and the proceedings cease to be specified proceedings. It is not appropriate to invoke public law procedures in private law proceedings (*Re CE (section 37 direction)* [1995] 1 FCR 387, [1995] 1 FLR 26.)

Family assistance orders (s 16)

D[5.18]

Whether or not the court makes a s 8 order, it may make a family assistance order requiring a CAFCASS officer or social worker to advise, assist or befriend a parent, the child or a person with whom the child is living or who has the benefit of a contact order. A family assistance order shall not be made so as to require a local authority to make an officer of the authority available unless (i) the authority agree (ii) the child concerned lives or will live within the local authority area.

D[6]

Public law proceedings

D[6.1]

Normally Art 8 of the Human Rights Act protects family life from state interventions. However this is a qualified right and the local authority or the NSPCC are prescribed by statute as being able to bring proceedings for the welfare of children.

A local authority may provide accommodation for any child within their area if they consider that to do so would safeguard or promote his welfare and in certain cases, such as where children have been abandoned or are in need, are under a duty to do so. However, such accommodation may not be provided where any person with parental responsibility who can arrange for his accommodation objects. The only means whereby a local authority may compulsorily obtain the care of a child is as a result of an order made by a court in care proceedings.

Articles 6 and 8 are engaged in every application and once the threshold test is satisfied the court uses a welfare checklist to balance the competing art 8 rights of the parties and the child. The family proceedings court will normally deal with these issues without need for an upwards transfer (*Re V (a child)* [2004] EWCA Civ 54, [2004] All ER (D) 52 (Feb)).

Directions appointments

D[6.2]

On receipt of an application in care proceedings the legal adviser must fix a date for a court hearing or directions appointment. The purpose of a directions appointment at which the parties, their legal advisers and a children's guardian may be present is to ensure that those facts which are and are not in dispute are clearly identified, that a guardian is appointed where appropriate if this has not already been done and that a timetable is set. The parties will be under a duty to disclose to each other and the court in written form the evidence on which they intend to rely. The magistrates may then read the evidence in advance of the hearing so that the oral evidence may be directed to matters in dispute. There may be more than one directions appointment during the course of the proceedings. The President of the Family Division of the High Court has intimated that care proceedings should where practicable be concluded within three months (this intimation must now be read in the light of the national protocol below). Other parties such as grandparents may apply for leave to join the application (or apply for a residence order). Their applications should be assessed with due regard to the statutory checklist: s 10(a) (*Re J (leave to serve application for Residence Order)* [2003] 1 FLR 114, [2003] Fam Law 27, CA).

In applying for leave to appoint an expert the applicant should specify:

(i) the category of expert evidence sought;
(ii) the name of the expert and their CV;
(iii) the expert's timetable for reporting and availability for attending court;
(iv) the relevance of the expert evidence to the issues of the case;
(v) an explanation if the report sought is not to be on a joint instruction. The normal expectation will be that an expert will be jointly instructed, with the guardian ad litem in public law and applicant in private law, acting as the lead party. The costs of a jointly appointed expert will be borne by the parties dependent on the reasonableness of the case (*Calderdale Metropolitan Borough Council v S* [2004] EWHC 2529 (Fam), [2004] All ER (D) 346 (Nov)).

The court may grant leave to the parties for example to have disclosure of documents (*Re B (disclosure to other parties)* [2002] 2 FCR 32, [2001] 2 FLR 1017).

The national protocol. Seeks to bring about a change in the culture of case management amongst judges and lawyers. Issues should be focussed earlier on in the process, documents necessary to resolving the issues should be identified early on, all parties should be clear on the timetable and the actions being taken by others, the number of directions hearings should be reduced and the settlement rate should increase. The process can be compressed into six stages:

Stage 1 [by 3rd day]	Application is made
Stage 2 [by 6th day]	First court hearing in FPC
Stage 3 [by 11th day]	Directions and allocations hearing
Stage 4 [between 15th and 60th day]	Case management
Stage 5 [by 260th day]	Pre final hearing review
Stage 6 [by 280th day]	Final hearing

Thus completing the process in a 40 week time period.

Applications

D[6.3]

Applicant. The local authority or an 'authorised person' (at present only the NSPCC).

Ordinarily a parent will be allowed to join proceedings as a party but this is not an absolute right. Notice has to be served even on an absent parent (*Re B (a child)(Parentage: knowledge of proceedings)* [2003] EWCA Civ 1842, [2003] All ER (D) 129 (Nov), sub nom AB (care proceedings: service on husband ignorant of child's existence), Re [2004] 1 FLR 527, [2004] Fam Law 17). In exceptional circumstances and after consideration of Arts 6 and 8 a parent, who has formed no family life with the child, may be excluded (*Re G* [2004] EWHC 1474 (Fam), [2004] All ER (D) 163 (May)).

D[6.4]

Grounds for application (s 31). The court must be satisfied (on the balance of probabilities):

(a) that the child concerned is suffering, or is likely to suffer, significant harm; and
(b) that the harm, or likelihood of harm, is attributable to:
   (i) the care given to the child, or likely to be given to him if the order were not made, not being what it would be reasonable to expect a parent to give him; or
   (ii) the child's being beyond parental control.

In some cases an order may result even though it is not clear which parent caused which injuries to their child (*Re O and N (care: preliminary hearing)* [2003] UKHL 18, [2004] 1 AC 523, sub nom Re O & N [2003] 1 FLR 1169, HL).

D[6.5]

The use of the terms 'is suffering or is likely to suffer' means at the date the local authority had initiated protective arrangements. If the need for these protective arrangements ceases because the child's welfare is satisfactorily provided for otherwise, it will not be possible to found *subsequent* jurisdiction on the situation at the time of initiation of those arrangements. It is only permissible to look back from the date of disposal to the date of initiation of protection where local authority arrangements had been continuously in place (*Re M* [1994] 2 AC 424, [1994] 3 All ER 298, HL).

D[6.6]

In order to establish that a child was likely to suffer significant harm in the future within the meaning of the Children Act 1989, s 31 so as to enable the court to make a care or supervision order, there has to be a real possibility of the risk, based on actual facts rather that mere suspicions (*Re H* [1996] AC 563, [1996] 1 All ER 1, HL). Once the threshold test has been conceded it is not necessary to hear lengthy evidence on issues of child protection (*Re B (threshold criteria in agreed facts)* [1999] 2 FCR 328, [1998] 2 FLR 968, CA).

A supervision order may be a proportional response to the circumstances of the case (*Re O (supervision order)* [2001] EWCA Civ 16, [2001] 1 FCR 289).

D[6.7]

Harm means ill-treatment or the impairment of health or development including, for example, impairment suffered form seeing or hearing the ill-treatment of another. It is not necessary for the harm to be proved to be due to a failure of care by one or more identified individuals but that it is attributable to an absence of care to the objective standard in the statute (*Lancashire County Council v A* [2000] 2 AC 147, [2000] 2 All ER 97, HL). Serious injury is still judged on the balance of probabilities, although the more improbable the event the stronger the evidence must be that it happened before, on that evidential burden, its occurrence will be established (*Re U; Re B (serious injury; standard of proof)* [2004] EWCA Civ 567, [2004] All ER (D) 197 (May); affd [2005] EWCA Civ 52, [2005] All ER (D) 385 (Feb).

D[6.8]

Development means physical, intellectual, emotional, social or behavioural development.

D[6.9]

Health means physical or mental health.

D[6.10]–D[6.15]

Ill-treatment includes sexual abuse and forms of ill-treatment which are not physical.

D[6.16]

Significant. Where the question whether harm suffered by a child is significant turns on the child's health or development, his health or development shall be compared with that which could reasonably be expected of a similar child.

D[6.17]

Appointment of a child's guardian (s 41). The court must appoint a guardian unless it is satisfied that it is not necessary to do so in order to safeguard the interests of the child.

D[6.18]

The guardian will be appointed from CAFCASS referred to at **D[4.2]**.

D[6.19]

The duties of the guardian include instructing a solicitor on behalf of the child and also preparing a report for the assistance of the court. The guardian's paramount consideration is to have regard to the need to safeguard and promote the best interests of the child.

D[6.20]

Welfare paramount and checklist. See **D[2]**.

D[6.21]

Delay. The court must draw up a timetable to dispose of the application. In child abuse cases the concentration should be on the factual issues which may establish the threshold test and not psychiatric or psychological assessment of the parties (*Re CB and JB (care proceeding guidelines)* [1998] 2 FCR 313, [1998] 2 FLR 211).

D[6.22]

Necessity for a court order. The court should ask itself whether an order would be better for the welfare of the child than making no order.

Orders of the court

D[6.23]

Care order. The local authority designated in the care order has parental responsibility for the child. Parents will retain their parental responsibility but the local authority may determine the extent to which the parents may meet their parental responsibility for him. The authority may only do this if it is necessary to safeguard or promote the child's welfare (s 33(4)).

D[6.24]

The court must consider a care plan when making a care order (s 31A). No order can be made unless the court has considered a care plan which may be challenged before the family proceedings court (*Re I (care proceedings; human rights claims)* (2004) 1 FLR 289).

Before making a care order the court must consider the arrangements made or proposed for contact with the child by his parents and other specified persons (s 34). There is a presumption (which is rebuttable) that there will be reasonable contact. The court may make an order regulating contact on application or of its own motion and may also make an order that there be no contact. In a matter of urgency and for no more than seven days a local authority may terminate contact without a court order. There is no power given to the court to impose conditions when making a care order (*Re T (a minor)* [1994] 2 FCR 721, sub nom Re T (a minor) [1994] 2 FLR 423, [1994] Fam Law 558, [1994] 21 LS Gaz R 40, CA). In *Re S (children: care plan)* [2002] UKHL 10, [2002] 2 AC 291, sub nom S (children: care plan) [2002] 2 All ER 192, HL the court said that when deciding whether to make a care order, the court should have before it a care plan which was sufficiently firm and particularised for all concerned to have a clear picture of the child's foreseeable future. However the court specifically disapproved the setting of 'starred milestones' in the order for the local authority to achieve.

D[6.25]–D[6.30]

Age limit. No care or supervision order may be made in respect of a child who has attained 17 years (16 if married).

D[6.31]

Duration. A care order, unless it is brought to an end earlier, will continue in force until the child reaches 18 years (s 91(12)).

D[6.32]

Supervision order. Places a child under the supervision of a probation officer or social worker for an initial period of one year. The order may be renewed for an aggregate maximum period of three years. The supervisor is to advise, assist and befriend the child and the order may require him to notify any change of address and to allow the supervisor to visit him.

D[6.33]

The order may include a requirement to comply with directions for intermediate treatment, and psychiatric and medical treatment (see **B[47.21]–B[47.24]**).

D[6.34]

Obligations may be imposed on a person with parental responsibility or with whom the child is living to take reasonable steps to ensure the child complies with the requirements made of him. The making of a supervision order brings to an end any earlier care or supervision order.

Interim orders (s 38)

D[6.35]

On an application for a care or supervision order or where in other family proceedings the court has directed the local authority to investigate the child's circumstances, the court may make an interim care or supervision order as a holding measure (*Re S (children: care plan)* [2002] UKHL 10, [2002] 2 AC 291, sub nom S (children: care plan) [2002] 2 All ER 192).

D[6.36]

The court must be satisfied that there are reasonable grounds for believing that the circumstances are as mentioned in the grounds for a care or supervision order set out at **D[6.3]**. Interim orders (which are renewable) may not extend for more than four weeks at a time except to extend for up to eight weeks from the making of the initial order.

D[6.37]

In deciding the period of an interim order, the court shall consider whether any party opposed to the making of the order was in a position to argue his case against the order in full. Where there is too much change in a case to make a final order, an interim order should be made (*Re C (a child)* [2001] EWCA Civ 810, [2001] 3 FCR 381). In *Re D (a minor: contact:interim order)* [1995] 1 FCR 501, [1995] 1 FLR 495 the court is advised to be cautious about making interim contact orders where principle of contact is in dispute/substantial factors unresolved, and to look upon interim orders as part of a coherent strategy – to be planned and implemented. For emergency protection orders see **D[9.16]**.

Exclusion requirement

D[6.38]

An exclusion order may be part of an interim care order and specify that:

(a) someone leave a dwelling-house in which he is living with the child concerned;
(b) someone be prohibited from entering a dwelling-house in which the child lives;
(c) someone be excluded from a defined area in which a dwelling is located (the dwelling must be where the child lives).

D[6.39]

The following criteria must be satisfied:

(1) there are reasonable grounds for believing that the child is suffering or is likely to suffer significant harm; and
(2) that the harm or likelihood of harm is attributable to the care given to the child, or likely to be given to him if the order were not made, not being what it would be reasonable to expect a parent to give him; and
(3) the court decides to make an interim care order on the basis of (1) and (2) being satisfied; and
(4) there is reasonable cause to believe that if someone is excluded from a dwelling-house in which the child concerned lives, the child will cease to suffer, significant harm; and
(5) that someone else living in the dwelling (who need not be a parent or a relation) is both:
    (a) able and willing to give the child the care which it would be reasonable to expect a parent to give him; and
    (b) consents to the exclusion requirements.

D[6.40]–D[6.45]

Duration. The exclusion requirement will usually be of the same length as the interim care order but will cease to have effect if the local authority removes the child from the dwelling in question for a continuous period of 24 hours.

D[6.46]

Undertaking. The court may instead of making an exclusion requirement accept an undertaking to the same effect.

Discharge and variation of care and supervision orders (s 39)

D[6.47]

A care order may be discharged or a supervision order varied or discharged on the application of:

(a) a person with parental responsibility for the child;
(b) the child himself;
(c) the local authority designated in the order.

D[6.48]

On discharging a care order a supervision order may be substituted. Further application may not be made within six months except by leave of the court (s 91(15)).

Appeals (s 94)

D[6.49]

Appeals lie to the High Court. Where the family proceedings court makes a decision which dismisses an application for a care or supervision order and the child was subject to an interim order, the court may make a care or supervision order respectively which will continue until the end of the period during which an appeal may be made or determined. Similar provisions apply where a care or supervision order has been discharged (s 40).

D[7]

Financial provision

D[7.1]

The family proceedings court may order a person to pay maintenance for a spouse. Maintenance for a spouse may be ordered in proceedings under the Domestic Proceedings and Magistrates' Courts Act 1978, ss 2, 6 or 7. Maintenance for a child may be ordered. Such applications are rare since the introduction of the Child Support Agency. **It is unclear what statutory changes, if any, will be made, following the announcement in late July 2006 that the government intends to abolish the Child Support Agency, in its current role. See also **D[7.47]**.

D[7.2]

Method of payment. Payment is normally to be made through the designated officer but exceptionally, at the wish of the payee, may be made direct to her. The court may instead direct that payment be made by standing order or direct debit or make an attachment of earnings order.

Financial Provision (DPMCA, s 2)

D[7.3]

No single lump sum may exceed £1,000, but an order may provide for lump sums, say for a wife and two children (£3,000) totalling more than that. A lump sum provision might be used, for example, to apportion savings or to purchase school uniforms etc. A lump sum may be ordered to be paid by instalments.

D[7.4]

When deciding what financial provision (if any) to make **for an applicant** it is the duty of the court to have regard to all the circumstances of the case, first consideration being given to the welfare while a minor of any child of the family who has not attained the age of 18 and in particular:

(a) the income, earning capacity, property and any other financial resources which each of the parties has, or is likely to have in the foreseeable

future, including in the case of earning capacity which it would in the opinion of the court be reasonable to expect a party to the marriage to take steps to acquire;
(b) the financial needs, obligations and responsibilities which each of the parties has or is likely to have in the foreseeable future;
(c) the standard of living they enjoyed before the occurrence of the conduct which is the ground for making the order (this may be different from the standard of living at the time of parting);
(d) the parties' ages and the duration of the marriage;
(e) any physical or mental disability of either party;
(f) the contributions made, or which are likely in the foreseeable future to be made, by each party to the welfare of the family including that made by looking after the home or caring for the family;
(g) anything else which the court considers to be relevant to take into account; this may include the conduct of each of the parties if that conduct is such that it would be inequitable to disregard it (see *Miller v Miller; McFarlane v McFarlane* [2006] 3 All ER 1, HL).

D[7.5]–D[7.7]

'First consideration being given to the welfare ... of any child', means that the child's welfare is not paramount but of first importance in deciding maintenance payments (*Suter v Suter and Jones* [1987] Fam 111, [1987] 2 All ER 336, CA).

D[7.8]

An order in respect of the wife will cease if she remarries and orders for children will cease normally when the child attains 17, or 18 years if the court specifies this. This may be extended if the child is being educated, or trained, even though the child may be in gainful employment at the same time. It may also be extended if there are special circumstances justifying it, for example, a disabled person unable to work.

Agreed orders (DPMCA 1978)

D[7.9]

DPMCA 1978, s 6. Either party to a marriage may ask the court for an order making financial provision simply on the ground that the other party has agreed to make that provision. In such a case there is no limit to the amount of any lump sum. The court before making such an order must be satisfied:

(a) that the respondent (or the applicant) has agreed to make the financial provisions detailed in the application for the order; and
(b) that there is no reason to think that it would be contrary to the interests of justice to make the order; and

(c) where there is financial provision for children, that the order would either provide or make a proper contribution towards the financial needs of the child.

D[7.10]–D[7.15]

If the court is not satisfied with the adequacy of any financial provision it may suggest some other provision and, if the parties consent, it may make an order accordingly. If the parties do not consent the application is to be treated as an application for an order under s 2 in the ordinary way.

D[7.16]

DPMCA 1978, s 7. Where parties to a marriage have lived apart for a continuous period of three months without either one having deserted* the other, the court may make an order for financial provision even though the grounds stated earlier do not exist and neither is there agreement about financial provisions. In applying for an order under these circumstances the applicant must specify in the application the aggregate amount of voluntary payments made by the respondent for the maintenance of the applicant and/or the children during the three months immediately preceding the application. This aggregate figure then sets the limit on the amount which the court may order. The court may make an order for periodical payments provided that the amount payable during any three-month period under the order will not exceed the aggregate sum referred to in the application. There is no power to include lump sums in this kind of order. If the court thinks that the best it can do in these circumstances would be inadequate it may treat the application as an application for an order under s 2 in the ordinary way.

[*To be repealed by the Family Law Act 1996, Sch 10 when brought into force.]

Variation of maintenance orders

D[7.17]

The court may vary the provisions of any maintenance order it has made. In respect of maintenance for a spouse, the commonest applications are to vary the financial provisions of the order where the husband's income has been reduced or increased or where the husband pleads that a child whom he is having to support is no longer a dependent eg holding down full-time employment..

D[7.18]

When dealing with an application to vary the amount of maintenance the court is generally concerned with considering a change of circumstances since the previous order was made. This is not an inflexible rule and the court has to look at the reality of the situation. The court may have to look afresh at the means of the parties and fix the amount of maintenance as they would do so when making a new order. It is not necessary to establish a change of circumstances since an order made in divorce proceedings was registered for enforcement in the magistrates' court where the payer clearly cannot afford the order and there was clearly some mistake in the fixing of the original amount*.It is a matter of good practice that courts record their reasons in variation proceedings (*Hackshaw v Hackshaw* [1999] 3 FCR 451, [1999] 2 FLR 876, [1999] Fam Law 697).

[*Such cases can, in appropriate circumstances, be remitted back to the county court to determine the variation hearing pursuant to the Maintenance Order Act 1958, s 4(4). See *Goodall v Jolly* (1983) 147 JP 513.]

Enforcement of an order

D[7.19]

If a payer falls behind in his maintenance payments the magistrates can grant a summons or a warrant to secure his appearance before the court for an inquiry into his means.

D[7.20]

If the court is satisfied that the payer has a good reason for failing to pay the instalments (such as ill health), and is satisfied that he has no resources with which to meet the arrears then it has the power to remit part or all of the arrears; but the recipient must be given an opportunity to make written or oral representations against such a remission, unless the court considers it unnecessary or impracticable to give her such an opportunity. The starting point for courts is that arrears over a year old should not be enforced unless there are special circumstances (*B v C* [1995] 2 FCR 678, [1995] 1 FLR 467). Courts can adjourn these cases to give the payer another chance to clear the arrears but if the court is not inclined to an adjournment it may make the following orders:

(a) Direct that payment be made by standing order or direct debit.
(b) Order the issuing of a **distress warrant** for the seizure and sale of his property.
(c) Make an **attachment of earnings order.** Such an order requires the employer to make weekly (or other periodical) payment into court of a fixed amount from the payer's wages.

D[7.21]

An attachment of earnings order will be able to follow him to his next job. If the court decides upon an attachment of earnings order it should inform the legal adviser before announcing this decision as the legal adviser has to obtain certain information as to the precise details of the job and works number (if any).

D[7.22]

The court must announce two figures. First, the **protected earnings rate**, which is the amount reasonable for the payer to retain having regard to his resources and needs.

D[7.23]

The second figure is the **normal deduction rate** which is the amount the court thinks reasonable to cover his liability under the order.

D[7.24]

(d) If the court is satisfied that the defendant either has wilfully refused to pay or culpably neglected to pay and an attachment of earnings order is inappropriate (because, for example, the defendant is likely to change his job to thwart an attachment of earnings order) the court can send the defendant to **prison** unless he pays the arrears immediately. The actual period of imprisonment is limited by the amount of arrears in accordance with this table (adapted from that used in criminal proceedings):

Arrears	Imprisonment
not exceeding £200	7 days
exceeding £200 but not exceeding £500	14 days
exceeding £500 but not exceeding £1,000	28 days
exceeding £1,000	6 weeks

D[7.25]–D[7.30]

Imprisonment may not be ordered in the absence of the debtor. Even where the debtor is arrested following the issue of a suspended committal order he should be informed of the nature of the proceedings and offered the opportunity of legal advice from the duty solicitor. An interpreter should be available where necessary (*Santa Cruz Ruiz v United Kingdom* [1998] EHRLR 208).

D[7.31]

If the defendant goes to prison and serves part of the sentence then the amount to secure his release is reduced proportionately.

D[7.32]

If the defendant serves the full sentence or part of it the arrears are not automatically wiped out, but the sanction of imprisonment is no longer available. Other civil rights of the person entitled to the arrears remain – see **D[7.33]** below.

D[7.33]

A person cannot be committed to prison twice for the same period of arrears but such arrears remain due from him and could still be enforced against him by, for example, a distress warrant (see (b) above) or by an attachment of earnings order (see (c) above).

D[7.34]

(e) **Make a suspended committal to prison** for the same reasons as applied in (d) above. The length of imprisonment will be determined in accordance with the table above.

D[7.35]

The sentence of imprisonment can be suspended for a fixed time to give the payer time to pay the whole amount or suspended whilst he pays a fixed sum regularly each week off the arrears (in addition to a sum as maintenance as laid down in the order).

D[7.36]

If the defendant fails to comply the designated officer sends him a notice inviting the defendant to provide within eight days written reasons why the suspended committal order should not be put into effect. If no written answer is received within eight days the committal warrant can be released. Since the inception of the Human Rights Act 1998, common practice is to issue an arrest warrant directing the defaulter to be brought before the court to show cause why the committal warrant should not be issued.

D[7.37]

If the defendant submits his reasons they are put before a single magistrate who can either direct that the matter be considered in open court or to be make directions similar to **D[7.36]** above.

D[7.38]

If the defendant goes to prison and serves part of the sentence the amount to secure his release is reduced proportionately.

D[7.39]

The serving of all or even part of the prison sentence does not automatically wipe out the arrears as a debt (see **D[7.32]-D[7.33]** above).

D[7.40]–D[7.45]

A defendant serving a sentence under (d) or (e) is entitled to apply for review of his committal to prison. It is first considered by a single magistrate who may either refuse a further review or direct that the application be considered in open court.

D[7.46]

Magistrates reviewing a committal order have wide powers. They can remit all or part of the committal, put the committal into effect, or allow it to continue on the same terms as before, or further suspend the committal on new terms. Generally arrears becoming due more than a year before commencement of an enforcement action are not enforced in the absence of special circumstances (*R v Cardiff Magistrates, ex p Czech* [1999] 1 FCR 721, [1999] 1 FLR 95).

D[7.47]

Where a maintenance assessment has been made by the Secretary of State for Work and Pensions in relation to an "absent parent" and that a sum or sums remain outstanding and unpaid he may apply, pursuant to the Child Support Act 1991, s 33 for a liability order. On an application for a liability order the magistrates' court must proceed on the basis that the maintenance assessment in question was lawfully and properly made. The magistrates' court is precluded from questioning any aspect of that assessment. Such an investigation is a matter to be pursued through the statutory appeal structure provided for by the 1991 Act (see *Farley (FC) v Child Support Agency* [2006] UKHL 31, [2006] 2 FCR 713).

Where the Secretary of State has failed to recover an amount owing under the Child Support Act an application may be made to the court for an order for disqualification from holding or obtaining a driving licence (Child Support Act 1991, s 39A).

D[8]

Domestic violence
Non molestation orders

D[8.1]

Non molestation orders provide a remedy to any associated person from molestation. Molestation includes, but is much wider than, violence and will cover any serious pestering or harassment which is of such a degree as to merit the intervention of the family proceedings court. Revelations to a newspaper do not constitute molestation (*C v C (non-molestation order: jurisdiction)* [1998] Fam 70, [1998] 2 WLR 599).

Who can apply?

D[8.2]

1 Associated persons. This includes husbands and wives, civil partners (within the meaning of the Civil Partnership Act 2004), divorced couples and cohabitants and former cohabitants. Other applicants may include a wide range of relatives, those who live or have lived in the same household (other than lodgers, tenants and employees) and those who have agreed to marry one another. In relation to a child the definition includes parents, natural parents and adoptive and those with paternal responsibilities. The court should take a purposive construction of associated persons (*G v F (non molestation order jurisdiction)* [2000] Fam 186, [2000] 3 WLR 1202, sub nom G v G (non- molestation order: jurisdiction) [2000] 2 FLR 533, [2000] Fam Law 703).
2 Authorised third parties.
3 Children under 16 with leave of the High Court.
4 The court of its own motion when dealing with an application in family proceedings.

D[8.3]

Criteria for grant. When considering whether or not to grant an application for a non molestation order the court shall have regard to all the circumstances including the need to secure the health, safety and well being of:

(a) the applicant;

(b) the person for whose benefit the order is made;
(c) any relevant child. A relevant child, includes any child whose interests the court considers relevant, any child who is living with or ought reasonably be expected to live with either party and a child who is the subject of adoption or Children Act proceedings. *Chechi v Bashier* [1999] 2 FCR 241, [1999] 2 FLR 489, CA emphasises that this is a discretionary order.

D[8.4]

Duration. The order may be for a specified duration or until further order but if made in the course of other family proceedings, it will expire if these proceedings are dismissed or withdrawn.

D[8.5]

Content of the order. The order may prohibit the respondent from molesting a named associated person(s) and relevant child. The court should endeavour to be specific as to what acts are prohibited so that the order is both understandable and enforceable.

D[8.6]

Variation. A non molestation order may be varied by:

(a) the person who applied for it;
(b) the respondent;
(c) the court itself where the order was made of its own motion.

D[8.7]

Ex parte applications. An application may be made in the absence of the respondent and if necessary to a single justice in exceptional circumstances. In addition to looking at all the circumstances the court must consider whether there is any risk of significant harm to the applicant or a relevant child and whether it is likely that the applicant would be deterred or prevented from pursuing the application. The court also has power to make an ex parte order where it has reason to believe that the respondent knows of the proceedings but is deliberately evading service.

D[8.8]

If an ex parte order is made then a hearing should be listed as soon as is just and convenient to allow for representations to be made.

D[8.9]

Power of arrest. A power of arrest must be attached where both parties have had notice of the hearing and the respondent used or threatened violence against the applicant or a relevant child, unless the court is satisfied that they would be adequately protected without such a power.

D[8.10]–D[8.15]

Where an ex parte order is made a power of arrest may be attached to the order where the respondent used or threatened violence against the applicant or a relevant child and they are at risk of significant harm from the respondent if the power is not attached immediately.

Enforcement

D[8.16]

A power of arrest is attached to ensure compliance with the order and to protect the applicant or relevant child. The power allows a constable to arrest without warrant a person whom he has reasonable cause to suspect has breached the non molestation order. The duration of the power will normally be the same length as the order it attaches to.

D[8.17]

If no power of arrest is attached the applicant may give evidence on oath of a breach and, if satisfied there are reasonable grounds, the court may issue a warrant for the arrest of the respondent.

D[8.18]

If arrested for a breach the respondent must be produced to the court within 24 hours (excluding Christmas day, Good Friday and Sunday). When the arrested person is brought before the court the attendance of the arresting officer is not necessary unless the arrest itself is in issue. A written statement from the arresting officer should normally be sufficient (*Practice Direction* 19 January 2000).

Sanction for breach

D[8.19]

Upon hearing a breach application the court may adjourn the case and may remand the respondent to a later date on civil bail, with or without conditions. If the breach is proved on the balance of probabilities the court may order the respondent:

(a) to pay a sum not exceeding £50 for every day he is in breach up to £1,000, or a sum not exceeding £5,000; or
(b) to be committed to custody for a period not exceeding two months or until he has remedied his default in such shorter period.

Breach of a non molestation order is also a criminal offence.

D[8.20]

Any committal to custody may be suspended upon condition of obedience to the order. However the Court of Appeal have indicated that in the case of a serious breach it must be understood that punishment will take place immediately (*Neil v Ryan* [1999] 1 FCR 241, [1998] 2 FLR 1068, CA).

Undertakings

D[8.21]

Where the court has the ability to make a non molestation order, and there have been no threats of violence or violence used, they may accept an undertaking from the parties. An undertaking is a promise by a party to the court that they will do or refrain from doing some defined act.

D[8.22]

Sanctions. The sanctions for breach of an undertaking are the same as those outlined above for breach of an order.

Occupation orders

D[8.23]

The family proceedings court shares a jurisdiction with the county court and the High Court to make declaratory and regulatory occupation orders. These orders deal with rights of occupation or exclude a person from all or part of the dwelling.

D[8.24]

These applications are unusual in the family proceedings court and should be the subject of detailed consultations with the legal adviser.

D[9]

Protection of children (Children Act 1989)

Police powers (Children Act 1989, s 46)

D[9.1]

Where the police have reasonable cause to believe that a child would otherwise suffer significant harm, they may remove the child to suitable accommodation and keep him in police protection for up to 72 hours. They must also inform the local authority, persons having parental responsibility for the child and anyone with whom he was living before he was taken into police protection.

Duties of the local authority (Children Act 1989, s 47)

D[9.2]

Where a local authority are:

(a) informed that a child is:
 (i) the subject of an emergency protection order (see **D[9.16]**), or
 (ii) in police protection, or

(b) have reasonable cause to suspect that a child is suffering or is likely to suffer, significant harm

the authority must make such inquiries as they consider necessary to enable them to decide whether they should take any action to safeguard or promote the child's welfare.

D[9.3]

The action which the local authority may take may include applying for one of the following orders.

Child assessment order (Children Act 1989, s 43)

D[9.4]

Only a local authority or the NSPCC may apply for this order. Where the court is satisfied that:

(a) the *applicant* has reasonable cause to suspect that the child is suffering, or is likely to suffer, significant harm;
(b) an assessment of the state of the child's health or development or of the way in which he has been treated is required to enable the applicant to determine whether or not the child is suffering or is likely to suffer significant harm; and
(c) it is unlikely that such an assessment will be made, or be satisfactory, in the absence of an order under this section

it may make a child assessment order.

D[9.5]–D[9.6]

Welfare of child and necessity for order. See **D[2]** and **D[4]**.

D[9.7]

Notice must be given where reasonably practicable to the child's parents and other persons specified in the Children Act 1989, s 43(11).

D[9.8]

The order must specify the date by which the assessment is to begin and will have effect for up to seven days from that date. It is then the duty of any person who is in a position to produce the child to do so to such person as is named in the order and to comply with court directions concerning the assessment.

D[9.9]

A child may be kept away from home only in accordance with directions in the order and only if it is necessary for the purposes of the assessment. Where the child is away from home, the order must contain such directions as the court thinks fit with regard to contact with other persons.

D[9.10]–D[9.15]

Assessment and emergency protection. A court cannot make a child assessment order where there are grounds for making an emergency protection order and it considers it ought to make such an order.

Emergency protection order (Children Act 1989, s 44)

D[9.16]

An emergency protection order authorises the removal of a child to accommodation provided by the applicant for the period specified in the order.

D[9.17]

Grounds. Any person may apply for an emergency protection order. The court may make the order where it is satisfied:

(a) (all applicants) there is reasonable cause to believe that the child is likely to suffer significant harm if he is not removed to accommodation provided by the applicant; or
(b) (local authority applicant) inquiries are being made because of the local authority's suspicion that the child is suffering or is likely to suffer significant harm (see **D[6.3]**) which are being frustrated by an unreasonable refusal of access and access is required as a matter of urgency; or
(c) (NSPCC) the applicant has reasonable cause to suspect that a child is suffering or is likely to suffer significant harm and inquiries into the child's welfare are being frustrated as in (b) above.

D[9.18]

The court may consider any evidence (including hearsay) which it considers relevant to the application.

X Council v B (emergency protection orders) [2004] EWHC 2015 (Fam) gives a review of relevant authorities in this area.

In *Re X: Emergency Protection Orders* [2006] EWHC 510 (Fam), [2006] Fam Law 627, Mr Justice McFarlane made the following observations together with some additional guidance:

(a) the 14 points made by Munby J in *X Council v B* above should be copied and made available to the justices hearing an EPO on each and every occasion such an application is made;
(b) it is the duty of the applicant for an EPO to ensure that the *X Council v B* guidance is brought to the court's attention;
(c) mere lack of information or a need for an assessment can never of themselves establish the existence of a genuine emergency to justify an EPO. The proper course in such a case is to consider application for a Child Assessment Order or issuing s 31 proceedings and seeking the court's directions under s 38(6) for assessment;
(d) evidence given to the justices should come from the best available source. In most cases this will be from the social worker with direct knowledge of the case;
(e) where there has been a case conference with respect to the child, the most recent case conference minutes should be produced to the court;
(f) where the application is made without notice, if possible the applicant should be represented by a lawyer, whose duties will include ensuring that the court understands the legal criteria required for both an EPO and an application without notice;
(g) the applicant must ensure that as full a note as possible of the hearing is prepared and given to the child's parents at the earliest possible opportunity;
(h) unless it is impossible to do so, every without notice hearing should either be tape recorded or be recorded in writing by a full note being

taken by a dedicated note taker who has no other role (such as clerk [legal adviser]) to play in the hearing;

(i) when the matter is before the court at the first 'on notice' hearing, the court should ensure that the parents have received a copy of the clerk's [legal adviser's] notes of the EPO hearing together with a copy of any material submitted to the court and a copy of the justices' reasons;

(j) cases of emotional abuse will rarely, if ever, warrant an EPO, let alone an application without notice;

(k) cases of sexual abuse where the allegations are inchoate and non-specific, and where there is no evidence or immediate risk of harm to the child, will rarely warrant an EPO;

(l) cases of fabricated or induced illness, where there is no medical evidence of immediate risk of direct physical harm to the child, will rarely warrant an EPO;

(m) justices faced with an EPO application in a case of emotional abuse, non specific allegations of sexual abuse and/or fabricated or induced illness, should actively consider refusing an EPO application on the basis that the local authority should then issue an application for an interim care order. Once an application for an ICO has been issued in such a case, it is likely that justices will consider that it should be transferred up for determination by a county court or the High Court;

(n) the requirement that justices give detailed findings and reasons applies as much to an EPO application as it does to any other application. In a case of urgency, the decision may be announced and the order made with the detailed reasons prepared thereafter;

(o) where an application is made without notice, there is a need for the court to determine whether or not the hearing should proceed on a without notice basis (and to give reasons for that decision) independently of any subsequent decision upon the substantive EPO application.

D[9.19]

Welfare of child and necessity for order. See **D[2]** and **D[4]**.

D[9.20]

Child's Guardian. See **D[3.24]**

Effect of the order

D[9.21]

(a) Directs any person in a position to do so to produce the child on request to the applicant.

(b) Authorises removal of the child to the applicant's accommodation and his retention there.

(c) Gives parental responsibility to the applicant which he may only exercise to the extent reasonably required to safeguard or promote the child's welfare.

(d) May contain directions as to any medical or psychiatric examination of the child.
(e) Presumes contact with parents and other persons specified in the Children Act 1989, s 44(13) subject to any more restrictive direction in the order.
(f) May require a person who has information relating to the child's whereabouts to disclose that information (s 48).
(g) May authorise the applicant to enter premises specified in the order and search for the child (s 48(3)).

D[9.22]

Where the court is satisfied that there is reasonable cause to believe that there may be another child on the premises who should be subject to an emergency protection order, it may authorise the applicant to search for that child and if the applicant is satisfied that the grounds for an order are satisfied the order has effect as if it were an emergency protection order (s 48).

Exclusion requirement

D[9.23]

As with interim care orders if the court is able and decides to make an emergency protection order but is satisfied that the reasons and grounds for making the order would be removed if someone is excluded from the dwelling in which the child lives and that someone else living there is both:

(a) able and willing to give to the child the care which it would be reasonable to expect a parent to give him; and
(b) consents to the exclusion requirement,

the court may make the requirement.

D[9.24]

The requirement may:

(a) specify that someone leave the dwelling-house in which he is living with the child concerned;
(b) specify that someone be prohibited from entering a dwelling-house in which the child lives;
(c) exclude someone from a defined area in which a dwelling-house is located (the dwelling-house must be where the child lives).

D[9.25]–D[9.30]

This allows the child to remain in its dwelling despite the making of the order.

D[9.31]

Undertaking. The court may, instead of making an exclusion requirement, accept an undertaking to the same effect.

D[9.32]

Warrant of entry. The intentional obstruction of a person exercising powers of search and removal of a child subject to an emergency protection order is a criminal offence. Where it appears to the court that a person has been or is likely to be prevented from exercising these powers by being refused entry to premises or access to the child, it may issue a warrant authorising the police to assist using reasonable force if necessary.

D[9.33]

Duration. An emergency protection order shall have effect for such period not exceeding eight days as may be specified in the order with special provision for public holidays. This period normally includes any period already in police detention. The order may be extended once for a further period of up to seven days.

D[9.34]

Discharge. The child, his parents, or anyone having parental responsibility or with whom the child was living prior to the making of the emergency protection order may apply to the court after 72 hours to have the order discharged unless they were present at the making of the order. There is no right of appeal in respect of the making of an emergency protection order.

D[10]–D[15]

Recovery order (Children Act 1989 s 50)

D[10.1]

Where it appears to the court that there is reason to believe that a child in care or subject to an emergency protection order or in police protection has been unlawfully taken away, has run away or is missing, it may make a recovery order.

D[10.2]

Application is by a person with parental responsibility by virtue of a care order or emergency protection order; or where the child is in police protection, for the purposes of s 46 CA 1989, the designated officer.

D[10.3]

The recovery order may:

(i) direct a person to produce the child;
(ii) authorise the removal of the child;
(iii) require disclosure of the child's whereabouts;
(iv) authorise a constable to enter specified premises to search for the child, using reasonable force if necessary.

D[16]

Child abduction

D[16.1]

Child Abduction Act 1984. It is a criminal offence triable either way for a person 'connected' with a child under 16 to take or send the child out of the United Kingdom without the appropriate consent.

D[16.2]

'Connected' persons include a parent, guardian, a special guardian of the child, or a person having custody, or in whose favour a residence order is in force, or a person reasonably believed to be the father of an illegitimate child.

D[16.3]

'Appropriate consent' is that of persons who are parents, guardians, a special guardian of the child, or in whose favour a residence order is in force, or any person who has custody of the child.

D[16.4]

Provision is also made for the protection of children subject to various court proceedings such as care and adoption. It is also an offence for other persons to take a child from the lawful control of any person having lawful control of the child.

D[16.5]

The Child Abduction Act 1984 provides certain defences for the person who has taken the child out of the jurisdiction.

D[17]

School attendance and truancy proceedings

(Education Act 1996)

D[17.1]

A magistrate who is a member of the local authority which is also the education authority should not adjudicate in this type of case.

D[17.2]

The educational duty of every parent or guardian of a child or young person of compulsory school age is 'to cause him to receive efficient full time education suitable to his age, ability and aptitude and to any special educational needs he may have, either by regular attendance at school or otherwise'.

D[17.3]

Compulsory school age is normally from 5 to 16. The actual date when a pupil reaches school-leaving age may be after his sixteenth birthday, for example, the date the term ends. Education legislation prescribes the exact dates and if there is any doubt in a particular case as to whether a 16-year-old has passed the date or not, consult the legal adviser. In this type of proceedings the pupil must be presumed to be of compulsory school age unless his parents prove the contrary.

D[17.4]

As against a parent there are two types of proceedings, which can only be brought by a local education authority:

(1) The local education authority can serve a school attendance order requiring the parent to register the child at the school named in the order. Before doing this the local education authority must have served on the parent a notice giving the parent at least 15 days in which to satisfy it that the child is already receiving efficient full time education suitable to his age, ability and aptitude and to any special educational needs he may have. If the education authority wishes to continue proceedings it must serve a notice stating the school it intends to specify in the order (or, if it thinks fit, several schools from which the parent can

choose one). Thus, the first set of proceedings is in effect for **failure to comply with a school attendance order.**

(2) The second type of proceedings is where the child or young person is a registered pupil at a school but has failed to attend regularly. This is an absolute offence and does not contravene art 6 of the ECHR (*Barnfather v Islington Education Authority* [2003] EWHC 418 (Admin), [2003] All ER (D) 89 (Mar); however, a child shall not be deemed to have failed to attend school regularly if:
   (a) he was absent with leave; or
   (b) he was absent through sickness or any unavoidable cause; or
   (c) he was absent on a day of religious observance kept by the religious body to which his parent belongs; or
   (d) his parents prove that the school is not within walking distance and the local authority have not arranged transport. If one of these defences is raised, consult the legal adviser.

The local education authority may issue a fixed penalty notice of £50 against a parent who fails to send their child to school. Payment is a bar to proceedings but non payment after 42 days may result in a summons to court.

D[17.5]

If convicted in either set of proceedings the parent can be fined on level 3. Note that the court is also empowered to make a parenting order. If the court is satisfied that the parent knows that the child is not attending regularly and fails without reasonable cause to ensure attendance this aggravated version of the offence is punishable by a level 4 fine and/or three months' imprisonment [**51 weeks when the CJA 2003, Sch 26 is brought into force]. The court may direct the local education authority to bring proceedings before the family proceedings court for an education supervision order.

For a prosecution under s 444(1A) see *R (on the application of P) v Liverpool City Magistrates* [2006] EWHC 2732 (Admin), (2006) 170 JP 453. In this case it was held that the parent bears an evidential rather than a legal burden when seeking to establish "legal justification".

Local education authorities may also apply for parenting order following a second exclusion in a 12 month period under s 20 of the Anti Social Behaviour Act 2003.

Education supervision orders

D[17.6]

The local education authority may bring proceedings for an education supervision order on the ground that a child is not being educated properly (where, for example, he is not complying with a school attendance order or is not attending regularly at a school at which he is a registered pupil, see above). Unless previously discharged, an education supervision order will last for one year initially but may be extended for periods of up to three years at a time until the child reaches school leaving age. The supervisor is under a duty to advise, assist and befriend and give directions to the child and his parents to secure that the child is properly educated. A parent who persistently fails to comply with a direction may be guilty of an offence (a maximum fine, level 3).

Care proceedings may be brought and the statutory grounds may be satisfied on evidence of non-school attendance alone (*Re O (a minor)* [1992] 4 All ER 905, [1992] 1 WLR 912).

D[17A]

Child safety order (Crime and Disorder Act 1998 (s 11))

D[17A.1]

This order may be made in the family court on application by the local authority. It is aimed at protecting children under 10 years who may involved in crime or in anti-social behaviour. The applicant must prove one or more conditions:

a) the child has committed an act which would have constituted an offence but for his age;
b) an order is necessary to prevent an act as mentioned in (a) above;
c) the child has contravened a curfew notice; and
d) the child has caused harassment alarm or distress to someone outside the child's household.

D[17A.2]

The order places the child under the supervision of a responsible officer for three months but this may be up to 12 months.

D[17A.3]

The court can impose conditions to ensure the child:

i) receives support, protection or control;
ii) is prevented from repeating the behaviour which resulted in the order.

If a child breaches the order the court may make a parenting order.

D[18]

Adoption proceedings

(Adoption and Children Act 2002)

D[18.1]

Under the Adoption and Children Act 2002, a child may only be placed for adoption in one of two ways, where there is consent of a parent or under a placement order of the court. During the placement with prospective adopters the local authority has a duty to manage, oversee and review the child's progress.

Consensual Placement

D[18.2]

An adoption agency may place a child for adoption if it is satisfied that each parent has consented to a placement (Adoption and Children Act 2002 s 19). CAFCASS will be involved in witnessing such consents to placement at the request of the adoption agency.

This route can not be used where there is a pending application for a care order or a placement order has been made. In such circumstances any application made by the local authority must be under the Adoption and Children Act 2002 s 22.

Placement Orders

D[18.3]

Freeing for adoption is abolished and replaced by a system of placement orders. This is an order authorising a local authority to place a child up for adoption with any prospective adopters chosen by the authority. The court may not make a placement order unless the child is subject to a care order or it is satisfied the conditions (Children Act 1989 s 31) for a care order are met or the child has no parent or guardian and each parent has consented to a placement order, or the court dispenses with that consent (Adoption and Children Act 2002 ss 21 and 52).

Once a placement order is made only a local authority may remove the child and it continues in force until it is revoked, the child marries, attains 18 years or the adoption order is made in respect of the child.

Consequences of a placement order

D[18.4]

(i) Parental responsibility for the child is given to the adoption agency and the prospective adopters for the duration of the placement. The parents' parental responsibility is not extinguished but it is shared with the prospective adopters and the agency. It is for the agency to decide on any necessary and proportionate restrictions of the parental responsibility of a parent or of a prospective adopter.
(ii) Any contact provision under the Children Act 1989 ceases to have effect but the court can order contact under s 26 either on application or of its own motion.
(iii) The child may not be given a new surname or removed from the UK for more than a month unless each parent consents or the court grants leave.
(iv) Any care order is 'suspended' whilst the placement order is in force, any supervision order or s 8 order ceases to have effect and there are prohibitions on certain orders being applied (s 29(3)–(5)).
(v) Once a placement order is made no parent or guardian may oppose the making of any adoption order unless the court grants leave. The court cannot grant such leave unless satisfied that there has been a change of circumstances since the placement order was made.

Applications for Placement Orders

D[18.5]

In order to avoid delay, a local authority **must** apply for such an order (s 22) when:

(i) a child is placed for adoption with them or is being provided with accommodation, no agency is authorised to place the child for adoption, the child has no parent or guardian or the conditions under s 31(2) of the 1989 Act (to make a care order) appears to be met and the local authority is satisfied that the child ought to be placed for adoption, or;
(ii) an application has been made and not disposed of on which a care order might be made or the child is subject to a care order but there is no authority to place him/her for adoption and the local authority is satisfied that the child ought to be placed for adoption.

Parental Consent

D[18.6]

Two of the key components of making a placement order are:

(i) consent of the parent or guardian, or alternatively,
(ii) dispensing with consent.

The issue of dispensing with parental consent is now dealt with at the early stages of the placement decision.

The court will consider the s 1 principles, which apply to the dispensing of consent, and consider the welfare checklist (see **D[18.19]**).

Consent to the placement is of central importance because it can have the effect of removing the parent from any subsequent adoption hearing unless the court gives permission to oppose.

Specified proceedings (ACA s 122)

D[18.7]

Applications to make or revoke placement orders are specified proceedings within s 41 Children Act 1989. Therefore the child will be a party and the children's guardian will be appointed by the court. The guardian will appoint a solicitor to represent the child.

Adoption orders

D[18.8]

An adoption order is an order giving parental responsibility for a child to the adopters. Any pre-existing orders for maintenance or orders under the Children Act 1989 are extinguished.

An adoption order can be made in respect of any child under the age of 18 years who is not, or has not been, married and can even be made even if the child has previously been adopted.

Applications for an Adoption Order

D[18.9]

Applicant must qualify for eligibility by virtue of age, domicile and residence.

D[18.10]

The Applicants. An application can be made either by a couple or one person. A couple may be married or living in an enduring relationship. A step parent or partner may adopt as a single applicant under the Adoption and Children Act 2002 s 51(2).

D[18.11]

Identity of the applicants. Where the applicants wish their identity to be confidential, they may apply for a serial number to be assigned to them. This number will be used instead of their names.

D[18.12]

Residence of the child with the applicants. Before an adoption order can be made the court must be satisfied that a probationary period where the child has been placed with the applicant has occurred. In the case of an agency adoption the period is 10 weeks, for a non agency parent or partner adoption the period is 6 months. Local authority foster parents may not adopt unless the child has its home with them for at least a year or the court gives its leave.

Application to the court

D[18.13]

An adoption application is made in a prescribed form.

D[18.14]

The court. An application can be made to the High Court, a county court or a magistrates' court but an application involving the *applicants* or *child* living abroad cannot be made to a magistrates' court. In respect of applications made or transferred to a county court, the case must be sent to a county court adoption centre or inter-country adoption centre as set out in the amended Children (Allocation and Proceedings) Order 1991.

Consent

D[18.15]

ACA 2002 s 52 is of general application to both placement and adoption.

'Consent' to the placement of a child for adoption or the making of an adoption order means:

> 'consent given unconditionally and with full understanding of what is involved; but a person may consent to adoption without knowing the identity of the persons in whose favour the order will be made'.

'Freely' has been omitted from the definition under ACA 2002 in recognition that many parents struggle against their own feelings in giving consent in the children's best interests.

The persons who have the right to consent are the parent 'having parental responsibility' or the guardian of the child (which includes a special guardian).

Those 'parents' who qualify are:

1. The birth mother.
2. The birth father, where he is married to the child's mother at the time of the child's birth or if he subsequently marries the mother.
3. An unmarried father if:
   i) he becomes registered as the child's father under the Birth and Deaths Registration Act 1953 or
   ii) he makes a parental responsibility agreement with the child's mother; or
   iii) he is granted a parental responsibility order by the court.

4. The child's adoptive parent, where the child has been the subject of a previous adoption.

Dispensing with Consent

D[18.16]

There are now only two grounds for dispensing with a parent's consent (ACA 2002 s 52(1)). These are:

Where the court is satisfied that:

a) the parent or guardian of a child cannot be found or is incapable of giving consent; or
b) the welfare of the child requires the consent to be dispensed with.

General Principles

D[18.17]

Whenever the court is making a decision in relation to placement orders, adoption orders or their revocation, contact under ACA 2002 s 26 (in relation to placements) or granting leave it must consider ACA 2002 s 1.

D[18.18]

Factors to consider therefore are:

1. The effect of the delay. ACA 2002 s 1(3) applies the general principle that delay is prejudicial to the child's welfare and s 109 lays down a statutory obligation on the court to draw up a timetable to minimise delay.
2. The whole range of powers and the 'no order' principle. ACA 2002 s 1(6) sets out 2 key principles which set out the context in which the welfare principle itself must operate.

(i) That the court or adoption agency must always consider the whole range of powers available to it in the child's case (either under ACA 2002or under the Children Act 1989) [see the Children and Adoption Act 2006 when in force] and;
(ii) The court must not make any order unless it considers that making the order would be better for the child than not doing so (the 'No Order' principle).

The Welfare Checklist and Other Factors

D[18.19]

ACA 2002 s 1 (2) provides that ' "the paramount consideration of the court or adoption agency must be the child's welfare throughout his life'.

ACA 2002 s 1 (4) states what the court or the adoption agency should consider in relation to the child's welfare: this checklist is very similar to the one used in the Children Act 1989.

The things that the court will consider include (among others) -

(a) the child's ascertainable wishes and feelings regarding the decision (considered in light of the child's age and understanding),
(b) the child's particular needs,
(c) the likely effect on the child (throughout his life) of having ceased to be a member of the original family and become an adopted person,
(d) the child's age, sex, background and any of the child's characteristics which the court or agency considers relevant,
(e) any harm (within the meaning of the CA 1989) which the child has suffered or is at risk of suffering,
(f) the relationship which the child has with relatives and with any person in relation to whom the court or agency considers the question to be relevant including –
  (i) the likelihood of any such relationship continuing and the value to the child of its doing so,
  (ii) the ability and willingness of any of the child's relatives, or of any such person, to provide the child with a secure environment in which the child can develop and otherwise to meet the children's needs,
  (iii) the wishes and feelings of any of the child's relatives or any such person regarding the child.

Procedural Requirements – Rules/Practice Directions

D[18.20]

A new single set of rules will cover all three levels of court (High Court, county court and magistrates' court).

The Family Procedure (Adoption) Rules 2005 (FPAR)

D[18.21]

These extend the application of the Civil Procedure Rules to some areas of adoption work and harmonisation with the CPR of all rules relating to family proceedings is in hand.

These rules are supplemented by a number of Practice Directions which are as follows:

- Who receives a copy of the application form for orders in the proceedings
- The first directions hearing – adoptions with a foreign element
- Forms
- Reports by the adoption agency or local authority
- Reports by registered medical practitioner ('health reports')
- Litigation friends
- Court documents
- Communication of information relating to the proceedings
- Service
- Service out of the jurisdiction
- Human rights
- Joining the Crown
- Disclosing information to an adopted adult
- Alternative procedure for applications (Part 8)
- Applications (Part 9)
- Civil restraint orders
- Interim injunctions
- Written evidence
- Depositions and court attendance by witnesses
- Change of solicitor.

The courts and all parties are subject to the overriding objectives, namely,

> 'to enable the court to deal with cases justly, having regard to the welfare issues involved'.

D[18.22]

FPAR rule 1. This means that court staff have a responsibility to support the judiciary in ensuring that:

1) the parties are on an equal footing
2) the case is dealt with fairly and in a timely way
3) the case is dealt with in ways which are proportionate to the nature, importance and complexity of the issues
4) an appropriate share of the court's resources are allotted to the case and
5) expense is spared.

D[18.23]

Rule 4 of FPAR 2005 lays down the court's duty to actively manage cases in order to further the overriding objective.

D[18.24]

This will include:

- monitoring timetables and directions which have been fixed by the judiciary
- assisting in progress of the case by referring back to the Judge or the legal adviser as necessary
- ensuring that family lists provide sufficient court time to cover as many aspects of the case as it can on the same occasion
- facilitating the attendance of the applicants at any hearing or hearing their evidence by telephone or any other method of direct oral communication.

D[18.25]

Part 10 of FPAR 2005 indicates that the Civil Procedure Rules 1998 (Part 3) apply in relation to the court's case management powers.

The Role of CAFCASS in Adoption and Placement

D[18.26]

If it appears that the parent is willing to consent and it is within the jurisdiction of the court then the court will appoint a reporting officer to witness the documents.

D[18.27]

The reporting officer:

1) Ensures that consent is given unconditionally and with full understanding
2) Investigates all circumstances relevant to consent
3) Writes a report/ makes an interim report if parent is unwilling to consent and the court will then inform the applicant.

D[18.28]

Placement / revocation of placement orders are specified proceedings and therefore a child's guardian will be appointed unless the court is satisfied it is not necessary to protect his interests.

D[18.29]

The court will have a new power to appoint a CFR (Children and Family Court Reporter) in an adoption case. On of his/her duties will be to advise the court whether the child should be joined as a party.

NB: the same officer may hold more than one role in relation to the child at the same time.

D[18.30]

The child will be a respondent and therefore a party joined in the proceedings where:

- permission has been granted to a parent or guardian to oppose the making of the adoption order (s 47 (3) or (5));
- he or she opposes the making of an adoption order;
- a child and a family reporter recommends that it is in the best interests of the child to be a party to the proceedings and that recommendation is accepted by the court;
- he or she is already an adopted child;
- any party to the proceedings or the child is opposed to –
  1) the arrangements for allowing any person contact with the child; or
  2) a person not being allowed contact with the child after the making of the adoption order;

- the application is for a Convention adoption order or a s 84 order;
- he or she has been brought into the United Kingdom in the circumstances where s 83 (1) applies (restriction on bringing children in);
- the application is for an adoption order other that a Convention adoption order and the prospective adopters intend the child to live in a country or territory outside the British Islands after the making of the adoption order; or
- the prospective adopters are relatives of the child.

D[18.31]

The court also retains a general discretion, at any time, to direct that;

- a person should be made/removed as a respondent.
- a child should be made a respondent where he/she;
  (a) wishes to make an application, or;
  (b) has evidence to give or a legal submission to make that will not be made by any other party, or;
  (c) there are special circumstances.

D[18.32]

The rules introduce a presumption that any child who has been joined in adoption proceedings should be represented by a guardian unless the court is satisfied that it is not necessary to protect his interests. Also, older children who hold divergent views from his/her guardian will be able to seek the leave of the court to instruct a solicitor directly.

Special Guardianship Orders

D[18.33]

ACA 2002 s 115 has inserted a new section – s 14A-G – into the Children Act 1989, which includes the new provision of Special Guardianship Orders (SGOs).

D[18.34]

They are intended to be another option for permanence available to the court.

They are deemed to be **Private Law Proceedings** and the principles of the Children Act 1989 will apply but applicants have to give 3 months' notice to their local authority unless the court makes the order of its own motion.

D[18.35]

The Children Act welfare checklist applies, not the ACA 2002 checklist.

Effects of Special Guardianship Orders

D[18.36]

SGOs are intended to meet the needs of children who cannot live with their birth parents but for whom an adoption order is not appropriate.

D[18.37]

The special guardian appointed by the order has parental responsibility for the child and is entitled to exercise that parental responsibility to the exclusion of any other person with parental responsibility with **two exceptions**:

1) It does **not** affect any of the rights, which a natural parent has in relation to a child's adoption or placement for adoption. Parents retain the right to consent, or not, to these applications.
2) It does **not** affect the operation of any rule of law which requires the consent of all those with parental responsibility, for example, the sterilisation or circumcision of the child.

Parents will retain their parental responsibility, but the exercise of that responsibility will be limited.

D[18.38]

The making of an SGO discharges all care orders.

The Local Authority has to investigate and write a report and the court may also appoint a CAFCASS officer and request a welfare report.

Disclosure of Information about a person's adoption

D [18.39]

Under ACA 2002 access to information is filtered through adoption agencies so as to provide an intermediary safeguard before disclosure is made.

Sections 54 and 56 to 65 (the disclosure group of sections) deal with different types of information.

D[18.40]

Section 54 *information,* which an adoption agency is required to disclose to prospective adopters.

Section 56 *information* or *'protected'* information, which an adoption agency must keep in relation to a person's adoption:

1) Information about the adopted person including his birth parents and siblings, his adoptive parents and siblings and other relatives.
2) Any information kept by the adoption agency (a) which is necessary to enable an adopted person to obtain a certified copy of the record of his birth or (b) which is information about an entry relating to an adopted person in the Adoption Contact Register.

It includes *'identifying'* information, which means information which identifies the person or enables the person to be identified.

D[18.41]

Section 58 *information* or 'background' information (which does not fall into either category).

The System for Disclosure

D[18.42]

In brief:

- The adoption agency is the single point of access for 'identifying information', including the information necessary to access a birth record.
- Protected information may only be disclosed by the agency pursuant to ss 57–65. The system for disclosure of protected information is subject to criminal sanctions imposed on adoption agencies who contravene the disclosure provisions.

D[18.43]

Certain background information must be disclosed to adopters and may be disclosed to certain persons for the purposes of the agency's functions.

D[18.44]

The adopted adult, has the right, at his request, under s 60:

- to receive from the agency the information disclosed to the adopters by the agency under s 54
- to receive from the adoption agency the information necessary to obtain his birth record ('the birth record information') unless the High Court orders otherwise. For the High Court to do so, there must be an application by the agency for permission not to disclose and the High Court must be satisfied that the circumstances are exceptional
- to receive from the court, which make the adoption order, a copy of -
  1) the application form for an adoption order (but not the documents attached);
  2) the adoption order and any other orders relating to the adoption proceedings;
  3) orders allowing a person contact with the child after the adoption order was made;
  4) any document or order referred to in the relevant Practice Direction. The court will remove any protected information from any such copy document or order before it is given to the adopted person.

Section E

The youth court

E[1]

Juveniles

(Children and Young Persons Acts 1933, 1963 and 1969)

E[1.1]

Children (those aged under 14) and young persons (those aged 14 or under 18) are juveniles. Cases involving juveniles are heard in the youth court apart from exceptional cases in criminal proceedings where the juvenile appears before the adult magistrates' court charged with an adult defendant. The adult court may also remand a juvenile, when no youth court is sitting.

Determining the age of the defendant

E[1.2]

If the exact age of a child (under 14) or young person (14 or under 18) is not known, his age will be the age that he appears to be to the court after it has considered all the available evidence.

E[2]

The youth court

E[2.1]

The magistrates who are members of the youth court are authorised to sit in that court because it is felt they are specially qualified to deal with juvenile offenders.

E[2.2]

Each youth court should (except in unforeseen circumstances) consist of three such magistrates, at least one of whom should be male and one female and the court should be presided over by the chairman or a deputy chairman of the panel. In *R v Birmingham Justices, ex p F* (1999) 163 JP 523, [2000] Crim LR 588 it was made clear that the court should consider representations before proceeding with a single sex bench. A district judge may sit alone in the youth court.

E[2.3]

Persons present during the hearing. Only the following are allowed to be present:

(a) members and officers of the court;
(b) parties to the case before the court, their solicitors and counsel, and witnesses and other persons directly concerned with that case;
(c) bona fide representatives of newspapers or news agencies;
(d) such other persons as the court may specially authorise to be present.

E[2.4]

Restrictions on reporting. The press may not report details of the name, address or school of a juvenile who is a defendant or witness in any proceedings before the youth court or any other details including the printing of a photograph which would identify him. An exception to this is when the court is dealing with an anti-social behaviour order. In such case the court may make an order under s 39 Children and Young Persons Act 1933 and give its reasons.

E[2.5]

These restrictions may be lifted:

(a) in order to avoid an injustice to a juvenile or in certain circumstances where a juvenile is unlawfully at large on application of the Director of Public Prosecutions; or
(b) the juvenile is convicted and the court, having listened to representations of the parties, believes it is in the public interest to do so.

Publication leading to the identification of an adult witness may also be prohibited under s 49 Youth Justice and Criminal Evidence Act 1999: see **I[1B.7]**.

E[3]

Criminal proceedings

E[3.1]

It shall be the principal aim of the youth justice system to prevent offending by children and young persons. Youth courts must have regard to this aim.

Age of criminal responsibility

E[3.2]

A child under the age of ten cannot be guilty of any offence (Children and Young Persons Act 1933, s 50).

Attendance of parent

E[3.3]

Unless the court considers it unreasonable to do so, it must insist on the attendance of the parent or guardian of a child or young person under 16 years. In respect of those who are 16 and 17 years' old, the court has a discretion. 'Parent' will include a local authority where the juvenile is in their care. At all stages of the proceedings, if a parent refuses to attend a warrant can be issued against him or her.

Remands (Children and Young Persons Act 1969, s 23)

E[3.4]

A juvenile may be remanded in the way described in Section I (Court procedure). Defendants who have attained 17 years are remanded in the same manner as an adult, although Youth Offending Teams must have bail support programmes in place for children and young persons remanded on bail while awaiting trial or sentencing. In areas covered by the street crime initiative (see **[J1.6]**) a 17-year-old may also be made subject to a condition of curfew with electronic monitoring. Where bail is refused in respect of a defendant under 17 years, he will generally be remanded into local authority accommodation. Where the juvenile is remanded into local authority accommodation the local authority may apply to the court to use secure accommodation in certain circumstances.

E[3.5]

Secure accommodation (civil application). Where a juvenile is remanded into local authority accommodation he may not be kept in accommodation provided for the purpose of restricting liberty unless the youth court (or magistrates' court) which remands him is satisfied:

(a) that:
  (i) the juvenile has a history of absconding and is likely to abscond from any other description of accommodation; and
  (ii) if he absconds he is likely to suffer significant harm; or

(b) that if he is kept in any other description of accommodation he is likely to injure himself or other persons.

E[3.6]

Where the juvenile is charged with an offence carrying 14 years' imprisonment or more or with an offence of violence or he has previously been found guilty of an offence of violence the criteria that must be established are that non-secure accommodation is inappropriate because:

(a) the juvenile is likely to abscond from such accommodation; or
(b) the juvenile is likely to injure himself or other people if he is kept in any such accommodation.

E[3.7]

This application is under the Children Act 1989, s 25. However, the welfare of the child is relevant, not paramount, in a remand situation (*Re M (a minor) (secure accommodation)* [1995] Fam 108, [1995] 3 All ER 407, CA).

E[3.8]

The maximum period of authorisation is the length of the remand or, in the case of committal to the Crown Court, 28 days.

E[3.9]–E[3.15]

Conditions. After consultation with the local authority, the court may require a juvenile remanded to their accommodation to comply with conditions analogous to those for conditional bail (see **J[1.55]**). The court may also impose requirements on the authority to ensure the juvenile's compliance with those conditions and may stipulate that he be not placed with a named person.

E[3.16]

Remand with a security requirement In some situations the remand may be to secure accommodation or prison accommodation, namely:

(a) he is charged with or has been convicted of a violent or sexual offence, or an offence punishable in the case of an adult with imprisonment for a term of 14 years or more; or
(b) he is charged with or has been convicted of one or more imprisonable offences which, together with any other imprisonable offences of which he has been convicted in any proceedings:
  (i) amount, or
  (ii) would, if he were convicted of the offences with which he is charged, amount, to a recent history of repeatedly committing imprisonable offences while remanded on bail or to local authority accommodation.

and (in either case) the court is of opinion that having considered all the other options only remanding him to secure accommodation would be adequate to protect the public from serious harm from him or prevent the commission by him of imprisonable offences.

E[3.17]

15 and 16-year-old males. 15 and 16-year-old males who meet the above criteria will normally be remanded to prison accommodation unless they are defined as vulnerable by reason of immaturity or propensity for self-harm, in which case they may be remanded to previously identified secure accommodation.

This differentiation between males and females was found to be justified in *R (SR) v Nottingham Magistrates' Court* (1986) 84 Cr App Rep 316, 151 JP 49.

E[3.17A]

Age at date of sentence If a defendant's case is retained by the Youth Court when the defendant is 17 years old and sentenced when he is 18 years old the Youth Court has its full power open to it: s 29 of the Children and Young Persons Act 1963 and *Aldis v DPP* [2002] EWHC 403 (Admin), [2002] All ER (D) 128 (Feb).

In *R v Ghafoor* [2002] EWCA Crim 1857, [2003] 1 Cr App Rep (S) 428 it was said that the starting point for sentencing was the age of the defendant at the date of the offence.

*Juveniles and committal for trial [**see below]*

E[3.18]

(a) If the charge is homicide the juvenile must be committed for trial (Magistrates' Courts Act 1980, s 24).

(b) If the offence is punishable by 14 years' imprisonment or more (or certain prescribed offences under the Sexual Offences Act 2003 eg sexual assault (s 3); or certain prescribed offences under s 5 of the Firearms Act 1968) he must be committed for trial if the magistrates consider that in the event of his being found guilty he could be detained for a term of two years or more, or in the case of an offender aged 10–15 years – where there is some unusual feature of the case – a sentence approaching two years (*R (on the application of H) v Southampton Youth Court* [2004] EWHC 2912 (Admin), [2004] All ER (D) 38 (Dec)). If the magistrates are not of that opinion he must be tried summarily (Powers of Criminal Courts (Sentencing) Act 2000, s 91) (*R v Mills* [1998] 2 Cr App Rep (S) 128, [1998] Crim LR 220, CA). Cases involving offenders under 15 years of age for whom detention and training was not available will only rarely attract a period of detention under PCC(S) A 2000, s 91 (*R (on application of M) v Camberwell Green Youth Court* [2004] All ER (D) 95 (Dec), DC). In order to place themselves in the same position as the Crown Court magistrates may have regard to previous relevant convictions when making this decision (*R (Tullett) v Medway Magistrates Court* [2003] EWHC 2279 (Admin), 167 JP 541). The Sentencing Guidelines Council issued guidance in July 2006 for offences of **robbery**. The guidelines apply to offenders who have not been assessed as dangerous. The sentencing ranges and presumptive starting points apply to three types of robbery namely (i) street robbery or "mugging" (ii) robberies of small businesses (iii) less sophisticated commercial robberies. The starting points are based upon a first-time offender aged 17 years who pleaded not guilty. In such cases it will be necessary to consult the legal adviser.

(c) A juvenile of 16 or 17 who faces a minimum sentence under s 51A of the Firearms Act 1968.

(d) If a juvenile is jointly tried with someone aged 18 or older, the juvenile must be tried summarily unless the magistrates consider it necessary in the interests of justice to commit both for trial (Magistrates' Courts Act 1980, s 24).

(e) [Having indicated a not guilty plea] the offence is a specified offence within the meaning of s 224 of the CJA 2003 and it appears to the court that if found guilty the criteria for the imposition of a sentence under s 226(3) [detention for public protection] or s 228(2) [extended sentence] would be met. For general guidance see *R v Lang* [2005] EWCA Crim 2864, [2006] 2 All ER 410.

The legal adviser should be consulted when this point arises.

[The following amendments will apply once the provisions of Sch 3 to the Criminal Justice Act 2003 are brought into force. NB: Committal proceedings will be abolished.]**

Allocation and the sending of juveniles to the Crown Court for trial

E[3.18A]

There is a general presumption that a juvenile will be tried in the magistrates' [youth] court unless certain criteria apply. In those circumstances the youth must be **sent** to the Crown Court. The criteria are as follows:

(a) The charge is one of homicide.
(b) The juvenile faces a serious complex fraud allegation and the prosecution has served a relevant notice under the CJA 2003.
(c) The case involves a child witness and the prosecution has served a relevant notice under the CJA 2003.
(d) [Having indicated a not guilty plea] the offence is a specified offence within the meaning of s 224 of the CJA 2003 and it appears to the court that if found guilty the criteria for the imposition of a sentence under s 226(3) [detention for life or public protection] or s 228(2) [extended sentence] would be met. For general guidance see *R v Lang* [2005] EWCA Crim 2864, [2006] 2 All ER 410;
(e) A juvenile aged 16 or 17 who faces a minimum sentence under s 51A (1) of the Firearms Act 1968;
(f) [Having indicated a not guilty plea] a juvenile is jointly charged with someone aged 18 or older, and the court considers it necessary in the interests of justice to send both for trial.
(g) [Having indicated a not guilty plea] if the offence is punishable with 14 years' imprisonment or more; or the offence is a prescribed under the Sexual Offences Act 2003 ie sexual assault (s 3), a child sex offence (s 13), sexual activity with a child family member (s 25), inciting a child family member to engage in sexual activity (s 26); or is a prescribed offence under s 5 of the Firearms Act 1968 – where s 51A(1) above does not apply; a juvenile **must be sent** for trial if the magistrates consider that in the event of his being found guilty he could be detained for a term of two years or more; or in the case of an offender aged 10–15 years – where there is some unusual feature of the case – a sentence approaching two years.

Given the complexity of these provisions it is advisable for the magistrates to consult with their legal adviser.

**Committal for Sentence

E[3.18B]

Under the old legislation committal for sentence was not available to a youth or adult magistrates' court. Under the new sentencing regime committal for sentence is available in limited circumstances:

(a) A juvenile **pleads guilty** to an offence punishable with 14 years' imprisonment or more; or the offence is a prescribed offence under the Sexual Offences Act 2003 ie sexual assault (s 3); a child sex offence (s 13); sexual activity with a family member (s 25); inciting a child family member to engage in sexual activity (s 26); and, the court is of the opinion that the offence or the combination of the offence and one or more offences associated with it, was such that the Crown Court should, in the court's opinion, have power to deal with the offender as if the provisions of s 91(3) of the PCC(S)A 2000 applied ("power to detain for specified period") the court **may** commit him in custody or on bail for sentence: s 3B Magistrates' Courts Act 1980. The court may also commit him to the Crown Court to be dealt with in respect of certain other offences: s 6 Magistrates' Courts Act 1980.

(b) On the summary trial of an information a juvenile is **convicted** of a specified offence and it appears to the court that the offender is eligible for a sentence under s 226(3) (detention for life or public protection) or s 228(2) (extended sentence) the court **must** commit the offender in custody or on bail to the Crown Court for sentence: s 3C Magistrates' Courts Act 1980. The court may also commit him to the Crown Court to be dealt with in respect of certain other offences: s 6 Magistrates' Courts Act 1980.

(c) Where a juvenile is sent to the Crown Court for an offence and the offender faces a further **related charge** which carries 14 years' imprisonment or more, or is a prescribed offence under the Sexual Offences Act 2003 (see (a) above), and the offender indicates his intention in due course to plead guilty to that offence or pleads guilty to that offence, in due course the court may commit him in custody or on bail to the Crown Court to be dealt with in respect of the offence pursuant to s 4A Magistrates' Courts Act 1980.

These procedural provisions are complicated and it is recommended that magistrates consult with their legal adviser before exercising any of the above powers.

E[3.19]

It is suggested that the chairman announces the decision as to whether the juvenile shall be committed [sent] for trial or tried summarily so as to make it clear that this point has been considered. This will prevent any suggestion being made that the juvenile was committed [sent] for trial and a summary trial not considered. *R v Allen and Lambert* (1999) 163 JP 841, CA suggests that it is undesirable for the Crown Court to remit back to the youth court cases committed to it.

Procedure

E[3.20]

The court has to consider two general duties, the welfare of the child and the principal aim of the youth justice system to prevent offending by juveniles.

E[3.21]

The court must take care to ensure that he understands the proceedings and the charge should be explained in simple terms appropriate to his age and understanding. If not represented, his parents should be allowed to assist him in his defence.

E[3.22]

Oath. In the youth court, the evidence of children under 14 years must be given unsworn, otherwise the defendant and all the witnesses use a modified form of oath which commences 'I promise before Almighty God to tell the truth' etc. This oath is also used by a juvenile who gives evidence in the adult court (Children and Young Persons Act 1963, s 28).

Evidence from a witness in need of special protection (a child victim of a violent or sexual offence) will give evidence via a live video link (*R v Camberwell Green Youth Court, ex p G* [2005] UKHL 4, [2005] All ER (D) 259 (Jan)).

E[3.23]

Remission to a local court. Where the court before which a juvenile appears is not the youth court for the area in which he resides it may (and if it is an adult magistrates' court, it must unless it exercises its limited powers of sentence) remit him to be dealt with by his local youth court. This would normally be done, for example, where reports are required and the case has to be adjourned in order to obtain them. The court may give directions as to whether the defendant should be bailed or kept in custody until he appears before the local court.

E[3.24]

Remission to the adult court. Where a juvenile attains the age of 18 before conviction or after conviction but before sentencing he may be remitted on bail or in custody to be dealt with in the adult court, but not for an indictable offence (*R (on the application of Denny) v Acton Youth Court* (2004) Independent, 24 May).

E[3.25]

Delay. A stay of proceedings even on the grounds of unjustifiable delay will not normally be acceptable in a Youth Court (*R (on the application of DPP)* *v Croydon Youth Court* (2001) 165 JP 181, 165 JPN 34) but see *R (on the application of Knight) v West Dorset Magistrates' Court* [2002] EWHC 2152 (Admin), 166 JP 705.

E[4]

Possible orders for juveniles

E[4.1]

See the Process of sentencing at **B[5]**, and also the notes on each type of sentence in the 'Sentencing' section at **B[8]–B[47]**.

E[4.2]

Payment of fines, costs and compensation. See **B[33]**.

E[4.3]

If a juvenile is found guilty of an offence in a magistrates' court (as opposed to a youth court) because he has been jointly tried in the magistrates' court with a defendant aged 18 or older, the magistrates' court can only impose one of the following:

(a) absolute discharge;
(b) conditional discharge;
(c) fine;
(d) bind over.

E[4.4]

Costs, compensation, endorsement and disqualification can also be imposed. If the magistrates' court considers some other sentence appropriate the juvenile must be remitted on bail or in care to a youth court which will usually be the youth court of the area where he resides.

E[4.5]

Binding over parent(s) or guardian(s). The court is required to bind over the parent or guardian of an offender aged under 16 years who has been convicted of an offence to take proper care of him and exercise proper control over him; in the case of 16 and 17-year-olds there is a discretion to do so. Although the consent of the parent or guardian is required, an unreasonable refusal will attract a fine of up to £1,000.

E[4.6]

Parenting orders. Where a juvenile has been convicted of an offence the court has a duty in the case of an under 16-year-old and a power in the case of a 16 or 17-year-old to make a parenting order if it considers it would be desirable in the interests of preventing further offending. If no order is made the court must state its reasons.

The order requires parents to control their child and prevent offending within a 12 month maximum period and to attend counselling or guidance sessions for up to three months. Such orders will not breach Article 8 of EHRC (*R (M) v Inner London Crown Court* [2004] 1 FCR 178, [2003] 1 FLR 994).

Orders must not conflict with the parent's religious beliefs, work or education.

Breach is punishable with a fine up to level 3.

E[4.7]

Fines. In relation to fines, it should be noted that in the case of 16 and 17-year-olds there is now a power for the court to order a parent to pay any fine. If the juvenile is ordered to pay a fine the amount of costs ordered may not exceed the amount of the fine. Also, where a local authority has parental responsibility for a juvenile who is in their care or is provided with accommodation by them, they are to be treated as the person's parent for the purpose of a parent's responsibility to pay a fine etc. Where a parent etc is responsible for payment it will be his means that are taken into account, not those of the juvenile: see also **B[33.7]–B[33.10]**.

E[4.8]

Intensive Support and Surveillance Orders (ISSPs) ISSPs are not orders in their own right but may be attached to other orders, and are available for persistent young offenders who appear in court and have been charged, warned or convicted on four or more separate occasions within the previous 12 months and who have received at least one community or custodial penalty. Young offenders can also qualify for ISSPs if they are at risk of custody because they have been charged with or convicted of an offence for which an adult could face a sentence of 14 years or more or has been guilty of repeat offending whilst on bail and are at risk of a secure remand under s 23 CYPA 1969 as substituted by Criminal Justice and Police Act 2001, s 130 (See **[E3.16]** and **[B 47.37]**).

Section F

Liquor licensing

Readers will wish to note that the Licensing Act 2003 is now on the statute book. Its effect will be to transfer responsibility for licensing to local authorities.

Magistrates' courts still hold an appellant function from a licensing authority and may be involved in closure orders.

F[1]

Appeals under the Licensing Act 2003

Background

F[1.1]

The Licensing Act 2003 makes provision for the grant of both personal and premises licences by local authorities.

F[1.2]

A personal licence is granted under section 111 to an individual and authorises that person to supply alcohol for a period of ten years.

F[1.3]

A premises licence under section 11 and may be granted in respect of any premises and authorises the premises to be used for one or more licensable activities.

F[1.4]

The licensable activities are defined in section 1 as,

(a) sale by retail of alcohol
(b) supply of alcohol by club
(c) provision of regulated entertainment and
(d) provision of late-night refreshment.

F[1.5]

The local authority will determine the application or licence under section 120 and must grant where the applicant is 18 all over, possesses a described licensing qualification, has not forfeited his personal licence within the previous five-year period nor been convicted of any relevant offence. In the case of the first three criteria the local authority must reject the application where they are not met.

Appeals

F[1.6]

In respect of any of the local authority's functions outlined above or variation or imposition of conditions the applicant has a right to appeal to a magistrates' court. Schedule 5 of the Licensing Act 2003 set out in detail the decisions against which an appeal from the local authority may be made.

F[1.7]

When the appellant considers the local authorities licensing policy to be incompatible or 'ultra vires' the provisions of the statute, an appeal to the High Court by way of judicial review may be appropriate

Notices

F[1.8]

An appeal is commenced by way of written notice being given to a magistrates' court, in the case of a personal licence to the court for the area in which the local authority concerned is situated and in the case of a premises licence, the magistrates' court for the area in which premises are situated.

Period of notice

F[1.9]

Notice of appeal must be lodged within the period of 21 days beginning with the date on which the appellant is notified of the local authority's decision. It is the appellant's responsibility to serve notice on all respondents and prove to the court that such notice has been given.

The hearing

F[1.10]

Whilst any justice of a local magistrates' court may hear and determine an appeal most courts will have appointed an appeals panel in accordance with guidance issued by the Justices' Clerk's Society. In potentially complex appeals the court may hold a pre-hearing review to identify the issues, the numbers of witnesses and a time estimate for the hearing together with other preliminary matters. At such a hearing the justices may make directions regarding disclosure by the parties to each other (*Rushmoor Borough Council v Richards* (1996) 160 LG Rev 460). The proceedings are civil proceedings and therefore hearsay evidence may be admitted. To shorten proceedings justices or their legal adviser may give directions as to the conduct of the case – including the filing of evidence and any skeleton legal arguments.

F[1.11]

The court's powers (section 181). On hearing the application the court may:

(i) dismiss the appeal; or
(ii) uphold the appeal and make any other decision which could have been made by the licensing authority; or
(iii) remit the case to the licensing authority to dispose of in accordance with the direction of the court, if , for example, the local authority has simply failed to process an application.

Procedure

F[1.12]

The appellant's case may be presented in person or by a representative qualified under the provisions of the Courts and Legal Services Act 1990. The appeal is by way of a rehearing on the merits of the case and is neither a review of the local authority's decision nor an appeal on a point of law. The court is, therefore, able to hear all the evidence that was before the local authority committee and any relevant evidence, which has arisen subsequent to the local authority's decision.

Order of speeches

F[1.13]

As the appeal is commenced by way of a complaint the order of proceedings is governed by the Magistrates' Courts Rules 1981 (rule 14). This means that the appellant will open the case and call evidence in support of the appeal. Any respondent will be permitted to cross-examine witnesses called by the appellant and the appellant may re-examine any of those witnesses.

F[1.14]

Subject to any questions the justices may have, at the end of the appellant's case the respondent will outline his case and call witnesses in support. Such witnesses may be cross-examined and re-examined and the respondent may make a closing speech leaving the appellant with the final address to the court.

The decision

F[1.15]

The court will have regard to the licensing authority's statement of licensing policy and any guidance issued by the Secretary of State under s 182 of the Act. The court will also make its decision with the aim of promoting the licensing objectives set out in the Act namely:

(i) the prevention of crime and disorder,
(ii) public safety,
(iii) the prevention of public nuisance, and
(iv) the protection of children from harm.

The court will give reasons for its decision and if the court departs from either the statutory guidance or the licensing statement it will give reasons for doing so. Justices hearing an appeal should not consider or engage in planning matters which fell properly within the jurisdiction of the licensing authority (*R (on the application of Blackwood) v Birmingham Magistrates' Court* [2006] AER (D) 324 (Jun)). Except in the case of a closure order there is no further statutory entitlement to appeal the decision of the magistrates' court.

Costs

F[1.16]

The court may make such order for costs as it thinks fit under s 181 of the Licensing Act 2003. Case law such as *Bradford Metropolitan District Council v Booth* (2002) suggests that public authorities need to be able to make honest, reasonable and sound administrative decisions in the public interest without fear of exposure to undue financial prejudice if they are successfully appealed.

In *Crawley Borough Council v Attenborough* [2006] EWHC 1278 (Admin), (2006) 170 JP 593, the justices varied conditions imposed by the Borough Council in relation to licensed premises run by the respondent. The justices ordered the local authority to pay all of the costs of the respondent. On appeal it was agreed that there was no practical distinction between the terms of s 64 of the MCA 1980 (civil proceedings) and s 181 of the Licensing Act 2003. The Divisional Court upheld the justices' decision to award costs having regard to the fact that they had considered all of the circumstances including the facts and the history of the case and bearing in mind the order was varied on appeal by the justices.

Just over one week later, in *R (on the application of Cambridge City Council) v Alex Nesting Ltd* [2006] EWHC 1374 (Admin), (2006) 170 JP 539, it was decided that although as a matter of strict law the power of the appellate court in such circumstances to award costs is not confined to cases where the local authority acted unreasonably or in bad faith, the fact that the local authority has acted reasonably and in good faith in the discharge of its public function is plainly a most important factor. In ordinary civil litigation the principle that costs follow the event does not apply in this type of case. Therefore, an award of costs should not routinely follow in favour of a successful appellant in this type of case, if anything, quite the contrary.

It is submitted that if there is a perceived conflict between the two authorities above, there was fuller argument in the latter case and therefore the approach adopted in *Alex Nesting Ltd* is to be preferred.

F[2]

Closure Orders: police powers to close disorderly and noisy on-licensed premises

(Licensing Act 2003, ss 161–171)

F[2.1]

Power. On licensed premises only

- closure for a period not exceeding 24 hours
- no entry to members of the public during closure
- purchases or supplies prohibited during closure
- contravention without reasonable excuse is liable to a fine not exceeding £20,000 or to imprisonment for a term not exceeding 3 months (**no increase is provided for by the Criminal Justice Act 2003, Sch 26), or to both.

F[2.2]

Grounds. Requires authorisation by a senior police officer who believes that:

- likely to be disorder in or near premises and that closure is necessary in the interests of public safety, or
- disorder already taking place and that closure is necessary in the interests of public safety, or
- public nuisance is being caused by noise from the premises and that closure is necessary to prevent nuisance.

F[2.3]

Duration.

- up to 24 hours (notice must be given in writing);
- may be cancelled by police at any time after the order has been made (notice must be given in writing);
- order may be extended by responsible senior police officer if he/she believes grounds continue to apply and that magistrates will not have considered the order by end of closure period;
- no such extension shall come into force unless notice is given by end of previous closure period.

F[2.4]

Consideration hearing by magistrates (ss 164–165).

- as soon as reasonably practicable (must have written notice);
- must be in 'open court';
- powers may be exercised by a magistrates' court (which can be exercised by a single justice);
- evidence given must be on oath.

F[2.5]

Powers. The court may:

- revoke the order and any extension of it if the order or extension is still in force; or
- order the relevant premises to remain, or to be, closed until the matter is dealt with by the licensing authority. In considering whether to exercise this power the magistrates will have regard to s 161 in determining whether the grounds for making the order are continuing, or are likely to continue;
- order the premises to remain or be closed until dealt with by the licensing authority under s 167 but subject to specified exceptions;
- order the premises to remain or be closed until determination by the licensing authority unless conditions specified in the order are satisfied.

F[2.6]

Appeal from the Justices. Any person aggrieved by the decision of the magistrates may appeal to the Crown Court (Licensing Act 2003, s 166).

Section G

Betting and gaming licensing

G[A1]

Gambling Act 2005

G[A1.1]

****The Gambling Act 2005** contains a new regulatory system to govern the provision of all forms of gambling in Great Britain, other than the National lottery and spread betting. The Act will repeal the Betting, Gaming and Lotteries Act 1963, the Gaming Act 1968 and the Lotteries and Amusements Act 1976 respectively. The 2005 Act will be brought into force in accordance with commencement orders made under s 358. To date, most of the provisions of the 2005 Act remain unimplemented. The target date for implementation is **September 1 2007**.

The following is a brief summary of the timetable for the implementation of the Gambling Act 2005 and the changes in procedure and jurisdiction the Act will bring. NB: The relevant order ie the Gambling Act 2005 (Transitional Provisions) (No 2) 0rder 2006 (SI 2006/1758) was laid before Parliament on 5 July 2006 and came into effect on 1 August 2006.

General changes and timetable

G[A1.2]

1. Creation of a Gambling Commission.
2. A two-tier jurisdiction with local authorities dealing with premises.
3. The Act removes all responsibility from licensing, betting and gaming justices for granting betting and gaming permissions, which they exercised previously.
4. Decisions of the licensing authority ie the relevant local authority may be the subject of an appeal to the local magistrates' court. Decisions of the Gambling Commission may be the subject of an appeal to the Gambling Appeals Tribunal (but not a magistrates' court).
5. 1 September 2006: Existing authorities that expire on or after the said date will be renewed automatically so that they are valid until 31 August 2007 (no fee chargeable).
6. If the holder of a permit or licence seeks variation of a condition then the holder must apply for renewal to the current licensing authority.
7. 1 January 2007: Gambling Commission will accept advanced applications for the new forms of licence.

8. 31 January 2007: Gambling Commission will accept advanced applications for permissions.
9. 27 April 2007: Cut off date for applicants to qualify for continuation rights.
10. 1 September 2007: Gambling Act 2005 fully implemented.

Betting and Bingo

G[A1.3]

1. Existing operators must make advanced applications to the Gambling Commission between 1 January 2007 and 27 April 2007.
2. Existing operators must also make advanced applications to the licensing authority for a premises licence between 31 Janauary 2007 and 27 April 2007.
3. If the existing licence expires before 1 September 2006 apply in the normal way. The licence will be renewed so that it has effect until 31 August 2007.
4. If the existing licence expires on or after 1 September 2006 it will be renewed automatically without the need for an application or fee.

Casinos

G[A1.4]

1. Similar time frames etc as above.
2. Certain continuation rights for existing licences which afford protection against the restrictions imposed under the 2005 Act.

Gaming in Pubs and Clubs

G[A1.5]

1. Responsibility for s 34 Licensing Act 1964 permits was transferred to local authorities in November 2005 by virtue of the Licensing Act 2003.
2. Permits granted before November 2005 will continue to have effect until they expire.
3. Between 1 August 2006 and 31 July 2009 all existing permits for non-gambling premises such as take away food shops will be allowed to run their course. From 1 August 2009 it will be illegal to offer s 34 gaming machines in such premises.
4. Section 285 of the Gambling Act 2005 takes over with an automatic entitlement to one or two machines (known as a "permission"), although more machines can be applied for.

5. Prior to 31 August 2007 apply to the existing authority as now if the permit is due to expire. Thereafter, any new permission application must be submitted to the new licensing authority.

Clubs

G[A1.6]

1. Parts II and III of the Gaming Act continue until 1 September 2007.
2. Registrations that continue after 31 August 2007 will be converted into new style permits; they will expire on the same date as the original 1968 permit.
3. Renewals due prior to 31 August 2007 will continue to be made to the Gaming Committee or a magistrates' court as appropriate.

G[1]

Betting licensing committee

(Betting, Gaming and Lotteries Act 1963)

G[1.1]

A betting licensing committee is a committee of magistrates appointed by the local magistrates at the Annual General Meeting of magistrates in October of each year.

G[1.2]

It comprises at least 5 and not more than 15 magistrates.

G[1.3]

Three constitute a quorum.

G[1.4]

The committee hears applications to grant, renew or cancel bookmakers' permits, betting office licences and betting agency permits. The last named are rare and are not dealt with in this book. If such an application does come before the committee the clerk to the committee should be consulted.

Applications for a bookmaker's permit or betting office licence

G[1.5]

**** See the summary on the proposed timetable for the implementation of the Gambling Act 2005 at the beginning of this section**

The applicant has to serve certain statutory notices and it is suggested that when the applicant has completed his presentation of the case the clerk to the committee should be asked if all the necessary notices have been served, including one upon HM Revenue and Customs.

G[2]

Betting licensing sessions – court procedure (Sch 1)

Evidence

G[2.1]

If no objection is made to an application to grant or renew a bookmaker's permit or betting office licence the committee can proceed without hearing the applicant.

G[2.2]

If the committee considers it appropriate they can require any evidence to be given on oath.

Objections

G[2.3]

The committee can only refuse to grant a bookmaker's permit or betting office licence on certain grounds which are set out on the following pages.

G[2.4]

An objector must serve the clerk with two written copies of the grounds for his objection, and the clerk is responsible for serving one copy on the applicant.

G[2.5]

Normally the objector must carry out this procedure within 14 days of the appearance of an advertisement in a newspaper advertising notice of the application.

G[2.6]

A similar procedure must be taken by an objector to a renewal of a betting licence. Normally the objector must do this before the closing date for receiving objections, which date will be specified by the proper officer in a newspaper advertisement in February giving public notice of the day in April when annual renewals are due to take place.

G[2.7]

If a late objection is made the committee has a discretion whether or not to hear it. If it is decided to hear the objection the applicant must be given sufficient time to consider the written grounds for objection. An adjournment may be necessary.

Court fees

G[2.8]

For granting a bookmaker's permit	£160
For renewing a bookmaker's permit	£20
For granting a betting office licence	£125
For renewing a betting office licence	£25

Costs

G[2.9]

The committee can order an unsuccessful objector to pay costs to the applicant and vice versa.

G[3]

Duration of permits and licences

G[3.1]

In 1997, the duration of licences and permits was extended to three years, and the present three-yearly cycle runs to 31 May 2009.

G[3.2]

Renewal applications for permits and licences can be dealt with by the clerk to the appropriate authority unless there are objections.

Not transferable

G[3.3]

A bookmaker's permit cannot be transferred to another person or limited company. The second person or company must apply for a new permit.

G[3.4]

A betting office licence cannot be transferred from one set of premises to another; a fresh application must be made for each set of premises. Nor can the licence be transferred from one person or company to another at the same premises; a new application must be made.

G[3.5]

Death of holder. The legal personal representatives of the deceased holder of the licence or permit can continue business under the licence for six months after his death. If they can satisfy the committee that further time is necessary to wind up the deceased's estate and there are no circumstances that make it undesirable, the committee can grant a further extension of six months and repeat this extension for a further six months when the extension runs out.

G[3.6]

Change of address. The holder of a bookmaker's permit is required to notify the horserace betting levy board of a change of his office address.

G[4]

Refusal of bookmaker's permit

G[4.1]

The committee must refuse to grant a new permit or renew an existing one if any one or more of the following grounds exist:

(a) the applicant (not being a body corporate) is under 21;
(b) the applicant is disqualified from holding a bookmaker's permit following a conviction for certain betting offences or a conviction of other offences involving fraud or dishonesty. A full list can be supplied by the clerk to the committee;
(c) the applicant (not being a body corporate) is not resident in Great Britain or was not resident during the six months prior to the application;
(d) the applicant is a 'body corporate' which is not incorporated in Great Britain;
(e) the applicant, during the previous 12 months, has been refused the grant or renewal of a bookmaker's permit or betting agency permit because the committee was not satisfied that he was a fit and proper person or the Horse Racing Levy Board do not approve of his application;
(f) the applicant has had his bookmaker's permit cancelled during the previous 12 months.

G[4.2]

The committee **may** refuse to grant or renew a bookmaker's permit on either of the following grounds:

G[4.3]

(i) That the committee is not and has not been satisfied that the applicant is a fit and proper person, despite the fact that with his application the applicant has to enclose two character references.

G[4.4]

If the applicant is a limited company the application has to include two character references in respect of two persons upon whose instructions or directions the company's employees are accustomed to act.

G[4.5]

The committee will usually rely on the police so far as the references are concerned.

G[4.6]

In deciding whether a person is a fit and proper person to hold a bookmaker's permit the committee must have regard to whether or not he has paid in full his bookmaker's levy to the Levy Board and to the circumstances in which any failure to pay arose; and also whether or not he has paid the general betting duty due from him to HM Customs and Excise.

G[4.7]

In assessing the applicant's character the committee must disregard any convictions under the Betting Act 1853 or any corresponding offences under local Acts of Parliament, or offences under the Street Betting Act 1906 committed on or before 1 December 1961, and certain convictions under the Betting and Gaming Act 1960 committed before 1 December 1961.

G[4.8]

(ii) The committee can refuse to grant or renew a bookmaker's permit if it is satisfied that being granted or renewed it would be managed by or carried on for the benefit of a person who would be refused the grant or renewal of a permit for any of the reasons mentioned above.

G[4.9]

Home Office Circular No 29/1999 provides detailed guidance on the above provisions.

G[5]

Grounds for refusing a betting office licence

G[5.1]

The committee **must** refuse to grant or renew a betting office licence if it is not satisfied on the following points:

(a) that the applicant will hold either a bookmaker's permit or betting agency permit when the licence comes into force or continues in force; this does not apply if the applicant is the Totalisator Board;
(b) that the premises are or will be enclosed;
(c) that the betting office will have its own means of access to the street without passing through premises where some other business is carried on.

G[5.2]

The committee **may** refuse to grant or renew a betting office licence on any or more of the following grounds:

(a) that the committee think that having regard to the layout, character, condition or location of the premises they are not suitable for a betting office;
(b) that the grant or renewal of a betting office licence is inexpedient having regard to the demand for the time being in the locality for the facilities etc and the existing number of betting offices already available in the locality;
(c) that the premises have not been conducted properly under the licence.

G[5.3]

If the committee refuses to grant or renew a bookmaker's permit or a betting office licence it must notify the applicant of the refusal forthwith.

G[5.4]

The applicant has a right of appeal to the Crown Court and the committee can be legally represented at such an appeal. The clerk to the committee should be consulted as the committee will wish to ensure that the use of public funds for their legal representation has been authorised.

G[6]

Cancellation of bookmaker's permit

G[6.1]

Any person can apply for forfeiture and cancellation of a bookmaker's permit, e g a dissatisfied punter.

G[6.2]

The application for forfeiture and cancellation must be made in the prescribed form and accompanied by two copies of the grounds on which the application is based. Upon receiving the documents the clerk to the committee must submit them to any one member of the betting licensing committee, who may resolve the matter in one of two ways:

G[6.3]

(a) If he considers that further consideration of the application is unnecessary or inexpedient before the next April meeting of the committee when the licence would come up for renewal he may direct that the application be refused but the applicant will be entitled to rely on the same grounds for presenting an objection at the annual meeting at which permits are renewed.

G[6.4]

Again, if the member of the committee considers that the matters raised in the application have been or ought to have been raised by way of objection when the permit was originally granted or last renewed, or if the matters raised are or have been the subject of proceedings for certain offences under the Betting, Gaming and Lotteries Act 1963 or offences involving fraud or dishonesty, then again the member of the committee may refuse the application for cancellation of the bookmaker's permit (this is because the court that dealt with the offences would have cancelled the permit if they thought it appropriate).

G[6.5]

As before, the applicant may use the same grounds to object to the renewal of the permit when it comes up for consideration at the next renewal meeting.

G[6.6]

(b) The alternative action the member of the committee can take is to direct that the application to cancel the bookmaker's permit be referred to the betting licensing committee. The clerk to the committee must then give the applicant, the bookmaker and the police 21 days' notice of the date when the betting licensing committee will meet to decide the issue. The clerk must also serve on the bookmaker a copy of the applicant's grounds for seeking cancellation of the bookmaker's permit.

G[6.7]

It may be that the police themselves are seeking the cancellation and are themselves the applicant; if they are not the applicant they are entitled to make representations at the hearing.

The hearing before the betting licensing committee

G[6.8]

The committee must refuse the application to cancel a bookmaker's permit if it is satisfied that the matters raised have been or ought to have been raised by way of objection when the permit was originally granted or renewed, or if the committee is satisfied that the matters raised are or have been the subject matter of proceedings for certain offences under the Betting, Gaming and Lotteries Act 1963 or offences involving fraud or dishonesty then the committee must refuse the application for cancellation as that aspect will have been already judicially considered by a court.

G[6.9]

The committee must not cancel a bookmaker's permit except for the following reasons:

(a) that the bookmaker is no longer a fit and proper person. A failure to pay bookmaker's levy to the Levy Board, or to pay general betting duty to HM Customs and Excise entitles the betting licensing committee to rule that the bookmaker is no longer a fit and proper person; or
(b) that the business is being managed by or carried on for the benefit of someone who would be refused a permit if he himself applied either because he would be held to be disqualified from holding a permit or because he was not a fit and proper person to hold a permit.

G[6.10]–G[6.15]

In coming to their decision as to whether to cancel a bookmaker's permit the committee must disregard any conviction for offences under the Betting Act 1853 or corresponding offences under local Acts of Parliament or offences under the Street Betting Act 1906 committed on or before

1 December 1961, or certain offences under the Betting and Gaming Act 1960 committed before 1 December 1961.

G[6.16]

If the committee decides not to cancel the permit it must give written notice to the applicant for cancellation, stating that his application for cancellation of the permit is refused without prejudice to his right to raise the matter again when the permit next comes up for renewal.

G[6.17]

If the committee decides to forfeit and cancel the permit there is a right of appeal to the Crown Court and the cancellation will not take effect until the appeal has been decided or abandoned.

G[6.18]

The committee has power to order an unsuccessful applicant for cancellation of a bookmaker's permit to pay costs to the bookmaker and vice versa.

Cancellation and forfeiture of betting office licences

G[6.19]

(a) a court is enabled to order the cancellation and forfeiture of a betting office licence held by a person convicted of managing a betting office in contravention of the rules set out in the Betting, Gaming and Lotteries Act 1963, Sch 4;

(b) provision is made for the cancellation of betting office licences. The three discretionary grounds upon which a licence can be cancelled are:
   - (i) having regard to their layout, character and condition, they are not suitable for use as a licensed betting office; or
   - (ii) they have not been properly conducted under the licence; or
   - (iii) they have not been used as a licensed betting office in the period of 12 months ending with the date on which the applications made and the licence has been in force for at least 12 months.

G[7]

Opening hours of licensed betting offices

G[7.1]

Licensed betting offices may remain open until 10 p.m., **only** during the months April to August inclusive. They have to remain closed:

(a) between 10 p.m. and midnight during April, May, June, July and August; and
(b) between 6.30 p.m. and midnight at any other time of the year.

G[7.2]

Betting offices are allowed to open on Sundays at the same times as on other days of the week.

G[8]

Bingo club licence

(Gaming Act 1968)

G[8.1]

****See the summary on the proposed timetable for the implementation of the Gambling Act 2005 at the beginning of this section**

A bingo club licence is a gaming licence (see below) which contains a restriction pursuant to the Gaming Act 1968, Sch 2, para 25, limiting the type of gaming to bingo. As it is a gaming licence the procedures and notes mentioned below also apply here except for grounds of refusal numbered (f) and (g) at **G[9.9]**, and for the compulsory restrictions mentioned at **G[9.16]**. The applicant must first obtain a certificate of consent from the Gaming Board which will be limited to bingo and then the applicant must apply to the betting and gaming licensing committee for the area in which the premises are situated. Reference should therefore be made to gaming club ('casino') licences below.

G[8.2]

The court fee for a bingo club licence is £3,800 (compared with £28,915 for a full gaming licence) and £7,500 for Gaming Board Consent.

G[8.3]

A gaming licensing committee is entitled to hear an application for a bingo hall licence under the Gaming Act 1968, Sch 2 even though the premises to which the application relates have not yet been built *(R v Gaming Licensing Committee, ex p Gala Leisure Ltd* [1996] COD 312).

G[9]

Gaming licence

(Gaming Act 1968)

G[9.1]

****See the summary on the proposed timetable for the implementation of the Gambling Act 2005 at the beginning of this section**

The Gaming Act 1968 is aimed at strictly controlling the issue of such licences. An applicant must first obtain a certificate of consent from the Gaming Board of Great Britain. Without this no applicant can proceed with the second step of his application which is to obtain a gaming licence from the betting licensing committee for the area in which the proposed premises are situated.

Method of application to gaming licensing committee (Gaming Act 1968, Sch 2)

G[9.2]

Application to a betting and gaming licensing committee may be made at any time.

G[9.3]

It is suggested that the betting licensing committee ask their clerk to confirm that the correct application procedure has been followed.

In computing the time in which a person may object to the grant of a licence the date of publication or service is not included and the latest date should allow for the expiry of the relevant time period (in this case 14 days). For example, a notice published on 26 January 2006, should specify that any person wishing to object should do so by 10 February 2006 (and not 9 February as in the instant case): *R (on the application of TC Projects Ltd) v Gaming Licensing Committee* [2006] All ER (D) 241 (Apr).

G[9.4]

The newspaper advertisement must be strictly limited to mentioning only prescribed matters; but an inadvertent misprint does not invalidate the advertisement (*R v Brighton Gaming Licensing Committee, ex p Cotedale Ltd* [1978] 3 All ER 897, [1978] 1 WLR 1140, CA).

G[9.5]

Procedure at the hearing. If no objection is made, or if objections have been withdrawn, the licence can be granted without hearing evidence.

G[9.6]

The committee can impose restrictions on such matters as the times when and the parts of the premises where gaming can take place; also on the types of gaming that can take place.

G[9.7]

If a licence is granted the court fee is £28,915 (and £8,000 for Gaming Board Consent).

G[9.8]

Grounds for refusing a licence. The committee can require evidence tendered by the applicant or an objector to be upon oath. The Act requires the committee to take into consideration advice tendered to it by the Gaming Board, and the advice may be based on a local, or a regional or even national viewpoint. If the Gaming Board's advice is in writing, the applicant is entitled to obtain a copy of it by writing to the clerk of the betting licensing committee.

G[9.9]

An application can be refused on any of the following grounds:

(a) The committee is not satisfied that a substantial demand *already* exists for the type of gaming proposed. The committee is expected to take into consideration gaming facilities existing in reasonably accessible areas, as well as inside their own area.
(b) The layout, character, condition, or location of the premises are unsuitable.
(c) The applicant is not a fit or proper person; or would merely be a front for others who are not fit and proper persons.
(d) Reasonable facilities to inspect the premises have been refused to the committee (or its representatives), the officials of the Gaming Board, police, local authority or fire authority.
(e) Gaming duties under the Finance Acts have not been paid.
(f) The premises are not in a prescribed licensed club area.
(g) There is direct access to the premises from other private premises not in the licence.

G[9.10]–G[9.15]

It is a mandatory ground for refusal where a disqualification order under the Gaming Act 1968, s 24 has been made prohibiting the holding of a licence for the premises.

G[9.16]

Compulsory restrictions. The committee must include restrictions banning bingo, dancing, music, or entertainments by live performers.

G[9.17]

The committee can award costs to be paid to an applicant by an objector, and vice versa.

G[9.18]

Duration of gaming licence. The licence will expire 12 months after it is granted. Application for renewal must be lodged not later than two months or earlier than five months prior to the expiry date.

G[9.19]

Appeal. An unsuccessful applicant, or one who is dissatisfied with a restriction that the committee has imposed on his licence, can appeal to the Crown Court.

G[9.20]

The Gaming Board can also appeal to the Crown Court against the grant of a licence, or because, in the Board's opinion, a restriction imposed on a licence is inadequate. No other objector has a right of appeal to the Crown Court.

G[10]–G[15]

Gaming machine registration certificates

(Gaming Act 1968, Part III)

G[10.1]

****See the summary of the proposed timetable for the implementation of the Gambling Act 2005 at the beginning of this section**

A bona fide members' club or a proprietary club can apply to its local gaming licensing committee for a registration certificate under the Gaming Act 1968, Part III of the Act which will entitle the club to use a maximum number of three gaming machines (jackpot machines) at the club premises. There is no need for the club to obtain the prior consent of the Gaming Board.

G[10.2]

A gaming machine is a slot machine for playing a game of chance in which the element of chance is provided by the machine itself. It offers a large or unlimited jackpot to winners. It should not be confused with an amusement with prizes machine which can also be a slot machine for playing a game of chance; an amusement machine must comply with the requirements of the Gaming Act 1968, s 34. For the procedure for applying for an amusement with prizes machine permit for licensed premises see Sch 9 to the Gaming Act 1968 as amended.

G[10.3]

The maximum stake for single play on a club or jackpot gaming machine is £1.The maximum prizes that may be offered are £250 (in a registered club); £500 (in a bingo Club); and £1,000 (in a casino).

G[10.4]

Method of application for gaming machine registration certificate (Gaming Act 1968 Sch 7). It is suggested that the gaming licensing committee ask the clerk to confirm if the correct procedure has been followed.

G[10.5]

Procedure at the hearing. The Gaming Act 1968 envisages the police being the only objector. If no objection is made by them, a registration certificate can be granted without hearing evidence. The committee can require evidence to be given on oath particularly in a contested application.

G[10.6]

Grounds for refusing. The committee must refuse a registration certificate if it appears that the machine or machines will be installed on premises which are frequented wholly or mainly by persons under 18 years.

G[10.7]

The committee **may** refuse on any of the following grounds:

(a) the club is not a bona fide members' club. A proprietary club can be granted a certificate. It is a matter for the committee's discretion in each application. The clerk to the committee should be consulted;
(b) the club has less than 25 members;
(c) the club is of a merely temporary character.

G[10.8]

The committee can order the applicant to pay costs to the police, or vice versa.

G[10.9]

Duration of registration certificate. Five years from date of issue.

G[10.10]–G[10.15]

Appeal. An unsuccessful club can appeal to the Crown Court, but the police have no right of appeal to the Crown Court against a certificate being granted.

G[16]

Registration certificate for members' club for gaming

(Gaming Act 1968, Part II)

G[16.1]

****See the summary on the proposed timetable for the implementation of the Gambling Act 2005 at the beginning of this section**

A miners' welfare institute or a bona fide members' club which has 25 or more members and is not of a temporary character can apply for a registration certificate under the Gaming Act 1968, Part II. Gaming must not be the principal purpose of the club, but bridge and whist clubs are expressly authorised to apply for such registration certificates. There is no need to obtain a certificate of consent before making the application to the gaming licensing committee. The gaming can include bingo.

G[16.2]

Effect of registration. The gaming licensing committee will not decide what types of gaming can take place under the registration certificate. That point is dealt with by the Gaming Act 1968 and regulations made under that Act. As already mentioned bingo is authorised. Generally speaking a banker's game will be illegal and so will any gaming in which each player does not have an equal chance of winning; but pontoon and chemin de fer will be legal.

G[16.3]

Only members of 48 hours' standing and their bona fide guests will be allowed to participate in the gaming. Anyone participating must be present in the gaming room. If a charge is imposed it must not exceed £2 per person per day, 'day' meaning 24 hours starting from noon. (No charge can be imposed on a guest.) In addition a club or institute, whether registered under the Act or not, may generally charge £6 per day for gaming consisting of whist and/or bridge where no other gaming (except by means of gaming machines) takes place on that day, or 60p for other gaming where the chances are equal (guests may be subject to these charges). A club registered under the Gaming Act 1968 may make both charges, i e £2 and £6 or 60p, as the case may be. A non-registered club may only make the charge for bridge and whist, or the 60p for equal chance games; pontoon and chemin de fer will be prohibited.

G[16.4]

Method of application to gaming licensing committee. It is suggested that the committee ask the clerk to confirm that the correct application procedure has been followed.

G[16.5]

Procedure at the hearing. If no objection is made or objections have been withdrawn, the committee can grant a registration certificate without hearing evidence. In a contested case the committee can require the evidence to be given on oath. The committee can order an objector to pay costs to the applicant and vice versa.

G[16.6]

The committee can impose restrictions limiting the gaming to a particular room or rooms.

G[16.7]

Grounds for refusing. The committee must refuse the application if any of the following apply:

(a) the club is not a bona fide members' club (eg it is in fact a proprietary club in which one or more individuals own the club and take the profits);
(b) the club has less than 25 members;
(c) the club is of a merely temporary character;
(d) the principal purpose of the club is gaming, but this does not apply to bridge and whist clubs.

G[16.8]

Duration of registration certificate. It will expire 12 months after it was granted. Application for renewal (which may be for a period of up to ten years) must be lodged not later than two months nor earlier than five months prior to the expiry of the certificate.

G[16.9]

Appeal. An unsuccessful club, or one dissatisfied with a restriction included in its certificate, can appeal to the Crown Court. If a certificate is granted the Gaming Board can appeal to the Crown Court against the grant.

Section H

Council tax

H[1]

Background

H[1.1]

The administration and enforcement of the council tax is regulated by the Council Tax (Administration and Enforcement) Regulations 1992.

H[2]

Recovery and enforcement

H[2.1]

The first action the courts are involved in is the issue of a summons by a single justice or a justices' clerk against the alleged debtor following a complaint by a local authority of non-payment. Prior to this the local authority will have served a demand notice on the liable person and when payment has not been forthcoming the authority must serve a reminder notice. If payment is not made within seven days of the issue of the reminder notice the whole amount outstanding becomes due after a further seven-day period. The final step the local authority takes before making a complaint for a liability order is the issue of a final notice. Such notice will state the sum outstanding and the amount of any costs reasonably incurred in obtaining the liability order. The court will fix a date when the applications for the liability order will be heard.

H[2.2]

A summons may be served on a person by delivering it to him; leaving it in his usual or last known place of abode; sending it to him by post to that address or leaving it or sending it by post to an address given by the person as an address at which the service of the summons will be accepted (eg a solicitor's office). In the case of a company service can be effected at the company's registered office.

H[3]

The court hearing

H[3.1]

The court hearing is conducted as a complaint and the complainant council may make out their case for a liability order on the balance of probabilities, whether or not the non-payer appears in court. In order to be successful the council must satisfy the court that:

(a) council tax has been set by resolution of the authority;
(b) a sum due has been demanded in accordance with the regulations as set out above; and
(c) a summons has been served.

H[3.2]

It follows that if the amount has not been demanded in accordance with the regulations or has been duly paid then this will amount to a defence. A complaint for a liability order made more than six years after the amount became due will not be valid.

H[3.3]

Reopening

It is noteworthy that the power to reopen and rehear a case under s 142 of the Magistrates' Courts Act 1980 does not apply to this type of civil proceedings (*R (on the application of Mathialagan) v Southwark London Borough Council* [2004] EWCA Civ 1689, [2004] All ER (D) 179 (Dec)).

H[3.4]

Nor can the power be used when a case has been dismissed (*Verderers of the New Forest v Young* [2004] EWHC 2954 (Admin), [2004] All ER (D) 14 (Dec)).

H[4]

Evidential requirements

H[4.1]

Much of the evidence may be produced by way of certificate, for example, a certified copy signed by the appropriate officer showing the council's resolution setting the amount of the council tax for the given local authority area. In addition:

(a) computer generated documents are admissible under the Civil Evidence Act 1995 so long as the document constitutes or forms part of a record compiled by the authority;
(b) direct oral evidence of any facts stated would have been admissible; and
(c) where the document has been produced by a computer it is accompanied by a certificate which:
    (i) must identify the document and the computer by which it was produced;
    (ii) give appropriate explanations to the contents of the document; and
    (iii) be signed by a person occupying a responsible position in relation to the operation of the computer.

H[4.2]

The only legitimate defences against the making of the liability order are outlined above and such matters as pending appeals at the valuation tribunal as to the correct banding, or disputes as to the amount owed, will not amount to a reason for the court to decline to issuc a liability order. The justices are obliged to prevent the claimant from putting forward irrelevant matters such as whether the defendant should have received council tax benefit (*R (on application of Williams) v Pontefract Magistrates' Court* [2002] All ER (D) 465 (May)).

H[5]

The liability order

H[5.1]

Where magistrates are satisfied that the local authority has made out its case then they have no further discretion but to issue a liability order,. This order will include an order for reasonable costs. A liability order gives the local authority the power to take enforcement action such as an attachment of earnings order, distress or deductions from income support. Matters which may be raised at a valuation tribunal are not relevant in liability order proceedings.

H[6]

Committal proceedings

H[6.1]

Following the failure of liability or other enforcement methods the local authority may apply to the court for a means inquiry to be held with a view to a committal to prison in default of payment of the outstanding council tax. A warrant of commitment may only be applied for if the local authority has first attempted to levy distress and have received a report that the bailiffs were unable to find sufficient goods on which to levy the amount outstanding. In order to secure the debtor's attendance the court may issue a summons or a warrant for his arrest. At the committal hearing the court will inquire into the defaulter's means and may impose a period of three months maximum to be served in imprisonment where they are satisfied that failure to pay is due to the person's wilful refusal or culpable neglect. Justices using this power should be satisfied of the criteria on a criminal standard of proof or a high civil standard (*R v South Tyneside Justices, ex p Martin* (1995) Independent, 20 September). The defaulter must be present before the court and although local authorities are not under a statutory obligation to exhaust all other remedies before making an application for committal, it may well be advisable for them to do so. Courts will therefore be keen to see such action being tried as clearer evidence that the defendant is culpable in his neglect to pay and not just unable to pay through impecuniosity or mismanagement.

H[6.2]

When dealing with a committal application then the magistrates may:

(a) issue a warrant for commitment;
(b) fix a term of imprisonment and postpone the issue of the warrant until such time and on such conditions as the court thinks fit; note that where a warrant is issued after postponement and, since the term of imprisonment was fixed, part-payments have been made, these payments will reduce the imprisonment in a proportion to the full amount outstanding;
(c) adjourn the application;
(d) dismiss the application;
(e) remit all or part of the sum owing. As a guideline payments should be able to be made within a three-year period (*R (on the application of Broadhurst) v Sheffield Justices* (2000) 164 JP 870). Previous case law

points to the fact that, as with rates enforcement, this may only be appropriate if the debtor cannot afford to pay; remission remains an option only up to the point at which a term of imprisonment has been fixed (*Harrogate Council v Barker* (1995) 159 LG Rev 889, 159 JP 809);

(f) theoretically the court might find wilful refusal or culpable neglect but not issue a commitment warrant as the matter does rest within its discretion: once a warrant of commitment has been issued or a term of imprisonment fixed, a charging authority may not take further steps to recover the debt under the liability order (Council Tax (Administration and Enforcement) Regulations 1992, reg 52).

H[6.3]

The Council Tax (Administration and Enforcement) Regulations 1992, regulation 47(2) makes it clear that on an application for commitment to prison being made the court shall, in the debtor's presence, inquire into his means and inquire whether the failure to pay which has led to *the application* is due to his wilful refusal or culpable neglect. In other words, the court's inquiries concern the period of time after the issue of the liability order but before the application for a commitment to prison. This in fact makes it even more important that local authorities pursue all available options to them under the authority's liability order before coming into court to ask for a commitment warrant to be issued.

H[6.4]

Although the council may only deduct 5% of debtors' benefit payments direct from income support a magistrates' court may order a payment in excess of this figure in appropriate circumstances (*R v Felixstowe etc Magistrates' Court, ex p Herridge* [1993] RA 83, 158 JP 307).

H[7]

Suspended commitments

H[7.1]

Where a commitment to prison is issued but postponed on terms it appears that the court must hold a further inquiry before the commitment warrant is issued to take the defaulter to prison. This was considered in *R v Faversham and Sittingbourne Justices, ex p Ursell* [1992] RA 99, 156 JP 765. The court considered that a further inquiry into a commitment warrant postponed on terms was necessary before that warrant could be issued. This was a further opportunity to enable the court to be satisfied that the conditions had not been met by the debtor as well as giving the debtor a further opportunity to explain his default.

H[7.2]

The role of a defaulter was considered in *R v Wolverhampton Stipendiary Magistrate, ex p Mould* (1992) Times, 16 November. This was a case under the community charge legislation. The role of the defaulter was defined as going beyond the mere giving of evidence. He could also:

(a) challenge the evidence given by the charging authority as to indebtedness and any steps to levy distress;
(b) challenge the information given about his means;
(c) submit that failure to pay was not due to wilful refusal or culpable neglect; and
(d) even if it was, that a warrant of commitment postponed on suitable conditions was to be preferred to immediate custody.

H[7.3]

Where the defaulter fails to attend, in the light of the European Convention on Human Rights, it is advisable to issue an arrest warrant rather than issue the warrant of commitment in the absence of the defaulter. Magistrates should adjourn hearing a warrant for committal case where they know the debtor has not been served with the relevant committal notice (*R v Doncaster Justices, ex p Hannan* (1999) 163 JP 182, [1998] 32 LS Gaz R 30, [1998] RVR 254, 142 Sol Jo LB 218).

H[7.4]

A number of cases have emphasised that before committing a debtor to prison the court must have considered all available alternatives to attempt recovery of the sum due (*R v Newcastle under Lyme Justices, ex p Massey* [1995] 1 All ER 120, 158 JP 1037, [1994] NLJR 1444, sub nom R v Stoke-on-Trent Justices, ex p Knight [1994] 1 WLR 1684).

Section I

Court room procedure

I[1]

The Human Rights Act

I[1.1]

The purpose of the Human Rights Act 1998 is to allow citizens of the United Kingdom to enforce their rights under the Human Rights Convention in the domestic courts.

The Act requires all courts and tribunals to give effect to Convention rights by interpreting existing legislation and laws, where possible, compatibly with the Convention.

I[1.2]

With regard to statute (primary legislation) the courts are required to interpret the legislation so as to uphold the Convention rights unless legislation is so clearly incompatible with the Convention that it is impossible to do so. If a Convention right is contravened by a provision in primary legislation which the court is unable to interpret compatibly it must give effect to the will of Parliament. However, in such circumstances an appeal may be made to the High Court for a *declaration of incompatibility* which leads to a fast track procedure in Parliament for the passing of a *remedial order* to cure the apparent incompatibility.

In the case of secondary legislation or precedent the court's duty is to give effect to Convention rights; firstly through the medium of interpretation or secondly through disapplying the relevant domestic law.

I[1.3]

Additionally, courts must take into account judgments, decisions and opinions of the European Court of Human Rights and the Commission. All public authorities have a positive obligation to act compatibly with the Convention. This includes magistrates' courts, local authorities, the Probation Service and justices' clerks.

I[1.4]

Advocates wishing to raise a Convention point in magistrates' courts should be prepared to identify the article of the Convention which it is suggested may be breached, the reason for the breach and the remedy required of the courts. Court may give directions requiring the parties to file skeleton arguments in support of any Convention arguments.

Procedural steps

I[1.5]

Step 1 Ask if a Convention right is engaged.

If no Convention right is engaged, the case must be decided on the basis of domestic law.
If the Convention is engaged move to step 2

Step 2 Identify the relevant article and its class

- Absolute Rights:
  Article 3: prohibition of torture, inhuman or degrading treatment
  Article 4(1): prohibition of slavery or servitude
  Article 7: prohibition of punishment without law
- Limited Rights:
  Article 2: right to life
  Article 4(2): prohibition of forced or compulsory labour
  Article 5: right to liberty
  Article 6: right to a fair trial*
- Qualified Rights:
  Article 8: right to respect for private and family life
  Article 9: freedom of thought, conscience and religion
  Article 10: freedom of expression
  Article 11: freedom of assembly
  * Parts of Article 6 such as art 6(1) confer limited rights. Other parts, such as art 6(3) confer qualified rights.

I[1.6]

The threshold is high for breach of an *absolute right* but once breached for any reason, a violation is established.

Limited rights contain definitive statements of the circumstances which *permit* a breach of the right. If the restrictions are not complied with, there has been a violation of the Article.

Qualified Rights *may* be breached if:

- the breach is prescribed by domestic law
- the law is clear and accessible
- the breach pursues a legitimate aim which is set out in the Article
- the measure is a proportional response

If these provisions do not apply there is likely to be a violation of the convention.

I[1.7]

A magistrates' court which finds a breach or potential breach of the Convention may grant such relief or remedy, or make that order within its powers and it considers just and appropriate. In essence this may mean a simple adjournment to provide more time to prepare for a trial or it may involve the exclusion of evidence which would have had an unfair effect on the trial itself.

In *R (Laporte) v Chief Constable of Gloucestershire* [2004] EWCA Civ 1639, [2005] 1 All ER 473 the High Court found that the police acted reasonably in stopping a coach party, in apprehension of a breach of the peace and did not violate their Article 10 rights. However their actions in forcibly returning the coach to London breached Article 5.

I[1.8]

Burden of Proof. Where a statutory provision imposes a burden of proof on a defendant the court must first ascertain if it is an evidential or a legal burden. An evidential burden can be discharged by some evidence which could result in a decision in the defendant's favour. A legal burden on the other hand may breach the presumption of innocence in Article 6 (*R v Johnstone* [2003] UKHL 28, [2003] All ER (D) 323 (May), HL and *A-G's Reference No 1* (2004)).

I[1A]

Reasons for decision

I[1A.1]

There are many statutory requirements to give reasons in court. Examples are the imposition of imprisonment or where a court orders the removal of press restriction normally applicable in court. Such requirements are outlined in the text of this work. Article 6(1) states: '… everyone is entitled to a fair and public hearing within a reasonable time by an independent and impartial tribunal established by law. Judgment shall be pronounced publicly …'.

I[1A.2]

The giving of reasons enables an aggrieved person to understand the decision and make an informed decision on the right to appeal. It also provides an explanation for the public at large and those observing the proceedings in court. Reasons need not be elaborate (*McKerry v Teesdale and Wear Valley Justices* (2000) 164 JP 355, [2000] Crim LR 594, CA).

I[1A.3]

However, a reasoned judgment at the end of a trial should cover the major issues in dispute, and any legal submissions, together with the findings of fact. In *Ruiz Torija v Spain* (1994) 19 EHRR 542, ECtHR the European Court stated: 'The court reiterates that Article 6(1) obliges the courts to give reasons for their judgments, but cannot be understood as requiring a detailed answer to every argument. The extent to which this duty to give reasons applies may vary according to the nature of the decision'. One area where it is clear the court will have to give reasons is where there is any suggestion that an inference from the exercise of the right to silence is to be drawn: see *Condron v United Kingdom* [2000] Crim LR 679, 8 BHRC 290, ECtHR.

I[1A.4]

One other area that would appear to be clear is that the courts must not resort to formatted or standard reasons. In *Yagci and Sargin v Turkey* (1995) 20 EHRR 505, ECtHR the European Court disapproved of the use of stereotyped reasons by a court when refusing bail.

I[IA.5]

The court, like all other tribunals and public authorities, must act compatibly with the European Convention. In general a rigorous approach to giving reasons for a decision will normally alert the court to any human rights issues. A structured approach to those issues should lead to a successful resolution of human rights problems in court.

I[1B]

Proceedings to be in open court

I[1B.1]

Magistrates conducting a summary trial must generally sit in open court (Magistrates' Courts Act 1980, s 121) and comply with the provisions of Art 6 of the ECHR that everyone is entitled to a fair and public hearing.

I[1B.2]

There may be exceptions such as governing the conduct of proceedings in a youth court (at **E[2]**) and a family proceedings court (at **D[1]**) including particular restrictions in adoption proceedings (at **D[18]**). Also, statute provides for a court to sit in camera when considering evidence in proceedings under the Official Secrets Act 1920. All these may be read into Art 6(1) of the Convention and are unlikely to be subject to challenge.

I[1B.3]

Power to clear court while child or young person is giving evidence in certain cases. Where, in any proceedings in relation to an offence against or any conduct contrary to decency or morality, a juvenile is called as a witness, the court may be cleared of persons other than members or officers of the court, parties to the case, their counsel or solicitors, and persons otherwise directly concerned with the case, but bona fide representatives of the press may not be excluded (Children and Young Persons Act 1933, s 37).

I[1B.4]

Apart from the statutory exceptions evidence must be given in open court except where it may be necessary to depart from this principle where the nature or circumstances of the particular proceedings are such that the application of the general rule in its entirety would frustrate or render impracticable the administration of justice (*A-G v Leveller Magazines Ltd* [1979] AC 440, [1979] 1 All ER 745, HL).

I[1B.5]

The High Court has commented on the magistrates' decision to hear mitigation in camera because embarrassing and intimate details of the defendant's personal life would have to be given by her and she had an overwhelming fear of revealing them publicly. The judges felt the magistrates' exercise of their discretion was unsustainable and out of accord with principle (*R v Malvern Justices, ex p Evans* [1988] QB 540, [1988] 1 All ER 371).

I[1B.6]

Non-disclosure of evidence given in open court. Sometimes where the court decides not to sit in camera there is a request that a witness may write down his name on a piece of paper or use a pseudonym. In criminal cases at least this should only be done where the criteria for sitting in camera are met and such a device is normally only encountered in blackmail cases. Such a power is not designed for the benefit of the comfort and feelings of defendants such as where publication of a defendant's address might cause him to be harassed by his former wife (*R v Evesham Justices, ex p McDonagh* [1988] QB 553, [1988] 1 All ER 371).

Reporting of court proceedings

I[1B.7]

Apart from the special provisions governing the youth and family proceedings courts referred to above, the press may report all legal proceedings held in public (Contempt of Court Act 1981, s 4(1)). There are certain exceptions to the general rule:

(a) *Children and young persons:* The court may direct that no newspaper may reveal the name and address or other specified particulars calculated to lead to the identification of any juvenile concerned in the proceedings either as a witness or a defendant, nor that any picture shall be published, except as permitted by the court (CYPA 1933, s 39). The court may not order that the names of the adult defendants should not be published although a report naming the defendant and linking it to the victim may breach the s 39 order (*R v Teesside Crown Court, ex p Gazette Media Co* [2005] EWCA Crim 1983, [2005] All ER (D) 367 (Jul)).
(b) After an allegation of rape and other sexual offences (e g see **A[53]**) has been made the general statutory rule is that no material likely to lead to the identification by the public of the complainant may be published or broadcast (Sexual Offences (Amendment) Act 1992).
(c) *Publication of matters exempted from disclosure in court:* Where a court has allowed a name or other matter to be withheld from the public in proceedings before the court, the court may give such directions prohibiting the publication of that name or matter in connection with the proceedings as appear to the court to be necessary for the purpose for which it was so withheld (Contempt of Court Act 1981, s 11). The order must be in writing and must state with precision its exact terms, extent and purpose.

(*d*) *Power to postpone publication of reports of court proceedings:* Where it appears to be necessary for avoiding a substantial risk of prejudice to the administration of justice in those proceedings or in any other proceedings pending or imminent the court may order that the publication of any report of the proceedings or any part of the proceedings be postponed for such period as the court thinks necessary for that purpose (Contempt of Court Act 1981, s 4(2)). The order should be no wider than is necessary for the prevention of prejudice to the administration of justice (*R v Horsham Justices, ex p Farquharson* [1982] QB 762, [1982] 2 All ER 269, CA) and must be in writing and must state with precision its exact terms, extent and purpose.

(e) Under s 46 Youth Justice and Criminal Evidence Act 1999 the court may prevent publication of any matter which may lead to the identification of an adult witness for the duration of that person's life, if it is satisfied that the quality of their evidence or their participation would be diminished by fear or distress related to public information.

I[1B.8]

Photographs and sketches in court. No person shall take or attempt to take a photograph, or make or attempt to make any portrait or sketch of a justice or party or witness to proceedings, in a court room or in a court building or precincts or entering or leaving them (Criminal Justice Act 1925, s 41).

I[1B.9]

Tape recorders. It is a contempt of court to use a tape recorder (other than for the purpose of making an official transcript) in a court without the leave of the court (Contempt of Court Act 1981, s 9). Guidelines for the decision whether to grant leave were given in a Practice Direction by the Lord Chief Justice in 1982 which may be summarised thus:

(a) Has the applicant a reasonable need to use the tape recorder?
(b) Is there a risk of a recording being used to brief witnesses?
(c) What is the possibility of distracting proceedings or distracting or worrying witnesses?

I[1B.10]

Abuse of the process. The jurisdiction exercised by magistrates, to protect the court's process from abuse is confined to matters directly affecting the fairness of the trial of the accused, and it does not extend to the wider supervisory jurisdiction for upholding the rule of law which is vested in the High Court (*R v Horseferry Road Magistrates, ex p Bennett* [1994] AC 42, [1993] 3 WLR 90, sub nom Bennett v Horseferry Road Magistrates' Court [1993] 3 All ER 138, HL). It must not be used, therefore, to exercise a disciplinary function over eg executive decisions made by a prosecuting authority.

The parameters of this power are narrowly drawn. Justices may only stay proceedings where it would be unfair to try the defendant or where the defendant cannot receive a fair trial. It may be an abuse of process if either (a) the prosecution have manipulated or misused the process of the court so as to deprive the defendant of a protection provided by the law or to take unfair advantage of a technicality, or (b) the defendant has been, or will be, prejudiced in the preparation or conduct of his defence by delay on the part of the prosecution which is unjustifiable.

Magistrates would be well advised to consult with their legal adviser before adjudicating on such matters. The defence should give advance notice of such application. Where notice is not given magistrates should look favourably on an adjournment application by the prosecution. In addition, the court should give directions for the filing of skeleton arguments by the parties. A skeleton argument should focus on the issues arising in the case and the relevant principles. An excessive citation of authorities is to be deprecated.

I[IB.11]

Principles. May be summarised as follows:

1. The discretionary decision as to whether or not to grant a stay as an abuse is an exercise in judicial assessment dependent on judgement, rather than on any conclusion as to fact based on evidence. Accordingly, in cases of delay it is potentially misleading to apply to the exercise of that discretion the language of burden and standard of proof, which is more apt to an evidence-based, fact-finding process (*R v S* [2006] EWCA Crim 756, (2006) 170 JP 434).
2. The applicant must identify the ground or grounds upon which he relies eg delay, manipulation of the proceedings or destruction of evidence.
3. Where there is no fault attributable to, or the prosecution have acted in good faith, it will be very rare for a stay to be granted.
4. Is there serious prejudice to the accused? No stay should be granted in the absence of serious prejudice to the accused. When assessing possible serious prejudice, the court should consider its powers to regulate the admissibility of evidence, and that the trial process itself should ensure that all relevant factual issues arising from eg delay or the destruction of evidence, are placed before the court for its consideration.
5. When assessing possible serious prejudice, the court can take into account its powers in relation to sentence, assuming there is a conviction or a guilty plea.
6. A permanent stay should be the exception rather than the rule.
7. If having considered all the relevant factors, the court's assessment is that a fair trial will be possible, a stay should not be granted.

I[2]

Misbehaviour in court

I[2.1]

Misbehaviour by members of the public:

(a) Where persons misbehave in court the first approach should be to attempt to calm down offenders by an appeal to reason and good manners. A court can also consider putting the case back for a 'cooling off' period and the chairman may also make mention in very general terms of the court's powers to maintain order.
(b) If this is not successful a court has power to order persons disrupting the court to leave the court room. If they refuse, and their removal is necessary to enable justice to be administered properly, the court may order a court security officer or the police to remove such persons using reasonable force if necessary.
(c) Where persons are misbehaving in court the magistrates should not exercise their power to **bind over** (Consolidated Practice Direction para 54 (2002)).

I[3]

Contempt of court

Charges

I[3.1]

(a) **Wilfully did insult AB being a justice of the peace (or a witness before the court, or an officer of the court, or a solicitor or counsel having business before the court) during his sitting or attendance in court or when he was going to or returning from the court; or**

I[3.2]

(b) **wilfully interrupted the proceedings of a magistrates' court; or**

I[3.3]

(c) **wilfully misbehaved in a magistrates' court.**

Contempt of Court Act 1981, s 12.

I[3.4]

Maximum penalty. Fine of level 4 and one month. Proceedings under s 12: offender may be ordered to be taken into custody by an officer of the court or a constable and detained until the rising of the court in addition to or instead of the penalty mentioned above. A person under 18 years may not be committed for contempt. A substantial prison sentence (12 months) was upheld in *R v D (contempt of court: illegal photography)* (2004) Times, 13 May where the defendant had photographed the interior of the Crown Court (see **I[1B.8]**).

Legal notes

I[3.5]

Wilfully insult. The word 'insult' has to be given its ordinary English meaning. A person who had *threatened* a defendant had not 'insulted' him and was not in breach of s 12 (*R v Havant Justices, ex p Palmer* (1985) 149 JP 609, [1985] Crim LR 658).

I[3.6]

Officer of the court. This term is not defined in the Act. It will apply to the justices' clerk and his staff, presumably whether or not they are concerned in the particular proceedings in which the insult occurs. If there is any doubt, the matter could certainly be resolved by simply alleging misbehaviour in court.

I[3.7]

Procedure. See *Practice Direction (Magistrates' Courts: Contempt)* [2001] 2 Cr App Rep 272. By the nature of such proceedings, feelings may be running high and it is a grave matter to punish someone for contempt of court. Accordingly magistrates should be careful not to act in haste. The court should allow time for reflection. If necessary the case can be put back to the end of the court list. If the offender is removed to the cells, he should have the opportunity of speaking to his solicitor or receiving other legal advice (legal representation is available for contempt proceedings). The offender should always be given the opportunity to apologise to the court and it may be that a genuine apology together with the brief period spent in the cells may suffice. If it is necessary to punish the offender imprisonment should be the last resort. Where a person has been in prison, for example, because he refuses to apologise he may apply subsequently to the magistrates to purge his contempt by apologising and the magistrates may then order his release from custody.

In the case of a contested contempt the overall trial process must be in accordance with Art 6 and this may mean involving a different bench to try the issue.

I[3.8]

Where the disorder in court is so overwhelming magistrates should retire immediately and allow the police to restore order. Where the offenders are subsequently dealt with, they should be dealt with individually.

I[3.9]

Witnesses. In addition to the powers outlined above, where a witness refuses to take the oath or to answer a question, he may be committed to prison for a period of up to one month (and ordered to pay a fine on level 4). He may be released immediately he changes his mind and decides to co-operate with the court. This advice may ensure his compliance.

I[3.10]–I[3.14]

Defendants. Disorderly defendants may be dealt with as outlined above. However, a court is naturally reluctant to deal with the case in the absence of a defendant. Accordingly, if the defendant has to be ejected the court should carefully consider adjourning the case for a 'cooling off' period. The more serious the case the less appropriate it will be to proceed in the defendant's absence. The defendant should be informed that he will be readmitted to the court any time he is prepared to conduct himself properly.

I[3.15]

Taking a photograph in court with a mobile phone is a contempt of court and has resulted in immediate prison sentences in the Crown Court (*R v D* (2004) Times, 13 May). See **I[1B.8]**.

I[4]

Plea before venue and mode of trial proceedings

I[4.1]

****The following will apply when the new allocation proceedings under the Criminal Justice Act 2003 are brought into force.** Schedule 3 of the CJA 2003 revises the procedures to be found in ss 4–8 and 17–25 of the Magistrates' Courts Act 1980. The revised procedure for adult offenders charged with an offence triable either way will be as follows:

Allocation – adult accused – Key points

1. Indictable only offences – no change – send to the Crown Court.
2. Summary only – unless linked to an indictable only or either way offence – no change – take a plea.
3. Either way offences – modified procedures. Committal proceedings are to be abolished.

For either way offences the court will apply a modified procedure **unless**:

1. Serious or complex fraud; vulnerable child witness; or offence linked to either situation and, the prosecutor has served a notice signifying Crown Court trial.
2. Either a third specified drug or domestic burglary offence when the offence becomes indictable only.
3. The offence is linked to an adult co-accused charged with an indictable only offence.

In 1–3 above the court must send the offender to the Crown Court for trial pursuant to s 51 Crime and Disorder Act 1998.

Procedure for either way offence:

1. Defendant to indicate plea.
2. If guilty, the court should normally decide whether it has power to sentence or to commit for sentence. Note, the plea must be unambiguous. If the accused pleads guilty and then qualifies the plea eg makes a statement which, if true, would amount to a defence to the charge, the court should then enter a plea of not guilty.
3. On a guilty plea, if there is a dispute as to the facts which is material to sentence the court should conduct a Newton hearing, unless, on either

version of the facts the sentencing powers of the magistrates' court are inadequate, when the justices should commit the defendant to the Crown Court for sentence.

4. [If the adult is jointly charged with a juvenile and the allegation is a specified offence within the meaning of s 224 of the CJA 2003, the court must ask the youth to indicate a plea. If the plea is one of not guilty, the court must inquire as to dangerousness. If the court determines that the juvenile is liable to be sentenced under the dangerousness provisions it must send the juvenile to the Crown Court pursuant to s 51A Crime & Disorder Act 1998. The adult should then be asked to indicate a plea. If the plea is one of not guilty he also must be sent to the Crown Court and for any related offence which is triable either way pursuant to s 51A(6)].
5. [Disregarding 4 above] If no plea or a not guilty plea is indicated the court will hear representations as to venue. The court is entitled to take into account the offender's previous convictions. The primary test is whether the court's sentencing powers are adequate. The court will make its decision taking the prosecution case at its highest. Personal mitigation is not relevant to the decision as to venue.
6. If the court determines Crown Court trial, it will immediately send the offender for trial pursuant to s 51 CDA 1998.
7. If the court determines summary trial, the defendant will be asked to elect where he wishes to be tried. Before making his choice, the defendant may ask for, or in some cases the court might decide to give an indication of sentence if he were to elect summary trial. If the court gives an indication it will express the sentence in general terms eg custody or a community penalty.
8. If the defendant elects trial at the Crown Court, the court will immediately send the defendant for trial pursuant to s 51. Any indication as to sentence will not be binding on the Crown Court.
9. If the accused elects summary trial, he will be asked to enter a plea. If the plea is one of guilty any indication as to sentence will be binding on the court unless the magistrates determine to commit for sentence under the dangerousness provisions (see s 3A PCC(S)A 2000).
10. Where there is more than one adult co-accused and a co-accused elects to be tried at the Crown Court, the court must send all defendants pleading not guilty to the Crown Court for trial, even if one or more co-accused have elected, or would have elected to have their cases tried summarily. The legislation reverses the rule in *R v Brentwood Justices, ex p Nicholls* (1990) 154 JP 487, HL.
11. If the defendant consents to trial in the magistrates' court and enters a plea of not guilty the court will proceed to summary trial. Any indication as to sentence will not be binding on the court even if the offender later changes his plea to one of guilty.
12. At a later date the prosecution can ask the court to review the mode of trial decision where (i) further information has become available since the decision as to venue was made; (ii) the court is satisfied that as its sentencing powers are inadequate. The power may not be exercised

where the court has determined a pre-trial issue eg the admissibility of bad character evidence or hearsay evidence.

Allocation guidance – SGC guidelines:

1. General presumption = summary trial.
2. Broad rule of thumb – if in doubt as to venue – send to the Crown Court.
3. Presumption that adult co-accused pleading not guilty should be tried together.

I[4.1A]

Current Procedures:

Where a person is accused of an offence triable either way, the magistrates cannot conduct committal proceedings or try the offence themselves until plea before venue proceedings have taken place. The court will invite the defendant to indicate his plea, having explained to him that he may be committed to the Crown Court for sentence if the court considers its powers are insufficient. If the defendant indicates a plea of guilty he will be treated as convicted and the court will proceed to sentence, or committal to the Crown Court for sentence. If the defendant fails to intimate a plea or intimates a plea of not guilty the court will hear representations on the seriousness of the case, both from the prosecutor and the defendant. The court at this stage is only concerned with the gravity of the offence and not with the character of the defendant, and previous convictions of the accused are, therefore, irrelevant and should not be mentioned. The prosecutor should therefore give the court an outline of the prosecution case so that the gravity of the offence can be ascertained, eg in an assault case: the description of the injuries caused and whether a weapon was used. The defence may then make representations if it wishes before the magistrates make their decision.

Once mode of trial has been decided there is no inherent jurisdiction to change it. Such procedure is prescribed by MCA 1980, s 25 (*R (DPP) v Camberwell Green Youth Court* [2005] UKHL 4, 2005] All ER (D) 259 (Jan)).

Although *R (on the application of C) v Grimsby and Cleethorpes Magistrates* [2004] EWHC 2240 (Admin), [2004] All ER (D) 494 (Jul) suggests that s 25 has no application in the magistrates' court to proceedings against juveniles it is submitted that this observation is per incuriam having regard to the decision of the Divisional Court in *H v Balham Youth Court* [2003] EWHC 3267 (Admin), [2003] All ER (D) 173 (Dec).

Matters to which the court is to have regard

I[4.2]

(a) the nature of the case;

(b) whether the circumstances make the offence one of a serious character;
(c) whether the punishment which a magistrates' court would have power to inflict for it would be adequate (*R v Flax Bourton Magistrates' Court, ex p Customs and Excise Comrs* (1996) 160 JP 481, [1996] Crim LR 907);
(d) any other circumstances which appear to the court to make it more suitable for the offence to be tried in one way rather than the other (Magistrates' Courts Act 1980, s 19(3)).

I[4.3]

If the magistrates feel able to deal with the case the defendant is given a choice of which court he wishes to try the offence. Before he makes his choice he *must* be warned that if he elects summary trial and pleads guilty or is convicted after a trial he may still be committed for sentence if the court is of the opinion that the offence (or the combination of the offence and other associated offences) is so serious that the magistrates' powers of punishment are insufficient, or, in the case of a violent or sexual offence, a longer sentence is necessary for protection of the public.

I[4.4]

In order to promote greater consistency of approach to the making of mode of trial decisions, the Lord Chief Justice has now issued guidelines, the essence of which is as follows, with the emphasis on more cases being dealt with by magistrates. Cases which are often tried at the Crown Court are noted in the National Sentencing Guidelines with the query 'are Magistrates sentencing powers appropriate?'

General guidelines

I[4.5]

(a) The court should never make a decision just for convenience or expedition.
(b) Where there is a dispute on the facts at this stage, the court should rely on the prosecution version.
(c) The defendant's antecedent and personal circumstances are irrelevant.
(d) The fact that the offences before the court are specimen offences is relevant.
(e) Offences to be taken into consideration are irrelevant.
(f) Complicated issues of fact and/or law will tend to make the case more suitable for the Crown Court.

I[4.6]

Except for the presence of one or more 'qualifying factors' either way offences should be tried summarily. Qualifying factors are features which indicate that trial at the Crown Court is more appropriate. These qualifying factors are set out in the articles of the relevant offences in Section A.

I[4.7]

Criminal damage offences. The offence is triable as an ordinary either way offence for the purposes of plea before venue if the value is over £5,000. The offence is triable as a summary offence if the value is under £5,000. See **B[9.4]**.

I[4.8]

Indictable offences only. Under the Crime and Disorder Act 1998, s 51 indictable offences (such as aggravated burglary and grievous bodily harm) only have an initial hearing in the magistrates' court to decide on bail and legal representation.

The case will then transfer straight to the Crown Court for a preliminary hearing (within eight days if the defendant is in custody).There will be no committal proceedings and any challenge to the evidence will be made to a judge at the Crown Court.

The section does not apply generally to persons under 18 years of age or corporations.

I[5]

Committal for trial at Crown Court

****Committal proceedings will be abolished once the new allocation procedures under the Criminal Justice Act 2003 have been introduced. See I[4.1].**

I[5.1]

Magistrates have no power to try the guilt or innocence of an adult accused charged with an offence triable only at the Crown Court or with an offence triable either way where either the magistrates themselves have declined jurisdiction in mode of trial proceedings or the accused has elected to be tried at the Crown Court. See **B[16]** for committal for sentence.

I[5.2]

Magistrates dealing with committal proceedings are referred to examining justices. They examine the prosecution case to decide whether there is sufficient evidence to put the defendant on trial by jury. The sole test for the justices to apply is whether the prosecution has adduced sufficient evidence to satisfy them that there is a triable issue to be put before a jury. This is normally done where the defendant is represented, by statements tendered by the prosecution being accepted by the defence lawyer. In this case the defendant is formally committed to stand trial at the Crown Court with a date for either a plea and directions hearing or a preliminary hearing. If the defence do not accept that there is a prima facie case the court will consider the prosecution evidence only.

I[5.3]

A magistrates' court will consider only documentary evidence and exhibits tendered by the prosecution, together with representations by both parties, when determining whether there is a case to answer. Evidence should be presented in accordance with s 5B-5E of the Magistrates' Courts Act 1980 and will be read out in full unless the court directs that it is summarised. No witness will be called to give evidence or be cross examined. The defence may make submissions that there is insufficient evidence to put the accused on trial by jury. If the court is of the opinion that the statements disclose evidence upon which a jury could convict of an indictable offence the defendant will be committed to stand trial at the Crown Court. If they are not of that view the defendant will be discharged.

General provisions concerning committal proceedings

I[5.4]

The hearing. The committal proceedings may take place before only one magistrate but any hearing must take place in open court unless for any part, or the whole, of the proceedings, the ends of justice would not be served by having a sitting in open court. The evidence shall be tendered in the presence of the accused unless his disorderly conduct has made it impracticable for him to remain in court or he is ill and is represented by an advocate and has consented to the evidence being tendered in his absence (Magistrates' Courts Act 1980, s 4). See *R v Liverpool City Magistrates, ex p Quantrell* [1999] 2 Cr App Rep 24, [1999] Crim LR 734.

I[5.5]

Publicity. Only certain formal matters may be contained in any report of committal proceedings including:

(a) the identity of the court and the names of the examining justices;
(b) the names, addresses and occupations of the parties and witnesses and ages of the accused and witnesses; and
(c) the offence or offences, or a summary of them, of which the accused is or are charged;
(d) where the court commits the accused or any of the accused for trial, the charge or charges, or a summary of them, on which he is committed and the court to which he is committed;
(e) any arrangement as to bail on committal or adjournment;
(f) whether legal representation was granted to the accused or any of the accused.

I[5.6]

These restrictions automatically apply unless an accused chooses to have the reporting restrictions lifted. Where there are several accused, and they are not unanimous in wanting restrictions to be lifted, the magistrates must decide whether it is in the interests of justice to do so. Further, the restrictions do not apply where the accused are all discharged in the proceedings or after the conclusion of the trial in the Crown Court.

Summary offences

(**Criminal Justice Act 1988, ss 40 and 41**)

I[5.7]

Where an accused is committed or sent for trial for an offence triable either way, the magistrates may also commit or send him for trial for any connected summary offences provided they are either imprisonable or endorsable. At the Crown Court, if the accused is convicted of the indictable offence, he may also plead guilty to the summary offences and be dealt with, the Crown Court having the same powers as the magistrates with respect to the summary offences. If he denies the summary offences he may not be tried for them in the Crown Court, but proceedings may then continue in the magistrates' court (Criminal Justice Act 1988, s 41).

I[5.8]

Certain summary offences including common assault, damage and taking without consent may be heard at the Crown Court if they arise from the same facts or evidence as an indictable charge being committed to the crown court or they are part of a series of offences of the same or similar character as the indictable charge (Criminal Justice Act 1988, s 40).

I[6]

Summary proceedings

I Not guilty plea

I[6.1]

When an accused person enters a not guilty plea, he is not necessarily proclaiming his innocence. This arises from two factors: firstly, it is not the function of the court to decide whether he is guilty or not, the court's function is to decide *whether the prosecutor has proved that he is guilty*. Secondly, there may be legal or procedural reasons why an accused should enter a not guilty plea as will be seen from the following circumstances. A plea of not guilty should be entered when:

(a) the accused disputes the facts;
(b) the accused hopes to show that some legal condition precedent to conviction has not been fulfilled, eg a notice of intended prosecution;
(c) the accused believes that the prosecutor's witnesses will be incapable of establishing the facts beyond reasonable doubt, for example because:
  (i) there is a question of legal competence;
  (ii) there is lack of corroboration in a case where the law requires it;
  (iii) evidence vital to the prosecution is legally inadmissible;
  (iv) the accused believes he can discredit a prosecution witness by cross-examination;

(d) the accused agrees the facts but wishes to show that as a matter of law they do not constitute the offence charged;
(e) the accused has a statutory defence;
(f) the accused has no recollection of the circumstances alleged by the prosecutor and wishes to hear evidence before deciding whether he should plead guilty.

Trial in absence. Section 11 of the Magistrates' Courts Act 1980 provides the general authority for proceeding in the absence of the accused subject, in the case of a summons, to its being served in accordance with the rules (*R (on the application of Durham County Council v North Durham Justices* [2004] EWHC 1073 (Admin)[2004] All ER (D) 260 (Apr)). The Divisional Court handed down broad guidance in *R v Ealing Magistrates Court, ex p Burgess* (1999) 163 JP 82, [2000] Crim LR 855 on hearing a trial in the defendant's absence. The Court indicated that the defendant must be given a fair opportunity (but not an unlimited opportunity) to be present. A defendant may waive his right to be present or to be represented (*R v Haywood* [2001] EWCA Crim 168, [2001] All ER (D) 256 (Jan); affd [2002] UKHL 5, [2002] All ER (D) 275 (Feb)) and may by his behaviour be said to have voluntarily absented himself (*R v Jones* [2002] UKHL 5, [2003] 1 AC 1) but not where the defendant is known by the court to be in custody at the time of his trial (*R (R) v Thames Youth Court* [2002] EWHC 1670 (Admin), (2002) 166 JP 613).

I[6.2]

Whatever the reason the accused chooses to enter a not guilty plea, once he has entered the plea all the facts relevant to the proof of guilt are said to be 'in issue' which means that the prosecutor must either prove those facts beyond reasonable doubt or (in some few cases) must establish facts which then place the burden of proving his innocence on the accused. An example of this last situation occurs where the police allege the uninsured use of a motor vehicle. Once they establish that the accused used a motor vehicle on a road it becomes the responsibility of the accused to satisfy the court that his use of the vehicle was insured. The prosecutor will establish his facts by the oral testimony of witnesses who may then be cross-examined, and/or by the production of witness statements of which the accused will have had prior notice in order to object to them if he wishes, and/or by formal admissions from the accused which should be written down and signed by him. If the accused wishes to give evidence he may use all or any of these methods of doing so. The basis on which a not guilty plea is entered is important to the sentencer in some cases. It is often urged in mitigation that the accused pleaded guilty consequently saving stress and inconvenience to witnesses, court time and expense. The court must take account of the stage in the proceedings that the guilty plea was entered and the circumstances in which it was given. If as a result the court imposes a punishment which is less severe than would otherwise have been the case, it must state, in open court, that it has done so. It should not be held against an accused that he pleaded not guilty if he clearly was justified in doing so. However, in some cases where the basis of a not guilty plea proves unjustified, the accused's proper course is to change his plea. An example of this would be where he wishes to plead a technical point and has been overruled.

I[6.2A]

No case to answer. There must be a sufficient case for the defendant to answer by the end of the prosecution case. If the prosecution have failed to prove an essential ingredient of the offence or the evidence adduced has been so discredited by cross- examination or is shown to be manifestly unreliable then if no reasonable tribunal could convict at that stage the case should be dismissed (*R v Galbraith* [1981] 2 All ER 1060, [1981] 1 WLR 1039 CA).

Where the court dismisses the case it must give reasons for its decision. The converse does not apply ie the court is not required to give reasons if it finds a case to answer (*Moran v DPP* [2002] EWHC 89 (Admin) (2002) 166 JP 467).

I[6.2B]

Amendment of charge or information. Justices have a discretion to allow the amendment of a charge or information under the Magistrates' Courts Act 1980, s 123. This may even allege a different summary offence after the 6 month limitation period and even as late as the close of the prosecution case, but only where they are satisfied the allegation arises out of the same facts and it is in the interests of justice to allow the amendment (see *DPP v Everest* [2005] EWHC 1124 (Admin), [2005] All ER (D) 363 (May)). However, it is impermissible to amend an information by substituting a different defendant where the six-month statutory time limit has expired (*R (on the application of Sainsbury's Supermarkets Ltd) v Plymouth Magistrates' Court and R (on the application of J Sainsbury's Supermarkets Ltd) v Plymouth Magistrates' Court* [2006] EWHC 1749 (Admin), [2006] All ER (D) 137 (Jun)).

2 Guilty plea

I[6.3]

A guilty plea must be unequivocal; when an accused purports to admit an offence but then adds words or offers an explanation redolent of a defence the legal adviser should normally be left to clarify the plea. If the defendant is unrepresented it might be advisable for the case to be stood back for the accused to seek independent legal advice from a solicitor. If the court concludes that the plea is equivocal it has no discretion but to substitute a plea of not guilty.

A guilty plea, however, is an admission of the offence charged and not necessarily of every fact which the prosecutor may allege as a circumstance of it. A guilty plea to assault, for example, would not indicate an acceptance of the prosecution's allegations of the number of blows struck or their severity. Where there is a dispute about an important circumstance of the offence either side may call evidence notwithstanding the guilty plea. The court can also decline to sentence until the matter has been resolved by evidence. This procedure is known as a **Newton hearing**. There are one or two exceptions. The legal adviser should be consulted where the question of a Newton hearing is being canvassed. Evidence may also be called if there is a dispute relating to an ancillary matter, such as the amount of compensation or liability for back duty. The evidence should be confined solely to deciding the issue in question and, if the prosecution cannot establish its version of the facts beyond a reasonable doubt, the defence version must be accepted.

The other aspect of the question is that the court must sentence only on the basis of the case put forward by the prosecution and not on the basis of conclusions it might draw that the case is in reality more serious. For example, if a person is accused of two cases of theft from his employer the court must not infer that in fact this was a common occurrence and sentence accordingly. Sometimes the inference might be inescapable. The important thing is that it does not affect the sentence for the offence charged. There are exceptions to the above rule e g in the case of sample or specimen charges or offences admitted and taken into consideration. Magistrates should clarify the legal principles with their legal adviser.

I[6.3A]

Application to change a plea of guilty to not guilty. A magistrates' court may allow a defendant to withdrawn his plea of guilty at any time up to sentence being passed (*S (an infant) v Manchester City Recorder* [1971] AC 481, HL). The onus lies on a party seeking to vacate a guilty plea to demonstrate that justice requires that this should be permitted.

For the principles and procedures governing the exercise of the discretion see *R v South Tameside Magistrates' Court, ex p Rowland* (1984) 148 JP 202. For a more recent authority see *DPP v Revitt* [2006] EWHC 2266 (Admin), [2006] NLJR 1476.

3 Legal Advice

I[6.4]

The legal adviser has a duty to advise on matters of law and matters of mixed law and fact. Justices who refuse to act on his advice in a straightforward matter (eg a driver's liability to disqualification) may run the risk of being ordered to pay the costs of a consequent appeal. The justices are entitled to invite the legal adviser to retire with them if they think that a matter may arise on which they will seek his advice. In a case of any complexity it is wise to invite the legal adviser to retire at an early stage in order that he can give such advice as the occasion may require during the justices' discussions. If the legal adviser has taken a full note of the evidence he may be called upon to refresh the justices' memory from it. However, so far as it is practical to do so, the legal adviser should be asked to give his advice openly in court. This will not always be a practical way to give advice, especially in complicated matters, or where reference to books may be necessary, or where a discussion with one or more of the justices may be involved. The justices' clerk has the right to advise the justices even though he is not sitting with them in court so that, if he is available, he may always be sent for if necessary. It should be noted, however, where representations have been made to the court which the justices' clerk has not heard they should be repeated in the presence of the justices' clerk before he gives his advice to the bench. It is especially useful to bear this in mind when sitting with an inexperienced legal adviser. Equally, where the legal adviser finds it necessary to give advice in the retiring room on a point not canvassed with the advocates then the legal adviser should return to court telling them of the advice given and allowing them to address the bench if they have anything additional to contribute.

I[6.5]

For a fuller account of the role of the justices' clerk and his staff see **Section L**.

4 Consideration of guilt

I[6.6]

The question for justices to ask themselves at this stage is, 'Has the prosecutor satisfied the majority of us beyond reasonable doubt that the accused committed the offence with which he has been charged?' A reasonable doubt must not be a fanciful doubt nurtured by prejudice. The burden of proof, that is the degree to which a court should be convinced of guilt, is a matter of law and one on which the legal adviser can assist.

I[6.7]

When announcing the decision in court it is generally better to avoid using a reference to 'the case'. It is better to say, 'We find you guilty of theft' or as the case may be, rather than, 'We find the case proved'. The accused feels he has 'a case' too, and the latter expression of the decision sometimes creates the impression that 'the case' which the court has been concerned with has been the prosecution case. The former method of announcing the decision leaves nothing to doubt or prejudice and is especially to be recommended when there has been more than one charge or accused.

5 Reports etc

I[6.8]

Whatever the plea, once the guilt of the accused has been established the court may hear further information about him relevant to sentence. The prosecutor will give information about previous convictions or the fact that there are none. He will also indicate if the accused has admitted other similar offences which he wishes the court to take into consideration when determining the sentence. These will have been written down and should be put one by one by the clerk and the accused should be asked to signify his admission of each such offence separately. This is important because offences admitted and taken into consideration ('TICs' as these offences are usually known) may be significant in the sentencing decision and because (especially if there is a long list) it is very easy for the police to include in a list of outstanding offences some which a prisoner will admit through not giving the matter proper thought. Compensation may be ordered in respect of offences taken into consideration and this is another reason for being procedurally correct when dealing with them. The maximum amount of compensation depends on the number of substantive charges eg a plea of guilty to two charges of theft and 24 TICs means that the magistrates' powers to award compensation are limited to £10,000 (£5,000 per offence).

I[6.9]

Also at this stage the prosecutor will ask for any appropriate ancillary orders such as costs or the forfeiture of a weapon or drugs, etc. The chairman should make a written note of such matters so that they are not overlooked when the final sentencing decision is made.

I[6.10]–I[6.15]

Pre-sentence report. The court may at this stage consider a pre-sentence report and if one is not available the question of an adjournment in order to obtain one should not be overlooked. Although they need not do so if they are of the opinion that it is unnecessary, it is still a statutory requirement for a magistrates' court to consider a pre-sentence report before imposing any custodial sentence or a community sentence (except a probation order with no additional requirements, although the obtaining of a pre-sentence report is nevertheless still strongly advised).

I[6.16]

The pre-sentence report is to assist the court in determining the most suitable method of dealing with an offender. The responsibility for determining the seriousness of an offence remains solely with the magistrates. However, the pre-sentence report will contain impartial advice and information and will balance the aggravating and mitigating factors in the case and report on the nature of the defendants offending: *R v Salisbury Magistrates' Court, ex p Gray* [2000] 1 Cr App Rep (S) 267, 163 JP 732. The report may give advice in support of a particular sentence although it will bear in mind the ultimate responsibility of the sentencer. The Crown prosecutor may make representations on matters contained in the pre-sentence report.

I[6.17]

Short or fast-delivery reports. These reports have the same status as a pre-sentence report but can be requested by the court on the day if they are considering a lower end order such as a community order with a single requirement.

Note that the Youth Court must have a written report before it can make a reparation or action plan order but these are not classified as pre-sentence reports.

I[6.18]

Medical report. Where the offender is, or appears to be, mentally disordered, the court must, if it is considering a custodial sentence, obtain a medical report. Such a report is made orally or in writing by a doctor approved under the Mental Health Act 1983 as having experience in the diagnosis or treatment of mental disorder.

I[6.19]

Reports from other sources may be available, for example, a reference from an offender's employer or educational establishment etc. In any case where the court thinks fit it may adjourn and call upon the maker of a report to attend for questioning upon its contents.

I[6.20]

The court must give the accused or his solicitor and the Crown Prosecutor a copy of the pre-sentence report. In the youth court the report will be given to a parent or guardian. It is very important, however, that the accused is aware of the contents of any written report submitted to the court. It is not considered entirely satisfactory simply to hand a written report to an unrepresented defendant in court. He may have difficulty in reading, especially in the stressful situation of court proceedings, so that he may not absorb the contents of the report at all, or he may not have finished reading it by the time he is invited to comment on it. Furthermore, he may not understand the meaning of everything he reads and he almost certainly will have had inadequate time to gather his thoughts and to express a useful opinion about anything contained in the report. The better practice, therefore, is that the probation officer (or youth offending officer) has discussed the contents of the pre-sentence report and especially the implications of any proposal therein, with the offender before the case is dealt with in court.

6 Guilty plea by post procedure

I[6.21]

This is a quick and effective procedure for dealing with summary cases, in the absence of the accused (specified proceedings). The procedures outlined below only apply to offences dealt with in the adult court and those offences which do not carry a term of imprisonment of more than three months.

I[6.22]

A summons is served on the defendant along with a witness statement of evidence. The defendant may plead guilty in absence on the basis of the evidence supplied and the clerk to the court reads the statement (or if directed by the court a summary) in open court before the court decides to accept the plea.

I[6.23]

The legal adviser will then read any statement in mitigation from the defendant and any statement of means is considered along with the driving licence, in endorsable cases. The court may then pass sentence or adjourn if it requires the defendant's attendance, for example if it is considering a disqualification. This may be done in the absence of a prosecutor.

I[6.24]

Failure to respond. If the summons and statements are properly served but the defendant fails to respond the proceedings become non-specified and the prosecution may use the evidence in the statements to prove the case against the defendant at the first hearing.

I[6.25]

Not guilty plea. Where the defendant indicates in writing that he wishes to plead not guilty but attends court to give evidence the statement may be used at an adjourned trial date unless the defendant has indicated he wishes any of the prosecution witnesses to attend court. Note that the police will be able to ask for costs in writing against a defendant who has either pleaded guilty or been convicted on the statements served. There is also a hybrid procedure of serving the defendant with a statement of facts, upon which he may enter a guilty plea, and witness statements which will be used if he fails to enter a plea.

7 Appeals

I [6.26]

There are three common forms of appeal from the Magistrates' Courts

I[6.27]

Appeal against conviction and or sentence to the Crown Court. Notice for such an appeal must be lodged within 21 days of the date of sentence. This time limit may be extended with the consent of the Crown Court (s 108 MCA 1980).

I[6.28]

Appeal by way of case stated to the High Court on a point of law. The justices may be asked to state a case within 21 days of their decision. There is no power to extend this period. Once an application for a case stated is made the right to appeal to the Crown Court normally ceases (s 111 MCA 1980).

I[6.29]

Application for judicial review. This application must be lodged with the High Court as soon as practicable and in any event within 3 months of the grounds for the appeal arising (Supreme Court Act 1981, ss 29, 31; Civil Procedure Rules 1998, Part 54). If successful the High Court may make quashing, prohibiting and mandatory orders to correct or prevent an error in law or a failure to exercise jurisdiction. See for example *R (on the* *application of Durham County Council) v North Durham Justices* [2004] EWHC 1073 (Admin), [2004] All ER (D) 260 (Apr).

I[7]

The Criminal Defence Service

Introduction

I[7.1]

The Legal Services Commission is responsible for the provision of a Criminal Defence Service. This includes advice and assistance at a solicitor's office, police station advice and assistance, advocacy assistance in the magistrates' courts including representation by the court duty solicitor and finally magistrates' court representation.

Representation orders

I[7.1A]

See reg 3 of the Criminal Defence Service (General) (No 2) Regulations 2001 as amended. Circumstances in which a representation order is available in a magistrates' court include:

(a) any person who is to appear before a magistrates' court or a youth court in respect of an offence; this includes an application for the removal of a disqualification from driving (*R v Crown Court at Liverpool, ex p McCann* [1995] RTR 23);
(b) a person who is to appear before a magistrates' court to answer a complaint for failure to pay a sum due or obey a court order where such failure carries a risk of imprisonment or for a binding over order or breach;
(c) a person who is committed for trial or for sentence to the Crown Court;
(d) a person who proposes to appeal to the Crown Court against a decision of a magistrates' court;
(e) proceedings where following a conviction of a child or the making of an anti-social behaviour order, an interim order or sex offences prevention order or the court makes a parenting order. This includes appeals against and variations of parenting orders;
(f) proceedings under the Football Spectators Act 1989 for banning orders and references to the court;
(g) orders under Part 1 of the Anti Social Behaviour Act 2003 (closure of premises).

Where a representation order is granted, new regulations will provide that the order extends to the Crown Court if the proceedings continue there.

I[7.2]

The Criminal Defence Service Act 2006 (CDSA) received the Royal Assent on 30 March 2006. It is anticipated that the majority of the Act's provisions, together with secondary legislation, will be brought into force on 2 October 2006. The CDSA 2006 makes a number of amendments to the Access to Justice Act 1999. A major amendment is the requirement that the power to grant a right to representation may only be exercised where a person is **financially eligible**, under regulations, to be granted such a right. The Government stated during the passage of the CDSA 2006 that these powers would be exercised, in the first instance, in relation to criminal proceedings, in magistrates' courts.

Financial Eligibility

I[7.2A]

The Criminal Defence Service (Financial Eligibility) Regulations 2006 set out the criteria which must be satisfied before individuals involved in criminal proceedings in a magistrates' court may receive publicly funded representation.

Individuals in receipt of certain "passported" benefits such as income support, income-based jobseeker's allowance and guarantee credit under s 1(3)(a) of the State Pension Credit Act 2002 are **automatically eligible**, as are those under the age of 16 years or under 18 years and in full-time education. If the individual has a partner, the partner's resources are to be treated as those of the individual, unless the partner has a contrary interest in the proceedings.

An individual is **financially eligible** for a representation order if his gross annual income, adjusted to take account of any partner or children, is **£11,590 or less**. An individual is **ineligible** if his gross annual income, as adjusted, is **£20,740 or more**. Where it falls between these amounts, the representation authority will calculate the individual's annual disposable income, making deductions in respect of any income tax, national insurance, council tax, housing expenses, child care costs, maintenance and cost of living expenses, from the applicant's adjusted income. The individual is financially eligible if his **annual income does not exceed £3,156**.

Where there is a material change in an individual's financial circumstances, he must notify the representation authority of the change if he has been granted a representation order, and he may make a renewed application if his previous application has been refused because he was financially ineligible.

Regulations will provide for a review of the decision to refuse representation on the basis that the applicant is financially ineligible, on the grounds that his income has been miscalculated or that he cannot afford to pay for legal assistance notwithstanding that he is financially ineligible. Regulations will provide, in some cases, for the application to be renewed to the representation authority or the Legal Services Commission.

Regulations to be made contain provisions about the withdrawal of representation orders. The representation authority must normally withdraw an order where an individual fails to provide evidence of means that has been requested. Where a subsequent application is made following the withdrawal of a representation order, the same representative must be selected unless the representation authority considers there are good reasons why a different representative should be selected.

I[7.3]

An application **must** be made in the prescribed form. There will be new application forms:

- CDS14 – Application for Legal Aid
- CDS15 – Financial Statement
- CDS16 – Review on Grounds of Hardship
- CDS17 – Statement of Truth.

The forms must be fully completed within two working days of charge. It is likely the court will return incomplete forms or refuse to grant representation. The court will make a decision within two working days unless the applicant's means are complex.

The CDS14 form must be accompanied by the following evidence of means:

- One pay slip for employed applicants
- For applicants on benefits, a National Insurance number or evidence of their benefits
- P11D where benefits in kind are received
- A recent bank statement where the main income is a private pension
- Evidence where the applicant pays more than £500 in childcare costs per month
- Evidence of housing costs where the amount exceeds £500 per month.

Where the applicant is remanded in custody he/she will be required to provide details of his/her financial circumstances. If unable to provide a wage slip, the CDS17 form will be accepted as evidence. If claiming a "passported" benefit, the applicant must provide his/her National Insurance number.

This may be considered by the representation authority who may make an order provided that it is satisfied that (i) the applicant is financially eligible (see above); and, (ii) it is in the interests of justice that a representation order should be made. Representation is considered in the Access to Justice Act 1999, s 14 and Sch 3. A parent or guardian may apply on behalf of a defendant under 17 years.

The Legal Services Commission has posted full guidance, including the new forms, on its website (www.legalservices.gov.uk).

A representation order may be backdated to cover urgent work undertaken and may in certain circumstances outlined in reg 17 of the Criminal Defence Service (General) (No 2) Regulations 2001 be withdrawn.

I[7.4]

It should be noted that a magistrates' court may only make an order for the services of a Queen's Counsel with one junior counsel where the proceedings are a trial involving substantial, novel or complex issues of law or fact, such as murder or where the prosecution is brought by the Serious Fraud Office.

I[7.5]

Two or more co defendants must be assigned the same representative unless there is a conflict of interest.

Interests of justice

I[7.6]

The Justices' Clerks' Society has reissued guidance in relation to the interests of justice test. The document is entitled "Guidance on the Consideration of Defence Representation Order Applications" (Ref: 53.0010, issue 08/06) and is to be found on the JCS website via www. secretariat@jc-society.co.uk.

As to whether it is in the interests of justice that a representation order should be made, the factors to be taken into account include:

(a) the offence is such that if proved it is likely that the court would impose a sentence which would deprive the accused of his liberty or lead to loss of his livelihood or serious damage to his reputation; or
(b) there is a substantial question of law involved; or
(c) the accused may be unable to understand the proceedings or state his own case (because of his inadequate knowledge of English (*R (Matara) v Brent Magistrates' Court* (2005) 169 JP 576), mental illness or other mental or physical disability); or
(d) the nature of the defence is such as to involve the tracing and interviewing of witnesses or expert cross-examination of a witness for the prosecution; or
(e) where it may be in the interests of a third party, e g the victim of a sexual offence who might be distressed at being cross-examined directly by the accused, or who might be spared an appearance in court if the accused is given proper legal advice as to his plea.

I[7.7]

These criteria, which are used in the assessment of whether or not it is in the interests of justice that representation should be granted, are largely self-explanatory. A motorist who wishes to raise a plea of special reasons based on an allegation that a drink had been 'laced' would need an expert witness and would need to cross-examine witnesses to the incident. Such a driver should be granted representation (*R v Gravesend Magistrates' Court, ex p Baker* (1997) 161 JP 765). In *R v Liverpool City Magistrates Justices, ex p McGhee* (1993) 158 JP 275, [1993] Crim LR 609 it was pointed out that 'expert' in (d) above meant that the cross-examiner should be expert, it was not necessary that the witness should be an expert.

I[7.8]

Guidance was also given on (a) above in that it was pointed out that the likelihood of a community sentence was not a sentence which deprived the accused of his liberty. However, in view of the Practice Direction on the subject of failure to answer bail which could result in a custodial sentence a grant should therefore follow (*R (on the application of Evans) v Chester Magistrates Court* [2004] All ER (D) 260 (Mar)).

Section J

Remands in custody and bail

J[1]

Remands in custody and on bail

'Remand'

J[1.1]

When a case is adjourned to a fresh date the defendant may be remanded to ensure his attendance at the next hearing. The accused may be remanded in custody or released on bail. The prosecution will very often ask the court for a 'remand', when in fact it is seeking an adjournment. The other party to the case frequently does not object to the adjournment, but it should be remembered that the final decision rests with the court. Although the court may have been presented with a *fait accompli* where an agreement has previously been made between the parties, the magistrates should always be scrupulous to ensure that an adjournment is necessary. They should hear representations from both sides and make their decision judicially, taking all the relevant considerations into account. While it may not be possible to prevent an adjournment, the court may be able to avoid future adjournments. If magistrates do not keep a tight hold on the course of proceedings, it will not be surprising that undue delays occur in the administration of justice.

Bail and the Human Rights Act 1998

J[1.2]

Some sections of the Bail Act 1976 have been subject to challenge under the ECHR, for example the power to remove bail based solely on a police officer's belief that a defendant will breach a bail condition (Sch1, Part 1, para 6). It is now established that while there is no need for a full inquiry following an arrest for breach of bail conditions, Art 5 does apply to any remand in custody (*R v Havering Magistrates' Court, ex p DPP* [2001] 3 All ER 997, [2000] All ER (D) 2307).

However, the Bail Act as outlined before should comply with Convention requirements if the overall concepts of fairness and proportionality are borne in mind. For example, a defendant may be remanded in custody on substantial grounds that he will commit a further offence, but that must relate to a serious offence based solely on the facts of the individual case.

See *MB v Switzerland* (2001) 37 EHRR 1000, ECtHR for the application of Article 5 to the defendant's rights on arrest and production before a court.

J[1.3]

Remand on unconditional bail. The accused is released with an obligation to surrender to the custody of the court on a certain day at a specified time. If he fails to do so, there are two consequences: the court can immediately issue a warrant for his arrest and he may be prosecuted for the criminal offence of failing to answer his bail.

J[1.4]

Remand on conditional bail. The accused is on bail but with conditions attached to that bail, to ensure that he appears at court on the appointed day at the appropriate time or does not commit offences in the meantime or does not interfere with the witnesses in the case.

J[1.5]

Remand in custody. Where bail is refused, the defendant is detained in prison or in police cells until his next appearance in court.

J[1.6]

Juveniles. The remand of juveniles on bail is largely the same as that outlined below for those aged 17 and above. The exception is the condition of electronic monitoring of a curfew which can be imposed for 17-year-olds and adults. Elsewhere, in order to impose such a condition the court must be satisfied that the offender has reached the age of 12, and has been charged with:

- a violent or sexual offence or an offence carrying more that 14 years' imprisonment in the case of an adult, or
- (an) imprisonable offence(s) which, together with other such offences where there has been a conviction in any proceedings, mean that he has a recent history of repeatedly committing imprisonable offences while on remand (bail or local authority).

The court must have been informed by a YOT that imposing an electronic monitoring requirement will be suitable for this individual. The court must have been notified that electronic monitoring is available and be satisfied that the necessary provision can be made under those arrangements.

For remand of juveniles with a security requirement, see **E[3.16]–E[3.17]**.

When must the court remand?

J[1.7]

Where the court is acting with a view to committal for trial or sending an accused to the Crown Court for trial the accused must always be remanded on bail or in custody.

J[1.8]

If the offence is triable either way, the court must always remand where the accused was initially arrested by the police and brought to court in custody or bailed for his appearance, or he has previously been remanded in the proceedings.

J[1.9]

Where the offence is purely summary, the court always has a discretion whether to remand or simply adjourn the case.

J[1.10]–J[1.15]

In the case of juveniles (under 17) the court may remand if it thinks it is necessary to do so in those cases where it must do so when the defendant is 17 or over.

Length of the remand – before conviction

J[1.16]

In custody. A remand in custody is not normally for longer than 8 clear days, ie the day when the decision to remand is made and the day when the defendant is next due to appear in court, are excluded. Therefore a remand in custody may be from the Monday of one week to the Wednesday of the next.

J[1.17]

There are three major exceptions:

(a) If the defendant is to be kept in police cells, the maximum period is 3 clear days or 24 hours in the case of a juvenile.
(b) Where the accused is already serving a custodial sentence and will not be released in the intervening period, he may be remanded for up to 28 days.
(c) The court may remand a defendant present before the court who has previously been remanded in custody for a period not exceeding when the next stage of the proceedings is reached or 28 days, whichever is the less. In exercising this power the court will have to have regard to the total length of time which the accused would spend in custody if it were to exercise the power. This would not affect the right of the defendant to apply for bail during this period.

J[1.18]

On bail. Unless the accused consents, a remand on bail cannot be for more than 8 clear days. However, defendants always do consent to longer remands and that is why, as mentioned above, it is important for the magistrates to exercise control over the granting of adjournments. It should be remembered that bail is always granted to a fixed date and so it is not possible to adjourn a case *sine die* where the accused is remanded. An exception to this rule is a committal or send to the Crown Court although a plea and directions hearing may be specified.

Length of remand – after conviction

J[1.19]

A remand after conviction (for further inquiries and pre-sentence reports) cannot be for longer than 3 weeks if in custody, or should not be for longer than 4 weeks on bail.

Committal or send to the Crown Court

J[1.20]

When a magistrates' court commit or sends proceedings to the Crown Court for trial (or commits for sentence) the court may order the accused to be kept in custody until his trial (or sentence) or it may grant him bail.

Remands in the absence of the accused

J[1.21]

An application for a remand for not more than 8 clear days may in prescribed circumstances be heard in the absence of the accused. The conditions to be complied with before this is possible are as follows:

(a) the court is adjourning a case before conviction; and
(b) the accused is present before the court;
(c) he is legally represented before the court (although his solicitor need not necessarily be present in court).

J[1.22]

The accused must be asked whether he consents to future remands being determined in his absence. If he does, the court may remand him for up to three occasions in his absence. This means that the defendant must be brought before the court every four weeks. If the accused withdraws his consent or for any reason ceases to be legally represented, arrangements will be made by the justices' clerk to bring him before the court at the earliest opportunity, even though the period of his remand has not expired.

J[1.22A]

Video remands. The Crime and Disorder Act 1998, s 57 provides for the use of video conferencing between the prison and the court for defendants previously refused bail in person. No consent is required and the defendant's next physical appearance before either the magistrates' court or the Crown Court will be for trial or plea and sentence.

J[1.23]

If the defendant has been remanded on bail or in custody and cannot appear because of accident or illness, the court may further remand him in absence. A court can always further remand in absence an accused who is on bail. *R (on the application of Grimshaw) v Leeds Magistrates' Court* [2001] EWHC Admin 880, [2001] All ER (D) 350 (Oct) is authority for a remand in the absence of the accused where he has not been produced due to a mistake.

The decision whether to remand in custody or on bail

J[1.24]

Presumption of liberty. The general principle is that an accused man has a right to be released on bail where he has not been convicted of the charge or where his case has been adjourned for pre-sentence reports. This means that the accused never has to apply for bail, it is up to the prosecution to object to his right to bail (although in practice the defence are referred to as making an application for bail). Therefore, it is no reason for remanding an accused in custody that he has not applied for bail. However this right to bail does not apply to a committal to the Crown Court for sentence.

J[1.25]

Grant of opposed bail. Where the court grants bail following a prosecution objection to bail the court must state its reasons for doing so.

J[1.26]–J[1.30]

Exceptions to the right to bail. An accused can only be denied his right to bail if the court finds that there is an exception to that right. These exceptions are set out in the Bail Act 1976, Sch 1. They differ according to whether or not the offence is punishable by imprisonment (whether or not the accused himself is liable to imprisonment because of his age etc). In taking these decisions the court must also have regard to any misuse of controlled drugs by the defendant so far as it is relevant.

J[1.31]

A defendant need not be granted bail if he is charged with an either way or indictable offence and it appears to the court that he was on bail in criminal proceedings at the date of the offence.

J[1.32]

Imprisonable offences. The exceptions to the right to bail are:

1 Where the court has substantial grounds for believing the accused would:
   (a) fail to answer bail; or
   (b) commit further offences on bail; or
   (c) interfere with witnesses or otherwise obstruct the course of justice.

J[1.33]

Each of the exceptions must be substantiated by a reason given by the court such as:

(i) the nature and seriousness of the offence or default (and the probable method of dealing with the accused for it);
(ii) the character, antecedents, associations and community ties of the defendant;
(iii) the accused's previous record when granted bail (e g committing offences on bail or absconding);
(iv) (except when remanding after conviction for a report) the strength of the evidence against the accused;
(v) any other relevant reasons.

Note that where the prosecution objects to bail but the court nevertheless grants bail it must provide reasons for granting bail. A written record must be kept.

J[1.34]

2 Remand in custody for the accused's own protection (or in the case of a juvenile, welfare). Used only in exceptional circumstances and with strong reasons e g the accused is a high suicide risk.

J[1.35]

3 Where the accused is already in custody as a result of a prison sentence.

J[1.36]

4 Where there has been insufficient time to gather information to make the bail decision.

J[1.37]

5 Where the accused has absconded or breached the conditions of his bail in the same proceedings already.

J[1.38]

6 Where the case has been adjourned for reports or inquiries and it is impracticable to gain the information or prepare reports without remanding the accused in custody.

7 A defendant need not be granted bail, unless there is no significant risk of offending while on bail, or the defendant declines to take up an offer of a "relevant assessment, or having agreed to one, fails to comply with such an assessment. It is a precondition that:
   (a) the defendant be aged 18 or over;
   (b) the presence of Class A drugs has been detected in his body; and
   (c) either he has been charged under s 5(2) or s 5(3) of the Misuse of Drugs Act 1971, or the court is satisfied that his misuse of Class A drugs caused or contributed to his behaviour, or his offending was wholly or partly motivated by his intended misuse of a Class A drug.

** Note the Criminal Justice Act 2003, s 19, which imposes restrictions on the granting of bail to persons who have tested positive for a Class A drug, is in force but only in areas notified by the Secretary of State.

8 A person who has been charged with or convicted of an offence specified in s 25 of the Criminal Justice and Public Order Act 1994 (murder, rape and certain specified sexual offences) and has previously been convicted within the United Kingdom of any such specified offence as mentioned in s 25(3) shall be granted bail only if the court or police constable considering the grant of bail is satisfied that there are exceptional circumstances which justify it. Magistrates would be well advised to consult their legal adviser.

J[1.39]

Non-imprisonable offences. The exceptions to the right to bail are:

(a) having been previously granted bail in criminal proceedings the accused has failed to surrender to his bail; and the court believes, in view of that failure, that the defendant, if released on bail (whether subject to conditions or not) he would again fail to surrender to custody;
(b) remand in custody for the accused's own protection (or in the case of a juvenile, welfare);
(c) where the accused is already in custody as a result of a prison sentence;
(d) where the accused has already absconded or breached the conditions of his bail in the same proceedings and this leads the court to find that there are substantial grounds for believing the defendant would fail to surrender to custody, commit an offence on bail or interfere with witnesses or otherwise obstruct the course of justice.

General considerations

J[1.40]-J[1.45]

It is not common for a court to have to deal with a remand of a non-imprisonable case and it is even less common for the court to consider a remand in custody. Therefore the following remarks are confined mainly to remands of imprisonable cases.

J[1.46]

The usual grounds for the police objecting to bail are exceptions (1) (a)–(c) above (failure to surrender, further offences or interference with the course of justice). It is worthwhile to examine these a little more closely.

J[1.47]

Failure to surrender to custody. The accused may fail to surrender because he knows he will be convicted of a serious charge and will receive a custodial sentence.

In considering this objection to the right to bail, the bench might have regard to the likely sentence that will be imposed, in which case the accused's record will be relevant. Then, the circumstances of the defendant: Is he a 'local' man? How long has he lived in the district? Does he have anywhere else to move to? Are all his friends and relations in the area? The court must also consider whether bail with a condition of finding a security or surety would suffice instead of a remand in custody.

J[1.48]

Further offences on bail. A defendant may consider that he will receive a custodial sentence and that he might as well be 'hung for a sheep as a lamb', in other words the final sentences he receives will not be materially affected whether he is sentenced for one or several offences. This is particularly the case with the 'professional' burglar or the youth with a penchant for taking the cars of other people without their consent.

J[1.49]

Interference with the course of justice. In certain situations, a defendant released on bail would interfere with the course of justice. This has three main aspects. First, he might 'tip off' a co-accused who could then abscond or destroy evidence. Second, the co-accused might collaborate to concoct a consistent but false story. Third, the defendant might intimidate the prosecution witnesses, eg in disputes involving a domestic background. The court must consider whether conditions attached to bail would be sufficient to prevent this occurring, eg of non-association with co-accused, or with the prosecution witnesses.

J[1.50]

Mistakes commonly made in finding these exceptions are that the bench fail to announce that they find substantial grounds for believing etc and that they announce reasons but no exceptions, e g the defendant is remanded in custody because of his character and antecedents and the nature and seriousness of the offence. These are reasons for finding one of the exceptions (1) (a)–(c), but they are not in themselves exceptions to the right to bail.

J[1.51]

Custody time limits. The Prosecution of Offences Act 1985, s 22 provides for restrictions on the period for which a person charged with an either way, indictable or summary offence may be remanded in custody. The maximum period of a custodial remand is 70 days between his first appearance and the start of a summary trial or committal proceedings, as appropriate. Where, in the case of an either way offence, summary trial is decided upon within 56 days the summary trial must commence within 56 days of the first appearance. Time limits also apply to proceedings before the Crown Court.

NB: An offence "triable either way" includes an offence which, although triable only on indictment in the case of an adult, is in the case of a juvenile person under 18 years of age triable summarily or on indictment under s 24 of the Magistrates' Courts Act 1980 (grave crimes procedure) (*R v Stratford Youth Court, ex p S* (1998) 162 JP 552).

J[1.52]

The court may extend the custody time limits on receipt of an application either orally or in writing but the court must not grant an extension *unless* satisfied that the need for it is justified by virtue of one of three criteria:

(a) illness or absence of the accused, a necessary witness, a judge or magistrate; or
(b) a postponement occasioned by the ordering by the court of separate trials in the case of two or more accused or two or more offences; or
(c) some other good and sufficient cause.

The procedure for an application to extend time limits may be informal but the prosecution must still satisfy the court and the defendant be given an opportunity to test the application (*Wildman v DPP* [2001] EWHC Admin 14, (2001) 165 JP 453).

A successful application to vacate the trial by the defence is relevant to a reconsideration of a refusal to extend custody limits (*R (on the application of DPP) v Crown Court at Blackfriars* [2001] EWHC Admin 56, [2001] All ER (D) 205).

However, custody time limits were not extended when the defence requested an adjournment to consider disclosure which was two months late as the fault was that of the prosecution (*R (on the application of Holland) v Leeds Crown Court* [2002] EWHC 1862 (Admin), [2003] Crim LR 272).

J[1.53]

The court must also be satisfied the prosecution has acted with all due diligence as well as expedition. See *R v Central Criminal Court, ex p Johnson* [1999] 2 Cr App Rep 51. The fact that a trial could not proceed because of the illness of a victim is irrelevant if the prosecution have failed otherwise to act with due diligence (*R v Central Criminal Court, ex p Bennett* (1999) Times, 25 January). This approach was rejected by the High Court in *R v Leeds Crown Court, ex p Bagoutie* (1999) Times, 31 May as leading to absurd results so that it does not matter that the prosecution has not acted with all due diligence if there is good and sufficient cause in the eyes of the court. However, in complex matters where the defendant is asking for extensive disclosure the prosecution could expect reasonable notice of such enquiries to enable it to comply (*R (on the application of Smith) v Crown Court at Woolwich* [2002] EWHC 995 (Admin), [2002] All ER (D) 05 (May)).

J[1.54]

Where a custody time limit has expired the accused must be released on bail with or without conditions. However, a new charge will attract its own custody time limit (*R v Crown Court at Leeds, ex p Wardle* [2001] UKHL 12, [2002] 1 AC 754).

Conditional bail

J[1.55]–J[1.60]

A custody sergeant at the police station may grant an accused conditional bail and may do so for the same reasons as a bench of magistrates who may decide that the defendant cannot be released on unconditional bail. It is only if conditional bail would be inadequate that custody should be contemplated.

J[1.61]

Conditions are only to be attached to bail where it appears to the bench necessary to do so for the purpose of preventing the accused:

(a) failing to surrender to custody; or
(b) committing an offence while on bail; or
(c) interfering with witnesses or obstructing the course of justice; or
(d) from being harmed, i e for his own protection or in the case of a juvenile for his welfare.

J[1.62]

Conditions may also be imposed to enable a pre-sentence report to be prepared, or requiring a defendant to attend an interview with a legal representative before the next court hearing. The court must give its reasons for imposing conditions on the bail.

In the case of a person accused of *murder* the court granting bail **shall**, unless it considers that satisfactory reports on the accused's mental condition have already been obtained, impose conditions: (a) a requirement that the accused shall undergo examination by two medical practitioners for the purpose of enabling such reports to be prepared; and (b) a requirement that he shall for that purpose attend such institution or place as the court directs and comply with any such directions which may be given to him for that purpose by either of those practitioners. One of the practitioners must be approved for the purposes of s 12 of the Mental Health Act 1983 (Bail Act 1976, ss 6A, 6B).

When notified that arrangements for assessment are available in a given area, a person over 18 who has tested positive for a specified Class A drug and who the court is satisfied that his offending was motivated by drug misuse or that misuse contributed to the offending a court **must** impose a condition to undergo assessment and follow up if the defendant consents (Bail Act 1976, s 3(6D)). If the offender does not consent see **J[1.38]**.

J[1.63]

Commonly imposed conditions are:

(a) residence (absconding);
(b) curfew (fresh offences);
(c) reporting to a police station (absconding);
(d) non-association with specified people (interference with the course of justice);
(e) a security or surety (absconding).

Other conditions may be imposed provided they are reasonable and are enforceable, including a 'doorstep' condition for those on a curfew condition (*R v Chorley Justices* [2002] EWHC 2162 (Admin), 166 JP 764, sub nom R (DPP) v Chorley Justices [2002] 43 LS Gaz R 34).

J[1.64]

It must be emphasised that conditions are not to be imposed as a matter of course; they can only be imposed to prevent one of the occurrences mentioned above. If a condition is imposed it must relate to the mischief which is feared (a *guide* is given by the words in brackets above). Conditions must not be imposed which have no relevance to the reason given by the court, eg a surety because the bench fears fresh offences.

J[1.65]

Conditions may also be imposed to require defendants to comply with hostel rules where residing at a bail or probation hostel on remand or for assessment. Electronic monitoring of defendants on bail to enforce a curfew is also permitted. Electronic monitoring of children over the age of 12 is also permitted subject to the same restrictions imposed on the use of secure accommodation: s 3AA of the Bail Act 1976 (see **J[1.6]**).

J[1.66]

Sureties. With one exception, mentioned below, no one has to deposit money or valuables to secure a person's release in remand proceedings. However, a third party may agree to stand as surety for an accused. A surety is a person who agrees to forfeit a sum of money fixed by the court (called a recognisance and pronounced 'reconnaissance') if the accused fails to surrender to custody. A surety's obligations are to ensure that the accused surrenders to custody; he is not there to ensure that the accused complies with the conditions of his bail. The court should specify that the person standing surety is to secure the accused's attendance at the next hearing or for each occasion to which the case may, from time to time, be adjourned.

J[1.67]

In deciding whether to accept a person as a surety, the court should in particular have regard to:

(a) the surety's financial resources;
(b) his character and any previous convictions of his;
(c) his proximity (whether in point of kinship, place or otherwise) to the person for whom he is to be surety.

J[1.68]

Forfeiting the recognisance of a surety. If the accused fails to answer to his bail, the surety should be informed by the court that it is considering forfeiting his recognisance. Standing surety is a solemn obligation. The court will start from the basis that the whole amount is to be forfeited. The culpability of the surety will be investigated to see what steps he took to ensure the defendant's attendance. However, a surety should not forfeit his recognisance if he is not to blame for the defendant's failure to surrender when required to do so. When forfeiting a recognisance the court must take into account the surety's ability to pay.

J[1.69]

Depositing a security. An exception to the rule that an accused does not have to deposit money or valuables is where the court believes a security is necessary to ensure the defendant surrenders to custody. The usual security is money, but it could be a valuable item such as motor car, provided it is readily convertible into money.

In the case of a security the law presumes that the sum deposited by way of security should be forfeited and it is for the person who deposited the security – on receipt of a court notice – to show cause why the sum should not remain forfeited.

J[1.70]–J[1.75]

The effectiveness of conditions. The usefulness of some conditions is questionable. A condition of reporting to the police at anything longer than 24-hour intervals is generally of little value and such a condition should be not imposed to make the accused more readily available for questioning. Nor should a condition be imposed for its nuisance value to the accused. A condition of depositing a passport is of little value, especially where the accused can travel within the EU without a passport.

Appeal by the prosecution

J[1.76]

The Bail (Amendment) Act 1993 (as amended) gives the Crown Prosecution Service the right to appeal to a Crown Court Judge where a court grants bail to a person who is charged with or convicted of an offence punishable by imprisonment. Notice must be served within two hours of the decision and the hearing (see *R (Jeffrey) v Warwick Crown Court* (2003)). Such an appeal must be commenced within 48 hours of the date of the decision. See *R v Crown Court at Middlesex Guildhall, ex p Okoli* (2001) 165 JP 144, [2000] Crim LR 921.

Where bail is refused

J[1.77]

Making a further application. At the first hearing after that at which the court decided not to grant the defendant bail (which normally would have been the first time the case was remanded) he is entitled to apply for bail as of right. At any subsequent hearings the court need not hear any arguments as to fact or law which it has heard previously.

J[1.78]

The court must, however, always consider the matter of bail on each occasion on which the case is remanded. As the liberty of the accused is at stake, it is suggested that any doubt whether to allow a fresh application should be resolved in the accused's favour.

J[1.79]

Appeals. The defendant may appeal to the Crown Court against the imposition of bail conditions relating to residence (other than to a bail hostel), sureties and securities, curfew and contact with other persons. Such an application may only be made following the determination of an application to vary the bail conditions made in the magistrates' court. There is no concurrent power to appeal to the High Court.

Application to a Crown Court Judge in chambers. Where the magistrates have heard a full application and refused bail, their legal adviser will supply the accused with a certificate to that effect. He then has a right to make a bail application to a Crown Court Judge in chambers.

Bail in cases of murder, manslaughter and rape

J[1.80]

See **J[1.38]** and **J[1.62]**.

Reconsideration of bail

J[1.81]

Where a court or a constable has granted bail for an indictable or either way offence the prosecution may apply to have that decision reconsidered by the court who may:

(a) vary the conditions of bail;
(b) impose conditions on unconditional bail;
(c) withhold bail.

This may only be done on the basis of fresh information not previously available to the court or constable who granted bail.

Prosecution for failing to surrender to custody

J[1.82]

The law is that the accused is released on bail with a duty to turn up at court on the appointed day at the appointed time. If he fails to do so the first consequence is that a warrant may be issued for his arrest. Secondly, he may be prosecuted for the criminal offence of failing to surrender to custody.

J[1.83]

Where bail has been granted by a police officer for an accused to surrender either to a police station or a magistrates' court, any failure to surrender to custody should be initiated by charging the accused or laying an information. On the other hand, an accused who fails to answer to bail granted by the magistrates themselves should be brought before the court following his arrest. The court will then initiate proceedings following an express invitation by the prosecutor. The prosecutor will conduct the proceedings and, where the matter is contested, call the evidence. Any trial should normally take place immediately. In the meantime the defendant can expect to have bail revoked. In cases which cannot or are unlikely to result in custodial sentences a trial in the absence of the defendant may be a pragmatic solution. The bail offence should be dealt with immediately in normal circumstances (Revised Practice Direction (2004)).

J[1.84]

The offence is triable only summarily where bail was granted by magistrates and proceedings are begun on the invitation of the prosecution. The accused must be asked whether he pleads guilty or not guilty. Where a prosecution is contemplated the legal adviser should be consulted to ensure the correct procedure is followed.

J[1.85]–J[1.90]

Defence. It is a defence to such a charge if he proves (that it is more probable than not) that he had a reasonable excuse for not answering his bail, or that having a reasonable excuse for failing to surrender to custody at the appointed time and place, he surrendered to custody at the appointed place as soon after the appointed time as was reasonably practicable. It is not a defence that the accused was not given a copy of the decision to grant him bail.

J[1.91]

Penalty. A maximum penalty of 3 months' imprisonment** and a fine on level 5 in the magistrates' court or the accused may be committed for sentence to the Crown Court**, where the maximum penalty is 12 months' imprisonment and an unlimited fine. In *R v Clarke* [2000] 1 Cr App Rep (S) 224, CA the Court of Appeal upheld a prison sentence for the offence. Any such sentence will normally be consecutive to the sentence for the substantive offence (*R v White* (2002) Times, 9 December).

**At the time of writing it is anticipated the power to commit to custody for an offence under the Bail Act 1976 will be retained but the sentence will be treated as a form of contempt of court. Any sentence would be served first before any sentence such as custody plus under the Criminal Justice Act 2003. There is no provision in the Criminal Justice Act 2003 to amend or remove the power of the magistrates' court to commit for sentence under s 6(6)(a) or (b) of the Bail Act 1976.

J[1.92]

Failing to comply with a condition. Failing to comply with a condition of bail is not an offence (see *R v Ashley* [2003] EWCA Crim 2571, [2003] All ER (D)

106 (Aug)). It does mean, however, that a police officer can arrest the accused forthwith and bring him before the court. His failure to comply with the condition may in itself constitute an exception to the general 'right to bail'. If a defendant is arrested in breach of a bail condition the court should ask if he admits or denies the breach. If a denial is recorded the magistrates should hear evidence or a statement of the arresting officer's 'reasonable grounds' for arrest. If they are of the opinion that the defendant was in breach of his bail conditions he may be further remanded either in custody or on bail. If there is no breach of condition there is an entitlement to bail on the same conditions. Only after a finding of breach does the consideration of the reasons for breach become relevant (*R (Vickers) v West London Magistrates Court* [2003] EWHC 1809 (Admin), [2003] All ER (D) 211 (Jul)). Such hearing must be within 24 hours of arrest although there is power for the case to be put back in the list during that time period *(R (Hussain) v Derby Magistrates' Court* [2001] EWHC Admin 507, [2001] 1 WLR 2454).

Bail pending appeal

J[1.93]

The policy of the Court of Appeal has for long been against the granting of bail pending the hearing of an appeal against a custodial sentence, unless there are exceptional circumstances. The appellant's remedy is to apply for an expedited appeal. It is generally felt to be unsatisfactory that a person sentenced to custody is released in the hope of a successful appeal and is subsequently required to return to prison to serve his sentence. Therefore, only exceptional circumstances will lead to the granting of bail (*R v Watton* (1978) 68 Cr App Rep 293, [1979] Crim LR 246, CA). The court considering the application is not concerned with whether it would have imposed the same sentence, but only whether the sentence was reasonable. Where the sentence is clearly appropriate for the offence, then personal matters which are the basis for an appeal for clemency should not influence the court considering the bail application.

Disqualification of justices to be removed

J[1.94]

When in the course of any bail application, a magistrate had been told of the accused's previous convictions, that magistrate could not hear the trial of the case if the accused subsequently pleaded not guilty (there was no such restriction if he pleaded guilty). The restriction which is to be found in s 42 of the Magistrates' Courts Act 1980 will be removed by virtue of Sch 37, Part 4 of the Criminal Justice Act 2003. The change reflects the law relating to the admissibility of bad character evidence in criminal proceedings which is to be found in Part II, Chapter I of the Criminal Justice Act 2003.

J[2]

Summary of procedure at a remand hearing

J[2.1]

1 Prosecution (or defence) applies for an adjournment. Bench decides whether to grant the application (length of adjournment may vary depending whether accused will be remanded in custody or on bail).

2 As the presumption is that an accused will be remanded on bail, the prosecution must put forward any exceptions to the right to bail. It is not necessary for evidence to be called and strict proof given.

3 Where the accused has had a previous application for bail refused, the court must consider whether he may put forward further arguments in support of bail.

4 The accused then makes his application for bail.

5 The bench consider whether there are any exceptions to the right to bail, that is:
   (a) can the accused be released on unconditional bail?
   (b) if not, would conditional bail suffice?
   (c) is there an exception to the right to bail?

6 The bench announces its decision:
   (a) if the remand is in custody:
      (i) the chairman will specify the exception to the right to bail which applies together with the reasons for applying that exception where appropriate;
      (ii) the accused is given a record of the decision and a certificate of refusal of bail after a full hearing;
      (iii) the court may inquire whether the accused will consent to further applications being heard in his absence or having heard representations from the parties, fix a date up to 28 days ahead, when it expects the next stage in the proceedings to take place.
   (b) If the remand is on conditional bail, the chairman will announce the conditions and the purpose of those conditions. If sureties are required they may be taken in court or the accused remanded in custody until a security is deposited or a surety is taken.

J[3]

Decision to refuse bail

(See the exceptions (1) (a)–(c), at **J[1.32]**)

J[3.1]

You are refused bail in this case because we find that there are substantial grounds for believing that if released on bail you would:

[fail to surrender to custody]

[commit an offence while on bail]

[interfere with witnesses or otherwise obstruct the course of justice]

and in reaching our decision we have had regard to:

[the nature and seriousness of the offence [and the probable method of dealing with you for it]]

[your character, antecedents, associations and community ties]

[your record as respects the fulfillment of your obligations under previous grants of bail in criminal proceedings]

[the strength of the evidence of your having committed the offence]

You will therefore be remanded in custody to appear at this court on [*date*] at [*time*].

J[4]

Decision to grant bail with conditions

J[4.1]

The court grants bail in this case. You will be released with a duty to surrender to the custody of this court on [*date*] at [*time*]. The bail will be subject to the following conditions:

You are:

[to reside at [*address*] in the meantime]

[to remain indoors at that address between the hours of p.m. and a.m.]

[to report at police station between the hours of and on [*specify days*]]

[not to associate with the following persons]

[to provide a security or surety[ies] in the sum of [*each*]]

The court considers it is necessary to impose the condition[s] to prevent you:

[failing to surrender to custody]

[committing an offence while on bail]

[interfering with witnesses or otherwise obstructing the course of justice]

Section K

Justices in the Crown Court

K[1]

Justices in the Crown Court

K[1.1]

The Crown Court is part of the Supreme Court of Judicature and exercises both civil and criminal jurisdiction. There are three kinds of professional Judges: High Court Judges, circuit Judges and recorders. The most serious cases are dealt with by a High Court Judge sitting alone but when circuit Judges and recorders deal with appeals they may sit with between one and four justices according to the type of case involved.

K[1.2]

The following Judges should be addressed in court as 'My Lord' (or 'My Lady' as the case may be):

(a) any circuit Judge or recorder when he is sitting as a High Court Judge;
(b) any Judge in the Central Criminal Court;
(c) any circuit Judge holding office as honorary Recorder of Liverpool or Manchester.

K[1.3]

Subject to the above rule, the following Judges should be addressed in court as 'Your Honour':

(a) a circuit Judge;
(b) a retired circuit Judge sitting as a deputy;
(c) a recorder;
(d) a deputy circuit Judge.

K[1.4]

When justices sit with a circuit Judge or recorder, the justices are as much a part of the court as is the professional Judge and the decision of the court is the decision of the majority of those on the bench. Only if there is an equality of votes does the Judge or recorder have a second or casting vote. The Judge or recorder must preside and his rulings on legal matters will bind the justices.

K[1.5]

The rules which prescribe the number of justices who must sit in the Crown Court and their qualifications are complicated and liable to be changed by the Lord Chief Justice or the Lord Chancellor and such changes may affect all Crown Court centres or only one. Moreover, where the parties agree the Judge has a discretion to continue the case without justices.

K[1.6]

Justices may deal with cases at the Crown Court even though the case arose in a part of the country for which they do not act as justices; for example, a justice for one county may sit at the Crown Court to hear an appeal from the decision of a court in a neighbouring county. Note, in the magistrates' court the justices now have jurisdiction to try any summary or either way offence committed in any part of England and Wales (s 2 Magistrates' Courts Act 1980 as amended by s 44 Courts Act 2003).

Where justices sit in the Crown Court to hear an appeal that sitting or sittings count as part of the annual returns made to the Lord Chancellor via the relevant local advisory committee.

K[1.7]

On appeal if the prisoner is found guilty in the Crown Court then the bench decides what sentence to impose (technically all persons before the Crown Court are prisoners; those who have been bailed must surrender to custody at the beginning of the hearing and thus become prisoners).

K[1.8]

There is no jury present when the Crown Court hears an appeal against conviction and/or sentence (see s 108 MCA 1980), or when the court hears an appeal from the decision of a Betting and Gaming Licensing Committee.

When the Gambling Act 2005 becomes law appeals from decisions of the relevant local authority will lie to the local magistrates' court (ss 202–206). The same legislation makes no provision for appeals from magistrates' courts to the Crown Court.

Under the Licensing Act 2003 the only statutory provision for an appeal from a decision of the magistrates' court to the Crown Court is in relation to a closure order (s 166).

K[2]

Procedure

K[2.1]

The clerk of the court in the Crown Court wears a gown but does not perform the same functions as does a legal adviser in a magistrates' court. He does not act as legal adviser to the court, although in practice he may from time to time draw the Judge's attention to some legal or procedural matter.

K[2.2]

The proceedings begin with the arraignment of the prisoner if he is to stand trial or in other cases with the announcement of the case by the clerk of the court. When the prisoner is arraigned he is addressed in rather more formal terms than he would be when charged before a magistrates' court, but the arraignment is simply the charging of the prisoner and asking for his plea. The charge is called an indictment and if there are several offences alleged then each is called a count, so that one indictment may contain several counts.

K[2.3]

If there is a guilty plea no jury is required. If any of the counts is denied and not withdrawn by the prosecution a jury is summoned. Justices no longer sit on trials following a not guilty plea but the following description is given for information. Each member of the jury takes the juror's oath separately because the prisoner may object to an individual sitting as a juror. The prisoner may object to a juror if he gives a reason for his objection. The bench will decide whether the reason is sufficient for dismissing the juror. The jury is then charged with the duty of deciding on the evidence the question of the prisoner's guilt or innocence. After this the trial proceeds in the same way as the hearing of a criminal charge in the magistrates' court until counsel have made their final speeches (the prosecution has a closing speech immediately before that of the defence) when the judge will sum up the evidence for the jury and instruct them, if necessary, on any legal points involved in the case. The clerk then gives the jury to the charge of the jury bailiff who not only ensures that they have no communication with anyone but also acts as their messenger to the court, so that, for example, he will warn the court that the jury has completed its deliberations and wishes to return, or that the jury wishes to have further guidance from the Judge.

K[2.4]

Frequently while a jury is 'out' on one case the court will occupy its time by dealing with another, perhaps a guilty plea or prisoner committed for sentence.

K[2.5]

When the jury returns the foreman will be questioned by the clerk of the court and will be asked for its verdict on each count separately. When this has been done the jury may be discharged and it remains for the Judge to decide the appropriate sentence if there has been a verdict of guilty to any count.

K[3]

Sentencing

K[3.1]

On an appeal against conviction and/or sentence from a magistrates' court (see s 108 MCA 1980) where the appeal is unsuccessful the sentence may be increased as well as reduced. The Crown Court may also award costs which the justices did not award (*Johnson v RSPCA* (2000) 164 JP 345, [2000] 20 LS Gaz R 42).

K[3.2]

The maximum sentences which may be imposed at the Crown Court are generally greater than those which may be imposed in a magistrates' court. They are noted in the appropriate sections of this book. Until the amendments envisaged by the CJA 2003 are brought into force imprisonment may not be imposed on persons under 21 years.

K[3.3]

In certain circumstances (eg for breach of community penalty) a 'nominal sentence' of imprisonment for one day may be imposed.

K[4]

Expenses

K[4.1]

Justices who attend the Crown Court are entitled to be paid travelling, subsistence and loss of earnings allowances at the same rates applicable in the case of attending the magistrates' court. These rates are changed from time to time and can be obtained from the court's administration.

K[5]

Disqualification

K[5.1]

A justice must not sit at the Crown Court on an appeal from the decision of a magistrates' court of which he was a member. He may sit on an appeal from the decision of a licensing committee (ie betting or gaming) of which he is himself a member, provided he did not form part of the meeting of the committee whose decision is in question (see **K[1.8]**). Normally arrangements will already have been made between the Crown Court staff and justices' clerk's office which will ensure that a justice is not called to the Crown Court who is disqualified, but in any case of doubt the justice should inform the Judge with whom he is sitting before the case begins.

Section L

The role of the justices' clerk

L[1]

The justices' clerk

L[1.1]

Some justices' clerks continue to hold independent public office. They may not be dismissed without the approval of the Lord Chancellor, who must in turn consider any representations made to him by the magistrates for the local justice area concerned. Although more recently some justices' clerks are appointed on a fixed-term contract they are still the holder of an independent public office.

L[1.2]

The justices' clerk must be distinguished from those of his assistants ("legal advisers") who on his behalf give advice to justices in court when the justices' clerk is not personally in attendance. Both however are obliged to act compatibly with the ECHR.

Functions of the justices' clerk

L[1.3]

Some of the functions of the justices' clerk will be seen from the following extract from the Courts Act 2003, which is not an exhaustive statement:

> 'The functions of a justices' clerk include giving advice to any or all of the justices to whom he is clerk about matters of law (including procedure or practice) on questions arising in connection with the discharge of their functions, including questions arising when the clerk is not personally attending on them … The powers of a justices' clerk include, at any time when he thinks he should do so, bringing to the attention of any or all of the justices of the peace to whom he is clerk any point of law (including procedure or practice) that is or may be involved in any question so arising.'

L[1.4]

It should be noted that the term 'justices' clerk' is used in the Act where it is also defined so as to exclude a member of his staff.

The Courts Service and Structure

L[1.5]

The office of justices' chief executive was abolished by the Courts Act 2003. The Courts Act 2003 unified the court structure by abolishing magistrates' courts committees and bringing magistrates' courts within the Courts Service ("Her Majesty's Courts Service"). The Head of the Courts Service locally is the Area Director although the judicial independence of the magistracy and justices' clerks (including legal advisers, whose advice in individual cases the justices' clerk is responsible for) is preserved by s 29 of the Courts Act 2003.

Advice in court

L[1.6]

Although the extract from the Courts Act 2003 above refers solely to the justices' clerk himself, it is recognised that in practice he may delegate his advisory functions to legal advisers who are either professionally qualified as barristers or solicitors or are qualified under the Justices' Clerks (Qualification of Assistants) Rules 1979 as amended. This is recognised by a Practice Direction on the role of the clerk from the Lord Chief Justice reissued in July 2002 which states:

> 'V. 55
>
> 1) A justices' clerk is responsible for:
> a. The legal advice tended to the justices within the area;
> b. The performance of any other functions set out below by any member of his/her staff acting as legal adviser;
> c. Ensuring that competent advice is available to justices when the justices' clerk is not personally present in court;
> d. The effective delivery of case management and the reduction of unnecessary delay.
>
> 2) Where a person other than the justices' clerk (a 'legal adviser'), who is authorised to do so, performs any other functions referred to in this direction he/she will have the same responsibilities as the justices' clerk. The legal adviser may consult the justices' clerk or other person authorised by the justices' clerk for that purpose before tendering advice to the bench. If the justices' clerk or that person gives any advice directly to the bench, he/she should give the parties or their advocates an opportunity of repeating any relevant submissions prior to the advice being given.
>
> 3) It shall be the responsibility of the legal adviser to provide the justices with any advice they require to properly perform their functions whether or not the justices have requested that advice, on:

i) questions of law (including ECHR jurisprudence and those matters set out in section 2 (1) of the Human Rights Act 1998)
ii) questions of mixed law and fact;
iii) matters of practice and procedure;
iv) the range of penalties available;
v) any relevant decisions of the superior courts or other guidelines;
vi) other issues relevant to the matter before the court;
vii) the appropriate decision-making structure to be applied in any given case. In addition to advising the justices it shall be the legal adviser's responsibility to assist the court, where appropriate, as to the formulation of reasons and the recording of those reasons.

4) A justices' clerk or legal adviser must not play any part in making findings of fact that may assist the bench by reminding them of the evidence, using any notes of the proceedings for this purpose.

5) A justices' clerk or legal adviser may ask questions of witnesses and the parties in order to clarify the evidence and any issues in the case.

6) A legal adviser has a duty to ensure that every case is conducted fairly.

7) When advising the justices the justices' clerk or legal adviser whether or not previously in court, should:
i) ensure that s/he is aware that of the relevant facts;
ii) provide the parties with the information necessary to enable the parties to make any representations they wish as to the advice before it is given.

8) At any time justices are entitled to receive advice to assist them in discharging their responsibilities. If they are in any doubt as to the evidence which has been given, they should seek the aid of their legal adviser, referring to his/her notes as appropriate. This should ordinarily be done in open court. Where the justices request their legal adviser to join them in the retiring room this request should be made in the presence of the parties in court. Any legal advice given to the justices other than in open court should be clearly stated to be provisional and the adviser should subsequently repeat the substance of the advice in open court and give the parties an opportunity to make any representations they wish on the provisional advice. The legal adviser should then state in open court whether the provisional advice is confirmed or if it is varied the nature of the variation.

9) The performance of a legal adviser may be appraised by a person authorised …to do so. For that purpose the appraiser may be present in the justices' retiring room. The content of the appraisal is confidential, but the fact that an appraisal has taken place and the presence of the appraiser in the retiring room, should be briefly explained in open court.

10) The legal adviser is under a duty to assist unrepresented parties to present their case, but must do so without appearing to become an advocate for the party concerned.

11) The role of legal advisers in fine default proceedings or any other proceedings for the enforcement of financial orders, obligations or penalties is to assist the court. They must not act in an adversarial or partisan manner. With the agreement of the justices a legal adviser may ask questions of the defaulter to elicit information which the justices will require to make an adjudication, for example to facilitate his or her explanation for the default. A legal adviser may also advise the justices in the normal way as to the options open to them in dealing with the case. It would be inappropriate for the legal adviser to set out to establish wilful refusal or neglect or any other type of culpable behaviour, to offer an opinion on the facts, or to urge particular course of action upon the justices. The duty of impartiality is the paramount consideration for the legal adviser at all times, and this takes precedence over any role he or she may have as a collecting officer. The appointment of other staff to "prosecute" the case for the collecting officer is not essential to ensure compliance with the law, including the Human Rights Act 1998...'

Family proceedings: Note, the Practice Direction of 1981 was revoked and the above direction was issued with the concurrence of the President of the Family Division. However, the above Practice Direction is entitled ("... crime: consolidated"). Although it applies with modification to family proceedings courts, the role of the justices' clerk and legal adviser in family proceedings is somewhat modified to reflect the procedures and responsibilities under eg the Children Act 1989 and the Family Proceedings (Children Act) Rules 1991.

L[1.7]

In court the legal adviser's duties are both advisory and executive. He may, if the justices so desire, perform those many tasks which ensure the smooth progress of the court's business. For example, he may decide the order in which cases are called, identify, caution and charge defendants, take their pleas and put to them other offences for the court to take into consideration. He may deal with the swearing of witnesses, he may deal with such matters as the explanation of a sentence such as a supervision requirement and confirm the defendant's consent to the requirement. He is empowered to take recognisances which have been fixed by the court, dealing with the arrangements for paying monetary penalties and the questioning of witnesses or defendants on the justices' behalf, including the conduct of a means inquiry. When the justices' clerk (or one of his legal advisers) performs these or any other similar tasks, he carries out those functions on behalf of the justices. There are at least three good reasons why he should carry out most, if not all of these executive functions: his legal knowledge, experience and professional ethics will usually mean that he can perform these functions more effectively than a justice can; there will be more uniformity of procedure if these functions are left to the legal adviser; the less the chairman has to worry about procedural tasks, the more of his attention he can give to listening and decision making.

L[1.8]

The extent to which the legal adviser exercises these tasks, however, varies from court to court and even in the same place it may change according to which chairman is sitting or whether the justices' clerk himself or one of his staff is in court. Whatever the legal adviser does he should be careful to avoid giving to the general public the impression that he and not the chairman is in charge of the court's affairs. The conduct of the court is always the responsibility of the chairman in consultation with his colleagues on the bench; but a wise chairman will usually leave the general conduct of business in court to the legal adviser.

L[1.9]

The Lord Chief Justice has warned that justices who fail to take the clerk's advice on a legal point may be ordered to pay the costs of any resulting appeal. This warning arose in a case where justices insisted on finding 'special reasons' in spite of advice given to them in court by the clerk and later in writing.

L[1.10]–L[1.15]

If the justices retire the legal adviser should not retire with them as a matter of course: either the chairman should specifically and audibly invite him to join the justices or the legal adviser should remain in court and be seen to have been sent for. **NB**: There is not the same prohibition on the legal adviser retiring immediately to join the justices in family proceedings eg in order to assist in the drawing up of the justices' reasons.

L[1.16]

If the justices retire the legal adviser may join them. All too often justices are themselves unaware that a point has arisen in their discussion upon which they need advice, and unless the legal adviser is with them to hear their discussion he too will be unaware that they need advice. Moreover, if he is present during their discussion the legal adviser may be able to help by reminding them of parts of the evidence they may have overlooked, or by explaining the legal significance of particular evidence, or by correcting errors of recollection. In the event that the justices are later asked to state a case the clerk will find it a considerable advantage to have listened to the justices' discussion in the retiring room. Once the legal adviser is satisfied that he can be of no further assistance to the justices he should return to his place in court.

L[1.17]

If the justices do not send for the clerk when they retire, he is entitled to go to advise them if he considers it necessary to do so, but will inform the parties as to what he is going to say to the justices, giving them an opportunity of making representations before that [provisional] advice is given. See *Clark v Kelly* [2003] UKPC D1, [2004] 1 AC 681 on the legality of the justices' clerk's advice and its compatibility with Article 6 of the ECHR.

Delegation

L[1.18]

Apart from his duty to provide justices with advice when they sit in court, the justices' clerk may perform those judicial functions of a single justice which are prescribed by the Justices' Clerks Rules 1999. Amongst the more important judicial functions which a justices' clerk can perform are: the issue of a summons, a witness summons, a distress warrant or a warrant for arrest following a defendant's failure to appear at court so long as no objection is raised on behalf of the accused. The justices' clerk may adjourn a case and grant bail to an accused in his absence with the consent of the prosecution and in the same terms as previously imposed.

L[1.19]

The justices' clerk may take a plea, fix a trial date and commit a criminal case to the Crown Court for trial pursuant to MCA 1980, s 6(2) where the defendant is on bail (the latter function will lapse when the allocation procedures under the CJA 2003 are brought into force). He may authorise a legal adviser to exercise these functions and under the Children Act 1989 to conduct directions appointments and appoint guardians ad litem. Delegation should be by specific authorisation and in writing.

Delegation in relation to the grant of legal representation in criminal proceedings is currently governed by the Access to Justice Act 1999 and regulations made thereunder. The Criminal Defence Service Act 2006, from a date to be appointed, envisages that responsibility for the grant of representation will ultimately shift to the Legal Services Commission. However, in the first instance it is anticipated that magistrates' courts will retain the power to grant or refuse representation. The Act and regulations envisage that those functions are administrative in nature and will be delegated to court staff via the Area Director. See **Section I[7]**.

L[1.20]

The justices' clerk and those of his assistants with delegated powers have case management powers which can be exercised as if by a single justice. Often referred to as 'Narey Courts' the justices' clerk may sit alone in an early first hearing court where simple cases can be listed and a guilty plea is anticipated. Where the case is more complex or a not guilty plea is anticipated the case can be listed for an early administrative hearing where the justices' clerk can deal with trial listing, conditional bail variation (with the consent of the prosecution and the defence) and warrants of arrest in the event of a non-appearance by the accused.

Section M

Applications to a justice

M[1]

Applications to a justice

M[1.1]

It would probably surprise most newly appointed magistrates to learn that a single justice may issue a document such as a warrant to enter premises either at a courthouse or at home. Fortunately it would be exceptional if any one magistrate found himself called upon to perform anything more than a small number of such duties away from the courthouse. This section does not catalogue all of the "out of hours" magisterial functions but gives general advice and deals with some of the more common 'doorstep' applications.

M[1.2]

It sometimes happens that the press will telephone a magistrate seeking an opinion or comment, especially if he is senior court chairman or of a branch representative of the Magistrates' Association. It is unwise to deal with such a request immediately. In most cases the magistrate will refuse to make any initial response. Normally it would be appropriate to refer the inquiry to the justices' clerk or to the chairman of the bench. As a magistrate be very careful (having declined to make any comment, or words to that effect) that you are not drawn into a conversation, isolated parts of which may make tomorrow's headlines. Words spoken conversationally can take on a whole new meaning when reduced to journalistic print. There will be times however when it may be proper to make some statement to the press. In such cases ask the caller to ring again in 30 minutes and use that time to discuss the matter with the justices' clerk, the chairman of the bench or a senior colleague; this will help you to collect your own thoughts on the matter and then it might be helpful to prepare and retain some written note.

M[1.3]

You should invariably refuse to enter into any discussion of a case with any person who has been involved in a decision of the court. A persistent telephone caller can be warned that he is liable to prosecution for making annoying telephone calls. A persistent member of the public should be advised to put his complaint in a letter addressed to the justices' clerk or Area Director. If a magistrate should receive any letters he/she should hand them to the justices' clerk and not reply personally.

Children

M[1.4]

(Emergency procedures under the Children Act 1989 are referred to in **Section D**.)

Warrants

M[1.5]

A warrant is a document signed by a magistrate which authorises the person named in the warrant to carry out the action specified.

M[1.6]

Signing a warrant is an extremely serious matter and a magistrate would be well advised always to refer the applicant to the courthouse where the application can be made in the presence of a legal adviser. If that is not possible, the justices' clerk or a legal adviser should be telephoned for advice. The following notes are intended to give a broad description of the procedure. **They should not be taken to encourage the hearing of an application in the absence of a legal adviser.**

M[1.7]

Some benches go as far as appointing an out-of-hours panel of volunteer magistrates who are given special training. Even so, in such cases a legal adviser is always contacted first about the proposed application.

M[1.8]

For the purposes of this section warrants fall into three categories: warrants to enter premises (and, usually, search for goods which may then be seized); warrants to arrest an individual; and applications under the Proceeds of Crime Act 2002.

M[1.9]

An application under s 42 or Sch 5 of the Terrorism Act 2000 to search premises may be made to a justice of the peace or a district Judge. Applications for warrants of further detention under Sch 8 may only be made to a designated district Judge authorised by the Lord Chancellor.

M[2]

Warrants to enter premises

1 The applicant

M[2.1]

Usually a police officer. If it is not, the magistrate should check whether any authority is needed by the applicant, e g in the case of an official from a supplier of Gas or Electricity (see **M[2.31]**). As a sensible precaution, a police officer should be asked to produce his warrant card, and anyone else evidence of his identity, and where appropriate, his authority to bring proceedings.

2 Authority for issuing a warrant

M[2.2]

A warrant of entry may only be issued where a statute gives authority to do so. When considering an application the magistrate should ask the applicant under what Act and section he is applying for a warrant. The warrant and supporting paperwork should indicate the Act and section.

M[2.3]

Applications by the police generally fall into one of two categories:

M[2.4]

Search for unlawful articles. These are powers of search for goods which generally it is an offence knowingly to possess, e g warrants to enter and search for:

(a) stolen goods – Theft Act 1968, s 26;
(b) drugs – Misuse of Drugs Act 1971, s 23;
(c) obscene articles – Obscene Publications Act 1959, s 3;
(d) firearm or ammunition – Firearms Act 1968, s 46.

M[2.5]

Search for evidence. Until the Police and Criminal Evidence Act 1984, there was no power to issue a warrant to search for *evidence*, e g of a murder, unless the object of the search was also an 'unlawful article' so that a warrant could be issued under the powers described above. The Police and Criminal Evidence Act 1984, s 8 (as amended by the Serious Organised Crime and Police Act 2005) now provides a general power to search for evidence of an offence. However since the Police and Criminal Evidence Act 1984 also gives the police considerable powers of search without a warrant in connection with the arrest of a defendant, an application for a warrant to search for evidence will very often entail the power to enter the premises of a possibly innocent third party to look for evidence implicating the accused.

Issuing a warrant to search for evidence of an indictable offence (Police and Criminal Evidence Act 1984, s 8)

M[2.6]

The application must be made by the police and the magistrate must have reasonable grounds for believing:

(a) that an indictable offence has been committed; and
(b) that there is material on premises specified in the application which is likely to be of substantial value (whether by itself or together with other material) to the investigation of the offence; and
(c) that the material is likely to be relevant evidence; and
(d) that it does not consist of or include items subject to legal privilege, excluded material or special procedure material; and
(e) that any of the following applies:
    (i) that it is not practicable to communicate with any person entitled to grant entry to the premises;
    (ii) that it is practicable to communicate with a person entitled to grant access to the premises but it is not practicable to communicate with any person entitled to grant access to the evidence;
    (iii) that entry to the premises will not be granted unless a warrant is produced;
    (iv) that the purpose of a search may be frustrated or seriously prejudiced unless a constable arriving at the premises can secure immediate entry to them.

M[2.7]

Reasonable grounds for believing. The magistrate himself must have reasonable grounds for believing etc and his judgment will be based on the information supplied by the officer. It is advisable for a short note to be kept by the magistrate of the reasons for granting or refusing a warrant (which can be attached to the application). In the Code of Practice issued for guidance to the police, the officer must take reasonable steps to check that the information is accurate, recent and has not been provided maliciously or irresponsibly. An application may not be made on the basis of information from an anonymous source unless corroboration is sought. The identity of an informant need not be disclosed but the officer should be prepared to deal with any questions from the magistrate about the accuracy of previous information provided by that source or other related matters. 'Belief' is something more than suspicion and implies an acceptance that something is true even though formal, admissible evidence may be lacking. It may be helpful to consider the reference to this matter made when considering the offence of handling stolen goods at **A[49]**.

M[2.8]

Indictable offence means an offence which, if committed by an adult, is triable on indictment, whether it is exclusively so triable or triable either way. The definition also includes a "relevant offence" as defined in s 28D(4) of the Immigration Act 1971: s 8(5) PACE 1984.

M[2.9]

Relevant evidence means anything that would be admissible in evidence at a trial for the offence.

M[2.10]

Premises. The premises referred to above are:

(a) one or more sets of premises specified in the application (a "*specific premises warrant*"); or
(b) any premises occupied or controlled by a person specified in the application, including such sets of premises as are so specified (an "*all premises warrant*").

If the application is for an "*all premises warrant*", the magistrate must also be satisfied:

(a) that because of the particulars of the offence referred to in the application, there are reasonable grounds for believing that it is necessary to search premises occupied or controlled by the person in question which are not specified in the application in order to find the material referred to in the application; and
(b) that it is not reasonably practicable to specify in the application all the premises which he occupies or controls and which might need to be searched.

The warrant may authorise entry to and search of premises on more than one occasion if, on the application, the magistrate is satisfied that it is necessary to authorise multiple entries in order to achieve for which he issues the warrant.

M[2.11]-M[2.15]

Legal privilege means in essence communications between a legal adviser and his client or communications between them and a third party in contemplation of legal proceedings. The legal adviser can supply a full definition.

M[2.16]

Excluded and special procedure material. This includes material held in confidence such as personal or business records, human tissues or fluids taken for the purpose of diagnosis or treatment and journalistic material. A magistrate cannot issue a warrant in respect of excluded or special procedure material; application can only be made, where applicable, to a circuit Judge.

M[2.17]

May issue. Even where all the criteria have been fulfilled, the magistrate still has a discretion.

3 Procedure (for search warrants issued to the police for evidence under the Police and Criminal Evidence Act 1984, s 8 and under other statutes)

M[2.18]

(1) The application may be made by a constable but it must have been authorised by an inspector or more senior officer, or in a case of urgency, the senior officer on duty. Where the officer is not known to the magistrate, a warrant card may be produced to establish identity.

M[2.19]

(2) Except in a case of emergency, if there is reason to believe that a search might have an adverse effect on relations between the police and the community, the local Police Community Liaison Officer should have been consulted.

M[2.20]

(3) The application must be supported by an information in writing stating:

(a) the ground on which he makes the application;
(b) the enactment under which the warrant would be issued; and
(c) if the application is for a warrant authorising entry and search on more than one occasion, the ground on which he applies for such a warrant, and whether he seeks a warrant authorising an unlimited number of entries, or (if not) the maximum number of entries desired;
(d) to identify, so far as is practicable, the articles or persons to be sought; and
(e) to specify the matters set out in **M[2.20A]** below.

M[2.20A]

The matters which must be specified as in (d) above are:

(a) if the application relates to one or more sets of premises specified in the application, each set of premises which it is desired to search and enter;
(b) if the application relates to any premises occupied or controlled by a person specified in the application:
  (i) as many sets of premises which it is desired to enter and search as it is reasonable practicable to specify;
  (ii) the person who is in occupation or control of those premises and any others which it is desired to enter and search;
  (iii) why it is necessary to search more premises than those specified under (i) above; and
  (iv) why it is not reasonably practicable to specify all the premises which it is desired to enter and search.

M[2.21]

(4) The constable must answer on oath any questions which the magistrate may ask him. Apart from questions designed to ensure that the grounds for the application have been made out, e g under the Theft Act 1968, s 26, the magistrate might usefully inquire whether the officer has had the same application previously refused by another magistrate. The police cannot 'shop around' for a magistrate willing to sign the warrant. A second application can only be made where it is based on additional grounds. Finally, there is a discretion whether to issue a warrant.

M[2.22]

(5) The police will usually have prepared a warrant and two copies beforehand. If he is prepared to issue the warrant, the magistrate should read it carefully and check that it covers the matters referred to in (3) above.

M[2.23]

(6) The justices' clerk should retain the information and the police must forward to him, after three months at the latest, the warrant either unexecuted or endorsed as to whether the articles or persons sought were found; and whether any articles were seized, other than the articles which were sought.

M[2.24]

(7) A note of reasons for grant or refusal should be retained

4 Procedure for warrants issued to persons other than police officers

M[2.25]

The provisions outlined above might usefully be taken into account where relevant. For non-police warrants the information is laid on oath. The applicant will usually produce a prepared information and swear to it in the following words: 'I swear by Almighty God that this is my information and that the contents thereof are true to the best of my knowledge and belief.' If he prefers it, he may substitute for the words, 'I swear by Almighty God …' the words, 'I solemnly and sincerely declare and affirm …'. If the wording on the information is not sufficient a further written statement should be appended to the information.

M[2.26]–M[2.30]

As a matter of practice the informant signs the information and the magistrate should retain this and forward it to the justices' clerk.

Warrants of entry for gas and electricity suppliers

M[2.31]

The provisions are complex and are summarised below. It is good practice for all such applications to be considered at a courthouse in the presence of a legal adviser from whom advice may be obtained. Those subject to the application should receive notification of the date and venue of the application.

M[2.32]

Applications may be made, for example, for entry to read a meter or to cut off the supply following non-payment of a bill. An electricity supplier may cut off the supply where the customer has not paid within 20 working days of a demand in writing and after two working days' notice of the supplier's intention to do so. However this power is not available where there is a genuine dispute about the amount owed. (Note – this procedure only applies to a bill for electricity supplied and would not include monies owed on an article supplied by way of a credit sale such as a cooker. Nor is it relevant that there is a genuine dispute about the quality of service since the customer may use a separate procedure to obtain compensation.) The relevant periods where a gas supply is concerned are 28 days after the demand in writing and seven days' notice of intent to cut off the supply.

M[2.33]

Right of entry. An officer of the supplier after one working day's notice (electricity) 24 hours' notice (gas) may at all reasonable times, on production of some duly authenticated document showing his authority, enter the premises for the purpose of cutting off the supply. No notice is required for entry to read a meter except where a warrant is to be applied for.

M[2.34]

Warrant of entry. No right of entry may be exercised except with the consent of the occupier of the premises or under the authority of a justice's warrant (except in cases of emergency).

M[2.35]

Requirements. There must be a sworn information in writing and the applicant must satisfy the justice:

(a) that admission to the premises is reasonably required for the specified purpose;
(b) the applicant has a right of entry to the premises;
(c) the requirements of any relevant enactment have been complied with; and in particular
(d) the relevant notices have been given, including notice of the hearing.

M[2.36]

The justice might also ensure that:

(e) there is no genuine dispute about the amount owed; and
(f) the amount owed is in respect of the supply of gas or electricity.

M[2.37]

Code of practice. Gas and electricity suppliers operate a Code of Practice (of which the clerk of the justices may be able to supply a copy) under which it is undertaken to provide assistance to domestic customers to meet their bills and the suppliers may refrain from cutting off the supply from those who are particularly vulnerable during the winter months; nevertheless where default has occurred, the suppliers may resort to the procedure outlined above.

M[2.38]

Duty to repair damage etc. Where a right of entry has been exercised the supplier must ensure that the premises concerned are left no less secure by reason of the entry and must make good or pay compensation for any damage caused in entering the premises or making them secure.

5 The warrant

M[2.39]

If the magistrate is satisfied with the application he will sign the warrant (which will normally have been prepared in advance by the applicant). This is handed back to the applicant and is his authority to enter and search etc. A magistrate who has issued a search warrant should say nothing to anyone about it, not even to a member of his own family. This is so that no suspicion falls on him in the event that it may appear that the occupier of the premises was expecting a search.

6 Who may sign

M[2.40]–M[2.45]

Any magistrate may sign a search warrant provided he is not on the Supplemental List (ie retired from active work on the bench).

M[3]

Warrants of arrest

M[3.1]

Magistrates will frequently have encountered these during sittings at court, e g for failing to answer bail. The procedure is very similar to that for issuing warrants of entry. However, it is virtually inconceivable that it should be necessary to approach a magistrate at home. The Police and Criminal Evidence Act 1984 provides wide powers of arrest without warrant even for minor offences where there is doubt about the identity of the arrested person or an arrest is necessary to prevent harm to him or the public. Accordingly, a magistrate would be unwise to issue such a warrant unless he has the advice of his justices' clerk or a legal adviser. Such applications should, as a matter of practice, be heard at the courthouse.

Proceeds of Crime Act 2002

M[3.2]

Minimum amount. Section 294 of the 2002 Act allows a customs officer or constable to seize and apply for forfeiture of cash which is not less than £1,000 and is obtained through or intended to be used in unlawful conduct (see the Proceeds of Crime Act 2002 (Recovery of Cash in Summary Proceedings: Minimum amount) Order 2006, SI 2006/1699).

Search power The police or customs may search a person or premises for tainted cash. An authorisation may be given by a single justice ex parte. A search warrant under this provision does not authorise entry to premises.

Detention of seized cash Application may be made to any magistrate in England and Wales who may extend the officers right to detain cash for 48 hours, for up to three months. In calculating the 48 hours for which seized cash may initially be held, Saturdays, Sundays, Christmas Day, Good Friday and bank holidays should be ignored. The applicant must serve notice on anyone from whom the cash was seized, sent to or by. Service of the notice need not be proved.

Grounds for detention order A magistrate may make the order for three months detention if he is satisfied that there are reasonable grounds for the officer's suspicion and the continued detention is justified for the purposes of investigation of its origins or use. Further extensions which may be for a total period of two years, must be made by a full court. Application for the release of detained money may also be made.

Forfeiture The police or customs may apply for detained cash to be forfeited and a magistrates' court can make an order if it is satisfied that the cash is recoverable property or intended for use in unlawful conduct.

Legal Notes

Cash means notes and coins, postal orders, cheques or travellers cheques, bankers drafts and bearer bonds and shares.

Minimum Amount Cash is only subject to the act if it is a minimum sum of £1,000, singly or as part of a larger sum. The amount may be estimated to preserve evidence.

Unlawful Conduct includes conduct which is unlawful under the criminal law in the UK and conduct which occurs outside the UK if it would have been unlawful in the UK.

Legal Aid A criminal legal representation order is not available. Civil legal aid may apply subject to means.

Right of Appeal. May be made against the decision of a magistrates' court ordering forfeiture of cash by either party whether the application is dismissed or approved. In this case an appeal lies to the Crown Court: s 299.

M[4]

Miscellaneous

Recognisance

M[4.1]

A recognisance of a surety for bail should not be taken unless the proposed surety produces a certificate stating the amount and conditions of bail. The surety should be questioned so as to satisfy the magistrate that he has, or can easily obtain, the sum mentioned in the certificate. If the certificate states that a specific person is to be surety, evidence of identity should be required. The clerk or an officer in charge of a police station may take these recognisances and, in any case of doubt, the surety should be referred to one of these persons.

Certificate of good repute

M[4.2]

A magistrate should not sign a certificate of good reputation or good character. If approached to do so he should refer the applicant to a legal adviser.

Passports and driving licences

M[4.3]

A magistrate should neither endorse an application for a passport, nor sign the photograph therewith unless he knows the applicant sufficiently well to meet the criteria on the form. Similar considerations apply to applications for a photocard licence.

Removal to suitable premises of persons in need of care and attention (National Assistance Act 1948, s 47 and National Assistance (Amendment) Act 1951, s 1)

M[4.4]

The following provisions are for the purposes of securing the necessary care and attention for persons who:

(a) are suffering from grave chronic disease or, being aged, infirm or physically incapacitated, are living in insanitary conditions; and
(b) are unable to devote to themselves, and are not receiving from other persons, proper care and attention.

M[4.5]

Where the proper officer (formerly the medical officer of health) certifies in writing to the local authority that he is satisfied after thorough inquiry and consideration that in the interests of any such person residing in the local authority's area or for preventing injury to the health of, or serious nuisance to other persons, it is necessary to remove him from his residence, the local authority may apply to a court for an order of removal.

M[4.6]

If the proper officer and another registered medical practitioner certify that in their opinion it is necessary in the interests of that person to remove him without delay, the local authority or the proper officer where duly authorised may make an application to a single justice having jurisdiction for the place where the person resides. The justice being satisfied on oral evidence under oath of the allegations in the certificate and that it is expedient so to do, may order his removal to a hospital where one is available or to some other place in, or within convenient distance of, the local authority area. If the justice thinks it necessary, the order can be made without notifying or hearing the person concerned.

M[4.7]

Duration of the order. The order may be for a period of up to three weeks. After it has expired the local authority would have to make a full application to a court.

M[4.8]

It should be noted, however, that as an emergency ex parte application can also be made to a magistrate sitting in a courthouse; accordingly, applications should normally be considered there except where circumstances dictate otherwise.

Statutory declarations

M[4.9]

It is necessary to make sure that the clause at the end of the form is properly completed and dated. It is not necessary to read the document, nor need the magistrate be concerned to establish in his own mind the truth of the contents of it. His signature on the document simply attests that he was present and heard the maker of the document declare that the contents are true.

M[4.10]–M[4.15]

The words for a statutory declaration are:

> **'I, AB, do solemnly and sincerely declare and affirm that the contents of this declaration are true to the best of my knowledge and belief, and I make this solemn declaration conscientiously believing the same to be true and by virtue of the provisions of the Statutory Declarations Act 1835.'**

M[4.16]

A Holy Book is not required for a statutory declaration.

M[4.17]

Any magistrate, including those on the Supplemental List, may sign a statutory declaration.

Warrants to search for and remove mental patients

(Mental Health Act 1983, s 135)

M[4.18]

A justice to whom it appears that there is reasonable cause to suspect that a person believed to be suffering from mental disorder:

(a) has been, or is being, ill-treated, neglected or kept otherwise than under proper control in any place within the jurisdiction of the justice; or
(b) being unable to care for himself, is living alone in any such place;

may issue a warrant authorising his removal to a place of safety with a view to making an application under the Mental Health Act 1983 or other arrangements for his treatment or care.

M[4.19]

Application is by way of an information laid on oath by a social worker specially approved by the local authority for the purposes of the Mental Health Act 1983. The patient need not be named in the information.

M[4.20]

Warrant authorises a constable to enter (if need be by force) any premises specified in the warrant and if thought fit to remove him to a place of safety.

M[4.21]

Place of safety means residential accommodation provided by a local authority or a hospital, police station, mental nursing home, or residential home for mentally disturbed persons or any other suitable place where the occupier is willing to receive the patient.

M[4.22]

Duration. The detention in a place of safety may not be for more than 72 hours.

Administration of oaths etc in certain probate business

M[4.23]

Justices of the peace are empowered by the Courts and Legal Services Act 1990, s 56 to administer oaths and take affidavits in non-contentious probate matters. The Judicial Studies Board has issued the following guidance for the assistance of magistrates' courts:

'(a) The oaths envisaged in this Act are those which are non-contentious and of a probate nature, ie, civil proceedings, and should not therefore be of great urgency requiring their administration out of court hours. Each court should therefore publish set hours during which these oaths will be administered.

(b) Justices should be discouraged from administering these oaths outside court hours and away from supervision by suitably qualified court staff.

(c) Justices should not administer oaths for documents which are to be used in court proceedings [including civil proceedings], and court staff should look at document headings with great care, to ensure that there is no court name or reference number thereon which might indicate a current court action.

(d) The wording of the oath to be taken is different from a court witness oath and is 'I swear by Almighty God that the contents of this my [affidavit] [and the exhibits annexed thereto] are true'.

(e) Be prepared for the oath to be sworn by members of all religions in the appropriate form – another reason why 'out of hours oaths' should be discouraged.

(f) An interpreter may be needed and he should be sworn first, taking the appropriate oath.

(g) A deponent may wish to affirm, in which case he will do so in the appropriate form – again a reason for oaths to be administered in the court setting, as justices will not necessarily know the correct wording.

(h) Every alteration to the document has to be initialled by the administering justice.

(i) Any exhibit has to be dated and signed and must clearly indicate that it is the exhibit annexed to the affidavit produced and sworn by the deponent on that same occasion.

(j) The jurat or attestation shall state the date and place the oath or affidavit is taken or made [Courts and Legal Services Act 1990, s 56(2)].

(k) No justice shall exercise the powers conferred in any proceedings in which he is interested [Courts and Legal Services Act 1990, s 56(3)].

(l) In the event of any person being sufficiently handicapped to make it impossible for him or her to attend court to swear a document, arrangement could be made by the clerk to the justices for a justice and member of the court staff to attend upon that person at their home, or a mutually convenient place. This should not occur frequently, but should be provided for by courts.'

Index